DIVISIVE DISCOURSE

The Extreme Rhetoric of Contemporary American Politics

Second Edition

By Joseph Zompetti
Illinois State University

cognella® | ACADEMIC PUBLISHING

Bassim Hamadeh, CEO and Publisher
Kassie Graves, Director of Acquisitions and Sales
Jamie Giganti, Senior Managing Editor
Jess Estrella, Senior Graphic Designer
Angela Schultz, Acquisitions Editor
Alexa Lucido, Licensing Associate
Kaela Martin, Associate Editor
Berenice Quirino, Associate Production Editor
Mandy Licata, Interior Designer

Cover image copyright © Depositphotos/klemsy.

Printed in the United States of America

ISBN: 978-1-63487-883-8 (pbk) / 978-1-63487-884-5 (br)

CONTENTS

In dedication to
TWW,
who helped me learn the art of debating,
and
12 AM,
who will forever be with me.

ACKNOWLEDGMENTS

A book of this scope, magnitude, and content could not be completed without the help and influence of many, many people. First, I want to thank the editorial staff at Cognella Academic Publishing. They are a group for whom I have been delighted to work. They offered much-needed guidance throughout this project without trampling on my plans or ideas. While writing this book was a challenge, they made producing it into a reality relatively easy.

I also must thank my awesome colleagues in the School of Communication at Illinois State University. They were extremely supportive throughout this process. While fiscal belt-tightening has become the norm for most of higher education, somehow my school found the resources to allocate a graduate research assistant in the spring of 2014 and 2016 to help me with some of my research. Thus, I am grateful to Scott Mitchell and James Ndone for their hard work in helping with part of the research of this volume. My colleagues also were very patient and understanding when I would come into work with a grumpy and irritable demeanor, after putting in successive long nights to finish the initial draft of this book. Plus, for the second edition of this book, my School of Communication and the College of Arts & Sciences (as well as the provost's office) were able to afford funding my sabbatical for this project. All of them deserve more than my gratitude. Over the years I also benefited from important conversations with Alauna Akins, Steve Hunt, Lance Lippert, John Baldwin, and Megan Koch, who helped with some of my arguments in this book.

Additionally, I need to thank my students. I have taught COM 303 (Controversy in Contemporary Society) for many years, and in that class we focus on the discourse of contemporary American political muckrakers. This book naturally is a result of those semesters, the discussions I have had with my students, our experiences and frustrations with political rhetoric, and the need for an in-depth analysis of issue-based extremist political rhetoric. In particular (but not in any particular order), I want to thank Bill Breault, Kelsey Brennan, Rebecca Sack, Hillary St. John, Andrew Sample, Taylor Bauer, Haley Palmer, Lynn Rossi, James Ngube, Nick Hebert, Jill Glazer, Kathren Sammis, Morgan Basso, Nicole and Jennifer Hughes, Mia Volpe, Kate Rich, Joe Oliver, Michael Rumfelt, Jessica McAdam, Mitch Combs, Chelsea Oshita, Rebecca Hemmer, Brad Johnson, Tyler Arnieri, Mariah Clarke, Megan Cavanaugh, Zoe Clemmons, and

Kellian Reed. Some of my recent graduate students who did not take the COM 303 course helped me in other ways, mainly by providing suggestions and research; they are Scott Mitchell, Amber Pineda, Chad Woolard, Jake Nickell, Nathan Stewart, Brian Sorenson, and Shanna Carlson.

Finally, those closest to me deserve special acknowledgment. My girlfriend, Buffy, when not slaying vampires, always found time to support me. Because she works in an orthopedics office, her ideas were very helpful for the chapter on healthcare. Plus, my parents have been instrumental in my political development. Ever since I can remember, my parents instilled in me a commitment to our community. Both of my parents exemplified the idea of community and political engagement—they volunteered and offered their services to political campaigns. I remember quite vividly canvassing neighborhoods as a young child, helping my parents register people to vote in our neighborhood. As a result, my parents instilled in me at an early age the value of being politically engaged. To this day, I value and appreciate that experience. While they, at the time, inculcated certain political values into me, I now know that they really were trying to impress upon me critical thinking. As a result, I am forever grateful.

In the first edition, I said this about my little baby girl, Midnight: "My four-legged daughter, Midnight, stayed up with me on countless nights. As she nestled herself next to me as I would pound away on my computer, I always felt the comfort of her little heart beating next to me. She has been inspirational in ways I really cannot describe." I miss her terribly. She passed away on January 29, 2017.

PREFACE TO THE SECOND EDITION

Although it has only been two years, much has happened since January 2015, when the first edition of this book was published. We have witnessed the election of Donald Trump as president of the United States; the Ferguson, Missouri, riots over the killing of Michael Brown and the subsequent attention given to other police shootings; the intensification of ISIS in the Middle East; the concomitant wave of Syrian refugees; the commandeering of coral reefs as islands by the People's Republic of China (D. Watkins, 2015); more muscle-flexing from North Korea; an agreement between the United States and Iran concerning potential Iranian nuclear proliferation; continued drug-related crimes and deaths in Mexico; the voluntary removal of the United Kingdom from the European Union (aka "Brexit"); the legalization of homosexual marriage by the U.S. Supreme Court; and the rampage against drug traffickers by the new president of the Philippines (Woody, 2016). In addition, the entire continent of Africa has, well, been largely unnoticed by the popular international press, as usual, despite a civil war in The Gambia (Barry & Searcey, 2017), unanswered terrorism by Boko Haram in Nigeria ("Suicide Attack Hits Nigeria's University," 2017), violence and uprisings in northern Africa as those countries struggle in the post–Arab Spring world, and mass poverty, disease, and violence all over the continent (Aizenman, 2016). What we do know for certain is that two areas have emerged in the past two years that definitely deserve our attention in terms of divisive discourse: the status of race relations in the United States and the precipitating international conflict areas concerning the Syrian refugees and the so-called Iranian nuclear deal.

Obviously, we could devote entire books to the subject areas above. My decision to focus on race relations and foreign policy as it relates to Syrian refugees and Iran is predicated on the following factors: First, I know that my students care about these topics. Well, they care about the first topic, at least. Many of my students have no idea what is occurring with Syria or with Iran. However, I know that once my students are knowledgeable about the realities of the Middle East, the issues confronting Syria and Iran are suddenly significant to them. Second, I currently live in the middle of Illinois—not too far from Ferguson, Missouri, and definitely not too far from Chicago (which currently has the highest shooting and murder rate in the United States). While my university is populated by less than 10% African-American students, issues of race—and definitely issues of race-related shootings—are very salient among our students and faculty. Plus, given the recent racial predicaments at the University of Missouri, issues of campus-related racial incidents have hit our radar in very significant ways (Izadi, 2015).

As such, this edition includes two very important new chapters, as well as significant updates to the previous chapters. Reviews and remarks from the first edition collectively suggested that there be a section on how to actually engage in productive and meaningful dialogue, and this edition attempts to address that concern by incorporating ways to engage in contentious conversations in the revised Introduction.

A quick note about the last edition and this edition—while most reviews of the first edition have been positive, one in particular noted that I occasionally use terms to describe individuals who are, by their nature, divisive. In other words, it is argued that I use words that are polarizing while I am simultaneously arguing against polarization. On one hand, I could say that polarization is inevitable (and it is). Regardless of what words are used to describe a situation or a person, some may find such words objectionable. This is the reality of sensitivity. On the other hand, I could say that I simply "call it like I see it." In other words, if someone appears to be extremist, I should label them as such. Of course, some labeling terminology is worse than others. To call Ann Coulter, for example, a "moonbat" instead of an "extremist" may conjure certain presumptions about my perspective, if not my objectivity. However, I do not claim to be objective (actually, I do not think anyone should claim such an absurd position), but I do claim to try to be balanced. If I call Ann Coulter a moonbat, I am also likely to call Keith Olbermann a moonbat. So there it is. If that is polarizing to some, I apologize. Yet, in order to reduce or fight against divisive discourse, we must have a lexicon to name it when it occurs—and moonbattery unfortunately happens to occur. Plus, if my choice of certain descriptors causes conversation about this overall issue, those descriptors, in part, are functioning as I intend them to.

I sit here typing on my laptop on inauguration day—the day that Donald J. Trump becomes the 45th president of the United States. For many, it is a day of rejoicing and jubilance, just as many celebrate whenever their person wins a contest. For others, today is a day of shock and fear about the future. It is a divisive time. The rhetoric from all sides during the election was tumultuous. The rhetoric of today is not much different. What will be the political rhetoric of tomorrow? We can presume that vitriol will continue. But books like this can hopefully help us navigate the minefields of divisive discourse for "a more perfect union"—a democracy worth sustaining and fighting for.

INTRODUCTION

Politics is about words and power. The way power is communicated forms the core of virtually all political study, whether the scholar who studies politics admits it or not (Welsh, 2013; Wolfsfeld, 2011). Of course, the relationship between communication and politics is quite varied and diverse; the subject area includes the way politics is taught, discussed among peers and family, communicated by public officials, reported by the media, and so forth. Despite these various intersections between politics and the word, the manner in which most conversations about politics occurs in contemporary America is rife with bitterness, vitriol, and animosity (Crowley, 2006). We would do well to listen to one of this country's Founding Fathers and the second president, John Adams, who said, "Abuse of words has been the great instrument of sophistry and chicanery, of party, faction, and division of society" (1819, p. 377). Indeed, the abuse of words, and the venom they invoke, is a major contemporary issue in American politics.

This is a book about divisive discourse in contemporary American politics. As I will argue, political division is a consequence of extremist rhetoric. According to Gutmann (2007), extremist rhetoric "tends toward single-mindedness on any given issue," and "it passionately expresses certainty about the supremacy of its perspective on the issue without submitting itself either to a reasonable test of truth or to a reasoned public debate" (p. 71). Although many scholars debate about whether polarization occurs among the political parties, citizens, political pundits, or all of the above, there appears to be a consensus that political extremism in some form is widespread and growing in the United States (Stryker, 2011).

The polarizing rhetoric exuding from news media, Internet junkies, and political pundits dominates the conversations concerning politics (Evans, 2003; McCarty et al., 2008; Pildes, 2011). And, when citizens engage in political discussions, they often mimic the language and positions they hear from those sources. As a result, talking about politics often brings out the worst in us. Of course, we will naturally have disagreements with others, which may breed hostility or, to the other extreme, may cause us to recoil at the thought of talking about politics at all. For most of us who have political opinions, those perspectives are closely linked to our overall identity as a person. Those political thoughts categorize us from others, and they frame the way we see others and the world around us. Hence, when we talk about politics, the nature

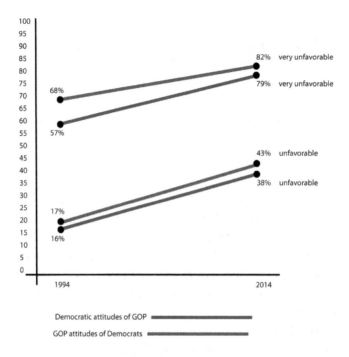

Figure 1: Acrimony & Hostility between Groups Growing.

of the discussion becomes very personal, which makes it challenging to discuss politics in abstract terms. Other folks who may not have given much consideration to political ideas may find discussing them intimidating or overwhelming. A knowledge deficit concerning political issues, then, can contribute to polarizing ideas particularly when a person uses the shorthand that they parrot from political pundits, politicians or online sources. Finally, controversial issues are often seen as a form of competition where one side believes they are right—and so others must be wrong—and then the discussion about the issues becomes a sparring match to see who can win. Such conversations can be enjoyable for some, but are more often than not frustrating to most people, leading to low-quality discussions that really do nothing for us.

What seems to be occurring, and important for my overall position in this book, is that polarization is occurring, and even increasing, among the major political parties and extremist political commentators (see Figure 2); but, at the same time, the American people are influenced by polarizing political forces, yet are much more moderate in their beliefs (Brownstein, 2007; Dimaggio et al., 1996; Evans, 2003; Fiorina, 2011; Heatherington & Weiler, 2009; McCarty et al., 2008; Stryker, 2011; Thomas & Beckel, 2008). The 2016 presidential election intensified the division, the extreme discourse that permeated the campaigns made most Americans feel it was the most polarizing political moment in recent history, so much so that Lee Drutman of *The New York Times* called it "the Divided States of America." Yet, John Avlon (2004) states it simply: "As Congress has grown more partisan, however, the electorate has grown steadily more

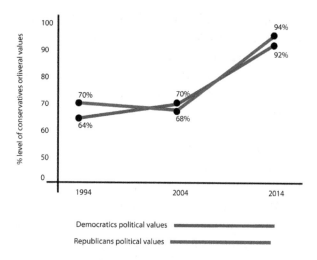

Figure 2: GOP More Conservative and Democrats More Liberal.

Centrist" (p. 14). One reason that citizens may not be highly polarized is that they lack the knowledge, skills, or motivation to be even tangentially involved politically. And, while Americans may generally have moderate political beliefs, the way we discuss them is often highly polarizing. But one thing is for sure: we should be concerned "to the extent that polarization is accompanied with greater incivility in political discourse" (Stryker, 2011, p. 8). This is because "emotionally extreme," ideological, and uncivil discourse on political news shows increased political polarization "by helping partisans think even less of their opponents than they already did" (Mutz, 2006, p. 240).

Divisive political discourse has a number of negative consequences, such as the president exerting more power, less bipartisanship, added intensity over key social

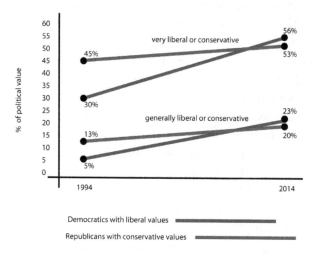

Figure 3: More Polarized than Before.

issues and political initiatives, and heightened voter apathy (Binder, 2014; McCarty et al., 2008). Political polarization "fosters an environment in which citizens distrust politicians, 'hate politics,' and fail to vote," in large part because citizens "do not see the link between their vote and the decisions made by those who hold power" (Rimmerman, 2011, p. 35). In fact, many young people in America reason that their distaste with politics stems from the detachment they feel when trying to grasp the dynamics of politics (Bauerlein, 2009; Rimmerman, 2011; Rountree, 2013). Part of their feeling of detachment relates to their perception of two sides bitterly mudslinging against each other—hyperbolized talk, extreme name-calling, negative campaign advertisements, mischaracterizations, and misleading positions (Ansolabehere & Iyengar, 1995; Rimmerman, 2011; Stryker, 2011). In short, American youth—as well as other segments of the population—are turned off by what John Avlon calls "wingnuts," who are the people "on the far-right wing or far-left wing of the political spectrum. They are the professional partisans and the unhinged activists, the hard-core haters and the paranoid conspiracy theorists" (Avlon, 2010, p. 2). Wingnuts might include journalists, entertainers, public officials, news correspondents, etc. Their prominence on the airwaves, televised and print news, and the Internet (Avlon, 2010) allows wingnuts to dominate our public political discussions, even to the point of "rising decibels of hate" (Tolchin, 1996, p. 5).

IDEOLOGY AND POLITICAL DISCOURSE

I will frequently use the word "ideology" throughout this book. For our purposes here, ideology is a value-neutral term—neither good nor bad—as it simply describes a world view or framework that guides our beliefs, decisions, and actions (Finlayson, 2012; Hawkes, 2003; Hollihan, 2009; Therborn, 1980). Of course, ideologies can become extreme if they are dogmatically accepted because ideologies "provide a series of reasons for thinking one sort of thing rather than another," especially "when seeking ways to persuade others to share the same perspective" (Finlayson, 2012, p. 758). This occurs when holders of certain ideologies fail to engage in critically questioning their beliefs, and when they blindly accept their ideology to explain the world around them without considering alternative options. People who engage in divisive discourse typically rely on ideology to justify their points of view, and they expect their listeners will fall back on ideology to blindly accept such points of view (Heatherington & Weiler, 2009). There is also the notion of "constraints," which means that because we hold an ideological perspective on one issue (e.g., we believe in strong gun rights), we are likely to hold similar ideological perspectives on other issues (e.g., if we are conservative on guns, we will be conservative on healthcare), meaning that our ideology that frames our point of view on one issue *constrains* our ability to view other issues differently (Noel, 2013). What's more, as Huckfeldt (2001) argues, when citizens discuss these ideologies, there is a "multiplier effect" as the arguments and positions of the political radicals are passed on from conversation to conversation (p. 425).

Recent Discussions on Divisive Discourse

The discussion about how polarized America is, if at all, and the reasons behind it is teeming with virulent studies and interesting positions. Some argue that we are engaged in a "culture war" since Americans are pitted against each other over moral, social, and cultural concerns (Fiorina, 2011), and others argue passionately that division in politics is mostly an economic phenomenon, such that Americans vote in their economic self-interests, as varied as those may be (Ansolabehere et al., 2006; Mueller, 2003). What is interesting for our purposes, however, is not a rudimentary discussion of American politics. Rather, I will explore how political pundits on the extreme left and right characterize their positions with the broader liberal or conservative beliefs in an effort to sway as many people as possible to their respective ideologies. I will investigate later how these polarizing die-hards try to persuade the moderate middle of America. Suffice it to say for now, politics is already a complicated field of study. It simply does not help us, or democracy, when extremists confuse labels, identities, and categories when addressing political issues. For example, it is common for either polarizing side to use labels such as "Socialist," "Communist," "Nazi," "Hitler," "Anti-Christ," and so on to characterize the other political polarity (Avlon, 2010; Jeffreys-Jones, 2010). Not only are such terms inaccurate; they also muddy the very important conversation we should have regarding politics. Even more significantly, these rhetorical ploys and others will be examined in this book because they escalate as one political group wields them at another (Kingwell, 2012). Also, this type of rhetoric damages our democracy. If we want a knowledgeable citizenry who can participate in a civil conversation about important policies in our society, we need to be on alert for the divisive discourse that is used by polarizing figures (Thomas & Beckel, 2008).

Political ideology and its polarizing influence, perceptions by American voters, the political system, and its impact on media messages are frequently discussed. Morris Fiorina (2011), in perhaps the most cited book on the subject, passionately argues in *Culture War* that the mainstream belief that political polarization overwhelms the totality of American politics is flawed. Instead, he claims that extremist attitudes and policy actions may exist in government or with public officials, but most American citizens and voters are moderates, or centrists. Mainly as a response to Fiorina's earlier edition of *Culture War*, Abramowitz and Saunders (2005) claim that deep divisions exist between Republicans and Democrats, so much so that the categorizations of "Red" and "Blue" states are justified. By using data from the American National Election Studies, the authors note that the evidence does not support Fiorina's claim that polarization is largely a myth concocted by social scientists and media commentators. While most Americans are moderate in their political views, there are sharp divisions between supporters of the two major parties that extend far beyond a narrow sliver of elected officials and activists. Red state voters and blue state voters differ fairly dramatically in their social characteristics and political beliefs. Perhaps most important, there is a growing political divide in the United States between religious and secular voters. These divisions are not a result of artificial boundaries constructed by political elites in search of electoral security. They reflect fundamental changes in American society and politics that have been developing for decades and are likely to continue for the foreseeable future. (Abramowitz & Saunders, 2005, p. 19) Later, Abramowitz (2010) challenges the argument that most Americans are moderates. Instead, Abramowitz argues that the key distinction to be made when analyzing political polarization is whether citizens are politically engaged or not. He claims that the more ideologically partisan citizens are also the most engaged, and, as a corollary, the most politically engaged Americans become the most polarized. Additionally, Abramowitz also claims that highly partisan or polarized citizens are not necessarily a bad thing, especially if such ideological biases encourage people to be more politically engaged. That, in turn, stimulates and revitalizes American democracy.

In a related way, Heatherington and Weiler (2009) argue that ideological polarization is the highest it has ever been in America. They examine a number of contemporary issues to reveal the degree to which polarization has infiltrated policymaking. To make sense of how citizen perceptions, public officials, and policy implementation all center around heightened polarization, the authors argue that authoritarian attitudes, mainly from political parties and government officials, congeal these different variables together. McCarty, Poole, and Rosenthal (2008) agree that political polarization has increased in America and that it is now at a crisis level. They argue, instead, that recent economic and social trends mold our political situation that allows, if not encourages, polarization to manifest itself.

However, authors such as Cal Thomas and Bob Beckel (2008) vehemently claim that the majority of Americans are not polarized, but political parties, the mass media, political consultants, and public officials are extremist. They suggest that polarization is nothing new in U.S. politics, but the severity and intensity of contemporary polarization is unique and very alarming. The authors passionately urge Americans to be able to identify the professional polarizers and, moreover, choose a path of bipartisanship and "common ground."

The Dynamics of Polarization

Ronald Brownstein (2007), in his book *The Second Civil War*, argues that political polarization has increased and widened in the past decade. But Brownstein notes that the spike in polarization is not so much the result of too many ideologues, but rather the consequence of having too few principled politicians to challenge the hyperpolarized political crusaders. Admitting that the "polarization of American politics is an enormously complex, interactive phenomenon," Brownstein targets his critique mainly on structural factors, such as the empowerment of interest groups, special interest lobbies, the no-compromise nature of contemporary political parties, as well as the overall political system (p. 19). Regardless of the cause or causes of polarization, Brownstein agrees that political division is spiraling downward and is a serious threat to American democracy.

Galston and Nivola (2006) attempt to clarify the different dynamics of American political polarization. By looking at the political "fissures" that exist in society, the authors claim that "the preponderance of evidence does suggest that some significant fissures have opened in the nation's body politic, and that they extend beyond its politicians and partisan zealots" (p. 2). The trouble is, of course, that polarization can occur with politicians, media pundits, party officials, and voters. And in terms of potentially polarized voters, we must distinguish between their division in extreme polarity, fissures in ideology, reactions to divisive ballot choices, and influence from media, officials, and parties. In other words, reviewing political polarization and its causes and implications is a complex discussion. Some scholars look at the relationship between political parties and partisan elites on the overall political system (Azzimonti, 2013; Bartels, 2002). Others look at the partisan dynamics between political parties and politicians (Hayes, 2005; Layman et al., 2010; Lauderdale, 2013). And, of course, many scholars examine the impact of partisan politics on the American voting public (Abramowitz & Saunders, 1998; Ansolabehere et al., 2006; Baldassarri & Bearman, 2007; Carmines et al., 2012; Carsey & Layman, 2006; Dimaggio et al., 1996; Evans, 2003; Heatherington, 2001; Schreckhise & Shields, 2003). This attention to the consequences of political polarization is examined by Somin (2004). Somin argues that reliance on media messages, claims made by political parties, and knowledge accrued from inadequate schooling results in a massively uneducated and ignorant electorate. While not specifically addressing political polarization or rhetoric, Somin offers us an important connection between political knowledge (or lack of knowledge) and its impact on American democracy. Somin reports that a democracy requires an educated citizenry because the citizenry needs to actively participate—in an informed way—in order for democracy to function and survive. If hyperpolarization exists in the rhetoric of extremist media personalities, at best, the amount of political knowledge among the citizenry might be a chimera; if an increasing number of Americans are turned off by partisan media, at worst, the citizenry is becoming more and more ignorant about politics. Thus, we must be very vigilant and cognizant of the relationship between media messages and American citizens if we believe that democracy is worthwhile.

Partisan Media

In 2008, Jeffrey Berry and Sarah Sobieraj looked at how news media engage in fallacies and other sensationalizing techniques to provide ideologically political messages. The rise and widespread dissemination of polarizing discourse in the media is a complicated phenomenon. The authors argue that the "growth of certain kinds of advocacy organizations and media outlets, coupled with the development of cable TV and the Internet, has had a profound impact on our political system. The competition for viewers, listeners, readers, and donors among politically oriented organizations, media corporations, and web sites leads many of them to promote a highly polarized view of American politics" (p. 2). Although Berry and Sobieraj do not analyze the specific rhetorical tactics used by partisan media, they do report that the media have tremendous influence on the American public, so much so that "American politics is surely more coarse than the norm; candidates for office have a strong incentive to ally themselves with sharply ideological groups; and bipartisanship in policymaking seems to have become more difficult to achieve" (p. 5).

In 2011, the same authors extended their investigation of partisan media. Sobieraj and Berry (2011) focus on what they call "outrage discourse" from partisan media sources, which includes "efforts to provoke a visceral response from the audience, usually in the form of anger, fear, or moral righteousness through the use of overgeneralizations, sensationalism, misleading or patently inaccurate information, ad hominem attacks, and partial truths" (p. 20). The authors show that "outrage" discourse from media sources has an effect on citizens' political attitudes and behaviors. They also point out that while both liberals and conservatives use such tactics, conservative media "use significantly more outrage speech than liberal media" (p. 30). Bill Press (2010) agrees, suggesting that conservative polarized discourse, what he calls "toxic talk," dominates radio talk shows. Press focuses on big-name wingnuts, such as Rush Limbaugh and Glenn Beck, but he also examines local radio talk show hosts.

Additionally, Levendusky (2013) examines how partisan media, or the media that are influenced by political ideologies, reinforce political polarization. He describes how audiences of partisan media "align their news consumption with their ideological and partisan leanings by watching these shows" (p. 4). Because individuals consume media messages for which they are already affiliated, Levendusky posits that partisan media do not actually create polarization among audiences. However, when ideologically

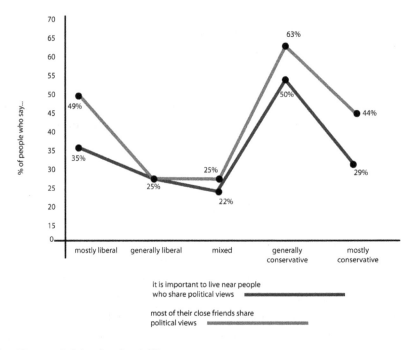

Figure 4: Ideological Silos.

predisposed citizens choose to watch like-minded media, two consequences occur (p. 4). First, the relationship between audience and media source constructs a "silo" effect, whereby political messages "echo" between people who already agree with one another; a proverbial "preaching to the choir" phenomenon (Lencioni, 2006). As Rountree (2013) articulates, "users of new media might just as well bookmark their favorite narrow, biased, ideologically driven websites, reinforcing their own views and shutting down dialogue that crosses the political spectrum, undermining those who seek compromise, and promoting simplistic and negative views of their opponents" (p. 434). Additionally, while this relationship does not necessarily create political polarization among viewers, the messages from partisan media do reinforce or amplify political cleavages (p. 33). The polarization that occurs as a result of partisan media is therefore likely to breed intolerance and less respect between different political perspectives. Levendusky claims that this implication may have damaging results for American democracy.

Polarizing Discourse

By now it should be clear that much has been written about the nature of political division in contemporary U.S. politics. However, the connection linking political partisanship with rhetoric, or *how* such partisan ideologies are persuasively communicated, is rarely discussed. However, one book that examines political discourse is written by communication professor Thomas Hollihan. Hollihan (2009) writes about contemporary American political campaigns, including their use of extremist rhetoric. In so doing, he draws heavily from a variety of political communication frameworks to understand the role communication plays in modern campaigns.

In a similar way, Hart et al. (2013) want to "determine how language affects our perceptions of others," particularly in the area of electoral politics (p. 3). Their focus is on the tone of political rhetoric, which they define as the "tool people use to create distinct social impressions via word choice" (p. 9), because "certain words, when drawn upon often enough, leave people with shared but often elusive perceptions of others" (pp. 9–10). They analyze eight distinct political tones: accommodating, balanced, urgent, assertive, resilient, measured, neighborly, and wandering. They argue that "political tone provides a handy barometer of how politicians cope with changing circumstances, political tone is a subtle yet tangible force that can be assessed scientifically … and tone helps explain voters' intuitive, often inchoate, reactions to political events" (p. 21). Ultimately, they conclude that political tone is "mysterious" (p. 233), yet it "blends politics with humanity" (p. 233) that serves to "treat leaders' remarks as indices of [our] essential beings" (p. 231).

Finally, as I have already mentioned, John Avlon (2010) discusses the nature of so-called "wingnuts" in current U.S. politics. Although Avlon does not explicitly address rhetorical techniques or tactics used by wingnuts, he does offer examples of some of the extremist discourse employed by wingnuts. Avlon's book is not a careful study of wingnut communication, but it does offer us a thorough account of how wingnuts generally operate, particularly in the media. In fact, it is Avlon's work that largely motivated my interest in extremist rhetoric. The wingnuts of our day engage in polarizing narratives, characterizations, and political positions that influence us in "many different dimensions" (Galston & Nivola, 2006, p. 3).

One of the purposes of this book is to challenge this way of thinking. By learning about the techniques used in ideological, extremist rhetoric, hopefully we will be better, more critical consumers of information. At the end of the day, we may continue to believe what some so-called "wingnuts" say, but hopefully our adherence to their position will have been critically thought out. My dad is fond of saying, "Even a stopped clock is right twice a day!" And, on occasion, so are partisan pundits. However, the point is that when we agree with the promoters of divisive discourse, we should agree with them based on the merits of their particular arguments, not just because the wingnut "lucks out" or happens to be correct every now and then.

How to Engage in Controversial Discussions

Some friends of mine as well as other reviewers who read the first edition of this book asked me if there are guidelines, rules, or "best practices" for engaging in discussions about controversial issues. I highly doubt that there is a magic bullet or superior methodology to adopt for these discussions, but I do believe, based on my experiences as well research for this project, there are some significant suggestions worth considering if people are willing to entertain these sorts of conversations. And, even if there is no perfect solution, something must be done, and we need to play our part. According to a recent study by Weber Shandwick (2016), 79 percent of American voters "say incivility in government is preventing action" on key issues, and "76 percent say incivility makes it difficult to even discuss controversial issues" (n.p.). This is consistent with earlier studies, such as the ones conducted by CBS News (2011) and the Center for Political Participation at Allegheny College (2016), except that the problem seems to keep worsening.

To begin, I think there are some substantial differences between situations where one is discussing controversial political issues with family, friends, or associates, either intimately or in a public venue, and a situation where a teacher is encouraging these conversations in a classroom. The knowledge of one's audience is different, the stakes are different, and ultimately there are different power dynamics involved. Nevertheless, there are a set of ideas that could be useful for any sort of situation entailing conversations about controversial, and potentially polarizing, topics.

For our everyday discussions, it may be difficult to establish ground rules that are mutually beneficial and mutually agreeable. Of course, when we can, establishing boundaries or ground rules for discussion can help reduce the amount and degree of uncivil discourse (Wiebe, 2003). However, some parameters for discussion can exclude important views, and even some people, from the conversation. As Wiebe (2003) reminds us, "Rules on civility and deliberation that suit some people ... block access for those who bring a different background, style, and intelligence to public life" (p. 35). At family gatherings, some might resort to a policy that bans all talk relating to politics or religion, which silences everyone. Unfortunately, this sort of boundary is becoming more and more prevalent. If a family cannot talk about these issues, it is unlikely that we will be able to have meaningful discussions elsewhere—after all, family members theoretically love one another! Just because topics may be difficult does not mean we should avoid them. Instead, it would be much better if our families learned *how* to talk about contentious matters.

The same can be said for our friends, co-workers, and others. If we can develop the skills to more civilly discuss polarizing politics, these conversations can be more meaningful, productive, and ultimately more beneficial for our democracy (Barber, 1998). When we encounter folks whom we do not like, obviously these discussions become even more challenging. What follows is a list of suggestions that can improve the civility of our conversations and provide a framework, much like what Rood (2013) calls "rhetorical civility," a "way of being" that commits "to understanding and being understood, respecting and being respected" (p. 344).

1. Listen. Probably the most important suggestion I can offer is that we should simply listen more. When I was a kid, a priest I knew said that the difference between hearing and listening is that hearing is when audible sounds go in one ear and out the other, while listening is when they enter and then stick. By listening, I am not talking about hearing. Listening also means that we are generally interested in what the other person has to say. "Most of us don't listen with the intent to understand. We listen with the intent to reply" (Covey, 2004, p. 239). We should really listen to understand. Plus, "careful listening is also the quickest way to find any possible common ground … this is because in order to understand and describe another's belief, one must interpret it" (Langerak, 2014, p. 17). One of my students reminded us during class one day that sometimes people just need to vent—they need vocalize their frustrations, hopes, fears, anger, excitement, and passion. When they do, we should let them. And while we do, we should carefully pay attention to what other people are experiencing because we might share some of their beliefs or, at the very least, we can better understand their position and social location from which their perspective emanates.

2. Think before responding. A suggestion very close to the first is that we should think before responding. My father used to tell me, "Think before you engage your mouth, son!" And it has always been sage advice, although I cannot claim that I have always heeded it. The point is that heated discussions often begin, and then are exacerbated by, emotional, knee-jerk reactions to statements other people make. If we first take a pause before responding to them, we will be less likely to contribute to the uncivil nature of such discussions.

3. Think of the other person as someone special. My idea of treating someone as special is similar to Langerak's (2014) notion of "respect" (p. 93). This can be extremely challenging, particularly if we are speaking with a person we really dislike, but if we can somehow see that person as important to us, we will be less likely to demonize them. If or when they call us names or belittle us, we may be able to let such offenses slide or even forgive them if we see them as someone significant to us. In other words, we can think of others as partners, collaborators, and colleagues, rather than as enemies, rivals, or adversaries—"we shouldn't aim to *destroy* or *eviscerate* or *annihilate* the other side; we must persuade them to consider a different perspective. That's not easy, but it's necessary" (emphasis in original, Mallicote, 2017, n.p.).

4. Remember that people are seldom wrong 100% of the time. This means that even when we vehemently disagree with someone, they are not always incorrect. We make mistakes, too, and we can take positions that are incorrect or in need of alteration. Plus, if we can identify a moment when the other side may be correct about something, that may be an opportunity to consider a compromise or some type of middle ground.

5. We can always learn something. This is related to suggestion number four, but it bears its own iteration. No matter how despicable we might think a position is, or even a person, we can probably learn something from them and possibly even agree with them. This may not always be the case, but if we approach a contentious discussion with this thought in mind, it may make the conversation more civil.

6. Anticipation. We should anticipate potential disagreements and carefully consider how to respond to them. This obviously requires us to be well-informed about contentious issues, and it means that we need to understand opposing viewpoints. But, if we have thought through these sorts of issues, we will be more even-tempered when discussing them with others.

7. Be well-informed. If suggestion number six is true, we need to be knowledgeable. We should question facts, evidence, and sources of information. "If someone actually believes outlandish conspiracy theories—that government leaders are lizard people, or the moon landing was faked—then imagine how many arguments devoid of facts slip past unchallenged in an online post or in a televised political speech" (Schackner, 2016, n.p.). Since the 2016 presidential election, there has been considerable attention paid to "fake news" and inaccurate information, particularly when spread online and through social media. According to many reports, so-called "fake news," or news that presents inaccurate, fabricated, or faulty information, is not only growing in prevalence (Weber Shandwick, 2017); during the 2016 presidential election, it was apparently consumed more than mainstream, more reputable information sources (Silverman, 2016). Plus, "misinformation can grease the wheels of incivility" (Herbst, 2010, p. 95). A free resource that outlines solid strategies for dealing with and avoiding problematic information online was recently published by Mike Caulfield (2017). Facebook also recently posted its "Tips to Spot False News," where they offer suggestions such as be skeptical of headlines, look closely at the URL, investigate the source, examine the photos, and explore additional sources of information to collaborate the information in other sources.

8. Diversify our exposure to information. This is a corollary to suggestion number seven. We should limit our involvement in echo chambers and question the veracity of information. We should obtain multiple sources for an issue instead of relying on just one that may be inaccurate or too slanted.

9. Try to remember that the bogeyman is not underneath every bed. Some comments are not racist, sexist, homophobic, etc., or are at least not intended to be. I am not suggesting that we should condone bigoted behavior or speech, but I am suggesting that occasionally a person's speech may not be as hateful as it seems. If we immediately react as if it is, chances are the tensions will only escalate, a possible learning moment will be lost (for us and them), and any chance at a reasonable conversation will be lost (French, 2017).

10. What if there is a bogeyman underneath the bed? If something offensive is said, we should interrogate why the statement was made and why the specific words were chosen for the particular comment (Barnett, 2017). Opening up the comments for added discussion can be a powerful learning moment. Of course, we should also be direct in our objection to such offensive remarks, but questioning the speaker as to why they said them, what they really meant by them, etc., could yield important insight and contain making tensions worse (Birnie, 2016). Regardless of the technique, it is important to remember that "Neither ignoring nor capitulating in the face of incivility will move a conversation" (Herbst, 2010, p. 95).

11. Challenge ourselves to see the world from the perspective of others. This is what Willer (2016) calls "moral reframing." Living in our own bubbles causes "blind spots" that prevent us from accessing other perspectives, or even acknowledging their existence in some cases (Thompson, 2017). Calum Matheson, a professor at the University of Pittsburgh, cautions, "You can live in a bubble where all the news you hear conforms to what you already believe" (cited in Schackner, 2016, n.p.).

12. Slow down the conversation. Often these controversial discussions can become derailed and unhinged quickly. By slowing the pace, exploring the facts behind the issues, and carefully reflecting on the nature of the discussion, the overall tenor of the conversation should improve.

13. "Be in the moment" (Headlee, 2015). This means we should focus on the conversation and pay close attention to what the other person is saying. We should not multi-task, think about other things, or look at our cell phones. Not only is this type of behavior disrespectful; it also increases the likelihood that we will miss something important in the conversation.

14. Engage in interpersonal communication. As much as possible, discussions about controversial issues should occur face-to-face so that we can have a better sense of another person's intent by means of reading their non-verbal cues. It is also more personable, meaning that we will be less likely to blow up over a single comment. Additionally, even a brief, ten-minute face-to-face interaction with a person can substantially improve rapport, reduce stereotypes, and encourage empathy (Broockman & Kalla, 2016).

15. Choose our words carefully. Words have consequences, and they shape our reality. We should be able to communicate without escalating tensions. In other words, "speaking truth to power need not entail the use of extreme language" (Anderson, 2017, n.p.).

16. Remember the Golden Rule. While this can be difficult, especially if we feel attacked, treating others as we would like to be treated is sound advice (Anderson, 2017). Even if the other person becomes hostile or believes they are winning the argument, or if they stoop to demeaning or offensive behavior, these things do not mean we should reciprocate. If a discussion devolves to this point, a polite bowing-out of the conversation is probably the best route to take. But if we try to "create a climate of civility," others are more likely to reciprocate our behavior (Birnie, 2016, n.p.).

17. Avoid the quicksand of the "blame game." Blaming and issues of culpability are the driving force behind political disagreements (Mantilla, 2013). When we also consider that a person's identity is intricately connected to the political views they espouse, the blame game can quickly become personal, or it can be perceived as being personal. Carolyn Lukensmeyer (2017) of the National Institute for Civil Discourse reminds us that we all have a part to play in improving civility. While it is easy to point fingers, all of us have either committed uncivil acts, communicated in uncivil ways, or stood idly by while others were uncivil when we had the power to stop them or address their behavior.

18. It is okay to want to convince others about our views. Now, what if we really want to persuade someone in one of these conversations? Not all political conversations occur just to improve our knowledge about the issues or our understanding of another person's perspective. We often engage in these talks because we feel passionately about an issue, and we want to convince others that our point has value. We may advocate a position because we strongly believe that society urgently needs to adopt our point of view. When this happens, we should first remind ourselves that such persuasion is unlikely to occur in a single setting—changing a person's political views typically involves a long process with multiple conversations, multiple forms of evidence, and a sufficient degree of patience from both parties. Additionally, it bears noting that political persuasion is rarely successful if we advocate as if we are speaking to a mirror. In other words, the reasons why we believe something may not, and probably will not, be sufficient to persuade someone who currently disagrees with our position. Understanding a person's core political ideology or philosophy can be helpful here. According to Willer (2016), if you want to move conservatives on issues like same-sex marriage or national health insurance, it helps to tie these liberal political issues to conservative values like patriotism and moral purity. And we studied it the other way, too. If you want to move liberals to the right on conservative policy issues like military spending and making English the official language of the United States, you're going to be more persuasive if you tie those conservative policy issues to liberal moral values like equality and fairness. (Willer, 2016). In other words, we should consider how others view the world, perhaps even trying to see the world through their eyes, and then we can determine a persuasive course of action.

19. Understand argument. By "argument," I do not mean squabbling, bickering, or fighting. I mean the purposeful construction of a position that is supported with evidence and reasoning. I will discuss this more later. But, for now, a climate where argument is accepted, understood, and critiqued is needed for civil discussions about democratic politics. We must teach and learn the skills of proper argument in order to participate in fruitful and meaningful dialogue. As Susan Herbst (2010) suggests, we need to create a *"culture of argument* and debate; through nuts-and-bolts techniques well known to many educators" (emphasis in original, p. 126).

20. The big picture. Ultimately, we need to ask ourselves, what kind of a world do we want to live in, and how can we produce it? Too often our political discussions become side-tracked over minute details, random tangential side issues, or squabbles over irrelevant tidbits. By focusing on the forest instead of staring at the trees, we can continually calibrate ourselves in these conversations to keep us balanced and on the right track. Being centered, focused, and reflective not only will improve the quality and civility of our conversations; these practices will also enable us to participate in more meaningful and productive dialogue that is vital for a vibrant and functioning democracy.

For a quick ten-point list of suggestions, we can consider what the group Be Civil Be Heard (BCBH), recommends: (1) be attentive, (2) acknowledge others, (3) be inclusive, (4) listen, (5) respect other views, (6) speak out with courage, (7) act with compassion, (8) give and accept constructive criticism, (9) treat your environment with respect, and (10) be accountable ("Ten Tenets of Civility," n.d., n.p.). I like and appreciate the brevity of this list, and I particularly applaud the added element of "give and accept constructive criticism."

Obviously, not all of these suggestions will be helpful in each instance, and there may be the occasion when none of them will work. Clearly there are discussions that simply should not happen, or they should not continue. While unfortunate, this is a reality. However, my hope is that we can try to minimize those instances as much as possible, primarily by educating ourselves on how to have more civil discussions.

The Political Spectrum (of Ideology)

Additionally, one of the key aims of this book is to challenge our assumptions about political ideology as a whole. Typically, we rely on our friends, family, media, and so on to frame political options and choices for us (Gerber et al., 2013; Schreckhise & Shields, 2003). Instead, we should spend a little bit of time to research what options exist, and then choose for ourselves. For example, political beliefs in the United States are usually described along a "spectrum" or a continuum of some sort (see Figure 5). On one end, we have liberals, the left wing (or just the "left"), or Democrats; on the other end, we have conservatives, the right wing (or just the "right"), or Republicans.

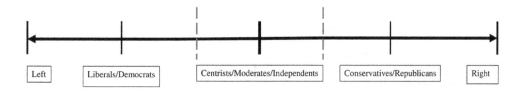

Figure 5: The Political Spectrum.

In this schema, we can see why the terms "left" and "right" are sometimes used to characterize people who believe in liberal and conservative ideologies, respectively. The origin of this description comes from the French Revolution, when supporters of the king in the *Ancien* Régime (their early parliament) sat on his right side, and the supporters of the revolution sat on his left. Once the National Assembly was formed, the ideological demarcations continued; thus, over time, the political affiliation became naturally associated with left and right (Gauchet, 1996). It also shows how conservatives and liberals are aligned, politically, *vis-à-vis* each other. In other words, the two major political ideologies tend to be "polarized" as they reside on either side of the poles of the political spectrum (Galston & Nivola, 2006). The majority of Americans, however, tend to lie somewhere in the middle of the spectrum—known as centrists, or moderates (Abramowitz & Saunders, 2005; Fiorina, 2011). In fact, the centrists comprise approximately 80 to 90% of the citizenry, which begs the question as to why wingnuts are so influential in our society, a question we will turn to later (the space between the dotted lines in Figure 5; Fiorina, 2011). For now, the political spectrum is meant to provide a guide for how we can view where certain political affiliations fit in comparison to others.

Before we move on, we need to question this political spectrum a bit more. Not only are most Americans in the center of the spectrum; they also aren't easily characterized by these political labels. For example, most of our voting-aged youth do not identify themselves neatly as either conservative or liberal (Hollihan, 2009). In fact, most of them feel at home in terms of fiscal issues (such as taxes, federal debt, budget issues, etc.) with the conservatives, and with social issues (such as homosexual rights, abortion, racial tolerance, etc.), they tend to be more liberal (Ellis and Stimson, 2012; see Figure 6). However, we also know that young voters are introduced to partisan ideology at a young age, which calcifies over time, thereby creating a hardened ideological allegiance among the electorate (Galston & Nivola, 2006).

Similarly, there are some Americans who affiliate in the opposite way (Abramowitz & Saunders, 2005; Hollihan, 2009), such that they might be more liberal with fiscal issues (such as the so-called "preferential option for the poor") but more conservative in terms of social issues (particularly abortion and homosexual marriage). An example of this group might be some Roman Catholics or the elderly (see Figure 7).

And, of course, many Americans are what we call "single-issue" voters. In other words, they believe that there is a single issue that over-determines other issues, and with that single issue, they engage in activism, advocacy, and voting behaviors in an effort to advance their agenda regarding that issue (Abramowitz & Fiorina, 2013; Carmines & Stimson, 1981; Hollihan, 2009). For example, some citizens are deeply

Fiscal Issues	Conservative
Social Issues	Liberal

Figure 6: Youth political affiliations.

Fiscal Issues	Liberal
Social Issues	Conservative

Figure 7: Some religious groups' political affiliations.

concerned about the environment, others are concerned about military entanglements, and still others might be concerned with the economy. Whatever the issue, many Americans focus on the issue that means the most to them. Their particular position on the single issue might fall within the traditional "liberal" or "conservative" camp, but these Americans are not necessarily liberal or conservative *in toto*. And, of course, there is a significant percentage of American voters who identify with the two major political parties—the Republicans and the Democrats—for a number of reasons, including that they have always affiliated with the respective party, their friends and family belong to the political party, or the particular political party does an adequate job with its campaigning strategies to sufficiently convince citizens to vote accordingly (Abramowitz & Saunders, 1998, 2005; Beck et al., 2002; Carmines et al., 2012; Carsey & Layman, 2006; Hollihan, 2009; Klofstad et al., 2013). Similarly, one of the reasons individual states are often described as "red" or "blue" states is because Americans tend to populate near like-minded individuals. This concept is known as "sorting," and it be problematic for, say, a conservative, who happens to live in a "blue" state, because it will be challenging for a conservative to overcome the inertia of liberals in that state (Bishop, 2009).

Plan of the Book

Before we can have a close examination of some of the radical rhetoric of key topics in U.S. politics, we need to understand some theories that can help us in our pursuit. In Chapter One, I draw on several perspectives that provide a framework for identifying and interpreting extremist language. For example, I will look at rhetorical fallacies, rhetorical strategies of manipulation and spin, and other discursive techniques used by political pundits. Regardless of the issue, we should be able to use some of these principles to uncover the outlandish and even ridiculous claims made by wingnuts.

In Chapters Two through Six, I will analyze specific political issues where divisive discourse occurs. From immigration to homosexual rights, and from foreign policy to healthcare, we will look at how various political commentators engage in polarizing rhetoric. They will undoubtedly use some of the techniques we explore in Chapter One—fallacies, discursive manipulation, etc.—for their purposes of persuading Americans to adopt their political positions. I will investigate many of these different, contemporary political issues because each will demonstrate specific examples of divisive discourse. Some of the polarizing pundits will be the same, regardless of issue, and some will be unique to a particular issue. Nevertheless, I will offer many instances of their wingnutty comments so that we can see how the extreme political polarities try to frame, influence, and corrupt our civic conversations.

By the very nature of this project, I will be looking into the ways political pundits talk about controversial issues. Of course, I have my own personal political beliefs, but throughout the book, I will carefully attempt to be as neutral as possible. By focusing on the tactics and techniques of discourse rather than the content, my hope is that the conversations generated by this book will be about how political issues are discussed instead of what is being discussed. In order to do this, I will try to include examples from both sides of the political spectrum when analyzing these issues. However, some argue that extremists on the right engage in more invective and vitriol than those on the left (Avlon, 2010). The reasoning, I suppose, is that conservatives are just crazier. Yet I disagree. I believe the preponderance of conservative examples of extremist discourse is a matter of time and technology. When George W. Bush (president 43) was president, many liberals were in the spotlight, as they criticized his persona and policies. Thus, because we currently have a Democrat president, it makes sense that the pundits will most likely be conservative. Plus, in the age of Obama, vituperative rhetoric reverberated and transmitted much more quickly and easily, with social media becoming more dominant in how we obtain our news. So, while there probably is more extremist discourse (in terms of volume and degree) from the right at the moment, the pendulum might swing the other direction now that a Republican president has been elected.

CONCLUSION

According to Somin (2004), the "American electorate does not have adequate knowledge for voters to control public policy," and "Democracy demands an informed electorate" (p. 1). This is a troubling thought, and while Somin's comment is a bit dated, not much has changed since 2004. Moreover, our political predicament of ignorance and apathy is exacerbated by the dominant radical rhetoric of wingnuts, who "see politics as ideological bloodsport, an all-or-nothing struggle for the nation's soul. They find purpose by dividing America into 'us against them,'" which is "good for business. ... But it can be murder on a democracy" (Avlon, 2010, p. 2). This book is an attempt at changing this frustrating situation. As such, I hope you will find this book useful in many ways. For the political novice, this book should provide a baseline of information to enhance your ability to participate in political conversations. For readers already inclined or predisposed to polarizing ideologies, hopefully this book will help you critically question your beliefs. At the end of the day, you may still believe what you currently believe, but perhaps you will gain skills to defend your beliefs in a way that respects and appreciates other political perspectives so that we can have meaningful and productive conversations about our democracy. For readers who find themselves somewhere in the middle of the political spectrum, this book should offer a panoply of ideas on how to avoid falling into the rhetorical traps of extremists. Ultimately, my hope is that this book enhances our democratic skills, reinvigorates our participatory potential in politics, and provides ideas on how we can have civil discussions about political issues. The purpose, in short, is to try to make as many of us as possible "politically enlightened." Walter

Parker (2003) discusses this important goal of "political enlightenment" because "it is aimed at the realization of democratic ideals. Unenlightened action undermines them" (p. 34). No one enjoys being yelled at, cursed at, or called names that serve only to distract us from the real issues. Again, hopefully this book will help—at least a little bit—to curb this tendency in our political conversations.

IMAGE CREDITS

CHAPTER ONE

Theoretical Foundations

In this chapter, I will explore various perspectives that can help us recognize divisive discourse as well as aid in our interpretations of extremist rhetoric. In other words, I will examine and describe rhetorical *theories* that will benefit us in our analysis of polarizing talk. Theories are guiding perspectives that permit us to see the world in a specific way. In essence, they bring order to the chaos of our world, such that if our surroundings or circumstances are confusing or complicated, theories can aid our efforts at making sense of it all. As such, theories function like colored sunglasses. If we wear yellow glasses, we will see the world with a yellow tint; if we wear green glasses, the world will appear green, and so on. The color of the glasses, like a theory, shapes the way we see the area around us. Another analogy often used to explicate theories is a toolbox. Each theory is like a specific tool in the toolbox. Thus, if we have a particular problem, we will choose the best tool to address that problem. For our purposes, the goal, of course, is when we choose a particular theory, we want it to help us make sense of language in insightful ways.

RHETORIC

Since we are concerned with rhetoric, we need to immerse ourselves into some productive rhetorical tools, or theories. But first, I should discuss what I mean by some important terms, such as rhetoric, discourse, signification, and argument. Aristotle

(1926) defined rhetoric as "the faculty of discovering the possible means of persuasion in reference to any subject whatever" (p. 1355). While other various definitions have appeared throughout the ages, Aristotle's conception of rhetoric still applies today. Notably, almost everyone agrees that rhetoric involves persuasion. But persuasion can be viewed artistically, with an emphasis on aesthetics and style when appealing to an audience, or persuasion can be considered a set of skills, where the rhetor employs specific, even formulaic principles when addressing audiences. Whether seen as an art (Aristotle, 1926) or a skill (Cicero, 1949), the persuasive function of rhetoric suggests that language is used to compel or convince others of a belief, attitude, value, or behavior.

Moreover, Aristotle's definition provides us another very important component to rhetoric: the "possible *means*" of persuasion. This signifies that rhetoric involves the method or procedure of persuasive communication. Aristotle posited that there were four essential ways of engaging in—or the means of—persuasion: *ethos, pathos, logos,* and identification. Also known as "rhetorical proofs," these four components can be used separately, but are more effective collectively, by a rhetor aiming for adherence from his or her audience. *Ethos,* or credibility, implies that the expertise, reputation, or goodwill of a rhetor can be persuasive. For example, we frequently trust expert testimony in judicial proceedings because the witness is an authority figure in the area under investigation. The second proof, *pathos,* is an appeal to emotion. *Pathos* appeals rely on fear, excitement, sorrow, sympathy, etc. to convince an audience to embrace the rhetor's message. In a somewhat antithetical manner, *logos* appeals rely on reasoning and evidence to persuade others. Finally, identification (see Burke, 1969) utilizes methods of connecting with an audience by means of locating common ground or establishing resonance with the audience so that it and the rhetor have a sense of camaraderie and rapport. Understanding Aristotle's definition of rhetoric not only helps us comprehend the essence of rhetoric, but it also provides a foundation for the different ways we can examine the "toxic talk" (Press, 2010) of political radicals.

Aristotle's description of rhetorical proofs enables us to see what constitutes effective persuasive discourse. In other words, a persuasive message that lacks a rhetorical proof is all but guaranteed to fail. However, *ethos, pathos, logos,* and identification only go so far in characterizing the way rhetoric functions in political communication. To be sure, they are the necessary ingredients to support (i.e., forms of "proof") an effective rhetorical message. Yet there are two other structural components of which we must be aware. The general approach to persuasion—the manner by which we attempt to reach a broad-based goal—is considered a "rhetorical strategy" (Oswald, 2004). In contrast, "rhetorical tactics" are the specific tropes, techniques, and choices that are "governed by those strategies" for the purpose of constructing a single message or group of messages (Bowers et al., 2010, p. 21). According to de Certeau, a rhetorical tactic "operates in isolated actions, blow by blow," such that it "takes advantage of 'opportunities' and depends on them" by accepting "chance offerings of the moment" (de Certeau, 1988, p. 36–7). While de Certeau emphasizes the situational and even impromptu nature of tactics, I will consider tactics that are tied to purpose-driven strategies but are nevertheless still "isolated actions" that often are deployed in a "blow by blow" fashion in the process of polarizing argument. Since I will be investigating particular statements and passages from radical rhetors, I will be most concerned with the types of rhetorical **tactics** employed in polarizing discourse. The overarching rhetorical **strategy** will almost always be the "solidification" or "polarization" of an ideological perspective to an audience (Bowers et al., 2010, p. 22). Hence, focusing on tactics will best suit our needs for this book.

DISCOURSE

Related to rhetoric is the concept "discourse." Discourse is the body or field of related statements or utterances that belong to the same genre or category. Foucault (1982) referred to discourses as *"epistemes,"* or bodies of knowledge. For example, statements concerning politics could be considered part of a political discourse, arguments about religion would comprise a religious discourse, etc. This is why "rhetoric" is often used synonymously with "discourse," because discourses are constituted by rhetorical utterances. Every *episteme* involves power, either by attempting to compel people to adhere to its concept or because it is structured and/or sustained by forces of power. The *episteme* of healthcare, for instance, might include arguments trying to persuade individuals that socialized medicine is an ideal program, or the *episteme* may be supported by—and therefore benefit—the insurance industry. In either case, the healthcare discourse would be premised on notions of power. As such, the discourse relies on rhetoric for its existence (ontology) as well as advancing knowledge (epistemology).

SIGNIFICATION

Of course, both rhetoric and discourse only exist and function so long as meaning exists. People must agree on the meaning of symbols (i.e., verbal and non-verbal means of communicating) in order to have a productive method of communication. Ascribing meaning to a symbolic word or concept is called "signification." Signification is a process used to establish understanding for the items we use to communicate (Barthes, 1987). For example, the word "democracy" probably means something specific to Americans—guaranteed freedoms and *rights*, the separation of powers, a tradition of balancing majoritarian with counter-majoritarian interests, and so on. However, in some authoritarian societies, such as the former Soviet Union, "democracy" was used to describe their political culture as they sought to provide *equality* among their citizenry, especially through their workers' councils (Molyneux, 2003). Thus, a single word—democracy—can have a vastly different meaning depending on how a group of people agree on what the word or concept suggests to them. Signification, then, is a very important process for us to remember as we examine the types of polarizing rhetoric that occur between political extremists.

ARGUMENT

Another important theoretical concept for our purposes is "argument." Most people think they know what an argument is, typically a verbal altercation of some sort. However, an argument is simply a statement of justification, support, or proof. Of course, arguments can be deployed in heated verbal exchanges, but they are also obviously utilized in civil, rational discussions. Borrowing from Toulmin (2003), we can say that an argument is a structured way to support an opinion or a position. Toulmin calls the position we hold a "claim." Each claim is justified, supported, or proven by the sum of reasoning (known as "warrants") and evidence (known as "data" or "grounds"). This can be visualized in Figure 1.1. Toulmin adds additional components for more complicated arguments, such as "backing" (reinforced support for warrants), "qualifier" (hedges absolute or universal claims to the particular circumstance at hand), and "rebuttals" (preemptory statements against anticipated counter-arguments), which we can see in Figure 1.2.

Aristotle (1926) can also help us understand the nature of "argument." Aristotle introduces us to the argument form known as a "syllogism," which is an argument consisting of two premises and one conclusion. The premises combine to produce the conclusion, as in Figure 1.3. This is similar to Toulmin's argumentative structure if we simply replace the words in the model, such that the conclusion could be seen as a

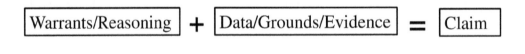

[Source: Toulmin, Stephen E. (2003).]

Figure 1.1: Basic Toulmin Model.

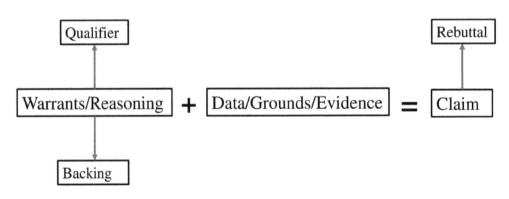

[Source: Toulmin, Stephen E. (2003).]

Figure 1.2: Extended Toulmin Model.

claim, premise one could be data, and premise two could be warrants. In any case, the Aristotelian syllogism is important for us to consider because while Aristotle's formula lays the groundwork for formal logic, we can see syllogisms in everyday, informal argumentation. For example, if we say that democracy protects individual rights (premise one) and democracy is part of the United States political system (premise two), then American democracy is worth protecting (conclusion).

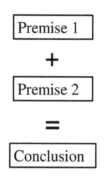

Figure 1.3: Aristotelian Syllogism.

If we remove a premise—say, premise two in this example—the syllogism still makes sense. The argument would look like this: democracy protects individual rights, therefore American democracy is worth protecting. Obviously, if a rhetor were to say this syllogism, the audience could infer that America is a democracy; indeed, it is the only way the argument would make sense at all. In other instances, we could bypass the first premise or even the conclusion, allowing the audience to participate in the argument process by supplying the missing component. Aristotle calls this version of a syllogism—a truncated syllogism—an "enthymeme." To be sure, most of us do not engage in the formulaic presentation of a syllogism, but we do engage in enthymematic argumentation all of the time. As we will see later in the book, political extremists use enthymemes quite frequently, either because their argument rests on a number of assumptions (or missing premises) or because their argument depends on already commonly shared beliefs that their audience can provide.

FALLACIES

Not only do wingnuts use enthymemes frequently, they also deploy fallacies with some regularity. "Fallacies" are flawed reasonings, coming from the Latin *fallax* and *fallere*, meaning "deceptive" and "to deceive," respectively (Paul & Elder, 2004). Being able to recognize fallacies is vital for us to be proficient critical thinkers, as well as to identify some of the rhetorical strategies used by polarizing political blowhards who use fallacies to "camouflage" deceptive reasoning (Paul & Elder, 2004, p. 7). It is important to note that not all fallacies are problematic, as some are very useful in persuading audiences as part of worthwhile and genuine arguments. Hence, not all fallacies contribute to polarization, but many often do, as they can amplify the differences between people's perspectives. However, fallacies can also be employed to deceive audiences by misdirecting their attention.

There are a large number of fallacies, far too many to cover for our purposes, but Paul and Elder list forty-four prominent fallacies (2004, p. 9). Even with this focused attention, we need to narrow the list more for it to be theoretically meaningful in our analysis of divisive discourse. Thus, the most common fallacies used by wingnuts are:

- Faulty generalizations
- Slippery slope fallacy
- Appeals to authority
- Appeals to tradition
- False dilemma/dichotomy (including the "us vs. them" mentality)
- Vilifying the opposition
- Oversimplifying the issue
- Constructing red herrings

- Fallacies of causation
- Ad hominem attacks
- Appeals to fear or pity
- Appeals to righteousness
- Straw person arguments
- Ignoring the evidence
- Use of vague or ambiguous language
- Bandwagon fallacy

Faulty generalizations include representations that are based on too few examples, unrepresentative examples, or glittering generalizations of the rhetor's proposal or position (Paul & Elder, 2004, p. 11). For instance, Glenn Beck (2010a) is fond of criticizing universal healthcare because England's healthcare system is replete with problems. Beck's generalization is both based on too few examples (he only discusses England's system), and it is unrepresentative (other countries' universal healthcare systems are arguably much stronger than England's). When Beck combines this fallacy with overstating the benefits of the current American healthcare system, he also engages in a glittering generalization of the U.S. system by ignoring its worrisome issues. Incidentally, a glittering generalization like Beck's is also the fallacy of "ignoring the evidence," which illustrates how some forms of reasoning can fit multiple types of fallacies.

There are many fallacies of causation, but two significant ones are the *post hoc ergo propter hoc* (i.e., *post hoc*) fallacy and the fallacy of signs. The *post hoc* fallacy means "after this, therefore because of this," and it suggests that just because B happens immediately after A that somehow A *caused* B. However, this is a temporal fallacy because A and B may be unrelated (Fearnside & Holther, 1959). An example might be when someone claims that more gun control laws reduce violent crime by citing historical examples. In those instances when violent crime did lessen, it does not necessarily mean the reduction was triggered by stricter gun laws (incidentally, both the pro-gun control advocates and the anti-gun control advocates use *post hoc* rationales for their position on this issue). This is fallacious since other alternate causes or intervening variables may have caused the drop in crime. The argument from sign (also known as the "fallacy from sign") is more commonly known as "where there's smoke, there's fire." Ideologues typically employ this fallacy to suggest that the opposition's position is absurd (which would also be a *reductio ad absurdum* fallacy). A political pundit could, for example, argue that conservatives oppose the Fair Minimum Wage Act of 2013 because it restricts businesses, which means that conservatives are obviously very dogmatic in their allegiance to the free market, even to the point of being sexist or violating people's rights. However, conservatives could claim that their opposition to the law is not based on a pro-business stance, but rather the belief that duplicate laws are unnecessary, especially since in this case, the U.S. already forbids wage disparity.

The slippery slope fallacy—which sometimes can also be a *reductio ad absurdum* fallacy—hyperbolizes the negative consequences of a particular position. When some conservatives argue that legalizing gay marriage will result in people marrying their dogs, this is clearly a slippery slope since the chance of that happening is virtually zero (Lunsford & Ruszkiewicz, 2007). An *ad hominem* fallacy is known as "attacking the person" fallacy, and it is committed when a wingnut engages in name-calling or beats on the opposition's persona rather than addressing the issues at hand. We will see many instances of this fallacy later in the book.

Appealing to authority can be a fallacy, although not always, especially when the authority is misplaced or when it ignores counter evidence that may be more specific, more abundant, or more authoritative (Fearnside & Holther, 1959). When a forensics expert testifies in court, it is an appeal to authority, and it may be perfectly justified. However, if the defense asks a renowned physicist about criminal forensics, the physicist is an expert, but in the wrong field. Appeals to authority are also problematic when counter evidence clearly outweighs the authority's opinion. The dozen or so scientists who argue that climate change is not anthropogenic—while experts in some situations—are clearly outweighed by the thousands of climatologists and meteorologists from all over the world who disagree (Fanelli, 2014). Similarly, appeals to fear or pity can also be legitimate (after all, the Aristotelian notion of *pathos* is based on emotive appeals), but when they are taken to the extreme or premised on faulty reasons or run against more accurate and genuine warrants, then they are fallacious (Lunsford & Ruszkiewicz, 2007). Misrepresentations or tugs at gut-level and knee-jerk emotions mean that these types of arguments can be easily manipulated by skillful political rhetors.

Appeals to tradition are often used by pundits from both poles of the political spectrum. Conservatives are known for appealing to the Founding Fathers, whereas liberals can be expected to reference historical struggles for civil rights. By themselves, these arguments are not necessarily troublesome, but when they are exaggerated or sloppily applied to a current issue, they can easily be deceptive (Fearnside & Holther, 1959). Similarly, appeals to righteousness play to the audience's proclivity for desiring to do what is right, ethical, or moral. The assumption here is that neither the rhetor nor the audience can be wrong or culpable for a situation, although the opposition clearly can be blamed. Political hucksters use these fallacies incessantly.

In a related way, extremists often create a false dilemma or a false dichotomy. This usually occurs by means of establishing a forced choice (as if the audience can only choose between the two options offered by the rhetor). This fallacy is tantamount to stacking the deck in poker. By framing a situation in this false way, the pundit can manipulate the audience down the path that the wingnut desires in an effort to "seduce those who don't know much about a subject" (Lunsford & Ruszkiewicz, 2007, p. 494). President Bush's (2001) famous statement of "either you are with us or you are with the terrorists" when describing the War on Terror is a good example of this false dichotomy. Political spinsters typically characterize their position in contradistinction to opposing viewpoints. This "us vs. them" mentality is fallacious since if the rhetor's perspective is right or moral, then the opposition must be wrong or immoral. The false dilemma fallacy is sometimes used in conjunction with the straw person fallacy. Also known as simply the "straw" fallacy, the straw person argument takes its name from the construction of straw figures—like scarecrows—as a form of misdirection, requiring others to tear down the straw argument before proceeding to more relevant issues. According to Paul and Elder (2004), a straw fallacy "is literally not real, though it may look like it is," because the argument "is a false or misleading representation of someone's reasoning" (p. 27).

Similar to the "us vs. them" argument, the fallacy of vilifying one's opponent is frequently an effective, albeit deceptively manipulative, maneuver. This could also sometimes be considered an *ad hominem* attack, or it could be described as "name-calling." By (mis)characterizing the opposition by using absolute negative words, the rhetor constructs them as villains. Language such as "evil," "Hitler," "Nazi," or "Fascist" often accompany this fallacy. There is, however, a subtle and important distinction between *ad hominem* attacks and name-calling, but it may be considered more of a difference in degree. Name-calling is simply what it sounds like—it labels a person something, and the label is usually negative. An *ad hominem* attack may employ name-calling during its use, but an *ad hominem* is an actual attack against the person (as opposed to addressing the issue or content of an argument). Thus, an *ad hominem* attempts to deface, undermine, or otherwise destroy the opposition through verbal warfare, whereas name-calling may not reach such gravity.

Idealogues, by definition, are dogmatic in their ideological beliefs. As I have noted, they are extremists. As such, they refuse to listen to other perspectives, quite literally to a fault. "In order to avoid considering evidence that might cause them to change their position, manipulators often ignore evidence" so that they "avoid having to consider it in their own minds, because it threatens their belief system of vested interests" (Paul & Elder, 2004, p. 30). The previous example about climate change exemplifies this type of argument. Many conservatives simply ignore the overwhelming consensus of evidence that stipulates otherwise. In a related way, many skilled rhetors oversimplify issues to their advantage. Both conservatives and liberals tend to oversimplify any issue dealing with the economy, partly because economic arguments can be complex and confusing and in part because by oversimplifying the situation, radicals can portray events to support their position. In a verbal sleight-of-hand, political blowhards also utilize vague or ambiguous language when simplifying convoluted issues. Vague descriptions allow rhetors to backpedal later if they are placed in a corner, or the ambiguous language helps rhetors avoid specific elements that could jeopardize their overarching position (Fearnside & Holther, 1959).

Also known as a *non-sequitur* (that which does not follow), red herring fallacies provide wingnuts the opportunity to "divert from the issue by focusing on what is irrelevant (but emotionally loaded)" (Paul & Elder, 2004, p. 37). When extremists cannot defeat counter-arguments, they occasionally deflect the discussion to an emotionally charged issue instead. When gun control advocates are unable to overcome the position of Second Amendment supporters, they may point to isolated examples of when poor, innocent children have died as a result of gun discharges.

Finally, if an issue enjoys popular support or is based on commonly held assumptions, polarizing pundits may employ the bandwagon fallacy. This fallacy appeals to an audience by referring to the irrelevant happenstance that many people, or even a majority, support the issue. Children who claim to their parents that "everyone is doing it, so it must be okay" are guilty of the bandwagon fallacy. Glenn Beck (2010a) argues that liberals who support subprime mortgages so that low-income families can purchase a home engage in the bandwagon fallacy; after all, if everyone is buying a home, it must be a legitimate practice in which everyone should be able to partake. In this way, the bandwagon fallacy urges "people to follow the same path everyone else is taking" (Lunsford & Ruszkiewicz, 2007, p. 499). As such, this argument type is prone to manipulation by media and politicians who select what they want Americans to consider.

The list of potential fallacies could go on and on. However, I have chosen to delineate the most commonly used fallacies by the divisive political crackpots. As I explore the specific issues of polarizing rhetoric throughout this book, we should be able to identify these fallacies relatively easily. In almost every partisan comment or position statement, at least one fallacy is apparent. As I mentioned earlier, some remarks may be considered as more than one fallacy, and some fallacies overlap or are mutually reinforcing with one another. When these occur, we should explore the relationship between fallacies or be able to suggest that one fallacy is more important in the particular context than other fallacies.

RHETORICAL SPIN

Fallacies, as Paul and Elder (2004) argue, are used by skillful manipulators to spin issues to their ideological positions. But other types of rhetorical spin also exist. In their acclaimed book *Un-spun*, Jackson and Jamieson (2007) write about the various ways communicators can manipulate language to hoodwink audiences. They examine various discourses, ranging from public relations campaigns, politicians' messages, and the way stores try to sell products. From their analysis, Jackson and Jamieson delineate the following overarching methods of rhetorical "spin":

- If It's Scary, Be Wary—Appeals to fear or danger can cloud or judgment (p. 26)
- A Story That's Too Good—When something appears to be too good, we should investigate further because they typically are too good to be true (p. 30)
- The Dangling Comparative—"A dangling comparative occurs when any term meant to compare two things—a word such as 'higher,' 'better,' 'faster,' 'more'—is left dangling without stating what's being compared" (p. 32)
- The Superlatives Swindle—Superlative words, such as "greatest" or "biggest" or "smallest" can serve as warning signs that the underlying claim is misleading (p. 33)
- The "Pay You Tuesday" Con—As a typical political tactic, some deceivers may try convince us of a program without referring to future costs, or by presuming future payments will be made by a different administration (p. 36)

- The Blame Game—This is a very common technique where someone blames another while attempting to misdirect attention away from a weakness or problem
  (p. 37)
- Glittering Generalities—This occurs when very attractive words are used to
  describe a project or proposal; they are used generally to distract us from the
  troubled substance underneath the flashy language (p. 39)
- Misnomers—"Language does our thinking for us" because "puffery is so common
  that much of the time we aren't fooled and can even make fun of it" (p. 44–45).
  Wingnuts use bloated and arbitrary language, like the so-called "death tax," in
  order to frame an issue. "A simple rule of persuasion holds, 'Frame the issue, claim
  the issue'" (p. 47). Labels such as "pro-life" or "pro-choice" in the abortion debate
  are excellent examples of this tactic.

Many of these techniques are used by polarizing political rhetors. By referring to these
manipulative methods as "spin," Jackson and Jamieson (2007) explain how "spinners
mislead by means that range from subtle omissions to outright lies. Spin paints a false
picture of reality by bending facts, mischaracterizing the words of others, ignoring or
denying crucial evidence, or just 'spinning a yarn'—by making things up" (Jackson &
Jamieson, 2007, p. vii). These skills of spin will undoubtedly help us when we examine
the divisive discourse of political pundits.

Additionally, political extremists utilize rhetorical strategies or linguistic efforts to
achieve certain goals (Bowers et al., 2010). As I discussed earlier, rhetors use specific
rhetorical "tactics" to accomplish their particular goals because they are the specific
persuasive techniques used to maximize the chances for success in convincing an audience (Del Gandio, 2008, p. 65). According to Jason Del Gandio (2008, p. 66), there are
a number of rhetorical tactics used in radical political discourse:

- Tell emotional stories
- Juxtapose shocking images
- Use official government reports
- Evoke sense of community and togetherness
- Link radical ideas to traditionally accepted norms and principles
- Repetition of message
- Foster audience's desires, imaginations, and dreams

- Use scientific facts or statistics
- Use thought-provoking analogies and metaphors
- Emphasize hypocrisy, bias, and inconsistencies
- Embrace collective identities, like race, religion, class, and gender
- Provide long lists of objectionable material from the opposition
- Use passion and energy with sense of urgency
- Create a vision of a better world

- Naming the issue
- Frame the issue

- Labeling and characterizing the opposition
- Use of propaganda techniques

This is clearly not all of the possible rhetorical tactics, but this list does offer us perspective on the most important tactics used by idealogues. Sobieraj and Berry (2011) describe components that constitute what they call "outrage discourse," which they define as:

> political discourse involving efforts to provoke visceral responses (e.g., anger, righteousness, fear, moral indignation) from the audience through the use of overgeneralizations, sensationalism, misleading or patently inaccurate information, ad hominem attacks, and partial truths about opponents, who may be individuals, organizations, or entire communities of interest (e.g., progressives or conservatives) or circumstance (e.g., immigrants). Outrage sidesteps the messy nuances of complex political issues in favor of melodrama, misrepresentative exaggeration, mockery, and improbable forecasts of impending doom. Outrage talk is not so much discussion as it is verbal competition, political theater with a scorecard. (p. 20)

And Conway, Grabe, and Grieves (2007) identify the following as rhetorical tactics:

- Name-calling—"gives a person or idea a bad label to make the audience reject them without examining the evidence. This is, by definition, a negative device. The terms conservative, liberal, left, right, progressive, traditional, or centrist were treated as name calling" (p. 203)
- Glittering generality—"captured the use of virtue words that make the audience accept an idea or person without examining the evidence" (p. 203)
- Transfer—"involves using prestige or authority of one idea or person and transferring that to another to make it acceptable or add stature to it" (p. 203)
- Plain folks—"occurs when the host presented himself, another person, an institution, or idea as one of the people" (p. 203)
- Bandwagon—"suggests that because everybody approves or disapproves of an idea or person, the audience should hold the same opinion" (p. 203)
- Testimonial—"involves a respected (or disrespected) person endorsing or rejecting an idea or person" (p. 204)
- Card Stacking—"constitutes the selective use of facts, half-truths, and or lies to convince the audience to accept or reject an idea or person" (p. 204)
- Fear appeals—"a prominent focus on danger, a threat to life, social order or the American way of life" (p. 204)

Different versions of rhetorical tactics also exist. The "vision for a better world" tactic and the "passion and energy with a sense of urgency" approach, when combined, can yield what Lemuel (2010) claims is a form of "prophetic voice" (p. 46). In other words, the ideologue can establish a messianic persona who predicts apocalyptic doom if we travel the road of the opposition versus the portrayal of a form of "promised land" so long as the audience embraces the rhetor's vision. These tactics can be used in various ways and occasionally are deployed simultaneously with overlapping functions. For example, if a huckster articulates a "vision of a better world," not only is he providing a positive image of the ultimate conclusion of his position, but he also may be denigrating the alternative advanced by his opposition, thereby "labeling and characterizing the opposition." Rhetorical tactics, then, can be slippery and savvy at the same time.

Some other rhetorical tactics of spin include framing an "us vs. them" dichotomy, oversimplifying the issues, divide and conquer, and muddying the waters. The "us vs. them" dichotomy is also a fallacy, which I described above. However, it is a very common rhetorical vision statement by polarizing pundits. By characterizing one's position as morally just, on the side of truth, and yielding the maximum benefits, it automatically juxtaposes the ideological position in contrast with the polar opposite ideology. And, obviously, most audiences will want to side with the ideology that is moral, truthful, and beneficial. Extremist rhetors are also known for oversimplifying the issues. In part, oversimplification is a product of our instant-gratification, Twitter and ticker-tape-headline generation. But spinsters utilize this quick, shallow-level thinking to their advantage. Political and economic issues are typically complex problems with multiple causes and various implications. Radical rhetors, however, typically distill these issues to a singular cause (usually the opposing ideology) and an equally oversimplified ideology (that is usually a broad, sweeping generalization of the rhetor's ideology). Additionally, pundits can establish and maintain control as well as minimize threats from others by incorporating a "divide and conquer" tactic. Amy Gutmann (2007) explains this technique when she describes demagogy: "The opposite of a sound democratic argument is demagogy: manipulation and deception in order to divide and conquer the democratic populace. Extremist rhetoric is a common tactic of demagogy: it divides in order to conquer" (p. 72). Hence, by pitting one group against another, which weakens both, the extremist rhetor can secure a position of strength. Finally, muddying the waters is often used as a tactic that is intended to deceive and engage in misdirection. Usually, this tactic is used to (mis)represent an opposing ideology's position in an overly complicated, confusing, and incoherent manner. In this way, citizens may fail to understand, and consequently will fail to embrace, the other polarity, instead following the rhetor's ideological position (which will probably be oversimplified).

CONCLUSION

All in all, I have discussed various theoretical perspectives to help us identify and understand the rhetoric of extremists. By knowing about arguments, fallacies, strategies vs. tactics, and methods of rhetorical spin, we can recognize and examine divisive discourse in a meaningful and productive way.

I want to end this chapter by again referencing Del Gandio (2008), who illustrates the dynamic importance of rhetoric when thinking about our political culture. As such, he lists four important maxims for rhetorical activism:

- Change the rhetoric and you change the communication.
- Change the communication and you change the experience.
- Change the experience and you change a person's orientation to the world.
- Change that orientation and you create conditions for profound social change. (p. xiv)

These maxims demonstrate the process of how the use of rhetoric can change the way we think about the world and contemporary social issues. In this way, these maxims, as well as this chapter's exploration of theoretical perspectives, allow us to review specific issues for which wingnuts engage in divisive discourse.

IMAGE CREDITS

- Fig. 1.1: Copyright in the Public Domain.
- Fig. 1.2: Copyright in the Public Domain.
- Fig. 1.3: Copyright in the Public Domain.

CHAPTER TWO

Galvanizing Over Guns:
Second Amendment Discourse

So far, I have noted the overall context of divisive discourse in contemporary American politics. We now know that extremist political pundits engage in rhetoric that polarizes political conversations. In order to make some sense of this polarizing discourse, I described the concepts of rhetoric and discourse, signification, and argument. In so doing, I detailed how the use of fallacies and rhetorical tactics can be used to promote ideological perspectives. In this chapter and subsequent chapters, I will explore specific issues discussed by polarizing pundits where they use the rhetorical tactics mentioned in Chapter One. In other words, in each chapter, I will describe a controversial political issue, report on some of the comments made by wingnuts, and apply some of the theoretical items from Chapter One. By looking at the divisive discourse in this way, I intend to demonstrate the potency of polarizing rhetoric in our current political discussions.

There is perhaps no other contemporary issue that reveals the frequency and magnitude of divisive discourse than gun control. As Charles Krauthammer, the conservative commentator, explains, "Every mass shooting has three elements: the killer, the weapon and the cultural climate. As soon as the shooting stops, partisans immediately pick their preferred root cause with corresponding pet panacea. Names are hurled, scapegoats paraded, prejudices vented. The argument goes nowhere" (Krauthammer, 2013, p. 160). Gun rights defender, Dana Loesch, calls liberals who want more regulations "gun grabbers" who use mass shootings as an "opportunity" to "exploit people" (2014, p. 20). At the same time, however, gun violence is a serious problem in America. Indeed,

"In 2010, there were more than 31,000 firearm deaths in the United States: 62% were suicides, 36% were homicides, and 2% were unintentional. Almost as many Americans die from gunfire as die from motor vehicle crashes (almost 34,000 in 2010)" (Miller et al., 2013). The nature of the debate, of course, is to what degree should individuals have the right to purchase, possess, and use guns compared to the degree to which the government should regulate gun ownership. The foundation of this debate rests on the meaning of the Second Amendment of the Constitution, enacted in 1791, which states, "A well regulated Militia, being necessary to the security of a free State, the right of the people to keep and bear Arms, shall not be infringed." Thus, for over 220 years, Americans have discussed the legality of gun ownership in various contexts and the possible necessity of some degree of governmental regulation. In this chapter, we will describe the rhetorical context of gun politics, explore some of the key arguments, examine the provocative rhetoric used, and discuss the argumentative tactics employed by pundits on both sides of this debate.

THE CONTEXT OF GUN POLITICS

At various points in U.S. history, the nature of gun ownership became more acute than usual. Fears of unrest, notable examples from abroad concerning armed citizens, mass shootings, gun accidents, and so on have all spurred timely discussions about gun ownership and control. To help us understand how debate emerges at some points rather than others, we can use the concept of Bitzer's "rhetorical situation" (1968).

According to Bitzer, all discourse is framed by a situation, which he defined as a "complex of persons, events, objects, and relations presenting an actual or potential exigence which can be completely or partially removed if discourse, introduced into the situation, can so constrain human decision or action as to bring about the significant modification of the exigence" (p. 3). Thus, for Bitzer, an "exigence" would be the rhetorical problem (in this case, heated debate about guns), the "audience" consists of people who can serve as agents of change, and "constraints" are any obstacles that might limit decision or action. In other words, when a rhetor (i.e., a speaker or politician or pundit) is confronted with a pressing social issue (exigence), he or she typically tries to overcome any discursive obstacles (constraints) in order to persuade people who can make a difference (audience).

Since Bitzer said all rhetoric involves situations, how can we make sense of when an exigence is important enough to stimulate controversy? In other words, Americans have wrestled with the issue of guns for over 200 years, but only at certain points in history has the political rhetoric about guns become divisive. What makes those particular moments important?

Another element to consider when applying the concept of a "rhetorical situation" is the ancient Greek notion of *kairos*. *Kairos* can simply mean "time," but it can also mean a "unique" moment in time—a particular moment that arises when an issue becomes most salient. In other words, *kairos* can concern "that what is said must be said at the right time" (Poulakos, 1983, p. 40–41). Therefore, if something tragic, problematic, or unexpected occurs, a *kairotic* moment may exist. If it does, then we can apply the concepts of exigency, audience, and constraints to understand more clearly how the rhetorical controversy happens as a rhetorical situation.

Clearly, when a shooting tragedy occurs, a *kairotic* moment emerges. Typically, gun control advocates—usually a position held by liberals—use the tragedy (or *kairotic* moment) to initiate rhetorical positions with the aim of increasing gun control. In response, gun advocates—usually a position held by conservatives—view the tragedy and the gun control advocates' response to it as a *kairotic* moment in which to respond and refute the claims made by pro-gun control promoters. Both sides of this debate see an exigence (the tragedy and the response to it), attempt to persuade an audience (the American people, lawmakers, etc.), and try to overcome possible constraints (media coverage, previous credibility concerns, money to fund public activism, etc.).

As I will discuss in the rest of this chapter, several *kairotic* exigencies have occurred in recent American history. The school shootings at Columbine, Virginia Tech University, Northern Illinois University, Sandy Hook, University of California at Santa Barbara, Seattle Pacific University, and Umpqua Community College in Oregon, were all tragedies that sparked widespread media and public attention. Gun control activists spared no time to use these tragedies for the purpose of arguing for stricter gun control laws. At the same time, gun owners and the National Rifle Association (NRA), the well-funded and influential gun lobby, responded with arguments about how, while these episodes were tragic, the existence and use of guns were not the cause of these horrendous acts. As we will see shortly, both sides of the gun debate engage in polarizing discourse that utilizes fallacious and manipulative reasoning. But knowing how these *kairotic* moments triggered salient exigencies will help us to better understand how such polarizing rhetoric transpires.

THE NATURE OF THE GUN DEBATE

In their very passionate article on gun control, Kates et al. (1994) characterize gun discourse as "a struggle between modern enlightenment and, at best, morally obtuse and intellectually benighted atavism. There is no time for arid, academic discussion; the need for gun control is too urgent to require--or allow--equivocation, doubt, debate, or dissent. ... Moreover, there is no point to discussion, detached reflection, or dissent in a struggle between the forces of light and darkness. Evidence or perspectives that might induce skepticism or produce delay are per se invalid inventions of the Neanderthal racist gun lovers" (p. 518–519). In short, the authors provide a gloomy forecast for the possibility of a civil discussion concerning guns in this country. While Kates et al. appear to blame gun advocates for unenlightened dogmatism, the truth is that the issue of guns in America raises the blood pressure of almost everyone involved in the conversation.

Of course, most of the arguments concerning guns rely on certain interpretations of the Second Amendment. The amendment begins with "a well regulated militia."

Gun control activists argue that this means that (a) the amendment presupposes that militias, not individuals, are given gun rights, and (b) whomever is granted gun rights should be "well regulated" (Aborn, 1995). Gun owners quickly retort that the amendment must be read in its total context, which means that the last part of the amendment that states "right of the people ... shall not be infringed" makes it clear that individuals have the right to "keep and bear arms" and that this right is absolute—it shouldn't be infringed (Hattem, 2014). Both sides of the controversy use the historical context of the amendment to support their respective interpretations. Given the Revolutionary War and the fight against the British monarchy's laws imposing firearms restrictions on the colonists, the gun control promoters argue that the Second Amendment was intended to ensure that colonists could retain the ability to confront the redcoats (Watts, 2011). However, gun owners argue that militias at the time were hodgepodge, unorganized groups of men (i.e., individuals) who needed guns to protect America from the tyranny of Britain (Dreier, 2013; Wilmouth, 2008). Over the years, Supreme Court decisions have not helped to resolve this chasm. In *United States v. Miller* (1939), the Court reasoned that the Second Amendment protected gun rights for collective groups, i.e., organized militias that became modern-day National Guard units. Later, Second Amendment jurisprudence was rearticulated by the court in *District of Columbia v. Heller* (2008), which stipulated that individuals have a recognized, constitutional right to keep and bear arms (Hatt, 2011; Winkler, 2009; Winkler, 2011).

When *kairotic* moments have emerged, typically when a tragedy of some kind occurs, gun control supporters argue that the existence of guns is the common denominator among gun-related incidents. In other words, if guns were not allowed to be purchased or used by average citizens, then the particular tragic event would not have happened. The pro-gun side of the debate vehemently argues that if individuals want to wreak massive damage to other human beings, they will find a way to do so regardless of the existence of guns. This is the proverbial "guns don't kill people, people kill people" argument, although those on the opposite side, like Dennis Henigan (2009) equate this argument to the "cars don't kill people, people do," yet most Americans have no problem whatsoever requiring driver training, compulsory driver's tests, and enforced traffic laws. But, pro-gun advocates opine that trained gun owners can deter or prevent gun tragedies, and they often cite studies that supposedly prove that areas that have more guns also have less crime. In response, gun control promoters cite competing studies that actually conclude the opposite in that they depict more crime in areas that have more guns. The anti-gun folks also argue that guns do not deter violent gun-related crimes since deterrence relies on individuals to be rational and knowledgeable that other citizens are actually armed. Ironically, it is the extremely conservative windbag Charles Krauthammer who clearly makes this argument when he writes, "While law deters the rational, it has far less effect on the psychotic" (Krauthammer, 2013, p. 162). So, perhaps there is a chance for common ground to be reached between the conservatives and liberals on this issue.

The "rationality" position to rebuff the deterrence argument raises another issue—the mental health of individuals. Current law is supposed to prevent individuals with a history of mental illness from buying and owning firearms. However, such individuals

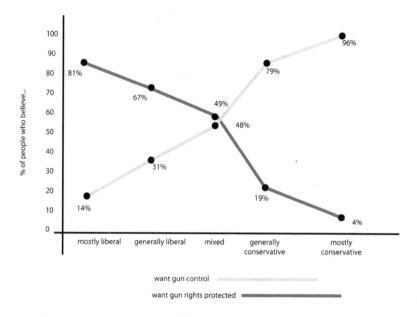

Figure 2.1: Conservatives Don't Want Limits on Gun Ownership.

invariably find ways of obtaining guns. Many people suggest that our country needs to address mental health concerns more vigorously, which, in turn, could reduce violent gun-related tragedies. And the pro-gun activists claim that if mentally ill people can obtain weapons when the law prohibits them from doing so, then that speaks to the weakness of prohibition laws in general. Thus, if making guns illegal fails to prevent individuals from obtaining the weapons, then we should protect the rights of law-abiding citizens to have their guns.

In response, gun control advocates claim that prohibition laws need to be strengthened, not dismissed. What is concerning to many is the relative ease in which people, including felons, can purchase guns online and at gun shows (Carroll, 2016; Sherman, 2016). Known as "loopholes," people can circumvent current laws by purchasing firearms at gun shows or online (Giffords & Kelly, 2014). Another way of improving these laws is to require extensive background checks before individuals can purchase weapons. Such background checks, while not a panacea, would substantially improve the safeguards that would check felons and mentally ill people from acquiring guns (Wintemute, 2013). The overwhelming majority of Americans support such background checks because they could help reduce gun-related tragedies while still protecting a law-abiding individual's right to own a gun (Giffords & Kelly, 2014). The pro-gun position retorts by arguing that background checks risk a slippery slope—that each instance of gun control means the government can eventually outlaw all possession of firearms. Gun advocates also argue that regulations like background checks to not stop criminals from obtaining guns, which means that adding more gun control only punishes "law-abiding Americans" (Loesch, 2014, p. 67).

THE DIVISIVE DISCOURSE OF GUNS

Recent *kairotic* moments have stimulated divisive debate between the pro-gun and anti-gun camps. Mass shootings in schools have captured most of our attention, although other tragedies have also occurred, such as the Aurora theatre shooting (Crummy and Steffen, 2012), the 2009 Binghamton shooting at an immigration center (McFadden, 2009), the rampage shooting at Fort Hood in 2009 (Kenber, 2013), the 2011 shooting in Tucson that injured Gabby Giffords (Joslyn and Haider-Markel, 2013; Lacey and Herszenhorn, 2011), the 2012 controversy resulting from the shooting of Trayvon Martin (Kaduce and Davis, 2013), the 2014 Las Vegas shooting of police officers (Pearson et al, 2014), the mall shooting in Washington State in 2016 (Mele, 2016), the Thanksgiving Day, 2016, shooting in Louisville, Kentucky (Sanchez, 2016), the 2016 shooting at an Orlando gay club that was attributed to an ISIS-inspired terrorist (Ellis et al., 2016), and countless other incidents. And, of course, the litany of recent school shootings—Columbine (1999), Virginia Tech (2007), Northern Illinois University (2008), Seattle Pacific University (2014), University of California at Santa Barbara (2014), Reynolds High School in Oregon (2014)—has heated up the Second Amendment debate. By many accounts, the tragic shooting incident at the Sandy Hook Elementary School in Newtown, Connecticut, fostered a nationwide discussion about gun control, background checks, and mental health issues, thereby triggering a moment of *kairos* for extremist rhetoric (Dreier, 2013; Gerney & Parsons, 2013; Omero et al., 2013; Parsons & Johnson, 2014).

In order to make sense of this "culture war," we need to examine the rhetoric from both sides of this debate. This analysis purposefully singles out the dichotomous views on guns, even if the issue itself is more complex (Harcourt, 2004). We are primarily concerned with how guns are discussed in American society, not the constitutional, sociological, or political implications of particular views on the right to bear arms. As such, I will examine four threads common to the vituperative gun debate: (1) safety/killing arguments, (2) rights/tyranny arguments, (3) self-defense/"stand your ground" arguments, and (4) other fallacies. Incidentally, Dennis Henigan (2009) explores many of the common arguments—what he calls "myths"—from gun defenders; and, on the other side of the debate, a key text that address point-by-point the common arguments is John Lott's (2010) book, now in its third edition (See also Lott's other book, 2003). These books are worth a quick read for those interested in this topic.

Since guns have been a part of the American cultural fabric for over 220 years, we will begin with looking at the rhetoric from those who believe we should change this dynamic. As noted by the renowned constitutional scholar Erwin Chemerinsky (2004),

> Both sides of the debate over the Second Amendment have arguments based on the constitution's text, the framer's intent, tradition, and social policy. One side emphasizes the preamble to the Second Amendment, that it is about protecting a well-regulated militia, while the other side stresses the latter

part of the Amendment concerning the right of individuals to keep and bear arms. Each side has a strong argument of what the framers intended. (p. 479)

In other words, the anti-gun perspective wants to reduce, eliminate, or impose more regulations on guns, which would be a stark divergence from our historical legacy. As such, most arguments from this vantage point are premised on the severity of crimes, murders, suicides, and other violent acts that involve guns. Indeed, gun-related tragedies provide the basis for most, if not all, of anti-gun advocates.

Safety/Killing Arguments

First, gun control proponents claim that gun-related incidents, while each are tragic, also manifest into modern-day massacres. For example, many argue that the shooting at Sandy Hook Elementary School was a "massacre" (Rachel, 2013) and an example of the much larger "deadly epidemic of gun violence" (Dreier, 2013, p. 95). Other shootings are characterized as "rampages" that cause "traumatic death" (Diaz, 2013, p. 172), "crisis" (Parsons & Johnson, 2014), "mass killings" (Dreier, 2013, p. 92), and the "impulsive acts of unstable people" (Dizard et al, 1999, p. 13). Nancy Pelosi (D-Rep, California), the House of Representatives minority leader, has even referred to guns as "weapons of war" (Mantel, 2014, np). Gun law advocates use the power of naming to define the debate, meaning that if such incidents are "mass killings," it is much more difficult to respond to the arguments; after all, most rational people do not favor "mass killings." This rhetorical tactic is also known as "loaded language," and by portraying all incidents involving guns in a like manner, this tactic is also a fallacious generality since obviously, not all gun-related events reach the level of "mass killings."

One of the reasons that American shootings are so noteworthy, according to gun control promoters, is that the United States is the only Western, industrialized country with such lax gun laws. As a result, so they argue, the United States has more gun-related violence and shootings. Of course, this "causal" argument is an example of a *post hoc ergo propter hoc* (after this, therefore because of this) fallacy. In other words, just because Y happens immediately after X doesn't mean that X caused Y. Other intervening variables (or causes) may exist. In this case, the United States might have more shootings than other countries because we have worse mental health treatment, or our open society creates more opportunities for gun violence, or even the graphic violence portrayed in video games, television, and the movies fosters such violent shootings. All of these alternate-cause arguments are frequently voiced by pro-gun advocates. However, the gun control crowd retorts by saying that other industrialized countries have similar mental health treatment and open, porous societies, and, of course, all Western nations have the same exposure to violent games and media. Additionally, radical rhetors, like Michael Moore, claim that guns create a cultural climate of violence, which would explain the desire for violent films and video games (Egberto, 2014; Wilshire, 2007, p. 43). Michael Moore, famous for his politically themed documentaries, is a passionate ultra-liberal who speaks his mind concerning conservative views. Moore's answers to the Right's alternate causality arguments also suffer from the *post hoc* and generalization fallacies since the presence of guns does not necessarily cause an overall violent culture, especially when other variables certainly exist.

Additionally, the anti-gun folks claim that the mere existence of guns, or the practically unfettered availability of guns, cultivates more gun-related deaths, whether those incidents are intentional (e.g., mass shootings, suicides, etc.) or unintentional (e.g., accidents, crimes going awry, etc.). This correlation appears to make intuitive sense, for the presence of violent use of guns requires the actual availability of guns to begin with; or, as Diaz (2013) simply opines, "More guns means more shootings" (p. 35). Instead of guns causing violent use, however, which is another *post hoc* fallacy, we could see this claim as a necessary but not sufficient argument. In other words, it is necessary that guns be available for violent use to occur, but the presence of guns alone does not adequately explain gun-related tragedies. Interestingly, though, a recent "mega study" from the University of California, San Francisco, focuses on this argument with laser-like specificity. By combing through a litany of other studies and investigations, the scholars of the study report that unequivocally, people with the "ability to get to a gun are three times as likely to commit suicide and twice as likely to be the victim of a homicide than people without access" (Zadrozny, 2014, np).

The NRA and conservative pro-gun adherents, of course, have a different take on the "guns cause violent use" arguments. First, the NRA calls the recent UCSF mega-study "snake oil research" because the entire study was conducted with a "propaganda" research agenda, which naturally corrupts the way research questions and analysis are conducted (Zadrozny, 2014, np). Gun advocates also reiterate that the guns themselves are not the culprit; rather, evil or mentally ill people who commit the crimes are at fault (Doc Vega, 2013). This obviously is the same argument made above concerning the comparisons of the U.S. to other countries, and, as such, falls prey to the same fallacies. Another important pro-gun argument on this particular issue is an overarching defense of guns. If guns are useful for hunting and self-defense, then gun defenders can proclaim the protection benefits that gun possession bestows. Not only do guns offer a means to engage in self-defense, but they also can provide a deterrent before violent crimes even begin (Gerney et al., 2013; Homsher, 2004; Kates, 1992). In fact, one of NRA CEO Wayne LaPierre's famous mantras is the only way to "stop a bad guy with a gun is with a good guy with a gun" (Sappenfield, 2014). One study that is used to support the claim that guns save lives comes from criminologists Gary Kleck and Marc Gertz who wrote in 1995 that, "400,000 people a year use guns in situations where the defenders claim that they 'almost certainly' saved a life" (p. 180). Finally, gun laws, conservatives argue, do not reduce the number of violent crimes; instead, they infringe on the rights of law-abiding citizens. This position, taken by Republican Florida Senator Marco Rubio, among others, is a way of shifting or deflecting the debate. Instead of focusing on the tragedies of violent gun use, right-wing pundits misdirect our attention to violations of the Second Amendment (Morrison, 2014).

Anti-gun advocates do not typically point out the fallacious reasoning employed by gun defenders (perhaps because liberal extremists also utilize fallacies), but they do respond to these gun-defense arguments. Gun control promoters, of course, reiterate that more guns increase the risk of violent use. The liberal blowhard Arianna Huffington (2008) says that conservatives "play politics with our safety" (p. 309) by their "demented demands" allowing for more access to guns, which makes the "job of al Qaeda sleeper cells, domestic terrorists, school shooters, David Koresh wannabes, and bloodthirsty lunatics everywhere a whole lot easier" (p. 308). This is especially true, apparently, when a gun has already been used in a situation—introducing another gun/shooter to the episode only heightens the likelihood of more people being hurt (Wilstein, 2014). In a related way, when pro-gun folks claim that guns can reduce or deter violent incidents, the opposition argues that not only do more guns create more violence, but we also do not need guns to reduce or stop gun-related attacks. When Jon Meis, an engineering student, witnessed a gunman shoot fellow students, Meis waited for the shooter to add more ammunition, then stepped up and reacted to the culprit with pepper spray (Sappenfield, 2014). Liberal radical Al Sharpton relates this notion of more gun use to the issue Marco Rubio addressed regarding the infringement of law-abiding citizens. Sharpton responds by saying, "Our society grows increasingly unsafe with the proliferation of guns everywhere. Moral people should reflect a moral society" (Sharpton, 2013). By extension, if the anti-gun position is the "moral" position, then the pro-gun arguments are immoral, or at least contribute to immoral beliefs and behaviors. This rhetorical tactic is a form of demonizing the opposition by (mis)characterizing them in a negative light. In other words, regardless of actual substantive merits or drawbacks to the availability of guns, arguing the point is not a moral claim.

For those comporting to maintain the status quo, or a modified version of the current system that reduces governmental regulations on guns, most of the arguments are premised on the individual rights interpretation of the Second Amendment. Most pro-gun claims spin off from that core premise. Indeed, the Second Amendment is viewed as sacrosanct and the foundation of gun rights activists.

Rights/Tyranny Arguments

Perhaps due to the influence and intense pressuring of the NRA (Davidson, 1993; Giffords & Kelly, 2014; Spitzer, 2008), most pro-gun supporters base their perspectives about guns on the Second Amendment, which, of course, is the core principle of the NRA (Dreier, 2013; Spitzer, 2008). Part of the narrative of the Second Amendment, and one of the reasons it is so powerful as a persuasive perspective, is that the amendment to bear arms is not just a constitutionally based right; it is a logic that is divinely derived and directed. The Second Amendment is believed to be sacrosanct, so much so that the NRA argues that blind citizens should be allowed to conceal and carry (Stein, 2014). Gun trumpeter, Dana Loesch, says the "Second Amendment is also the teeth against domestic tyranny, the epitome of big government, as well as tyranny abroad" (Loesch, 2014, p. 103). Glenn Beck, who is arguably one of the zaniest conservative extremists alive and who preaches his points of view to millions of followers, explains this dogma of Second Amendment doctrine by saying, "The words contained in our

Constitution, while written by our founding fathers, come directly from God—as do the rights they grant us" (2007, p. xxiii). He goes on to say that we should put our "trust in God" and "our faith in the Constitution" (p. xxiii). According to Beck, the Second Amendment is vital for not just preserving gun rights, but also every other right in America. By using a slippery slope fallacy, Beck claims that if we "successfully weaken" the Second Amendment, "it's only a matter of time before all of our other rights begin to fall away, like dominoes" (2009, p. 35). Given that the Second Amendment, according to Beck, is the backbone of American liberty, any law, regulation, or perspective that threatens it should immediately be rejected. While offering zero evidence, Beck scares his followers into believing that Obama is coming to take away all of their guns, and in so doing, he fallaciously crafts massive paranoia in the minds of gun lovers (Amato & Neiwert, 2010, p. 41–43). Of course, by portraying liberals (and the president) as Fascist gun haters (Butterfield, 1995; Israel, 2012), Beck is also demonizing the opposition to guns, which elevates his position among the choir to whom he is preaching (Beck, 2009, p. 35). This type of rhetoric is why the polarizing liberal and former MSNBC commentator (until he and the network parted ways; See Bauder, 2011; Goodale, 2012; Mirkinson, 2012) and current TV personality, Keith Olbermann said, "You, Glenn Beck, you personally are encouraging Americans to shoot other Americans" (Olbermann, 2011, p. 62). Outlandish, outrageous, and extreme, to be sure, but this sort of tit-for-tat exchange illustrates the downward-spiraling nature of divisive discourse.

Another conservative pundit, Sarah Palin, also engages in the sanctimonious veneration of the Second Amendment. Sometimes labeled as the "new Glenn Beck" (Larson & Porpora, 2011, p. 756), Palin, like Beck, worries that liberals systematically attack the rights enshrined by the Second Amendment (PolitiFact, 2014). To respond to such threats, "mama grizzly"—as she calls herself—urges gun owners to "not retreat, reload!" (Engles, 2012, p. 122). Furthermore, since gun opponents have proposed more "gun free zones," especially in the wake of all of the recent school shootings in general, and the Sandy Hook massacre in particular, Palin does not let such proposals go unchallenged. In fact, by calling gun free zones "stupid on steroids" (Delmore, 2014; Reilly, 2014), Palin emphasizes her condescending sarcasm juxtaposed with her militant, motherly persona (Gallagher, 2010; Harp et al., 2010). Incidentally, all of this is somewhat ironic since the "The Gun-Free School Zone Act of 1990" was enacted when George H. W. Bush was president (Krouse, 2002). Yet, gun advocates raise a strong point—gun-free zones tend to be where mass shootings occur, such as in schools, malls, movie theatres and so on (Loesch, 2014, p. 38). After the Newtown school shooting, political commentator and law professor, Glenn Harlan Reynolds, observes,

> Policies making areas "gun free" provide a sense of safety to those who engage in magical thinking, but in practice, of course, killers aren't stopped by gun-free zones. … Gun-free zones are premised on a lie: that murderers will follow rules, and that people like my student are a greater danger to those around them than crazed killers. That's an insult to honest people. Sometimes, it's a

deadly one. The notion that more guns mean more crime is wrong. In fact, as gun ownership has expanded over the past decade, crime has gone down. (Reynolds, 2012, np)

However, philosophy professor Firmin DeBrabander points out the intuitive notion that more guns heighten the risk of violence, especially since,

> Hardened, resolved, well-armed criminals—or strung-out drug addicts—are hardly fearful of guns in the hands of private citizens. … In a world where more and more people must walk the streets armed … they would hardly consider themselves safe. Guns are a sign of insecurity—at the very least, they are no deterrent to criminals who are resolved, ruthless, and well armed. If we do not address the underlying causes of crime, it is not hard to see that a plethora of guns is a toxic ingredient added to the mixture. (2015, p. 148–149)

And here, DeBrabander (and this point is echoed by others) makes an important point that often is overlooked—gun violence, while certainly a problem, is also a symptom of much larger issues, such as crime, mental illness, etc. (See Giffords & Kelly, 2014).

As a polarizing pundit who frequently employs what Jeremy Engles (2012) terms a "rhetoric of violence," Sarah Palin is known for her unique, if not outrageous, political blather. Perhaps her most violent rhetoric was illustrated with regard to the 2011 Tucson, Arizona, shooting. At the time, Gabby Giffords (D-Rep.), along with eighteen others, were shot by a lone gunman. After the incident, the shooter blamed his actions on Sarah Palin's confrontational discourse (Balz, 2011; Dunn, 2011). More specifically, the gunman claimed he was fulfilling what he thought was an urgent call from Palin, as she placed on her Facebook page key political contests for the upcoming election in crosshairs—a simulated visual of targeting the districts as if looking through a rifle scope. The visual display that literally took aim at liberal candidates received an array of criticism for its violent meaning, and as a result, Palin removed it from her Facebook account. But by the time it was deleted, the damage had already been done in terms of influencing Jared Lee Loughner, the alleged gunman. Of course, Palin denied any responsibility for the tragedy because, as she saw it, it was the "act of a crazy man," and her so-called "crosshairs" were not intended to be images of a rifle scope, but rather should have been interpreted as merely spotlighting the important elections (Dunn, 2011; Engles, 2012). Additionally, Palin characterized the attacks against her as a form of "blood libel," which is a reference to a concept going back to the Middle Ages that "justified Christian persecution of Jews by claiming that they engaged in murder, in particular of children, and used the blood in their rituals" (Engles, 2012, p. 122). Thus, by first placing the crosshairs online, then using the rhetorical tactic of denial, then deflection, Sarah Palin implemented important techniques of polarizing discourse.

Additionally, the NRA's Wayne LaPierre resorts to vilifying the group's opposition by likening them to Hitler and fascist Nazi Germany. Simply put, the NRA and other gun advocates claim that any encroachment on the right to bear arms, but especially registration or background checks, will justify the government's confiscation of firearms, and the confiscation, as illustrated by Nazi Germany, will allow and foster tyranny (Harcourt, 2004). More specifically, by reviewing the historical analogy of Hitler, "it teaches that totalitarian governments will attempt to disarm their subjects so as to extinguish any ability to resist crimes against humanity" (Halbrook, 2000, p. 532). Even worse, LaPierre describes how the Jewish underground was unable to wage an effective resistance to the Nazis after their Fascist government confiscated all of the citizens' firearms (LaPierre, 1994, p. 86–87). Although this "logic" is fallacious in that it utilizes generalizations, demonization of the opposition, labeling, and a deductive rationale, it is also historically accurate, which might explain its persuasive efficacy (Harcourt, 2004).

The grounding of pro-gun advocacy in the rhetoric of rights and the Second Amendment permits the anti-gun perspective to debate the legal implications of "rights" in the context of citizen ownership of firearms. Since gun advocates tend to base their positions on the Second Amendment, their opposition have a few different options in terms of refutation: (1) they can argue over interpretations of the Second Amendment, (2) they can dispute the historical implications, including the role of militias in early America and the historical analogue to Nazi Germany, (3) they can argue about how victims of gun tragedies also have rights that are violated when they are killed or injured, or (4) they can ignore the Second Amendment position entirely, a strategy that is not very wise since it creates the framework for the entirety of pro-gun sentiments.

Regarding the interpretation of the right to bear arms, the amendment was long held to provide protection for state militias to have firearms, not individuals, until the 1968 Gun Control Act stirred controversy over the legality of individual possession by citizens. As a result of that legislation, Orinn Hatch (R-Sen, Utah) commissioned a 1982 report regarding the history of the Second Amendment, and its conclusion clearly pronounced that the amendment unequivocally protects individual rights (Lepore, 2012). Of course, it was not until 2008 in the *Heller* decision that the Supreme Court agreed with such an interpretation. Before 2008, the formal, declarative interpretation of the Second Amendment was that it guaranteed collective rights to bear arms—the kind of possession necessary for militias or national guards for the pursuit of collective protection—and not individual possession. Even now, "most constitutional scholars agree that the Founding Fathers' original intent behind the Second Amendment was to equip state militias with the firearms needed to protect and defend the nation's newly formed government, not to take arms against it" (Press, 2012, p. 130).

Nevertheless, after the 1968 Gun Control Act and the Republican sweep in the 1994 midterm elections, it was through the efforts of Orinn Hatch (D-Sen, Utah), Newt Gingrich (R-Rep., Georgia), James McClure (R-Sen, Idaho), Howard Volkmer (D-Rep, Missouri), and Republican House candidate Oliver North (Virginia) that the individual rights interpretation of the Second Amendment gained more and more currency (Carter, 2012; Jelen, 1998; Lepore, 2012). Up until this moment, most gun advocates relied on two arguments—that guns are necessary for sport and hunting, and guns are important for self-protection and self-defense (Jelen, 1998, p. 232). So, whether gun control adherents liked it or not, they had to now develop arguments against the logic that the Second Amendment concerned individual rights. This is extremely important since, as we have seen, articulating the amendment as an individual right allows gun activists to discuss the significance of gun rights with other individual rights, and framing the Second Amendment as an individual right makes it more challenging to propose gun control initiatives—federal legislation that threatens individual rights is typically held to a much higher standard than other laws.

Therefore, many gun control defenders felt the need (and still do) to attack the individual-rights framing of the Second Amendment. This argument strategy requires controllists to offer a different interpretation by advancing several rhetorical tactics. Naturally, many easily referred back to the former interpretation—that the Second Amendment is about collective possession and security, not individual rights. Certainly, there was ample history and jurisprudence to support this perspective, not the least of which included the arguments initially proffered by the 1939 *Miller* Supreme Court decision. Additionally, some Second Amendment scholars remind us that the Founding Fathers of the Constitution, after just experiencing British tyrannical rule and the concomitant Revolutionary War, feared the idea of a standing army, so the architects of the Second Amendment arranged for a constitutional provision for defense forces, albeit militias (Dizard, Muth, and Andrews, 1999). Furthermore, the idea that individual gun ownership needs protection so that individuals, by themselves, can counter tyranny is a non-sequitur, at least in the modern context. Individual use of guns to fight against tyranny today would look quite a bit different than in the late 1700s, as well as the fact that our individual citizens simply would pose no match against the tanks, aircraft carriers, and drones of the modern American military (Nuckols, 2013).

In terms of comparing American gun control to the policies of the Nazi regime in the mid-1930s, gun control promoters respond with a couple of different arguments. The first points out how pro-gun folks are using a false analogy. Sure, it is true that the Nazis enacted a compulsory firearms registration policy that led to a total confiscation. However, to relate that to twenty-first-century America is fallacious. So far, gun registration has an altogether different purpose in the United States, and every other industrialized country has stricter gun control laws than the U.S. without any signs of creeping toward Nazi-like Fascism. Of course, that does not mean that confiscation of weapons, repression, and genocide could never occur. However, we have multiple checks to prevent tyranny in the United States—voting, separation of powers, impeachment proceedings, etc.—all of which not only illustrate a different context than 1930s Germany, but also reduce the chances of repressive fascism to emerge (Nuckols, 2013). The bottom line: guns are not as essential to protecting our way of life as the pro-gun advocates suggest.

Another complication to the pro-gun perspective that is exploited by the opposition is that even if the Second Amendment is interpreted to protect individual rights, it does not mean that such rights are absolute (Nuckols, 2013). In other words, almost all individual rights in the United States have certain limits. For example, our freedom of speech is limited in that we cannot yell "fire" in a crowded theatre, our First

Amendment rights to worship are limited in that we cannot engage in human sacrifices (even if our deity demands it), and even our rights to own private property are limited when the government demonstrates a need for our land, known as eminent domain. Thus, the Second Amendment, too, is not absolute. After all, the amendment itself stipulates "a well regulated militia," meaning that even if we concede that individuals should have the right to bear arms, such a right should still be "well regulated." These sorts of arguments are speculative and require methodical constitutional interpretation by our courts. Usually, when rights come into some sort of conflict (such as when one individual right collides with another), the courts enact some type of criteria to negotiate the tension, such as a balancing test (Zucca, 2008). Additionally, some gun control advocates argue that more gun-wielding individuals in the streets is tantamount to the Wild West, which threatens our democracy because issues are resolved by, or at least are based on, firepower instead of civil discourse (DeBrabander, 2015).

Interestingly, one of the social impacts of this conflictual absolutist discourse is that when one person's sacred right is in tension with some else's revered constitutional right (e.g., one person's right to bear arms vs. another person's right to not be placed in unnecessary danger), then polarizing rhetoric and even physical altercations can result. Known as "rights talk," this phenomenon concerns our "increasing tendency to speak of what is most important to us in terms of rights, and to frame nearly every social controversy as a clash of rights" (Glendon, 1991; Spitzer, 2008, p. 18). For instance, although the right to bear arms is now deemed a constitutionally protected right by the Supreme Court, victims of gun-related tragedies believe their rights from being needlessly subjected to a violent situation are also violated, such as Mr. Martinez, who recently blamed pro-gun entities like the NRA and Congress for his son's death in the University of California, Santa Barbara, shooting (Pennacchia, 2014; Tomlinson, 2014). Not surprisingly, if our conversations inevitably boil down to a clash of rights, then ultimately, any resolution will simply be a matter of ideological affiliation, and society as a whole loses.

In the end, the argument thread regarding the Second Amendment results in speculation, legal interpretation, and identification with a particular ideology. Both sides of this debate use analogies, sometimes faulty ones, to support their speculation, interpretation, and identification. In other instances, the different sides in the gun debate rely on historical, and often revisionist, perspectives. Regardless, both the pro-gun and the anti-gun positions do not solely advance these particular arguments, but instead also levy claim about self-defense.

Self-Defense/"Stand Your Ground" Arguments

Another common argumentative thread in the gun debate is self-defense. Both sides utilize self-defense claims to justify their positions. While multiple variations of this type of argumentation exist, I will examine just the main contentions in order for us to see how the polarizing rhetoric of guns occurs.

If we begin by looking at the pro-gun proponents, we will notice that they frequently use the claim of "self-defense" to support why they believe they need guns. In an uncertain and violent world, they argue that owning firearms equalizes the playing field either by deterring violent attacks against them or by providing a means to counter the criminals who wield guns during these violent episodes. Underlying this claim is a fundamental *pathos* appeal—the fear of crime. Since many Americans worry that they may become victims of crime, the prospect of possessing a gun to reduce such a risk is enticing. In fact, it is known that the NRA often contends with gun control measures by calling them "soft on crime," meaning that adoption of such laws takes away our ability to confront crime head-on, by ourselves (Spitzer, 2008). Despite the fact that most objective research emphasizes how the presence of guns makes people less safe, the gun lobby and its followers fervently believe that gun possession is a "common sense" way of addressing violent threats or possible attackers (Diaz, 2013, p. 57).

In response, gun control extremists use the rhetorical tactic of naming and labeling to diffuse the pro-gun view. For instance, instead of referring to laws that restrict the possession of guns as "gun control," the anti-gun crowd names its perspective "gun safety" (Ball, 2013; Beck, 2013). This appropriates and reclaims the pro-gun rhetoric of "self-defense" to characterize guns as the central problem, not criminals. Additionally, this sort of linguistic maneuver is used to portray the pro-gun activists as "demented and blood-thirsty psychopaths" who feel no shame when others "rain death upon innocent creatures" (Kates, 1992, np). In this way, the gun control advocates reframe the debate by shifting the attention away from an individual's response against crime to the more rhetorically powerful tactic of characterizing their opponents as irresponsible and the culprits behind the means of such crime in the first place. In response, the gun lobby and its followers rely on their standard self-defense arguments, as well as attempt a bit of rhetorical reframing themselves. For example, Charlton Heston, who is a celebrity actor and spokesperson for the NRA, makes this comment:

> Heaven help the God-fearing, law-abiding, Caucasian, middle class, protestant, or even worse evangelical Christian, Midwest or southern or even worse rural, apparently straight or even worse admitted heterosexual, gun-owning or even worse NRA-card-carrying, average working stiff, or even, worst of all, a male working stiff, because then, not only don't you count, you're a downright nuisance, an obstacle to social progress. (Heston, 1999, p. 201)

This type of sarcasm makes a poignant case—the characterizations and labeling conducted by the anti-gun folks demonstrates their low-level, extreme, and inappropriate tactics. Of course, the statements by both sides also demonstrate how gun discourse quickly becomes polarizing.

A recent issue relating to guns and self-defense are the so-called "stand your ground" laws. These laws, made famous by the 2012 shooting of Trayvon Martin in Florida, essentially change prior laws that require would-be victims to retreat when they are otherwise unable to engage in self-defense. With "stand your ground," a person may carry a gun and use it when, or if, they feel threatened. Taking Sarah Palin's words in a different direction, these laws are essentially self-defense on steroids. Of course, pro-gun advocates celebrate these laws as a reaffirmation of the Second Amendment's protection of individual rights. As a result, they argue that stand your ground measures empirically reduce instances of rape, citing a study that reveals that "in states that passed a 'stand your ground law' rapes declined by 5.9 per 100,000 residents between 2000–02 and 2009–11" (Bronars, 2013, np). And, in a related way, advocates claim that these laws "curb violent crime and make citizens feel safer" (Goodnough, 2005, np).

An incident that highly politicized the concept behind these laws was the Trayvon Martin shooting, where during an evening on "patrol," a neighborhood watch volunteer, George Zimmerman, fatally shot seventeen-year-old Trayvon Martin, who was unarmed, wearing a dark hoodie, and in possession of a drink and some candy. Zimmerman's defense, and the arguments which subsequently yielded his acquittal, were legally based on self-defense law, but subsequent trial arguments and even the judge's instructions to the jury referred to Florida's stand your ground law (Follman & Williams, 2013). By claiming that Zimmerman felt threatened by Martin—because there had been a series of burglaries in that neighborhood, it was dark out, and Martin failed to respond civilly to Zimmerman—the Florida law worked in his favor; since Zimmerman felt he was at risk, it was deemed legitimate for him to deploy his gun to counter the perceived threat.

Consequently, decades of behavior that were previously ruled as "criminal," such as shooting to death an unarmed kid in the middle of a housing subdivision, are now considered to be perfectly legal (Kaduce & Davis, 2013). As a result, many scholars have emphatically expressed how stand your ground laws unravel the rule of law that was used in previous cases, as well as legitimizing murder under the guise of "self-defense" (Lave, 2013, p. 859–860). Furthermore, there appears to be zero evidence that stand your ground laws create any sort of deterrence from violent crimes (Bronars, 2013). Therefore, political idealogues, such Al Sharpton, who is a famous civil rights activist and an MSNBC television show host, have rushed to the defense of African American youth everywhere who might fall prey to these circumstances. Sharpton worries that these laws have no objective legal basis and instead justify fatally shooting unarmed kids simply because a gun owner happens to "imagine" a threat (Sharpton, 2014b). Additionally, by using multiple *pathos* appeals, generalizations, and speculation, Sharpton criticizes these laws:

> 'Stand your ground' and similar self-defense rules have created a dangerous space where any shooting can be excused by simply stating that you feared for your life. It has allowed an individual's ingrained biases to potentially be protected under the law, no matter who gets hurt in the process. ... That means mothers and fathers are burying their young because someone or multiple people felt 'threatened.'. And that means jurors across the country may very well fail to convict people who kill others because the burden of proof is virtually impossible to achieve. (Sharpton, 2014a)

As we can see, both sides of this debate use fear as a motivating emotion to warrant their positions concerning this legal doctrine.

Similarly, a new law in Georgia, known as the "guns everywhere" bill, literally permits registered gun owners to conceal and carry their weapons anywhere in the state of Georgia, including bars, restaurants, banks, churches, and schools (Benen, 2014). Interestingly, this law was passed less than a year after the Sandy Hook massacre, which prompted a nationwide discussion about limiting the prevalence of guns, especially in or near schools, not increasing them. The NRA's Wayne LaPierre also advocated for more guns in schools immediately after the Newtown shooting, which turned off most centrist Americans (Giffords & Kelly, 2014, p. 147). Again, proponents and critics of Georgia's new law primarily rely on the *pathos* appeal of fear to substantiate their respective positions.

Other Fallacies

Related to the pro-gun position regarding self-defense, there is a fallacious argument that depends on compelling like-minded subscribers to the Second Amendment. By framing their perspective in terms of a group of individuals versus those that oppose them, the defenders of gun rights construct an "us vs. them" dichotomy. An excellent example of this rhetorical framing can be seen with pro-gun extraordinaire Charlton Heston:

> This debate would be accurately described as those who believe in the Second Amendment versus those who don't but instead it is spun as those who believe in murder versus those who don't. A struggle between the reckless and the prudent, between the dim-witted and the progressive. Between inferior citizens who know, and elitists who know what's good for society. (Heston, 1999, np)

In this case, Heston not only breaks up the debate into an acknowledgeable dichotomy, but he also portrays the opposition in very negative terms. The "us/them" split, then, helps to frame ideological positions, one of which sounds very appealing to an audience, and another which is named in such a way as to reject it outright. After all, most folks would rather be part of a group known as "prudent" and "in the know" rather than "dim-witted" and "elitist."

It is not surprising that Charlton Heston uses this sort of language, particularly since the NRA engages in this rhetorical tactic all of the time (Brady, 2006; Rachel, 2013). Case in point: in a mass mailing conducted by the NRA to support a candidate in a congressional election, the NRA said, "This is the litmus test on where your congressman stands on guns and hunting rights—either he is for us or he is against us" (Davidson, 1993, p. 67). This rhetorical dichotomization is problematic since rarely are controversial issues so clear-cut, nor are the labels used typically an accurate representation of the believers. This dichotomization also exists when liberals compare gun owners to criminals since a variation of this occurs when pro-gun advocates frame an image of law-abiding citizens with guns versus violent criminals or those who are concerned more with criminals' rights than they are with the law-abiding citizens (Diaz, 2013). Similarly, participants in the gun debate use name-calling, or *ad hominem* attacks, on their opponents without clearly describing an us/them situation. An *ad hominem* attack is a fallacy because it directs one's position against the opposition's persona rather than their arguments. For example, issue ideologue and conservative pundit Glenn Beck said this about the gun control point of view:

> Nothing illustrates the battle between the good forces of individual liberties and the destructive, idiotic forces of collectivism better than the ongoing battle over the meaning of those 27 little words. Normal people understand the natural existence of the right to bear arms, the plain language guarantee-ing us that right, and the clearly documented history that led to its enshrine-ment in the Bill of Rights. (Beck, 2009, p. 35)

Calling the anti-gun crowd "destructive and idiotic" is not a response to their argu-ments, but rather is a low-blow about who they are as people. Not to be outdone by any political extremist, Rush Limbaugh, the famous conservative hack who dominates talk radio, called gun control defenders "dangerous," "evil," and a "threat to our country" (Wilson, 2011, p. 237–238).

Of course, the pro-gun side of the debate is not the only culprit of name-calling. The liberal commentator of political fanaticism Rachel Maddow, who hosts her own weeknight show on MSNBC, calls gun advocates "insane" and "paranoid" because they make the world a more dangerous place (Brown, 2011). Furthermore, in a fundraiser in San Francisco, President Barack Obama exclaimed his now-famous gaffe that politi-cally inferior believers "get bitter, they cling to guns or religion or antipathy to people who aren't like them or anti-immigrant sentiment or anti-trade sentiment as a way to explain their frustrations" (Obama, 2008; Rubin, 2014, p. 111). Obama's suggestion that some people "cling to guns or religion" was immediately attacked as a demeaning, condescending, and *ad hominem* attack against Middle America (*Christianity Today*, 2008; Smith, 2008). Conservative Dana Loesch had this to say: "In Obama's mind, guns are only for bitter, frustrated bigots who aren't as enlightened as he is and can't afford to outsource their family's security" (2014, p. 48). Naturally, the liberal website *Daily Kos* defends the president's comments by suggesting that Obama never identified a particular group with his comments, which could equally apply to liberals or anti-gun extremists (Great Quail, 2008). Nevertheless, name-calling is frequently used in controversial issues, and it certainly polarizes the issues unnecessarily.

Both sides of the debate also use fear as a powerful motivator when attempting to persuade people to their position. We have already seen how some gun advocates use fear appeals, particularly the fear of crime, to justify more support for the right to bear arms. For instance, the NRA is fond of saying comments like "nothing less than the future of our country and our freedom will be at stake" (Millhiser, 2012; Sherfinski, 2014). But they are not the only ones using *pathos* appeals grounded in fear. Calling the pro-gun positions "demented demands," the liberal media provocateur Arianna

Huffington said, when referring to the elapse of the assault weapons ban, that it makes "the job of al Qaeda sleeper cells, domestic terrorists, school shooters, David Koresh wannabes, and bloodthirsty lunatics everywhere a whole lot easier" (Huffington, 2008, p. 308). As a result, she claims that conservatives and the NRA have been "sabotaging homeland security" (p. 309). Fear appeals, especially if they are unwarranted, intensify debates and only serve to polarize controversial issues even more.

Another kind of fallacy that appears frequently in the gun discussion is the use of generalities. Generalities, also known as sweeping assertions or broad claims, characterize a position in a negative manner, typically due to a few, singled-out instances that may be worse than other examples. Therefore, generalities provide inadequate, unfair, and inaccurate pictures of what an opponent believes or says. For example, we know that the gun control promoter and liberal commentator Lawrence O'Donnell uses generalities by pointing to one example of gun use during the Boston Marathon bombing to characterize all of the NRA positions as unfounded (*The Huffington Post*, 2013). Additionally, the anti-gun liberal agitator Ed Schultz describes gun advocates as "hiding behind the Second Amendment," especially when

> tonight is ... a time we as a people come to grips with a changing society. We need to be the Founding Fathers on how we deal with the sickness in our country called 'gun violence.' Hiding behind the Second Amendment doesn't cut it anymore. Hiding behind the Second Amendment can no longer be the shield for access. The people who wrote that document owned slaves, oppressed women, and were short on tolerance. (Feldman, 2012, np)

But, as with other fallacies, the anti-gun crowd does not engage in this rhetorical tactic alone. The pro-gun cohort also uses generalities to portray its opposition as flimsy and irresponsible. When Obama advocated restrictions on stand your ground laws after the shooting of Trayvon Martin, Republican Senator Ted Cruz (Texas) generalized Obama's position as an indication of Obama declaring war on the Second Amendment. He said, "It is not surprising that the president uses, it seems, every opportunity that he can to go after our Second Amendment right to bear arms. This president and this administration have a consistent disregard for the Bill of Rights" (Beamon, 2013, np). The extremely conservative instigator Ann Coulter generalizes frequently. She also typically fails to provide backing or footnotes to support her generalities. In one such instance, Ann Coulter refers to studies that prove the benefits of conceal carry laws; yet, she offers no such proof (Coulter, 2007). In a much more inflammatory instance, Coulter attempts to deflect the problems of gun violence by blaming gun tragedies on black-on-black crime. She tries to argue that "on the gun crimes, we keep hearing how low they are in Europe and, 'Oh, they're so low and they have no guns.' If you compare white populations, we have the same murder rate as Belgium. So, perhaps, it's not a gun problem, it is a demographic problem, which liberals are the one are pushing" (Edwards, 2013, np). As frightening as such rhetoric is, Ann Coulter's liberal counterpart, Michael Moore, uses the same rhetorical tactic, but in reverse: "Nearly all of our mass shootings are by angry or disturbed white males. None of them are committed by the majority gender, women. Hmmm, why is that?" (Egberto, 2014, np). No one probably knows why this is because both Moore and Coulter are overgeneralizing these problems by basing them on isolated cases.

Finally, we should also note how pro-gun advocates use hyperbole to justify some of their positions. Instead of providing substantive claims about why assault weapons should remain legal, they resort to attacking the nature of "governmental control" and even equate such control to a form of "slavery" (Nimmo, 2012). This rhetorical tactic combined with an appeal to patriotism constructs a powerful pro-gun narrative. As Diaz explains, "The NRA ... [rhetorical] style combines a vehement 'patriotic' meanness with a ruthless willingness to say or do anything to defeat even the most modest proposal to regulate guns ... this is largely cynical play-acting to whip up gun owners and raise funds" (2013, p. 29). This misplaced sense of patriotism has a particular allure for many gun sympathizers. Plus, this tactic has the added benefit of also being a form of the us/them fallacy. After all, if people agree with the pro-gun position, they are patriotic. If they do not, then they clearly hate America and are un-patriotic. This type of simplistic thinking tends to work in many circles. My guess is that the tenor of the gun debate often becomes so polarized and so heated that minimalist tactics like "you're either with us because we're the good guys, or you're against us because you're part of the evil side" become a fallback position for average Americans just trying to make sense of it all.

One final comment should be made about the victims of gun shootings. Many passionately argue that victims have become political pawns in the overall discussion about gun control. Not surprisingly, mostly conservative talking heads argue that victims should be mourned but should not be politicized for a liberal agenda (Huckabee, 2015). In response, after the Umpqua Community College shooting, President Obama said that tragedies should be politicized because the needless violence continues and something needs to happen to curtail it (Fabian, 2015). But the victims are not the only ones who are politicized. Occasionally the media also focus on the shooters, in part as victims themselves, but mainly as evil-doers. While not a perpetrator of gun violence, one of the terrorists of the Boston Marathon bombing is a case in point. *Rolling Stone* magazine received considerable criticism for placing one of the brothers, Dzhokar Tsarnaev, with a rock star image on the front cover in a way that glamorized him (Brown, 2013; Cannold et al., 2013). Needless to say, media representations and political posturing contribute to the overall divisive discourse concerning guns in America.

CONCLUSION

Statements about guns provide an excellent example of divisive discourse. There is perhaps no better case of polarizing political rhetoric than the gun debate. As Cornell and DeDino express, "Few issues in American constitutional law are as bitterly divisive as the meaning of the right to keep and bear arms" (2004, p. 487). Of course, it does not help that many statements on this issue are based on faulty logic, ideological vehemence, and a paucity of facts. Indeed, probably the "absence of facts is precisely what makes it possible for many patently foolish perspectives on guns and gun control to survive in the United States" (Diaz, 2013, p. 26–27). The use of slippery slope, *post hoc*, and *ad hominem* fallacies, generalizations, and nefarious labeling and use of hyperbole complicate this polarizing debate even further.

Fortunately, there are many participants in this discussion that are calling for a more tempered debate. Some urge us to focus more on substantive arguments and rely less on inflammatory discourse (Rachel, 2013). Still others implore us to recognize the problems in the rhetoric of guns so that we can eliminate them and focus on the important policy considerations instead. These advocates argue that unless we change our perspectives, the polarizing positions on guns will undermine our democracy. They are specifically addressing the distinctions made about assault weapons, but Dizard and colleagues also make this point in general:

> But in the polarized atmosphere in which we currently find ourselves, the nuance and reasonableness needed to come up with such distinctions have virtually no public voice. The prospects for sensible regulation of ownership and use are continually frustrated by the impassioned shouts from the pro-gun and anti-gun extremes. Our democracy is weakened when we persist in framing issues in terms that admit no nuance, contingency, or compromise. (1999, p. 8–9)

This argument may be a fear appeal itself, but we should take note that polarizing rhetoric concerning important political issues is very serious. We should hope that calmer heads will prevail with such controversial issues. And, for our part, we can begin to notice the particular rhetorical tactics used to emphasize the divisiveness in this discourse.

IMAGE CREDIT

- Fig. 2.1: Adapted from: "Conservatives Don't Want Limits on Gun Ownership," http://www.people-press.org/files/2014/06/6-12-2014-Political-Polarization-Release.pdf, pp. 61. Copyright © 2014 by Pew Research Center.

CHAPTER THREE

The Rhetoric of Religion: Divisive Religious Discourse in Contemporary Politics

---

In the previous chapter, I analyzed some of the polarizing rhetoric that envelops conversations regarding gun control. For this chapter, I will dive into another incendiary pool of discourse—discussions about the intersection of religion and politics. For many Americans, religious faith may be a deeply personal matter, and others may not find religion all that relevant to political issues. For people of faith, their religious belief system may constitute the core of their identity, meaning that even civil discussions easily turn into statements that can be perceived as personal attacks. Indeed, the common perception among Americans is that the United States has a "separation" between church and state, such that the comingling of the two realms should be verboten. Given the intense, even ideological, basis for both political and religious beliefs, dialogue about the combination of both topics is often, as we would expect, extremely incendiary, if not mephitic. As Chuck Donovan argues, "Few topics spur more court battles than the separation of church and state" (2011, n.p.). To be sure, each realm (the political realm and the religious realm) in itself invites ideological invective, so merging the two naturally yields a massive field of landmines where a single misstep by a conversant can ignite an explosion from another party who may feel attacked or, at the very least, may feel like his or her position and beliefs need to be defended at all costs. A recent Pew Research poll highlights the polarizing nature of religion in America:

> There are deep divisions in the political typology over religious beliefs, views of the Bible and social issues such as homosexuality and abortion. And while

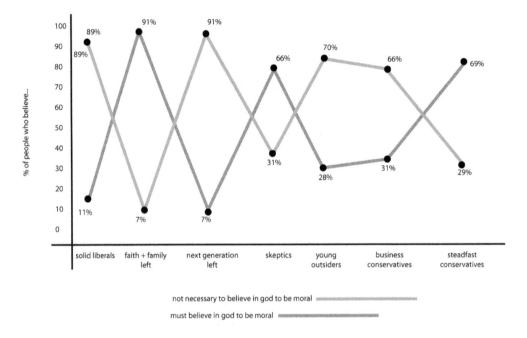

Figure 3.1: Religious polarization, Dimock et al. (2014), p. 53.

the right and left differ over these issues, in many cases they also divide both parties' coalitions. On fundamental views related to belief in God, 53% of the public says it is not necessary to believe in God in order to be moral and have good values, while 45% believes it is necessary. While overall opinion is fairly evenly split, opinion among the typology groups is not: Large majorities of all groups are on one side or the other of this question. (Dimock et al., 2014, p. 53)

A breakdown of this religious polarization can be seen in Figure 3.1.

It is no wonder, then, that many people simply refuse to talk about religion, and certainly religion and politics together, such that we often hear phrases like, "It is not proper to discuss politics or religion at the dinner table," or even, "If you want to keep friends, never talk religion or politics with them."

However, as I have suggested earlier in this book, the very nature of democracy requires a concerted commitment by citizens to engage in civil deliberations about the potentially perilous issues threatening society. In other words, if we refuse to talk about religious and/or political issues, our democracy is in danger. Silence simply is not an option—no matter how vehemently some Americans plea to avoid religion and politics as conversation topics. And, of course, when people are not silent and engage in bitter, contentious diatribes, we need to be alert to their tactics and learn how to separate the wheat from the chaff (to use a religious allusion) in these politico-religious discussions.

THE CONTEXT OF RELIGIOUS, POLITICAL RHETORIC

Although religion is a matter of deep, personal conviction, it is also a national issue that dates back to the origin of the United States. As most readers will no doubt know, one of the reasons America fought a revolution against England was in response to religious oppression. As in England, the colonies were expected to commit to the Church of England (the Anglican faith) without exception as a matter of religious uniformity, and if a person wasn't even a Christian, well, they had serious troubles with the British (Gingrich, 2005). This last point is important since most of this country's Founding Fathers were deists—not Christians, and certainly not Anglicans (Johnson, 2009). People who resisted the Church of England—believers and non-believers alike—faced egregious persecution, even to the point of death (Hutson, 1998). Of course, the Puritans who eventually dominated the religious views in the New World fostered their own forms of persecution, including anti-Quaker laws and consequences for so-called heathens that included the death penalty (Hutson, 1998). But, as we know, the American political founders, such as Madison, Adams, Jay, Franklin, Hamilton, Washington, and Jefferson, used their status as prominent land owners and political leaders to create a more religiously tolerant nation (Morris, 1973).

Of course, like the issue of guns in America, the debate about religion begins with the Constitution. The First Amendment stipulates that "Congress shall make no law respecting an establishment of religion, or prohibiting the free exercise thereof." And that is it; one sentence that has sparked much controversy and polarized bickering since the eighteenth century. And although many disputes, court decisions, and controversies have erupted over the potential confusion of various interpretations of the Establishment Clause, it should, at a minimum, mean this: "Neither a state nor the federal government may set up a church. Neither can pass laws that aid one religion, aid all religions, or prefer one religion over another" (Ohio Len, 2005). Readers should notice that the word "separation" does not exist in the First Amendment, nor does the word "wall," so arguments about the "separation of church and state" or the "wall between church and state" are phrases that, through multiple iterations and generally in times of crisis, have formed a mental shortcut in the minds of many Americans. However, if we want to give some credit to the Founding Fathers in terms of understanding the rationale of religion's role in American politics, we need to consult Thomas Jefferson. In 1802, Jefferson wrote a letter to a Baptist organization to clarify the government's position—and his firm belief—on the relationship between religion and the state. He wrote:

> Believing with you that religion is a matter which lies solely between man & his god, that he owes account to none other for his faith or his worship, that the legitimate powers of government reach actions only, and not opinions, I contemplate with sovereign reverence that act of the whole American people which declared that their legislature should make no law respecting an establishment of religion, or prohibiting the free exercise thereof, thus building a wall of separation between church and state. … Adhering to this expression

of the supreme will of the nation in behalf of the rights of conscience, I shall see with sincere satisfaction the progress of those sentiments which tend to restore to man all his natural rights, convinced he has no natural right in opposition to his social duties. (my emphasis)

Jefferson's clarification does, indeed, help contextualize the meaning behind the so-called Religion Clauses—the Establishment Clause and the Free Exercise Clause.

With Jefferson's description, we can see how the language of separation and a "wall" came to existence. This is extremely important since virtually every argumentative position involving religion in American politics is grounded on the Religion Clauses. Simply put, the Establishment Clause means that the government and its institutions (i.e., the states, municipalities, public schools, etc.) cannot impose a single religion or any sort of religious faith, doctrine, or influence in the public sphere. On the other hand, the Free Exercise Clause provides the liberty to believe and act in accordance with one's own faith free from intrusion, discrimination, or persecution. Even the language of the Clauses helps to characterize their legal impact in terms of liberty—the Establishment Clause is a freedom from (otherwise known as a negative right), and the Free Exercise Clause is a freedom to (also known as a positive right). This distinction is important, as we will see later, in that there are times in our history when the two clauses are mutually supporting and other times when they are conflicting. As such, First Amendment jurisprudence is a recipe for potential clashes, disputations, and offensive crusades, while simultaneously providing a framework for respect, liberty, and tolerance. The potential for this issue to erupt into partisan bickering is also very relevant for us today. As Lunceford (2012) suggests,

> Current events have brought the idea of what it means to be an American and how this intersects with religion to the forefront. For many, defining what it means to be an American requires strict adherence to a kind of orthodoxy that was never present with the founding fathers themselves. As the discourses of American exceptionalism have been told and retold, a kind of revisionism has crept in, framing this exceptionalism in terms of America's founding as a Christian nation. (p. 20)

The religion-politics relationship has been, and will continue to be, not only a defining characteristic of America as a nation; it will also be marked with significant clashes. For example, a piece of legislation was proposed in the North Carolina legislature to make Christianity the state's official religion—arguing that the Tenth Amendment provides states a shield from federal government imposition (Maddow, 2013). And with the Supreme Court case concerning the religious freedom of Hobby Lobby in relationship to the contraceptive mandate in the Affordable Care Act, the question of the nexus of religion and politics in our national conversation will not fade any time soon. In *Burwell v. Hobby Lobby Stores* (2014), the Court ruled that business owners have the First Amendment protection to not be compelled to follow federal law (in this case, the

ACA) if there is a religious objection, such as providing health insurance to employees that includes contraceptives or abortion procedures.

As a framework for contentious debate, the First Amendment helps establish the rhetorical situation (Bitzer, 1968). To recall, a rhetorical situation requires three elements—a problem (exigence), constraints (issues that can challenge or frustrate resolution to the problem), and an audience (people involved who are potential agents of change). For politico-religious disputes, we often see rhetorical problems take the shape of some sort of religious infringement with constraints that range from other, conflicting rights or societal concerns, and the audience involved in these situations can be justices of the Supreme Court, other judges, lawmakers, religious leaders, and, of course, citizens. Political discussions involving these change agents generally stereotype them into groups: Christians (any group self-proclaiming to be Christian), the Religious Right (extreme right-wing Republicans who are also very devout in their Christian religious beliefs, often using those beliefs to guide their political philosophies), Dominionists (radical right-wing Christians who believe they must control the political realm in order to satisfy biblical prophecies, which probably means facilitating some sort of apocryphal eschatology), sectarians (individuals who are closely aligned with a particular type of religious belief, or sect), secularists (persons who may or may not be religious but believe there should be a clear separation between church and state, such that the "state" is free from any religious influence and vice versa), and non-believers (people who tend to not believe in religion). Typically, when a conflict emerges, it is met with a corresponding *kairotic* moment (i.e., the element of *kairos*) that enables change agents to potentially resolve religious and political tensions. Of course, these *kairotic* moments may also escalate into blithering banter between extreme blowhards of any religious or non-religious stripe.

Not only does the Constitution provide a justification for both sides of the debate to polarize; the nature of religion seems to also encourage divisive discourse. This should not be surprising given that religion requires adherents to have a significant commitment, if not an absolute allegiance. As Mike Lofgren notes, "Compromise is a dirty word if you are doing God's bidding. ... If the world is divided between the Children of Light and the Children of Darkness, then compromise in the spirit of traditional representative government becomes difficult" (2013, p. 134). Thus, if American multiculturalism and religious diversity promise space for everyone, but everyone believes they are right, tension and conflict will naturally occur. When we add secularists and non-believers to the mix, the discussion dynamics will become even more convoluted. In terms of deeply religious Americans, they oppose, if not resent, any governmental imposition into their affairs. One way of preventing such an imposition is to enter into the political realm and construct legal protections. At the 1992 National Republican Convention, Pat Buchanan exclaimed, "It is about what we believe. It is about what we stand for as Americans. There is a religious war going on in our country for the soul of America. It is a cultural war, as critical to the kind of nation we will one day be as was the Cold War itself," and later in the speech, Buchanan noted, "Millions of political extremists on both the left and the right believe in a culture war and they have enlisted in it. The culture war is primarily being waged over the issues of abortion, gay marriage, school prayer, and, more recently, stem-cell research" (quoted in Thomas & Beckel, 2008, pp. 78–79). As the insertion of religion into politics became more pronounced after 1992, including the 2000 and 2004 presidential campaigns, when issues like abortion and same-sex marriage were highlighted in so-called swing states, American politics saw a practical marriage between a candidate's religious and political views as he or she ran for office. Indeed, "there is now a de facto religious test for the presidency: Major candidates are encouraged (or coerced) to share their feelings about their faith in a revelatory speech, or a televangelist like Rick Warren will dragoon the candidates (as he did with Obama and McCain in 2008) to debate the finer points of Christology, offering himself as the final arbiter" (Lofgren, 2013, p. 129). Knowing this, we can identify key political issues that are now forged as a tight relationship between the religious and political affiliations. During each election campaign, each controversy that erupts, and each crisis in a news cycle, we should be able to locate important politico-religious issues that provide fodder for divisive discourse.

THE LEGAL NATURE OF RELIGIOUS, POLITICAL RHETORIC

To begin our examination of religious divisive discourse, it might be helpful to look at the Supreme Court cases that established an early precedent concerning the Religion Clauses. If we ignore the Court's decision to outlaw bigamy—and by extension polygamy—in its 1879 decision of *Reynolds v. United States*, we will see that the Supreme Court did not really begin dealing with questions of church and state until 1947, in its landmark decision of *Everson v. Board of Education*. The Everson case not only was the benchmark case that signified the Court's entrance into the separation of church and state quandary, but it also marked the first decision dealing with the Establishment Clause. Most of the Court rulings that have relevance for our purposes in terms of polarizing political rhetoric are premised on the Establishment Clause—in fact, most of the church/state Court rulings deal with the Establishment Clause. However, as I will note below, there are a few Free Exercise Clauses that are either directly pertinent for understanding divisive discourse or are tangentially related by providing some elements of the overarching legal context on this issue.

Establishment Clause Cases

Everson v. Board of Education (1947) was the first time the Court took up the question about the nature and extent of government involvement in "establishing" religion. More specifically, before 1947, the federal government largely left the relationship between church and state up to the individual states. The Supreme Court in *Everson*, however, ruled that the federal government prohibited violations of the Establishment Clause and used the Due Process Clause of the Fourteenth Amendment to prohibit such violations uniformly among all of the states. As a result, the Court used its *Everson* precedent to rule in *McCollum v. Board of Education Dist. 71* the following year. In *McCollum*, the Court decided that religious instruction in a public school in Illinois was a violation of the Establishment Clause and therefore unconstitutional.

A few years later, in 1952, the Supreme Court ruled in two additional important First Amendment religion cases. In *Burstyn v. Wilson*, the Court decided that the government has no legal justification to censor a motion picture because it is offensive to religious beliefs. In the other decision, the Court ruled in *Zorach v. Clauson* that a school district that allows students to leave school for part of the day in order to receive religious instruction did not violate the Establishment Clause since the government was not directly sponsoring any religion and the instruction did not occur on public school grounds.

The 1960s, perhaps due to some of the larger cultural changes occurring in the United States, witnessed several Religion Clause cases. The 1961 *Torcaso v. Watkins* decision ruled that applicants for public office cannot be forced to swear they believe in the existence of God because such action would violate the Establishment Clause. A year later, in *Engel v. Vitale*, the Court decided that any sort of prayer—regardless of religion or sect—given in public schools violates the Establishment Clause since such prayer would be a direct sanctioning by the government of a particular religious view. The *Engel* case became an enormously important precedent on which the Court relied in future religious-based disputes. Based on *Engel*, the Court also established a clear logic that public schools function as a government entity. As such, the Court ruled in *Abington School District v. Schempp* (1963) that public school-sponsored prayer reading violates the Establishment Clause. And in 1968, the Supreme Court decided in *Epperson v. Arkansas* that public school districts cannot prevent the teaching of evolution because doing so, in that case, would be a *de facto* promotion of a religious view (the Court's reasoning was that the alternate explanation to evolution relied on a conception of God, although as we know now, the theory of evolution does not necessarily preclude a role from a deity).

Until this point, First Amendment jurisprudence involving religion dealt with the Establishment Clause. Except for the *Reynolds* decision in 1879, all of the major Supreme Court cases concerned the Establishment Clause, not the Free Exercise Clause. While the Court established precedent and ruled in accordance with how it viewed the First Amendment for each case, it had yet to essentially "solve" the question of when and if the government or any of its institutions could favor any sort of religious activity. This changed in 1971. In *Lemon v. Kurtzman*, the Court reasoned that in order to attempt to settle when government mandates avoid the Establishment Clause, a test needed to be adopted. The nature of the case concerned the state of Pennsylvania's financial support to nonpublic schools—which happened to be Roman Catholic—for payment for secular instruction in those nonpublic schools as well as financial support for secular supplies. The Court ultimately ruled against Pennsylvania, reasoning that the result of the pecuniary sponsorship (i.e., non-secular instruction and supplies) did not forgive the state from violating the initial action of supporting religious schools.

In so doing, the Court argued that the state was establishing religious preference, even if the result was secular. To decide this case, however, the Court adopted what is now known as the three-part *Lemon* test. In order to determine if a government action does not violate the Establishment Clause, these three components must be met: (1) the governmental action must have a secular purpose (which Pennsylvania met in this case), (2) the action's primary purpose must not be to inhibit or to advance a religion (which the Pennsylvania law violated), and (3) there must be no excessive entanglement between government and religion (and the very fact that government money trickled down, eventually, to secular practices, by definition, meant entanglement had occurred in this case). What is interesting about the *Lemon* decision, besides establishing this important test, is that it lays the presumption against the state at first. In other words, the government must prove, *prima facie*, it does not violate the Establishment Clause, as opposed to allowing governmental action in all matters and then proving that such actions violate the Establishment Clause. By framing the test in this way, the Court provides an affirmative value against government-established religious practice, a perspective that seems fully in line with what Jefferson (1802) discussed in his elaboration of the First Amendment.

After *Lemon*, the Court had a string of cases that either ruled based on the *Lemon* three-prong test or referred to it indirectly for the Court's perspective. In *Stone v. Graham* (1980), the Court decided that any posting of the Ten Commandments in public schools violates the Establishment Clause. In 1985, the Court ruled in *Wallace v. Jaffree* that a "moment of silence" in public schools violates the Establishment Clause when the silence's purpose is to promote prayer. In a ruling that upheld the Court's earlier precedent in *Epperson* (1968), it decided in *Edwards v. Aquillard* (1987) that a public school's teaching of "creation science" violates the Establishment Clause because such curriculum has a clear "religious motivation." The Supreme Court continued its line of preserving the Establishment Clause when it ruled in *Allegheny County v. ACLU* (1989) that it is unconstitutional to display a nativity scene inside a public governmental building. In 1992, the Court decided in *Lee v. Weisman* that it is unconstitutional for a public school district to have clergy perform prayer at a graduation, even if such prayer is "nondenominational." The *Lee* decision is interesting given that almost a decade earlier, in 1983, the Court ruled in *Marsh v. Chambers* that chaplains conducting prayer in state legislatures and other official government bodies (other than schools) is permissible because the clergy's role in such practices was part of longstanding tradition and, as such, posed no unique or demonstrative threat to opposing religious beliefs. After the *Lee* decision, in 1993, the Court ruled in *Church of Lukumi Babalu Ave., Inc. v. Hialeah* that a city cannot forbid the killing of animals during a religious practice (in this case, a practice of the Santeria religion) provided that the religion has been an established belief and the practice is not threatening to other beliefs or the safety of humans.

In *Zelman v. Simmons-Harris* (2002), the Court upheld a voucher-based school funding system in Ohio, even though some of the money went to fund the attendance of religious schools. To determine if this violated the Establishment Clause, the Court constructed a five-prong test similar to the *Lemon* test but with slight deviations.

In order to be considered free from violation, a program must meet all five prongs: (1) the program must have a valid secular purpose, (2) the financial assistance must go to parents, not schools, (3) a variety of different beneficiaries (i.e., parents of diverse religious backgrounds) must be covered, (4) the program must be neutral, on face, with respect to religion, and (5) there must be sufficient non-religious options.

Free Exercise Cases

Again, while not as relevant or predominant as the Establishment Clause cases, the Free Exercise rulings are still, nevertheless, important for appreciating the overall legal context of divisive church and state discourse.

Conclusion

Knowing the legal principles behind the debate involving the Religion Clauses provides important context for appreciating the overall rhetorical situation. This legal background should also help us when viewing specific *kairotic* moments. As a result, since we have an understanding of how the intersection of religion and politics relates to the rhetoric of controversial issues, we should be able to examine the specific issues and the specific comments involved in tumultuous and polarizing discourse.

THE DIVISIVE DISCOURSE OF RELIGION

It should be obvious at this point to see how die-hard believers of any religious or anti-religious group can enter the conversation and use the Constitution to help frame their arguments. In this chapter, I will explore some of the rhetorical tactics that these true believers use, which contribute to the overarching toxic, verbal exchanges of religious polarization. In so doing, I will try to provide additional context of the particular rhetorical situation as I analyze specific, pernicious discourse. Instead of organizing this discourse by argumentative threads as I did in the previous chapter, I believe it will be more useful to look at this discourse by topic theme, including the controversies surrounding public prayer, tax exemptions, holy days, school curricula, prayer in schools, public religious displays, Islam, and issue-specific areas of contention, such as stem cell research, the teaching of evolution, religious exemptions in the Affordable Care Act, and LGBTQ+rights.

Public Prayer

As we just learned, the Court has dealt with the idea of public prayer, sectarian or otherwise. The Supreme Court has established its perspective regarding public prayer—if it is a relatively new occurrence, it is considered unconstitutional. According to the decision in *Lee v. Weisman*, a public prayer does not explicitly need to refer to a particular faith, religion, or sectarian belief. If it is a prayer of any kind, with the purpose of invoking a moment of prayer of any sort, such an action violates the Establishment

Clause. However, if such a prayer is a longstanding part of a larger secular event—such as a prayer before a session of a state legislature—then the Court has ruled that the traditional and historical nature of the prayer is not unconstitutional since the American people have experienced the prayer for many years (meaning any offense incurred by the prayer would be minimal at best) and the larger secular nature of the legislature's work grossly overshadows any minimal or residual religious implications emanating from the prayer.

This underlying distinction—a relatively sudden exposure to public prayer versus a historically established prayer of a larger secular activity—was acknowledged recently in a case the Court agreed to hear. In early May 2014, the Supreme Court ruled in *Town of Greece v. Galloway* that a public, open meeting can begin with an explicitly Christian prayer. Relying on the precedent established in *Marsh v. Chambers* (1983), the majority opinion's rationale rested essentially on the premise that as long as the name of "Jesus Christ" was not mentioned all of the time or recurring during every opening prayer, then the municipality's open meeting does not violate the Establishment Clause (Olsen, 2014). In fact, Justice Kennedy, in writing the majority opinion, argues "Absent a pattern of prayers that over time denigrate, proselytize, or betray an impermissible government purpose, a challenge based solely on the content of a prayer will not likely establish a constitutional violation" (Kennedy, 2014, p. 794–795). The opinion of the Court also claimed that the occasional reference to Jesus was not overly imposing since Americans are tolerant people. Indeed, Thomas G. Hungar, who represented the town of Greece, argued before the Court that "Americans are not bigots, and we can stand to hear a prayer delivered in a legislative forum by someone whose views we do not agree with," especially since this "is the tradition of this country and that is why it doesn't violate the Establishment Clause" (cited in Markoe, 2013, n.p.). As a result, although some might be offended by the content of the prayer on occasion, Justice Kennedy responds that such an offence "does not equate to coercion" (Epps, 2014, n.p.). Besides, as others have argued, public prayer, especially in this context, is common and part of American tradition (Burke, 2014).

The Court's line of reasoning, while perceived as insensitive to opponents, was clear, direct, and unapologetic. If a non-believer or an adherent of absolute secularism objects to prayers of this sort, Justice Kennedy argued that these people can exit the meeting if they feel so inclined (Burke, 2014). To Kennedy, and the concurring justices, opening a public meeting with a prayer was merely "ceremonial," which should not be viewed as an intrusion or an imposition by the government in religious affairs. In fact, Kennedy claimed that ceremonial "prayer is but a recognition that, since this nation was founded and until the present day, many Americans deem that their own existence must be understood by precepts far beyond the authority of government" (Olsen, 2014, n.p.). The ceremonial aspect of these prayers is a pivotal point in the Court's rationale. In other words, if the prayer is simply ceremonial or part of an expected tradition, citizens should not be surprised, nor offended, by its content. Additionally, if a community believes prayer is important, the occasional reference to a particular sect or religious belief should not be offensive; after all, someone will always be unhappy since the government cannot please Muslims, Christians, Buddhists, Hindus, Baha'i, and atheists alike (Markoe, 2013). Accordingly, Justice Kennedy emphasizes that "legislators need not—indeed cannot—monitor prayers for sectarian content" (Epps, 2014, n.p.). Finally, since the ceremonial aspect of this form of prayer does not violate the Establishment Clause, as stipulated by Justice Kennedy, it "is merely the continuation of a long American tradition, practiced by Congress and dozens of state legislatures, and is intended to 'invoke divine guidance' and place governmental institutions in a 'solemn and deliberative frame of mind'" (cited in Abcarian, 2014, n.p.).

With these arguments, the Court relied on generalizations, insensitivities, and spin. By claiming that meeting invocations are part of the national history, the Court's reasoning is based on the fallacy of generalizing from a paucity of examples. The Court may point to the prayers by Congressional chaplains over the years, or an incident or two of invocations like the *Town of Greece*, but many—and perhaps even most—public meetings, particularly governmental public meetings, do not involve prayer. And, of course, even if public prayer has been widespread, it does not, by itself, make it constitutional. Such an argument, for example, was once used to justify slavery, but the U.S. government eventually came to its senses in 1864 with the passage of the Thirteenth Amendment. Additionally, the *Greece* decision is rhetorically problematic because of its insensitivity to those who disagree with or oppose the town's use of prayer. In Savage's (2014) description of the case, he quotes Justice Kennedy's attitude toward the secular opposition: "Justice Anthony M. Kennedy, who spoke for the court's conservative majority, said those who 'feel excluded or disrespected' by such religious invocations could simply ignore them. 'Adults often encounter speech they find disagreeable.'" In essence, the bulk of the majority opinion rested on the idea that folks who might be offended are not held captive, regardless of the fact that the offense must occur first before an offended party would be able to respond with exiting the meeting. Finally, the court engaged in spin—if not explicit manipulation—of some of the facts of the case. Kennedy claims the prayers referring to "Jesus" were infrequent, yet the dissent introduced evidence of a prayer that included, "It is in the solemn events of next week that we find the very heart and center of our Christian faith. We acknowledge the saving sacrifice of Jesus Christ on the cross. We draw strength, vitality, and confidence from his resurrection at Easter" (Seeman & Merriam, 2014, n.p.). Indeed, Justice Breyer in his dissenting opinion noted that "during the more than 120 monthly meetings at which prayers were delivered during the record period (from 1999 to 2010), only four prayers were delivered by non-Christians. And all of these occurred in 2008, shortly after the plaintiffs began complaining about the town's Christian prayer practice and nearly a decade after that practice had commenced" (Breyer, 2014, n.p.).

Opponents to the decision, of course, believe the Court is overreaching. While the majority opinion claimed that the occasional reference to "Jesus" was not imposing, others felt differently, as Epps (2014) sarcastically emphasized: "The majority decided that prayers to Jesus, invitations to bring Him into our lives, and mentions of His death and resurrection are pretty much fine, as long as they don't happen every single month" (n.p.). Overall, proponents of the "wall" of separation between church and state typically believe that the government should err on the side of secularism, not particular faiths, when laws become entangled with religious beliefs and practices. In this case, the town of Greece was using a public prayer before its municipal meetings, most of which referred to Jesus. There can be no question that when such prayers occurred, it signified a preference for Christian beliefs (Markoe, 2013). Secularists also argue that even if the prayers did not specifically mention "Jesus," any invocation that refers to "God," "Supreme Being," or "Creator" implies at least a deistic religion, thereby excluding agnostics or atheists. For the *Greece* decision, the minority argued that the prayers provide "favoritism" for Christianity, which is a direct violation of the Establishment Clause (Siebold, 2014). The Court's emphasis, or favoritism, of Christianity is even more pronounced if we look at the decision from a different perspective. David Savage, paraphrasing and quoting the dissenting opinion from Justice Kagan, offers another point of view:

> The majority might view the case differently if a "mostly Muslim town" decided to open its meetings with Muslim prayers or a Jewish community always invited a rabbi to open its official proceedings … citizens … should not confront government-sponsored worship that divides them along religious lines. (2014, n.p.)

In so doing, the town of Greece invariably breaches the "wall," and it fosters exclusion and alienation toward non-believers (Esbeck, 2014). As Siebold (2014) declares, "The government should not invite members of the clergy to pray at public meetings. If you do, someone is always going to feel left out or offended. And it's more proof that we must continue to push for the separation of church and state" (n.p.).

With these arguments, the opposition to the *Town of Greece v. Galloway* ruling, like the majority opinion, utilize fallacious reasoning and manipulative spin. For instance, just as the majority opinion can be perceived as insensitive to non-believers, the opposing view displays its own insensitivity by declaring, "If people want to pray they should do it privately or in a church. The faithful are as free to pray as they have always been without making a public display out of a private, personal process" (Siebold, 2014, n.p.). Of course, one could say that expecting religious individuals to pray in private or church allows them a venue to pray without imposing on others (which conducting the invocation certainly does since non-believers are exposed to the prayers of others in public), which is less intrusive. However, the Court often rules, as it did in this case, that the religious liberty of an individual trumps conflicting claims that are not enumerated in the Bill of Rights. Notwithstanding the majority opinion's privileging of prayer, the dissent claims that public prayer has a higher threshold for offence than does normal speech since a person's "response to the doctrine, language, and imagery contained in those invocations reveals a core aspect of identity—who that person is and how she faces the world" (Epps, 2014, n.p.). In short, if a non-Christian or non-believer is present in the midst of a Christian invocation, he or she is essentially "outed," which immediately conjures feelings of exclusion, resentment, frustration, and so on. Imagine, for example, a Muslim woman, wearing a hijab, awkwardly trying to be inconspicuous during the public, Christian prayer. The ensuing feelings of anxiety and alienation would be obvious and likely would tarnish the rest of the meeting for believers and non-believers alike.

Moreover, what if the tables were turned? The question of who has the power to dictate if a prayer occurs—and what type of prayer—should give us pause before we agree with the majority too quickly. However, in an act of fallacious reasoning, Justice Kagan of the dissent offers a slippery slope perspective:

> "I would hold that the government officials responsible for the above prac-tices—that is, for prayer repeatedly invoking a single religion's beliefs in these settings—crossed a constitutional line," Kagan wrote. "I have every confidence the Court would agree." So why, she asks, should a town meeting be treated any differently? And what, she wonders, would happen if a predominantly Jewish community asked a rabbi to begin every gathering chanting from the Torah. ... Or a Muslim community to begin with the Islamic call to prayer. ... Or, for heaven's sakes, Satanists. After all, they, too, consider themselves a religion. And who is to say otherwise? (cited in Abcarian, 2014, n.p.)

Flipping the presumption of the type of prayer or religious belief provides us a different prism with which to view the impact of allowing public, sectarian prayers. However, the dissent in this case clearly offers a slippery slope fallacy, such that other variables or community norms would probably prevent the terminal point of indignation. As such, the opposition to the *Greece* ruling risk dissuading persons from their viewpoint precisely because arguments such as these border on the ridiculous. Finally, the dissent simply exclaims, "The only purpose of praying in public is for proselytizing. It has no place in any state-funded, subsidized or operated organization" (Siebold, 2014, n.p.). This overgeneralization may appeal to some who find any sort of government subsidi-zation of religion problematic, but this argument hardly rebuts how communities have historically engaged in prayer, which not only preserves individual religious liberties, but also offers a sense of community bonding at the public event.

Thus, both sides of this issue employ fallacious reasoning and even flimsy, if not far-cical, contentions. On the other hand, both sides also provide interesting and attractive positions that are appealing to many. The complexity of this issue demands that we pay close attention to the rhetorical situation, facts of the case, and the types of reasoning used in this debate. Furthermore, we will see some of these concerns in the next issue.

Tax Exemptions

While not an issue addressed above in the legal context of religious rhetoric, the tax-exempt status of religious institutions has generated controversy at different moments in American history. And tax exemptions provide a rationale for other religious exemp-tions, some of which I will mention later and we can see in Figure 3.2.

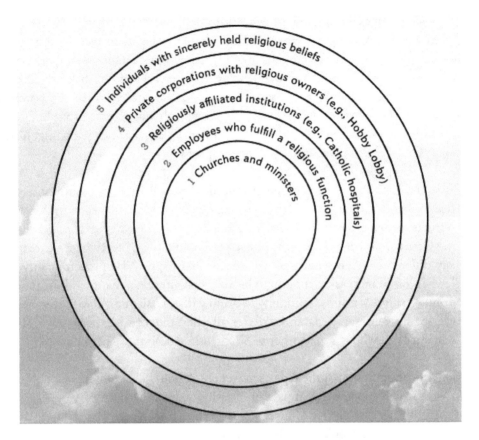

5. Individuals with sincerely held religious beliefs
4. Private corporations with religious owners (e.g., Hobby Lobby)
3. Religiously affiliated institutions (e.g., Catholic hospitals)
2. Employees who fulfill a religious function
1. Churches and ministers

Figure 3.2: Levels or Religious Exemptions, Stern (2014a).

Offering tax exemptions to any entity is likely to generate some controversy. When we add to that the highly sectarian and partisan views of religious institutions, we may face a powder keg ready to blow. Tax-exempt status for churches—including their property holdings, salaries, housing allowances, benefits, etc.—has a long tradition in this country, spanning over a hundred years. This historical legacy may dampen some of the volatile emotions and positions that surround this controversial issue; after all, it may have been around long enough that most Americans are simply numb to the idea. Or, because of the tradition established over the issue, the opposite may result. In fact, as Golden argues, "Some faith-related issues are so steeped in tradition and sentiment they cause near-instant polarization," such as "the tax-exempt status conferred to religious organizations" (Golden, 2013, n.p.). Indeed, the controversial aspect of religious tax exemptions has sparked new rounds of divisive discourse since the 1970 landmark Supreme Court decision of *Walz v. Tax Commission of the City of New York*, as well as some federal court cases in the past couple of years.

To understand the rhetorical situation of this imbroglio, we need to begin with the *Walz* decision. With *Walz*, the majority opinion, written by Chief Justice Burger, articulates a rationale primarily based on the idea that religious institutions are nonprofit entities and should enjoy tax-exempt benefits like other nonprofits. The Court reasons that no church and state violation occurs because all religions may obtain tax-exempt status, and allowing tax shelter for churches is no different than other nonprofit agencies. Along these lines, the Court suggests that an "exemption is neither the advancement nor the inhibition of religion" because the government "has not singled out one particular church or religious group or even churches as such; rather, it has granted exemption to all houses of religious worship within a broad class of property owned by nonprofit, quasi-public corporations which include hospitals, libraries, playgrounds, scientific, professional, historical, and patriotic groups" (Burger, 1970, p. 673). This position is reinforced with the presumably neutral claim that churches help their communities, therefore they should receive some support from the community: "The State has an affirmative policy that considers these groups as beneficial and stabilizing influences in community life and finds this classification useful, desirable, and in the public interest" (Burger, 1970, p. 673).

The dissent, led by Justice Douglas, relied on several opposing arguments, such as how tax-exempt benefits convolute notions of equality, they require more imposition of the government in order to determine what constitutes a "religion," they are not necessary to maintain community benefits, and they frustrate the harmony between religious institutions and the secular sphere. Moreover, since the state is in a position to decide the merits of an entity's claim to be a "religion," the *Walz* decision automatically forms an exclusion to those who do not qualify as a religion; therefore, "it is itself a signal of persecution" (Douglas, 1970, p. 725). Simply put, Justice Douglas argues that "a tax exemption is a subsidy" (1970, p. 705), and, as such, is a clear violation of the Establishment Clause.

A 2002 tax-exempt case involving megachurch pastor Rick Warren in California would have probably been decided as unconstitutional; however, before the judge could rule, Congress preempted it with the Clergy Housing Alliance Clarification Act of 2002, which *de facto* terminated the court case because the plaintiff no longer had grounds for the lawsuit (Wiener, 2009). In late 2013 and early 2014, federal courts wrestled with the same issue of whether clergy should receive tax shelter from their housing allowance bestowed by their church. Two cases that received the most discussion were in Kentucky and Wisconsin, both of which tackled the tax-exempt disputation. In the Wisconsin case, U.S. District Judge Barbara Crabb ruled that any type of tax exemption concerning housing allowances for clergy are unconstitutional based on the Establishment Clause (Laird, 2014; Left Coast Lucy, 2013). As we might expect, her decision created a firestorm of reactions, mostly from religious groups.

In these cases, along with the national discussion as a whole, the nature of religious institutions receiving tax-exempt status ignites passionate pleas from both sides of the debate. In terms of the arguments by supporters of tax exemptions for religious institutions, the major claims made are essentially extensions of Justice Burger's comments in the *Walz* majority opinion. To begin, one very common argument is the appeal to tradition (which is also a fallacy). Simply put, "For generations, churches have been exempt from income taxes" (Wood, 2012, n.p.), which includes Christian and non-Christian religious entities alike (Callahan, 2014), even dating back before the American Revolutionary War (Singham, 2013). Over the years, many advocates claimed that churches help their communities, primarily by serving the poor (Callahan, 2014; Thistle, 2013). In fact, not only do churches help their communities, but they also relieve some of the pressure for governmental social programs because churches serve "as an alternative to the governmental sector as a method for addressing society's problems" (Callahan, 2014, n.p.). Some opponents argue that church-based poverty programs risk abuse, but there are safeguards in place to prevent malfeasance (Callahan, 2014). Finally, because religious institutions are members of their communities, encouraging more churches promotes religious diversity, which in itself is a positive end (Smith, 2007). But this begs the question: How does tax-exempt status relate to religious-based social programs? Tax-exempt supporters reason that if religious organizations had to pay taxes, they would have fewer resources for social programs. Furthermore, they argue that tax-exempt status provides a "reimbursement," *per se*, for all of the good the religious entities do for their communities (Thistle, 2014). And in a related position, the clergy housing allowance cases provide an affirmative financial boost for smaller churches, which are important if we value religious diversity (Laird, 2014).

Because religious organizations are treated "neutrally" as a nonprofit, the IRS regulations for 501(c)(3) entities applies to them (Callahan, 2014). This means that in order to receive tax exemptions, a church cannot engage in politicking—it cannot speak from the pulpit to endorse a particular candidate or political party (Stanley, 2008). Advocates for tax-exempt status argue that this IRS provision helps secure a wall of separation between church and state. This is pivotal since many believe that the key hinge argument concerning tax exemptions is that they might violate the Establishment Clause. This is particularly salient to many when they consider that their tax dollars may be supporting—indirectly by offering a religious benefit via tax exemptions—a religious faith for which they find objectionable. For example, many Americans are suspicious of Islam, especially in a post-9/11 world. However, mosques are eligible for tax exemptions just as Christian churches are. This sort of entangling may be offensive to some. Nevertheless, supporters of tax exemptions suggest a more tempered approach. Instead of viewing the tax policy as providing a benefit to certain religious institutions, we should perhaps view the process as an investment in the community, especially if we believe that churches, mosques, temples, etc. are important contributors to their communities (Golden, 2013). Furthermore, because other religious groups (like Islamic, Jewish, Hindu, Buddhist, etc.) may receive tax exemptions just like a Christian denomination, it solidifies the government's "neutral" approach in this instance. In other words, no breach of the Establishment Clause occurs since the government is treating all religious entities—and all nonprofits, for that matter—equally (Callahan, 2014). Since the Establishment Clause is the primary concern here, it is imperative that supporters address this potential conundrum. One advocate for tax-exempt status for religious entities provides this rhetorical justification:

> There is said to be an old Arabian proverb: "If the camel once gets his nose in the tent, his body will soon follow." This expression is especially pertinent in the tax exemption context. Churches are tax exempt under the principle that

there is no surer way to destroy the free exercise of religion than to tax it. If the government is allowed to tax churches (or to condition a tax exemption on a church refraining from the free exercise of religion), the camel's nose is under the tent, and its body is sure to follow. But that's not just my opinion; it's the understanding of the U.S. Supreme Court. (Stanley, 2008, n.p.)

By using metaphor, this argument carries a rhetorically powerful component. Additionally, this argument is compelling to many because it addresses the Establishment Clause concern head-on. If we reduce or eliminate tax-exempt status for churches, it risks permitting even more governmental influence into religious affairs. This, of course, would violate the Establishment Clause. To take this argument further, even if tax-exempt status violates the Establishment Clause, the argument goes, having no tax exemptions would be much worse. Thus, if we balance the two options, granting tax exemptions appears to be the most constitutional practice. Of course, the use of metaphors may be problematic if the metaphor itself is confusing or an inappropriate fit. Plus, in this case, Stanley's claim is also an appeal to fear—that more state intrusion may take place—by means of a slippery slope fallacy. While somewhat nuanced, these carefully crafted arguments are purposefully composed in order to persuade the maximum amount of people.

Other arguments for tax-exempt status also exist. Some pastors do not receive salaries, suggesting that their work is *de facto* volunteerism and, as such, should not be taxed. In many communities, faith-based centers and churches fill-in the gaps left by government agencies who fail to provide crucial services. Similarly, many religious institutions do more than just charitable work in their areas—they offer shelters for victims of domestic violence, shelters for the homeless, food banks, child care, youth services, and so on. In these ways, religious groups claim they should be exempt from taxation due to the vital work they perform in communities throughout the nation.

Therefore, advocates for tax-exempt status appeal to the senses of Americans by employing appeals to tradition/history, fear appeals, metaphors, slippery slope arguments, and generalities claiming that all (or at least most) churches benefit their communities. These rhetorical tactics are pervasive and powerful. To summarize their overall position, a tax-exempt supporter vehemently contends:

In conclusion, churches have been tax exempt throughout our country's history because they are meaningful to the structure and functioning of society in the United States. Exemption furthers diversity in American culture, results in public benefit to society, and protects the constitutional guarantee of freedom of exercise of religion. (Callahan, 2014, n.p.)

This overarching rationale sets the stage for responses from those who oppose tax exemptions for religious entities.

Opposition to tax exemptions primarily respond to the arguments proffered by the pro-tax exemption position. Underlying the claims of opponents is a fundamental belief: religious groups operate like businesses (Mehta, 2012). If that is the case, special privileges for any religious benefit become moot. Given the multiple, even slippery, purposes for which religious organizations exist, the concern about potential politicking arises (Lynn, 2008). Tax-exempt opponents passionately argue that supporting religious groups who turn around and preach politics not only violates the Establishment Clause, but it also jeopardizes our democracy. The *Free Thought Today*, which is a newsletter published by the Freedom from Religion Foundation (FFRF), summarizes this notion:

> What ADF and rogue churches want to achieve would make Citizens United look like peanuts. Congregations could be turned into political machines. Tax-exempt donations could be funneled to politicians and campaigns with no accountability, no sunlight, no reporting, no limits. Politicians would be forced to openly pander in order to curry votes. Our democratic republic would be imperiled, and we would be at the mercy of a religious shadow government. (Free Thought Today, 2013, n.p.)

Obviously, this argument depends on generalities and fear and uses the slippery slope fallacy. And since mostly secular or non-religious groups oppose religious tax exemptions, it does not help the dispute that most of the churches guilty of politicking have been found to be affiliated with the so-called "Religious Right" (*Free Thought Today*, 2013). Even though a reasonable claim might be made that tax exemptions aid organizations that engage in political behavior, it does not follow that the terminal result of such aid would "imperil" our democracy. Furthermore, this also utilizes a *post hoc ergo propter hoc* fallacy. Just because we give some religious entities tax-exempt status does not mean that the status causes heightened politicking or the jeopardizing of democratic principles. Of course, advocates for tax-exempt status claim that the IRS checks any abuse emanating from politicking. However, while all nonprofit organizations must submit a form to be granted tax-exempt status, religious groups do not need to fill out the form because they are naturally given the status (Lynn, 2008). And while in theory, the IRS is duty-bound to monitor political activity, the agency has sworn off auditing religious entities since 2009, meaning that political behavior by religious groups can occur willy-nilly (*Free Thought Today*, 2013; Notte, 2013). Additionally, if the day comes when the IRS changes its "no-audit" policy, the agency's regulations are also easily circumvented (Wald et al., 1988). This issue of politicking can be seen as a very serious concern. The prevalence of this activity is quite significant, with conservative estimates stating that over 1,500 churches violate the "no-politicking" rule (*Free Thought Today*, 2013). And if tax-exempt status contributes to the extraneous political behavior of religious groups, even if indirectly, opponents argue the violation of the Establishment Clause is obvious.

Abuse from political activity is not the only type of abuse that is identified by opponents. Pecuniary malfeasance, along with morally objectionable behavior, also provide cause for concern. According to a vocal extremist on this issue:

> The puzzle this solved was that we all know that many so-called church leaders seem to live high on the hog from the money they get from their

often poor parishioners, having a luxurious lifestyle that seemingly depends on them being able to easily divert money given to the church for their own personal use, effectively treating the church's funds as if it were their personal account. (Singham, 2013, n.p.)

Furthermore, the tax-exempt status uniquely fosters this type of financial abuse because it permits multiple tax covers. Another secular radical on this issue argues that the "IRS rules expressly permit clergy to 'double-dip' by using tax-free money to buy a home, then deducting interest on the mortgage from their taxes," which means taxpayers end up paying for much more than we naturally bargain for (Laird, 2014, n.p.). Thus, by using incendiary language and framing abuse issues as "morally" problematic, opponents to religious tax exemption utilize key rhetorical tactics meant to tilt the debate in their favor.

Perhaps the most important concern from the opposition revolves around the implications for the Establishment Clause. With a fallacy of causation camouflaged by a fear appeal, opponents passionately argue that tax exemptions provide a "blatant favoritism for religion" (Laird, 2014, n.p.). But not only do tax exemptions establish a *de facto* endorsement for religion, they also open the door for intrusion on religious groups. For instance, if it is constitutional for the government to offer tax-exempt status for religious entities on the basis that all religious groups are treated equally, the same rationale can be used in reverse—the government could alter course and levy taxes on all religious organizations, provided that the taxes were applied equally (Laird, 2014). As such, the tax-exempt "benefit" that supposedly does not violate the Establishment Clause could permit a limitation of the Free Exercise Clause by imposing burdensome taxes on people's freedom to believe whatever faith they want. Finally, at least with the housing allowance cases, the opposition claim the government gives itself too much power. In order to determine if a clergy housing allowance is permissible under the tax-exempt code, the entity must be classified as a religion. In this way, the government becomes the arbiter of what is and is not a religion (Laird, 2014). This argument, too, uses an appeal to fear as a persuasive tactic. After all, if an audience dislikes religion, it may be persuaded that tax-exempt status promotes religion. However, if an audience embraces religion, it might be persuaded by the arguments that characterize how the government has too much power over religious groups. Either way, opponents of tax exemptions can deploy fear appeals regarding the church and state dilemma as a rhetorical tactic.

In their effort to achieve equal and fair conditions for religious groups, government policies of tax-exempt status actually create less equality among religious and non-religious groups. By offering this up as an argument against tax exemptions, opponents are using the argumentative tactic of "turn-around." Mentioned first by Aristotle when he discusses *topoi*, to turn an opponent's argument simply means that if the opposition's argument results in something good, we should argue that it is bad; if they argue that something results in something bad, we should argue that it results in something good. In terms of the debate surrounding tax-exempt status, the opposing side utilizes precisely this tactic—instead of preserving or promoting fairness among groups by offering tax-exempt status to everyone equally, the government actually fosters a climate of unequal relations and acrimony. This occurs in a couple of different ways. First, atheists tend to be offended by tax exemptions. Atheists generally oppose any privilege granted to a religious organization, and tax exemptions are no different (Laird, 2014). The Court has responded by allowing atheists to be considered a "religion," thereby permitting them to also enjoy tax-exempt status. However, atheists find this maneuver insulting and condescending since their core belief rejects the very idea of religion (Chumley, 2013). Second, tax exemptions can be viewed as unfair for the taxpayers as a whole. Since all religious groups have access to tax-exempt status, it means that taxpayers are supporting—indeed, they are subsidizing—religious organizations with whom they may disagree (Mehta, 2012). In other words, if a religious entity is counter to a citizen's beliefs or values, it is unfair to have that citizen subsidize the religion that he or she finds objectionable (Veith, 2013). Therefore, tax exemptions may run counter to the very philosophies of the citizens who should be enjoying religious liberties in the first place.

Finally, opponents to religious tax exemptions are quick to point out the enormous financial cost of such tax exemptions. A recent study claims that tax-exempt status for religious organizations costs over $71 billion dollars (Mehta, 2012). Eliminating just the clergy housing allowance's tax-exempt status could yield over $700 million per year (Laird, 2014). Given our current economic malaise, that hefty sum could go a long way to alleviate some of our financial hardships. Thus, the financial significance of this issue is frequently articulated by opponents to reject tax exemptions, even if they are found to be constitutional.

Although tax-exempt status for religious entities has a long tradition in the United States, it does not cease to generate controversy. As we have seen, both sides of the debate rely on the following persuasive tactics: appeals to fear, generalizations, fallacies of causation, slippery slope fallacies, and appeals to tradition. The use of these tactics exacerbates the divisive discourse that occurs between religion and politics.

Holy Days

Controversies surrounding holy days occur in various ways concerning several religious or spiritual events. For our purposes, however, I will briefly analyze two holy day disputes: the National (and State) Day of Prayer and the proposed Muslim holy day in New York City public schools.

The National Day of Prayer has a long history. It officially began in 1952, when President Truman ordered the day to be a countrywide exploration into different types of prayers (Trobee, 2014). But the National Day of Prayer has its origin dating back to the Continental Congress, which instigated invocations beginning in 1775, and soon after, President George Washington started the national Thanksgiving prayer in 1795 (Donovan, 2011). Now, there is even an invocation associated with Memorial Day (Easterbrook, 2011). As a result, most Americans have grown accustomed to some type of religious prayer associated with major national events. In fact, "State and federal courts nationwide have repeatedly upheld and recognized prayer proclamations as a deeply rooted part of American history and tradition" (Trobee, 2014, n.p.). Although these public prayers have a long history, they are not without controversy. For example, many religious pundits criticized President Obama's role in the National Day of Prayer by suggesting he did not take it seriously.

Despite Obama's prayer message where he calmly stated, "I ask all people of faith to join me in asking God for guidance, mercy, and protection for our nation" (Donovan, 2011, n.p.), one critic reported that "George W. Bush made the National Day of Prayer a very public event where religious leaders would come to the White House and offer prayers. The overarching theme of such gatherings and of the event itself was not focused on a specific religion, but on the idea that America is a country where prayer has value and worth. President Barack Obama reduced the public White House event to a memo in his first year in office" (Ibbetson, 2010, n.p.). While there has been a consistent legal validation of public prayers that are tied to holy days, recently there have been two federal appellate court cases that dealt directly with the problem of government-endorsed holy days and their potential clash with the Establishment Clause.

The first court case upheld the practice of public prayer by ruling the plaintiff lacked standing. In 2010, the secular, disruptive agitators known as the Freedom from Religion Foundation (FFRF) filed a lawsuit to stop the National Day of Prayer activities in the state of Indiana. The case, cited as *Freedom from Religion Foundation, Inc., v. Obama*, eventually made it to the federal appeals court in Wisconsin, where the court stated "that 'neither the statute nor the President's implementing proclamations injures plaintiffs,'" therefore the plaintiffs lack standing (Easterbrook, 2011, n.p.). The FFRF claimed that the National Day of Prayer was an endorsement by the government to present prayer to the public, thereby violating the Establishment Clause. Since major government leaders, including the president of the United States, take part in the National Day of Prayer, the FFRF said it was a form of coercion to non-believers and secular citizens. The court disagreed. The arguments proffered by the court essentially relied on the ideas that such prayers have a long history in the United States, that prayer is an important component to the founding principles of the country, and the proclamation of prayer does not force or require anyone to believe in religion or even take part in the ceremonial prayer itself (Donovan, 2011; Ibbetson, 2010).

About a year later, the second court case ruled virtually the opposite way than the Wisconsin *Obama* decision. In *Freedom from Religion Foundation v. John Hickenlooper*, the FFRF contested the State Day of Prayer in Colorado. Although the State Day of Prayer is sponsored by the National Day of Prayer task force and is "sponsored " by "National Day of Prayer events," the *Hickenlooper* court explicitly stated that its decision only affected the state of Colorado (Bernard, 2012). Nevertheless, *Hickenlooper* was a victory for the FFRF because Chief Judge Bernard ruled that a Day of Prayer has explicit religious intent, it is endorsed by the government without a secular purpose, and, as such, it violates the Establishment Clause.

Thus, we have a dichotomy between those who advocate for days of prayer and those who disagree and oppose them. Many supporters for days of prayer claim that most Americans pray, at least 90%; therefore, it is no big deal if the government provides for public prayer (Bornschein, 2012). While that statistic is probably debatable, the fact remains that many Americans engage in prayer. When lawsuits such as the ones issued by the FFRF occur, advocates for days of prayer, such as one of the *amicus curiae* briefs, worry that important, holy moments are trivialized into mere "ceremonialism" (Araujo, 2010). Furthermore, persistent affronts to days of prayer are perceived by supporters as absurd. Opponents often argue that the language in these prayers are offensive; yet supporters quickly point out that, "the address is chiseled in stone at the Lincoln Memorial on the National Mall. An argument that the prominence of these words injures every citizen, and that the judicial branch could order them to be blotted out, would be dismissed as preposterous" (Donovan, 2011, n.p.). Thus, these challenges not only are "legally flawed, but clog our court systems and represent a waste of judicial resources" (Sekulow, 2011, n.p.).

These knee-jerk opinions notwithstanding, advocates for days of prayer also levy extremist, arguably even fanatical, contentions. These advocates typically claim that God requires prayer, and, as such, having days of prayer are crucial for a genuine and meaningful relationship with God for both the individual as well as the country (Bornschein, 2012; Velarde, 2008). This ultimate appeal to authority is difficult to refute since the very existence of God is in dispute. But this fallacy does not deter advocates, who go so far as to exclaim God "actually prefers it when we come to have faith in him through prayer, instead of through logical arguments alone. God doesn't just want to satisfy a curiosity we have, He wants to enter into a friendship with us" (Bornschein, 2012, n.p.). They also postulate that "communication with the divine is the lifeline of America's survival and prosperity. It is more valuable to the body of this country than air is to the lungs. Without it we are doomed, and will die as a nation gasping in the dark" (Ibettson, 2010, n.p.). Setting aside for a moment the obvious religious and sectarian bias in such comments, I should also point out that many religious zealots, and not just the Religious Right, believe that capital-T "Truth" is on their side (Montgomery, 2014). With such obstinance, it is virtually impossible to find common ground or achieve compromise. This is particularly the case regarding the days of prayer controversy. Not only do supporters sometimes appear intransigent, but they also distrust the opposition. Conservative crusader Paul Ibbetson, who hosts a radio show called the "Conscience of Kansas" as a Tea Party representative, declares that anti-prayer activists use "deceptive" attempts in their arguments. He goes on to pronounce,

> To deny the simple acknowledgement of the value of communication with a higher power is nothing short of poisoning the seedlings from which organized religion grows. No matter how it is presented, the arguments forwarded by groups such as the Freedom from Religion Foundation are nothing more than the usual vomitous verbal spray of liberal propagandists who try to sell Godlessness as the freethinker's utopia. (Ibbetson, 2010, n.p.)

These *ad hominem* statements and fear tactics premised on "poisoning the seedlings from which organized religion grows" further polarize this issue. But this type of rhetoric is no doubt effective to those who are already inclined to favor a day of prayer. After all, it is this sort of commitment to a religious presence in our lives that enable some advocates to claim that it is our Judeo-Christian values that have "allowed people from all over the world to experience the freedom of making their life choice—including freedom of religion—and living out the consequences thereof. This has led to America being the most prosperous/blessed nation on earth" (Willis, 2014, n.p.). Finally, and to provide additional support for the claim that America is the most blessed nation on the planet, some supporters point out that a praying nation causes less crime. It is not uncommon to hear from prayer activists that "following a forty-day prayer vigil organized by the Orlando Police Department, a dramatic decrease in crime was reported. The goal was to reduce crime in Orlando by taking God's word outside of churches and onto the streets" (Bornschein, 2012, n.p.). While these fallacies are based on generalities (they only state one example) and a *post hoc* rationale (just because prayer increased, then crime decreased, does not mean one caused the other), believers in prayer find such claims very persuasive.

Of course, more concrete arguments, some of which are premised on fallacies and spin, are also made by day of prayer supporters. One of the most obvious efforts at spin comes from Sarah Palin. The former Alaskan governor and vice presidential candidate is fond of aligning herself with gun and God-loving Americans. During the 2010 presidential campaign, she noted that faith in God is a form of patriotism (Waters, 2010). Believing that the United States was founded on Christian principles, Palin seized some attention concerning the National Day of Prayer controversy:

> Sarah Palin joined Fox News's Bill O'Reilly recently to condemn the critics of the National Day of Prayer, saying that the Judeo-Christian belief was the basis for American law and should continue to be used as a guiding force for creating future legislation. According to Palin, the recent backlash against the National Day of Prayer is proof that some people are trying to enact a "fundamental transformation of America" and to "revisit and rewrite history" in order to shift the Christian nation away from its spiritual roots. (The Huffington Post, 2010, n.p.)

Sarah Palin and Bill O'Reilly are both known for their extremist political discourse. And with these comments, Palin is utilizing *non-sequiturs* to rely, instead, on impulsive beliefs that latch on to the appeals to Christianity. Additionally, by entering into the religious fray, their invective heightens the polarization.

In some ways, opposition to days of prayer, such as the FFRF, probably provide supporters with evidence that prayer should be increased, not decreased. In other words, if one believes that prayer is vital in order to have a solid relationship with God and it brings with it the benefits of a blessed country, reduced crime, and so on, it is not hard to imagine that extremist supporters of prayer will claim that more prayer is needed to hedge against waves of Godlessness occurring in the country. Lou Dobbs, the infamous provocateur extraordinaire, distressingly asks, "Why are we moving away from singing the praises of God for His bountiful blessings upon us and our beautiful country? It's as if there's almost a national silence, an aversion to public expressions of love of God and country" (2014, p. 3). Indeed, participants of the National Day of Prayer warn "of a continuing moral and spiritual decline, interceding for national repentance, and, in at least one case, expressing defiance toward the 'abortion president' and the contraception mandate that his administration has tried to foist on Americans" (Bohon, 2014, n.p.). And since the National Day of Prayer "is an exercise of constitutional freedom, a wonderful expression of goodwill and love by those who choose to pray for the continued success of our nation, out of a desire to honor the God in whom we believe," it presents an ideal opportunity, as award-winning Christian singer Lucinda Williams says, to "get right with God" (Williams, 2001, n.p.).

More sensible arguments for days of prayer mostly rely on legal reasoning. First, many advocates point out how Thomas Jefferson's clarification of the "wall of separation" of church and state was intended to restrict government intrusion into religion, not to restrict religion's influence in public life (Willis, 2014). This position is shared by the crazed, conservative huckster Newt Gingrich when he writes that the Religion Clauses are "designed to protect freedom *of* religion not freedom *from* religion" (2005, p. 50). This First Amendment rationale is strengthened when one considers Supreme Court precedent, such as its 1983 decision in *Marsh v. Chambers*. Derek Araujo, an attorney who wrote an *amicus* brief in support of the National Day of Prayer for the Seventh Federal Circuit Court of Appeals decision, clarifies how *Marsh* helps the arguments in favor of the National Day of Prayer:

> The courts have limited the doctrine of ceremonial deism to a small number of highly specific contexts. In these particular contexts, the courts have either held or suggested in dicta that a government religious practice is constitutional, despite the practice's prima facie violation of the Establishment Clause, on the grounds that the practice is longstanding and its religious impact is minimal. (Araujo, 2010, pp. 4–5)

Finally, perhaps the most reasonable argument made by supporters of the National Day of Prayer is that it is not coercive, which negates any risk of violating the Establishment Clause. As Judge Easterbrook of the Seventh Circuit Wisconsin decision argues, the prayer is a "proclamation" and therefore not a command "any more than a person would be obliged to hand over his money if the president asked all citizens to support the Red Cross or other charities" (Easterbrook, 2011, pp. 4–5).

As we know, Judge Easterbrook in the Wisconsin *Obama* decision ruled that the FFRF lacked standing, which meant the legal issue was remanded back to the state that already upheld the day of prayer (Sekulow, 2011). Opponents to the National Day of Prayer find public prayer problematic for multiple reasons, but Barry Lynn, the executive director of Americans United for Separation of Church and State, claimed that this *Obama* case marked "an ominous trend in the federal courts to deny Americans the right to challenge church-state violations" (cited in Bauer, 2011, n.p.). This argument is interesting because it does not take a position one way or the other concerning days of prayer; instead, it points out that ruling that the case had no standing necessarily eliminates any federal discussion on this matter. In so doing, the *Obama* decision stops the conversation. While arguments were made regarding the National Day of Prayer's repercussions to the particular state, the *Obama* case—and its sister case in *Hickenlooper*—forecloses the possibility of discussing any federal implications that may occur.

Other opposing arguments are much more direct against days of prayer. First, and most obviously, challengers to days of prayer report that the government simply has no place in matters involving prayer. Judge Steven Bernard of the Colorado *Hickenlooper* case says that government should leave the "prayer business" altogether, and instead, it should "leave that purely religious function to the people themselves and to those the people look to for religious guidance" (2012, p. 5). When the government fails to step out of the way of religion, religious "liberty protected by the Constitution is abridged when the State affirmatively sponsors the particular religious practice of prayer" (Bernard, 2012, p. 2).

Furthermore, all of the potential benefits that supporters believe prayer accrues are not precluded. Judge Bernard argues that his ruling "does not affect anyone's constitutionally protected right to pray, in public or in private, alone or in groups. No law prevents a [citizen] who is so inclined from praying at any time ... and religious groups are free to organize a privately sponsored [prayer event] if they desire the company of likeminded citizens" (2012, p. 2). And this makes sense. Believers do not need the government to tell them or even to offer an opportunity to pray because they have all of the liberties enshrined in the First Amendment—freedom of speech, expression, and religious exercise—in which to practice their faith. Additionally, the corollary to this argument is perhaps what makes this controversy so fragile and polarizing. While supporters of prayer days argue it is their religious right to do so, opponents claim that government-sponsored prayer days violate the Establishment Clause. Since the National Day of Prayer serves no explicit secular purpose, it is, instead, an "explicit call by government for religious exercise on the part of citizens" (Araujo, 2010, p. 2, 17). Araujo continues to clarify this position—days of prayer are not ceremonies or festive occasions solely, but instead, they are proclamations of "government exhortation to engage in prayer, a quintessentially religious activity, and attempts to influence individuals' decisions about whether and when to pray" (pp. 15–16). As such, proclamations of prayer have explicit religious intent; "their content is predominantly religious; they lack a secular context; and their effect is government endorsement of religion as preferred over nonreligion" (Bernard, 2012, p. 2). If this is true, days of prayer naturally violate the Establishment Clause.

As we know, supporters of prayer days base many of their arguments on the American history and tradition of prayer both in and out of the public sphere. However, a common response suggests that the Founding Fathers would probably find a National Day of Prayer problematic (Araujo, 2010, p. 22). In fact, a close study of the original documents and letters of the Founding Fathers reveals that instead of "composing a detailed and specific civil code listing permissible and unacceptable practices, however, the Framers composed the Constitution in terms of 'majestic generalities' the 'broad purposes' of which must be applied by future generations to the issues of each age" (Araujo, 2010, p. 23). Therefore, it is most likely more accurate to view the Constitution and other documents as elastic to accommodate the religious views of the nation that change over time. Finally, if a strict interpretation of the history argument prevails, opponents to prayer days warn Christians that their claim may backfire:

> Reliance upon historical longevity to shield government practices from Establishment Clause scrutiny is equally problematic. As the Supreme Court has noted, reading the Establishment Clause to permit any practice in existence at the time of the Framers would mean that the government would be free to discriminate against all non-Christians, in direct contradiction of the courts' present understanding of the Religion Clauses. (Araujo, 2010, p. 24)

If we can set aside for a moment the obvious slippery slope fallacy undergirding this particular argument, we may find some common utility in it. If any hope of resolution or compromise exists in this area of church/state relations, perhaps a careful analysis of the implications of the Establishment Clause will offer an opportunity for the rival positions to come together.

Challengers to days of prayer also claim that as a result of breaching the Establishment Clause because religion is endorsed during these prayers, religious (and non-religious) minorities are not being protected by the state. Protection of religious liberty, as advocated by Judge Bernard in the *Hickenlooper* decision, is equally important to the protection of free exercise, and, moreover, helps to secure religious tolerance (Bernard, 2012, p. 4). Thus, the conversation about public prayer is highly contentious. It has even recently been raised as a justification to permit Muslim holy days in New York public schools (Dara, 2014). As a result, we will probably not see a resolution to this dispute any time soon.

Curricula and Prayer in Schools

Naturally, one of the political sites of religious contestation is public schools. Their tie to state-based academic standards and funding make them prone to religious entanglement when matters of faith become associated to school activities. In particular, religious issues involving school prayer, school curricula, and the practice of stating the Pledge of Allegiance are areas in which to examine the relationship between religion and politics as well as to identify the extremist rhetoric surrounding public schools.

As we know, there have been several important Supreme Court cases that relate to the intersection of religion and schools. *Engel v. Vitale* (1962) ruled that state-sponsored school prayers recited in public schools are unconstitutional. One year later, in 1963, the Court relied on the precedent established in *Engel* and decided in *Schempp v. School District of Abington Township, PA* that Bible reading, which is state-sponsored, that occurs in public schools is unconstitutional. Furthermore, the Court ruled in *Wallace v. Jaffree* (1985) that even a state-allowed one-minute prayer or meditation in public schools is also unconstitutional. And, as I already discussed, the Court's *Lee v. Weisman* decision in 1992 forbids clergy-led prayers at high school graduation ceremonies. Based on the *Lee* precedent, the Court held in *Santa Fe Independent School District v. Doe* (2000) that not only are clergy-led prayers unconstitutional, but so too are student-led prayers at events such as public high school football games.

In all of these instances, the role of religion in public schools has been severely restricted, if permitted at all. The Court has consistently ruled in favor of protecting the religious liberties of minority religious views by invoking the Establishment Clause to prohibit state-based religious activities in public schools. The *Engel* and *Schempp* decisions have constructed a relatively firm precedent that protects schools from religious intrusion (Bobbitt, 1982). Nevertheless, many still advocate the importance of instilling Judeo-Christian values in our schools, primarily by having prayer.

Like many of the church/state cases of this type, supporters claim that prayer is part of American history. In particular, Justice Potter Stewart argued in his dissent in the *Schempp* case that it is somewhat hypocritical for the Court to forbid prayer in schools when the Court itself "opens its own sessions with the declaration, 'God Save this Honorable Court' and that Congress opens its sessions with prayers" (Stewart, 1963, p. 308). While the United States often begins important governmental sessions with prayer, it should also be noted that such prayers are never forced upon members. In the school setting, prayer proponents argue that the exercise of prayer is purely voluntary, which means it is not a coercive act (Bobbitt, 1982, p. 202). As such, by forbidding prayer in schools, the Court is actually restricting the free exercise of religion from those students who believe in prayer (Bobbitt, 1982, p. 204). In this way, the Establishment Clause, which is used to justify the banning of school prayer, can conflict with and undermine the Free Exercise Clause (Bobbitt, 1982). The conflict between the Establishment Clause and Free Exercise Clause in this context is even more pronounced since prayer advocates claim that banning prayer means the government is, *de facto*, establishing its own religion of secularism. As Justice Stewart said in his dissent, "A refusal to permit religious exercises thus is seen, not as the realization of state neutrality, but rather as the establishment of a religion of secularism, or at least, as governmental support of the beliefs of those who think that religious exercises should be conducted only in private" (Stewart, 1963, p. 313). Others have argued since that secularism can be considered a religion, and, as such, it can be seen to be an established religion by the Court (Bobbitt, 1982).

More radical proponents for prayer in school also begin with the claim that prayer in school is a voluntary act, whereby students are not forced to believe in any particular religion. This premise is used by the instigating yakker Rush Limbaugh, who says that the "free-exercise clause of the First Amendment precludes any prohibition on voluntary prayer in school, or anywhere else for that matter. Prayer in school, again, has nothing to do with the establishment of religion" (Limbaugh, 1992, p. 278). This is important for the extremist position, which then lays out its second premise: that the Establishment Clause's intent was to prevent theocracy, not to eliminate any trace of religion in governmental affairs. Thus, if we map out these premises, we can see the larger position of the crusading true believers:

> Premise 1: Prayer in school is voluntary
> Premise 2: The Establishment Clause's (EC) only purpose is to prevent theocracy
> Conclusion: Therefore, prayer in school does not risk theocracy.

By combining this syllogism with the claims that prayer is beneficial, the more radical position constructs a position that favors prayer by also dodging criticisms from the opposition (i.e., that prayer in school establishes a preference for state-sponsored Christianity).

Thus, to make the syllogism worthwhile, the religious fringe must create a reason to accept prayer in schools; there must be a reason for its advantageous adoption. The guttersnipes of Rush Limbaugh and Glenn Beck quickly resort to the most extreme trump card they can possibly muster—without prayer, our Godless nation will result in a Nazi-like or Stalinist-type totalitarian society. Limbaugh claims that without God in our hearts and without presenting God to our children in schools, we will have to fill the vacuum left by the absence of God with something. As he argues, "Throughout history that substitute for faith has been a belief in a man-made god called the state. Untold crimes have been committed in its name. Hitler and Stalin being the most bloody recent examples. The separation of church and state in our Constitution is not there to protect Americans from religion. It is there to protect Americans from their government" (Limbaugh, 1992, p. 281). In a similar vein, Glenn Beck, in his typical reactionary way, pieces a string of cherry-picked historical moments together, and then pieces them together to create a picture of gloom-and-doom:

> Remember, Hitler learned an awful lot of stuff from a guy named Bernays. And Bernays was the guy who when Goebbels died, they found the book by Bernays on propaganda, an American author, an American that was with Wilson, in the office of Goebbels. It was on propaganda. They say they learned propaganda—Hitler learned propaganda from the Wilson administration. Well, one of the things that the Wilson administration and progressives did at the time was: they knew they had to destroy our faith. They knew they needed to get social justice in there. Well, Hitler took it a million miles farther. He set out to draw Christians to him by explaining the seeds (ph) in "Mein Kampf," where he spoke of the Creator and universe and of eternal providence. He also states his belief that the Aryan race was created by God and that it would be a sin to dilute it through racial intermixing. He tried to head off church resistance by professing in a speech that Jesus was the one true God. Well, one pastor who's going to be with us tonight has told us of the story when Hitler became chancellor of Germany. He met with all of the leading pastors and he openly tried to reassure them that the position of the church was secure. But he secretly was setting out to silence them. (Beck, 2010b, n.p.)

Limbaugh and Beck are clearly using historical allusions, fear appeals, and faulty analogies to amplify their reasons for why prayer should be in our public schools. As if these points were not damaging enough, another denizen of doom, the American Family Association of Kentucky, made this outrageous claim when it urged people to sign a petition to require the Kentucky State School Board to implement school prayer:

> The petition states that after the removal of prayer from public schools, teen pregnancy and violent crime rates spiked 500 percent, instances of STDs increased 226 percent and SAT scores plummeted for 18 consecutive years. Taken together, the petition said, these conditions "open[ed] the door for the AIDS epidemic and the drug culture. ... Florida and Mississippi have already put prayer (religious speech) back into their schools!" the petition states. "Students praying again will eventually turn our country back to God!... The American Family Association of Kentucky doesn't cite to any authority backing up these statistics." (Klein, 2013, n.p.)

In other words, if we do not allow prayer in school, we invite either a Nazi or Stalinist totalitarian government that also would cause dumber students and higher rates of sexually transmitted diseases. The apparent logic in these claims escapes me, but I suppose many people who already follow the nuttiness of Limbaugh and crew will naturally see these connections.

Opponents to school prayer provide arguments that are relatively straightforward, especially in light of Court precedent. As Philip Bobbitt makes clear, the law created by *Engel* simply forbids prayer in public schools since it violates the Establishment Clause (1982, p. 201). Even if the prayer is considered by many to be "voluntary," the trouble is that students are a captive audience who must be present for an "obligatory religious observance" (Bobbitt, 1982, p. 200). Any actions by the government, and by extension public school administrations, must be *prima facie* neutral, meaning that there can be no perception one way or another that any sort of religious imposition is taking place. In sum, Bobbitt clarifies the underlying rationale for opponents to public school prayer:

> For a state legislature to compose a prayer for distribution in the schools seems almost the paradigmatic establishment of an official religion. That it occurred in a context in which no recognized religion seemed to be favored, that it was recited in a public school, and that compulsion to conform was not proved—these facts were inessential. (Bobbitt, 1982, p. 202)

Thus, providing time for any sort of prayer, even if voluntary, is seen as unconstitutional under the Establishment Clause.

Related to prayer in schools are also disputes regarding the content of educational materials in schools, but the same Supreme Court decision applies. This is why a recent issue in Oklahoma public schools will probably fall in line with the *Engel* and *Schempp* line of cases. In suburban Oklahoma City, a public school district wants to adopt a book that teaches archaeology, history, and the arts through Bible stories. Supporters of the adoption argue that children do not need to believe in the Bible, and it is merely used as a metaphorical way to understand these other scholastic issues (McBride, 2014). However, not only does the book explicitly reference the Bible, it also "describes God as eternal, 'faithful and good,' 'full of love' and 'an ever-present help in times of trouble,'" and the book declares that the "'first pages of the Bible spotlight God's desire for justice and a just world,' the second chapter says, but adds, 'When humanity ignores or disobeys his rules, it has to suffer the consequences'" (McBride, 2014, n.p.).

Others, along these lines, have advocated that religious materials should be taught in public schools. For example, Michele Bachmann—who claims God told her to run as a Republican for the U.S. House of Representatives and president of the United States in 2012—passionately urges schools to teach biblical lesson plans (Roberts, 2011). She says it is important to counter an increasing threat of a "secular humanist" world (Syvret, 2011). This is important to note because Bachmann is affiliated with the rise of Christian Dominionism (Avidor, Bremer, & Young, 2012). Seder and Sherrill quote the creed of the Dominion, "Rapture Right":

> Christians have an obligation, a mandate, a commission, a holy responsibility to reclaim the land for Jesus Christ—to have dominion in the civil structures, just as in every other aspect of life and godliness. But it is dominion that we are after. Not just a voice. It is dominion we are after. Not just influence. It is dominion we are after. Not just equal time. It is dominion we are after. World conquest. That's what Christ has commissioned us to accomplish. We must win the world with the power of the Gospel. And we must never settle for anything less. (Seder & Sherrill, 2006, p. 3)

Another Dominionist claims, "Our job is to reclaim America for Christ, whatever the cost" (Hedges, 2006, p. 61). Any perceived threat to the Dominion cause means that it is also a threat to God's plan, so much so that "Dominionism … seeks to politicize faith. It has, like all fascist movements, a belief in magic along with leadership adoration and a strident call for moral and physical supremacy of a master race, in this case American Christians" (Hedges, 2006, p. 11). Bachmann also adds that preventing biblical instruction in schools violates Christian principles and treats Christians as second-class citizens. She argues that "Christians are discriminated against by these conventional interpretations of the Establishment Clause, which … have contributed to the treatment of Christians as 'second-class citizens.'… That's because, of course, under a 'liberal' … view of the First Amendment's Establishment Clause, the government cannot act in a way that does, or appears to, endorse a particular religion" (Posner, 2011, n.p.).

When it comes to the issue of teaching evolution in schools, the Religious Right, like Bachmann, pull no punches when it comes to describing how they believe it erodes our Christian nation. As a cheerleader for the Religious Right, Ben Shapiro attacks the secularist, areligious opponents to prayer and biblically based curricula, especially when liberals insist on teaching evolution as science and religious interpretations of human origins as solely faith-based:

> This type of rhetoric is all too common among secularists on the left. They paint a false dichotomy between religion and science. They say that religious people are anti-science, because science makes God irrelevant—therefore, religious people want to stop scientific progress. They point to the fact that many religious people are skeptical about the theory of evolution—as though skepticism of a scientific finding were in and of itself unscientific. (Shapiro, 2013, p. 241)

Rush Limbaugh has also engaged in this debate, arguing that both evolution and creationism require faith (Beutler, 2010). The implication there is that if both require faith, evolution is no more scientific than a religiously based notion of our origins. However, one thing that separates evolution and creationism is that evolution is predicated on secular beliefs, which is why many among the Religious Right call it *"evil*-ution" (Morris, 2000).

Public Religious Displays

Much like the other issues I have been addressing, the issue of whether religious displays can occur on public land or in public buildings has been in dispute. In terms of religious displays in public areas, there are essentially two contested issues—religious displays at holiday time and the display of the Ten Commandments. In *Stone v. Graham* (1980), the Supreme Court ruled that posting the Ten Commandments in public schools violates the Establishment Clause. The Court's ruling in *Lynch v. Donnelly* (1984) stipulated that a Christmas nativity scene in Pawtucket, Rhode Island, "simply recognized the historical origins of the holiday, one that has secular as well as religious significance" (Lupu et al., 2007, p. 1). In 1989, the Court decided in *Allegheny County v. ACLU* that a nativity scene in a government building violates the Establishment Clause. In 2005, the Supreme Court heard two different cases relating to religious displays. The first, in *McCreary County v. ACLU of Kentucky*, dealt with the Ten Commandments on display in Kentucky courthouses. The Court decided that since the posting of the Commandments was done rather recently, it violated the Establishment Clause because a "reasonable observer" might conclude that the courthouses intended "the religious nature of the document." The other case in 2005 was the *Van Orden v. Perry* decision. The Court used the same "reasonable observer" standard as it did in *McCreary*, but in the opposite direction. Since the display of the Ten Commandments in the Texas state Capitol had been present for over forty years, the Court said that any "reasonable observer" would not see them as predominantly religious, but rather could view them as part of tradition.

Thus, regarding religiously related displays in public areas, the Court tends to rule that they violate the Establishment Clause unless the displays have been a part of a long-lasting tradition; and the Court tends to use the so-called "reasonable observer" test to determine if a display appears religious or as part of a secular tradition. Most Americans disagree. According to the Pew Research Center, "83 percent of Americans said displays of Christmas symbols should be allowed on government property. In another 2005 Pew Research Center poll, 74 percent of Americans said they believe it is proper to display the Ten Commandments in government buildings" (Lupu et al., 2007, p. 1). On this issue, the provocative, radical instigator Michele Bachmann seems to be a part of the majority. At a Ten Commandments rally, Bachmann stated that the Ten Commandments should be placed prominently in our public areas, in part because "the founders of the United States—including George Washington and Thomas Jefferson—'recognized the Ten Commandments as the foundation of our laws'" (cited in Posner, 2011, n.p.). Sarah Palin agrees. Palin says that "those politically correct police … tell us that we must boot Christ out of Christmas, [but] we're saying no, enough is enough of being intimidated and scared of that political correctness. We want to exercise our freedom of religious expression" (Hoffmann & Concha, 2013, n.p.). However, Palin, never one to be called a "reasonable observer," took her position to a polarizing extreme: "If we were to allow our constitutional rights to be adversely affected by those who want to be politically correct, we will go the way of other nations, others states, other societies that have fallen because they don't have a strong foundation of freedom" (Hoffmann & Concha, 2013, n.p.). In this way, Palin polarizes the issue by using hyperbole and a slippery slope fallacy in order present an appeal to fear. As with most of the Religious Right arguments regarding church and state, the more distance we put between the public and religion, the more we have to fear.

Islam

Since 9/11, the United States has experienced what some are calling a new wave of "religious intolerance" (Areshidze, 2013; Nussbaum, 2012). While America prides itself for protecting religious liberties and maintaining a degree of religious pluralism, there have been, nevertheless, periods in our history when religious groups have been less than welcomed to our shores. To be sure, the historical examples of religious bigotry in our country are plentiful, which is why it is important to quote Martha Nussbaum at some length to summarize these moments of religious crisis:

> Despite conditions that emphasize heterogeneity and religious pluralism, however, prejudice and occasional violence against new religious groups have never been absent from the U.S. scene. The early settlers at times exiled people whose religious views were deemed heretical. … Jews, Quakers, Baptists, and Mennonites were welcome in some colonies, but not in all. In the nineteenth century, a surge of Roman Catholic immigration from Ireland and Southern Europe prompted an upsurge of virulent prejudice, as "nativism" became a popular political cause … anti-Catholic prejudice has remained a major factor in American political life until extremely recently: during the Cold War, for example, liberal journalist Paul Blanshard, in his best-selling book American

Freedom and Catholic Power (1947), warned Americans that Catholicism was as big a danger to American democracy as global communism. Meanwhile, smaller groups such as Mormons and Jehovah's Witnesses suffered not only prejudice but also outright violence. Anti-Semitism was extremely common until the 1970s, and has still not disappeared. (Nussbaum, 2012, p. 7)

But today, Nussbaum continues, "by far the largest number of troubling incidents concern Islam" (p. 8). According to a Pew Research poll, Americans seem to be split on their perception of if Islam is a violent religion or not, despite the repeated attempts at many to educate the populace that Islam is a peaceful religion with certain fanatical sects—like every other religion (Kaleem, 2013). But a more recent Pew Research poll shows that "roughly four-in-ten Americans (38%) say the Islamic religion is more likely than others to encourage violence among its believers, while half (50%) say it does not encourage violence more than other religions," with conservatives agreeing that there is a connection between Islam and violence more than liberals (Dimock et al., 2014, p. 59), as we can see in Figure 3.3. However, given our post-9/11 world, Nussbaum argues, "It's not rational to dismiss the fear of Muslim terrorism. … But it's simply not reasonable to believe that all one's neighbors are fiends in disguise" (2012, p. 237).

This fear—fear of terrorism, fear of the Other, fear of the unknown—has manifested itself in a couple of different ways in the religious-political realm. First, many polarizing pundits engage in "Muslim-baiting" to either prove a point or to provoke a controversy (Areshidze, 2013). For instance, regarding former president Obama, the ever-agitating

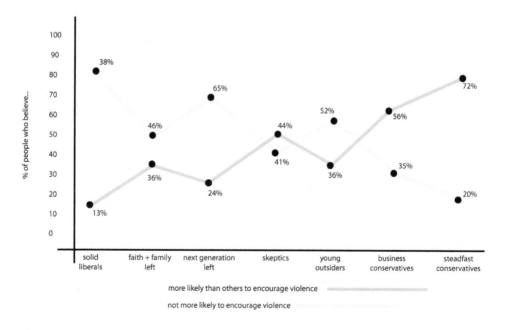

Figure 3.3: Americans' opinions about the relationship of Islam to violence (Dimock et al., 2014, p. 59).

political extremist Todd Starnes "not-so-subtly [hinted] that the president [had] an affinity for Islam—referring to Obama as someone who 'professes' to be a Christian, twice assailing him for calling the Muslim call to prayer 'one of the prettiest sounds on earth at sunset,' and suggesting that Obama [hadn't] secured the release on [sic] American pastor detained in Iran because the pastor had left the Islamic faith" (Brinker, 2014a, n.p.).

Additionally, the ideological blowhard Ann Coulter says many things to incite outrage. Feeding the misguided and ignorant paranoia that "all terrorists are Muslims," and if Muslims want to be considered peaceful, "Muslims might do their part by not killing people all of the time" (Coulter, 2007, pp. 212–213), Coulter actually claims that the Qur'an is a training manual for terrorists (Ohio Len, 2005). One wonders if she has even read the book. Seemingly disappointed that the Boston bombing was not perpetrated by Muslim fanatics for an apparent religious jihad, Coulter nevertheless found an opportunity to spout her invective. When she saw a picture of one of the bomber's widows, Katherine Russell, Coulter belittled Russell for seemingly converting to Islam since she wore a hijab. As a result, Coulter yelped, "I don't care if she knew about this. … She ought to be in prison for wearing a Hijab. This immigration policy of us, you know, assimilating immigrants into our culture isn't really working. They're assimilating us into their culture. Did she get a clitorectomy too?" (Hillcox, 2013, n.p.). This kind of vitriol, of course, serves no purpose other than inviting more anti-Muslim hysteria and placing Coulter's name in the headlines. In so doing, it also undermines the very nature of our First Amendment protections for religious liberty (Hillcox, 2013). After all, if a prominent commentator like Coulter is able to denigrate another person's faith with such carefree disregard, our so-called religious tolerance is vacuous of any worthwhile meaning.

Given Coulter's verbal assault on Islam, it should come as no surprise that other conservatives advocate anti-Muslim positions. In Georgia, a candidate for Congress, Jody Hice, argues that Islam does not even deserve First Amendment protections for religious liberty since it is not really a religion. Instead, Hice claims it "is a complete geo-political structure and, as such, does not deserve First Amendment protection" (Parton, 2014, n.p.). Setting aside for a moment that Christianity could also be considered a "geo-political structure," what is most troubling with this position is that some political conservatives do not want to extend religious protections toward Islam, namely the freedom to exercise and practice it.

Newt Gingrich, another divisive pundit, former Republican Speaker of the House and presidential candidate, has been very vocal against Muslims in America. When moderate Muslims wanted to build a community center—that had a prayer room—near the 9/11 Ground Zero, Gingrich and others vehemently opposed its construction. And New York Republican representative Peter King has been a vocal proponent for questioning anything Islamic. The proposed mosque/community center near Ground Zero has only encouraged King to be more outspoken. In an inquisition-like manner, King chaired a Homeland Security committee to investigate violent Muslims. According to Nussbaum, Peter King consistently claims that the "entire American Muslim community is suspect, not just a radical fringe. He has repeatedly alleged that

Muslim-Americans in general have failed to cooperate with law enforcement. And he once made the outrageous claim that '80 to 85 percent of mosques in this country are controlled by Islamic fundamentalists'" (Nussbaum, 2012, p. 51). Furthermore, Newt Gingrich suggests that "there should be no mosque near Ground Zero in New York so long as there are no churches or synagogues in Saudi Arabia. The time for double standards that allow Islamists to behave aggressively toward us while they demand our weakness and submission is over" (cited in Mantyla, 2010, n.p.). The presence of a Muslim building, even if it is an interfaith community center aimed at teaching how Islam is a peaceful religion, would be seen, according to Gingrich, as a "victory memorial" to the Muslim criminals who terrorized New York City (Areshidze, 2013). Even more shocking is that Gingrich says the center near Ground Zero will be like "Nazis putting a plaque near a Holocaust memorial" (cited in Patel, 2011, n.p.). Like Coulter, King, and Starnes, Gingrich is Muslim-baiting with no real substance. However, his comments were quickly challenged by political extremists from the other side of the spectrum. In response to Gingrich and King, Michael Moore began raising money for the building of the center (CNN, 2010). And Rachel Maddow characterizes the conservatives as irresponsible and un-American:

> I think the idea that you would decide on the basis of what religion is building somewhere, whether or not to build, is fundamentally un-American. That in America, religion is a private matter and that we do not prevent people from the free exercise of their religion. And so the idea that we'd be O.K. with a church there and not a mosque means that we are, anybody who's making that argument is making an un-American argument, as far as I'm concerned. (cited in Urken, 2010, n.p.)

As a result, the debate concerning the so-called "Ground Zero mosque" has become an ugly yelling match, with both sides throwing baseless accusations at the other.

In a related issue, Newt Gingrich has also advanced the proposal that the United States should outlaw *Sharia*, or Islamic, law. While running for president, Gingrich campaigned on his conspiratorial paranoia regarding the virtually impossible risk of *Sharia* law being imposed in the United States. He argues, "I believe *Shariah* [sic] is a mortal threat to the survival of freedom in the United States and in the world as we know it. ... I think it's that straightforward and that real" (cited in Shane, 2011, n.p.). Of course, this statement is in the context of Gingrich's overall position that "America is experiencing an Islamist cultural-political offensive designed to undermine and destroy our civilization" (cited in Patel, 2011, n.p.). Martha Nussbaum, herself a distinguished professor of law, points out the obvious: "The most obvious issue is redundancy: the Establishment Clause of the First Amendment to the U.S. Constitution would already preclude enforcing in U.S. courts the legal codes of any specific religion" (2012, p. 11). In other words, *Sharia* law cannot be imposed anywhere in the United States because it on-face violates the Establishment Clause. Nevertheless, the religious xenophobia stirred by propagandist gasbags like Gingrich has prompted places like Oklahoma to adopt an amendment to its state constitution that would outlaw "the legal precepts of other nations or cultures … international law or *Sharia* law" (cited in Nussbaum, 2012, p. 11).

While one state is trying outlaw an imposed religious code like *Sharia* law, another state is doing the opposite, except it is attempting to establish Christianity as its official state religion. North Carolina considered making Christianity its state religion in 2013. In part, over one-third of the citizens desire Christianity to be their official religion, but it would require a constitutional amendment to do so (Ungar, 2013). Arguably, the Establishment Clause does not apply to individual states since the First Amendment clearly states that "Congress shall make no law respecting an establishment of religion," although opponents might argue that the Supremacy Clause would override this. However, Supreme Court Justice Clarence Thomas argues this point about the Establishment Clause. Since individual states are not bound by the Establishment Clause, they may create an official religion for their respective state, such as Christianity (Stone, 2014). According to the logic of Thomas, the First Amendment "arguably goes beyond prohibiting a federal establishment of religion; it also can be read as preventing Congress from interfering with decisions by the states about whether they would have established churches or policies that preferred one denomination over another" (McGough, 2014, n.p.). Moreover, in Alabama, the chief justice of its state supreme court, Roy Moore, contends that First Amendment protections only apply to Christianity because religions like Islam and Buddhism do not refer to the "God the Creator" that is mentioned in America's founding documents. As Moore claims, "Buddha didn't create us. Muhammad didn't create us. It's the God of the Holy Scriptures . … They didn't bring a Koran on the pilgrim ship, Mayflower . …. Let's get real. Let's learn our history. Let's stop playing games" (Whitmire, 2014, n.p.).

It seems unlikely that talk of official state religions would occur in an America that was not preoccupied with a fear of Islam. And the initiatives to ban mosques and *Sharia* law are certainly a result of this suspicion of Islam. Because religion is so important to so many people, it is not surprising to see such polarizing discourse. However, Nussbaum (2012) cautions us from forgetting what is truly important to us as a nation:

> Respect for persons, then, requires not the stifling of all critical discussion but equal space for people to exercise their conscientious commitments, whether or not others approve of what they do in that space. (pp. 119–120). … Our current climate of fear shows that people are all too easily turned away from good values and laws, in a time of genuine insecurity and threat … irresponsibly manufactured fears threaten principles we should cling to and be proud of. (p. 244)

Islamophobia, which is also discussed in the Foreign Policy chapter, has become a serious problem throughout the world, and of course in the United States. We would do well to remember that we dislike it when others generalize our own issues of faith when we engage in the religious discourse of others.

Atheism

While the Supreme Court has ruled that atheism can be considered a religion, most Americans probably would disagree, and they certainly would not equivocate their own deeply seated religious notions with that of atheism (Chumley, 2013). In fact, most Christian Americans feel threatened by atheists, and they certainly do not trust atheists (Boesveld, 2011; Gervais et al., 2011). When the Pew Research Center (2014b) surveyed Americans about how they felt about different religious groups, atheists ranked only slightly higher than the lowest group—Muslims, who were frequently equated with terrorists—although, according to Metha (2012), politicians who are "gays/lesbians and Muslims have a better rating" than atheists (n.p.). On that point, atheists are distrusted as much as rapists (Matousek, 2012; Winston, 2011), and atheists are rated as "the least desirable group for a potential son-in-law or daughter-in-law to belong to" (Grewal, 2012, n.p.). However, a recent Pew Center (2017) survey reports that American sentiment toward Muslims and atheists are improving slightly.

As Arel (2016) points out, most people of faith feel that atheists do not share the same "morals or values" as they do. While to others this sentiment may seem absurd, to the devout faithful, particularly Christians, the idea of spiritualists and atheists co-habiting is simply nonsensical. The connections may appear peculiar, but it is the basis or framework for one's moral beliefs—not the morals or values themselves—that separates different religious belief systems. Although there is nothing philosophically or even theologically that prohibits Christians and atheists from having similar morals and values, many still insist on their incompatibility.

As I noted earlier, there is a fundamental misconception that America is a so-called "Christian" nation. Sarah Palin even said it was "mind-boggling" to think that America is not a Christian country (David & Loffman, 2010). As a matter of fact, according to Niose (2012), "the political agenda of religious conservatives gets much traction from the belief that America's religiosity is a primary, defining characteristic of the nation and its people" (p. 31). But none of the founding fathers were Christian in the sense that modern Christians claim to be, and most were deists, not Christians (Linker, 2006; Niose, 2012; White, 2013). Furthermore, our first president, George Washington, signed the 1797 Treaty of Tripoli that was also "unanimously ratified by the Senate" (Linker, 2006), which expressly pronounced that, "As the government of the United States of America is not in any sense founded on the Christian Religion" (Miller, 1931, n.p.). But as the nation has developed, the concept of religious inclusivity has become strained. Not only is Islam and other major religious faiths demonized, but so too are the beliefs by the non-religious (Edgell et al., 2006).

Nevertheless, many religious believers, particularly Christians, feel there is a "war on religion," in fact, they believe there is a "war on Christianity" (Banks, 2017; Hixon, n.d.). Recently, most of the predominantly evangelical, Protestant rhetoric about the war on Christianity entails the fear over the way LGBTQ+are being granted more rights in the United States (Brown, 2016). For example, in an episode on *Fox News*, wingnut Bill O'Reilly (2015) had this to say: "Here in the U.S.A., verbal attacks against Christians are the headlines. As we reported yesterday, some far-left people aided by a sympathetic media are now smearing Americans who oppose things like abortion and gay marriage. No question it is open season on Christians" (n.p.). Additionally, a conservative news outlet had this to say just last year: "Is there an increasing hostility to Christian values and religious freedoms in our country today? Here are seven representative examples, all from the last few weeks. Judge for yourself" (Brown, 2016, n.p.). And fundamentalist Christians believe "the new liberalism" of science and secularism are pushing out religious thought and freedom in America (Ordone, 2014). Given this perception, it is no wonder why religious believers, and Christians in particular, perceive non-believers and atheists as a threat to the country's morals and values (Cook et al., 2015). Yet during the Obama years, there was really no demonstrative evidence to support this notion of a "war on Christianity," or a war on religion. In fact,

> One of Obama's earliest executive orders kept open the doors of the Office of Faith-based and Neighborhood Partnerships started by his predecessor George W. Bush under a slightly different name. Over the course of eight years, beneficiaries of government-funded religious social services have won greater religious liberty protections and an interfaith college initiative has grown to include hundreds of campuses involved in service projects. (Banks, 2017, n.p.)

And Mary Elizabeth Williams, a self-identified Catholic, poignantly states:

> We Christians in America have it so easy. And for the privilege of being able to live in a free country and practice our faith, all we have to do is accept that our fellow Americans have a right to practice theirs—or not practice any at all! All we have to do is abide by the Constitution. (Williams, 2015, n.p.)

Nevertheless, many right-wing, conservative, and evangelical Protestant blogs report that there is an unrelenting attack on Christianity. Here is just one example: "One reason for these attacks is that Christianity is in direct opposition to the open sinfulness some people want America to embrace. ... These people see religion as the source of all the worlds [sic] evil" (Hixon, n.d., n.p.). And, of course, the response from atheists is not much more civil. Reacting to the way non-believers are portrayed, Saad (2009) argues, "it is both sad and astonishing that in the 21st century, the populace of the most advanced civilization in history can still hold such backward views," and science "has freed us from the shackles of barbaric, divisive, and infantile superstition" (n.p.). Characterizing the faithful as "barbaric," "infantile," and based on "superstition" certainly does not reduce the polarization of American religious rhetoric.

Yet the prevailing animosity toward Otherized religions and non-believers appears to be waning. According to Leonhardt (2015), who cites a relatively recent study by the Pew Research Center (2015), "a remarkable 25 percent of Americans born after 1980, the group often known as millennials, are not religious, compared with 11 percent of baby boomers and 7 percent of the generation born between 1928 and 1945" (see also Neuhauser, 2016; Shapiro & Pearson, 2015). In fact, as of 2012, some studies suggest that as many as 20 percent of Americans consider themselves atheist or agnostic (Hallowell, 2012).

Although younger generations of Americans seem to be altering the dynamic of the notion that America is a primary Christian, or even religious, nation, the discourse surrounding the rhetoric of religion is still pronounced. Indeed, "Unlike the division over the Vietnam War or the struggles for racial and gender equality of years past, today's culture wars are not focused on one major issue of foreign or domestic policy, but reflect a much more broad, deeply philosophical and *theological* disagreement over the very nature and future of humanity" (emphasis added, Niose, 2012, p. 209). In terms of divisive discourse, both devout believers and non-believers engage in vilifying the other side, and both intensely utilize victimhood rhetoric—believers cry that there is a "war on religion," and atheists feel discriminated against and persecuted.

Issue-Specific Areas of Contention

There are a number of specific issues where the intersection of religion and politics causes some degree of controversy. For example, I could analyze the relationship between political principles and religious practices, such as the Native American use of peyote (e.g., the 1990 Court case in *Employment Division, Department of Human Resources of Oregon vs. Smith*). Or, we could look into the religious, albeit moral, considerations of stem-cell research. Of course, an entire book could probably be written about the divisive discourse of these issues. But two important issues should be discussed and are not a part of this current chapter: healthcare, specifically the Affordable Care Act, and LGBTQ+rights. These two areas of contention have dominated the news headlines and forced virtually every American to question his or her belief systems.

CONCLUSION

After examining the many controversial matters relating to religion, we should also be cognizant that not only are there a multitude of issues, but there is also no shortage of polarizing rhetoric associated with these issues. Indeed, the interjection of firmly held religious ideologies into any political dispute is bound to create situations that invite contentious and turbulent discussions. Alan Abramowitz says it best:

> The rise of polarized politics in Washington is a direct result of profound changes that have taken place in American society and culture over several decades. These changes include … a deepening divide over religion and moral values. … Democratic and Republican voters today are far more divided by race, religious beliefs, ideological orientations and policy preferences than in

the past. Contrary to the views of those who see polarization as almost entirely an elite phenomenon, the deep divide between the parties in Washington and in many state capitols is largely due to the fact that Democratic and Republican elected officials represent electoral coalitions that differ sharply in their social characteristics and political orientations. The roots of polarization are in our changing society—and above all the growing racial and ethnic diversity of the American population. (Abramowitz, 2014, n.p.)

Because of this divisive discourse, we need to pay close attention to how specific religious issues develop into splintering wedges in our communities. This is why I will devote a chapter each to healthcare and LGBTQ+rights, since both are contemporary examples of how our religion and politics have triggered waves of discord.

Hopefully, through books such as this and future conversations with people who have engaged in meaningful self-reflection, we can progress as a society through these controversial issues. I do not mean to suggest that we should avoid these tough conversations, like our parents sometimes ask of us ("Don't talk about religion or politics," they implore). Instead, I agree with Mary Ann Glendon (1991), who firmly believes we should continue our discussions of these vitally important issues, but from a position of self-reflection, open-mindedness, and with a purpose to improve our communities, rather than from a position of dogmatic, ideological zealotry primarily aimed at winning a debate. In terms of these political and religious controversies, Brett Lunceford poignantly remarks that,

> religion cannot be easily removed from public deliberations that require citizens to deliberate concerning matters of virtue or ethics. What is needed is more discussion, rather than less. … The great hope of democracy is that despite their differences, people can come together and work for a common good. However, this is unlikely to happen if different factions retreat into their enclaves and refuse to find common ground. (2012, pp. 28–29)

IMAGE CREDITS

- Fig. 3.1: Adapted from: "Religious polarization," http://www.people-press.org/files/legacy-pdf/Beyond-Red-vs-Blue-The-Political-Typology.pdf, pp. 53. Copyright © 2011 by Pew Research Center
- Fig. 3.2: Adapted from: "Levels or Religious Exemptions," http://www.slate.com/blogs/outward/2014/07/10/one_chart_that_explains_religious_exemptions_controversy.html. Copyright © 2014 by The Slate Group LLC.
- Fig. 3.3: Adapted from: "Americans' opinions about the relationship of Islam to violence," http://www.people-press.org/files/legacy-pdf/Beyond-Red-vs-Blue-The-Political-Typology.pdf, pp. 59. Copyright © 2011 by Pew Research Center.

CHAPTER FOUR

The Rhetoric of Healthcare

The Patient Protection and Affordable Care Act (ACA), also known as Obamacare, has stirred tremendous turmoil. Even the name is contentious, since some conservatives refuse to call it the "Affordable Care Act" because it is "neither affordable or [sic] caring" (Cultural Limits, 2014, n.p.). Concerns about costs incurred by small businesses, choice of doctors, range of insurance options, the ability to cover young adults with adequate insurance, coverage of pre-existing conditions, so-called "death panels," heightened government bureaucracy, preventive care, religious oppositions, exemptions, and so on are only some of the issues raised with the ACA. The skeletal version of the legislation itself is well over 1,000 pages, and it covers a host of new reforms that have triggered an enormous amount of controversy.

But the ACA is not the only current controversial healthcare issue that brews divisive discourse. Given the longstanding legal framework for abortion, opponents—or Pro-Life advocates—always seem to find a way to restrict legal abortions, or even attempt to ban it altogether. There have also been some recent reports that the Veterans Affairs (VA) department (officially named the U.S. Department of Veterans Affairs) has mismanaged money and provided less than adequate healthcare for military veterans (Veterans Affairs, 1997). Given that Obama occupied the office of the president, the Republican political banter about the healthcare implications of our veterans has been highly politicized.

So, with issues involving abortion, individual health insurance, Medicare and Medicaid for mostly the elderly and low-income Americans, and healthcare for our veterans, the overall issue of healthcare in the United States has become a major hotbed for polarized rhetoric and even potentially violent vitriol (as in the case of abortion-related violence). Given the intensity, diversity, and breadth of healthcare issues, there is simply no way I can analyze each issue very carefully. However, in this chapter I will analyze the major claims of controversy in healthcare issues. The divisive discourse that occurs over healthcare in America is common and intense. People feel passionately about this subject. Healthcare concerns quality of life issues as well as potentially life-threatening decisions. Therefore, by examining the overall nature of healthcare controversies, I will outline the nature of polarized rhetoric about healthcare.

THE CONTEXT OF HEALTHCARE

I could write an entire book on the history and context of American healthcare. In fact, several books have already accomplished this (Altman & Schactman, 2011; Lawrence & Skocpol, 2012; Loker, 2012). For the current rhetorical situation, our emphasis should be on understanding the ACA (Bitzer, 1968). Almost all contemporary healthcare concerns today have some connection to the ACA. One possible exception might be the Veteran Affairs scandal, but even with that issue, many pundits use the larger climate of the ACA as an opportunity to attack Obama in other areas, such as the VA controversy. Thus, if we have some understanding of the rhetorical situation of the ACA, most other healthcare discourse can also be understood within that framework.

The Rhetorical Situation

The rhetorical situation of the ACA is unique in that it is largely a constructed situation. Audiences, according to some rhetorical scholars, can be created, but not in the actual sense, of course (Campbell et al., 2014). We can craft our messages to appeal to certain groups—to their whims, needs, desires. By targeting our persuasive points to specific people, we, in effect, are creating them as particular audiences. Theoretically, we can also create problems (exigencies), and I suppose we could create—although probably not intentionally—constraints. With our current healthcare controversy, we can see these components occurring in a largely synthetic fashion. Rising healthcare costs, cumbersome legal and bureaucratic hurdles, efforts at developing new medicines and tackling debilitating disease—these elements, among others, are part of our overall healthcare problem. Most rhetors involved in the healthcare controversy cast blame on their opponents, typically legal entities, corporations, or even sick individuals themselves, as conservative pundit Michael Savage likes to suggest that our personal lifestyle choices are to be blamed for the illnesses we contract, and we are therefore responsible for our own care (Savage, 2012).

It is possible that specific rhetors could construct these exigent circumstances, such as a company raising their drug costs because they claim that government regulations stifle research and development, which would then allow drug company officials to deliver messages about the harmful effects of governmental intrusion into healthcare. While the problem faced by sick individuals would be the high cost of medicine, the drug company could use its decision to increase the cost on consumers as a way to craft its political messages against the imposition of governmental regulations. These sorts of scenarios happen all of the time, but they are not always consciously constructed in this way. Probably more often than not, a problem that occurs for whatever reason is addressed by a rhetorical entity—a company, the government, even individuals—and the reacting entity is taking advantage of the exigence, instead of manipulating it. This is the essence of *kairos*—an emerging, timely moment that permits the rhetorical entity to capitalize on the exigence because the exigence his helpful or harmful in some manner. Thus, instead of creating the problem (e.g., let's say hypothetically rising drug costs), a rhetorical entity could observe the moment when rising drug costs are occurring and utilize that moment to levy arguments against the meddling of governmental restrictions on drug manufacturers.

In a related way, obstacles that appear during the rhetorical situation may either impede the rhetorical entity's persuasive messages or they may provide an opportunity. Rhetorical obstacles can include many things in this case, such as higher costs of doing business, a recalcitrant populace who is confused or uneducated or being swayed to an opposing point of view, legal and policy maneuvers (such as injunctions or Senate filibusters), or even the historical political realities of this particular crisis, such as a long history of efforts at trying to establish universal healthcare in the United States, which, at the same time, has always been at odds with America's spirit of individualism and freedom from government dependency (Altman & Shactman, 2011).

We will see many of these rhetorical situation elements appear as I discuss the rhetorical tactics of polarizing groups involved in the healthcare debate. Before I examine those tactics, however, I shall delve briefly into the historical development of American healthcare. The reason, of course, is that a basic understanding of the historical context of the problem area (i.e., the "rhetorical situation") will add depth to my analysis of the overall discourse of divisiveness regarding American healthcare.

The Crux of Healthcare in America

Before we explore some of the history of healthcare reform, we should quickly note how healthcare currently functions in the United States. Some of this description will not be entirely accurate depending on the time period one is exploring—for example, for many decades, insurance companies could reject claims (and even terminate an individual's insurance entirely) based on what they termed a "pre-existing condition," meaning that if a person suffered from a problem for some time before a crisis incident, the insurance company could reject any claims related to the malady because the individual already had a condition that should have been disclosed and treated that could have, theoretically, prevented the crisis incident in the first place (Jacobs & Skocpol, 2012). Today, under the ACA, insurance companies can no longer purge claims based on "pre-existing conditions." So, in this instance, knowing about pre-existing conditions

Government-Supported Health Care	Government-Free Health Care
Uses tax dollars to provide care for all	Imposes taxes on all despite individual condition
Believes citizens need help with HC costs	Believes individuals should be responsible for their own HC needs
Believes gov't should regulate costs and/or types of care	Believes gov't is a hindrance on HC innovation & development by businesses
Believes limits are needed to control costs	Believes gov't-imposed limits hurt businesses
Believes U.S. health care is weak & insufficient	Believes U.S. health care is best in the world
Believes gov't should help patients & doctors make decisions	Believes gov't should stay out of the decisions of patients & doctors
Believes gov't should impose limits on abuses & practices of insurance companies	Believes gov't regulations on any industry (incl. insurance) undermines effectiveness & innovation

Figure 4.1: U.S. Health Care Philosophy.

is in some ways irrelevant given our current situation with the ACA, yet understanding that the ACA disallows such a practice is important in terms of weighing the relative impact and benefits versus drawbacks to the ACA.

Another important component to understanding healthcare reform is simply knowing how insurance works. Insurance allows us to pay (hopefully minimally) into a system that will be there for us if we need it. It is analogous to contributing to a pool of money with friends and family so that when an individual finds themselves in trouble, that pool of money can be used to pay for the care they need. Insurance works the same way. However, if there are groups of individuals who do not pay into the system (which I will discuss in a moment) or if some individuals are chronically sick, the insurance pool of money plummets quickly. The healthy individuals who are paying a monthly premium are, in essence, paying for those who are not paying monthly premiums and those who require enormous resources from the insurance pool to cover their continuing treatments. What this means is that the smaller the pool of insureds, the less money there is for the entire group—if one or two people in a small insurance pool face a catastrophic illness (like cancer), the entire insurance pool could suffer, sometimes irreparably. Thus, a larger pool is usually a better option, which is why many liberals claim a government-managed healthcare system could be more resourceful and effective than private insurance since the entire population would constitute the insurance pool.

Other factors also contribute to this potential crisis. Some individuals do not pay into the system, yet either expect to receive benefits from it, or the way our system operates naturally services them regardless if they pay into it or not. If someone is unemployed, they are not paying monthly premiums into an insurance plan (private or government-sponsored, like Medicare). Many conservatives, for example, are concerned that so-called "illegal immigrants" will also be a drain on our health system because they will not being paying into the insurance pool, even if they are working (because if they are "illegal," they typically are paid cash for their services and the employers do not report their earnings).

So, one might ask, "If someone does not have insurance, what do they do if they become sick?" This is an excellent question. Former President George W. Bush said,

"People have access to healthcare in America . . . . After all, you just go to an emergency room" (Weiner, 2012, n.p.). And Mitt Romney said something similar when he ran for president:

> Well, we do provide care for people who don't have insurance," Romney told interviewer Scott Pelley. "If someone has a heart attack, they don't sit in their apartment and—and die. We pick them up in an ambulance, and take them to the hospital, and give them care. And different states have different ways of providing for that care. (Weiner, 2012, n.p.)

Of course, any individual in the United States—whether they have insurance or not, or if they are a citizen—can go to an emergency room for a crisis. However, to consider that "insurance" seems naïve. Obviously, emergency rooms only treat crisis events; they do not treat long term care, they cannot monitor, for example, individuals with diabetes in a consistent way, they cannot dispense necessary and daily medications for continuing or chronic ailments, etc. Plus, attending an emergency room is hardly "insurance." It constitutes medical care, to be sure, but it is not insurance since someone, other than a covered insured, will pay for the treatment. Furthermore, treating an ER room as a person's primary care location overloads already stressed emergency rooms. To provide some additional context to this situation, the Department of Health and Human Services reports that in 2006 that an estimated one-fifth of 120 million emergency room visits were done by uninsured people (Jacobs & Skocpol, 2012), and a more recent study explains that, "uninsured persons under age 65 were more likely to have multiple ER visits in a 12-month period than those with private insurance" (Garcia et al., 2010, p. 5). Renowned liberal commentator and senior editor of her own online magazine, Arianna Huffington, explains the trouble with using emergency rooms as insurance:

> Mandating emergency room care as a safety net for the poor isn't, of course, the best way to provide medical care for them. … If your only option is to go to the emergency room, then you'll only get medical care when you have an emergency and not receive the regular checkups, vaccinations, and preventive care that help avoid emergency room visits and, for the seriously ill, extended hospital stays. By turning the emergency room into the neighborhood physician, you also compound the difficulty of providing efficient urgent care because the ER becomes the first point of contact with a healthcare provider for that many more people. (The Huffington Post, 2008, p. 272)

Regardless of one's views about the use of emergency rooms, the point still remains that our country has many people who need healthcare. Estimates vary on how many Americans (before the ACA) were without health insurance. Arianna Huffington (2008) claims almost 90 million people were without insurance at different periods during 2007–2008. But according to a more conservative pundit, Chip Wood, just prior

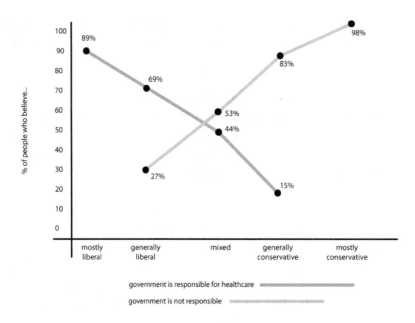

Figure 4.2: Ideological Views on Health Care.

to the adoption of the ACA, around 40 million Americans were uninsured (Wood, 2014). Notwithstanding the ACA, Obama and ACA supporters estimate that 8 million people now have insurance who previously did not (Walsh, 2014). Some claim the number is much lower, because, as politically conservative auger Joe Scarborough claimed on his MSNBC show, *Morning Joe*, Obama's officials have "cooked the books" by fudging numbers of Census data (Isquith, 2014b, n.p.). Even if the liberal estimates are correct, we still have tens of millions without insurance. In addition to the uninsured, we also have millions of Americans who are under-insured, meaning they technically have some form of insurance, but their coverage is minimal or grossly inadequate or extremely costly in order to obtain normal and necessary coverage (Huffington, 2008).

The Historical Context

As Stuart Altman and David Schactman (2011) discuss in detail, the history of contemporary healthcare in the United States involves, as a basic fundamental difference, a tension between a country that expects (or needs) its government to provide varying degrees of healthcare for its citizens versus an American philosophy of independence from governmental intrusion that relies, instead, on the belief that individual responsibility and self-reliance enable citizens to protect themselves as they see fit. At its core, the American healthcare debate is dominated by essentially two opposing sides (see Figure 4.2): One that believes individuals and families should prepare to protect their own healthcare needs and that government involvement restricts the freedoms of families and businesses to make the wisest choices possible for their particular needs (along with the notion that government-involved healthcare also imposes taxes on responsible families and businesses for the benefit of those who are less responsible) *versus* a philosophy that welcomes help from the government (and that acknowledges the need for taxpayers to fund such help).

The contemporary history of healthcare, dating back to President Nixon in the early 1970s, is a story of the two major competing philosophies of healthcare jockeying Congress, sometimes influencing the President and sometimes directed by the President, but always finding a way to codify one of the philosophies into law. According to Altman and Shactman (2011), Nixon's proposed national health insurance law during his second term was the closest to pass Congress, second only to Obama (p. 33). But Nixon was a conservative Republican. And while he was a paradox in many respects—like building relations with China and negotiating with unions—Nixon remained a rather stalwart conservative, typically rejecting larger governmental solutions to problems. Nevertheless, Nixon proposed a national health insurance law that was almost identical to the bill that the liberal senator, Ted Kennedy (D-MA), was recommending, in that it would ensure insurance coverage of some type to all Americans. Hence, some scholars suggest that Nixon's national healthcare plan was not as altruistic as it may seem. Since it was so closely aligned to the liberal proposal championed by Kennedy, some believe Nixon proposed his national healthcare initiative to "co-opt the healthcare issue from the Democrats, while, at the same time, claiming their [the Democrats] proposals would result in socialized medicine" (Altman & Shactman, 2011, p. 34). This was a bold and clever rhetorical maneuver by suggesting the opponent's plan is "socialism," while the President's plan was extremely close to the original initiative. In other words, if two rival groups propose two similar ideas, one way to differentiate themselves from the other party is to call the opposition a name or deflect one's position by pointing at someone else. Ultimately, a number of congressional side-stepping maneuvers and boiling self-interest prevented the Nixon initiative from passing. Altman and Shactman explain:

> Nixon's bill was too liberal for Republicans and not liberal enough for non-southern Democrats, who preferred to wait for the next election. By July of 1971, twenty-two health reform bills were filed. None were ever reported out of [congressional] committee. Everyone supported health reform, but only if the particular bill would benefit his or her constituency. (Altman & Shactman, 2011, p. 44)

As we shall see, not much has changed in 40 years.

The next president who argued for national health insurance was President Bill Clinton. Clinton. Given the lessons learned from Nixon's folly in being unable to legislate healthcare reform, Clinton tried to appease all parties while still advocating a form of universal healthcare. In other words, President Clinton wanted a version of healthcare to supplement existing inadequate health insurance as well as provide mandatory insurance to those who did not have it, primarily funded through tax dollars and employer contributions. This is an extremely liberal approach. However, in order to appeal to conservatives, Clinton proposed a new idea, called "managed competition." This component encourages free market competition among health insurance companies, drug companies, and others involved in healthcare by radically reducing the amount of government regulations for such competition with one major exception—these companies would not be allowed to abuse the system and engage in price gouging (or the unnecessary and/or arbitrary hiking of prices). In other words,

> Managed competition is a concept which capitated (also called prepaid) health plans compete against each other in a structured marketplace ... employers are mandated to pay a portion of the insurance premium for all employees, but they do not choose their specific plan. Instead, they submit their portion of the capitated payment to intermediaries ... who "manage" the competition among plans. ... Theoretically, with such standardization, plans have to compete on price and quality and not on selecting the youngest and healthiest enrollees. (Altman & Shactman, 2011, p. 73)

Ultimately, Clinton's plan was not conservative enough since the "managed" part of his plan meant that insurance companies were bidding within a structured framework, which is contrary to the openness of free market competition. Small insurance companies, in particular, were adamantly opposed to the initiative because they simply could not compete against the juggernaut companies who could steamroll over smaller companies in a managed environment. Furthermore, Clinton's proposal suffered from its own historicity. In other words, at the same time that Clinton was trying to generate support for his healthcare reform, Newt Gingrich was cheerleading his "Contract With America." As a Representative from Georgia, Gingrich rallied extreme Right wingers along with liberal southerners. His attacks on Clinton and powerfully persuasive, almost preacher-like, thumping against big government meant that Gingrich became an emergent obstacle—in the sense of a rhetorical situation—that Clinton had not anticipated and could not overcome in terms of his healthcare plan. When Clinton's bill arrived to the Senate, Republican senators utilized what is known as a "filibuster" that allows any senator to speak as long as they wish on a bill and "any senator can prevent a vote on a bill by speaking interminably" (Altman & Shactman, 2011, p. 77). Despite Gingrich's influence, he was not the sole reason for Clinton's failure. Altman and Shactman posit that ultimately Clinton's plan was "too much change and too much government," but it provided important lessons for future efforts (2012, p. 94).

Liberals lost any chance at enacting national healthcare after Clinton's failure, especially since George W. Bush became President, and then won re-election for his second term. Conservatives during the 2000s stressed market initiatives and so-called "medical savings accounts." In addition to the *status quo*, Republicans argued that individuals should begin separate savings accounts so they could have their own pools of money in the event of a health crisis (Heritage Center for Health Policy Studies, 2013). Of course, liberals argue that medical savings accounts might work for the wealthy, but low-income Americans typically have no money to place in savings accounts, or if they do, they do not have enough to generate a resource pool capable of grappling with a catastrophic illness (Huffington, 2008; Park & Greenstein, 2006). Thus, eight years of Bush made it virtually impossible to discuss healthcare, except for one issue: Drugs. This is a bit lengthy, but Altman and Shactman explain this very well:

> Many people were upset about the price of drugs. Between 1998 and 2002, prescription drug spending per person in the United States had increased more than 13 percent every year. Employers had been cutting back health benefits, especially to retirees, and many private Medicare plans … had reduced coverage or exited the market completely after cutbacks from the Balanced Budget Act of 1997. Nearly one quarter of Medicare beneficiaries had no drug coverage. … Controlling the presidency and both houses of Congress, the Republicans had their first unified government in over forty years. The opportunity existed to enact substantive change, and the Medicare program had long been in the crosshairs of Republican conservatives. Bush saw an opportunity to use the prescription drugs as an enticement to change the nature of the program and shift it back toward the private sector. At the same time, by providing a prescription drug benefit to seniors, he could usurp the Democrats' long-held advantage with the Medicare population. It was a win-win situation—seemingly too good to pass up. (2011, p. 180)

After a couple of years of wrangling with more liberal Republicans and attempts at compromising with Senate Democrats and special interest groups, the Medicare Modernization Act (MMA) was passed, also known as the Medicare Part D plan. It is a very complicated and lengthy piece of legislation, but it essentially does the following: Medicare beneficiaries could keep their current plan, they could choose traditional Medicare that also encompasses private drug-only policies, or they could choose private Medicare plans that also included some sort of drug coverage (Altman & Shactman, 2011). The proposal was largely a compilation of multiple compromises between liberals and conservatives. Private business interests, particularly those who could offer supplementary or primary insurance coverage under the parameters of the MMA, were well protected with this legislation. However, liberal interests, mainly due to the pressure of Senator Ted Kennedy (D-MA), were able to secure protections for low-income participants in the program, most of whom would be able to receive their medication for free or at a substantially lower cost. The way the MMA was able to pay for this was, in part, based on increasing the costs of more wealthy participants. The higher their incomes or levels of wealth, the higher their contributions to the plan must be (Altman & Shactman, 2011). Thus, a degree of compromise between conservative and liberal interests occurred with the passing of the MMA. Other provisions were also in the bill, but the description here provides an overall historical framework of healthcare reform during the Bush years. This also helps set the stage for perhaps the most controversial piece of health legislation in history—Obama's Affordable Care Act.

While not perfect, the MMA seemed to address at least one component concerning the rise of healthcare costs. However, pharmaceutical costs still continued to be a menace for millions of Americans, and the rest of the healthcare system was becoming more burdensome, expensive, and in many ways less efficient. At the same time, the economy was in shambles. As Altman and Shactman remark, "For the average worker, wages grew about 20 percent between 2000 and 2008, but health insurance premiums grew by almost 100 percent during the same period—five times higher than wage growth!...The country was already spending about 17.5 percent of its annual income on healthcare, and costs were increasing three to four times faster than national income" (2011, p. 203). Indeed, higher healthcare costs seemed particularly to pinch both individuals, whether employed or not, and their employers.

For individual citizens during the 2000s, healthcare became an enormous nuisance. As I have already discussed, most insurance companies were not covering pre-existing conditions, meaning that insurance companies could simply refuse to pay many claims. This resulted in millions of Americans forced to pay full price for coverage of grossly overpriced care that was, in some cases, dictated by large companies that could set their price without fear of retribution or of financial pressure from their insureds. After all, individual citizens—even groupings of concerned citizens and special interest groups—could yield very little economic pressure, if any at all, on insurance companies. Not only were insurance companies not covering conditions that they could deem as "pre-existing," but they were also increasing premium costs and deductibles, and, at the same time, they were in many cases lowering the extent to which they would cover certain procedures and services. If the economy weakens and wage growth stagnates, but healthcare costs skyrocket, individuals are forced to make extremely difficult choices, such as forgoing health concerns in order to pay for things like rent, food, clothing, education for their children, etc. And then, when a medical crisis happens to the family, they either find themselves with no insurance, or they have weak coverage that still costs them tremendously in the form of deductibles and services that the insurance company will not cover.

What happens when a person or family cannot pay their medical bills? As I have mentioned, some people, particularly the uninsured, may visit an emergency room for some coverage, but this does not involve long-term care or follow-up procedures. As we know, the number of uninsured ranged from 38 to 48 million Americans (Huffington, 2008; Jacobs & Skocpol, 2012). For millions of other Americans who work hard on their jobs, their insurance plans were overwhelmingly inadequate and the amount of coverage they used to enjoy plummeted. An extensive report conducted by the neutral think tank, Center for Economic and Policy Research, carefully explains this troubling dynamic:

> Between 1979 and 2008, the share of workers in the lowest quintile who had employer- provided health insurance fell about 25 percentage points. In the second quintile, the decline was almost 16 percentage points. Even in the top quintile, employer-provided coverage fell about six percentage points.

For workers in the bottom quintile, the decline in employer-provided coverage was about equally divided between workers who lost coverage provided through their own employer (about 13 percentage points) and those who lost coverage through their spouse or other relative's employer (about 12 percentage points). For workers in the second wage quintile, losses in own- employer coverage (down about 11 percentage points) were more important than those through a spouse or relative's employer (about 4 percentage points). (Rho & Schmitt, 2010, pp. 17–18)

Additionally, while coverage has decreased, costs have climbed sharply. In fact, contrasted to all other industrialized nations, the United States pays at least twice as much in healthcare, up to 16% of our Gross Domestic Product (GDP), compared to the next closest countries France, Switzerland and Germany who pay over five percent less of their GDP (Pearson, 2009, p. 1). As Pearson explains, "Americans spend more than twice as much as relatively rich European countries such as France, Germany and the United Kingdom" (2009, p. 2). As a result and at least in terms of cost, healthcare in the United States has become a real crisis. As Jacobs and Skocpol simply state, Americans "paid more for less" (2012, p. 27).

Rising healthcare costs have not just impacted individuals and their families, however. Employers, too, have suffered; they experienced a 131% increase in premium costs between 1999–2009 (Jacobs & Skocpol, 2012, p. 28). Particularly, small businesses have been struggling with finding ways to provide adequate health insurance for their employees at reasonable costs. With costs increasing sharply, companies have encountered unpleasant realities—either drop coverage altogether, procure cheaper and less extensive coverage, or cut wages or shift full-time employees to part-time status (and thereby not offer any coverage to part-time workers as well as save costs in general) in order to accommodate the healthcare costs. If an employee is moved from full-time to part-time status, or a company cancels their health insurance entirely, coupled with the rising costs of healthcare in general, it is not difficult to see how some families found themselves in dire financial straits solely because of healthcare. It is not an overstatement to say that this problem is extremely serious, especially since, "catastrophic healthcare costs are a leading cause of family bankruptcy in today's America" (Jacobs & Skocpol, 2012, p. 28). In fact, according to a study in *The American Journal of Medicine*, 62% of bankruptcies in 2007 were from medical expenses, and "Since 2001, the proportion of all bankruptcies attributable to medical problems has increased by 50%. Nearly two thirds of all bankruptcies are now linked to illness" (Himmelstein et al., 2009, p. 744).

One might wonder how this situation occurs in a wealthy country like the United States. Conservatives argue that some of the reasons healthcare costs have increased is due to higher governmental regulations that restrict open competition, exorbitant physician fees, unfettered malpractice lawsuits (which means the high cost of settlements are passed on to consumers), and poor choices by individuals in the healthcare system (Pitts, 2012). As a result, conservatives generally believe that government involvement in healthcare is the main reason why it is inefficient and costly, and, instead, we should have a market-oriented system where companies have a financial incentive to be efficient, productive, and cost-conscious. Thus,

> the standard list of potential conservative health-policy remedies includes more equitable tax treatment of all types of health-care spending, deregulation and decentralization of health-care decisions, a reform of Medicare toward a premium-support model, defined-contribution financing of health-coverage choices coupled with more targeted need-based subsidies, and market-based pricing. (Miller, 2013, n.p.)

This is why Sally Pitts, a right-wing, but relatively tempered, columnist says that "our healthcare system would drastically change for the worse under a Government run program. Government never provides better services for less cost than the free market can provide in any area of life" (Pitts, 2012, n.p.).

On the other side, liberals claim that allowing companies and the healthcare industry to run amok, unrestrained from regulations, under the auspices of an open free market system is part of the problem. In other words, in a free market system companies are driven by the profit motive, not mercy or compassion for sick individuals. Thus, a market system allows, if not encourages, skyrocketing prices, corner-cutting, and impersonal systems that do not address the problems of individuals since, if the company deals in large volume, particular issues and individuals do not raise much concern. Here is another way of looking at the problem:

> For more than sixty years, our democracy has encouraged—and subsidized—profit-making businesses, researchers, and medical professionals, unleashing them to create wondrous medical innovations and make money by offering advanced healthcare—and by selling insurance for fortunate segments of the population, especially privileged employees and their families. But many in the working and middle class are falling into growing cracks, as more and more employers and families are being priced out of secure access to healthcare. No wonder that seven or eight out of every ten Americans have been consistently insisting that the health system needed fundamental change or needed to be completely rebuilt. (Jacobs & Skocpol, 2012, p. 29)

As we know, Senator Barack Obama, Democrat from Illinois, won the presidential election in 2008. Part of his "hope and change" campaign platform included a pledge to overhaul healthcare in the United States. He frequently mentioned the devastating nature of high medical costs, lack of access to insurance, and inefficiency in most of America's healthcare related industries. Thus, Obama sought to establish healthcare reform that would theoretically tackle all of the issues related to the problems average Americans faced regarding healthcare.

The story and process that culminated into the eventual passage of the ACA was long, complicated, and extremely contentious. Because much of the *status quo* healthcare system relied on employer autonomy to determine their own coverage policies for their workers, insurance industry "best" practices and a lack of price controls, Obama's proposal would certainly include more government oversight and intervention into the free market and the healthcare industry. Naturally, Republicans would oppose these efforts, regardless of the particularities and intentions of the proposal. Worried about re-election threats and lack of support from constituents in their districts and states, even some Democrats had the potential to resist such an overhaul. The history of healthcare reform attempts since Nixon and the turbulent political climate meant that Obama's idea for healthcare reform—even without knowing the specifics—was problematic before it was debated, dissected, and described in congressional discussions.

Given this, there were a series of proposals, counter-proposals, considerations of very complicated and technical health-related policy concerns, and political obstructionism by the Republicans. Conservative Republicans despised the so-called "Obamacare" proposal so much that they attempted to repeal it nearly 40 times, and they refused at one point to fund it, which caused the federal government to shut down due to a lack of a budget, known in this procedural sense as a "continuing resolution," which provides funds for salaries and operating expenses for many of the nation's civil service jobs. The shutdown cost the government over $3 billion and deepened the effects of the economic recession (Senti, 2013). The partisan moonbat, U.S. Representative Michele Bachmann (R-MN), was among many Republicans who passionately wanted the shutdown to circumvent the already-adopted ACA because, as she said President Obama and the Democrats "buy love from people by giving them massive government subsidies" (Reilly, 2013, n.p.). Her statement about the continuing resolution and the ACA was not so much about funding issues in general as it was an attempt at using a political process to stall the implementation and operation of the ACA. By comparing the operation process of the ACA to "buying love," Bachmann was clearly using impassioned, politically motivated extremist discourse to accomplish the GOP's goal of thwarting Obamacare. This type of discursive intensity is what I will be analyzing below.

I will not go into detail about the operational aspects of the ACA and its history unless parts of it will help us understand the particular divisive comments made about the ACA and the larger, overall healthcare reform process. Hence, anyone interested in the nuances of the ACA's history and process of implementation should consult other sources. For our needs, we simply should know what the ACA does and what is intended to do.

The Nature of the Affordable Care Act

To understand and appreciate much of the vitriol that occurs in conversations about the ACA, I think it is important to know a little bit about the law. There are many places where one might go to explore what the ACA law does (see American Public Health Association, 2012; DPCC, 2009; DPCC, 2011; Department of Health & Human Services, 2014; Kaiser Family Foundation, 2013; ObamaCareFacts, 2014). Of course, there are many others, but these sources provide a reasonably straightforward and non-politicized explanation or summary of the ACA.

To begin, we should read one of these summaries. A person might wonder why I am choosing a summary account of the ACA rather than reporting on the entire legislation. I could do that, but the ACA bill is well over 5,000 pages when we consider some of the related regulations and other components, and some even suggest that the total count would be over 11,000 pages (Kessler, 2013b). In this case, a summary should be sufficient for our purposes, and instead of me combing through the behemoth, a more concise summary from a renowned authority on this topic. However, even with a summary of the ACA, it is very lengthy. Given the issue here about the ACA and its import to divisive discourse concerning healthcare in the United States, a summary, even if lengthy, is necessary:

> Overall approach to expanding access to coverage. Require most U.S. citizens and legal residents to have health insurance. Create state-based American Health Benefit Exchanges through which individuals can purchase coverage, with premium and cost-sharing credits available to individuals/families ... and create separate exchanges through which small businesses can purchase coverage. Require employers to pay penalties for employees who receive tax credits for health insurance through an Exchange, with exceptions for small employers. Impose new regulations on health plans in the Exchanges and in the individual and small group markets. ... Requirement to have coverage. Require U.S. citizens and legal residents to have qualifying health coverage. Those without coverage pay a tax penalty of the greater of $695 per year up to a maximum of three times that amount ($2,085) per family or 2.5% of household income. ... Exemptions will be granted for financial hardship, religious objections, American Indians, those without coverage for less than three months, undocumented immigrants, incarcerated individuals, those for whom the lowest cost plan option exceeds 8% of an individual's income, and those with incomes below the tax filing threshold. ... Requirement to offer coverage. Assess employers with 50 or more full-time employees that do not offer coverage and have at least one full-time employee who receives a premium tax credit a fee of $2,000 per full-time employee, excluding the first 30 employees from the assessment. ... Require employers with more than 200 employees to automatically enroll employees into health insurance plans offered by the employer. Employees may opt out of coverage. ... Treatment of Medicaid. Expand Medicaid to all non-Medicare eligible individuals under age 65 (children, pregnant women, parents, and adults without dependent children) with incomes up to 133% FPL based on modified adjusted gross income (as under current law undocumented immigrants are not eligible for Medicaid). ... Creation and structure of health insurance exchanges. Create state-based American Health Benefit Exchanges and Small Business Health Options Program (SHOP) Exchanges, administered by a governmental

agency or non-profit organization, through which individuals and small businesses with up to 100 employees can purchase qualified coverage. … Abortion coverage. Permit states to prohibit plans participating in the Exchange from providing coverage for abortions. Require plans that choose to offer coverage for abortions beyond those for which federal funds are permitted (to save the life of the woman and in cases of rape or incest) in states that allow such coverage to create allocation accounts for segregating premium payments for coverage of abortion services from premium payments for coverage for all other services to ensure that no federal premium or cost-sharing subsidies are used to pay for the abortion coverage. (Kaiser Family Foundation, 2013, pp. 1, 4, 5)

Immediately we can tell that the ACA involves many components. It tries to simultaneously increase coverage and reduce costs. This is not a simple or easy piece of legislation to implement. President Obama signed the ACA into law on March 23, 2010. Despite its problems, it has irrefutably benefited many Americans. Students may now receive healthcare benefits from their parents (or through governmental subsidies) until they are 26. Tens of thousands of people who suffer from a chronic illness no longer worry about their insurance ceasing due to a pre-existing condition. More and more people are enrolling into the ACA and participating in its insurance networks (Walsh, 2014). The ACA is far from perfect, but it seems that it is perceived by some as evil to the core, as we shall see below.

And the ACA's complexity is, in part, why there is so much misinformation, mischaracterizations, and distortions. One part of the ACA was recently challenged in a Washington D.C. circuit court due to its ambiguity. The ACA requires an "individual mandate," which means that everyone must have health insurance. If they cannot procure insurance, the government either provides subsidies or tax relief so the insurance is affordable, or, in extreme cases, minor penalties may occur. The ACA constructs a framework for this operation in the form of network exchanges among the states. The network allows consumers and employers to be exposed to a variety of plans and, theoretically, the competition among the states should drive costs downward. But the participation of the states in these exchanges is voluntary. When a state does not participate, it is up to the federal government to provide the subsidies. However, the ACA is unclear as to what point—and to what degree—the federal government should avail these subsidies to citizens. The D.C. circuit court ruled in *Halbig v. Burwell* (2014) that "people in the 36 states that use the federal health insurance exchange are ineligible for subsidized insurance" (Grim & Young, 2014, n.p.). What's more, the *Halbig* court's decision impacts 14 states and Washington D.C. since they are in the court's district area. The ruling provides those "states' officials the power to exempt large employers in the state from the PPACA's [the Patient Protection and Affordable Care Act] employer mandate" (Cannon, 2014, n.p.), meaning that the *Halbig* decision can trigger a sort of slippery slope where other businesses and even individuals will claim the ACA's conditions are too cumbersome, expensive, inefficient, or essentially any reason they provide. But opponents to the decision argue that blocking federal subsidies yields a massive 76% increase in premiums for over five million Americans (Carpenter, 2014, n.p.). Along those lines, another court took up this matter of subsidies with the ACA, on the same day. The 4th Circuit Court of Appeals in Washington D.C. said in *King v. Burwell* that "we find that the applicable statutory language is ambiguous and subject to multiple interpretations" such that the ACA "permits the federal exchange—and not just state-run exchanges—to provide subsidies" (Kapur, 2014, n.p.). With these two conflicting decisions, "U.S. judges have their work cut out for them," especially since at "stake is how millions of Americans pay for private health insurance, or if they can afford it all" (Reuters, 2014, n.p.). Additionally, the vagueness of some of the language and the overly specific and precise wording that exists in other places, coupled with its length and complexity, make the ACA ripe for spinning and manipulating political messages.

Of course, the ACA is a lightning rod for criticism, spin, and ideological volatility— so is abortion and the controversy over how our veterans are being treated. In short, the healthcare debate is a magnificent example of how the concept of a "rhetorical situation" can help us examine the polarizing rhetoric that seems omnipresent whenever the topic of healthcare emerges. We can trace who the actors are and place them within a larger context. By understanding the problem, the obstacles that arise and the way the audience is included and constructed regarding this issue, we can hopefully begin to see not only how these components relate, but also how to analyze the divisive discourse happening whenever the idea of change in our healthcare system is discussed.

THE DIVISIVE DISCOURSE ABOUT HEALTHCARE

Now that we have a general idea for how rhetorical situations can construct and reflect ideological beliefs, I want to explore the language used when "reflecting" such ideological perspectives. In short, this part of the chapter will delve into the actual discourse of healthcare. Although tied to the political realities of the particular historical moment, the rhetoric used to advance and defend healthcare beliefs in some ways stands on its own. In other words, the rhetoric can show us things that looking at political procedures and history cannot do. For example, unless a political figure explicitly addresses their intentions of an act, political and historical approaches cannot uncover the deeper, latent meanings of texts, much less the core motivations of rhetors. A rhetorical approach, however, can do this. It is not a science, to be sure, but a rhetorical approach uses material from other perspectives—like politics and history—and integrates them into a textual analysis. The rhetorical critic, then, can provide textual evidence to support their arguments about the text, which may include speculation about the essential, yet subjacent, elements that are pivotal for understanding a text's meanings.

One of the key magnetic areas that attracts radicals and political zealots is abortion. Perhaps no other single topic can raise one's blood pressure and heart rate faster than abortion. It almost goes without saying that everyone has an opinion or firm belief, one way or another, about abortion. Some even go so far as to engage in violence, as we have seen in the cases of bombing abortion clinics by the so-called "pro-Life" extremists (ADL, 2012a); and we know that some so-called "pro-Choice" radicals have roughed up and pummeled their opposition (Harden, 2014; Kabbany, 2014). In fact, occasionally abortion-related violence becomes so serious and troubling that the Anti-Defamation League refers to the violent acts as forms of "terrorism" (ADL, 2012a, n.p.), which could be considered a rhetorical tactic of hyperbole or even a fear appeal.

Those along the periphery who write for blogs, speak at events, participate in TV editorializing and occasionally appear as "legitimate" journalists generally jump at the opportunity to be involved in controversies like abortion. As such, we will begin looking at the discourse of division by examining briefly some of the rhetorical issues concerning abortion. The abortion controversy is enormous. But as I have said before, knowing the rhetorical situation for any social issue is vital, and some knowledge concerning the political process may be helpful, but most is not. Thus, I will occasionally draw upon other viewpoints to provide additional context. After all, history and politics and sociology, among others, are in many ways related fields to rhetoric. However, just to be clear, my focus solely concerns summaries of key positions so we may acquire a feel for the polarizing rhetoric used in the abortion debates.

Abortion

When Americans consider examples or types of controversy, they almost always include abortion as a quintessential polarizing topic. To be sure, abortion involves many deeply seated beliefs that are usually framed and viewed through an ideological prism. The divisive nature of abortion can involve religious convictions, appeals to hard science, sensitivity to women's issues, rallying cries for social movements, and so on. Just in terms of abortion's relationship with moral arguments, John Acton points out that, "perhaps more than any other political issue, abortion naturally produces extreme moralistic reactions. This is to be expected. To someone who is pro-life, abortion is an assault on human life. To someone who is pro-choice, attempting to restrict abortion is an assault on human autonomy. It is an issue with massive moral implications and virtually zero room for compromise" (2013, n.p.). Clearly, then, abortion offers us tumultuous discourse with profound intransigence from both sides.

Celeste Condit notes that the controversy surrounding abortion is uniquely rhetorical in nature, as both sides of the dispute strategically try to frame their position vis-à-vis the opposition (Condit, 1990, pp. 43–46). By initiating stories that deliver strong and persuasive viewpoints, rhetors who are engaged in the abortion debate not only utilize the current rhetorical situation to amplify their appeals, but they also incorporate historical notions that then offer a sense of "authenticity" or "legitimacy" to the overall persuasive position (Condit, 1990, p. 44). Therefore, the abortion debate is not just another "controversy" for us to study. Rather, it is an issue with potent framing tools that make it a unique cauldron of polarization.

The rhetoric surrounding abortion can be very intense and extreme. For instance, John Acton, who argues in favor of the sanctity of life, claims that his side of the debate is morally correct and on-balance better than those who argue for "choice":

> Current pro-choice rhetoric … does not shy away from levying accusations against specific individuals for being pro-life, while a quick glance at the rhetoric of actively pro-life representatives … shows that pro-life rhetoric usually focuses on the humanity of a fetus as opposed to the motivations behind abortion. (Acton, 2013, n.p.)

The notorious conservative pundit, Ann Coulter, echoes the moralist perspective of Acton (Media Matters, 2006). However, as she frequently does, Coulter cannot resist utilizing bombastic verbiage, such as this:

> A "moderate Democrat" is someone who experiences doubt when undergoing her third abortion. The party of compassion believes it is very important to have "choice" when it comes to killing babies. … Liberals will pass laws to protect children from "secondhand smoke" but not from being doused with poisonous saline solution or having their skulls crushed in the womb. This is why liberals are known as "compassionate."… Climbing out of the tree, feminists recently began acknowledging that abortion is evil—albeit a "necessary evil."… NARAL [National Abortion Rights Action League] believes abortion is a fundamental human right, the sine qua non of woman's equality. … The "no one is for abortion" line is just re-arranging the deck chairs on a sinking argument. It is not a surprise that the people who most fervently support abortion refuse to discuss it, a condition known as "abortion denial." (Coulter, 2007, pp. 38–39)

Given Coulter's proclivity for vivid language, sarcastic moralizing and outrageous conjecture—and, of course, all coupled with her tremendous popularity and media savvy—she is able to negotiate between unfettered literary liberties (i.e., borderline fabrication), personal attacks, and infuriating polarized partisanship. In addition to Coulter, members of the religious right engage in extreme, if not hostile, rhetoric against their opposition. For example, Pat Robertson, the famous Christian evangelical pastor and founder of the television station, *The 700 Club*, lashes out at Planned Parenthood and its founder, Margaret Sanger:

> Today on the 700 Club, Pat Robertson said that Margaret Sanger "was the one who set the stage for Adolf Hitler, she didn't copy him, he copied her."… Robertson said that the group founded by Sanger is "evil" and targets black people. "What they said was, they said 'what we've got to do in order to get

the black people in America to have abortions, we have to have some noted black leader who will come out for Planned Parenthood and we'll give him the Margaret Sanger award and therefore he will be our poster boy showing the black people they should have abortions," Robertson maintained, "it was strictly genocide." (Tashman, 2013, n.p.)

And by referring to abortion as "genocide," Robertson is emphasizing the ideological premise of the conservative argument——that abortion involves killing a "life." According to McGee, a word that is packed with ideological meaning is called an "ideograph." By referring to "images of the fetus," "babies" and "unborn children," conservatives use ideographs as the "linchpin of pro-[life] rhetoric" (Hayden, 2009, p. 114)

Another representation of conservative polarized discourse concerning abortion can be seen with a Republican state senator from Virginia, Steve Martin. Martin noted on Facebook, "I don't expect to be in the room or will I do anything to prevent you from obtaining a contraceptive … However, once a child does exist in your womb, I'm not going to assume a right to kill it just because the child's *host* (some refer to them as mothers) doesn't want it" (my emphasis, Bassett, 2014b, n.p.). Referring to a mother as a "host" is insensitive and objectifies the woman, especially in contra-distinction to a fetus who is presumed to have more legal rights than the mother, from a conservative perspective. Such a perspective can be articulated in a very dogmatic fashion, as we

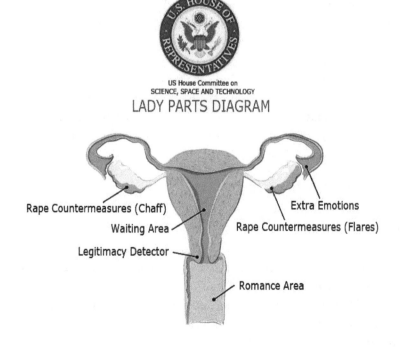

Figure 4.3: Lady parts diagram.

see from former Missouri Congressman Todd Akin, who said during an interview that even in the case of rape, women should not be allowed to have abortions. The reason, according to Akin, is that there exists a "legitimate" type of rape, especially since "the female body has ways to try to shut the whole thing down," meaning that if a woman truly dislikes rape or other sexual act, her body has some sort of natural defense system (Alter, 2014, n.p.). Like Martin, Akin's comments are incredibly insensitive, intense and extreme, not to mention clearly inaccurate. If the subject matter were not so serious, these statements could be considered humorous. For instance, in Figure 4.3, we can view a satirical anatomical diagram of how the female body can ward-off "illegitimate" sexual advances, fully armed with countermeasures, "extra emotions" storage, etc. To provide additional satirical impact, the diagram even uses the seal for the U.S. House of Representatives, thereby enhancing the ethos of the message. For another example of this type of discourse, we can also look at the statement by former Indiana Treasurer Richard Mourdock. Mourdock, a Republican, ran for the U.S. Senate in 2012. During a campaign debate, Mourdock professed that a pregnancy as a result of rape is a "gift from God" (Groer, 2012, n.p.).

But the conservative perspective, as exemplified by Coulter, Martin and Akin, is not the only troubling abortion discourse. Many so-called "pro-Choice" activists are also guilty of jumping to conclusions, reinforcing political stereotypes and failing to critically reflect by ignoring, even muting, opposing views. The conservative writer John Acton points out this problem:

> Unfortunately, the pro-choice community did not respond in a productive way. Instead, they responded with politically motivated and unfair attacks, the type of which only contribute to the polarization and gridlock which define today's political climate. ... The primary problem with this type of rhetoric is that it misconstrues the motivations of the "extremist Texas legislators" and other pro-life activists. To someone who is pro-life, the question of how the government should make laws regarding abortion has literally nothing to do with women's rights. Rather, it is a question of whether or not a fetus is a human being. (Acton, 2013, n.p.)

Additionally, while conservative abortion rhetoric utilizes ideographs such as "life" and "babies" to frame their rhetorical advocacy, liberal polarized rhetoric responds with ideographic representations of their own. Pro-Choice activists discuss the plight of women with arguments about rape and domestic violence. To pronounce this position even more, pro-Choice rhetors emphasize the impact of criminalized abortions on low-income women, forcing them to have so-called "back alley" abortions that oc-cur with more frequency than legal abortions and are much more dangerous (Bassett, 2014a). When discussing a 1973 *Ms. Magazine* article by Roberta Brandes Gratz, Sara Hayden notes how Gratz illustrated

her story with a crime-scene photograph of a woman who died as a result of an illegal abortion. Noting that "various abortion-law repeal and reform groups have used this photograph as one answer to the magnified fetus photographs so often displayed by antiabortion forces," Gratz argued that the woman imaged "has come to represent the thousands of women who have been maimed or murdered by a society that denied them safe and legal abortions." (Hayden, 2009, p. 117)

Finally, much pro-Choice rhetoric not only characterizes a world without *Roe v. Wade* as horrific to women, but also uses *ad hominem* attacks against the opposition, calling them "anti-woman" (Hulsey, 2014, n.p.), people who support "forced motherhood" and "female enslavement" (Stop Patriarchy, 2014, n.p.), and people who "peddle hate and intolerance" (Torres, 2014, n.p.). Pro-Choice rhetors also strategically use naming to reinforce the idea of "us vs. them" by saying any opposition to their positions is a "war on women" (Dvorsky, 2016, n.p.).

Like most divisive discourse, reality for most Americans is probably somewhere near the center of this polarized discussion. For many, abortion is seen as a tragic act that ends a life, or at least as *Roe v. Wade* (1973) stipulates, a "potential" for life, while others, who typically also dislike the act itself, also recognize that there are certain realities that people face—such as women who are raped (which is always illegitimate)—that may mean employing an abortion as a last resort. But even these more reasonable, potentially common-ground positions, such as former Vice President Joe Biden's personal belief that abortion is wrong but political belief that government should not interfere with a woman's right to choose, are automatically discarded by the polarized extreme (Davis, 2015). Conservatives claim that the "potential for life" argument trivializes actual life and erodes the seriousness of how abortions are actually a "genocide" (*Life Insight*, 2007). On the flip side, liberals say that pro-Life advocates engage in a "war on women" (NARAL, 2011). As such, both sides use highly charged hyperbole—"genocide" and "war" on women—to solidify their positions. Name-calling, or *ad hominem* attacks, are perhaps the most used rhetorical tactic by people engaged in abortion conversations. Tragically, calling each other names will not allow us to move forward. So, it is not surprising that Emily Hulsey argues that, "peppering the abortion debate with sensational buzzwords like 'revolting' and 'war on women' degrades it from something that should be taken very seriously to just another partisan agenda. Abortion is serious business, and it deserves sincere attention, empathy and respect from all sides" (2014, n.p.). But as we know, most polarized rhetoric fails to be empathetic.

Contraceptives

Related to the abortion discussion, and an issue that will serve as a segue into my analysis of the Affordable Care Act, is contraception. Like my examination of abortion, the issue of contraceptives is complicated and varied, so I will focus on an example that I believe is representative, not of the issue itself *per se*, but is illustrative of the nature of divisive discourse. The example, of course, is the controversial remarks made by Rush Limbaugh regarding Georgetown law school student, Sandra Fluke.

As we learned in Chapter Three on religious rhetoric, the recent Supreme Court *Hobby Lobby* (*Burwell v. Hobby Lobby Stores*, 2014) decision upholds the right of a publicly traded company to opt out of contraception insurance coverage on religious exemption grounds. But the *Hobby Lobby* decision was not the first time the issue of contraception insurance coverage under the ACA was in contention. In February 2012, congressional testimonials were scheduled so that the Congress could take those into consideration when funding portions of the Affordable Care Act. One of the people invited to speak to the congressional hearing was a Georgetown law student, Sandra Fluke. When she was called to speak, there was not a single woman present, and the event appeared to be a sham. The Democrats took the opportunity to hold their own, separate "unofficial" hearing by inviting Ms. Fluke to tell her story (Legge et al., 2012). In part, this is what Fluke reported:

> Without insurance coverage, contraception, as you know, can cost a woman over $3,000 during law school. For a lot of students who, like me, are on public interest scholarships, that's practically an entire summer's salary. Forty percent of the female students at Georgetown Law reported to us that they've struggled financially as a result of this policy. … Just last week, a married female student told me that she had to stop using contraception because she and her husband just couldn't fit it into their budget any more. Women employed in low-wage jobs without contraceptive coverage face this same choice. And some might respond that contraception is accessible in lots of other ways. Unfortunately, that's just not true. Women's health clinics provide a vital medical service, but, as the Guttmacher Institute has definitively documented, these clinics are unable to meet the crushing demand for these services. Clinics are closing, and women are being forced to go without the medical care they need. … These denials of contraceptive coverage impact real people. In the worst cases, women who need this medication for other medical reasons suffer very dire consequences. A friend of mine, for example, has polycystic ovarian syndrome, and she has to take prescription birth control to stop cysts from growing on her ovaries. Her prescription is technically covered by Georgetown's insurance, because it's not intended to prevent pregnancy. Unfortunately, under many religious institutions' insurance plans, it wouldn't be. … For my friend, and 20 percent of the women in her situation, she never got the insurance company to cover her prescription. Despite verification of her illness from her doctor, her claim was denied repeatedly on the assumption that she really wanted birth control to prevent pregnancy. She's gay—so clearly, polycystic ovarian syndrome was a much more urgent concern than accidental pregnancy for her. After months of paying over $100 out of pocket, she just couldn't afford her medication anymore, and she had to stop taking it. I learned about all of this when I walked out of a test and got a message from her that, in the middle of the night in her final-exam period, she'd been in the emergency room. She'd been there all night in just terrible, excruciating pain. She wrote to me: "It was so painful I woke up thinking I'd been shot." Without her taking the birth control, a massive cyst the size of a tennis ball had grown on her ovary. She

had to have surgery to remove her entire ovary as a result. On the morning I was originally scheduled to give this testimony, she was sitting in a doctor's office trying to cope with the consequences of this medical catastrophe. Since last year's surgery, she's been experiencing night sweats and awaking and other symptoms of early menopause as a result of the removal of her ovary. She's 32 years old. As she put it: If my body indeed does enter early menopause, no fertility specialist in the world will be able to help me have my own children. I will have no choice at giving my mother her desperately desired grandbabies, simply because the insurance policy—that I paid for, totally unsubsidized by my school—wouldn't cover my prescription for birth control when I needed it. Now, in addition to potentially facing the health complications that come with having menopause at such an early age—increased risk of cancer, heart disease, osteoporosis—she may never be able to conceive a child. Some may say that my friend's tragic story is rare. It's not. I wish it were. (Moorhead, 2012, n.p.)

The excerpt is long, I know, but I believe it is necessary to obtain a sense of Fluke's overall argument as well as to understand the nature of Limbaugh's response.

Fluke kept her testimony to the relevance of acquiring contraceptives at Georgetown law school, because Georgetown, as a Roman Catholic university, could opt out of providing coverage for contraceptives as a religious exemption. As a young woman, Fluke obviously spoke from her experience as someone who uses contraceptives, but not only because contraceptives prevent pregnancy. Fluke spoke about herself as well as many of her friends who use contraceptives for medical reasons. And since Congress was considering an amendment to allow religious organizations an exemption to covering contraceptives under the ACA, Fluke implored the lawmakers to reject the proposal in light of the impact the amendment would have on women's health.

Clearly, Fluke uses some *pathos* appeals in her testimony—mentioning the impact on financially struggling women, utilizing emotionally charged stories, etc.—but for the most part, she provides *logos*-centered arguments by emphasizing personal experience, referencing studies, and employing deductive reasoning when explaining the implications of contraception exemptions. Nevertheless, Rush Limbaugh seized the opportunity to pounce on Fluke's speech in order to fuel his larger attacks against the so-called "Obamacare." His vicious attacks against Fluke initially spanned the course of three days, so the amount of transcribed material from his show is quite lengthy. However, Legge et al. (2012) do a great job of synthesizing the material to capture the essence of Limbaugh's remarks, even though their synthesis is also a bit long:

Limbaugh intentionally misinterpreted Flukes' comments, ignoring entirely her testimony about the health benefits of contraceptive hormones and repeatedly suggested that the amount of contraceptive hormone pills a person takes is related to the amount of sex that they have. He focused on Fluke's sex life, suggesting that she and other women at Georgetown were having so much sex that they were going broke paying for birth control and that she wanted others, perhaps "the Pope," to pay for her birth control. Limbaugh reasoned, "What does it say about the college co-ed [Sandra] Fluke, who goes before congressional committee and essentially says she must be paid to have sex?" Then he asked, "What does that make her? It makes her a slut, right? It makes her a prostitute. She wants to be paid to have sex. She's having so much sex she can't afford the contraception. She wants you and me and the taxpayers to pay her to have sex" (Limbaugh apologizes, 2012, para. 4). This first day of comments did not go unnoticed by pundits and politicians who began to attack Limbaugh. Limbaugh was only emboldened by these attacks and renewed his narrative on Fluke, reiterating his charge that Fluke and other Georgetown students are "having so much sex that they're going broke." A brief sample of this day's extensive comments appears below:

[They are] "having so much sex that they're going broke."

"having so much sex that it's hard to make ends meet."

"Now what does that make her? She wants us to buy her sex."

"She and her co-ed classmates are having sex nearly three times a day for three years straight, apparently these deadbeat boyfriends or random hookups that these babes are encountering here having sex with nearly three times a day."

"She's having so much sex it's amazing she can still walk, but she made it up there." (Wilson, 2012)

Limbaugh then went on to suggest that because Fluke and other women want the government to pay for their sex, that he wanted something for it. "And I'll tell you what it is. We want you to post the videos online so we can all watch" (Wilson, 2012, para. 5). Day three (March 2) brought more comments regarding Ms. Fluke. "Does she have more boyfriends? Ha! They're lined up around the block." Limbaugh wondered, "Who admits to having so much sex, she can't pay for it?" (Wilson, 2012, para. 6)

Obviously, Limbaugh uses rhetorical tactics that are the opposite of Fluke's—he employs mostly *ad hominem* attacks on her personal character, engages in considerable over-generalizations primarily about the sexual behavior of female law students, and resorts to crude sexual innuendos instead of solid inductive or deductive reasoning.

To many, Limbaugh's reactionary comments concerning Fluke may sound outrageous, disgusting, "callous," and even perverted (Lowen, 2012). A large chunk of his advertisers certainly felt that way. Almost immediately, many of Rush's sponsors withdrew their support (Legge et al., 2012; Salzillo, 2014). In response, he issued an apology, stating that his intent is to illustrate "the absurd with absurdity" and that he "chose the wrong words" when describing Sandra Fluke, and he said "I sincerely apologize to Ms. Fluke for the insulting word choices" (Limbaugh, 2012a, n.p.). Two days later, Limbaugh elaborated on his apology by saying that we cannot expect "morality or intellectual honesty from the left," and he said he was sorry that he stooped to their level when attacking Fluke. Limbaugh said he "became like them [the Left], and I feel very badly about that." He went on to say that the "apology to her over the weekend was sincere," and then Rush pivots to "the hearing that started all of this" by attacking Obama and the ACA (Limbaugh 2012b, n.p.). Of course, Obama entered into the fray by denouncing Limbaugh's pejorative comments, and other Democrats called on advertisers to boycott Limbaugh for seemingly politicized reasons to curry additional pro-women votes for the November election (Riehl, 2012).

To some involved in this political issue, Limbaugh could never apologize or make up for what he said about Fluke. By attacking her use of contraceptives the way he did, Limbaugh was seen as attacking all women, what is known as a part-to-whole argument, or synecdoche (Marcotte, 2012). Additionally, by labeling Fluke a "slut," he engaged in what is known as "slut-shaming," or the condemnation of female sexual activity that is often accompanied with a double standard for male promiscuity (Beusman, 2013). And, according to Emily Yoffe, what Limbaugh said cannot really be considered an apology, mainly because he did not personally reach out to Fluke, and because his so-called "apology" was couched in politicizing the larger issue about contraception, instead of focusing on the personal damage done by his words (Yoffe, 2012). I think we should also add that just because someone says their apology is "sincere," as Limbaugh did, does not necessarily make it so. Of course, this points out one of the problems with gauging rhetorical intent in discourse. Hence, most people who study rhetoric will explain that intent is not only something that is difficult to ascertain, it also has little impact when compared to the effects rhetoric has on an audience. In other words, the consequences of rhetoric are usually more important than the speaker/writer's intent.

Nevertheless, we can learn a few things from the Limbaugh/Fluke incident. First, this ordeal demonstrates the potency of polarized pundits in general, and Rush Limbaugh in particular. We already know that for years Limbaugh has had one of the most popular political radio talk shows (Chafets, 2008; Press, 2010), and he "may be one of the most influential figures in contemporary American politics" (Bennett, 2009, p. 66). But what the Sandra Fluke dispute reveals is how Rush's words can yield major damage, and, at the same time, a rhetorical incident involving Rush captures tremendous attention by media sources, politicians and the general public (Butler et al., 2012). Second, we can obviously learn something about the power of rhetorical tactics. For Fluke, a reliance on tactful, reason-based testimony ultimately prevailed, but we also cannot discount the potency of Limbaugh's emotionally laden vitriol. What makes the Fluke episode so interesting and unique is that Limbaugh can generally escape condemnation for his outrageous remarks, but in this case, he could not avoid being placed under a microscope. Some political scholars argue that the Fluke incident is unique because Limbaugh was the target of an "Obama-orchestrated assault" (Shapiro, 2013, n.p.). However, given that the Democrats had no way of knowing what either Fluke or Limbaugh were going to say, it seems unlikely that there was some sort of Obama conspiracy, unless it was a reactionary strategy developed almost overnight. What seems more likely is that during a national election year, the discourse from political pundits is both amplified and scrutinized. As a result, these rhetorical exchanges are even more important to analyze. Ultimately, although the conservatives have had to endure the implementation of the ACA, they were successful in limiting both the contraceptives and abortion components of the bill. With the *Hobby Lobby* decision, the Supreme Court has all but ensured that companies and religious organizations may be exempt from providing contraceptives, if they so choose. And the Republicans were successful in passing a vital amendment to the ACA—known as the Stupak amendment since its proponent was House Democrat Bart Stupak (D-MI), who was a vehement pro-Life Democrat during the ACA debates. In order to secure all of the Democrats' votes, including those who were pro-Life as well as some key Republican swing votes, Nancy Pelosi (the Democratic Speaker of the House at the time) had to compromise by allowing the Stupak amendment to pass, even though Pelosi is staunchly pro-Choice. At the end of the day, the only realistic way the ACA would pass is with the Stupak amendment attached. Once the Stupak amendment passed the House, the ACA as a whole was passed with only a five-vote margin (Altman & Shactman, 2011).

The Patient Protection and Affordable Care Act (ACA)

Regarding healthcare, the most recent controversial issue has been the ACA. Also known, sometimes pejoratively, as "Obamacare," the ACA is an attempt at securing affordable health insurance for all Americans. Earlier in this chapter I already discussed the historical context of the ACA, the ACA's major components, and many of the arguments surrounding the ACA. I will try not to repeat those elements here. What is important for our purposes now is analyzing some of the specific rhetorical tactics used by both supporters and opponents of the ACA. Given that many of the arguments in favor of the ACA were already mentioned earlier, I will begin with what many of the opponents argue first, then I will trace some of the answers to those claims. Without delving into too many nuanced positions about specific components of the ACA, I will attempt to focus on the major rhetorical tactics used by both sides.

Opposition to the ACA has been fierce. The Republican-led assault on the ACA has generated much controversy, heated arguments, and even nearly 40 attempts at partial or complete repeal of the law since its passage in 2010 (Kessler, 2013a). With a combination of *pathos* and *logos* appeals, conservative opposition to the ACA has largely centered around four key arguments: (1) the ACA imposes an enormous bureaucracy, (2) the ACA undermines businesses, particularly small businesses who will end up absorbing much of the implementation costs of the law, (3) the ACA is "socialist" (or some variant thereof), and (4) the ACA erodes too much control and power of the patient. Other arguments have been levied as well, such as the ACA will cause a dearth of doctors (see de Gastyne, 2014) and the ACA will overburden Medicaid (see Clemmitt, 2014), but these four main arguments seem to occur most frequently and will serve our purposes for outlining some of the key rhetorical tactics used in this controversy.

The first major argument against the ACA is that it creates more bureaucracy. Mainly articulated by former Speaker of the House and presidential candidate, Newt Gingrich, this argument states that the ACA adds many regulations, control mechanisms, and requirements to our already overburdened healthcare system. With virtually no proof from the actual legislation and quite a bit of scare tactics thrown into the mix, Gingrich claims that

> Obamacare … comes with lots of bureaucrats in Washington, more regulations, IRS agents to wade through your medical bills, and boards of experts to tell you which treatments you may and may not have. Under Obamacare, the Department of Health and Human Services, the Food and Drug Administration, Medicare, Medicaid, and the rest of the healthcare bureaucracy will take over your doctor's office … you and your doctor will certainly make fewer choices about your care, while bureaucrats will make more. (Gingrich, 2013, p. 50)

Ultimately what Gingrich suggests is that Obamacare places too much control into the hands of Washington bureaucrats. More specifically, he worries about the degree to which the Director of the Department for Health and Human Services can determine "what, exactly, health insurance will cover … the secretary of HHS will 'determine what type of insurance coverage every American is required to have. She can influence what hospitals can participate in certain plans, can set up health insurance exchanges within states against their will, and even regulate McDonald's Happy Meals'" (Gingrich, 2013, p. 56). The fear generated by the image of a tyrannical government controlling the destinies of our health is echoed by arch-conservative Tom DeWeese, who warns that "ObamaCare with its avalanche of rules and regulations and the reporting required of every doctor, every step of the way in treatment can only result in short-cuts and less care in the medical procedures. The result will be a bureaucratic takeover of the system, as unqualified political hacks will make life-and-death decisions for patients. It will lead to the end of innovation and advancement of medical treatments" (2014, n.p.). The "avalanche of rules and regulations" is particularly problematic since such command and control policies are an affront to a market-based system. An approach that relies on the free market is what is typically advocated by conservatives. In fact, government intervention in pricing and insurance regulation is why Gingrich states that the "very regulatory system health professionals complain about has in fact been hiding the enormous inefficiencies that make American healthcare unnecessarily expensive" (pp. 49–50). Thus, the ACA as a whole runs contrary to a much preferred market-based system that, if left unmolested, would yield much lower prices, better efficiency, and less control in the hands of bureaucrats.

Democrats generally attack the underlying premise behind the bureaucracy argument. While Gingrich will ask, "Do you want a bureaucrat to make healthcare decisions for you?" liberals will use an Aristotelian *topoi* tactic, known as a turn-around, by flipping the question by asking, "Do you want an insurance company to make healthcare decisions for you?" (Moore, 2007, n.p.). Or, as Altman and Shactman state, "If insurance companies win, you lose" (2011, p. 320). Presumably in an ideal world, Americans would not want either entity to make vital healthcare decisions, but at least for now our system requires something to be put into place.

ACA opponents generally argue next that the law will undermine businesses, particularly small businesses. At first, this is a natural outgrowth of what Gingrich was saying—the bureaucracy of the ACA undermines free market principles, which in turn frustrates business initiatives. More specifically, however, the ACA has to somehow pay for extending health insurance to every American. One way the cost is offset is by requiring employers to purchase sufficient insurance plans for their employees. Naturally, that means that businesses' net growth will suffer. Michael Savage, by using his typical mischaracterizations and name-calling, explains that "the passage of socialized medicine in America is a blunder of major proportions. Businesses will have to reduce or cut benefits to remain solvent—or move jobs abroad" (Savage, 2010, pp. 137–138). Or, if businesses choose not to provide sufficient insurance for their workers (after all, the employer mandate provision in the ACA was gutted by Republican opposition before its passage), individual workers will be required somehow to secure coverage, presumably by adopting government-based health insurance (Carroll, 2009). This, in turn, will raise the costs on taxpayers. Moreover, if employers provide coverage, it is actually unlikely they will bear the brunt of the cost. Instead, they will most likely pass the costs on to the consumer, or they will lower wages and other benefits to their workers (Gonshorowski, 2014). In fact, "economists generally agree that, in the long run, employees—not employers—pay for a mandate out of their wages. They claim the market for wages is based on total compensation, and workers who receive health benefits eventually earn that much less in salary than those with no benefits" (Altman & Shactman, 2011, p. 48). Thus, the real argument posed by Republicans is a range of cost implications, not just an impact on businesses—either the ACA will undermine business profits, or it will require more taxes, or it will cause wages and other benefits to plummet for employees. In this way, conservatives utilize a *logos*-heavy position (typically relying on statistics and economic projections) that is supplemented with a healthy dose of fear appeals.

ACA supporters counter these arguments by utilizing their own set of rhetorical tactics, but they, too, are *logos*-heavy. By similarly citing a wealth of studies and statistics, liberals argue that overall and long-run market indicators suggest that the ACA will have a net-positive impact on businesses and the economy. The primary reason for this goes back to the argument discussed earlier in this chapter about the nature of insurance—when there are more (healthy) people in an insurance pool, the costs for the aggregate group are reduced. It is somewhat ironic that in order to reduce costs—something Republicans purportedly espouse—we need to insure as many people as possible. Simply put, "getting everyone—even healthy young people—to buy insurance is the only way to ensure that there is enough money for every American's care" (Clemmitt, 2014, p. 302). In addition, supporters claim that "all employers will benefit from more fluid job markets, healthier workers, and reduced costs—especially for employers who have already been providing healthcare coverage for their employees" (Jacobs & Skocpol, 2012, p. 135). Finally, there are some liberal commentators who utilize dogmatic, ideological positions that are either anti-free market or anti-big business/anti-insurance companies. For example, Ed Schultz, who generally champions the causes of the middle class, says, "Think about this: during the past eight years, there's been about a *428 percent increase in profits* for the insurance industry giants, while middle-class families have been getting financially butchered—and the Republicans want to blame big government!" (emphasis in original, 2010, p. 75). Similarly, liberal activist Al Sharpton argues, "It should be a right, not a privilege, to be healthy in America. … It's a shame that the people at the bottom, who are poor, are living in a nation that could see them well but would rather have people make money selling health than provide health to all of its citizens" (2002, p. 113–114). Hence, liberals attempt to defend the ACA by either using long-term market-based economic arguments, or by trashing the current profit-driven system. After all, because we have relied on the free market for so long, and healthcare prices have skyrocketed, perhaps it makes sense, according to liberals, to try a different approach altogether (Rivlin, 2013).

A third position articulated by conservatives is an extension of the first two, but given its frequency of use and polarizing potential, I am marking it as a separate argument entirely. The argument, of course, is the claim that the ACA is socialist. Many people who use this label do not appear to know what socialism really means (such as Glenn Beck), as they use it interchangeably with "Nazism" or "fascism" (see Milbank, 2010). But given the complexity of political and economic concepts such as these, it may be a purposeful rhetorical tactic of confusion or conflation of these systems. After all, if one's audience is also largely ignorant about the nuanced nature of these concepts (Olbermann, 2011), lobbing them against the ACA will simply reinforce the negative elements of the law, without any real, particular knowledge as to why.

I believe other conservatives use the label "socialism" intentionally to invoke images of a stale, repressive Soviet Union or to provide a cognitive shortcut that functions as a negative criticism of the law as un-patriotic or un-American. After all, if something is "socialist," it simply cannot be "American" at the same time. Semantically, and even economically, this argument makes zero sense. But we are dealing with political and philosophical argumentative positions. In other words, if a rhetor intentionally wants to change or reinforce an audience's political or philosophical beliefs, it does not matter if two concepts are semantically and economically compatible; it only matters what is politically or philosophically perceived to be incompatible. Thus, labeling Obama a "socialist" or calling the ACA "socialism" establishes a mental framework for some audience members that Obama and the ACA are perhaps "un-American," "evil," "tyrannical," or "oppressive." With this country's history of fighting the Cold War and McCarthyism, labeling something

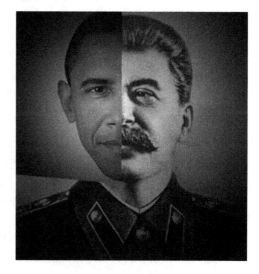

Figure 4.4: Obama as Stalin.

socialist carries significant semantic and cognitive impact (Jeffreys-Jones, 2010). Glenn Beck, for example, in the same breath when he refers to Obamacare as "socialist," says that "America is burning down to the ground" as a result of this healthcare reform (cited in Milbank, 2010, p. 1).

In a similar way, ultra-conservative radio talk show host Laura Ingraham says that the ACA "tramples" our constitutional rights by establishing a "new health-care regime [that] empowers the federal government to ration care based on 'cost effectiveness,' which ultimately intrudes upon our personal medical choices and the doctor-patient relationship" (Ingraham, 2010, p. 119). The word "rationing" conjures up images of the long lines in the former Soviet Union when Russians would stand for hours to receive their weekly rations of bread. This representation is very powerful, given our history vis-à-vis the USSR, since

> This is where forty years of Stalinism has gotten them ... standing in line for biscuits. What finally ripped open the Iron Curtain was not a grand, sudden revolutionary thrust at the Marxist-Leninist ideal, but the local, day-to-day contempt for the Communist system, one that idealize the masses but ignored and humiliated the individual human being. One of the strengths of democracy is the benefits it bestows on those leaders who best address such daily, kitchen table concerns. (Matthews, 1988, p. 48)

The image of the Soviet Union—with its socialist economy—implies that the medical rationing of Obamacare is equivocal. Take, for instance, the unapologetic conservative, Joe Otto, from the website *Conservative Daily*, who compares Obamacare to the Soviet Union in order to cement this analogy:

> One of the world's top communists, Joseph Stalin, told us what he would do: "Work for more government intervention and control of the business activities of the people. In this way the American people will accept Communism without knowing it." Don't you know that Stalin would love Obama and he would be very pleased with this President and his nationalization of just a few unimportant things, like housing, mortgages, financial and insurance industries during the his first year in office (Otto, 2013, n.p.).

Additionally, although he does not use the word "rationing," populist conservative Lou Dobbs agrees with Ingraham and Beck, since he notes how "Obamacare is a Frankenstein creation of a statist, socialist administration intent on raising taxes—taxes increasing now on those with higher income levels as well as small business owners" (Dobbs, 2014, p. 16). Even the sometimes "moderate" conservative, Bill O'Reilly, has stooped to this level. Since the premise of the ACA is to ensure that all Americans have health insurance, O'Reilly claims it is a form of wealth redistribution, and "income redistribution is a hallmark of socialism and we, in America, are now moving in that direction" (O'Reilly, 2014, n.p.). Like the word "socialism," the word "redistribution" conjures up ideas of Marxism, and is particularly powerful to shore-up support with the conservative base, since "The prospect of the electorate's splitting along class lines, with the grubby masses voting to divvy up the assets of the rich, strikes an elemental fear in the hearts of the right" (Chait, 2007, p. 127). In these ways, conservative, fanatical true believers reiterate the mantra of socialism however and whenever they can. Interestingly, none of them ever define the concept of socialism, nor do they ever point to a specific part of the ACA that is socialist in nature.

Despite the flimsy and unsupported conjectures by conservatives that Obamacare is "socialist," there still seems to exist a fair amount of Americans who believe it is socialized medicine. Joe Otto claims that "all signs point to Americans being fed up with BOTH PARTIES, the PRESIDENT, and especially, the horrible, horrible legislation known as Obamacare" (Otto, 2013, n.p.). There is even a website called "commieblaster" that devotes several sub-pages to the title "Obamacare Socialism" (Commieblaster, 2014). Of course, none of these conservative sources provide any evidence to support their claims. In fact, several recent polls actually suggest that more and more Americans are supportive of the ACA (Sakuma, 2014). In fact, a "CNN poll finds that 39 percent of Americans favor Obamacare, while 57 percent oppose it. That's awful, right? But it turns out only 39 percent oppose the law because it's "too liberal," while 12 percent say it "isn't liberal enough." That's a total of 51 percent who favor the law or don't think it goes far enough" (Sargent, 2014, n.p.). Interestingly, in one of the most conservative, popular magazines in America, *Forbes*, Mark Adomanis contributes an article that directly refutes all of the typical conservative analogies linking Obamacare to the Soviet Union. Specifically, Adomanis points to five major differences: (1) all medical employees were state-owned in the USSR, (2) all private health-related enterprises were banned, (3) Soviet 5-year plans rationed all healthcare "down to the number of surgeries and the amount of medication," (4) Soviet medical salaries were lower than other average wages, and (5) the Soviet system devoted 3% GDP or less to healthcare (compared to America's current 18%). All of this leads Adomanis to conclude, "I don't think you need to be an Obama partisan to suggest that nothing that is on offer here will come anywhere close to transforming our system into a fully socialized, Soviet-like one" (Adomanis, 2013, n.p.).

Of course, one might argue that just because Obamacare does not come close to the Soviet system does not mean it is not socialist, or at the very least, has some socialist components. Liberals generally point out, however, that the ACA does not even come close to socialism. The "links" to socialism that Republicans argue, such as "income redistribution" or how Obamacare increases taxes, etc., are either mischaracterizations (such as income redistribution), faulty analogies, or a misunderstanding of healthcare as a "public" versus "private" good (i.e., the idea that healthcare is public/government responsibility, like education, as compared to healthcare as a commodity, like purchasing a new car). One of the easiest ways to see how close the ACA comes to socialism is to ask self-identified socialists. According to the national secretary for the American Socialist Party, Greg Pason, "Obamacare cannot be considered socialist in any way ... the ACA program relies on private health insurance companies to manage health services. ... A socialized system would not include 'health insurance,' but would be an actual national health-care system which would be publicly funded through progressive taxation and controlled by democratically elected assemblies of health-care workers and patients" (cited in Smerconish, 2013, n.p.). Similarly, John Avlon asked a national board member of the American Communist Party, Dan Margolis, who says, "Obama is certainly no communist. ... There's no way that you could say that he's gone anywhere close to being a communist. The only similarity I can see is that Fidel Castro said the word 'change' and Obama uses the word 'change.'... The idea that Obama is somehow leading a socialist revolution in this country is just patently ridiculous. ... His policies aren't socialist" (Avlon, 2010, pp. 68–69).

So, there we have it. The old adage that says "if it walks like a duck and talks like a duck, it must be a duck" seems to apply here—the ACA simply does not walk or talk like a socialist duck. In fact, there are probably stronger arguments that the ACA goes the opposite direction—it reinforces and perpetuates capitalism! As Adomanis (2013) points out in his article, the "mandate" is not about entrenching governmental power, but rather it forces everyone to purchase private, corporate insurance. Given the size and power of the major health insurance companies, it would not take much for them to form an oligopoly or even a monopoly under the ACA, meaning that the new law allows, if not encourages, a form of monopolistic capitalism—arguably the worst type of free-market capitalism, and certainly not "socialism" (Nimmo, 2014, n.p.). In this way, the ACA promotes the capitalist free market. Furthermore, Paul Waldman reminds us that "the core of the Affordable Care Act ... was originally a conservative proposal," but apparently because Obama proposed it, suddenly Republicans have major objections to it (Waldman, 2014, n.p.). During the 2012 presidential campaign, Americans were told (or reminded) that former Governor—and Republican—Mitt Romney enacted virtually the same thing as the ACA on the state level in Massachusetts (Stephenson, 2011).

Finally, conservative opposition to the ACA worries that the law reduces the amount of power and control individuals and their doctors have over healthcare decisions. Obviously, this is also an extension of the bureaucracy argument, since as bureaucratic controls increase, individual autonomy decreases. However, this argument is often deployed individually or separately from the bureaucracy position, probably because the implications of the two arguments are slightly different—for the bureaucracy argument, the consequence is more tyranny; and for the lack of individual autonomy, the consequence is the fear of losing control, heightened distrust between a patient and their government-chosen healthcare provider, as well as intimations of a large, conspiratorial (probably socialist) government behemoth.

Simply put, Obamacare opponents argue that the law is riddled with new regulations and requirements, with the priority to save the government money and little to no intention of providing quality care (Ingraham, 2010). The conservative position is best summed up by the Heritage Foundation:

Obamacare moves American healthcare in the wrong direction by eroding the doctor–patient relationship, centralizing control, and increasing health costs. True healthcare reform would empower individuals, with their doctors, to make their own healthcare decisions free from government interference. … For a better life, Americans need a health care system that they, not the government, control. Consumers should have the ability to choose how to meet their health insurance needs in a free market for insurance. (Heritage Center for Health Policy Studies, 2013)

One of the specific items in the ACA that inflicts this sort of damage to individual autonomy is the so-called "death panels." Obamacare supposedly establishes a board, consisting of Washington bureaucrats, who decide which Americans should receive treatment, especially if patients are terminally ill. The implication is that the federal government would theoretically have the power to make life and death decisions, functionally providing state power to inflict euthanasia on Americans it deems as unworthy of expense.

The death panel issue originated with Sarah Palin, who wrote on her Facebook wall the following:

The Democrats promise that a government healthcare system will reduce the cost of healthcare, but as the economist Thomas Sowell has pointed out, government healthcare will not reduce the cost; it will simply refuse to pay the cost. And who will suffer the most when they ration care? The sick, the elderly, and the disabled, of course. The America I know and love is not one in which my parents or my baby with Down Syndrome will have to stand in front of Obama's "death panel" so his bureaucrats can decide, based on a subjective judgment of their "level of productivity in society," whether they are worthy of healthcare. Such a system is downright evil. … We must step up and engage in this most crucial debate. Nationalizing our healthcare system is a point of no return for government interference in the lives of its citizens. If we go down this path, there will be no turning back. (Palin, 2009)

Other outspoken conservatives quickly aligned themselves with Palin's position. Glenn Beck defended Palin by saying, "She is right. … Basically, they come up with the number of maximum treatment costs per year to keep you alive" (cited in Milbank, 2010, p. 99). Then, the extreme right-wing radio talk show host, Michael Savage, added his fear appeal to the concept, with "there's a 'death panel' that may just deny you the coverage you need in the name of 'medical rationing' … especially if you're a senior citizen" (Savage, 2010, p. 118). And John Wilson describes how Rush Limbaugh, who also supported Palin's "death panel" theory, engaged in "outrageous lies" about the concept:

Limbaugh persisted with the fake story of death panels: "Page 429: Advanced care planning consult will be used to dictate treatment as patients' health deteriorates. This can include an order for end-of-life plans. The order will be from the government." Nothing on page 429 says that the government can order death. In fact, it requires that a doctor's order "effectively communicates the individual's preferences regarding life-sustaining treatment." (Wilson, 2011, p. 181)

Of course, *PolitiFact* has discredited all accusations of "death panels" in the ACA (PolitiFact.com, 2009). Nevertheless, the fact that death panels is a fabrication does not really matter in the world of politics. The fact that an entire ensemble of conservative zealots reiterates the death panel conspiracy reinforces the concept of the "echo chamber," which I described in the Introduction chapter. Moreover, another implication of the death panel argument is that it allows pundits like Glenn Beck to extend his position just a bit farther, as he says "Your freedom is at stake. This is the moment. This is the bill. You must not allow this to pass," he said in November 2009. "It will be a nail in the coffin of America. … You must wake everybody up you know. This is the end of prosperity in America forever if this bill passes. This is the end of America as you know it. … This is the end of the American Constitution" (cited in Milbank, 2010, p. 100). Thus, Obamacare becomes the quintessential fear appeal, couched in threats against our freedoms and placed within a political context that justifies a particular, albeit nefarious, ideology.

Supporters of the ACA, however, clearly do not believe that death panels are a reality. They point to neutral fact-checkers, like *PolitiFact*, to prove that the death panels are a fabrication. Additionally, liberal blowhard and instigator Keith Olbermann responds to Palin's accusation with anger—not so much because she lies about the existence of the death panels, but because of the manner in which she makes her point. Olbermann yelps,

> You [Sarah Palin] have forfeited your right to be taken seriously the next time you claim offense at somebody mentioning your children. You have just exploited your youngest child, dangled him in front of a mindless mob, as surely as if you were Michael Jackson. You have used this innocent infant as an excuse to pander to the worst and least of us in this nation. You have used him to create the false image of "death panels." (Olbermann, 2011, p. 150)

Furthermore, he flips the argument about how government death panels reduce individual autonomy by pointing out the catastrophic nature of pre-ACA healthcare: "Death panels? We have them now. They're called Wellpoint and Cigna and United Healthcare and all of the rest" (Olbermann, 2011, p. 192). In other words, since insurance companies traditionally make decisions about how a person receives coverage or not—especially when they were able to not cover "pre-existing" conditions—they functioned as death panels already. In this way, Olbermann reinforces the classic tension between the polarizing sides in the healthcare debate—big government versus big business.

Ultimately, it is also important to note that many liberals also oppose the ACA. In the latest issue of the *International Socialist Review*, Helen Redmond details the holes and pitfalls of the legislation, and she pays particular attention to the areas that were promised to be provided (i.e., affordable insurance for all, maximized coverage, quality preservation, etc.) and then how those promises are not being kept. The ACA's botched attempts at solving our healthcare crisis began at the inception, and then the process, of the act's development. The bundled deals in order to reach a compromise, according to Redmond, doomed the proposal from being effective. She also focuses on how insurance companies are able to manipulate and circumvent ACA loopholes in order to profit from the healthcare needs of average Americans. She writes, the "ACA is a *massive swindle* that mostly benefits the insurers who are set to receive about $1 trillion in subsidy money from the American taxpayer. … It is a sick example of how crony capitalism rewards the corporations that are the cause of the health care crisis" (my emphasis, Redmond, 2014, p. 58). Ironically, as conservative Republicans continue to yelp about how Obamacare is socialism, the ACA is actually funneling money into large insurance corporations. As a committed leftist, Redmond believes the ACA does not go far enough, and we should have implemented a single-payer system from day one.

The American Health Care Act (AHCA)

The Republicans tried to repeal Obamacare over 60 times while Obama was in office (Cowan & Cornwell, 2017). Once Donald Trump was elected the 45th president of the United States, along with a Republican-majority House and Senate, the Republicans began discussing ways of dismantling and replacing Obama's Affordable Care Act. In fact, one of the key factors Trump articulated during his campaign was the removal of "Obamacare." In early January 2017, both the House and the Senate voted to repeal the Affordable Care Act since they finally secured enough votes to do so (Cowan & Cornwell, 2017). However, the measure stalled as the Republicans struggled to craft legislation to not just repeal the ACA, but also to replace it, in large part because Speaker Ryan promised to "repeal and replace" in one fell swoop (Bradner, 2017a). By March, the Republicans, led by Speaker of the House Paul Ryan and President Trump, finally announced a new healthcare provision, called the American Health Care Act (AHCA).

Learning about the AHCA, in its detail, is probably not all that important. However, here are most of the key components:

- Repeal Obamacare's individual and employer mandates.
- Decrease and modify premium tax credits by 2020.
- Keep some of Obamacare's more popular reforms, such as protections for enrollees with pre-existing conditions and the requirement that adult children can stay on their parents' plans until age 26.
- Increase the ratio that insurance companies can charge older enrollees for premiums compared to younger enrollees. This is called "age-band rating."
- Establish a Patient and State Stability Fund.
- Repeal funding for the Prevention and Public Health Fund by the end of 2018.

- Encourage people to use health savings accounts (HSAs).
- Restructure Medicaid funding.
- Repeal many of Obamacare's taxes.
- Prohibit federal funding for Planned Parenthood clinics, and prevent premium tax credits from being applied to any insurance plans that provide coverage for abortions, with certain exceptions. ("The American Health Care Act," 2017)

The reasons why we do not really need to study the details are, for one, we did not dive into all of the details of the ACA. Second, the AHCA has many "working parts," some of which are more important than others ("The American Health Care Act," 2017). Finally, the AHCA ultimately did not pass because it never actually came up for a vote. One of the reasons the bill never received a vote is because after the Congressional Budget Office, a non-partisan group that "runs the numbers" on legislation, provided the "numbers" on the bill, many legislators did not think the bill would fulfill its promise of saving expenditures (Potter, 2015, n.p.). The Democrats, obviously, opposed the bill on arrival. But they did not have enough votes by themselves to stop it. In an ironic turn of events, many Republicans actually opposed the legislation as well, but for very different reasons from those of their Democrat counterparts. The liberal Democrats strongly felt the bill did not do enough for working Americans, while many conservative Republicans, known as the Freedom Caucus, opposed the law because it was not conservative enough—they wanted to gut virtually all involvement by the federal government, thus encouraging market-driven healthcare processes (Pear et al., 2017). The defeat of the AHCA was widely seen as a major blow to Speaker Ryan, but even more so for Trump, who used the bill as his first major foray into pushing his domestic agenda as president (Berg, 2017; Thomas, 2017).

Interestingly, while healthcare discourse, as I have been discussing this entire chapter, has been polarizing overall, the rhetoric surrounding the AHCA was relatively civil by comparison to the rhetoric surrounding Obamacare. But this is not to say that no divisive discourse occurred. For example, Democrat minority Senate leader Chuck Schumer of New York called Trump "petulant," and said, "You cannot run the presidency like you run a real estate deal. You can't tweet your way through it. You can't threaten and intimidate and say I'll walk away" (cited in Moore, 2017b, n.p.). Schumer also called the AHCA "irresponsible" (Detrow, 2017, n.p.). Such personal jabs do not foster appropriate governing.

On the other side, we have House Speaker Paul Ryan, using the rhetoric of "choice" in his attempts to persuade the American people—and by extension members of the House and Senate—that the AHCA should be approved. Ryan gave a detailed presentation of the law to all mainstream media, with sleeves rolled-up and a 21st-century PowerPoint presentation that was later published in full in *USA Today* in an effort to reach as many Americans as possible. While the presentation itself tries to detail the AHCA's key provisions, Ryan nevertheless uses careful rhetorical tactics in his persuasive attempt. For example, one obvious tactic employed is the use of the word "choice."

Ryan juxtaposes Obamacare with the AHCA in a way that rhetorically frames the distinction as a socialist-vs.-capitalist decision. Regarding Obamacare, Ryan says,

> The collapsing law is driving up health care costs and driving out choices for American families. This year alone, premiums have gone up by double digits in 31 states. Choices have dwindled to the point that one out of every three counties in America has just one insurer to choose from. ... That's why we must end this law—repealing it once and for all. But rather than going back to the way things were, we must move to a better system that embraces competition and choice and actually lowers costs for patients and taxpayers." (emphasis added, Ryan, 2017, n.p.)

In contrast, the Republican-sponsored law tries "to give every American access to quality, affordable healthcare. For families, that means lower costs, more *choices and greater control.* Let me walk you through how our plan will help get us there" (emphasis added, Ryan, 2017, n.p.). And, finally, Ryan concludes his appeal with this: "Instead of mandates forcing you to buy what the government wants, you will have real *choices*" (emphasis added, Ryan, 2017, n.p.).

There are a couple of reasons why Speaker Ryan's "choice" rhetoric is important. Most obviously, the rhetoric of "choice" is typically a tactic used by liberals when they advance arguments about abortion, which we discussed earlier in this chapter. Thus, in at least a partial way, Ryan's presentation co-opts some of the potency of that traditional line of discourse. Second, when Paul Ryan says the AHCA offers Americans "choices" in their healthcare, he is using an enthymeme—if there are more choices with the Republican option, that must mean there are fewer choices with Obamacare and with whatever the Democrats advocate. For instance, Ryan has said that Obamacare is simply a "warmed-over substitute for government-run health care," also making it seem more socialist or communist (Detrow, 2017, n.p.). However, there is another component at work here—a sort of enthymeme-in-reverse. I am not sure anyone has examined this sort of thing before, but what Speaker Ryan is also not saying is an unquestioned assumption—and premise—that the Republican version of healthcare offers Americans a "choice" when it comes to limiting government influence; however, what he does not say, and oddly enough the Democrats never articulate in response, is that under the Republican version of healthcare, instead of the government deciding things on behalf of Americans, we instead have insurance companies exerting influence. In other words, under Obamacare, the "government" reduces individual choice, but under the AHCA (the Republican option), "insurance companies" reduce individual choice. Either way, "choice" is really an illusion, but both sides of the debate try to capitalize on the notion of choice to advance their particular ideological agenda.

Other Thoughts on Polarizing Healthcare Rhetoric

Ultimately, as we have seen, right-wing approaches to the ACA are based largely on perceived threats to individual and business freedoms. Michele Bachmann even worried that "President Obama [couldn't] wait to get Americans addicted to the crack cocaine of dependency on more government healthcare" (cited in Reilly, 2013, n.p.). Such seemingly outlandish claims would not be concerning if they occurred in a vacuum. However, they become echoed by other spinsters in their ideological silos and are used to justify even more radical positions. And, as former Republican National Committee chair and George W. Bush campaign manager Lee Atwater was fond of saying, "perception is reality" (Forbes, 2008). For instance, Will Bunch describes how another, but more recent than Atwater, former Republican National Committee chair, Michael Steele, lit a fuse that chained out among other conservatives:

> Michael Steele, the perpetually embattled chairman of the Republican National Committee who was elected to that job not long after Obama's inauguration, told reporters that health-care reform was "socialism" and that a "cabal" in Congress was backing it. The very next day, Glenn Beck—consciously or not—echoed Steele and called the package "good old socialism … raping the pocketbooks of the rich to give to the poor." Over time, of course, the rhetoric began to escalate when charges of "socialism" had lost their shock value. By August, Rush Limbaugh was casually telling his listeners that "the Obama health-care logo is damn close to a Nazi swastika logo," and by December, after months of nonstop attacks, Limbaugh was comparing Democratic health-care proposals to Nazis and Cuba and everything in between. The escalating radio hyperbole was not nearly as surprising, however, is the way in which the stark, apocalyptic tone then carried over to the Republican members of Congress … the right-wing politicians eagerly signed on to what was now cast as a political war of the worlds, a "Waterloo" with no retreat and no surrender. (Bunch, 2011, pp. 295–296)

Thus, extreme right-wing Republicans engage in what Arianna Huffington calls "rhetorical yoga" to advance their perspectives on Obamacare (Huffington, 2008, p. 297). Through distortions (and even outright fabrications), fear appeals, dichotomized us/them framing, allusions and analogies to communism and Nazism, along with reasonable contentions premised on deductive reasoning and statistical studies, conservatives play an important role in the divisive discourse regarding contemporary healthcare rhetoric.

But liberals and ACA supporters are culpable as well. After the passage of the ACA in 2010, President Obama received quite a bit of criticism. As a result, when he ran for re-election two years later, it was imperative that his campaign counter some prevailing sentiments about the law. Obama decided to "recruit two million supporters to help debunk attacks on the president's record and hit back at his Republican rivals. Called the 'Truth Team,' the new effort will engage Obama supporters online and in person, encouraging them to communicate with undecided voters about the president's record" (The Centrist Word, 2012, n.p.). In other words, Obama openly formed a propaganda component to his campaign specifically purposed to affect his image regarding his major policies, of which the ACA was paramount. Moreover, the Democrats also used scare tactics, like their opponents, but obviously in a different context. Concerned about the trajectory of American healthcare, liberals used certain rhetorical tactics to propel their healthcare reform ideas forward. For example, the "Democrats claimed that Republicans proposed 'ending Medicare as we know it,' turning it into a stingy voucher system that would force seniors to pay thousands of dollars more for their healthcare. 'Ending Medicare as we know it'—whatever it may mean—sounds terrifying to anyone over 65, as almost all seniors depend heavily on Medicare to finance their healthcare" (Rivlin, 2013, p. S17). Hence, with both ends of the political spectrum misleading the public, engaging in questionable rhetorical tactics and preferring name-calling over substantive policy analysis, it is no wonder that the former director of the Department of Health and Human Services, Kathleen Sebelius, said that "healthcare is one of the thorniest public policy issues of our day" (Sebelius, 2013, p. S13).

CONCLUSION

Given the relatively recent adoption of the ACA, the VA scandal, the Court's *Hobby Lobby* decision, and the ongoing disputes over contraceptives and abortion, it should come as no surprise that healthcare is a preeminent example of division and discord in contemporary American discourse. Despite the contentious nature of healthcare issues, recent implementation of the ACA in states that are embracing it reveals significant reductions in uninsured Americans, less hamstrung Medicaid procedures, and more effective handling of resources (Young, 2014). When referring to the 2012 presidential election, Alice Rivlin discusses how the polarization over healthcare occurs:

> We witnessed a shouting match in which each side tried to scare the voting public by depicting the other as advocates of drastic change that would wreck the American health system, alter the relationship between doctor and patient, and threaten all of the aspects of our healthcare system that people value most. But the reason each side scares voters by exaggerating the terrible consequences of electing the other is that both sides perceive that most people are pretty satisfied with their healthcare providers and afraid of drastic change. ... So the most effective campaign rhetoric is to depict the opposing candidate as an advocate of radical change. If candidates talked honestly about policies that they thought stood a chance of actual enactment, they would find the differences between them narrowing and compromise within reach. (Rivlin, 2013, p. S16)

And, as Rivlin suggests, if we can re-center our political discussions around policies instead of ideological dogma and personality attacks, we might stand a chance at facilitating meaningful, productive democratic discourse. However, if we are not careful, we place our democracy in jeopardy, "where the ongoing bi-partisan squawk took the place of rational discourse, apathy seemed the sane response to an insane amount of stupid talk" (Wiebe, 2010, p. 266). Since the American Health Care Act failed, we continue to live in a world of limbo concerning healthcare. My hope is that by learning the fallacies and rhetorical tactics of both sides of the debate, Americans will make the best decision they can as we move forward.

IMAGE CREDITS

- Fig. 4.2: Adapted from: "Ideological Views on Health Care," http://www.people-press.org/files/2014/06/6-12-2014-Political-Polarization-Release.pdf, pp. 68. Copyright © 2014 by Pew Research Center.
- Fig. 4.3: Source: https://www.balloon-juice.com/2012/08/20/lady-parts-diagram-and-open-thread/
- Fig. 4.4: Source: https://littledixiedynamite.wordpress.com/tag/joseph-stalin/

CHAPTER FIVE

LGBTQ+ Rights

For many Americans, no other contemporary issue is as controversial as LGBTQ+ rights; its contentious nature runs deeply in the American psyche. In one respect, the topic of LGBTQ+ rights lies at the nexus of two competing, crucial components of what defines America—our religious traditions and our philosophical belief in individual liberties. As we have been discussing in the previous two chapters, religious convictions in the United States are generally held in high regard. Likewise, protections for individual rights remind us of our history and one of the reasons this country began. When these two themes conflict, we are bound to witness a dispute of monumental proportions. And with the controversy surrounding LGBTQ+ rights, we have precisely that.

By most measures, Americans are deeply divided about whether LGBTQ+s should be allowed to marry or if they should receive special protections as a "suspect category," much like race and gender are afforded under our laws. Typically, the concern with extending such protections involves religious beliefs, but not always. As we will see in this chapter, other arguments are also levied to maintain the *status quo*, such as restricting the activism of the judicial branch, upholding the general will of the populace, preserving traditional notions of things like marriage, and, arguably, compelling state interests such as the welfare and protection of children. Of course, each of these claims is also refuted by those in favor of changing our society's views regarding LGBTQ+ rights. Hence, these arguments and others, as well as religious claims, lay the groundwork for this important, albeit polarizing, contemporary issue.

A NOTE ABOUT LANGUAGE

Even the naming and labeling of the groups involved in this issue signify why this contemporary issue is important for us to examine. At times, the word "gay" may refer to all homosexuals, but it is not an accurate term since it actually refers to male homosexuals. Female homosexuals, of course, are referred to as "lesbians." In terms of sexual orientation, individuals may be attracted to, or prefer to have relations with, the same sex, or they may have a proclivity for sexual relations with both sexes, which would classify them as "bisexuals." In addition, some people are born with genitalia from both sexes, so they might be named "hermaphrodites." Others may be born with certain genitalia to officially designate them either male or female, but by virtually any other indication, they believe themselves to be the opposite sex; when this occurs, the person is technically a "transsexual," but since our society apparently cannot discern the difference between sex and gender, they are typically called "transgender." Or, as Lyla Cicero (2012) puts it, the word transgender "calls into question the assumed match between biological sex and gender identity." More accurately, "transgender" individuals frequently engage in cross-gendered behavior—or they may play with traditional gendered expectations, such as dress—regardless of their sexual orientation or preferences. But, to be clear, transgender in common parlance also refers to individuals who feel trapped inside a sexual body to which they do not identify, and many undergo operations to transition from their born sex into the other. Given the complexity of classifying where individuals reside in this spectrum, even the term "LGBTQ+" does not quite capture the essence or range of sexual identities. Hence, acronyms have been utilized to help frame the discussions that involve all of these different groups. Initially, GLBT was used (gay, lesbian, bisexual, transsexual), but that acronym privileged "gay" since it came first. In response, the acronym changed to LGBT that places "lesbian" first. But that acronym is insufficient, too. A more recent acronym—LGBTQ—adds a "Q" to include "queer" (Petrow, 2014).

Once a pejorative term (and occasionally, depending on the context, may still be considered derogatory), the word "queer" has been rearticulated, or reclaimed, by many in the LGBTQ+/LGBTQ movement to capture varying sexual identities that are not easily categorized, as well as signify a political identity tied to LGBTQ+ politics. With the development of "queer studies" in academia as well as rhetorical maneuvers by certain movement leaders, some markers once thought to be offensive—such as "queer" or "fag"—are now deployed as a way to politically signify both the disenfranchisement and the power of LGBTQ individuals (Galinsky et al., 2013; Riggs, 2010). But, of course, not everyone who identifies as a member of the LGBTQ community agrees with using such politically loaded language.

As a "sexual minority," transgender individuals constitute approximately three-tenths of one percent of adults (Scherer, 2016). Another sexual minority, often referred to as "intersex," might be what we also consider as hermaphrodites, and they compose approximately two percent of adults (Cicero, 2012). Then there are folks who identify as "genderqueer," or a sexual identity simply based on difference, and androgynous, which is an individual who identifies as part female and part male. Thus, the labels of "transgender, genderqueer, androgynous, and intersex are all identities which call into question the gender binary" (Cicero, 2012). Lyla Cicero, a clinical psychologist and feminist-gender activist, also makes the case for adding two more letters—P and K. The "P" is for pansexual, to which Cicero herself identifies, in order to represent holistic inclusivity; as Cicero describes, pansexual "pulls the rug out from under the gender binary as well as earlier concepts of sexual orientation, by separating sexual/affectional orientation from binary notions of gender" (2012). And the letter K stand for "kink," or the identity for "those who practice bondage and discipline, dominance-submission and/or sado-masochism, as well as those with an incredibly diverse set of fetishes and preferences," which accounts for approximately 15% of adults (Cicero, 2012).

If we use the first letter of these labels and add them to our acronym, the new permutation becomes lengthy, unwieldly, and challenging to say or use—LGBTQIAPK. And some also add another "A" for allies, or those folks who may be heterosexual but act in solidarity with these other identity categories. As a result, some people simply use the acronym LGBTQ+ to utilize the more user-friendly original acronym with the "+" symbol to represent the other identity categories.

As I will explore in more detail later, another matter of linguistic import is the concept of marriage. Many people refer to homosexual marriage as "same-sex marriage," obviously because matrimony of this sort entails wedding two people of the same sex. However, a more recent phrasing of this concept is "marriage equality." As such, the name clearly de-emphasizes the nature of two people of the same sex marrying and instead places the importance on the question of equality. This rhetorical maneuver is clearly purposeful. There is nothing wrong or politically problematic from referring to same-sex couples marrying, but by emphasizing "equality," advocates for homosexual marriage shift the debate to one of fairness, tolerance, and equality, thereby reducing the propensity of defending why members of the same sex should be in a relationship in the first place (Lipp, 2013).

Since different individuals may self-identify in different ways, and since we generally want to be as accurate as possible when discussing controversial issues, I will try to reflect and utilize appropriate terminology in this chapter. In this book, I try to interchange identity categories in an effort to not exclude individuals. But, at the same time, I am also mindful of writing in a way that flows, makes sense, and allows the reader to absorb the text without too much strain. As such, I will frequently use the word "LGBTQ+" or the acronym LGBTQ+. I realize that the "+" can be perceived as an add-on or even as a footnote, relegating certain identities to a less privileged position. I apologize in advance if this offends anyone, for it is not my intent to be insensitive; actually, my intent is quite the opposite. As I have mentioned, it is important to note that some individuals wish to be identified with different terms, but if we are going to have a conversation about these issues, we must begin somewhere, and I hope that using the words LGBTQ+, same-sex, gays, lesbians, and LGBTQ+ will be an agreeable and minimally insensitive starting point.

THE CONTEXT OF LGBTQ+ ISSUES

Homosexuality has occurred as long as recorded history. In fact, many opponents to LGBTQ+ rights cite passages from the Bible to support their philosophical resistance to LGBTQ+ rights or status. Additionally, we know that homosexuality was practiced in ancient Rome, especially when we hear stories of Emperor Caligula and some of the parties that presumably occurred during that era. Similarly, we know that homosexuality existed in classical Greece, where it was not uncommon for young boys to have relationships and the famed island of Lesbos was rumored to be the origin of lesbians. Throughout the ages, homosexuality has encountered periods of acceptance and opposition. Of course, in recent history and in contemporary America, homosexuality is known as an important and divisive social issue.

The Historical Context

Many historians and members of the LGBTQ+ community argue that the starting point for the social conversation regarding LGBTQ+ rights in the United States began with the so-called Stonewall riots in 1969. Discrimination against LGBTQ+ folks and conversations regarding the LGBTQ+ community obviously pre-date 1969, but many consider Stonewall to be a "catalytic event" (Shaiko, 2007, p. 85) or those "moments in the life of a movement that provide the appropriate conditions for discourse" (Darsey, 2001, p. 303).

The Stonewall Inn was a bar in New York City owned by a suspected mafia businessman. It was frequented by drag queens and LGBTQ+ patrons looking to have a good time and perhaps "hook up" with other LGBTQ+ individuals. Like most bars at the time, Stonewall tried to maximize its profits by avoiding the hefty taxes levied on alcohol, which typically meant there was just enough liquor at the bar to serve the immediate orders, and the rest was stored in nearby cars. When bars like the Stonewall Inn were raided by the police, they could easily reopen the next day since not all of their liquor stockpiles would be confiscated (Duberman, 1993). But avoiding liquor taxes as well as providing a watering hole for LGBTQ+ people made taverns like Stonewall a target for police. And, like other bars, the Stonewall Inn had experienced its fair share of raids, but they were generally relatively peaceful and low-impact. Some speculate that the local police may have received kickbacks from the bar's owners, and the known mafia connections associated with the owner helped support that theory (Wolf, 2009).

However, in the early morning of June 28, 1969, something different and unexpected occurred at the Stonewall Inn. Unlike typical police visits, this evening was met with local police and federal agents from the Alcohol, Tobacco, and Firearms Bureau (ATF). In addition to rounding up liquor bottles that had no tax stamps, the police also harassed the LGBTQ+ clientele, even arresting some for solicitation (Duberman, 1993). When a wagon arrived to cart the arrested folks to jail, onlookers and Stonewall patrons who had avoided arrests taunted and vocalized their frustrations toward the officers.

According to Duberman (1993), "The mêlée broke out in several directions and swiftly mounted in intensity…the crowd had swelled to a mob, and people were picking up and throwing whatever loose objects came to hand—coins, bottles, cans, bricks from a nearby construction site. Someone even picked up dog shit from the street and threw it in the cops' direction" (pp. 197–198). Protests accompanied with violent clashes and outbursts between police and members of the LGBTQ+ community lasted for seven days. Several evenings during that week were characterized as "all hell broke loose." Although the police crackdown was harsh, they were not the only culprits or instigators. As at least one report suggests, "Trash baskets were again set on fire, and bottles and beer cans were tossed in the direction of the cops (sometimes hitting protesters instead); the action was accompanied by militant shouts of 'Pig motherfuckers!' 'Fag rapists!' and 'Gestapo!'" (Duberman, 1993, p. 209). While discrimination and abuse against gays and lesbians was not uncommon in the late 1960s, the Stonewall incident symbolized how agents of authority engaged in a concerted and direct anti-gay campaign. Additionally, the nature of the assaults were egregious (Vaid, 1995). Whereas previous anti-LGBTQ+ encounters generally involved slurs being bantered about along with charges—some of which were trumped-up—of violations of some sort of city ordinance (such as disorderly conduct, obstruction, resisting arrest, public indecency, etc.), the Stonewall incident represented abuse that was difficult to justify even by the most ardent law enforcement apologist. Even if the LGBTQ+ individuals involved had committed actual crimes, the treatment they encountered certainly was not commiserate with any behavior they could have arguably been doing.

Thus, Stonewall became a symbolic moment that characterized the brutal ways many LGBTQ+ people were treated. Protestors, movement organizers, sympathizers from the 1960s civil rights struggle, and activist LGBTQ+ individuals seemed to unite over the maltreatment of LGBTQ+ folks. Part of this struggle was exemplified by the political campaigns of Harvey Milk. Popularized by the recent film starring Sean Penn, Harvey Milk was an important figure in the struggle for LGBTQ+ rights, as he endured public and visible displays of anti-gay animosity when he ran for San Francisco mayor and as a member of the San Francisco Board of Supervisors (Kepner, 2004; Klarman, 2014). At first, the nascent LGBTQ+ movement was assimilationist in nature—focusing on electoral changes and seeking areas of compromise with the larger heterosexual culture. A prominent organization at the time that embodied this philosophy was the Mattachine Society. It was not long, however, before fragmentation within the movement occurred, especially when some LGBTQ+ people strongly believed that assimilationist strategies of compromise were actually methods of selling out and cooptation (Wolf, 2009). A more radical group splintered off from the Mattachine Society and called themselves the Gay Liberation Front (GLF).

The GLF probably proved to be too radical for the culture of the 1970s, but at the very least, the GLF and the Mattachine Society suffered from organizational difficulties, resource constraints, and communication problems (Wolf, 2009). Moreover, perhaps the most daunting obstacle to the budding LGBTQ+ social movement—and a problem that persists even today—was a unique component that impacts only gays and lesbians: the closet. Faced with the threat of housing and workplace discrimination, ostracization from peers, and rejection, even disowning, from family members, many LGBTQ+ folks hid their identity, largely out of necessity (Wolf, 2009). Many feared receiving mail from organizations such as the Mattachine Society or the GLF because they worried that word would get out that they were gay or lesbian, and the potential negative ramifications of that revelation simply outweighed, by far, any potential gain that could come from associating with these groups (Chauncey, 2004).

The camouflage that the closet provides LGBTQ+ people can be crucial for their individual well-being, but for a culture or social movement, large numbers of closeted individuals can be devastating (Sedgwick, 2007, p. 161). One of the most important elements for any social movement is recruitment of members and the rallying of support. A movement simply cannot exist, much less be successful, if it is occupied by phantom members (Chauncey, 2004). Thus, while Stonewall provided a crucial catalyst for some LGBTQ+ members to coalesce in protest against larger societal norms, as a community, LGBTQ+ individuals found it challenging to move forward in any meaningful and productive way.

Until the mid-1980s. Most LGBTQ+ people still remained closeted, but the 1980s ushered in a new material, medical, and rhetorical situation—AIDS (Jost, 2014). Of course, AIDS is a tragic syndrome that precipitates devastating, debilitating, and horrific disease due to lowered immune systems. But politically and culturally, the AIDS crisis brought a unique challenge and opportunity for the gay and lesbian community (Darsey, 2001). On one hand, AIDS was being rhetorically framed by many in society as the "gay disease," in large part because AIDS is relatively easily transmitted through anal sex, which is a common sexual practice among gay men. Being labeled the "gay disease" and associated almost entirely with the LGBTQ+ community, AIDS further intensified, in many cases, the proclivity for LGBTQ+ folks to remain in the closet (Chauncey, 2004). After all, even if they were healthy, LGBTQ+ people did not want to be blamed for the "scourge" that was known as AIDS.

However, the AIDS crisis also provided an interesting opportunity for the LGBTQ+ movement, particularly since a separate movement, ACT UP, formed specifically because of AIDS. It brought attention to the plight that many gay and lesbian Americans had to endure at the time (Vaid, 1995). But perhaps more important, when LGBTQ+ individuals were dying from the disease, heterosexuals began to see the humanity that occurs when a person sees a loved one die, or when a loved one is not permitted to attend hospital visiting hours because he or she is not a blood relative or a state-sanctioned spouse, or when a LGBTQ+ has to conduct funeral arrangements despite the fact he or she will not receive the loved one's life insurance or pension. In other words, the pain and agony LGBTQ+ people must endure—on top of the pain and grief they experience when a loved one passes—was something that heterosexuals never considered or understood until the AIDS crisis occurred. While the mistreatment faced by LGBTQ+ folks during the AIDS epidemic did not alter overall public opinion about the plight LGBTQ+ individuals faced, nor did it radically transform the laws regulating such things as hospital visitations and spousal benefits, what the AIDS crisis did do was raise awareness about these issues, and it helped the LGBTQ+ community reinforce some of its activist principles and societal complaints, which, over time, could help slowly alter the larger American culture.

HIV/AIDS is still a serious concern, but once the medical community was able to prove that AIDS is not a "gay disease" and then reassure the populace that individuals cannot contract HIV through casual contact, the syndrome became less of an automatic blemish placed on gays and lesbians simply for being LGBTQ+. Many in the LGBTQ+ movement wanted to use the AIDS crisis as a springboard to demand a cure (Stockdill, 2003). Others wanted to use the crisis as a way to highlight the way LGBTQ+ sexual practices are perceived in society. The latter philosophy became even more pronounced after the famous Supreme Court decision of *Bowers v. Hardwick* (1986).

When the Atlanta police entered the residence of Michael Hardwick in order to serve an arrest warrant, they found him engaging in sodomy with a consenting gay lover. The state of Georgia had an anti-sodomy statute on the books, which on-face was neutral in that sodomy was illegal for both heterosexuals and LGBTQ+ individuals. However, given the circumstance, the law was used to prosecute Hardwick, who happened to be LGBTQ+. Once the matter reached the U.S. Supreme Court, the issue became a lightning rod for LGBTQ+ advocates and opponents alike. Despite the law's original applicability to both heterosexuals and LGBTQ+ folks, the court case solely rested on whether sodomy should be condoned for LGBTQ+ couples. In fact, the justice writing the opinion of the Court, Byron White, said that the case concerned "whether the Federal Constitution confers a fundamental right upon LGBTQ+ people to engage in sodomy" (White, 1986, p. 1). As such, the Supreme Court case was a legal—and cultural—testament about LGBTQ+ conduct.

The *Bowers* decision ultimately ruled against Michael Hardwick and LGBTQ+ individuals in general. The main argument was simply that the Court believed that there is no "fundamental right to engage in LGBTQ+ sodomy" (White, 1986, p. 2). Sodomy, regardless of one's views on the actual practice, is simply not a protected right under the Constitution, even if the practice is between consenting adults. The *Bowers* decision had the unrelated effect of minimizing the Court's overprotection of privacy protections. However, the main result of the decision was that LGBTQ+ sexual conduct, which frequently takes the form of sodomy, was deemed illegal by the highest court of the land (Eskridge, 2004).

Although the original anti-sodomy law was facially neutral and it is difficult to enforce anti-sodomy laws, especially when such acts occur in the privacy of one's bedroom, the impact of the *Bowers* decision was felt by LGBTQ+ folks all over the country (Jost, 2014). Sexual conduct was deemed inappropriate because it was declared unlawful (Rimmerman, 2002). Additionally, the *Bowers* decision provided a legal and cultural rationale for varying governmental jurisdictions "to authorize a wide variety of bans and limitations on the lives of gay people, including the ability to parent children, serve in the military, and secure financial and legal protections for their relationships" (Keen and Goldberg, 2000, p. 14).

Bowers v. Hardwick (1986) was a pivotal case, in part because it "was a controversial decision. No decision of the Supreme Court upholding a statute against constitutional attack has been subject to the immediate and overwhelming criticism that *Bowers* was" (Eskridge, 2004, p. 36). In fact, the Supreme Court decision that later overruled *Bowers*, the *Lawrence v. Texas* (2003) case, has been touted as so vital that it "may even assume an importance for gay people that *Brown v. Board of Education* has had for people of color" (Eskridge, 2004, p. 36). Thus, resistance to *Bowers* and a larger, organized effort at limiting, if not eliminating entirely, laws that strike at the heart of LGBTQ+ identity and existence—their sexual behavior—seemed like it was not only the obvious way forward for the movement, but also the most important.

However, because of the actions of three homosexual couples in late 1990, the inertia and orchestrated efforts directed against *Bowers* and anti-sodomy laws came to a grinding halt. In December 1990, the three couples sought marriage licenses in Hawaii. When they were declined, the couples filed a lawsuit in 1991. Two years later, in May, the Hawaii Supreme Court said that marriage was "a civil right," which "was the first time in U.S. history that a court came remotely close to approving 'gay marriages'" (D'Emilio, 2007, p. 39). The decision in *Baehr v. Lewin* (1993) became extremely important since it ruled that denying marital rights *de facto* constructed a sex classification "in the same way that a ban on interracial marriage constitutes a race classification" (Klarman, 2014, p. 56). By creating a separate classification—in this case for a denial of a right—the government is also creating an identity classification worthy of equal protection under the Fourteenth Amendment. And the Supreme Court ruled in *Eisenstadt v. Baird* (1972), *Zablocki v. Redhail* (1978), and *Turner v. Safley* (1987) that marriage is a fundamental right. While the court decision was vital for those three couples, it immediately spurred a political backlash, mostly from religious conservatives who feared that allowing gay marriage in Hawaii would cause it to happen everywhere.

Almost immediately, conservatives began proposing legislation or constitutional amendments in individual states that would forbid same-sex marriage (Klarman, 2014). The influence of Pat Robertson and the so-called "moral majority," especially during the 1996 presidential campaign, did not bode well for marriage equality advocates. In fact, the Republican frontrunner, Bob Dole, co-sponsored a bill in 1996 to help galvanize Christian and conservative support—the Defense of Marriage Act (DOMA). DOMA passed both the House and the Senate, where arguments in support of the measure largely focused on anti-gay rhetoric and conservative prompts for moral action against homosexual "perversion," and it was subsequently signed by President Clinton (Klarman, 2014, p. 61). DOMA codified into federal law that marriage should be a union between a man and a woman.

The political backlash against the *Baehr* decision came full circle when, in 1997, the Hawaii state legislature agreed on a state constitutional amendment authorizing the option of limiting recognition of marriage to heterosexual couples. In that November, when the measure went up for a vote, Hawaiians overwhelmingly voted in favor of the amendment by a margin of 69% to 31% (Klarman, 2014). Similar actions against same-sex marriage occurred in other states, such as Colorado.

However, in Colorado, the state constitutional amendment that prohibited same-sex marriage ordinances on the municipal level was overturned by the state's Supreme Court. In 1994, the Colorado high court ruled in *Romer v. Evans* that the amendment—"imposing a broad and undifferentiated disability on a single named group"—was "so discontinuous with the reasons offered for it that the amendment seems inexplicable by anything but animus toward the class that it affects" (Klarman, 2014, p. 69). In other words, the court said the amendment targeted a particular group with prejudice. The *Romer* decision, then, became an enormous victory for the LGBTQ+ rights movement in general, and the battle for marriage equality in particular. And even though it was a state Supreme Court case, the *Romer* decision established an important precedent for other courts to follow.

Also in 1996, Vermont became the first state to recognize domestic partner benefits to state employees, although same-sex marriages were still illegal. But in the 1999 decision, the Vermont Supreme Court ruled in *State v. Baker* that the same-sex marriage prohibitions should be invalidated since they ran contrary to the spirit of the state's constitution (Klarman, 2014). The *State v. Baker* decision did not quite legalize same-sex marriages, but it was another important victory for the LGBTQ+ movement. However, there were many citizens who vehemently disapproved and, given the popularity of the political maneuver in other states, demanded a constitutional amendment to overrule the *Baker* decision. Instead of immediately instigating amendment discussions, the state legislature encouraged public town hall meetings. For the most part, the electorate in Vermont were divided. In the end, however, it appeared that the majority wanted some sort of provision allowing homosexuals to marry. In the spirit of compromise, the Vermont state legislature passed a law in March 2000 permitting what it called "civil unions," and it was the first state to offer some sort of marital union for gays and lesbians (Klarman, 2014).

Understanding the essence of civil unions (CU) is important because the term has been used and bantered about without much attention to its actual, legal meaning compared to the concept of "marriage." At the most basic level, an easy way to distinguish civil unions from marriage is that civil unions are recognized at the level of individual states, whereas marriage is federally recognized (GLAD, 2014; Klarman, 2014). The state/federal distinction is crucial for a number of reasons. First, civil unions cannot access federally based rights, such as Social Security benefits, unless the federal government decides to do so. Second, there is a sort of "limbo" land "with regard to governmental functions performed by both state and federal governments, such as taxation, pension protections, provision of insurance for families, and means-tested programs like Medicaid" (GLAD, 2014).

Next, unless all states recognize civil unions, a couple cannot take their union to another state. In other words, they are not portable (GLAD, 2014). Similarly, if a couple receive a civil union in a CU state, but then moves to a non-CU state, the couple cannot receive a divorce in the new state. Of course, perhaps they would have a *de facto* divorce since the new state may not recognize the CU in the first place. This is the next problem with civil unions—their ambiguity creates much uncertainty and potential legal difficulty.

Finally, marriage has an important symbolic meaning for couples who love one another, and they see it a "fundamental sign of their equality and full citizenship" (Chauncey, 2004, p. 166). For these reasons, most gays and lesbians desire marriage equality, not civil unions, since civil unions are, in essence, "separate and unequal" (Chauncey, 2004, p. 141). Further compromise is seen as reinforcing the feeling that homosexuals live as "second-class citizens" in their own country (Rimmerman, 2002, pp. 1, 45). Nevertheless, the adoption of civil unions in Vermont as a result of the *Baker* decision was a crucial victory. And it demonstrated an important benefit of civil unions over marriage—namely, that civil unions risk less political backlash than full-fledged marriage (Klarman, 2014).

However, although civil unions are not the same as marriage, and even though homosexuals "would have preferred marriage, gay rights groups viewed civil unions as a big victory—a cause for celebration" (Klarman, 2014, p. 79). Vermont became ground zero for the national debate over gay rights. While LGBTQ+ activists claimed that civil unions and the *Baker* decision were victories, conservatives were calling the actions in Vermont part of a new "moral war," whereas same-sex marriage advocates were saying that Vermont was "a beacon of hope" (Klarman, 2014, pp. 82–83).

Although the LGBTQ+ movement had largely shifted its energies almost entirely toward securing same-sex marriage rights, by this time, another issue related to LGBTQ+ rights was resurfacing. Despite the U.S. Supreme Court's 1986 ruling in *Bowers v. Hardwick* that LGBTQ+ individuals deserved no protections against antisodomy laws, most states by the turn of the millennia had either removed their sodomy laws completely or stopped enforcing them (Gill, 2012). However, responding to a report (that would later turn out to be false) that a dangerously armed man was in a house, Houston police entered the premises only to find John Lawrence engaging in sodomy with another male (Klarman, 2014). Both men were arrested. Lawrence appealed the arrest, which ultimately came to the U.S. Supreme Court. In 2003, the Court's decision in *Lawrence v. Texas* overturned the *Bowers* decision on due process grounds. In *Lawrence*, Justice Kennedy argued, "To say that the issue in *Bowers* was simply the right to engage in certain sexual conduct demeans the claim the individual put forward, just as it would demean a married couple were it said that marriage is just about the right to have sexual intercourse" (in *Lawrence*, 2003, p. 567). In any case, *Lawrence* decriminalized sodomy for consenting adults, thereby removing state-based legal injunctions on sexual identity and sexual behavior.

But the *Lawrence* decision was more than just a legal decision lifting the criminalization statutes against sodomy. Justice Kennedy also said, "When homosexual conduct is made criminal by the law of the State, that declaration in and of itself is an invitation to subject homosexual persons to discrimination in both the public and in the private spheres" (in *Lawrence*, 2003, p. 575). In other words, the Court makes clear that there is a legal presumption against state-based decisions that promote discrimination averse to LGBTQ+ individuals. Legal scholar Andrew Koppelman elucidates this legal provision: "If a state singles out gays for unprecedentedly harsh treatment, the Court will presume that what is going on is a bare desire to harm, rather than mere moral disapproval" (Koppelman, 2005, p. 154).

Given the momentum and changing public opinion toward homosexual marriage, gay and lesbian couples continued to fight for the right to marry (Gill, 2012; Klarman, 2014). The next major victory occurred in Massachusetts in 2003. In *Goodridge v. Department of Public Health*, the Massachusetts Supreme Judicial Court ordered that same-sex marriage licenses must be accepted. This ruling was significant because the Massachusetts court was the first judicial body to do so, which made the decision, as one lawyer put it, like "the Berlin Wall coming down for the gay community" (Klarman, 2014, p. 91). Furthermore, in 2008, the California Supreme Court, in its decision *In re* Marriage Cases (2008), ruled much like the Vermont *Baker* decision in that same-sex couples have a right to receive benefits under the state's notion of "domestic partners," and, as such, do not need to be afforded the opportunity to marry (Jost, 2014). And in *Varnum v. Brien* (2009), the Iowa Supreme Court ruled in favor of same-sex marriages by dismissing arguments that favor so-called "traditional" marriage, although the Court provided little analysis or reasons for doing so except that its state constitution declares that "people are born 'free and equal' and are entitled to equal 'privileges and immunities' to confer the right of marriage upon same-sex couples" (in Klarman, 2014, p. 126).

Same-sex marriage issues became important in Arkansas, Arizona, Maine, New Jersey, Oregon, Ohio, and elsewhere (Klarman, 2014). It was, simply put, a "vexing issue" that was "a more potent issue for voters than either abortion or gun control" (Klarman, 2014, p. 104). But public opinion was slowly becoming more amenable to marriage equality and LGBTQ+ rights. For instance, the "number of states with anti-discrimination laws covering sexual orientation rose from eight in 1993 to twenty in 2008" (Klarman, 2014, p. 119).

Unrelated to marriage, but still very important to LGBTQ+ rights, was the Clinton military policy of "Don't Ask, Don't Tell" (DADT). Passed in 1993, DADT was Clinton's attempt at compromising with conservatives and military leaders at the time to functionally disallow homosexuals to serve—the argument being, *inter alia*, that homosexuals in the military were bad for morale (Lynch, 2008). The measure was intended to reduce the discrimination gays and lesbians encountered in our armed forces. However, since DADT was implemented, "about thirteen thousand service members had been discharged because of their sexual orientation, including eight hundred who were deemed 'mission-critical' troops, such as fifty-nine Arabic-speaking linguists" (Klarman, 2014, p. 157). DADT also exemplifies the potency of language and naming. After all, simply declaring one's self as a homosexual puts their identity into concrete reality with, in this context, serious consequences. After repeated statements threatening to use his executive powers to nullify DADT, President Obama finally convinced the House and Senate to repeal DADT in December 2010 (Jost, 2014).

In July 2010, a U.S. District Court in *Gill v. Office of Personnel Management* (2010) held that the Defense of Marriage Act (DOMA) was unconstitutional on equal protection grounds since the law "bears no reasonable relation to any interest the government might have in making heterosexual marriages more secure" (Tauro, 2010, n.p.). As a response, in 2011, President Obama announced that he believed DOMA was

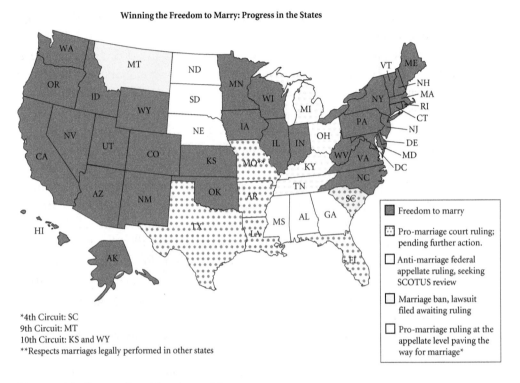

Figure 5.1: Same-Sex Marriage Map.

unconstitutional and, as such, he directed the Justice Department to no longer enforce any of DOMA's provisions (Klarman, 2014). Obama's position influenced a proposal in the Senate to repeal DOMA, which eventually occurred later that year. And in *United States v. Windsor* (2013), the Supreme Court upheld the striking down of DOMA.

Also in 2011, Hawaii, Illinois, Delaware, and Rhode Island adopted civil union provisions, and New York legalized full-fledged marriage for same-sex couples (Klarman, 2014). At the time of this writing (see Figure 5.1), eight states and Washington, D.C., have some form of same-sex recognition, and twenty-six states have some form of a same-sex marriage ban as a result of constitutional amendments (Jost, 2014). Moreover, the Supreme Court recently ruled in August 2014 that the state of Virginia cannot move forward with its ban on same-sex marriage (Mears, 2014). And, as we will discuss in a moment, in 2015, the Supreme Court ruled that same-sex marriages are constitutionally protected nationwide.

Throughout this timeline, conservatives initiated several proposals to block same-sex marriages or civil unions. Many efforts included some sort of state constitutional amendments or court actions to prevent same-sex marriage to some degree. At the federal level, some politicians, such as Michele Bachmann, proposed a federal constitutional amendment (i.e., the "federal marriage amendment," or FMA) to either outright prohibit same-sex marriages or *de facto* prohibit them by enshrining the definition of marriage as a man and a woman into the amendment. Rumblings of the FMA began as early as 2003 (Cahill, 2004; Talent, 2004), but some politicians hint at proposing it even today (Jost, 2014; Klarman, 2014).

In terms of contemporary marriage rulings, many states have permitted same-sex marriages or some variant thereof. In most of those cases, there was considerable backlash, mainly from conservative groups. They cried that by using the courts, homosexuals and their supporters were encouraging judicial activism (Klarman, 2014). In response, the conservatives looked to state legislators to pass laws or state constitutional amendments that would trump the juridical rulings. In other states, the backlash to the pro-homosexual court cases was minimal, and the court decisions remained the law of that state and provided precedent for other states and judicial districts. But, as we will discuss later, the U.S. Supreme Court legalized same-sex marriage in 2015, with their decision in *Obergefell v. Hodges*.

The Framework of LGBTQ+ Issues in America

Given this historical trajectory, LGBTQ+ rights in the United States have largely centered on the following areas: discrimination (including individual liberties), medical issues (e.g., HIV/AIDS), and same-sex marriage (including spousal benefits). Opposition to these issues has typically been based on legal, religious, and consequential grounds. In other words, many who resist increasing LGBTQ+ rights argue that the law prevents it, that religious principles oppose it, and/or that granting LGBTQ+ rights can have negative impacts, such as jeopardizing children, devaluing the institution of marriage, risking promiscuous lifestyles, etc. As we shall see, the rhetoric surrounding LGBTQ+ issues is premised primarily on legal and religious grounds, entailing arguments about individual liberties, morality, and cultural change.

The Rhetorical Situation

As we know, a rhetorical situation is determined by three components—an audience, constraints, and exigencies (Bitzer, 1968). Regarding LGBTQ+ issues, the main audience groups involved are the LGBTQ+ community, opponents to LGBTQ+ rights, and the larger general populace. Resistance to pro-LGBTQ+ initiatives mainly emanates from (culturally and politically) conservative groups, Republicans, Christian organizations (particularly evangelical Protestant denominations), and legal advocates who argue in favor of preserving the *status quo*. According to Persily, "all things being equal, religiosity and conservative ideology is associated with opposition to homosexuality and gay rights, while youth and education are associated with support" (2006, p. 15). These claims, of course, are generalities since in every demographic and religious group we can find folks who are both supporters and opponents to LGBTQ+ issues. For example, many Americans are unaware of the log cabin Republicans—conservative Republicans who also identify as LGBTQ+. While they are LGBTQ+ in terms of their sexual orientation or identity, they believe that the government should not endorse or support LGBTQ+ lifestyles while simultaneously believing strongly in other Republican principles (Log Cabin Republicans website, 2014). And with many LGBTQ+ folks still living in the closet, it is difficult to determine or identify specific target audience groups for LGBTQ+ discourse. After all, if members of a key target audience are unable to be identified, it will be equally difficult to ascertain the effectiveness of rhetorical messages to such closeted individuals, presuming they maintain their private discretion of identity.

A number of rhetorical obstacles exist, depending on the audience group and the issue. For example, gays and lesbians who remain in the closet not only impact the composition of an audience group, but they also establish a specific obstacle. Persuasive messages are difficult to transmit when potential audience members are reluctant to open themselves to the message. Another obstacle—for supporters and opponents alike—is public opinion. Public opinion regarding LGBTQ+ issues has slowly changed over time, but homophile movements have generally encountered resistance from the larger culture to pro-LGBTQ+ initiatives (Persily, 2006). However, public opinion has also changed over time to be more LGBTQ+-friendly (Brewer, 2003; Brewer and Wilcox, 2005; Klarman, 2014; Pew Research Center, 2014a; Yang, 1997), and some states are more receptive to LGBTQ+ rights than others. Finally, legal constraints can also be viewed as a rhetorical obstacle. Given the way many laws have been worded, it has been extremely challenging for LGBTQ+ individuals to promote change. For example, it took well over a decade before LGBTQ+ advocates could challenge the anti-sodomy precedent established in the *Bowers* decision. Another example is the lack of federal rights available to gays and lesbians until same-sex marriage is legalized. In other words, LGBTQ+ people are denied over one thousand federal rights simply because they cannot enter into matrimony—rights that married heterosexuals enjoy all of the time (Wolf, 2009, p. 35). The manner in which the law is structured creates a rhetorical obstacle in that arguments in favor of sharing spousal Social Security benefits, for example, cannot occur without first addressing the issue of marriage equality.

As I have discussed in previous chapters, exigencies can often be the rhetorical obstacles that are just seen from a different perspective. In other words, while some federal rights are restricted to LGBTQ+ people due to the legal constraints from the prohibition on same-sex marriage, such legal constraints can also be opportune exigencies for those who resist gay and lesbian initiatives. But rhetorical exigencies are also opportunities or *kairotic* moments in their own right. For example, despite years of anti-gay sentiments, a family member may be open to pro-LGBTQ+ rhetoric once one of his or her family members comes out of the closet. Generally speaking, "as Americans have gotten to know more gay people, they have also become more comfortable with them" (Persily, 2006, p. 14). Of course, the opposite can also happen—in the face of proximate exposure to homosexuality, some individuals, including close family members, may intensify their opposition to the LGBTQ+ identity, even to the point of engaging in backlash. Cognitive dissonance, then, may emerge as an exigent circumstance that could influence certain rhetorical messages (Holmberg, 2014). And some LGBTQ+ advocates argue that "research conducted over the past two decades has consistently shown that heterosexuals are less prejudiced against gay people if they know someone who is gay," but they interpret recent studies to suggest that personal contact does not reduce prejudice like it once did (Herek, 2009b; Morales, 2009).

Of course, rhetorical obstacles and exigencies are issue-dependent. Many Americans may not care too much about sodomy between consenting adults that occurs in the privacy of their own home because the issue itself is not very visible, nor does it directly impact the lives of the average American (Persily, 2006). An issue like marriage, however, has more salience because it arguably implicates the marriage that heterosexuals enjoy, or same-sex marriage may impact children, and so forth (Lewis and Oh, 2008). Thus, as we explore some of the specific rhetoric that occurs concerning particular LGBTQ+ issues, we should be able to see how the exigencies and obstacles of the rhetorical situation implicates the overall effectiveness of the discursive arguments.

THE NATURE OF LGBTQ+ ISSUES

Contemporary disputes regarding the LGBTQ+ community mainly focus on the issue of marriage equality. Of course, when President Obama repealed the military policy of "Don't Ask, Don't Tell," the issue of LGBTQ+ individuals serving in the military was a salient issue at the time (Hereka, 2009; Lusero, 2009). But in terms of a pressing dispute that has captured the public's attention with any sort of duration and import, it has been the issue of same-sex marriage (Pew Research Center, 2014a).

Americans appear to be very divided over the issue of same-sex marriage (see Figure 5.2). In some instances, there is a sizable show of support (Brewer, 2003; Brewer and Wilcox, 2005; Pew Research Center, 2014a; Yang, 1997). In other instances, there seems to be major resistance to the idea of LGBTQ+ rights, including even a "backlash"

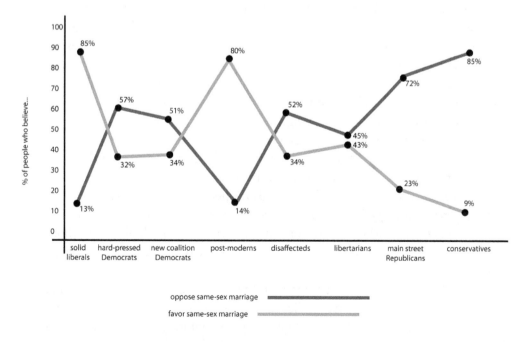

Figure 5.2: Public opinion on LGBTQ+ity issues.

to the gains of some pro-LGBTQ+ policies in other locales (Klarman, 2014). As such, marriage equality has become the prime area for discussion and dispute. Given that same-sex marriage tends to be the key issue that is currently identified with LGBTQ+ rights, I will examine the divisive discourse surrounding LGBTQ+ issues with a focus on same-sex marriage.

Additionally, LGBTQ+ rights—and marriage equality in particular—are interesting issues to examine because for the most part, adopting laws that promote LGBTQ+ rights, including marriage, is an attempt at altering the *status quo*. Thus, the burden of proof is on the promoters of gay and lesbian rights. The onus is on them to prove that additional protections or LGBTQ+ rights are necessary.

However, much of the divisive rhetoric occurs in response to calls for additional LGBTQ+ rights. Opponents have been extremely vocal in their resistance, and they generally make no apologies for their extreme views. Although the *status quo* is typically on their side (since supporters are proposing things such as anti-discrimination laws and same-sex marriages), the people who want to maintain the current system use inflammatory language, fallacies, and other rhetorical tactics to substantiate their position. I do not mean to suggest, however, that advocates for LGBTQ+ rights do not also engage in divisive discourse; they do. I will examine some of their rhetorical tactics as well. But since pro-LGBTQ+ rhetoric tends to advocate for tolerance, respect, and equality, their arguments are generally less incendiary than anti-gay rhetoric.

One other important consideration that involves public opinion as well as scientific evidence is the issue of immutability. Immutability is the question of whether homosexuality is natural or a choice. Quite simply, while "antigay voices say that homosexuality results from bad influences, recruitment, or seduction, queer activists make a case for biological determinism, insisting that they were 'born gay'" (Rohy, 2012, p. 102). And the question of immutability is vital because once "sexual orientation is seen as immutable, it becomes more difficult to justify discrimination against homosexuals as a necessary deterrent to immoral choices" (Klarman, 2014, p. 70).

If homosexuality is a choice, it buttresses many of the claims and policy proposals from conservatives, and typically religious conservatives. The argument is relatively simple: if homosexuality—or sexual orientation—is a choice, that must mean individuals can choose "not" to be LGBTQ+ if they want. This notion reinforces the conservative Christian point of view that homosexuality is a "sin"—a sin is something that a person can choose not to do. This idea also supports the conservative proposal for more "reparative therapy," also known as "conversion therapy." Reparative therapy is a form of rehabilitation whereby the individual undergoes counseling and psychological work to convert from homosexuality to heterosexuality (Chauncey, 2004; Khan, 1998; Santinover, 1996).

Much of the opposition to the immutability thesis is derived from studies that essentially report two things. The studies either suggest that homosexuality is, in fact, a choice or social construction or they critique or refute the immutability studies. The first set of research is primarily based on data from identical twins. When one twin is homosexual and the other is not, researchers argue that the sexual orientation or proclivities of each twin, being different when homosexuality occurs, proves that the sexual preferences are, as such, preferences (Family Research Institute, 2013c). Moreover, some studies critique the immutability thesis (Knight, 2004). One study argues that genetic linkages, which are crucial for immutability to occur, cannot be replicated, and when they have occurred, they are not statistically significant (Baron, 1993). The most often cited study by Byne and Parsons (1993) claims that sexual orientation is a composite of multiple variables, most of which are psychological in nature. Therefore, Byne and Parsons argue that homosexuality is not biological, but rather a product of social or cultural construction.

Pro- homosexuality advocates, however, generally argue that their sexual identity is immutable, natural, and unyielding. The first thing most LGBTQ+ advocates argue is that the opposing side rests almost all of their positions on the Byne and Parsons (1993) study, yet other studies have occurred since 1993 that have seriously discredited their position (Halley, 1994; Hamer et al., 1993). And, by extension, those studies that discredit Byne and Parsons also tend to emphasize the immutability thesis. If homosexuality is not a choice, much of the steam behind conservative Christians' argument evaporates. Socialist lesbian-feminist Sherry Wolf (2009) and my father—two folks who probably would not normally agree with each other on many issues, and seems odd to write them in the same sentence—both make the same point: if homosexuality is a choice, why would so many people intentionally choose to be mistreated and discriminated against?

Plus, Edward Stein (2014) simply says that the evidence suggesting that homosexuality is a choice is not very compelling, especially when one considers that the consensus of the scientific community argues that homosexuality is innate (Bailey and Pillard, 1991; Gooren, 1990; Halley, 1994; LeVay, 1991). Furthermore, at least one legal scholar believes that proving immutability is unnecessary. Instead, LGBTQ+ people and legal advocates should emphasize the equal protection connection to LGBTQ+ rights. And, lest we forget, they should also then view homosexuality not as a "sin" that needs to be changed in reparative therapy, but rather as an oppressed group that deserves equal protection under the law. Surveys show that believing homosexuality is not a personal choice but, rather, is fixed at birth or in early childhood has become more common (Wilcox et al., 2007). And, in contrast to the conservative argument about how choice means ability to change, if homosexuality is seen as immutable, it strengthens the argument for why discrimination should not be tolerated (D'Emilio, 2009).

One would think, as D'Emilio (2009) suggests, that if an identity is immutable, discrimination would immediately be de-justified. However, Wolf (2009) notes that clearly, race is an immutable characteristic, yet discrimination still exists against racial minorities. Moreover, there is a potential, albeit rhetorical, risk at stake with the immutability thesis. If homosexuality is an immutable "condition," then there is the danger that politicians and medical personnel could seek and attempt "to 'cure' homosexuality not only with psychoanalysis and aversion therapies but also with hormones, neurotropic drugs, and brain surgery" (Byne and Parsons, 1993, p. 236). Such a solution is similar to the sorts of human medical experiments conducted by the Nazis during World War II. And, as the former president of the Southern Baptist Theological Seminary, Dr. Albert Monier, Jr., notes, a biological explanation for homosexuality does "'not alter God's moral verdict on homosexual sin.' Christians…ought to consider the possibility of a genetic or hormonal 'treatment' administered to a mother to alter her child's sexual orientation" (quoted in Wolf, 2009, p. 216). Thus, the immutability perspective, while initially appearing useful in terms of altering public opinion and supporting anti-discrimination policies, poses certain risks if taken too far.

President Donald Trump has surrounded himself with friends, advisors, and cabinet members who have a history of advocating anti-LGBTQ+ positions. Most notably, Trump's vice president is former governor of Indiana Mike Pence. As governor, Pence championed the Religious Freedom Restoration Act of Indiana, which quickly became a model for other states to use religious liberty as a way to justify discrimination against LGBTQ+ people. Pence has also been an ardent supporter of reparative therapy (also known as conversion therapy), which uses a variety of practices, including shock therapy and psychological re-programming, in an attempt to "cure" the condition of homosexuality (Signorile, 2016). Not surprisingly, Pence has also opposed marriage equality, saying that it risks "societal collapse" and that confronting it is part of "God's idea" (cited in Signorile, 2016, n.p.). In addition, Trump appointed former presidential candidate and neurosurgeon Ben Carson as the Secretary of Housing and Urban Development. Carson has continued to defend his comments that likened homosexuality to pedophilia and incest (Signorile, 2016); he uses the slippery slope fallacy when he says, "Allowing same-sex couples to wed will lead to acceptance of pedophilia and bestiality" (Brinker, 2014). And Carson has repeatedly said he believes homosexuality is a choice. To support his position, Carson uses the *post hoc ergo propter hoc fallacy*, as he elaborated during a CNN interview: People "go into prison straight—and when they come out, they're gay. So, did something happen while they were in there? Ask yourself that question" (cited in Bradner, 2015, n.p.). Moreover, Trump appointed Newt Gingrich, also a former presidential candidate and a former Republican Speaker of the House, to his presidential transition team. At one time, Gingrich candidly expressed how he thought the movement for LGBTQ+ rights and those Americans who are supportive of such rights constitute a "gay fascism" (Signorile, 2016, n.p.; see also Auerbach, 2008). Another member of Trump's transition team, Ken Blackwell, former Ohio secretary of state, characterized homosexuality as a "compulsion," just like kleptomania (Signorile, 2016).

Thus, President Trump is greatly influenced by close associates who strongly oppose LGBTQ+ rights. During the Republican National Convention in the summer of 2016, the Republic Party also adopted a clear anti-LGBTQ+ agenda, despite for the first time having a LGBTQ+ on the platform committee (Juzwiak, 2016). The platform added a condemnation of redefining sex discrimination to include sexual orientation and other LGBTQ+ identities; it included an explicit statement opposing the Supreme Court's marriage equality decision; and the platform "[tipped] its hat" to conversion therapy by stating, "We support the right of parents to determine the proper medical treatment and therapy for their minor children" (cited in Juzwiak, 2016, n.p.).

The extreme anti-LGBTQ+ positions taken by the national Republican party model some of the initiatives occurring at the state level. In Texas, a Tea Party state senator, Konni Burton, proposed legislation that functionally would "out" LGTBQ+ students, especially to their parents. The law would require that teachers and other K–12 school employees who fail to "disclose a student's sexual orientation or gender identity to parents could face discipline," even when the student objects (Wright, 2016). Opponents to the bill worry that the added pressure and anxiety that would occur to these students puts them at "risk for abuse, neglect or suicide," especially if they come from homes that are not tolerant of their closeted identities (Wright, 2016). Another example comes from a Texas neighbor. The Arkansas state legislature recently passed a bill that actually permits discrimination against LGBTQ+ people (Holden, 2015). The bigoted law gained support under the guise that it was creating more certainty for Arkansas businesses, who previously had the discretion to promote workplace fairness or not. With the new legislation, which the governor has agreed to not sign or veto so that the bill naturally becomes law, all businesses in Arkansas can freely discriminate without fear of legal recourse (Holden, 2015).

However, Trump's allegiance may not be completely aligned with the RNC's platform. Although the Republican National Committee does not want employment discrimination laws to extend to LGBTQ+ identities, Trump "promised that he would sign the First Amendment Defense Act (FADA), which would allow for discrimination against LGBT people by government employees and others" (Signorile, 2016). While Trump did not sign the FADA, he did sign its functional equivalent as an executive order (LaBarbera, 2017). Then, after the shooting tragedy of a gay nightclub in Orlando, Florida, by a Muslim extremist, Trump declared he would do "everything" in his "power to protect our LGBTQ+ citizens from the violence and oppression of the hateful, foreign ideology, believe me" (cited in "Trump Vows to Protect," 2016, n.p.). And during the presidential campaign, Trump compared his foreign policy ideas on fighting Islamic terrorists to that of Hillary Clinton. In so doing, he now famously said that we should "ask *the gays* what they think and what they do, in, not only Saudi Arabia, but many of these countries, and then you tell me—who's your friend, Donald Trump or Hillary Clinton?" (emphasis added, cited in Mandell, 2016, n.p.). Of course, many in the LGBTQ+ community found Trump's reference to "the gays" both comical and insulting, but in classic Trump fashion, the linguistic gaffe spawned nearly 50,000 tweets using the phrase "ask the gays," which obviously generated more campaign publicity for the businessman-turned-politician.

Liberals, fearful of rollbacks to social policies, perceive the anti-LGBTQ+ discourse of the Republican platform and Trump's advisors with caution and concern. Some use the rhetorical tactics of fear appeals and the slippery slope fallacy to emphasize their points. For example, Signorile (2016) utilizes both: "I'm not going to sugarcoat this at all. We are in for a full-blown assault on LGBTQ rights the likes of which many, particularly younger LGBTQ people, have not seen. Progress will most certainly be halted completely, likely rolled back. And it's already underway" (Signorile, 2016, n.p.). Plus, early during the 2016 presidential campaign, Democrat contender Bernie Sanders vilified the Republicans, claiming that the conservatives were using the issue of marriage equality to divide Americans. Sanders, during a campaign stop in Iowa, said, "Why do you think working class people in America vote against their economic self-interest? … I think the Republicans have done a brilliant job over the years—they're very smart guys—in dividing people on a million different issues. In other words, the media's endless game of gotcha—just like the GOP's opposition to same-sex marriage—is nothing more than a distraction" (cited in Badash, 2015, n.p.).

THE DIVISIVE DISCOURSE INVOLVING LGBTQ+ ISSUES

Debates concerning homosexuality involve many issues, such as the essence of LGBTQ+ behavior (or the immutability debate, which I discussed above), adoption rights, hate crimes, employment and housing discrimination, same-sex marriage, the repeal of anti-gay laws, etc. Primarily because analyzing all of these issues would take a book in itself, I cannot analyze their rhetoric in their entirety or with much depth. I will attempt, however, to focus on some of the main themes that exist. The first issue that is complex and current that must be examined is the rhetoric concerning same-sex marriage.

Marriage Equality

Proponents of same-sex marriage levy several arguments to justify state-sanctioned marriage for homosexual couples. As an overarching rhetorical maneuver, advocates have generally switched the terminology from "same-sex" marriage to "marriage equality." The linguistic rearticulation emphasizes, of course, the nature of equality of the issue, which also rhetorically frames the position in such a way that makes it, on-face, difficult to challenge. After all, who openly argues that they are against equality? The problem for opponents of same-sex marriage, then, is that they either need to challenge the new moniker or find a way to articulate arguments opposing "equality" on some grounds. For the most part, those opposed to homosexual matrimony take the latter approach, almost as if they ignore completely the presumption that "same-sex" marriage is really a debate about "marriage equality." At least so far, the strategy of dismissing or ignoring the rearticulation does not seem to be hurting the opposition's positions.

Opposition to same-sex marriage has remained relatively constant in its rhetorical tactics, and several key arguments tend to recur. In no particular order, I will note and discuss the following tactics: same-sex marriage (SSM) undermines the traditional institution of marriage, it harms the children involved, it violates legal principles, it risks a slippery slope to other damaging acts, it supports "big" government and violates federalism, it violates religious liberties, and some other miscellaneous arguments.

SSM Destroys the Institution of Marriage

Republican senator Orinn Hatch (UT) worries that unless we pass a Federal Marriage Amendment to the U.S. Constitution to define marriage as a bond between a man and a woman, "The inescapable conclusion is that absent an amendment to the Constitution, same-sex marriage is coming whether you like it or not … it is going to be imposed on America." Hatch is so concerned about how homosexuality will be "imposed" on Americans, he says, "I don't know of anything that is more important to *morality*" (Hatch, 2004, p. S7877, emphasis added). When a U.S. senator characterizes a social issue in this manner, we know that it must be important.

Typically, one of the first arguments heard by opponents of marriage equality is that it undermines traditional marriage. Since the beginning of recorded history, humans have maintained a special, if not sanctified, place for a recognition of a committed union between a loving couple, and throughout time, the term "couple" has typically been known to be between a man and a woman. Senator Hatch speaks about this point as well: "For a simple and compelling reason, traditional marriage has been a civilizational anchor for thousands of years. Society has an interest in the future generations created by men and women. Decoupling procreation from marriage in order to make some people feel more accepted denies the very purpose of marriage itself. Marriages between men and women are the essential institutions to which future generations are produced and reared" (Hatch, 2004, p. S7879). For Christians, the Bible refers to marriage as a union that is endorsed by God, giving matrimony even more of a special status—a status sanctified by divine providence. And if the union is considered to be between a man and a woman, a state-based and a religious-based recognition of such a union should endorse only those committed relationships that occur between a man and a woman. In short, nowhere in this historical record is there a place for same-sex unions.

Since marriage has held such an esteemed position throughout history—both by governments and religious entities—it is considered an "institution" in itself. This means that marriage is more than a simple act or exchange of vows. It is instead a symbolic and material connection between two people that, as a result of their bond, yields certain privileges (Rauch, 2008). Moreover, by viewing "heterosexual marriage within the domain of nature, it is protected from contact with things that threaten its sacred status," unless, of course, the state permits something like same-sex marriage (Edwards, 2007, p. 247). Thus, there is no other relationship or type of human connection like (opposite-sex) marriage. Marriage is seen not only as a special recognition of two people's love for each other, but it is also a bond recognized by others to have a special status. This, in part, is why it is often referred to as "traditional" marriage, as it solidifies and carries notions of so-called "traditional" values (Haider-Markel and Joslyn, 2005). But we know that when we look at the histories of cultures, traditions are not static or universal (Oakeshott, 1965). Cultures change. This is particularly true with marriage. Bigamy and polygamy were allowed in the United States until the Supreme Court ruled in 1879 to make them illegal (*Reynolds v. U.S.*). And before the 1967

Court decision in *Loving v. Virginia*, interracial marriages were illegal in America. So, the so-called "tradition" and "institution" of marriage is not as stable or unchanging as some people say (Culbertson, 2007; Wax, 2005).

The status marriage acquires means it is given special rights, responsibilities, and considerations. In the religious context, marriage is seen as a sacrament with/from God. In a secular context, marriage permits a host of rights, such as health insurance coverage, spousal benefits from Social Security, hospital visitation rights, joint banking and tax privileges, etc. By some measures, there are nearly 1,050 federally based rights associated with marriage (Wolf, 2009). In addition to the rights acquired with marriage, there are also responsibilities associated with the couple's bond. It is expected that married couples function and engage in their communities in a responsible manner. They are expected to raise their children properly, and they are expected to be strong role models for others. After all, marriage requires a strong and dedicated commitment that is not to be taken lightly. Couples entering into such vows are expected to be reminders to the rest of the community about the importance of honesty, loyalty, and commitment since that is what marriage requires.

Homosexuals, however, complicate this understanding and framing of marriage. In order for the symbolic importance of marriage to occur and have meaning, many people argue that it must remain between a man and a woman. In the first place, opponents of same-sex marriage say the institution of marriage has always been between a man and a woman. As such, due to its history, it is important for us to remain consistent. Secondly, the image and expectation of marriage fall apart if it is no longer between a man and a woman. Traditional gender roles in parenting, community activities, and neighborly relations are complicated if not performed by the union of a man and a woman.

Another argument opponents make is that a homosexual marriage devalues and erodes the meaning of so-called "traditional" marriages (Banks, 2014). By sanctioning the bond of a same-sex couple, the distinctive status granted to the exclusive union of a man and a woman is altered—it no longer is "special" in the sense that now another relationship permutation (that of a man and a man, or a woman and a woman) is permitted. Of course, there are a number of other issues that already dilute the concept of "traditional marriage," such as divorce, separations, open marriages, etc. (Bailey, 2012).

Additionally, since marriage should be between members of the opposite sex, it enables procreation. As Ralph Richard Banks proclaims, "Even as the formal rules have fallen away, some of the meanings they generated continue to shape our understanding of marriage. For all the many ways in which our images and ideals relating to marriage have changed, the view of marital sex as procreative persists" (Banks, 2014, p. 4). Many claim that marriage is primarily a bond that exists in order to have a stable, structured family, which, of course, presumes that children are a result of the marriage bond. Homosexuals—unless they adopt—obviously cannot procreate. Some opponents to same-sex marriage, like Australia's former prime minister John Howard, find this to be extremely troublesome, going so far as to say that allowing same-sex marriages risks "the survival of the species" (Rohy, 2012, p. 101). In contrast, marriage equality advocates say that even "if traditional heterosexual marriage is the ideal setting for raising children as

Republican senators claimed, the government is still not justified in depriving same-sex couples of the benefits of marriage" (Liu and Macedo, 2005, p. 211).

SSM Hurts Children

Opponents to same-sex marriage also claim that among the other symbolic reasons for why marriage is important, there is also the material reality that married couples are expected to procreate and become responsible parents. Of course, not all heterosexuals have children—and some medically are incapable of procreation—but the ideal of marriage as a precondition to parenting is a longstanding belief. But despite the fact that the "American legal system frequently has been hostile to lesbian and gay parents and their children" (Patterson and Redding, 1996, p. 29), opponents to same-sex marriage continue to worry that permitting gay and lesbian parents will inflict catastrophic damage to their children.

One argument is that same-sex marriage obviously means that homosexuals will be parents. Gays and lesbians can be parents, of course, "through prior straight relationships, sperm donation, surrogate mothers, or adoption" (Rohy, 2012, p. 105). Marriage, obviously, is not a precondition for parenting, but permitting same-sex marriage will make it easier for homosexuals to confront current laws that restrict or prohibit gay and lesbian adoptions. Same-sex marriage also allows a gay or lesbian parent to have custody rights over children from previous heterosexual marriages. In any case, the idea that same-sex marriage could occur means that more children will be parented by homosexual parents. Opponents to same-sex marriage claim that homosexual parenting increases the likelihood that their children will "turn out" gay, that more molestation and incest will occur, and that the overall well-being of the children is at risk because of heightened psychological issues (because apparently, having homosexual parents creates mental disorders), and the children must face the burden of having homosexual parents during social and school events.

Initially, one of the concerns of homosexual parenting is that the children will also be gay or lesbian. The argumentative syllogism looks something like this:

> Premise 1: Married LGBTQ+s will have children (by some means).
> Premise 2: Gay and lesbian parents will teach their children about the LGBTQ+ lifestyle.
> Conclusion: Ergo, children in same-sex households will end up being gay or lesbian like their parents.

Of course, this syllogism rests on the premise that being gay or lesbian is a bad thing. Otherwise, why does it matter if children become homosexual? Additionally, this argument is simply fallacious because it equates one's identity with their parenting style; thus, it is a hasty generalization as well as a fallacy of equivocation. The argument also simply does not stand up to the scrutiny of common sense. In just about any heterosexual household, the children do not always embrace the lifestyle habits of their parents. In fact, in many cases, the children reject the behaviors of their parents through some sort of rebellious actions. Thus, the claim that homosexual parents—simply by being homosexual —somehow translates to creating homosexual children simply does not pass muster.

Moreover, the evidence does not support the claim that same-sex marriages will create or convert children to become homosexual. According to Patterson and Redding,

> Overall, then, results of research to date suggest that concerns about disruption of sexual identity among children of gay and lesbian parents are not warranted. Although studies have assessed over 300 offspring of lesbian or gay parents in many different samples, no evidence has been found for disturbances in the development of sexual identity among these individuals. Fears about difficulties with sexual identity among children of gay and lesbian parents have not been supported by the results of empirical research. (Patterson & Redding, 1996, p. 41)

Plus, if the immutability arguments are true (i.e., the notion that homosexuality is natural and genetic), children will be homosexual or heterosexual regardless of their parents' sexual proclivities. Without going into those arguments here, I want to stress that the conversion, on-face, simply is not compelling. Clearly, homosexual children emerge from stable, traditional, heterosexual parents, and there are countless examples of same-sex households with heterosexual children. As such, the conversion argument, whether it be the claim that homosexual parents will convert their own children to homosexuality or the conversion argument about adult gays and lesbians attempting to recruit heterosexuals, is a rhetorical tactic that not only misdirects us from the larger and more important issues, but also perpetuates fear that has no basis in reality.

Another argument made against homosexual parenting is that children in same-sex households are much more likely to be molested or victims of sexual abuse than are children in traditional, heterosexual households (Family Research Institute, 2009). This argument clearly relies on a fear appeal. No one, I submit, would endorse, condone, or accept a situation where children are abused in any fashion, especially sexual abuse. Therefore, the claim that gay and lesbian marriages increase the risk of molestations or incest is a serious accusation and, if true, definitely worthy of concern. However, the only value or substance to this argument is its reliance on fear. As I examine below under "non-marriage issues," this argument about homosexuals molesting their children has very little basis, and the studies have serious methodological flaws (Herek, 2006; Patterson and Redding, 1996).

Linda Harvey, a noted writer, speaker, and director of Mission America, which is an organization whose purpose is to "stamp out" homosexuality, has this to say about the proximity of homosexuals to children:

> Adults proudly living a homosexual life are disastrous role models. ... Children living in a home headed by homosexual adults are exposed to the same poor

examples in triple intensity and intimacy. ... LGBTQ+ adults are typically high consumers of pornography, another element poisonous to the young. Children from such homes have more problematic lives as young adults. ... Students are sometimes blank slates for the indoctrination plans of homosexual political activists, teachers and others. These innocent minds are taught to affirm sexual perversion, but often in concert with the entire platform of destructive, leftist causes. ... Now to the dynamite question: yes, some homosexually-identified adults do have sex with underage teens and even children. ... There is a contingent within homosexual circles pushing for adults to gain more access to minors, sometimes disguised as support for "questioning" kids. ... Exposure of kids to pornographic material is fine with these folks. It's "censorship" if we don't allow children to explore textual and visual pornography that steals their innocence and seduces some into an early sexual debut. ... Children quickly learn from homosexual adults that Christians are the "enemy." Much effort is devoted to smearing and demonizing believers, who form the main obstacle to unrestricted sexual license. ... By demonizing conservative views, "gay" activists mount a wall preventing many kids from hearing the whole story. (Harvey, 2014, n.p.)

Linda Harvey's reasons for why homosexuals do not "mix" with children are all based on unfounded fear appeals, along with hasty generalizations and causation flaws. Reading her objections appears, for the most part, that her experiences and references support reasonable claims against homosexual relationships with children. On the other hand, when read more closely, we can reveal how she uses virtually no evidence to support her accusations, and in many cases, she blatantly utilizes conjecture and fantasy-based ideas to frame her perspective.

Finally, opponents to same-sex marriage are also concerned about the overall well-being of children from gay and lesbian parents (Kennedy and Newcombe, 2004; Lutzer, 2010). These children must be able to explain why they have two fathers or two mothers, they must face ridicule on the playground concerning their family, and they have to somehow reconcile the differences between their homes and the lifestyles and home lives of their peers who come from traditional-marriage families (Family Research Institute, 2009). As if the psychological lessons and problems children face simply by being children is not enough, with same-sex marriages, these children also have to endure the psychological trauma inflicted upon them by their gay or lesbian parents (Family Research Institute, 2009). Again, these claims are largely based on methodologically flawed studies, which I detail below.

It is important to point out, however, that advocates for same-sex marriage counter these claims by saying, "Research findings suggest that unless and until the weight of evidence can be shown to have shifted, parental sexual orientation should be considered irrelevant to disputes involving child custody, visitation, foster care, and adoption" (Patterson and Redding, 1996, p. 29). And same-sex marriage advocates cite their own studies: "In a survey of married same-gender couples in Massachusetts, the first state to allow civil marriage for same-gender couples, 24% of the respondents noted that their children had previously been explicitly teased or taunted about having a gay or lesbian parent, but 93% of respondents stated that marriage has made their children happier and better off" (Perrin et al., 2013, p. e1381). Apparently, there was a study conducted in England that "compared 39 families with lesbian mothers to 74 heterosexual parents," and evidently, "No difference was found between the groups in emotional involvement" (Saint Louis, 2013). Moreover,

> Extensive data available from more than 30 years of research reveal that children raised by gay and lesbian parents have demonstrated resilience with regard to social, psychological, and sexual health despite economic and legal disparities and social stigma. ... Because marriage strengthens families and, in so doing, benefits children's development, children should not be deprived of the opportunity for their parents to be married. Paths to parenthood that include assisted reproductive techniques, adoption, and foster parenting should focus on competency of the parents rather than their sexual orientation. (Perrin et al., 2013, p. e1374)

Of course, the studies proponents use suffer from some similar methodological issues as do the studies from the Family Research Institute. Some even argue that pro-marriage equality studies are flawed because they focus only on affluent lesbian couples, which excludes problematic sample groups (Saint Louis, 2013). However, having said that, recently, the American Academy of Pediatricians announced that same-sex marriage is actually, on balance, positive for children. This endorsement for marriage equality is extremely important since the Academy of Pediatricians carries a great deal of *ethos*. According to the *New York Times*,

> The academy cited research finding that a child's well-being is much more affected by the strength of relationships among family members and a family's social and economic resources than by the sexual orientation of the parents. "There is an emerging consensus, based on extensive review of the scientific literature, that children growing up in households headed by gay men or lesbians are not disadvantaged in any significant respect relative to children of heterosexual parents," the academy said. (Saint Louis,   2013, n.p.)

A large body of evidence demonstrates that children raised by gay or lesbian parents fare as well in emotional, cognitive, and social functioning as peers raised by heterosexuals.

When the *logos*-based appeals are stripped down, we find that both sides of this debate are using arguments based on emotion rather than reason. On one side (the advocates for marriage equality), we have people claiming that individuals who love each other are the necessary precondition for good parenting. On the other side (the opponents to same-sex marriage), we have fear based on uncertainty and moral claims that can either be debated themselves or clearly cannot be imposed on everyone, especially in a country that prides itself with a separation of church and state (Boston, 2013).

Incidentally, in March 2016, a federal district judge ordered an injunction against the state of Mississippi's law that banned same-sex couples from adopting children (Reilly, 2016). Because the ruling happened in federal court, the judge's ruling considers Mississippi's law "unconstitutional, making gay adoption [now] legal in all 50 states" (Reilly, 2016, n.p.). Of course, the U.S. Supreme Court could grant *certiorari* to the case and overturn the federal judge's decision, but if or until that occurs, same-sex adoption is now a constitutionally protected right nationwide.

SSM Violates Legal Principles

In addition to the other arguments about traditional marriage, opponents claim that same-sex marriage simply violates established legal principles. Marriage has been codified as an institution between a man and a woman. The consequence of allowing same-sex marriage is that it obviously alters the conception of the status of marriage as solely a bond between a man and a woman. Gary Segura explains that,

> the opposition argument begins with two assertions at its core. First, homosexuality is fundamentally morally inferior to heterosexuality and represents the sinful outcome of perverse choices. Second, homosexual unions, by being inherently non-procreative, are fundamentally inferior to heterosexual unions. To grant legal status and recognition to inferior unions to immoral people undermines the importance of the institution, thereby eroding the foundation of civil society. (Segura, 2005, p. 190)

In this way, we really cannot separate the moral position from the legal one; at least one point of view about homosexual rights cannot divorce moral claims from legal principles.

While on one hand, conservatives can argue that current laws prohibit same-sex marriage and other LGBTQ+ activities, thereby prohibiting moves toward same-sex marriage now, opponents to same-sex marriage also worry that the judicial system—with its counter- or anti-majoritarian role in American democracy—has and will make decisions based on its interpretation of laws and not base its decisions on the will of the people. A similar conundrum was faced by those who opposed interracial marriages during the debates about the Supreme Court's 1967 decision of *Loving v. Virginia* (Eskridge, 1996). The Court ultimately ruled that any prohibition to allowing mixed-race couples from marrying were deemed unconstitutional on equal protection grounds. Today, homosexuals and conservatives alike face a similar battle. Conservatives should be careful, however, when making the claim that judges are activist and are ignoring the voices of the people, for as Bill Mears suggests, "It is time for the Supreme Court to affirm what more than thirty courts have held in the past year: marriage discrimination violates the Constitution, harms families, and is unworthy of America" (Mears, 2014, n.p.). There are different ways of interpreting the will of the people, but I believe the main point here is that relying on the law to resolve this issue—by itself—is naïve and unproductive.

SSM Causes a Slippery Slope

A common fear is that same-sex marriages will permit other types of marriages. After all, to "say that marriage is no longer between one man and one woman opens the door for marriage to mean anything" (Kennedy and Newcombe, 2004, p. 65). Once the revered and special status of marriage is redefined to include same-sex marriages, there is nothing to prevent further deterioration of the status by continuing to redefine it even further (Corvino, 2005; Eskridge, 1996). Some make extremist arguments, claiming that same-sex marriages will legally permit polygamy, incestuous marriages, and even marriages with pets. Hence, some opponents engage in the obvious fallacy of "slippery slope" arguments, primarily to invoke fear into people concerning what might eventually result from allowing same-sex marriages. Marriage equality advocates retort that the slippery slope argument engages in "abstract analysis" that does not prove how same-sex marriages will "entail a commitment to accept other forms" (Wax, 2005, p. 1081). Interestingly, proponents of same-sex marriage typically fail to point out how the "slippery slope" argument is, in fact, a fallacy, and as a result, they fail to capitalize on the troubling nature of how this particular argument is formed. Of course, there are legal and practical issues used in refuting the slippery slope claim, not the least of which is that things like polygamy and marrying an animal are illegal (Cahill, 2004; Rauch, 2008). Permitting same-sex marriages overturns no court precedent—nor would allowing same-sex marriage establish a precedent—that would automatically or even necessarily result in other types of matrimony. The challenges faced by the homosexual community to obtain marriage rights many decades after interracial marriages were legally permitted is a testament to how allowing one sort of marriage does not trigger a slippery slope.

SSM Perpetuates Big Government and Violates Federalism

Since same-sex marriage requires the endorsement of the government, it means the government must also monitor and oversee the process of same-sex marriages. Just like heterosexual marriages, same-sex marriages will require licenses, medical tests, and forms necessary to attribute all of the federal rights that accompany matrimony. The very nature of adding another type of matrimony, which would also by definition increase the number of marriages, means the government must be more involved. Some conservative critics of any liberal initiative argue that expanding the size of the federal government is problematic.

Another troubling issue with granting same-sex marriages is that it is allowed currently on a state-by-state basis. Individual states are passing legislation to either permit or prevent same-sex marriage, and many states have court decisions that either allow or deny the marriages as well. If the federal government passes a same-sex marriage law, or if the Supreme Court decides that same-sex marriages should be protected rights, the federal action would trump the initiatives by the states. In any case, some same-sex opponents use the rhetorical tactic of fear and hasty generalization to argue this point. An example comes from Craig James of the Family Research Institute, who worries that when a court decision permits same-sex marriage, it is "overriding ... the will of the people." Furthermore, when the government sanctions these marriages, everyone "should be alarmed" because such decisions "could pave the way for Big Government tyranny" (quoted in Tashman, 2014a, n.p.).

SSM Violates Religious Liberties

For many opponents to same-sex marriage, the most important issue is how such marriages contradict, frustrate, or even violate religious doctrine. This is really an entirely other issue, which I simply do not have the space to explore. But briefly speaking, this issue is about whether granting same-sex marriage status infringes upon a religious organization's religious liberties when such an organization disapproves of same-sex marriage. Much like the religious freedom exemptions claimed by Hobby Lobby and others regarding healthcare issues, the proposal for "marriage conscience protection" is guaranteed to be a lively debate in the near future (NeJaime, 2012). In response to the marriage conscience protection proposal, Peter Dolan suggests states adopt a "refuse and refer" position so that wedding service providers can decline same-sex marriages on the basis of religious objection grounds while simultaneously preserving the "dignity" of same-sex couples (Dolan, 2013). But marriage equality advocates argue that "religious liberty becomes a shield to deflect accusations of bigotry, even while justifying blatant anti-LGBT discrimination" (Brinker, 2014b, n.p.). Additionally, a pastor from the United Church of Christ argues that marriage amendments that forbid same-sex marriages denies his "religious freedom by prohibiting" him "from exercising this right" (Boggioni, 2014, n.p.).

Other "SSM Is Evil" Arguments

Some opponents, like the Alliance Defending Freedom, also fear that same-sex marriage is a stepping stone for other, larger social and cultural agenda items by gays and lesbians. In fact, they worry that "redefining marriage is ultimately part of a larger effort to redesign society in order to give social approval of homosexual behavior" (ADF, 2014, n.p.). Opponents, then, see homosexual marriage as an assault on society. As part of the "culture war," marriage equality threatens the reconsidering of other issues, and then accepting them. While there is literally zero evidence to support this claim, it is like many other arguments from same-sex opponents—it relies on the fear of the Other. Opponents fear LGBTQ+ enclaves, bars, households, and any sort of general LGBTQ+ activity. This fear provides the basis for many of their rhetorical claims.

Fear appeals, then, are a prominent and serious rhetorical tactic by same-sex marriage opponents. All of us can be motivated to alter our beliefs or behaviors because of marriage. But while "threat and efficacy clearly are important for fear appeal effectiveness, these two ingredients alone are not sufficient. Additionally, empirical results regarding fear appeal effectiveness are not conclusive. However, the literature conventionally agrees that more effective fear appeals result from a higher fear arousal followed by consequences and recommendations to reduce the negativity" (Williams, p. 1). Fear appeals are powerful motivators because "fear is more powerful than reason. Fear can sometimes be evoked easily and absurdly for reasons that live in mankind's evolutionary past" (Williams, p. 2). Nevertheless, since fear is an emotional component that resides in an individual, broad-based fear appeals in rhetorical messages are not as effective as we might think (Denzin, 1984). If someone is already predisposed to a particular emotion or fear, receiving a fear appeal only intensifies what already exists within that individual. Fear appeals are, after all, fallacies.

A fear appeal, then, is literally a rhetorical tactic that "preaches to the choir." And some studies suggest that using fear appeals on audiences that already have a high level of fear are most likely ineffective or could trigger reactions that are opposite to the intention of the message, known as the "boomerang" effect (Byrne and Hart, 2009; Muthusamy et al., 2009; Witte, 1992; Wolburg, 2006). An individual who is not predisposed to a particular fear will most likely not be affected by the message whatsoever, in large part because "different people fear different things" (LaTour and Rotfeld, 1997, p. 47). Simply put, "fear levels cannot be meaningfully increased by message inductions" (Muthusamy et al., 2009, p. 337). But despite their questionable effectiveness, fear appeals still provide the basis for many arguments used by same-sex marriage opponents.

Even with the fear-mongering, the fallacies, and the other polarizing rhetorical tactics used by opponents of same-sex marriage, some arguments are presented in reasonable ways, even if many people might disagree with their conclusions. For example, and by way of wrapping up this section, conservative pundit Laura Ingraham makes the following appeal:

> Family is the basic building block of our society, and stable families are a crucial part of ensuring our future. A healthy American democracy depends on a moral people to guide it. Families are where the morals and virtues that touch all aspects of public life are first taught and best learned. Families lay the interior foundation that will propel the next generation on to greatness or into oblivion. (Ingraham, 2010, p. 33)

It is probably unsurprising that Ingraham presents us with a fear appeal, coupled with a slippery slope, tied into a false dichotomy.

The Contemporary Climate after the *Obergefell* Decision

A major event since early 2015 is, of course, the legalization of same-sex marriage. In June 2015, the United States Supreme Court decided in *Obergefell v. Hodges* that so-called "gay marriage" is now a constitutional right across the country (Gerson, 2015). In a 5–4 decision, the Court ruled that "the Equal Protection Clause of the 14th Amendment does not allow states to ban same-sex marriage" (Allen, 2015, n.p.). Since the Court's 2013 ruling in *U.S. v. Windsor*, there have been over 80 challenges requesting that the Supreme Court make a final decision on the issue of marriage equality (McCarty, 2015). In fact, the Court ultimately decided to hear the *Obergefell* case (originating from Ohio) since its legal merits were similar to three other cases (from Kentucky, Michigan, and Tennessee), which allowed the Court to consolidate the petitions into a single, unified case (McCarty, 2015).

The *Obergefell* decision is considered a landmark ruling because it settles "once and for all … one of America's most divisive social questions," especially since same-sex marriage was permitted in only 37 of the 50 states (Sanchez, 2015). Of course, marriage equality has been a divisive issue for many years, but the *Obergefell* case brought it to a boiling point. The Supreme Court granted *certiorari* in early 2015 and rendered its decision in June—in those six months, southern state courts, like Alabama, were making same-sex marriage illegal so that in the event the U.S. Supreme Court ruled the other way, at least the states could prevent as many as possible in the meantime (Geidner, 2015). However, given that it was "just eleven years after Massachusetts became the first state to allow gay couples to wed," *Obergefell* reflects the overall changing social landscape in this country, as at least 60 percent of Americans now support same-sex marriage, according to a recent Gallup poll (Sanchez, 2015, n.p.). Of course, conservatives railed against the Court's decision, including one of the Court's own justices, Antonin Scalia, who feared that the ruling would be a "threat to American democracy" (cited in Sanchez, 2015, n.p.). And Ted Cruz, who was running for president at the time of the ruling, cringed that the Court's decision marks "the darkest 24 hours in our nation's history" (cited in Hunter, 2015, n.p.). Similarly, two other Republican presidential candidates found the *Obergefell* decision reprehensible. Mike Huckabee said the Supreme Court "can't overrule God" (Kohn, 2015, n.p.), and Rick Santorum said stopping gay people from marrying was about "the survival of our country" (Hunter, 2015, n.p.). Both Huckabee and Santorum have reportedly signed a pledge that reads: "We will not honor any decision by the Supreme Court which will force us to violate a clear biblical understanding of marriage as solely the union of one man and one woman" (Kohn, 2015, n.p.).

Other conservatives clearly objected to the decision. Those objections were almost entirely premised on religious grounds. The Family Research Council was quoted as saying that "no court can overturn natural law. Nature and Nature's God, hailed by the signers of our Declaration of Independence as the very source of law, cannot be usurped by the edict of a court, even the United States Supreme Court," and they promised they would not relinquish their strict objections (Sanchez, 2015, n.p.). Furthermore, the notorious Evangelical pastor, John Hagee from Cornerstone Baptist Church, declared that "the Supreme Court has made America the new Sodom and Gomorrah. … God will have to judge America or is going to have to apologize to Sodom and Gomorrah" (cited in De Leon, 2015, n.p.).

While the Court's *Obergefell* decision became "law of the land," many places refused to grant or authorize same-sex marriage licenses (Lawler, 2015). Municipal or county clerk offices became the new battleground over so-called "religious liberty" almost overnight. The now infamous example comes from a rural county in Kentucky, where the elected county clerk, Kim Davis, refused to grant marriage licenses to same-sex couples because same-sex marriage violated her Christian beliefs (Lawler, 2015). Presidential candidate Mike Huckabee immediately flew to Kentucky to meet with Davis. In so doing, Huckabee politicized an already highly contentious issue, especially when he urged like-minded Christians to "resist and reject" the Court's decision (Lawler, 2015). The American Civil Liberties Union (ACLU) filed a lawsuit against Davis on behalf of four couples whose licenses were refused, and the Kentucky governor ordered her to comply with the Supreme Court's ruling (Lawler, 2015). Davis remained steadfast in her principles. As a result, she was held in contempt of court and placed under arrest by U.S. marshalls (Robertson, 2015).

It was perceived by many that Kim Davis was arrested for her religious faith, rather than the fact that she failed to do her job and was violating a court order (Gerson, 2015). Mike Huckabee even characterized the episode, in his typical hyperbolic manner, as "the criminalization of Christianity in this country" (Huckabee, 2015, n.p.). Huckabee declared that "Kim's stand for religious liberty is a pivotal moment in our nation's history" (Huckabee, 2015, n.p.). Huckabee's statement, as he was now on a first-name basis with Mrs. Davis, emphasized his solidarity with her position. The preacher-turned-politician also railed against holding Davis in jail without bond (which is standard practice when someone is held in contempt of court), saying that it "seems even more ludicrous when you consider many of the America's most evil and notorious serial killers, murderers, rapists, mafia bosses and presidential assassins were actually let out on bail" (Huckabee, 2015, n.p.). Of course, he is using a faulty analogy (since, again, contempt orders do not permit bail), and his argument is red herring—enticing like-minded followers to magnify Davis's victimhood as if her penalty rivals that of a murderer or rapist. Similarly, Todd Starnes of *Fox News* hyperbolized the "criminalization of Christianity" theme with a faulty equivocation: "So our government allows illegal aliens to roam our streets but incarcerates a good-hearted Christian lady?" (cited in Williams, 2015). Davis's actions that were premised on her conscience and principles became headline news, and she instantly became a "martyr" and a "lightning rod" for religious Christians, particularly extreme Christian politicians (Robertson, 2015). Thus, as a matter of conscientious objection or civil disobedience, many Christians firmly felt that Davis's position was reasonable, courageous, and virtuous. Simply put, "sometimes the law is wrong, and people are bound by conscience to say so, and even behave as such" (Antle, 2015, n.p.).

On the flip side, many Christians argued that the position Davis took was harmful to religious liberty in the United States. Since Davis was an agent of the court (as county clerk) and an elected representative, she was taking her personal beliefs and imposing them on everyone in the county, whether they agreed with her or not (Robertson, 2015). As Brandan Robertson, a self-proclaimed Christian who writes for *The Huffington Post*, argues:

> It is easy to spin Kim Davis's story as one of persecution. It's easy to get on FOX News and warn pastors that this is what's coming for them if they refuse to perform same-sex marriage. But to do so would be dishonest. Because the reality is that Kim Davis is not being persecuted for her faith, she is reaping

the consequences of refusing to do her job as an agent of the state. Davis is welcome to hold her beliefs as tightly as she would like, but when she is at work, she needs to do her job. If her job violates her conscience, then she should quit, because imposing her beliefs on the people of Rowan County is not an option. It's a violation of one of the highest and most sacred American values: Religious Liberty. And all those who seek to protect and defend American's rights to freely practice their faith without fear of government regulation should be standing firmly against Davis's actions. (2015, n.p.)

Moreover, Laura Coates explains, "Although her [Davis's] religious convictions appear steadfast, her actions are completely unlawful. Her argument is based on the erroneous and naïve premise that the judiciary is powerless when its orders conflict with your personal conscience" (2015, n.p.). And Leonard Pitts echoes this distinction between individual religious belief and community responsibility when a person hold public office: "You have a right to your religious conscience. You do not have a right to impose your conscience upon other people. And if conscience impinges that heavily upon your business or your job, the solution is simple: Sell the business or quit the job. Otherwise, serve your customers and keep your conscience out of their affairs" (2015, n.p.).

For those who supported Davis's position, the double standard of liberals who were bashing her, as well as the hypocrisy of arresting her for contempt, caused frustration and ire. As Antle (2015) explains,

Conservatives have been quick to point out that Davis' jailing is not a fate that befell Gavin Newsom, when as San Francisco mayor he had government clerks issue marriage licenses to some 3,200 same-sex couples in 2004, back when marriage was still legally defined as a union between a man and a woman. Indeed, it's not hard to imagine a hypothetical county clerk in another time refusing to issue marriage licenses until marriage was no longer defined in such a discriminatory, heteronormative way. Others have pointed to the existence of sanctuary cities, which fail to cooperate with federal authorities in the enforcement of immigration laws. Yes, there are important legal differences between sanctuary cities and what Kim Davis is doing. But many people who think America's immigration laws are unjust, racially discriminatory, or guilty of breaking up families would cheer efforts to defy or resist them, rather than call for jailing those involved in sanctuary cities. (2015, n.p.)

Of course, such analogies are not necessarily equivalent, nor are they directly germane to the issue at hand. Particularly when one compares the so-called "principled" actions of sanctuary cities for immigrants, the nature and degree of the controversial issues differ—one is a religious principle, and the other is a human rights principle, and both range in importance depending on one's perspective. Yet given the sensitivity many Americans have to their religious beliefs, even a hint of hypocrisy is enough to stimulate a reaction.

However, the other side of the debate points out that Davis herself is hypocritical—namely that her conscientious and principled advocacy for the "sanctity of marriage" (because it is arguably threatened by same-sex couples) was not as pure and devout as she was portraying. Apparently, Davis was in her fourth marriage, having been divorced three times prior (Collins, 2015; de Vogue, 2015). Responding to the charge of hypocrisy, Davis explained that since her mother-in-law died four years prior, she "heard a message of grace and forgiveness," and so she "surrendered" her life to Jesus Christ. She continued, "I am not perfect. ... No one is. But I am forgiven" (cited in de Vogue, 2015). The issue of Christian forgiveness is outside the realm of this chapter, but suffice it to say that to non-Christians—and perhaps even to many Christians—the claim that one commits sins but they are forgiven not only smacks of arrogance; it also exemplifies the height of hypocrisy. In other words, instead of being a response to the double-standard argument, it actually comes across as being the epitome of hypocrisy. After all, when a person says that something should not be done, but it is somehow okay for them to do it, such a statement is, by definition, hypocrisy. Now, whether or not it is acceptable for Davis to by hypocritical and it not be fine for others is a different question. The main point to be made here, for our understanding of divisive discourse, is that charges of hypocrisy and the perception of hypocrisy are often used in polarizing rhetoric, and they definitely inflame the contentious issue, particularly when charges of blame, victimhood, vilification, and *ethos* are involved.

The Kim Davis incident essentially came to a close in early autumn 2015. The federal judge who found her in contempt of court released her in early September—five days after her arrest—under the stipulation that she could no longer issue marriage licenses to anyone, thereby requiring other personnel in the clerk's office to uphold the *Obergefell* decision's allowance of same-sex marriages (Hanna, 2015). At that time, largely encouraged by folks like Mike Huckabee, Kim Davis filed an appeal, which functioned as a counter-suit, alleging that her religious and civil rights had been violated by the federal court judge's order (Siemaszko, 2016). However, by summer of 2016, Davis and her attorney withdrew her appeal because the state of Kentucky passed a new law permitting clerks to issue marriages licenses without affixing the clerk's signature to the formal license (Siemaszko, 2016). Davis had always maintained that "To issue a marriage license which conflicts with God's definition of marriage, with my name affixed to the certificate, would violate my conscience" (cited in de Vogue, 2015).

NON-MARRIAGE ISSUES

Same-sex marriage, of course, is not the only issue related to the struggle for LGBTQ+ rights. LGBTQ+ people face discrimination, threats, and violence. Gays and lesbians encounter difficulties in the workplace (Barron, 2009), in housing (Kravis, 2012/2013), when trying to adopt children (Wald, 2006), when trying to serve in the military (*Harvard Law Review*, 2014), etc. They are also at risk from hate speech and violent acts. Simply put, LGBTQ+ individuals are often treated, at best, as second-class citizens. While improvements and gains have been made in some areas, such as serving in the military, gays and lesbians are still mistreated in many areas of their lives.

Discrimination

LGBTQ+ people face discrimination in many ways. A recent example that illustrates the difficulties LGBTQ+ folks encounter is with the Boy Scouts. In 2012 and 2013, the Boy Scouts of America wrestled with the problem of whether they should permit openly gay adult men to be Boy Scout leaders. After much debate and input from members and other organizations (like churches), the "Boy Scouts of America's national council adopted the policy accepting openly gay Scouts but retaining a ban on gay adult Scout leaders" (Yu, 2013, n.p.). Thus, by allowing gay kids to be in the Scouts but also banning adult leaders who are openly gay, the organization hoped that such a compromise would settle the controversy. Unfortunately for them, many church and faith-based groups were angry at the decision because they had hoped for a policy that prohibited all openly gay males from being involved in the Scouts. In fact,

> Churches of various faith denominations in Alabama, Georgia, Kentucky, Idaho and other states have ended Scouting programs because the policy goes against church teachings .... The United Methodist churches and the Catholic Church, the next two largest sponsors, have not formally opposed the policy shift, although individual churches and dioceses have sharply questioned the move. ... Baptist leaders reportedly will encourage the denomination's nearly 46,000 U.S. churches to stop sponsoring Scout troops at the annual Southern Baptist Convention. (Yu, 2013, n.p.)

Additionally, the Assemblies of God said many of their churches and programs would engage in a "mass exodus" from Scouting activities (Yu, 2013). One can probably understand the religious objection to certain behaviors, but given the sheer quantity of youth-based Scouting organizations and programs that are church-sponsored, the reactions by church leaders is devastating to not only the Boy Scouts, but also the openly gay males who want to participate. From a rhetorical and argument perspective, the religious reaction to the Boy Scouts' decision seems strange. Its threats of retreat and boycotting of Boy Scout activities can certainly provide political pressure on the national council to change its mind, but to prohibit involvement in a beneficial organization simply because some gays might be present is a straw person argument—a diversion from the real issue. In this form of misdirection, the religious reaction forgets that any involvement in any activity could include LGBTQ+ people; it is just in this particular instance, the Boy Scouts are explicitly stating that such a possibility might exist. But any time a young man joins a school swim team or the chess club, there might be homosexuals present. So the real issue here is not the potential exposure to LGBTQ+ identity. The real issue is that religious groups are taking a political stand to gain visibility to their position that homosexuality is morally threatening and unjustified. This type of rhetorical tactic attracts national media attention and broadcasts the moral argument to anyone listening. And given that the Boy Scouts are a national organization with enormous impact on young people, choosing their membership policy as a grandstanding issue allows faith-based groups to politicize their moral objections into the national limelight. However, since then, in July 2015, the executive committee of the Boy Scouts rescinded the ban (M. Berman, 2015). Yet the polarizing rhetoric continues, whether the Boy Scouts are inclusive of openly LGBTQ+ troop leaders or not. For instance, the outspoken Evangelical Christian preacher Franklin Graham immediately went to Facebook after the latest Boy Scout announcement, where he spouted, "We shouldn't shift as the winds of cultural change blow through society; we need to stand for God's truth and things that are morally right. This move is bending to LGBT activist groups and would put young, innocent boys at risk" (cited in Tashman, 2015). Subtly calling gay troop leaders sexual predators and pedophiles certainly does not advance civility in our discussions about LGBTQ+ rights.

Another area where LGBTQ+ people are stigmatized and devalued concerns their relations with children. Some opponents of LGBTQ+ rights have questioned whether gays and lesbians should be near children. The claim, like most deductive syllogisms, rests on two premises:

Premise 1: LGBTQ+ people commit immoral acts, like molestation, on children.
Premise 2: Our religious beliefs condemn LGBTQ+ lifestyle.
Conclusion: Ergo, we should keep LGBTQ+ people away from children.

When viewed this way, the opposition argument appears weaker. By diagramming it, we now know that the opponents are not condemning it for the legal reasons (i.e., one should not assault another, or one should not engage in sexual acts with minors). Nowhere in the literature from the Family Research Institute (FRI), for example, invokes the legal prohibitions against such behavior. However, its literature is replete with moralistic and religious undertones to cast the LGBTQ+ as a child predator.

In one report by the FRI, it looks at a single country with reports of sexual abuse against children, who were mainly boys, in situations where the perpetrator was of the same sex. Here is an excerpt of the report:

FRI has been tracking Pakistan; it may be the future of the West. Why? Not because of its Islamic religion or the bombings on Islam's behalf, but rather its widespread male homosexuality. Looking at press reports from 2003–2008, we found that Pakistan averaged one child rape and murder per 1.5 million inhabitants/year and 43% of the victims were boys. ... Sexual abuse of children in Pakistan is all across society. ... Punjab Minister for Law and Parliamentary Affairs, Rana Sanaullah, said the "majority of children admitted to Madrassas to get religious education were [sexually] abused." Since only 6% of the 4 million Pakistani Madrassas students are girls, the sexual abuse was overwhelmingly homosexual. And the trend is continuing. Pakistan registered 70 rape and murders of children in 2012; 28 (40%) of the victims were boys. All told, 618 rapes were recorded by Sahil: 260 (42%) were of boys being forcibly sodomized. If Western homosexuaity gains the status and prevalence it has in Pakistan, stories such as the gang rape of the kinder-gartener will start to grace our news. (Family Research Institute, 2013d, n.p.)

When a report is littered with statistics, references to authority figures (e.g., the Minister for Law and Parliamentary Affairs), and causal claims that conveniently omit other possible causal variables, the report seems genuine and convincing. These types of rhetorical tactics are not only purposeful, they are quite effective. Of course, most of the people who read the FRI's literature are already inclined to agree with its position on homosexuaity, so these types of reports serve to reinforce anti-gay beliefs. For others who may be on the fence with their opinions on homosexuaity, these rhetorical tactics can be enormously effective since they appear to be based on strong *logos* arguments (i.e., the use of statistics, authoritative reports, etc.).

In a similar report, the FRI argues that LGBTQ+ individuals are much more likely to molest young children than are heterosexuals; and, consequently, LGBTQ+ folks themselves are more likely to have been sexually abused as children. The FRI uses a study that seeks to look at prevalence rates of child sexual abuse (CSA) solely, not any sort of causal connection between the sexual identity of the predator and any resulting orientation development of the victim. Nevertheless, the FRI argues and tries to clearly connect how LGBTQ+ people are both predators and sexual deviants:

> If homosexuals reported a higher rate of having been molested by adults (today termed child sexual abuse [CSA]), it would 'fit' a model of 'homosexu-ality being acquired through molestation.' Sure enough, almost all studies have reported male and female homosexuals as more apt to say they were molested as kids. ... Now a large random survey has been published that included both homosexuals and heterosexuals. The results are as they should be if 'common sense' is correct: 33,902 adults—the largest random sample to date on this issue—were asked if they had been molested by an adult ... the results were dramatic: those who engage in homosexual sex were "sharply," as the authors put it, more likely to report molestation. ... For the most stringent definition of molestation, the differences were eight times more for men! This study validates 'common sense' about how homosexual tastes are acquired and maintained. The data show that it is very much more likely for a homosexual to have been molested as a child than for someone who is heterosexual. (Family Research Institute, 2013a, n.p.)

This study and these statistics not only allow the FRI to make its broad-based claims about LGBTQ+ predators; they also enable the FRI to advocate against certain policies and initiatives, like the proposal by the Boy Scouts to allow LGBTQ+ troop leaders (Family Research Institute, 2013a).

More recently, the FRI presented its findings of yet another "study." In this report, the FRI trolled through Google news stories and, as it admits, conservative-leaning news sources to ascertain the level or frequency of molestation that occurs from LGBTQ+ parents. As a result, the FRI claims:

> It is well-documented that those who engage in homosexuality are—as a group—much more likely to molest children than are heterosexuals ... children with homosexual parent(s) were about 50 times more apt to report being victims. In reports by journalists and their editors captured by Google News, homosexual parent(s) were about 40 times more apt to be incest perpetrators. ... the evidence seems to support the traditional understanding of homosexuality as a detriment to children. (Family Research Institute, 2014, n.p.)

Of course, a main problem with such an argument is the statistical "sampling" (i.e., it is not random or neutrally selected, nor is there a justification for why the news stories reviewed were important compared to other sources). Additionally, as Herek points out, studies such as these ignore "that many pedophiles and child molesters aren't even capable of relationships with adults and that their sexual attractions are directed solely at children" (Herek, 2006, n.p.). And Cahill cites Stevenson (2000) to report that "90% of pedophiles are men, and 95% of these individuals are heterosexual. ... Gay men desire consensual sexual relations with other adult men. Pedophiles are usually adult men who are sexually attracted to pre-pubescent children. They are rarely sexually attracted to other adults" (Cahill, 2004, p. 35).

Studies like these are not the only form of "evidence" the FRI uses to substantiate its claims. With the presupposition that there is a "link between homosexuality and pederasty," the FRI provides a report of how homosexuality is linked to, if not a cause of, pedophilia:

> In late February of 2008, FRI interviewed George Finch, Coordinator of Professional Practices in the Oregon education bureaucracy. Finch keeps the records and does much of the investigation of teacher-pupil sexual encounters for the state. Notes taken at the time of the interview recount Finch as saying: "that most of the molestations by male teachers in the elementary grades involved male homosexuals, and he only knew of two instances (in over a decade) by female teachers, one of a boy and one of a girl. At the high school level he noted that boys, especially, were loath to testify, but that it ran about 70% heterosexual/30% homosexual for male teachers and about 50/50 for female teachers. Finch noted that few girls were willing to testify about involvement with female teachers at the HS level, since he believed 'they were exploring their sexuality, and were often friends with the teacher with whom they had relations.'" (Family Research Institute, 2013b, n.p.)

Personal testimony or personal experiences are forms of evidence that can be quite compelling for a larger argument that they support (Cameron & Cameron, 1996). However, if they are anecdotal in nature, cannot account for other variables, and the source of the anecdotes can be questioned, the personal testimonies are a weak form of evidence. And again, when such forms of "evidence" are presented to an audience that is friendly and already largely agrees with the underlying premise of the position—known as "confirmation bias"—then such reports appear to be more legitimate, or at least fairly well-received, than other types of reports (Nickerson, 1998). Nevertheless, the FRI often uses anecdotes, and when they are combined with studies and other anecdotes, they contribute to a larger package of evidence. Individually, each form of evidence may be discounted or refuted, but when combined with other types of evidence, the bundle of support is much stronger. And when combined and uncritically released, it permits broad-based claims such as, "homosexuals also do a poor job of raising healthy, well socialized children" (Family Research Institute, 2009, n.p.).

Hate Crimes

LGBTQ+ people, of course, have been victims of terrible and often brutal attacks. It is one thing to be a victim of an assault; it is quite another to be a victim who is targeted precisely because of his or her sexual identity. It is sometimes difficult to prove if an attack occurred because it was motivated by one's animus toward another's identity, or if the attack was premised on other reasons, such as a financial, drug-related, or some other sort of crime. However, some assaults are so brutal as to defy any other explanation other than a perpetrator's simple hatred toward the identity of the victim. And, of course, there are the occasions when the culprits of the crime admit that their actions were motivated by their hatred of LGBTQ+ individuals. In any case, hate crimes against LGBTQ+ people exist, are often horrific in nature, and point to the extremes some individuals will go to express their negative views about fellow human beings who happen to have different sexual orientations.

In 1994, Congress passed federal hate crime legislation as part of a larger bill known as the Violent Crime Control and Law Enforcement Act. The specific hate crimes portion is known as the Hate Crimes Sentencing Enhancement Act (28 U.S.C. 994), which "defined a hate crime as 'a crime in which the defendant intentionally selects a victim, or in the case of a property crime, the property that is the object of the crime, because of the actual or perceived race, color, religion, national origin, ethnicity, gender, disability, or sexual orientation of any person'" (ADL, 2012b, pp. 13–14). Unfortunately, this law only applies to federal crimes, meaning that individual states also need to enact their own hate crimes laws in order for aggravating circumstances based on hatred or animus to be included in sentencing guidelines for non-federal crimes. According to a Congressional Research Service report in 2010,

> Many states have enacted some form of ethnic intimidation law or bias-motivated sentence-enhancement factors in attempts to curtail hate crimes.

> … State hate crime statutes vary in the protection offered to victims. At least 10 states and the District of Columbia have enacted hate crime laws that cover gender identity and sexual orientation. At least 21 states have criminal legislation that addresses gender-identity motivated crimes. There appear to be at least 25 states that protect potential victims of sexual orientation. (Smith and Foley, 2010, p. 1)

Although the 1994 law provides federal guidelines for hate crimes analysis, it fails to specifically account for animus against LGBTQ+ folks, and, as noted, it only applies to federal crimes. As of 2010, there are only twenty-one states that have hate crimes laws that apply to anti-LGBTQ+ crimes.

> In order to at least partially rectify this problem, Congress passed in 2009 the Local Law Enforcement Hate Crimes Prevention Act (LLEHCPA), which authorizes the Department of Justice to investigate and prosecute certain bias-motivated crimes based on the victim's actual or perceived sexual orientation, gender, gender identity, or disability. Currently, the federal government can only investigate hate crimes motivated by the victim's race, color, religion, and national origin. It will also provide local authorities with more resources to combat hate crimes and give the federal government jurisdiction over prosecuting hate crimes in states where the current law is inadequate. (Lewis, 2009, n.p.)

While individual states still need to pass their own hate crimes bills, the LLEHCPA provides resources for states and local authorities to pursue avenues related to hate crimes.

As part of the LLEHCPA, Congress passed, and President Obama signed into law, the Matthew Shepard and James Byrd, Jr. Hate Crimes Prevention Act (formerly the Local Law Enforcement Hate Crimes Prevention Act of 2009). According to acting assistant attorney general for the Civil Rights Division of the U.S. Department of Justice, Jocelyn Samuels, the "investigation into Matthew Shepard's death found strong evidence that his attackers targeted him because he was gay. In the case of James Byrd Jr., the three men responsible for his killing were well-known white supremacists. His brutal murder stands as one of the most nightmarish recent incidents of racially motivated violence." If we recall, Matthew Shepard was the twenty-one year old University of Wyoming student who was beaten, tortured, and left to die by being strung up to a roadside fence in October 1998 simply because he was gay. Despite the brutal nature of these crimes, none of the convicted perpetrators were sentenced with a hate crime. So, the 2009 Shepard-Byrd Act provides the judicial mechanism to apply heightened sentencing guidelines based on the commission of a hate crime. Samuels additionally notes that the "law also marked the first time that the words, 'lesbian, gay, bisexual and transgender' appeared in the U.S. Code" (Samuels, 2013, n.p.).

Recently, Stephen Jimenez, a reporter, reinvestigated the Matthew Shepard murder and uncovered some new evidence, namely interviews with the convicted murderers.

Jimenez's book explores the underlying reasons behind the motivations of Shepard's murder. Accordingly, Jimenez claims the murder was not motivated behind any bigotry or hatred toward Shepard's sexual orientation; rather, it was a crime involving drugs and money (Jimenez, 2013). This new account is very interesting given the nature of Shepard's death and the way it was reported. To some, "Shepard's story has been elevated close to legend, and Shepard himself to a near-messianic figure who suffered for the ultimate benefit of the rest of us" (Gumbel, 2013, n.p.). Since he was gay, the brutal nature of his death was emphasized as a quintessential example of a hate crime. If Jimenez is correct, Shepard's murder was not caused by a hatred of homosexuality, but was just a tragic and gruesome murder over cash. However, the Matthew Shepard Foundation claims that efforts "now to rewrite the story of this hate crime appear to be based on untrustworthy sources, factual errors, rumors and innuendo rather than the actual evidence gathered by law enforcement and presented in a court of law" (quoted in Nichols, 2013, n.p.).

But even if we discount the Matthew Shepard murder as something other than a LGBTQ+ hate crime, we know of many other examples. For instance, there is the Scotty Joe Weaver murder. He was "beaten, cut, and strangled to death," and he "was nearly decapitated" by one of his roommates who apparently had had enough of Weaver's homosexuality (Herek, 2007b). Then there is the Lawrence King murder, where a fifteen-year old King was murdered in his middle school's computer lab because he had recently come out of the closet. A fellow student with whom King allegedly flirted shot him (Herek, 2008). Additionally, if we look at data nationwide, we know that numbers of hate crimes against LGBTQ+ people are disturbingly high:

> Prevalence data are available from a survey conducted with a national probability sample. And they show that such victimization is alarmingly common: About 1 in 5 sexual minority adults report they have experienced a crime against their person or property based on their sexual orientation … 13% of respondents said they had been hit, beaten, physically attacked, or sexually assaulted because of their sexual orientation … 21% had experienced either violence or a property crime … 23% had been threatened with violence. (Herek, 2007a)

Egan and Sherrill support this concern by saying, "Gays and lesbians have achieved protection from discrimination in states that account for 37% of the U.S. population and in most big cities. But in the rest of the nation, gay people—and particularly transgendered people—lack protection from discrimination in employment, housing, public accommodations, or credit" (Egan and Sherrill, 2005, p. 229). Moreover, not only are the instances of LGBTQ+ hate crimes high, but the manner in which they are performed are also tragic. In fact, based on a study done by Miller and Humphreys (1980), we know that,

> seldom is a LGBTQ+ victim simply shot. He is more apt to be stabbed a dozen or more times, mutilated, and strangled. In a number of instances,

the victim was stabbed or mutilated even after being fatally shot. ... The homicides of LGBTQ+ and bisexual men were objectively more violent than murders of heterosexuals. Stabbing and other sharp-force injuries were the most common cause of death among the LGBTQ+ and bisexual victims. ... The bodies of LGBTQ+ victims, on average, evidenced more injuries from blunt weapons, more fatal stab wounds, and injuries to more areas of the body than the heterosexual victims. LGBTQ+ and bisexual men were more likely than heterosexual men to have injuries in the face, head, neck, back, arms, and legs. The percentage of cases with multiple causes of death—overkill—was greater among the LGBTQ+ and bisexual victims, although the difference was not statistically significant. (Herek, 2007b, n.p.)

If the violent acts against LGBTQ+ people tend to be "overkill," then it stands to reason that most violent crimes against gays and lesbians would be classified as "hate crimes." The violence against them is obviously motivated by deep-seated fear, anger, and confusion. Simply put, "LGBT people also remain the objects of great hate-inspired violence" (Egan and Sherrill, 2005, p. 230). As such, the crimes are more brutal and terrifying than the typical attacks against heterosexuals.

Of course, the Family Research Institute responds by saying that hate crimes and violent assaults against LGBTQ+ individuals are exaggerated. It claims that attacks against LGBTQ+ folks are not based on hate, nor are they prevalent or brutal. It cites a study that reports that "around half of anti-homosexual harassment reports in 1995 involved only slurs or insults, thus not rising to the level of actual or threatened physical violence" (Family Research Institute, 2009, n.p.). However, if around half of the incidents "only" involved slurs, that still leaves the other "half" who experienced very brutal and overkill attacks.

In 1990, the United States Congress passed legislation called the Hate Crime Statistics Act. The law requires that the federal government collect data annually about crimes relating to race, religion, sexual orientation, or ethnicity. Before its passage, Senator Jesse Helms (R-NC), who was notorious for his extremely social conservative and anti-gay views, wanted to add this language to the bill in the form of an amendment (and therefore called the "Helms Amendment"): "It is the sense of the Senate that: the homosexual movement threatens the strength and survival of the American family as the basic unit of society; State sodomy laws should be enforced because they are in the best interest of public health; the Federal Government should not provide discrimination protections on the basis of sexual orientation; and school curriculums should not condone homosexuality as an acceptable lifestyle in American society" (Herek, 2008, n.p.).

Helms was unable to secure enough votes for his amendment, but the pressure he was able to mount stimulated controversy over the Hate Crime Statistics Act. As a form of compromise to prevent the Helms Amendment, the rest of the Senate agreed to include this language into the act instead, which they felt was a compromise and much more accommodating to LGBTQ+ people: "SEC. 2. (a) Congress finds that: the American family life is the foundation of American Society, Federal policy should encourage the well-being, financial security, and health of the American family, schools should not de-emphasize the critical value of American family life. (b) Nothing in this Act shall be construed, nor shall any funds appropriated to carry out the purpose of the Act be used, to promote or encourage homosexuality" (Herek, 2008, n.p.). Thus, Congress used a piece of hate crime legislation, which is supposedly intended to serve the interests of minority groups such as LGBTQ+ people, to pre-empt a major issue for LGBTQ+, and more specifically homosexual, folks—that of same-sex marriage. Congress intentionally placed language into this hate crimes bill that codifies language in opposition to same-sex marriage. On one hand, it pacifies extremists like Helms, but on the other hand, it thwarts efforts for the LGBTQ+ movement to move forward in its agenda. Incidentally, this also illustrates how politically, one issue can affect other issues.

General Anti-LGBTQ+ Rhetoric

Seeing or hearing anti-gay rhetoric is not uncommon; however, it is somewhat surprising the frequency and degree to which we experience such rhetoric from our politicians and political pundits. For example, in a recent Illinois Republican primary campaign, one candidate, who ultimately won the primary election, openly stated, "I am not in favor of gay rights." Susanne Atanus explained her belief, not from a legal or political perspective, but rather from an extremist, if not perverted, religiously moral perspective. She said, "God is angry. We are provoking him with abortions and same-sex marriage and civil unions. Same-sex activity is going to increase AIDS," and, she claims, that tornadoes, autism, and dementia are "God's punishments for marriage equality" (Lachman, 2014, n.p.).

Atanus is an obvious example of a contemporary politician who uses extremist rhetoric for largely divisive purposes. In other words, her remarks, while she may genuinely believe them, are also clearly politicizing—and polarizing—in nature. Her position on homosexuality galvanizes others who agree with her position, and the result of which might help explain her rise in popularity sufficient to win the election.

But this sort of divisive and extreme rhetoric from a politician is not unique to Atanus. A Tea Party candidate in Oklahoma, Scott Esk, also engages in hateful speech against LGBTQ+ people to curry favor with his base and people who oppose homosexuality:

> Esk first claims that Leviticus 20:13 gives people the right to judge others, and goes on to claim that it is man's role to put others to death for atrocities such as homosexuality. Then he goes on to claim that if we don't start killing off homosexuals that God may send a series of "calamities" to nations who do not. So, in other words, every time there is a natural disaster, Esk has given himself the right to claim that it's because we don't follow an Old Testament Bible verse and stone gays and lesbians to death. Jerry Falwell would be SO

> proud of this man. And then it gets worse. Bates asks Esk if he indeed believes that homosexuals should be put to death, and he responds, "I think we would totally be in the right to do it." (Simpson, 2014, n.p.)

Clearly, someone who is a candidate for public office should not endorse killing citizens because of their identity. LGBTQ+s commit no crimes (by being LGBTQ+), and if they do, the crimes certainly do not warrant a death penalty. This sort of divisive discourse is precisely what continues to polarize Americans over social issues. If Esk has a problem with homosexuality, he should articulate his positions in respectful and civil ways, especially if he becomes a state legislator in Oklahoma.

In a recent interview with a CNBC reporter, Texas governor Rick Perry likens homosexuality to alcoholism when he says, "Whether or not you feel compelled to follow a particular lifestyle or not, you have the ability to decide not to do that. ... I may have the genetic coding that I'm inclined to be an alcoholic, but I have the desire not to do that, and I look at the homosexual issue the same way" (quoted in Topaz, 2014). This contentious claim raises the issue that homosexuality is not innate, or if it is, it can be somehow controlled or repressed, much like alcoholism. This position, then, justifies a faith in "reparative therapy," which is a process to convert or transform homosexuals into heterosexuals, or at least homosexuals who can control their impulses to be "homosexual" (Sullivan, 2014).

Similarly, U.S. representative Michele Bachmann (R-MN) has articulated polarizing remarks about gays and lesbians. Purportedly, Bachmann said that homosexuals have "bullied the American people and they have so intimidated politicians that politicians fear them and they think they get to dictate the agenda everywhere" (quoted in Clifton, 2014, n.p.). By "bullying," Bachmann is claiming that gays and lesbians are imposing their views onto others, even "targeting our children" (Avidor et al., 2012, p. 29). According to Avidor et al., "Michele Bachmann's crusade against gay marriage included radio appearances, hysteria-laced e-mails to 'Death Penalty for homosexuals as Prescribed [sic] by the Bible,' signs at an antigay rally at the state capitol, and an e-mail bragging about shutting down the legislature over this 'earthquake issue'" (Avidor et al., 2012, p. 27). In this way, Bachmann utilizes the rhetorical tactic of creating an us/them dichotomy, thereby further polarizing the issue.

In terms of political pundits, similar rhetoric exists. Kyle Mantyla (2014) reports on the discourse of Bryan Fischer, a conservative radio host. Mantyla writes,

> On his radio program today, Bryan Fischer spent an entire segment delivering a convoluted exegesis of the Old Testament in an effort to explain that God will eventually get fed up with America's tolerance of homosexuality and will use radical Islamic groups like ISIS to carry out his wrath. Just as God used the Israelites to destroy the Canaanites as punishment for their utter debauchery and then used "pagan armies" to punish Israel when it fell into sin, Fischer explained, so too will God use Islamic radicals to inflict his judgment upon America. Asserting that the people of Sodom and Gomorrah are

"just like the Gay Gestapo is today" and that America is celebrating behavior that God calls an abomination while persecuting those who stand for God's values, Fischer warned that "God eventually is going to run out of patience with the United States." And when that day comes, he said, God "will use pagan armies to discipline his people if they turn from him in rebellion and disobedience and descend into debauchery," pointing to the rise of ISIS to raise the possibility that "God will use the pagan armies of Allah to discipline the United States for our debauchery." (Manytla, 2014, n.p.)

Fischer provides an example of how discussions of gay rights are really a metaphor for any aspect of society for which we disagree. If the underlying premise of our beliefs about homosexuality also happens to be negative, our outrage or frustrations about other, perhaps more complicated, social issues becomes manifest when compared to homosexuality. If we can link the two concepts somehow, particularly by fallaciously suggesting homosexuality as the cause and the other concept the effect, we can not only strengthen our predisposition against homosexuality, but we can also reinforce our position about the other concept as well. In this case, of course, Fischer uses his animosity toward homosexuality to buttress his position on ISIS and militant Muslims.

Another pundit who is adamantly opposed to LGBTQ+ rights is Ann Coulter. Speaking at a conservative dinner, Coulter discussed how LGBTQ+ people do not need special rights (Smith, 2010). She also says that "I think the one thing we can all agree on is that there is definitely a 'mandate' against gay marriage. In fact, a clear majority of us are uncomfortable with the word 'mandate' because it sounds like Wayne asking Stephen out for dinner and a movie" (Coulter, 2007, p. 115). In typical Coulter sarcastic tone, she concludes her feelings on the subject by calling someone out (although just two pages earlier, she argues that Republicans are morally superior to Democrats because "we don't make a sport out of outing political opponents who happen to be gay"), with this brief comment when answering Chris Matthews' question:

> Matthews: How do you know that Bill Clinton is gay?
> Coulter: He may not be gay, but Al Gore—total fag.
> (Coulter, 2007, p. 116)

While her arguments are not that extreme—after all, she mainly just opposes same-sex marriages—Coulter uses her sarcastic wit to further polarize. Susan Estrich concurs: "When Ann calls us immoral, there are only two issues she is addressing. We know what they are. They come from the political playbooks, not from Scriptures. Abortion and gay rights. Women and homosexuals. Wedge issues. Intended to divide" (Estrich, 2006, p. 113).

Ann Coulter is not the only ideologically conservative instigator to use sarcasm to justify homophobic remarks. Rush Limbaugh is also known to use humor as a rhetorical ploy. In fact,

Many of his "jokes" are full of homophobic fears of gay men, such as "When a gay person turns his back on you, it is anything but an insult; it's an invitation."... He has a particular obsession with what he calls "anal poisoning," which is Rush's peculiar verbal invention. ... Democratic honcho Terry McAulifffe, Limbaugh warned, "will die of anal poisoning because he is so close to drilling Hillary. ... A variation of this anal attack is Rush's frequent use of the term "butt boy." He said about NBC reporter Andrea Mitchell "she does come off like a 'butt boy,'" and also referred to Ed Henry of CNN as a "butt boy." But Limbaugh's favorite butt reference is the classic "bend over, grab the ankles" to describe the experience of being screwed over by a dominant force. In 2008 he declared about the Democratic leaders in Congress, "Dingy Harry and Pelosi [are] bending over and grabbing the ankles at every MoveOn.org meeting or at every Daily Kos convention. (Wilson, 2011, p. 60)

I suppose if Limbaugh's listeners are fifth graders, some of this language might be funny, but most of Limbaugh's followers, I fear, take him seriously. Noted Limbaugh expert John Wilson says that Limbaugh's alleged humor is "good business" since it appeals "to the baser instincts of his conservative audience" (Wilson, 2011, p. 63).

One of the premises of anti-gay rhetoric is that LGBTQ+ people impose their will and agenda on the rest of society. This breeds resentment, of course, since LGBTQ+ individuals are a minority. For example, Erwin Lutzer, former minister of The Moody Church, says, "The radical gay movement let it be known that its agenda would proceed regardless of research, science, and dialogue; and that intimidation would be one of its weapons to achieve its aims, no matter what" (Lutzer, 2010, p. 20). This notion of "forcing their agenda" has significant rhetorical impact and justifies an emotional response (Kennedy and Newcombe, 2004, p. 29). As I have examined above, the Family Research Institute has nothing positive to say regarding LGBTQ+s. One of the reasons it opposes homosexuality is because it claims that the homosexual lifestyle is extremely dangerous:

Participants in both gay and lesbian 'marriages' offer each other something quite different. They see shared biological intimacy and sexual risk-taking as a hallmark of trust and commitment. Being exposed in this way to the bodily discharges of their partner increases the risk of disease, especially so if that partner was 'married' to someone else before or engaged in sex with others outside the relationship. The evidence is strong that both gays and lesbians are more apt to take biological risks when having sex with a partner than when having casual sex. The evidence is also strong that gays disproportionately contract more disease, especially AIDS and the various forms of hepatitis, from sex with 'partners' than they do from sex with strangers. (Family Research Institute, 2009, n.p.)

Therefore, many opponents suggest that the LGBTQ+ lifestyle is evil and threatening to the species since they cannot procreate. Kennedy and Newcombe even say that we are living in "scary times" because of homosexuality (2004, p. 32). The head of the FRI, Tony Perkins, advocates placing homosexuals into concentration camps in order to prevent them from jeopardizing the future of humanity (Fletcher, 2014). As such, the FRI continues to spew its scorn and hatred through its websites and other media.

In terms of sodomy, many view homosexuality as a problematic, to put it mildly, practice or behavior. The *Bowers v. Hardwick* decision heightened the visibility of sodomy and its ramifications on the LGBTQ+ community. Of course, *Bowers* also criminalized sodomy. Thus, "Disorderly conduct and anti-sodomy laws were used to break up gay organizations and arrest individuals looking for or engaging in gay sex" (Jost, 2014, p. 281). In terms of discourse, extremist, typically ultra-religious, rhetoric undergirded these attacks on gays and lesbians. A brief excerpt from the well-read and highly influential *Christianity Today* illustrates the sort of inflammatory vitriol used on this subject:

> homosexual practice is wrong, and it is not homophobic to say so. No faithful Christian, or any advocate of virtue, should acquiesce on this issue just because discussion of it is couched in the twisted terminology of "gay rights." ... Nor is the issue one of equal rights or unfairness or discrimination or bigotry. Advocates of "tolerance" for practicing homosexuals in the military and society at large are generally disingenuous in this appeal: It really cloaks what amounts to a political validation of an unnatural, unhealthy, and ungodly lifestyle. ... Sodomy, no matter how it is legitimized, is still a filthy practice at odds with human anatomy. (Webster, 1993, p. 23)

This sort of logic is why some anti-gay individuals make claims such as the "homosexual community, by militance and secret political maneuvering, is designing a program to increase the tidal wave of homosexuality that will drown our children in a polluted sea of sexual perversion—and will eventually destroy America as it did Rome, Greece, Pompeii, and Sodom" (LaHaye, 1978, p. 179).

Some religious leaders also illustrate extremist rhetoric against the LGBTQ+ community (Herman, 1997). Pat Robertson, the Baptist minister who founded the influential Christian Broadcasting Network, predicted that the "widespread practice of homosexuality 'will bring about terrorist bombs, it'll bring earthquakes, tornados and possibly a meteor'" (Wharton, 1998). But Robertson is not alone. For example, Richard Land, a former Southern Baptist Convention official, linked "the rise of gay rights and Nazi Germany" and allegedly claimed that "conservatives need to stand up to 'the gay thought police' or face Nazi-style persecution" (Tashman, 2014b, n.p.). And religious leaders at a prayer breakfast reportedly said that "gay marriage" is "an evil akin to Nazi Germany, and homosexuality [is] evidence of a nation on the brink of collapse" (quoted in Klarman, 2014, p. 182). This is, of course, ironic since the Nazis targeted homosexuals for internment and execution like other minorities and Jews. For some conservatives, it is easy to characterize LGBTQ+ people as painting "homosexual behavior as a form of barbarity, one step above bestiality. Gays and lesbians, like other enemies of Christ, are not fully human; they are 'unnatural'" (Hedges, 2006, pp. 114–115). This language is clearly problematic because it labels the opposition as the "enemies." Additionally, Todd Starnes, the conservative radio personality from Fox News Radio Network, writes that allowing LGBTQ+ behavior "will somehow threaten their religious beliefs. In fact, some have argued that we are not far from a day … when pastors will be 'brought up on charges of hate speech against LGBTQ+s'" (quoted by Brinker, 2014a, n.p.). Indeed, some LGBTQ+ individuals have become more aggressive in their tone and rhetorical tactics, but it is unlikely that they stoop to the level of the hate-ridden language exhibited by anti-gay rhetoric.

Of course, the most outrageous religious rhetoric against LGBTQ+ people comes from the hate-filled discourse of the Westboro Baptist Church (WBC). Hailing from Topeka, Kansas, the WBC wields cherry-picked Bible verses to support its mission (WBC, "Compendium of Bible Truth on Fags") to take "forth the precious from the vile, and so is as the mouth of God (Jer. 15:19). In 1991, WBC began conducting peaceful demonstrations opposing the fag lifestyle of soul-damning, nation-destroying filth" (WBC website). The WBC uses Leviticus 20:23 ("therefore I abhorred them") to justify the name of their website: "godhatesfags.com." But the "bigot takes his arguments where he can find them. … Any text can be made to say anything and the more sacred the better," so the WBC's rhetorical tactic of manipulating Bible passages should not really surprise us (Bronner, 2014, p. 34). The WBC has been enormously controversial, particularly with their protests, including protesting the return and memorial services of fallen U.S. military personnel because, as the WBC claims, their deaths represent "God's punishment for the United States' toleration of homosexuality" (HuffPost Politics, 2013, n.p.). The founder of the WBC, Fred Phelps, died in 2014, but the group continues its anti-gay agenda. Although not very strong in numbers, the WBC's extremism attracts a high degree of visibility. Its impact on American anti-gay culture can be summed up by the description of the WBC by the Southern Poverty Law Center: the "WBC is arguably the most obnoxious and rabid hate group in America" (SPLC, 2014).

Transgender Issues

Although transgender individuals have existed for millennia, only recently have they been in the spotlight in U.S. culture. Popular culture icons like Caitlyn Jenner and Laverne Cox have brought issues faced by the transgender community to public discourse (Scherer, 2016). Steinmetz says that Caitlyn Jenner is "the most famous transgender woman in the world," so I shall begin our examination of the divisive discourse concerning transgender identity with her (Steinmetz, 2015, n.p.). Caitlyn Jenner's "announcement" was called a "global media event," as Caitlyn agreed to "an April interview with Diane Sawyer" that had over 17 million viewers, which resulted in *Vanity Fair*'s website shattering "traffic records when a corseted Caitlyn was introduced on the magazine's cover in June" (Steinmetz, 2015, n.p.). Within four hours, Caitlyn Jenner had over two million Twitter followers (Pilkington, 2015).

Overall, 2015 was a key year for the transgender community. As Steinmetz explains:

Jenner's rebirth as Caitlyn was the most visible high point of a banner year for the transgender community. The Secretary of Defense called the ban on transgender people's open military service "outdated" and directed that the policy be reviewed. A measure to add nondiscrimination protections for LGBT people to the Civil Rights Act was introduced in Congress with nearly 200 co-sponsors. And critically acclaimed shows like Transparent that feature transgender story lines with respect and depth have chiseled away at the stigma of being trans. (2015, n.p.)

But, in the same year, "at least 21 transgender women [had] been murdered in America, making it the community's deadliest on record" (Steinmetz, 2015, n.p.). Furthermore, we know that the "transgender homicide rate [had] hit an historic high in the US, when more than 1,700 murders of transgendered individuals were reported around the world between 2008 and 2014" (Florêncio, 2016, n.p.). Moreover, "almost one in six transgender people have annual incomes of below $10,000—four times the rate of the general population," and nearly half of all black trans women "are incarcerated at some point in their lives; 27% are HIV positive; 29% (or five times the national average) are unemployed; and almost half experience being turned away from housing and many end up homeless" (Pilkington, 2015, n.p.).

As individuals struggle with their identity, they may not have had the opportunity to undergo the proper surgical and hormonal procedures to complete the transition from one sex to the other. During this process, a sort of identity limbo occurs, but it does provide the individual some flexibility to shuttle between the identifications of both sexes. This process is known as "passing." As Steinmetz explains,

> When it isn't obvious that a transgender person is transgender, they're often said to "pass." There is what is called "passing privilege," referring to the easier, safer, more accepted lives that such transgender people can often lead. But the notion that transgender people are successful only when they hide who they are is much criticized. So is the term itself. As one transgender woman told me, "Passing has a connotation that you're pretending to be something you're not, and we're just being ourselves." (2015, n.p.)

Yet for many other Americans, they struggle with the concept of transgenderism. As Steinmetz explains, "People doubt that they really are who they say they are, whether that's a parent insisting that it's all 'just a phase' or protesters in Texas asserting that transgender women are really men out to terrorize their daughters in the restroom" (2015, n.p.).

The static notion of a gender binary has been shattered, and signs of gendered rethinking are happening throughout American society. As Sapolsky notes,

> In fact, it's headline news. Bruce Jenner, a male gold medalist in the 1976 Olympics and a cover boy on a Wheaties box, is now Caitlyn Jenner, a 2015

cover girl on Vanity Fair. Laverne Cox, a transgender actor, is nominated for an Emmy for outstanding actress. America has seen openly transgendered individuals serve as a mayor, state legislator, judge, police officer, a model for a global cosmetics brand, and a high school homecoming queen. Even amid the appallingly high rates of discrimination and violence against the transgendered, there is a growing recognition that gender designation need not be permanent. (2015, n.p.)

As a result, some even question whether there is such a concept as "gender" (Sapolsky, 2015). Of course, the problematization of gender, or the inclusion of multiple gendered identity categories, is nothing new. In early Native American societies, for instance, the notion of *berdache* was an integral, revered, part of a community, constituting a third gender, but often associated with a community or tribe's sage or spiritual advisor (Thayer, 1980).

Part of the disconnect regarding transgender individuals in U.S. society is that our brains have been hardwired to conceptualize sex (and gender) as a binary system, an either/or categorization schema. Sapolsky (2015) describes how this occurs cognitively: "So we think categorically. And dichotomized gender is one of the strongest natural categories the brain has. The categorization is crazy fast—neuroimaging studies show the brain processes faces according to gender, within 150 milliseconds—that's 150 thousandths of a second—before there's conscious awareness of gender" (n.p.). Thus, as Sapolsky continues, "Automatic categorization by gender is deeply ingrained" (2015, n.p.).

Some in the transgender community have also been critical, or at least extremely cautious, of Jenner's "coming out." Many are frustrated with how long it took Caitlyn to announce she was a woman; some say that with her money and status, she should have been supporting the transgender community; and others bemoan how she has not recognized the hard work of other transgender individuals who made Jenner's announcement easier and more palatable to American society (Pilkington, 2015). Of course, others have come to Caitlyn's defense, such as Mara Keisling, who is the executive director of the National Center for Transgender Equality, when she says that "no story is typical," and that the transgender community needs to support its own (Pilkington, 2015, n.p.).

Some feminists have been very critical of Caitlyn Jenner's transgender identity announcement. For instance, Elinor Burkett, who claims to have been a feminist advocate for decades, says she "winced" at Jenner's proclamation, lamenting, "People who haven't lived their whole lives as women, whether Ms. Jenner or Mr. Summers, shouldn't get to define us. That's something men have been doing for much too long" (2015, n.p.). As Burkett's piece in *The New York Times* continues, her irritation becomes even more obvious:

Their truth is not my truth. Their female identities are not my female identity. They haven't traveled through the world as women and been shaped by all that this entails. They haven't suffered through business meetings with men talking to their breasts or woken up after sex terrified they'd forgotten to take their birth control pills the day before. They haven't had to cope with the onset of their periods in the middle of a crowded subway, the humiliation of discovering that their male work partners' checks were far larger than theirs, or the fear of being too weak to ward off rapists. (Burkett, 2015, n.p.)

Burkett even flippantly ends her article as she castigates Caitlyn's identity by means of a *reductio ad absurdum*: "Bruce Jenner told Ms. Sawyer that what he looked forward to most in his transition was the chance to wear nail polish, not for a furtive, fugitive instant, but until it chips off. I want that for Bruce, now Caitlyn, too. But I also want her to remember: Nail polish does not a woman make" (Burkett, 2015, n.p.). By framing Jenner's trajectory from a man—to trans—to woman, Burkett character-izes Jenner's story as imbued with a "hefty dose of male privilege." But obviously Burkett's critique does not apply to most transgender individuals, and it certainly does not account for the psychological anguish Bruce Jenner must have endured before transitioning into Caitlyn.

However, as we might expect, a large swath of the American public was not very accepting of, or happy with, Jenner's pronouncement (Rothkopf, 2015). To many social and religious conservatives, Caitlyn Jenner's popularity is "a reminder that they are los-ing the culture wars," so much so that they are painting "an apocalyptic view of America" (Costa & Rucker, 2015, n.p.). According to the former education secretary during the Reagan administration, William Bennett, people feel pressured to accept transgender people for fear of being called a "bigot." He said it is "like American culture is being dragged kicking and screaming not only toward acceptance but approval" (cited in Costa & Rucker, 2015, n.p.). Former preacher and presidential candidate Mike Huckabee combined sarcasm with sexism in his reaction to Jenner's announced identity: "I wish that someone told me that when I was in high school that I could have felt like a woman when it came time to take showers in P.E." (cited in Costa & Rucker, 2015, n.p.). And Rush Limbaugh—always with an opinion—actually tried to avoid the issue entirely when he said, "We should not be lionizing this. We should not be encouraging this," although he did characterize transgenderism as "really marginal behavior" (cited in Costa & Rucker, 2015, n.p.). Yet another conservative radio talk show host, Steve Deace, took the issue of Jenner and transgender identity head on, as he advised the Republican party to confront the issue. He warned that if they do not address this cultural shift, "[they] might as well just forfeit the 2016 election now." He further noted, "If we're not going to defend as a party basic principles of male and female, that life is sacred because it comes from God, then you're going to lose the vast majority of people who've joined that party" (cited in Costa & Rucker, 2015, n.p.). And former pastor and founder of the Idaho Values Alliance, Bryan Fischer, refused to identify Jenner as a woman, and then said, "If you want one snapshot of just how corrupt—how morally corrupt, how morally bent, how morally twisted, how morally confused, how morally bankrupt—we have become," Fischer said, "all you've got to do is take a look at the cover of *Vanity Fair* magazine" (cited in Costa & Rucker, 2015, n.p.). Finally, the extreme conservative writer

George Neumayr prophetically likened this cultural shift in America as a harbinger to a Brave New World, since issues like Jenner's transitioning exemplifies "all things perverse" (cited in Costa & Rucker, 2015, n.p.).

Another highly visible and discourse-generating event concerning transgender individuals in the past couple of years is the controversy concerning Chelsea Manning. President Obama "commuted all but the last four months" of Chelsea Manning's sentence in early 2017, functionally granting Manning a pardon (Gauthier, 2017, n.p.). While Manning was released from military prison after serving 6 years of her 35-year sentence, she has had to forfeit any claims to a military pension. Chelsea Manning, formerly known as Bradley Manning, was placed into military incarceration after being convicted for releasing highly sensitive and classified documents to WikiLeaks. When Manning was on tour in Iraq, he accessed "750,000 documents total, including 150,000 diplomatic cables, to notorious anti-American hacking group WikiLeaks" (Qazvini, 2017, n.p.). While in prison, Bradley Manning legally changed his name to Chelsea, and in 2013, Chelsea filed a lawsuit against the U.S. military so that she could receive treatment for "gender dysphoria"—the official medical name and diagnosis of altered gendered identity—including hormone therapy and "gender-reassignment surgery" (Blake, 2016).

Liberals generally praised Manning for being a champion of government transparency and accountability, while conservatives largely viewed her as a traitor (Gauthier, 2017). Liberals hailed Manning as a whistleblower for justice—for example, Ben Wizner, who is a director at the ACLU, yowled, "When a soldier who shared information with the press and public is punished far more harshly than others who tortured prisoners and killed civilians, something is seriously wrong with our justice system. ... This is a sad day for Bradley Manning, but it's also a sad day for all Americans who depend on brave whistleblowers and a free press for a fully informed public debate" (cited in Tate, 2013, n.p.). But even if Manning's actions helped improve government transparency, they also placed many military personnel in jeopardy. According to David French, who writes for the *National Review*, Manning "disclosed details of American military operations, the identities of American military allies, and placed sensitive American diplomatic relationships at risk . ... We may never know exactly how much damage he did" (cited in Qazvini, 2017, n.p.). However, when Bradley Manning stole the documents, he was just an Army private who knew nothing about what he was uncovering (Qazvini, 2017), which begs the question of how he could obtain such access in the first place.

Several tweets, as compiled by Gauthier (2017) from political conservatives, exemplify their extreme reaction to Manning's commutation:

[Tweet: Paul Ryan (17 Jan 2017)] Chelsea Manning's treachery put American lives at risk and exposed some of our nation's most sensitive secrets.

[Tweet: Judith Miller (17 Jan 2017)] Obama commutes sentence of Chelsea Manning. How many people died because of manning' [sic] leak?

[Tweet: John McCain (17 Jan 2017)] @POTUS's commutation of #ChelseaManning's sentence is a grave mistake that will encourage further acts of espionage

[Tweet: Piers Morgan (18 Jan 2017)] Would Chelsea Manning be released if she was Russian?

[Tweet: Ann Coulter (17 Jan 2017)] Chelsea Manning pardon [sic] is considered a favor to LGBTs. What's the argument here? The LGBT community doesn't care about national security?

[Tweet: Mark Dice (17 Jan 2017)] Putting on a wig and makeup doesn't make someone a women if they have a penis and a Y chromosome. Sorry. RE: Chelsea Manning

[Tweet: Mark Romano (18 Jan 2017)] Why did Obama commute "Chelsea" Manning's sentence. Because it would piss people off. He is an agitator, he gets off on this kind of crap!

[Tweet: Matt Walsh (17 Jan 2017)] The Chelsea Manning commutation is just another example of LGBT privilege

But vitriolic tweets are not the full extent of the conservative backlash to Obama's decision regarding Manning, which happened just three days before Obama left office. For example, Texas Senator and former presidential candidate Ted Cruz suggested that Obama was "determined to do as much damage as humanly possible" before exiting the White House, especially since he "has such little respect for the American people and the verdict they rendered on Election Day that he continues to wreak havoc, and in the instance of this commutation, to disregard the safety and security of American service men and women all across this country" (cited in Weaver, 2017, n.p.). Republican Senator from South Carolina and former presidential candidate Lindsey Graham said that Obama's decision was "a slap in the face" to veterans because by "granting clemency, in my view, slapped our men and women who serve honorably in the face" (cited in Weaver, 2017, n.p.). Another Republican senator and former presidential candidate, Marco Rubio from Florida, scowled, "It is shameful that President Obama is siding with lawbreakers and the ACLU against the men and women who work every day to defend our nation and safeguard U.S. government secrets" (cited in Weaver, 2017, n.p.).

While in prison, Chelsea Manning reportedly tried to commit suicide on two different occasions (Blake, 2016). An ACLU attorney told *The Washington Times* that he was worried that Chelsea was not receiving proper healthcare, particularly mental healthcare associated with her transitioning into a woman (Blake, 2016). Another perspective claims that both suicide attempts, along with a hunger strike, were strategically used by Manning to pressure the military to pay for the gender-reassignment surgery (Qazvini, 2017). After

Bradley Manning declared that he was Chelsea in 2013, since he felt he was a female "since childhood," the military said they would still view him as a male and he "would be treated like any other prisoner," including the requirement that Manning wear a "distinctive clothing" reflective of a male identity (Pearson, 2013). Initially, the Army said that, as a military prisoner, Manning "must still complete their sentence without hormone therapy or sex-reassignment surgery provided by the Army" (Pearson, 2013, n.p.).

The conservative outrage over the military's decision to fund Manning's reassignment surgery was palpable. Not only do conservatives generally oppose government-funded support for anything related to the LGBTQ+ communities; they also do not take too kindly to the idea that military veterans were put at risk by the actions of a transgender individual who will benefit from such a government program. And, yet, that is precisely how Chelsea Manning's reassignment surgery has been characterized. As John Hayward, who writes for the extreme right-wing source *Breitbart*, declared, "gender-reassignment treatments for someone who is going to spend most of the rest of his/her life in prison for exposing national security secrets" demonstrate the "realm of absurdities that our hyper-legalized mousetrap bureaucratic and legal systems somehow force to happen automatically—while the sane, normal, honorable, and productive are taxed and regulated into the dirt—grows larger. We can only wonder what remarkable precedents the Manning decision will set, and how much they'll cost us" (2015, n.p.). Medically speaking, there is also substantial opposition to funding Manning's surgery in particular, but also to the process of reassignment surgery in general. Renowned psychiatrist and former director of the Johns Hopkins psychiatry department Dr. Paul McHugh leads the charge against proscribing and endorsing reassignment surgery for gender identity disorder (GID). McHugh writes, "At Johns Hopkins, after pioneering sex-change surgery, we demonstrated that the practice brought no important benefits. As a result, we stopped offering that form of treatment in the 1970s" (2015, n.p.).

McHugh explains in more detail that when Johns Hopkins first began reassignment surgeries, they initiated a long-term study to compare post-operation patients with GID patients without surgery. McHugh reports, "Most of the surgically treated patients described themselves as 'satisfied' by the results, but their subsequent psychosocial adjustments were no better than those who didn't have the surgery. And so at Hopkins we stopped doing sex-reassignment surgery, since producing a 'satisfied' but still troubled patient seemed an inadequate reason for surgically amputating normal organs" (McHugh, 2014, p. A13). McHugh also points to another study conducted in Sweden where they concluded that about ten years after reassignment surgery, transgender individuals "began to experience increasing mental difficulties. Most shockingly, their suicide mortality rose almost 20-fold above the comparable non-transgender population" (McHugh, 2014, p. A13). Thus, McHugh argues that other forms of treatment are a more optimal route, especially given the high risk that surgery can actually increase a patient's depression and suicidal tendencies.

Others, including Samantha Allen of the *Daily Beast*, disagree. She argues that taxpayer-supported hormone treatment and gender-reassignment surgery categorically are the same as treatments for other socially agreeable conditions, such as depression

(Allen, 2016). Despite being an internationally awarded psychiatrist and the former director of the psychiatric department at Johns Hopkins University, Dr. Paul McHugh is labeled by Samantha Allen an "anti-LGBT physician." Allen does not directly refute McHugh's claims, but she does cite statements from both the American Medical Association (AMA) and the American Psychological Association (APA). In 2008, the AMA passed a resolution (Hudson, 2008) that emphatically proclaimed, "An established body of medical research demonstrates the effectiveness and medical necessity of mental health care, hormone therapy, and sex reassignment surgery as forms of therapeutic treatment for many people diagnosed with GID [gender identity disorder]" (AMA House of Delegates, 2008). Then, several years later, the APA passed a similar resolution, stating that the APA Board "recognizes that appropriately evaluated transgender and gender variant individuals can benefit greatly from medical and surgical gender transition treatments" (APA Board of Trustees, 2012, n.p.). Samantha Allen also points to a San Francisco report that documents how much the city has spent supporting hormone treatments, and the city has "not seen much strain on their bottom line" (Allen, 2016, n.p.). Moreover, Allen claims that gender reassignment surgery costs less than $20,000. While all of that may be fine and good, Allen ignores the fact that these practices still cost money for the taxpayer, not the health insurance company or the individual electing the transitioning process. Instead, she ends her article with faulty analogies and a *reductio ad absurdum*: "If you're OK with Uncle Sam paying for prisoners to receive antidepressants or knee surgery or a CPAP machine, there's no reason to get worked up over Chelsea Manning's medical treatment" (Allen, 2016, n.p.).

Another highly contentious issue related to the transgender community is the debate over segregated bathrooms that has been largely highlighted by the recent controversy in North Carolina. In March 2016, the North Carolina legislature enacted House Bill 2, or "the bathroom law," which regulated how transgender individuals can use public bathrooms (Berman, 2017). After a year of its implementation, the state has experienced massive protests, boycotts from various groups, and a noticeable negative financial impact of the legislation. While protests have been serious and important, the economic burden incurred from the law is probably the most important detriment to the bill. As Berman (2017) reports, a number of high-ticketed events have been pulled in direct response to the law: "The NBA pulled its All-Star Game from North Carolina, the NCAA withdrew a number of sporting events—including men's basketball tournament games that would have been played there this month—and Bruce Springsteen, Pearl Jam, Ringo Starr and Cirque du Soleil performances were all scrapped" (Berman, 2017, n.p.). Additionally, PayPal was planning on opening an expansion center near Charlotte, but withdrew its business shortly after the bathroom bill became law, costing a "massive" $2.6 billion and at least 400 jobs (Berman, 2017). Plus, PayPal was the "first major domino to fall," as Deutsche Bank withdrew its 250-job planned expansion as well (Berman, 2017). A number of alternative and compromise laws have been discussed since the bill's inception, but all have failed to gather any traction (Berman, 2017). All told, the Associated Press has estimated that North Carolina will lose approximately $3.7 billion in revenue and lost jobs as a direct consequence of the bathroom bill. As a result, on March 30,

2017, North Carolina lawmakers repealed the bathroom law, angering social conservatives and elating liberals all across the nation (Berman & Phillips, 2017).

It remains to be seen whether the retraction of North Carolina's law will impact the decision by other states to have similar regulatory bathroom laws for transgender individuals. For instance, Republican legislators in Wisconsin introduced a bill that would "prohibit transgender students in K–12 schools from using bathrooms or locker rooms that correspond with their gender identity," supposedly aimed at protecting the "privacy of all students in bathroom and locker rooms" (Schulte & Sager, 2015). Similarly, conservatives in Houston, Texas, removed a trans-inclusive bathroom law because it was argued that the ordinance allowed "predatory men to go into women's restrooms" (Schulte & Sager, 2015). But "in 17 states and about 200 cities," they "have passed antidiscrimination legislation to protect people from discrimination in employment, city services, housing and public accommodations, based on sexual orientation, gender identity, race and a dozen other categories" (Schulte & Sager, 2015).

Clearly, many conservatives, particularly religious conservatives, oppose special treatment for transgender individuals because, at a minimum, they do not feel that such practices should be legitimized. Furthermore, many conservatives advance the argument that permitting transgender individuals into public bathrooms, locker rooms, and other similar facilities risks children becoming prey for sex-crazed predators. This argument is also highly misogynistic in that it frequently is articulated as "protecting" young women from predator trans-males. For instance, at the 2016 Texas State Republican Convention, Dan Patrick, the lieutenant governor of Texas, claimed, "Women need protection in the bathrooms, the changing rooms, the shared showers. We will stand up for women and girls in America and in Texas," he thundered to more cheers. "You deserve your privacy, you deserve your dignity, you deserve your comfort and your safety when you go to the ladies' room" (cited in Scherer, 2016, n.p.).

On the other hand, when a transgender individual enters a public bathroom, the discrimination they are likely to face generates massive anxiety and humiliation. According to Scherer (2016):

> A 2016 analysis of a survey of more than 2,000 transgender college students found the rate of suicide attempts increased 40% among those who said they had been denied access to a bathroom. In a separate survey of 100 transgender people in Washington, D.C., 70% said they had been denied restroom access or harassed, and 58% said they had avoided going out in public because they feared being able to find a bathroom. "At some point they had just decided it wasn't worth it to go out in public and have to deal with the bathroom situation," says Jody Herman, a scholar at UCLA's Williams Institute, who authored the study. (2016, n.p.)

This controversy is unlikely to vanish anytime soon, and given the polarized perspectives on the access of transgender individuals to public bathrooms, the divisive discourse is unlikely to wane, either.

CONCLUSION

Sentiment concerning homosexuality and LGBTQ+ issues are very contentious in contemporary America (Chauncey, 2004). Same-sex marriage, in particular, is extremely volatile. As Klarman points out, "Opposition to gay marriage remains strong. … Powerful political constituencies not only continue to resist gay marriage, but they regard the issue as one of the most important in politics today" (Klarman, 2014, p. 219). And marriage equality is controversial among homosexuals, too. Some argue that marriage conforms too much to mainstream culture and politics, and its struggle occurs at the expense of more important and radical pursuits (Rimmerman, 2002; Vaid, 1995). Others claim that the institution of marriage is patriarchal, heteronormative (i.e., it perpetuates heterosexual ideology and power dynamics), and restrictive, and as a result, it should be abandoned as a socio-cultural structure altogether (Ettelbrick, 1989; Jost, 2014; Kim, 2011). In any case, same-sex marriage is a fiercely debated topic.

While many LGBTQ+ people wanted their movement to tackle more non-marriage issues or wanted to completely ignore the pursuit for marriage equality, there can be little doubt now that the fight for marriage rights galvanized the movement, heightened awareness for LGBTQ+ issues, and yielded very significant gains for gays and lesbians. Although Al Franken said this as a comedic moment in a larger political discussion, his remark is poignant for our understanding of this larger issue: "Gay marriage wasn't about marriage. It was about [being] gay" (Franken, 2005, p. 126).

Unfortunately, many of the discussions about same-sex marriage, or about LGBTQ+ rights as a whole, hover around the nature of LGBTQ+ folks and their identities, and not whether freedoms or legal protections should be re-examined. Too often, the heated and extremist rhetoric that occurs on this topic is about people's preferences or ideological beliefs about identity instead of viewing LGBTQ+ individuals in a larger cultural and humanistic context. For instance, "Politicians and advocacy groups on both sides of the issue seek first and foremost to define it in terms that will be most attractive to the public. Advocates of same-sex marriage emphasize certain themes (civil rights, citizenship, equality, and fair treatment), and opponents highlight different values (public sentiment, traditional values, protection of children, and religious belief)" (Rom, 2007, pp. 21–22).

I have spent considerable time investigating the rhetoric of those opposed to homosexuality. But, to be fair, LGBTQ+ advocates also utilize the rhetorical tactics of creating an us/them dichotomy, fear, name-calling, and other fallacies. After reading a considerable amount of material on this issue, I believe that pro-LGBTQ+ rhetoric has become much more calm and reasonable in recent years, while anti-gay rhetoric has become much more incendiary. Nevertheless, it is important to point out that LGBTQ+ advocates "insist that respect for a person is identical with accepting his or her political claims for equality in all areas of life. Even principled opposition is therefore tantamount to bigotry, 'homophobia,' and the equivalent of race-hatred" (Santinover, 1996, p. 21). Thus, many LGBTQ+ folks frame the debate in a way that makes it difficult for opposing viewpoints to be heard, especially if all other perspectives are labeled "homophobic." Not every argument against same-sex marriage or anti-discrimination laws is based on hatred or fear of gay people. Even if some opposition perspectives are repugnant or based on homophobia, it is a hasty generalization fallacy (also a fallacy of composition) to assume that all arguments are that way.

Some have suggested that incendiary and bloviated discourse about LGBTQ+ people is premised on the fear of heterosexuals, as if they "feel their power slipping away" (Stern, 2014a). However, there may be a more complicated dynamic at work, which is why this is worth quoting at some length:

> The bigot always directs his hatred against those who threaten (or might threaten) his privileges, his existential self-worth, and the (imaginary) world in which he was once at home. ... But the bigot's goal is always the same: to transform a living, disenfranchised, exploited, and persecuted subaltern into an object for his use, an Other whose fixed traits render him unholy, unnatural, or inferior. ... The bigot's frustration is understandable. Intellectuals, experts, politicians, and other outsiders seemingly have no respect for the bigot's opinions and traditions. The atheist, the foreigner, the homosexual, and the other subversives are all seeking to change the natural order of things. The open society threatens the bigot's hegemony and thus he engages in a politics that seeks to narrow the public sphere. Participation should be limited to those who are like him. Those unlike him are only conspiring against him anyway. (Bronner, 2014, pp. 5–8)

And while we may not change a bigot by calling him a bigot, we can, perhaps, try to understand a little of how his bigoted attitude originates and operates.

Additionally, I worry that even using the term "bigot" isn't helpful here. It may not be fair to consider all anti-gay rhetoric as "bigoted"; if we do, we run the very likely risk that we begin thinking the person is a "bigot" rather than their comments being "bigoted." In other words, this type of discourse encourages *ad hominem* attacks. This likely will only perpetuate polarized discourse rather than abate it. Thus, while we need to understand each other's points of view, we should also be self-reflective and critical of *how* we try to understand those perspectives, and we must be vigilant in how we deploy language in our conversations regarding controversial issues. The issues involving LGBTQ+ identities are complex, but we tend to react based on predispositions, stereotypes, and sound bites. But through all of the complicated laws and ideological arguments, "Discrimination and invasions of liberty whose justification boils down to penalizing a group of despised citizens are unhealthy for the polity" (Eskridge, 1996, p. 143). In other words, we all suffer when one of our groups is being harmed—that just simply is not the society we are supposed to be. Ultimately, as Gill argues, what "matters most, therefore, is not whether religious or secular justifications are used in the course of public advocacy, but how these reasons affect the individual's free exercise of conscientious belief, or how they affect religion in general, broadly conceived as the search for core and transcendent meaning in life" (Gill, 2012, pp. 9–10).

IMAGE CREDITS

CHAPTER SIX

The Inflammatory Rhetoric of Immigration

Another significant social issue in the United States is immigration. To be more precise, the issue in dispute concerns "illegal" or "undocumented" or "unauthorized" immigration. I place these words in quotation marks because they, too, are in dispute and lie at the heart of the matter. As a nation of immigrants, the United States has a bittersweet history with immigration. Today, the main issue is generally a question of maintaining legal paths to citizenship while limiting or controlling "illegal" immigration, or the immigration of non-citizens into the United States that occurs outside of legal or authorized procedures.

It seems like everything about immigration is contentious. Even the oft-cited quote relating to immigrants on the Statue of Liberty is disputable. As most know, the quote comes from Emma Lazarus (see Figure 6.1) and her poem "The New Colossus":

Figure 6.1: Immigration Cartoon.

Not like the brazen giant of Greek fame,
With conquering limbs astride from land to land;
Here at our sea-washed, sunset gates shall stand
A mighty woman with a torch, whose flame
Is the imprisoned lightning, and her name
Mother of Exiles. From her beacon-hand
Glows world-wide welcome; her mild eyes command
The air-bridged harbor that twin cities frame.
"Keep ancient lands, your storied pomp!" cries she
With silent lips. "Give me your tired, your poor,
Your huddled masses yearning to breathe free,
The wretched refuse of your teeming shore.
Send these, the homeless, tempest-tost to me,
I lift my lamp beside the golden door!"
(National Park Service, 2014)

The "new colossus" to which Lazarus refers is, of course, the radiant Statute of Liberty. Many pro-immigrant groups cite the Lazarus poem—"Give me your tired, your poor, your huddled masses yearning to breathe free"—as an ideological basis for their immigration advocacy. It illustrates a beacon of hope for immigrants fleeing the plight of their home nations, something Lazarus knew all too well, as she worked to help diasporic Jews who sought refuge in the United States.

However, the iconic image of the Statue of Liberty may be interpreted differently. The Statue was a gift from France, thanking America for its support during the turbulent French Revolution. As such, the Statue illustrated the meaning behind freedom and liberty, hence its name—the Statue of Liberty. Lazarus' poem was not engraved into the Statue until 1903, seventeen years after its placement in 1886 on Bedloe's Island in New York Harbor. Given this, some anti-immigrant groups insist on clarifying the historical record:

Once again history was twisted so that one group of people who wanted to convince the children of the world the Statue of Liberty was all about immigration. This was all one big lie that was taught in schools since 1903. This was a distortion by the progressives to make you think America was willing to take anyone, from any place in the world or universe. The truth is, the statue was a celebration of the Declaration of Independence. In fact, we don't call it the statue of immigration, we call it the statue of liberty. Lady Liberty is stepping forward. She is meant to be carrying the torch of liberty from the United States to the rest of the world. (Frea, 2010, n.p.)

Figure 6.2: Emma Lazarus.

Of course, "The New Colossus" involves the welcoming of immigrants, especially since most immigrants at the time traveled through Ellis Island, which is also in New York Harbor (Koed, 2005). However, by clarifying the original meaning behind the Statue as a symbol of freedom from France, anti-immigrant activists can distance the symbolic, albeit rhetorical, value of the Statue of Liberty. In this way, the common argument that the United States is a nation comprised of immigrants who welcome all immigrants can be deflated.

Thus, even the poem at the base of the Statue of Liberty can be disputed in the much larger divisive discourse concerning immigration. For decades, Ellis Island and the Statute of Liberty were seen as images of America's immigrant beginnings. However, our contemporary reality presents a different immigrant context. To be sure, immigrants have always been a subject of concern in American discourse. The Irish potato famine triggered waves of Irish immigrants in the mid-1800s. Then came other European groups, such as the Italians. Many of the immigrant groups were Catholic, which sparked massive anti-Catholic sentiment. In fact, "It was in the nineteenth century that anti-alien movements had their greatest impact in American history" (Bennett, 2001, n.p.). Bennett's statement may be a bit of an overstatement, particularly when we view the anti-immigrant movements today along America's southern border. Nevertheless, it is important to note how immigrants have not always been warmly welcomed. Not much changed in the twentieth century, either, as Beirich points out:

> Nativist backlashes have occurred many times in American history, perhaps most notably in the 1920s. At that time, the Ku Klux Klan had as many as 4 million members and recruited largely on the basis of anti-Catholic (and, more specifically, anti-Irish and anti-Italian) sentiment. The anti-immigrant movement of the period ultimately resulted in the passage of the racist Immigration Act of 1924, which outlawed all Asian immigration and instituted national origin quotas favoring Northern European immigrants. (Beirich, 2014, n.p.)

Of course, many other immigrant groups faced animosity when they landed on America's shores—the Chinese, Jews, Japanese, Koreans, Eastern Europeans, etc., all encountered turbulent transitions as they immigrated to the United States.

This brief and partial snapshot of immigrant reaction in America helps us frame the overarching issue of immigration. The dispute touches the nerve of most Americans, but perhaps for different reasons, hence the controversy. In general, there is a prevailing dialectical tension between securing the preservation of a certain way of life versus tugs of compassion for fellow humans who yearn to have a better life. The conflict becomes particularly acute when there is a perception that immigrants who want a better life threaten the quality of life of citizens. Like many political and social issues, instead of Americans engaging in a civil conversation to seek accommodating solutions to this conflict, we more often than not engage in divisive discourse. The rhetorical tactics used in this incendiary immigrant discourse are the subject of this chapter.

THE CONTEXT OF IMMIGRATION

In order to understand better the polarizing rhetoric levied back and forth between groups engaging in the immigration conversation, we need to acquire a contextual basis for the issue. We already know that anti-immigrant feelings have been expressed throughout American history, so the dispute about immigrant compassion versus nativist notions of security is nothing new. However, the current context of American immigration involves some unique components, and the contemporary dispute is as acerbic as ever.

Notes on Language and Labels

The names we use in the immigration debate are extremely important in the way the nature of the dispute becomes framed. For instance, someone may enter the United States and apply for citizenship by following all of the proper procedures, or someone may cross the border without a visa or proper documentation. By doing the latter, the person violates federal law. As such, many Americans refer to such individuals as "illegals" since they are breaking the law. However, the federal law is only a misdemeanor, and characterizing them as "illegal" becomes quite pejorative (López, 2014). But we also know that mainstream media were as likely to use the term "illegal" as their conservative counterparts," because the "term 'unauthorized' was used only 21 times in the 5,500 articles examined and the term 'undocumented' was used in 11% of stories" (Long, 2013b, n.p.).

Technically, anyone who is not a citizen may be referred to as a "non-citizen," an "alien," or simply an "immigrant" (Núñez, 2013). The word "alien" is frequently used, but it carries a negative connotation since it implies something invasive, like an extra-terrestrial alien who invades Earth (Johnson, 1996–1997). Other words in this debate are also loaded: "illegal," "undocumented," "unauthorized." All of the words used in the immigration discussion, in a vacuum, could be useful and descriptive labels. However, we should be careful when throwing around adjectives since "an adequate analysis of reference may not be able to make much progress if it restricts itself only to linguistic forms outside of their functional context (Ommundsen et al., 2014). This is particularly important since politicians and pundits know that "framing has important consequences in shaping public opinion on undocumented immigration," (Merolla et al., 2013, p. 790) which is why they use words like "illegal" or "undocumented." It has indeed been argued that what is distinctive about names is nothing about their form but rather than in using a linguistic form as a name we escape the ontological commitments implied when that same linguistic form serves as a description or as a categorization" (Carroll,

1980, p. 309). In other words, when we banter over naming the people who cross our borders, we often forget that those people are…people (Bean and Stevens, 2003).

Another interesting discursive move that has appeared rather recently is the term "Latinx." As part of the "linguistic revolution" for more gender inclusivity, activists and academics had been using "@" as a suffix to be gender neutral in Spanish words (Ramirez & Blay, 2016). Thus, instead of "*amigas* or *amigos*, it was *amig@s*" (Padilla, 2016). However, the suffix "@" was not adequately inclusive for gender-queer and "gender-nonconforming people" (Padilla, 2016). A new gender term for Spanish, "Latinx," emerged. No one really knows when the term "Latinx" exactly began, but according to Padilla (2016), it seems like it originated around 2004 and has gained more prevalence thanks to social media. In addition to conservative voices who rail against so-called "political correctness," many Spanish-speaking people oppose this linguistic maneuver. As Guerra and Orbea (2015) argue, this discursive shift "is a blatant form of linguistic imperialism—the forcing of U.S. ideals upon a language in a way that does not grammatically or orally correspond with it." They later continue by saying that Latinx is "the forced and unnecessary giving of incompatible segments of U.S. culture" by purposefully altering the centuries-old Spanish language. To be gender inclusive, Guerra and Orbea (2015) say we should simply stick to the word "*Latino*," since, as they posit, "gender in Spanish and gender in English are two different things," especially since in Spanish, even "inanimate objects are given gendered" endings. Their approach, then, presumes that although the *–o* and *–a* suffixes in Spanish are "gendered," they already presuppose inclusion; for example, "*los Cubanos*" might be interpreted by English speakers as "the male Cubans," but to native Spanish speakers, all they hear is "the Cubans."

Despite this caveat, it is almost unavoidable that the rhetorical, albeit political, tactic of naming will occur. As Derrida notes, "If *the* political is to exist, one must know who everyone is, who is a friend and who is an enemy, and this knowing is not in the mode of theoretical knowledge but in one of a *practical identification*: knowing consists here in knowing how to identify the friend and the enemy" (Derrida, 1994, p. 116). As we discuss our political opinions, values, and beliefs, we invariably position our perspectives in contrast with others. Mental and verbal shortcuts require labeling not only the countervailing positions, but also the people proffering them. This jockeying is a natural development based on our linguistic restrictions—English, for example, can only describe so much—and our cultural and political proclivities. This notion is supported by Kenneth Burke, who claims, "We discern situational patterns by means of the particular vocabulary of the cultural group into which we are born. Our minds, as linguistic products, are composed of concepts (verbally molded) which select certain relationships as meaningful" (Burke, 1984, p. 35). Thus, labeling ideas, as well as each other, is an outgrowth of our identities and cultural makeup.

Additionally, the immigration dispute involves a number of various and complicated concepts, at least in the American context. For example, the United States has many different visa categories (Kato and Sparber, 2013). According to the Immigration Policy Center,

The United States provides various ways for immigrants with valuable skills to come to the United States on either a permanent or a temporary basis. There are more than 20 types of visas for temporary nonimmigrant workers. These include L visas for intracompany transfers, P visas for athletes, entertainers and skilled performers, R visas for religious workers, A visas for diplomatic employees, O visas for workers of extraordinary ability, and a variety of H visas for both highly-skilled and lesser-skilled employment. Many of the temporary worker categories are for highly skilled workers, and immigrants with a temporary work visa are normally sponsored by a specific employer for a specific job offer. (Immigration Policy Center, 2014, n.p.)

The U.S. also has a guest worker program (also known as seasonal workers; Vaughns, 2005; White, 2007), a *de facto bracero* program (a specific seasonal worker program between the U.S. and Mexico; Bauer, 2004; Martin, 2003; Rosenberg, 2012; Tallman, 2005), and asylum/refugee allowances (Lim, 2013; Planas, 2014; Ray, 2013).

In addition, refugees are people who are unable "to return to their home countries because of a 'well-founded fear of persecution' due to their race, membership in a social group, political opinion, religion, or national origin. Refugees apply for admission from outside of the United States, generally from a 'transition country' that is outside their home country" (Immigration Policy Center, 2014, n.p.). Asylum is the category for people who already reside in the United States but seek special status in order to not return to their home country for the same reasons as a refugee (Lim, 2013; Ray, 2013). In other words, an asylee and a refugee have virtually the same sort of status, except an asylee is already located in the United States, whereas a refugee is attempting to enter the U.S. The amount of refugees permitted to enter the U.S. is determined each year by the president in consultation with Congress. For example, in 2013, the number was seventy thousand (Immigration Policy Center, 2014).

Finally, once someone has entered the U.S. legally (usually under the auspices of a visa program), he or she may seek citizenship, although the method is long and cumbersome. The Immigration Policy Center summarizes the process:

> In order to qualify for U.S. citizenship through naturalization, an individual must have had LPR status (a green card) for at least 5 years (or 3 years if he or she obtained the green card through a U.S.-citizen spouse or through the Violence Against Women Act, VAWA). There are other exceptions for members of the U.S. military who serve in a time of war or declared hostilities. Applicants for U.S. citizenship must be at least 18 years old, demonstrate continuous residency, demonstrate "good moral character," pass English and U.S. history and civics exams, and pay an application fee, among other requirements. (Immigration Policy Center, 2014, n.p.)

Overall, there is a set limit of people the United States permits to enter into the country each year, which, of course, impacts the number of people eligible for citizenship status.

The U.S. does not have quotas, *per se*, but it does have country "preferences" and will decline visas or citizenship status on the basis that too many have already been permitted within a given year (Herreras, 2010). To understand this dynamic, and also to help frame the larger issue of immigration, we should note how the U.S. sets limits on immigration:

> Numerical limits placed upon the various immigration preferences, the INA also places a limit on how many immigrants can come to the United States from any one country. Currently, no group of permanent immigrants (family-based and employment-based) from a single country can exceed 7% of the total amount of people immigrating to the United States in a single year. (Immigration Policy Center, 2014, n.p.)

Thus, individuals certainly have the opportunity, or potential, to achieve citizenship status as an authorized immigrant, although the process takes time and only offers a set number of possible citizenship allotments per year. This procedure will be important when we examine the immigration rhetoric below since some people argue that so-called "illegal" immigrants should be confronted and quashed under the assumption that such people have the alternative to become "legal" citizens. Of course, such arguments neglect to account for the limits placed on legal immigrant statuses each year. Because of this, I will try to use the term "unauthorized immigrant" when referring to non-citizens who are in the country "illegally" or without proper immigration authorization.

The Rhetorical Situation

To ascertain the rhetorical situation, we should identify the exigencies, constraints, and audiences (Bitzer, 1968). At any point in U.S. history, we could examine a particular rhetorical situation. For our purposes, I will explore the rhetorical situation in our contemporary context. The majority of immigrants, particularly illegal/undocumented immigrants, come from Latin American, Hispanic countries (Phillips, 2002). This partially frames the immigration debate since arguments focus on particular Latin American countries and the identities of the immigrants fleeing those countries. Plus, with the majority of immigrants traveling from Hispanic countries, anti-immigrant groups can base some of their arguments on the fear of Spanish as a threat to English-speaking citizens.

For many years, particularly since 9/11, anti-immigrant fervor has intensified (Phillips, 2002). The emotional, almost visceral, reaction to the image and idea of immigrants happens with many Americans and is compounded by exposure to certain media outlets. Josue David Cisneros (2012) explains the relationship between affect and the perception of immigration:

> The critical focus on affect and emotion demonstrates an attempt to move beyond the role of representation alone by focusing on the place of emotion

and, importantly, bodily experiences (affect) in constituting identifications and motivating people to belief or action. In sum, the affective dimensions of politics and culture speak to "how bodies are mobilized (called to action) at a material level for both good and ill. Yet affect does not take shape entirely separate from representation; rather, discourses participate with embodied experience, public culture, and historical memory to articulate affinities and emotional investments. Dominant attitudes, about immigration, for example, are articulated, developed, contested, and internalized through affective investments/associations, which are also themselves shaped by both public and personal experience .. ... Concern for affect moves us beyond a focus on ideology as pure representation ... by illustrating that ideology is articulated through a confluence of signs, bodies, and histories. Though bodies motivate certain affective responses ... bodies are also taken up into and influence systems of belief ... bodies, beliefs, and representations get "stuck" together into ideologies. (pp. 137–138)

With the amount of Mexican immigrants rising sharply, particularly in the American Southwest, most of the anti-immigrant sentiment has been directed at Spanish-speaking, predominantly Mexican, immigrants. Anti-Mexican views have intensified despite the fact that the majority of the American Southwest once belonged to Mexico, but through the American occupation with the Treaty of Guadalupe Hidalgo in 1868, the territory officially became part of the United States. The causes for the mounting Mexican immigration include deplorable economic conditions in Mexico, lack of job prospects (mainly a result of NAFTA), and the growing influence of drug cartels (Chacón, 2014). The potential for opportunities in America are perceived by many Mexicans as something worth sacrificing for, as illegal/unauthorized attempts at crossing the border can be perilous.

Figure 6.3: Ceded Territory from Mexico, 1848.

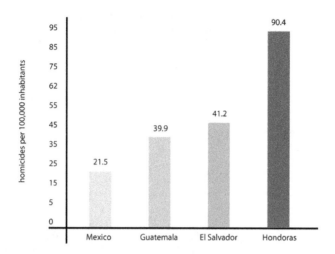

Figure 6.4: Honduras Leading Murder Capital.

As frustrations, fear, and animosity toward Spanish-speakers from Mexico grew, another development occurred in the past two years. Almost out of nowhere, massive amounts of women and children from other Spanish-speaking countries—namely Honduras, El Salvador, and Guatemala—arrived in Texas by bus, train, and via smuggling operations (Gao, 2014; Gonzalez-Barrera et al., 2014). Induced mainly by drug cartels that promise opportunities in America and inaccurately explain that if caught, the immigrants will still be able to stay in the U.S., these Central Americans may pay their life savings for a trip to the U.S. Even if the trek to America is uncomfortable—cramped like sardines—and ultimately a swindle since the individuals will face detention and/or deportation, the hope and dream of American refuge is worth the sacrifice (Foley, 2014; Ross, 2014). Honduras is now the murder capital of the world, and El Salvador and Guatemala (and Honduras, too) are experiencing severe economic turmoil—some of the most severe in all of Latin America (Gao, 2014; Gonzalez-Barrera et al., 2014). Thus, women and children (many of whom are unaccompanied minors) are flocking to the U.S. with the prospect of living a better life.

The Central American immigrants provide an interesting and unique exigency for our understanding of the broader rhetorical situation of immigration. As we will see below, Congress has been at a crossroads in determining what to do about immigration. Given how Congress hems and haws over immigration, President Obama issued some executive orders to deal with the immigration crisis—also labeled a "humanitarian crisis" with the murders and deplorable conditions from the Central American countries (Lakoff and Ferguson, 2006; Parsons et al., 2014; Ross, 2014). Nevertheless, the influx of Central American immigrants offers an emergent exigency. With a 2008 law called the William Wilberforce Trafficking Victims Protection Reauthorization Act (TVPRA), signed by President George W. Bush, for immigrants coming from a country other than Mexico, U.S. border officials must detain the immigrants, process

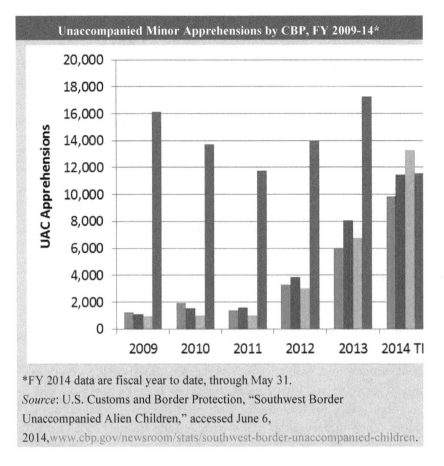

*FY 2014 data are fiscal year to date, through May 31.
Source: U.S. Customs and Border Protection, "Southwest Border Unaccompanied Alien Children," accessed June 6, 2014, www.cbp.gov/newsroom/stats/southwest-border-unaccompanied-children.

Figure 6.5: Unaccompanied Minors.

them, and provide a judicial proceeding (Govtrack.us, 2014; York, 2014). These procedures are important to protect the due process rights of the immigrants. For Mexican immigrants, all judicial procedures are waived, and the immigrants are deported back to Mexico expeditiously. Many politicians, including Obama, have offered to amend the Bush law so that Central American immigrants can more swiftly be deported in lieu of judicial proceedings, just like Mexican immigrants.

Given that Central American immigrants—particularly unaccompanied minors and unrelated women—have been flocking to our border rather unexpectedly, both President Obama and the Republican Congress viewed this humanitarian crisis in a politicized way. The president, despite promises to *La Raza* and pro-immigrant politicians (Arizona Republic, 2014; Ferdman, 2014; Gilchrist, 2014a; Velasquez, 2014), did not grant immediate amnesty to the Central American immigrants. Instead, Obama played politics with the 2006 TVPRA Bush law. Obama hoped to amend it so that all immigrants would be treated like Mexican immigrants—i.e., they would all have expedited judicial proceedings and then be quickly deported back to their home countries (Khalek, 2014; Meckler, 2014; Welch, 2014). The Republicans, despite the clear

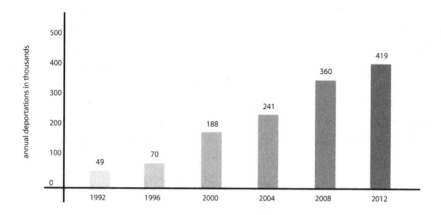

Figure 6.6: Annual Deportations Increasing.

message from Obama that the immigrants would be deported, worried that Obama would still provide some degree of amnesty (Hawkins, 2014). At the very least, the Republicans argued, Obama was being too lenient. They argued that the presence of the Central American immigrants was proof that the border is too porous and unguarded; thus, they provided evidence for a strict, enforcement-only approach to immigration control (Vaughns, 2005).

Hence, the new so-called "humanitarian crisis" breeds an exigency for our federal politicians to advocate for their ideological positions. As most exigencies, the Central American immigrant episode provides an exigent opportunity, but it also offers a massive constraint—neither Obama nor the Republicans could advance their pre-planned agenda or articulate their standard talking points. The emergent crisis requires flexible rhetorical positioning, for which Obama was quite skilled (Kienpointner, 2013). As constraints, the Central American immigrants caused Obama to shift his position on amnesty. The Republicans are trying to pivot back to a strong, draconian stance against immigration, but Obama's rhetoric regarding Bush's TVPRA altered the discursive landscape and created an obstacle for Republican advocates.

In terms of the audience, it seems like the politicians are throwing accusations and *ad hominem* attacks at each other without much regard for public opinion or the views of the immigrants themselves. Of course, we (meaning the American hierarchy) would never consult with the immigrants about our immigration policy. Our arrogant policy-making positions are geared for political maneuvering and issue camouflage, not public outreach. There have been no town hall meetings, no calls for public input, and when he had meetings scheduled in Texas, Obama didn't even bother to visit the border, claiming that it would be "political theater" and he doesn't "need photo ops, we need action. The ball is in Congress's court to do this right" (Zezima and Nakamura, 2014, n.p.). Additionally, Obama claimed he did not need to visit the border because his secretary for homeland security, Jeh Johnson, had been to the border. Obama argued that Johnson had "now visited, at my direction, the border five times. He's gone for a sixth this week.

He then comes back and reports to me extensively on everything that's taking place. So there's nothing that is taking place down there that I am not intimately aware of and briefed on" (*Real Clear Politics*, 2014). Ironically, of course, the president castigated his opponents for playing "theater" with this crisis, yet he politicized it himself by spinning the episode into a framework where he painted the Republicans as petty. In any case, the new whirling immigration debate among our politicians is scarcely sensitive to the public; rather, it appears targeted at each other. As such, the general discourse on immigration hardly benefits from the rhetoric emanating from our politicians.

The Historical Context

I briefly sketched some of the current developments of immigration in the United States, but in order for some of these issues to make sense, and in an attempt to clarify the overarching ideological positions on immigration, a tracing of some of the history regarding immigration in America is warranted. I obviously cannot go into detail with all of the aspects of immigration history in the United States, but I will highlight some of the most significant for our discussion about the divisive discourse that surrounds immigration.

Immigration policy dates back to the origins of the country. In 1790, the United States passed the Naturalization Act, which outlined the process to become a naturalized citizen. Since 1790, the U.S. Congress has periodically revisited and amended the Naturalization Act. The first attempt at enacting broad, sweeping immigration legislation, however, did not occur until 1882 with the passage of the Immigration Act. Among other things, it imposed a tax on all incoming immigrants, and it allowed for the screening of immigrants to prevent the "convict, lunatic, idiot, or person unable to take care of himself or herself without becoming a public charge" (Migration Policy Institute, 2013b). A few laws were passed in the late 1800s and the early 1900s restricting the amount of Chinese immigration. In 1921, Congress passed the Emergency Quota Act, which established certain quota caps on immigrants coming from certain countries. Due to labor shortages from World War II, the U.S. passed the *bracero* agreement with Mexico (allowing temporary agricultural laborers to work in the U.S.) and the Magnuson Act, which allowed Chinese nationals the opportunity to become U.S. citizens, functionally negating some of the earlier laws that restricted Chinese immigration. The 1952 Immigration and Nationality Act streamlined several immigration laws and updated and codified the quota system. The 1950s and 1960s saw an acknowledgement for American refugee policies with the Refugee Relief Act of 1953 and the Migration and Refugee Assistance Act of 1962. While quotas based on nationality were still maintained, the 1965 Immigration and Nationality Act also permitted naturalization for family members. Finally, the Refugee Act of 1980 formerly defines refugee and formalizes, through congressional statute, a new system for processing and admitting refugees (Migration Policy Institute, 2013b).

In terms of contemporary immigration policy, we should probably begin with the Immigration Reform and Control Act (IRCA), which was enacted in 1986. After seven long years of investigations, reports, and studies, a congressional committee called the

Select Commission on Immigration and Refugee Policy proposed what it considered was the panacea to immigration woes. Until this point in time, the United States had not really had a comprehensive immigration policy; growing concerns about immigrants from Mexico and Latin America necessitated a look at thorough policy reform. The Select Commission suggested the U.S. do many things, but after Congress deliberated, the IRCA eventually consisted of three key initiatives—sanctions against employers who hire illegal workers, enhanced paths to legal citizenship, and heightened border security. The employer sanctions "addressed future influxes of undocumented migrants by sanctioning (and in some cases prosecuting) employers who hired individuals without work authorization," and the "legalization provisions, considered 'the most ambitious amnesty program in U.S. history,' were intended to capture the then estimated three to twelve million undocumented migrant population by affording them opportunities to regularize their immigration status" (Vaughns, 2005, p. 163). The enhanced border security provision required the immigration agency at the time, the Immigration and Naturalization Service (INS), to increase border protection by 50% of 1986 levels (Migration Policy Institute, 2013a). When President Reagan signed the IRCA into law, he said, "Future generations of Americans will be thankful for our efforts to humanely regain control of our borders and thereby preserve the value of one of the most sacred possessions of our people—American citizenship" (Tumulty, 2013, n.p.).

We know, of course, that the IRCA did not live up to the hype Reagan gave it. In fact, an "estimated 3 million to 5 million illegal immigrants were living in the United States when the 1986 Immigration Reform and Control Act (IRCA) was passed. Now there are upward of 11 million. And the question of who gets to be an American, far from being settled, has been inflamed" (Tumulty, 2013, n.p.). While the IRCA was the first time the government imposed sanctions against employers who hire immigrants illegally, the law lacked enforcement teeth since in 2006, "not a single employer was fined" (Tumulty, 2013, n.p.).

After the IRCA, immigration became a more politicized issue between the Republicans and the Democrats. As a result, no other broad, sweeping legislation has been passed since 1986, although a number of piecemeal laws have been adopted. For example, the Immigration Act of 1990 established a ceiling of allowing 700,000 immigrants for three years, and then 675,000 every year thereafter (Vaughns, 2005). Then, in 1996, the Illegal Immigration Reform and Responsibility Act added more felonies to the list for which the U.S. government can deport an immigrant if such crimes are committed. Also in 1996, Congress passed the Personal Responsibility and Work Opportunity Reconciliation Act, which limits the amount of public services immigrants may receive (Migration Policy Institute, 2013a).

Nothing happened for almost a decade after, as Congress could not seem to agree on how to proceed regarding immigration. As a result of 9/11, Bush and Congress eliminated the INS and merged immigration and border security under the Department of Homeland Security with the creation of a new agency, the Immigration and Customs Enforcement (ICE). In 2005, Congress did manage to pass the REAL ID Act, which requires states to verify a person's citizenship for things such as driver's licenses. The law also adds restrictions to asylum qualifications (Migration Policy Institute, 2013a). A year later, in 2006, Bush signed into law the Secure Fence Act, which authorized the construction of a 317-mile fence along America's southern border (White House Fact Sheet, 2006). And although he campaigned to initiate immigration reform, Barack Obama was elected president in 2008 but was unable to muster enough support to pass sweeping immigration reform.

Contemporary Climate

Because the federal government has been unable to enact immigration reform, the state of Arizona decided to pass its own laws to clamp down on illegal immigration. In 2008, Arizona passed a law to strengthen sanctions against employers who hire illegal immigrants, although since the law passed, it has been rarely enforced, with only three businesses having faced penalties for violating the law (Hansen, 2013). In 2010, with growing fears and concerns associated with the rising amount of unauthorized immigration, Arizona lawmakers adopted S.B. 1070, which essentially does two things—it requires law enforcement officers to check an individual's citizenship status if the officer reasonably suspects a person might be an unlawful alien, and the law makes it a crime if an individual fails to produce the appropriate papers regarding their immigration status. The Arizona law is very controversial. Many people agreed with Arizona's position that the state should take immigration policy into its own hands, which is why Utah, Indiana, Georgia, and Alabama followed Arizona's lead and passed their own immigration laws. On the other hand, the federal government reacted to Arizona by arguing, under the doctrine of federal preemption, that immigration should be under the purview of federal jurisdiction. Ultimately, the Supreme Court ruled on Arizona's actions. While the Court upheld Arizona's employer sanctions law in *Chamber of Commerce v. Whiting* (2011), the Court also struck down the other provisions in *Arizona v. United States* (2012), ruling that "immigration law is the prerogative of Congress and the executive branch, and that states may not adopt laws or enforcement policies that conflict with federal law" (Cole, 2012, p. 4).

While the Supreme Court declared that immigration policy was the terrain of the federal government, the federal government simply is not doing anything about immigration. Virtually everyone agrees that the system is broken, although for different reasons. Individual states, particularly along the southern border, are in a conundrum because they may be experiencing the brunt of the pressures stemming from immigration, yet they are unable to be solution-oriented as long as the *Arizona v. United States* decision stands.

In the meantime, the Republican-controlled House and President Obama had been log-jammed over immigration. A number of Republican ideas had been proposed, almost all of which attempted to boost enforcement and restrict more immigration. Based on the ideological premise of reinforcing stricter immigration laws, the Republicans contrasted themselves with liberal policies—also premised along ideological lines—that tended to be more accommodating to immigrants while generally favoring the enforcement of current laws. For example, President Obama consistently pushed for the Development, Relief, and Education for Alien Minors (DREAM) Act, which provides economic assistance, primarily for education, to youth living in the United States whose parents are immigrants. Although the president's argument was that children have no culpability in their parents' decisions and education benefits the children as well as our communities, the Republican-controlled House of Representatives refused to pass the DREAM Act, largely because they felt that providing such assistance would provide a magnet for additional immigrants to cross our borders illegally so that their children can receive such benefits. Since Congress failed to pass the DREAM Act, President Obama, in 2012, authorized an executive order called the Deferred Action for Childhood Arrivals (DACA) program, which grants "temporary relief to undocumented youth who have grown up in the United States" so that they can "continue pursuing their educational and professional ambitions without the fear of deportation" (Rendeiro, 2014, n.p.).

One bipartisan initiative, sponsored by Democrat representative Henry Cuellar (TX) and Republican senator John Cornyn (TX), is called the Helping Unaccompanied Minors and Alleviating National Emergency (HUMANE) Act. It is intended to revamp the 2008 TVPRA. "The HUMANE Act would treat all unaccompanied migrants equally and offer all a voluntary return to their home countries," and it "speeds up the adjudication process" (Kiefer, 2014). The HUMANE Act failed to pass because many Republicans felt the law was still too lenient on immigrants (Telford, 2014). And because the law "speeds up" the process, many Democrats call the initiative the "rocket docket," believing that the law was too strict and violated the due process rights of immigrants (Kiefer, 2014; Lee, 2014).

Since Congress has failed to pass comprehensive immigration reform, and given the current humanitarian crisis with Central American immigrants, President Obama stated he would issue an executive order, although the specifics of the executive action are unclear. Initially, Obama said the executive order would occur by the end of summer of 2015, but he recently announced any executive action will be postponed until after the November midterm elections (Mejia, 2014). Clearly, the president's delay is a political move in an attempt to shield some Democrats who are running in tight races this coming November; however, by postponing the executive order, Obama was reneging on his earlier promise to handle the current immigration debacle in an expeditious manner (Ferdman, 2014; Velasquez, 2014). Additionally, by blatantly protecting Democrats running in contested elections, Obama was also signaling that those races are more important than the Latino voters for whom the president's immigration policy would notably impact the most. At the time of this writing, immigration policy is in a holding pattern and will most likely not be broached until sometime after 2017. President Obama ended his office with a push for a few immigration policies via executive orders. Most notably, one of Obama's orders protected five million immigrants from deportation, although the action does not provide a path toward citizenship (Knoll & Kille, 2014).

Now that Donald Trump is president, the situation involving immigration has changed considerably. During the 2016 presidential campaign, Donald Trump made several comments related to immigration that generated considerable controversy. Perhaps the most well-known Trump idea during the campaign was to "build a wall" along the U.S.-Mexico border. Despite the exorbitant cost, infeasibility, and geographical complications due to the Rio Grande, one of Trump's signature agenda items was proposed as follows: "On day one we will begin working on an impenetrable, physical, tall, powerful, beautiful southern border wall" (cited in Hing, 2016, n.p.). And although Trump said Mexico would pay for the wall, Mexico, of course, has refused such an arrangement (Bennet & Bierman, 2017).

Another Trump campaign item concerning immigration was deportation. The idea of deportation, trumpeted by many Republicans, is to expunge so-called "illegal" immigrants by sending them back to their home country. The notion of deportation is largely code, however, for removing Hispanic people, mainly Mexicans, since virtually no politician would suggest deporting undocumented Irish or Israeli immigrants, for example. Nevertheless, the idea of deportation remains popular, especially among conservatives. On the campaign trail, Trump kept reiterating something along the lines of this: "Day one, my first hour in office, those people are gone" (cited in Hing, 2016). Trump even referred to Mexican immigrants as "drug dealers," "criminals," and "rapists" (Gabbatt, 2015; Kaufman, 2015a). Trump claimed that "if you look at the statistics of people coming, you look at the statistics on rape, on crime, on everything coming in illegally into this country it's mind-boggling" (cited in McLaughlin, 2015, n.p.). He also stated in a different speech, "We are going to get them out, and we're going to get them out fast" (cited in Bennett & Bierman, 2017, n.p.) because "the US has become a dumping ground for everyone else's problems" (Gabbatt, 2015, n.p.). The newly elected Democratic senator from California, Kamala Harris, responded, "Directing a deportation force to break up immigrant families contributing to our country is not a show of strength. … It damages our communities and erodes local economies" (cited in Bennett & Bierman, 2017, n.p.).

Of course, Trump wanted to tackle one of Obama's signature initiatives, DACA (the Deferred Action for Childhood Arrivals), which was the president's 2012 executive order version of the DREAM Act. Trump declared that under his administration, it will not matter how long someone has been in the U.S. or if they have family as citizens. If they are a so-called "DREAMER," Trump implored, "they will have one route and one route only—to return home and apply for re-entry like everybody else under the rules of the new legal immigration system" (cited in Hing, 2016). Trump's polarizing, anti-immigrant invective triggered much controversy. During one of the Democrat presidential debates, former governor of Maryland Martin O'Malley called candidate Trump an "immigrant-bashing carnival barker," to which Trump later rebuked via Twitter, "O'Malley is a clown" (cited in Chaitin, 2015, n.p.).

While not specifying a causal connection between immigrants and crime, Trump played on the fear of immigrants and the associated belief that immigrants cause crime. The fear of immigrant criminals is unfortunately pervasive—"through the media, politicians desiring to restrict immigration have been able to represent undocumented immigrants as undeserving criminals and possible terrorists" (Chavez, 2013, p. 10). During the campaign, for instance, Trump emphatically pronounced, "Gangs will disappear, and the gangs are all over the place" (cited in Hing, 2016). What is interesting, however, is that the federal government has no way of accurately describing or reporting the nature of crimes committed by immigrants:

> The federal government does not have any way of tracking the overall criminal behavior of immigrants, U.S. Immigration and Customs Enforcement, the agency that detains and deports illegal immigrants, admitted in the information provided to the Senate. "ICE is unable to statistically report on the number of aliens who have been arrested for criminal offenses," the agency said. (Dinan, 2015, n.p.)

Furthermore, just about every metric indicates that immigrants, even Mexican immigrants, do not contribute to higher crime rates; they may, in fact, actually lessen crimes in some circumstances (Bump, 2015; Lopez, 2015). Nevertheless, this type of logic is why Trump also signed an executive order to publish on a weekly basis the crimes committed by undocumented immigrants (Kentish, 2017).

Although Trump promised these sweeping immigration changes on "day one" of his administration, nothing happened so quickly, largely because Trump—whether he knew it during the campaign or not—realized the realities of Washington politics once in office. Yet on January 24—just four days after the oath of office—Trump tweeted, "Big day planned on NATIONAL SECURITY tomorrow. ... Among many other things, we will build the wall!" (cited in David et al., 2017, n.p.). The next day, Trump signed an executive order authorizing the construction of his wall along the southern border. However, the order's force of authorization could only go so far because the President does not have budgetary authority—only Congress does, even though the order stated, "identify and, to the extent permitted by law, allocate all Federal funds" (Lind, 2017). This means, of course, that the executive order may have authorized the construction of the wall, but until Congress officially approves its funding, nothing will happen (Bennett & Bierman, 2017; Davis, 2017). Trump repeatedly noted during the campaign that Mexico would pay for the wall, but he never explained how, exactly, the U.S. would compel Mexico to provide funds (Lind, 2017), nor has Trump, since his election, proposed any measure to require Mexican payment, and neither has his press secretary, Sean Spicer (Min Kim, 2017). Nevertheless, Trump remained optimistic, stating that "I just signed two executive orders that will save thousands of lives, millions of jobs and billions and billions of dollars," as well as, "I truly believe we can enhance the relation between our two nations, to a degree not seen before, certainly, in a very, very long time. I think our relationship with Mexico is going to get better" (cited in Min Kim, 2017). But the cost of the wall is a serious issue because the Government Accountability Office (GAO), a non-partisan arm of the government that studies budgetary concerns, noted that the wall "could cost $6.5 million per mile to build a single-layer fence, and an additional $4.2 million per mile for roads and more fencing," and those figures "do not include maintenance of the fence along the nearly 2,000-mile border" (Davis et al., 2017).

Indeed, immigration has been a signature issue for both candidate Trump and president Trump. During his first week in office, he made this clear when he said to Homeland Security personnel, "A nation without borders is not a nation. … Beginning today, the United States of America gets back control of its borders" (cited in Bennett & Bierman, 2017, n.p.). After becoming president, Trump has also promised to eradicate or punish so-called "sanctuary cities"—municipalities that provide refuge to unauthorized immigrants—either by withholding federal funds or by making such actions illegal (Kentish, 2017; Page, 2017). Regardless, Trump has yet, at the time of this writing, done anything concrete regarding sanctuary cities.

Just like the reaction during his campaign statements, Trump's rhetoric and executive orders once in office also generated condemnatory reactions. Many opponents portrayed Trump's actions as "mean-spirited, counterproductive and costly" (Davis, 2017). Moreover, some of the most striking criticism originated from the American Civil Liberties Union. An ACLU attorney, Joanne Lin, noted that Trump's policies are "setting out to unleash this deportation force on steroids, and local police will be able to run wild, so we're tremendously concerned about the impact that could have on immigrants and families across the country," and, more troubling, "after today's announcement, the fear quotient is going to go up exponentially" (cited in Davis, 2017, n.p.).

Framing the Debate

Both sides of this issue frame their positions in a certain way before articulating their arguments. In scholarly literature, frames are cognitive schemas that allow us to interpret our world in certain ways (Baker, 2008), especially because language is an ideological construct that, in turn, molds our perspectives that we use to see and understand the world (Petrovic & Kuntz, 2013). We can think of discursive framing much like we would view a picture frame—a picture can exceed the borders of a frame, but we only see what appears within the frame. Thus, frames are rhetorical because they help in the persuasion process. As such,

> The power of a given frame to attract and mobilize constituents depends in part on its "resonance" with the life-experiences of potential constituents. The conditions for this resonance are: (1) ideational centrality/narrative fidelity—the frame must draw on traditions, values, folktales, and so on, that are already present in the culture of the constituency; (2) empirical credibility—the frame must have an apparent evidential basis; and (3) experiential commensurability—the social problems that the frame attempts to address must have penetrated constituents' lives. (Babb, 1996, p. 1034)

As such, rhetoric serves to frame what we think and believe in our social and political world. With the contemporary issue of immigration, we can see discursive framing at work; in fact, there are a few different types of frames that exist.

For the pro-immigrant side of the dispute, some liberals frame the debate in terms of racism. This occurs when opposing positions are characterized as motivated by racism. Racial framing is quite effective and persuasive, as we can see with the following:

> The "illegal alien" rhetoric is highly popular with racial demagogues. Stressing illegality provides a way to seed racial fears without directly referencing race. Scapegoating unauthorized immigrants carries a façade of neutrality insofar as it purports to refer to all persons present in the United States without proper authorization. Ostensibly, this would include the German citizen here on a tourist visa who takes a job, or, the Canadian who enters as a visitor but decides to live in Aspen indefinitely. Yet these are not the faces that come to mind when the term is bandied about. Rather, the usual suspects—the unavoidable suspects when Tea Party patriots spit out the phrase at rallies on the southern border—are undocumented immigrants from Latin America, especially Mexico. Indeed, often it seems the term is not limited to immigrants at all, but rather expresses an alarm that applies to almost all persons of Latino descent, most of whom are US citizens. By constantly drumming on the crises posed by "illegals," the right fuels a racial frenzy but can deny its intention to do any such thing. (López, 2014, pp. 122–123)

Therefore, any argument against immigrants can be labeled "racist." As Aviva Chomsky notes, "Noncitizens make easy targets and convenient scapegoats" (Chomsky, 2007, p. xi). By constructing the debate in terms of a false dichotomy, pro-immigrant rhetoric stacks the deck in its favor. For example, one Hispanic, pro-immigration group, the League of United Latin America Citizens (LULAC), formerly had a website that displayed this language:

> Those who oppose immigrants' rights often blame immigration and immigrants for an array of social problems, from unemployment to the poor quality of public schools to urban sprawl and congestion. … While such problems are all too real, blaming immigrants for causing them is a scapegoat that is ultimately rooted in racism as it serves to divide people who might otherwise make common cause. (quoted in Johnson, 2008)

The racism frame can be quite persuasive, as most people desire to avoid charges of racist inclinations. Of course, the topic of immigration itself is a racially charged one. It certainly does not help that, according to the Southern Poverty Law Center, many hate groups "consistently try and exploit any public discussion that has some kind of racial angle, and immigration has worked for hate groups in America better than any issue in years" (Associated Press, 2006, n.p.).

Figure 6.7: Mexicans in Their Homeland.

Anti-immigrant groups also frame the debate in specific ways. Several frames are utilized by anti-immigrant individuals in order to portray immigrants as "criminals, terrorists, and welfare cheats—and accused of everything from increasing crime and invading communities to stealing the jobs of hard-working citizens to destroying the environment" (Phillips, 2002, n.p.). In particular, anti-immigrant rhetoric frames immigrants as an illegal problem, a security problem, an amnesty problem, and an undocumented problem (Lakoff and Ferguson, 2006). As "illegals," immigrants are portrayed as criminals and as deviants, as if they are naturally bad people, instead of as human beings who may need compassion or opportunities to improve themselves (Huber, 2009). The security frame paints immigrants as risks who may jeopardize the national security of the United States. The amnesty frame suggests that "the fault lies with the immigrants, and it is a righteous act for the US Government to pardon them" (Lakoff and Ferguson, 2006, n.p.). Finally, some anti-immigrant groups characterize immigrants as "undocumented," primarily to appear benevolent and compassionate. However, calling immigrants "undocumented" implies that they "should be docu-mented," and, as such, reinforces the underlying premise of the illegality frame (Lakoff and Ferguson, 2006, n.p.).

Therefore, the extremes of the immigration debate try to frame the topic in ways that suit their respective ideological positions. Because partisan participants in the immigration conversation are trying to persuade their followers and others who may be vacillating in their beliefs, framing is a technique that is intimately connected to the way we make sense of our world. It is what Benford and Snow call "meaning work—the struggle over the production of mobilizing and countermobilizing ideas and meanings" (Benford & Snow, 2000, p. 613). Naturally, linguistically framing the dispute in these ways impedes solution-oriented discourse (Phillips, 2002). In so doing, rhetorical framing reinforces the polarization that often occurs when discussing immigration in everyday discourse.

THE DIVISIVE DISCOURSE INVOLVING IMMIGRATION ISSUES

As we know, immigration has become a very pertinent and current social, political, and economic issue. The amount of illegal or unauthorized immigrants in the United States is estimated to be between eleven and twelve million people. The overwhelming majority of these immigrants come from Latin America, and most of those emanate from Mexico. As such, immigration-related issues along our southern border are extremely important. The rhetorical tactics used by pundits and advocates on both sides of the issue have intensified and become more heated. I shall examine the different rhetorical tactics employed. For structural and organizational purposes, I analyze these tactics as they are used to support the main thematic arguments used in the immigration debate.

Incidentally, for simplicity's sake, I will frequently refer to the polarized positions in this debate as "pro-immigration" (or "pro-immigrant") and "anti-immigration" (or "anti-immigrant"). I mean no offense by using these labels, should anyone be offended. I am quite aware of the power of language, especially naming, as I described in the earlier part of this chapter. However, I am merely using them as a way to succinctly represent the major claims made by extremists involved in the immigration dispute. Furthermore, since the United States permits several hundred thousand immigrants per year to enter the country and since we have several million who are unauthorized, I will approach the argumentative themes by first identifying how anti-immigrant groups rhetorically frame the controversy. After all, if we have immigrants entering our country now (unauthorized and authorized), the burden is on those who have concerns.

Before examining the arguments and rhetorical tactics used in this debate, I want to point out that both sides of this issue have access to multiple scholarly studies that can be used to justify their perspectives. According to Phillips, "One study's data on the costs and taxes paid by immigrants can easily refute another's, and the accuracy of such data is difficult to ascertain. Subtle methodological distinctions between various studies often fail to translate into effective arguments. They usually boil down to ideological differences in the sponsoring organizations' or authors' perspectives" (Phillips, 2002, n.p.). The use of studies in virtually all social issues, but immigration in particular, points to the persuasive seduction as well as pitfalls of using deductive arguments. In essence, we have:

Premise 1: Studies prove that illegal immigration is harmful.
Premise 2: Illegal immigration is increasing.
Conclusion: Therefore, we should curb illegal immigration.

Or, the opposite can be illustrated:

Premise 1: Studies prove that unauthorized immigration is helpful to the economy.
Premise 2: Our current economy is in trouble.
Conclusion: Therefore, we should allow more unauthorized immigrants into the country.

Either way, these deductive arguments demonstrate how the argument makes sense structurally, but if one of the premises is faulty (i.e., the premise relying on studies), then the entire argument becomes suspect. Additionally, there are conflicting studies that lump together illegal and legal immigrants without distinguishing between the two. There are reports with outdated numbers and sometimes no real numbers at all. There are government reports, academic studies and statements by groups that have a clear agenda, either for or against illegal immigrants. The claims can inflame the debate, even though many make no distinction between legal and illegal immigrants and aim vitriol at anyone of Hispanic descent. Others have little to no basis in reality. (Davidson et al., 2010, n.p.)

Questions about methodology and accuracy of the studies are extremely important, especially when comparing and contrasting the studies, since they often contradict one another. Given this, it is also necessary for us to view the other types of rhetorical tactics used. It is crucial that we not become distracted or embroiled in the studies cited for particular arguments to the extent that we might overlook other tactics that are used.

Most of the arguments against immigration are economic in nature. The root of this concern primarily resides with the notion that immigrants drain our economy in various ways. Most immigrants tend to be "low-skilled" laborers (i.e., they lack formal or advanced education), so when they enter the United States, there is a risk that they will be a drag on social services, like welfare, and they will not contribute much to the overall economy since they lack the skills necessary for high-paying, high-contributing occupations. Other economic consequences also occur; anything that puts a strain on society without contributing much in return may be considered problematic for the economy. And that is precisely the premise behind many of the anti-immigration arguments. Yet focusing or over-relying on economic considerations may overlook other important factors in the immigration debate, not the least of which may be the contributions immigrants can make to society in both economic and non-economic ways (Phillips, 2002).

Jobs

The most frequently used argument against immigration, particularly unauthorized immigration, is the impact on American jobs. The presumption here is that if immigrants enter the United States, they obtain jobs that citizens would otherwise receive. This claim is particularly persuasive during periods of economic stress, like the recent historic recession (Bunch, 2011; Gomez, 2014; Phillips, 2002). A right-wing, anti-immigration group, the Federation of American Immigration Reform (FAIR), summarizes the perception that unauthorized immigrants steal American jobs: "An estimated 1,880,000 American workers are displaced from their jobs every year by immigration; the cost for providing welfare and assistance to these Americans is over $15 billion a year" (Garling, 2000, p. 7). This statistic is quite old, yet it remains on FAIR's seminal document on the impacts of immigration. Furthermore, the study that FAIR cites comes from a Rice University report that FAIR commissioned (see FAIR, 2013). It is not uncommon for conservative and liberal entities to cite friendly individuals or groups that are aligned in ideology, but the average consumer of information does not understand this unless he or she digs below the surface.

Other conservative provocateurs reinforce the idea that so-called illegal immigrants take jobs away from hard-working Americans. The crazed radio talk show host Michael Savage says that "illegal aliens take jobs from American citizens in an economy where the unemployment rate among citizens remains close to 10 percent and real unemployment is closer to 20 percent" (Savage, 2010, p. 191). And Savage's conservative kin, Glenn Beck, makes similar statements. Beck is fond of responding to the counterargument made by liberals that immigrants do jobs that Americans either don't want to do or cannot do. In response, Beck says, "If every illegal alien left the country tomorrow, we'd still build new homes and grow fruit and (reluctantly) vegetables … by leveling the playing field," and he concludes that when "fair jobs become available, Americans line up to do them" (Beck, 2010a, pp. 137–138).

Of course, liberals rebut these claims by suggesting that immigrants take jobs Americans do not normally want to do (Camarota & Zeigler, 2009). This is particularly true for low-skilled jobs for at least two different reasons. First, most Americans strive to land occupations that require more advanced skills because such jobs pay more. Second, even if some tension exists between immigrants and natives over low-skilled labor, such jobs tend to be plentiful, indicating actual threats to American jobs posed by immigrants are minimal (Kane & Johnson, 2006).

Furthermore, a pro-immigration position argues that unauthorized immigrants not only do not hurt Americans' jobs, but the immigrants benefit the economy as a whole. Interestingly, even the conservative think tank the Heritage Foundation illustrates this point. It claims that both low- and high-skilled immigrants help the economy because they "boost national output, enhance specialization, and provide a net economic benefit." The Heritage Foundation relies on an Economic Report of the President to show that "the benefits and costs of immigration shows the benefits of immigration exceed the costs":

> Studies show that a 10 percent share increase of immigrant labor results in roughly a 1 percent reduction in native wages-a very minor effect; Most immigrant families have a positive net fiscal impact on the U.S., adding $88,000 more in tax revenues than they consume in services; and Social Security payroll taxes paid by improperly identified (undocumented) workers have led to a $463 billion funding surplus. (Kane and Johnson, 2006, n.p.)

What's more, apparently, millions of Americans also prosper as a result of immigrant-owned businesses that provide nearly "$780 billion to the US economy" (Hillcox, 2013, n.p.).

Ultimately, the impact of immigrants on the American economy is complex. The first thing to which we should pay attention is the type of studies used to justify the economic arguments made. With no shortage of studies from which to choose, advocacy groups can avail themselves of any number of reports to support their positions. Without questioning the methodology and potential bias of such studies, arguments can, and are, easily skewed and manipulated for ideological purposes.

Additionally, the complexity of this issue can be seen in other ways. It probably depends on if someone is referring to low-skilled jobs or high-skilled jobs. It also makes a difference depending on the geographical location in the United States (the Southwest, for example, is probably harder hit in some ways than other parts of the country), what the overall state of the national economy is like, and how other minority groups are being treated (Camarota & Zeigler, 2009). The potential economic ramifications on other minority and marginalized groups is the subject of the next argumentative thread.

Wage Suppression

This contention is a variation of the "immigrants take the jobs of Americans" argument. Also referred to as "wage depression," this argument claims that low-skilled immigrants work jobs at wages extremely lower than the average wage. When this occurs, it drives the overall levels of wages downward. In this way, the salaries of citizens, particularly in low-skilled occupations, are suppressed, or squeezed.

It is not surprising that we see the Federation for American Immigration Reform (FAIR) at the forefront of this position. In 2000, FAIR analyst Scipio Garling reported that "half of all wage depression among high-school dropouts in America is attributable to job competition from immigrants. Because too much immigration keeps wages low, wage increases in low-immigration cities have been 48 percent higher than in high-immigration cities" (Garling, 2000, p. 7). FAIR updated its analysis in 2013 by noting,

> If the hiring of illegal alien workers is prevalent in a sector of the economy, as it has become the case in seasonal crop agriculture, the willingness of foreign workers to accept lower wages because of their illegal status acts to

depress wages and working conditions for all workers in that occupation. This in turn makes employment in that sector less attractive to U.S. workers who have other options. The result is a form of circular logic, i.e., the more that illegal aliens are able to take jobs in a sector of the economy, the less attractive the sector becomes to U.S. workers, and the greater appearance of validity to the lie that only illegal aliens are willing to take jobs in the sector. (FAIR, 2013, n.p.)

And, citing Census Bureau data, Camarota and Zeigler report that in "high-immigrant occupations, 57 percent of natives have no more than a high school education. In occupations that are less than 20 percent immigrant, 35 percent of natives have no more than a high school education. And in occupations that are less than 10 percent immigrant, only 26 percent of natives have no more than a high school education" (Camarota & Zeigler, 2009, n.p.). Of course, conservative extremists like Glenn Beck make similar points when they claim "minorities and the poor are hit the hardest by illegal labor entering the market" (Beck, 2010a, p. 137). Thus, in low-skilled and low-education careers, unauthorized immigrants seem to have a wage-suppression effect.

However, when we look at this argument carefully, we should note that, again, the distinction between low-skilled and high-skilled occupations is important. First, wage suppression rarely, if ever, occurs for high-skilled jobs. But even when wage suppression does happen in low-skilled contexts, it has a "negligible" impact (Davidson et al., 2010). Apparently, wage suppression does not occur often, but the positive contributions made by immigrants to the overall economy in the form of lower-priced goods and services and lower costs to employers outweigh those instances of wage suppression (Davidson et al., 2010).

Furthermore, some studies suggest that immigrant labor may actually improve the wage conditions for workers as a whole (Postrel, 2005). A study conducted by Ottaviano and Peri reports,

> It turns out empirically and theoretically that immigration, as we have known it during the nineties, had a sizeable beneficial effect on wages of US born workers. For a flow of migrants that increases total employment by 10%, with a distribution among skills just as the one observed in the nineties, US-born workers experience an increase of 3–4 percentage points of their wage. This happened because US-born and Foreign-born workers are not perfectly substitutable even when they have similar observable skills. (Ottaviano & Peri, 2005, p. 28)

Hence, the wage-suppression argument suggests that we should look carefully at the types of studies groups use to support their arguments, and we should closely examine the methods used by these studies to question the veracity of their findings.

Divide and Conquer

Some arguments in the immigration debate emphasize how immigrants distract from important issues affecting other racial minorities, namely African Americans. Similarly, anti-immigrant discourse also pits "legal" immigrants against "illegal" immigrants, "perpetuating a false divide in immigrant communities" (Phillips, 2002, n.p.). The purpose of this type of rhetoric is to pit "low-wage workers of color against each other" (Phillips, 2002, n.p.). The rhetorical tactic of divide and conquer is a very powerful maneuver, and one used mainly to maintain the dominant power of hegemonic structures (Hall, 1986). As Gramsci argues, "Reality is the deep and bottomless abyss that capitalism has dug between proletariat and bourgeoisie and the ever growing antagonism between the two classes" (Gramsci, 1975, p. 134). In other words, systems of power, like capitalism or dominant culture, have their interests served when marginalized power groups are at odds with one another, as opposed to confronting the hegemony. After all, if peripheral groups—like immigrants versus African Americans—are struggling amongst themselves, elites are shielded from contestations of power.

This "divide and conquer" argument, as I call it, is primarily an anti-immigrant position since it tries to show how mainly conservative groups attempt to place a wedge in between similarly disenfranchised groups. Here is an example of anti-immigrant rhetoric that engages in the divide and conquer tactic:

> Illegal immigration is not a victimless crime; it robs our poor, our minorities, and our most vulnerable of opportunity. With about 12-million already here, and over 100-thousand rushing across the border currently, illegal immigrants young and old are typically poorly-educated and looking for jobs available to unskilled workers. These are the starter jobs that are needed by America's poor, minorities and vulnerable who also need low-skill starter jobs. The black unemployment rate is about double the overall unemployment rate. For young black people it's even higher. They are hurt worse than most others by the flood of illegal immigration. It's made even worse when those who break the law to be here are rewarded with housing, health care, food, education, legal aid and more at the expense of American taxpayers. And when millions of Americans wish they had a job, they don't need illegal competition that makes it harder to get that job. (Istook, 2014, n.p.)

In this way, statements by anti-immigrant entities can utilize a variety of sub-arguments to heighten the wedge between marginalized groups. Quite simply, they try to "drive wedges between groups of immigrants based on differences such as legal status or national origin," as well as other minority groups. "Fueled by racial, ethnic, and economic tensions, anti-immigrant sentiment has been extremely effective at pitting low-wage workers of color against each other" (Phillips, 2002, n.p.).

Welfare

Many who advocate anti-immigration arguments fear that immigrants are a drain on welfare. Also known as the "bottomless cornucopia" argument, the claim is that immigrants utilize a variety of social services, all of which are funded by tax dollars. Of course, social services are not "bottomless" because tax dollars eventually evaporate, but the services are still, nevertheless, perceived to be "bottomless" (Gilchrist, 2014b). Rhetorical characterizations of "free-riders," "moochers," or "leeches" are common with this sort of argument.

Conservative pundit Michael Savage claims that "not all illegals are actually doing productive work. In fact, a significant percentage of them are not here to work. They're here to work the system" (Savage, 2010, p. 191). By citing the ultra-right wing and anti-immigrant think tank the Center for Immigration Studies, Savage reports that "illegal households created a net fiscal deficit at the federal level of as much as $400 billion," such that the "middle class must pick up the tab" (Savage, 2010, p. 191).

Other anti-immigrant sentiments make similar arguments. FAIR's Scipio Garling says that the "immigrant rate of using means-tested welfare programs (at 20.7 percent) is nearly fifty percent higher than native rate of usage (at 14.1 percent). That gap between the native and immigrant rate of welfare usage has doubled in the last ten years" (Garling, 2000, p. 8). And conservative poster boy Glenn Beck says that illegal immigrants are "50 percent more likely to use welfare than citizens" (Beck, 2010a, p. 139). Concerning a topic that most conservatives already oppose—welfare—the idea that immigrants utilize it more than citizens means that conservatives really become incensed.

However, if we were to prevent, somehow, all unauthorized immigrants from receiving any sort of welfare, it probably would yield no net economic advantage. Karl Rogers notes that studies suggest how "barring illegal immigrants from welfare does not achieve any significant change in welfare costs because the vast majority of welfare is claimed on behalf on their U.S.-born children, who are American citizens" (Rogers, 2011, p. 101).

Furthermore, unauthorized immigrants pay all sorts of taxes that then are used to fund welfare and other social services benefits (Davidson et al., 2010). Liberal talk show host Bill Press notes that undocumented workers "pay sales taxes, just like all the rest of us. If, as many do, they get a paycheck using a fake Social Security number, they pay payroll taxes and the FICA tax—which, not being citizens, they will never get back" (Press, 2010, p. 170). This means that even if immigrant workers are "paid under the table" by employers who do so illegally, the immigrants still pay a substantial amount in taxes. Immigrants pay enough in taxes, in other words, that "in aggregate and over the longer term, tax revenues of all types generated by immigrants—both legal and unauthorized—exceed the cost of the services they use" (Press, 2010, p. 170). Simply put, "Unauthorized immigrants pay considerably more in taxes—typically through payroll withholding—than they receive in social services" (López, 2014, p. 122).

Finally, like most arguments on this topic, much misinformation occurs. Conservatives are fond of reporting how illegal immigrants suck up the resources regarding food stamps. However, most illegal immigrants do not even quality for food stamps, and, if they do, it is because someone in their family is a citizen, like children who were born in the United States. Additionally, any instances of illegal immigrants receiving food stamps have been extremely exaggerated (Davidson et al., 2010). Thus, while some unauthorized immigrants undoubtedly find access to food stamps, the larger nature of the problem is exaggerated. But, as with most components of the immigration issue, certain aspects probably depend on one's perspective.

Healthcare

A version of the welfare argument concerns healthcare, which is also largely funded through tax dollars. Depending on one's point of view, whether immigrants are seen as paying their share in taxes goes a long way toward shaping the healthcare argument as well.

By drawing on right-wing sources, Glenn Beck announces that America "spends more than $4.7 billion a year on health care for illegal aliens" (Beck, 2010a, p. 139). Similarly, FAIR reports, based on its own studies, that "forty-three percent of immigrants under 65 have no health insurance, and the cost of their healthcare is passed on to the public: the annual bill to taxpayers for immigrant Medicaid is $14 billion and for Medicare $6.1 billion" (Garling, 2000, p. 7).

But we know the issue is more complex than what is portrayed by Beck and others. For instance,

> Federal law prohibits undocumented immigrants from enrolling in Medicaid and CHIP (Children's Health Insurance Program), although Medicaid will cover a medical emergency. How much money this costs taxpayers is unclear, since some states, including Utah, don't ask the immigration status of people whose emergency is covered by Medicaid. (Davidson et al., 2010, n.p.)

And in terms of immigrants clogging and draining emergency room resources, we simply do not know the full impact of immigrants' impact since hospitals do not keep accurate records of citizenship status. Furthermore, most of the conservative evidence relies on data that does not distinguish between illegal and legal immigrants (Davidson et al., 2010, n.p.).

What we do know, however, is that the use and costs of healthcare for immigrants is far lower than that of U.S. natives (Stimpson et al., 2013). In fact, immigrants paid into Medicare nearly $14 billion in 2009 as a result of payroll taxes (Zallman et al., 2015). We also know that in general, immigrants pay a substantial amount in taxes that not only positively impacts healthcare costs, but also helps compensate for other welfare programs. For instance, according to the Institute on Taxation and Economic Policy (ITEP), immigrants "pay billions of dollars each year in state and local taxes" (2017, n.p.).

More specifically, the ITEP report notes that "undocumented immigrants contribute significantly to state and local taxes, collectively paying an estimated $11.74 billion a year" (2012, n.p.). Furthermore, many studies have documented and reported that immigrants have an insignificant impact on the healthcare infrastructure because they either use medical services less than American citizens or because they offset their use by paying taxes (see Goldman et al., 2006; Huang et al., 2006; Ku, 2009; Mohanty et al., 2005; Ortega et al., 2007; Prentice et al., 2005; Stimpson et al., 2010; Tarraf et al., 2012).

Education

Like the debate about welfare and healthcare, "illegal" immigrants are said to suck up education resources, especially since many immigrants arrive into the U.S. with their children who are eligible for public schooling. According to FAIR, "the estimated cost to the American taxpayer for the education of immigrants' children is over $30 billion a year" (Garling, 2000, p. 8). Additionally, according to Glenn Beck, "We're also spending about $30 billion each year to educate illegal aliens in our schools—money that we could probably use to figure out how to educate our own children since we're doing such a miserable job at it right now" (Beck, 2010a, p. 139).

Yet, like the welfare and healthcare debate, the education issue resides mostly on the taxation issue—if immigrants pay their share in taxes, would the drain on educational resources really be a problem? According to the pro-immigrant study conducted by Lee Davidson and associates, immigrants pay more than enough to cover their use of education costs. Plus, the overall impact on education is not very significant since information from the Congressional Budget Office in December 2007 indicate that only about 4 percent of children who are school-age can be classified as "illegals" (Davidson et al., 2010, n.p.).

Housing Pressures

In some locales, particularly larger cities, immigrants are perceived to place undue stress on housing (Garling, 2000). Mounting population intensity causes urban areas to expand, causing what is known as "urban sprawl," which "increases traffic, saps local resources, and destroys open space," and, if unexpected or if there is improper preparation, the sprawl can threaten the "environment, health, and quality of life" of communities (Bhatta, 2010, p. 29). Of course, there are many causes to urban sprawl (such as economic growth, changing agricultural developments, geography changes, legal disputes, etc.), and the impacts to sprawl are occasionally positive, such as pressure to improve transportation, attractive prospects for foreign investment, added multicultural benefits, etc. (Bhatta, 2010). In the context of American immigration, however, urban sprawl and other housing pressures are rarely characterized in positive terms, in part because arguments "blaming immigrants for dwindling resources can be very powerful to people frustrated with traffic jams, overcrowded classrooms, and long unemployment lines in their communities" (Phillips, 2002, n.p.).

Crime

Another common argument from immigration opponents is that immigrants increase crime rates. The thinking here is that immigrants enter into the U.S. and, when faced with poor job prospects or other economic concerns, resort to crime. Some immigrants may already be prone to crime when they arrive. For example, it is suspected that many immigrants are already members of gangs, such as the infamously violent MS-13 (Hodges, 2014; The Inquisitr, 2014). Additionally, even if immigrants themselves are not criminal, the strain on the economy caused by their presence in the United States may encourage others, like poor U.S. citizens, to engage in criminal activities. Simply put, conservative, anti-immigrant sentiment claims that "if you're in the country illegally and you commit another crime, it's a crime that could have, and should have, been prevented by more stringent enforcement of immigration laws. It's a crime that's an affront to decent, law-abiding American citizens everywhere. The blood of the victims of these crimes is on the hands of America's elected officials, legislators, and judges" (Savage, 2010, p. 200).

It is no doubt difficult to ascertain the underlying motives of immigrants, but right-wing groups use the number of illegal immigrants in our jails and prisons as evidence of their criminal activity. Glenn Beck, for example, reports that "about 17 percent of all those in federal prison are illegal aliens—an astonishing number when you consider that they represent only three percent of the population" (Beck, 2010a, p. 139). Interestingly, although the argument is the same, the evidence used by Michael Savage differs by way of inflation: "Criminal aliens are increasingly becoming a burden on our Federal prison system as well, accounting for more than 29 percent of all prisoners in Federal Bureau of Prisons facilities" (Savage, 2010, p. 191). Similarly, FAIR declares that "one fourth of the federal prison population is foreign-born, and the INS must deport over 30,000 criminal aliens every year" (Garling, 2000, p. 7).

The idea that immigrants commit crimes reinforces the idea that they are "illegals," even if crossing the border is just a civil infraction (Butterfield, 2005; Cravens, 2013). Thus, it probably does not worry conservative groups that different sources for whom they typically look for evidence differ on the statistics of immigrant criminals. Yet, like most political and social issues, we must carefully question the evidence used by groups, especially if such groups have ideological predispositions. In this case, "Many specific claims about illegal aliens and crime on the Internet seem to lack credible sources." For instance, a common claim "cited as a source for '12 Americans killed each day by illegals' is a 2006 letter from Rep. Steve King of Iowa in which he makes this claim but cites no source" (Davidson et al., 2010, n.p.). In this way, Davidson et al. note that the number of immigrants in prison are proportionate to their overall population size, and violent crime along the Mexican border has remained stagnant, even while crimes within Mexico have exponentially increased (Davidson et al., 2010, n.p.). Citing several studies, López summarizes that "undocumented immigrants from Latin America commit far fewer depredations, not far more, than citizens" (López, 2014, p. 122). Indeed, Spenkuch (2013) has extensively studied the relationship between immigrants and

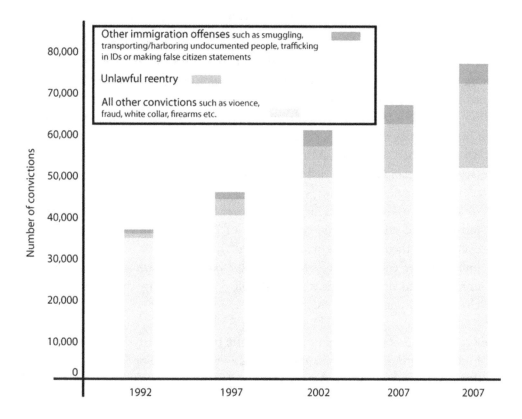

Figure 6.8: Federal Crimes.

crime, and he notes that "there is no clear evidence for an effect of immigration on violent crime, independent of whether immigration and crime are measured in logs or levels" (p. 19). Spenkuch also claims that, "While immigrants are known to have lower levels of education, lower wages, and higher unemployment rates than natives, previous studies have not found a relationship between immigration and crime, or proxies thereof" (2013, p. 22). A study that examines immigrant neighborhoods in New York City found that, "there is no evidence that crime rates are higher in places with higher immigration rates. Indeed, immigration status alone often means decreased crime rates" (Long, 2013a n.p.). According to researchers Davies and Fagan (2012),

> In short, the results presented here support the emerging consensus that immigration does not lead to higher rates of crime, and in some instances protects against crime. The story of immigration and crime in NYC comprises many chapters that reflect the unique experiences of different racial and ethnic groups. Each of the groups has added to the revitalization of the city in its own unique way, through repopulation, participation in niche economies, and entrepreneurial spirit. (p. 119)

Other studies support the findings of Spenkuch (see Bersani, 2014).

Terrorism

Like the argument concerning crime, many immigration opponents portray immigrants as terrorism threats. As Chavez (2013) notes, "Through the media, politicians desiring to restrict immigration have been able to represent undocumented immigrants as undeserving criminals and possible terrorists" (p. 10). Chavez also explains that this "Latino Threat Narrative" is very effective "precisely because its basic premises are taken for granted as true" (2013, p. 45). This is clearly and obviously an appeal to fear. The "label 'terrorist' scares and intimidates citizens" (Artz, 2011). A former assistant secretary of homeland security made the assessment that immigrants

> seeking to cross our borders illegally do present a threat—including potential terrorists and criminals. The current flow of illegal immigrants and people overstaying their visas has made it extremely difficult for our border and interior enforcement agencies to be able to focus on the terrorists, organized criminals, and violent felons who use the cloak of anonymity that the current chaotic situation offers. (Verdery, 2006, p. 2)

Based on these sorts of hypothetical assessments by an authority in the government, anti-immigrant groups frame their arguments about terrorism. For example, Dan Stein, president of the Federation for American Immigration Reform (FAIR), is a die-hard, anti-immigrant radical who speculates that

> today we found out once again that our failure to control illegal immigration and our inability to manage the current caseload of people applying for immigration benefits poses a lethal risk to the nation ... terrorists can and will take advantage of the same unenforced immigration policies that have flooded this country with illegal immigrants—we now have irrefutable proof that the terrorists understand where we are vulnerable. We can be certain that there are many more terrorists who entered the country illegally or overstayed visas. (Stein, 2007, n.p.)

It is not uncommon for these accusations to happen without evidence (Keating, 2014). The outspoken conservative, Ann Coulter, for example, characterizes Mexican immigrants as an "immigrant crime wave" (Man, 2015, n.p.). Coulter even resorts to the hyperbolic *absurdio* when she yelps, "Were we short on rapists? By definition, we're talking about people who have no right to be here. If Mexico is sending us 2 rapists—THEY'RE SENDING US RAPISTS" (cited in Man, 2015, n.p.). In fact, while FAIR argues for tougher security along our southern border, the evidence linking immigration to terrorism cited here by Stein was the capture of six Islamic radicals in New Jersey who were plotting to attack Fort Dix (Stein, 2007). There was zero evidence that the terrorists came into the country via our southern border, regardless of how vehemently anti-immigration advocates argue otherwise (Liberty Counsel, 2007). Even the acclaimed author Brigitte Gabriel (2008) argues that terrorists are aligning with the Latino gang MS-13 to threaten a WMD-style event, but all she provides is innuendo and conspiratorial dot-connecting, rather than any hard, demonstrable proof. What's more, it is more likely that they entered through Canada. But the enthymeme is powerful—if immigrants can cross over our borders illegally, it means we have unprotected and porous borders; therefore, an unsecure border poses a security risk. In our post-9/11 world, a "security" risk naturally entails potential terrorist threats (Camarota, 2002).

There are other examples of when anti-immigrant rhetoric emphasizes the potential risk of terrorism. For instance, the polarizing conservative pundit Phyllis Schlafly argues that,

> the terrorists are foreigners, most or all of whom should not have been allowed to live in our country.... It should be repeated over and over again: The terrorism threat is from illegal aliens who are allowed to live in our midst—and this is a failure of our immigration laws and our immigration officials .... The policy of opening our borders to anyone who wants to sneak into our country illegally—or to remain illegally after entering legally—must be exposed and terminated. This is the most important security precaution our government must take. (Schlafly, 2001, n.p.)

This sentiment, separated from the context of the larger report, seems to suggest that all immigrants—including the ones from Mexico and Central America—are terrorism threats. As such, our borders should be protected more. However, in this report, Schlafly is specifically discussing the 9/11 terrorists, who were "the plotting foreign terrorists" who "crossed our borders and lived in our country illegally" (Schlafly, 2001, n.p.).

Schlafly is not the only conservative muckraker who makes the terrorism argument. In fact, Texas governor Rick Perry recently said our border with Mexico risks inviting terrorists from ISIS (Keating, 2014). And Newt Gingrich "links the threat of terrorism to the immigration debate, arguing against 'amnesty' for undocumented workers" (Parker, 2007, n.p.). Ultimately, the terrorism argument is an appeal to fear, since Bill O'Reilly, who makes this argument often,

> is a classic scaremonger ... he knows how the idea of Hispanic foreigners infiltrating homes with murder in mind plays to his audience. Unfortunately, this is the same kind of subtle racism that makes people buy the argument that because brown, Middle Eastern Muslims attacked us on 9/11, we would invade a country full of unrelated brown, Middle Eastern Muslims. (Amann, 2006, p. 33–34)

Notably, most of the fear appeals used regarding terrorism utilize examples of legal immigrants who are then extrapolated to portray illegal immigrants as the ones posing a national security threat (Beck, 2010a). Even reports that Middle Eastern terrorists have teamed with Mexican drug cartels to smuggle weapons and threaten the U.S. Army Base at Fort Huachuca are based on "anonymous" sources and specious claims with no factual evidence (Carter, 2007).

While not explicitly refuted by pro-immigrant groups, the argument about terrorism is fuzzy and specious. There is no evidence that terrorists enter into the United States from the south. On the contrary, we have documented instances for when immigrants entered into the U.S. via Canada (Camarota, 2002; Wucker, 2008), and the border with Canada is a considerable risk:

> Canadian security officials have long-admitted that there are approximately 50 terrorist groups operating in Canada. The border between Canada and the Lower 48 states is 4,000 miles long, and was patrolled by 300 Border Patrol agents on 9/11 (now increased to 1,000 agents). Throw in the additional 1,000 mile border between Canada and Alaska and you have a huge hole in the dike. (Nunez, 2004)

Additionally, some argue that instead of blaming unauthorized immigrants, we should make available more avenues for legal immigration (American Immigration Law Foundation, 2007; Ross, 2014). Plus, it seems that much of our post-9/11 terrorism hysteria in the context of illegal immigration is unfounded—the 9/11 foreign perpetrators had all entered the United States legally (Aviva Chomsky, 2007; deLespinasse, 2003, n.p.).

Diseases

Another claim is that immigrants carry diseases, and then bring those diseases into the United States. Michael Savage notes that "many illegals carry diseases that would otherwise cause them to be declined entry. This means that in many areas emergency rooms and hospitals are taxed beyond their limits dealing with diseases that are resistant to conventional treatments" (Savage, 2010, p. 207). The current problem of Central American minors fleeing across our borders only heightens the disease rhetoric. A venomous anti-immigrant Facebook group recently posted, "Your children are required to have their imms up to date. Yet these illegal children are NOT! Be prepared for outbreaks of once vaccine controlled diseases!" (Anti-Illegal Immigration/Stop Supporting, Start Deporting, 2014). Another vitriolic group announced this: "In recent days, health and violent crime concerns have been raised. As previously reported by The Inquisitr, a scabies outbreak halted flights of hundreds of illegal immigrants into the San Diego area. Reports that several cases of Swine Flu, Tuberculosis, and a scabies outbreak have also been announced" (*The Inquisitr*, 2014). And yet another conservative extremist group posted on its website that unauthorized immigrants "are a parasitic disease upon the fabric of America—whether or not they are bringing with them TB, Cholera, Typhoid, Typhus, Smallpox, Yellow Fever, Spanish Flu, Malaria, Measles, or

AIDS. Their very arrogant presence, along with our do nothing federal government, is truly sickening" (Whitley, 2014, n.p.).

It is one thing to characterize an entire group of people as "disease-spreaders," but it is quite another to implement laws to correspond to such apparent threats. Because of the recent and seemingly problematic nature of Central American immigrants, many municipalities have passed laws banning certain facilities to these immigrants due to "health and safety concerns." In fact, some Texas cities and "lawmakers in Vassar, Michigan; Hazleton, Pennsylvania; and Murrieta, California have made similar claims that undocumented immigrants are diseased and are refusing to house them" because "[they] have no assurances that these children have been screened for diseases, or that there have been background checks conducted on them or the people who are seeking to take custody of them," especially since "illegal immigrants carrying deadly diseases such as swine flu, dengue fever, Ebola virus and tuberculosis are particularly concerning" (Lee, 2014, n.p.).

But, like all controversial issues, there is another side of this story. First, most of the minors travelling from Central America are already vaccinated (Lee, 2014). Additionally, the most dangerous diseases referenced as a problem among immigrant populations could be discounted since

> tuberculosis, mainly an upper respiratory disease, it is not only treatable and curable, but the Department of Health and Human Services screens and quarantines the children who test positive for TB. In fact, the first step once kids are intercepted by border agents is to perform health screenings on each individual. The general population is likely safe from swine flu because the vaccine for it is part of the trivalent influenza vaccine that's administrated annually. Measles and chickenpox vaccines are available and already required. … Hand, Foot, and Mouth disease is a benign infection that can be picked up anywhere like the playground and in daycare centers. (Lee, 2014, n.p.)

Thus, like the portrayal of immigrant groups in the past (Lee, 2014), the recent waves of immigrants into the United States are sometimes characterized as disease-prone and virulent invaders of our country.

Invaders

Finally, all of these argumentative themes have one thing in common: immigrants, particularly those who are unauthorized, are perceived as invaders into our country. As an invasion, it is natural for many Americans to want to enhance security protections. But before heightened security can occur, anti-immigrant rhetoric must first persuade a sufficient amount of Americans that immigration is, in fact, an invasion.

A number of online sources characterize immigration as an "invasion." For instance, it is not uncommon to witness this sort of discourse: "They are NOT 'Undocumented Immigrants.' They are Foriegn Invaders!!! [sic] They are perverting the 14th Amendment of the Constitution of the United States for their gain (freebies from the gov't for their children)" (Anti-Illegal Immigration/Stop Supporting, Start Deporting, 2014). This is also seen from a recently formed group, the Mothers Against Illegal Aliens, who have this to say:

> The United States of America is under "Martial Law" in every respect of this issue (the invasion of our southern border) because we the People of the United States of America are being FORCED to ACCEPT the LAWLESSNESS OF OUR OWN GOVERNMENT! It is no different if soldiers were marching down our streets! The PEOPLE of the United States of America do not have a choice or a say in the violations of our Constitution that the GOVERNMENT IS ENGAGED IN! Protest as we may, the American People are being ignored and abandoned as is our RULE OF LAW! We are UNDER MARTIAL LAW!!!! WE ARE BEING FORCED to accept this violent corruption of our laws by our own President, Congress, Courts, and Public Agencies by their use of tax payer money! Religious institutions are aiding and abetting the corruption that is being fomented by our government by using GOVERNMENT GRANTS to set up Resort Like Housing for these ILLEGAL ALIENS ALL ACROSS THE COUNTRY, the government is taking whatever in -your-face action they need to accomplish their treason! What will it take before our Representatives listen to the Majority and put an end to this lawlessness? (Mothers Against Illegal Aliens, 2014, n.p.)

And this sentiment is echoed by the so-called "Minutemen," who view their role as a constitutional posse to protect our southern border. According to the Minutemen's founder and organizer, Jim Gilchrist, they are positioned to

> stop an invasion. This offensive is an invasion, not led by troops, but by divisions of mothers, children and young adults marching north from Central America and Mexico. It is an offensive that shows no signs of slowing down but instead is spreading to other nations, putting America in even greater peril. Patriots around our nation are sounding the alarm as the Middle East and parts of Africa also pour their legions into Mexico that so they, too, can march north into the United States. (The Inquisitr, 2014)

But, as we know, since language and framing is so vital to the way we interpret our social reality, we should remember that "the word 'invasion' is used by the Minutemen and right-wing bloggers to discuss the wave of people crossing the border. Right-wing language experts intent on keeping them out suggest using the world 'aliens' whenever possible" (Lakoff and Ferguson, 2006, n.p.).

English Only

Another controversial issue related to immigration is the concept of "English Only." For some Americans, the idea that everyone should speak English seems commonsensical. If people live in the United States, the argument goes, they should speak the common language. But since many newcomers do not speak English, there are Americans who ardently believe that they should be required to speak English. There are, however, several variants of the English Only debate. At the extreme is the position that everyone should be required to speak English, period. Typically this argument entails compulsory English in all schools, all government and business dealings, and so on. Another version of the pro-English Only position is to minimize, if not eliminate entirely, expectations of language learning classes in K–12 other than English. In other words, we should not encourage bi- or multi-lingualism and, instead, we should privilege the teaching of English Only. Perhaps the most moderate version of the English Only position is the adoption of English Only in all government transactions and documents. Of course, there are folks who believe we should make English the "official" language of the United States, which would *de facto* make English the only language used in government policies as well as symbolically delegitimize other languages, such as Spanish, throughout the nation.

Arguments opposing English Only tend to be rather straightforward. One argument is a version of the old adage, "if it ain't broke, don't fix it." In other words, since there are virtually no significant problems occurring from newcomers and visitors speaking languages other than English, we do not need to alter anything. And, not only is there no real threat to English, as this argument goes, but immigrants groups generally become fluent in English during their second and third generation of living in the U.S. Indeed, the "rapid decline in use of Spanish in the Latino second and third-plus generations suggests that concerns about a threat to the prevalence of the English language are unfounded" (Chavez, 2013, p. 62). This argument is typically associated with the claim that proponents of English Only use the issue to inflame tensions and symbolically heighten awareness of differences and divisions among people in the country. This suggests that English Only adherents only raise this issue as a result of xenophobia, and they purposefully discuss English Only as a means of spreading fear and animosity. Another counter argument to English Only is that encouraging other languages prepares our youth for a more globalized world. Welcoming multiple languages, rather than restricting them, will only make us more competitive. Finally, some who oppose English Only call it "racist" as it intentionally demonizes and minimizes the languages of others. Using inflammatory labels generally exacerbates the issue and makes English Only advocates even more embittered.

One English Only proponent that received quite a bit of media attention is former Republican Speaker of the House and former presidential candidate, Newt Gingrich. In 2007, when speaking to the National Federation of Republican Women, Gingrich proposed that we require all government documents and policies be written in English, that we teach our children English Only, and that we require English competency for citizenship (*Associated Press*, 2007). Such suggestions are not necessarily divisive, but the manner in which Gingrich characterized these initiatives was:

> The American people believe English should be the official language of the government .... We should replace bilingual education with immersion in English so people learn the common language of the country and they learn the language of prosperity, not the language of living in a ghetto. (Gingrich, 2007b)

According to the *Associated Press*, Gingrich also stated back in 1995 that bilingualism poses "long term dangers to the fabric of our nation" and that "allowing bilingualism to continue to grow is very dangerous" (2007, n.p.).

Gingrich's 2007 comments elicited widespread negative reactions. Most critics of the remarks noted how Gingrich was contrasting English (as the language of prosperity) to that of Spanish (the language of the ghetto) in a way that arrogated English and viciously belittled Spanish. For instance, a couple of days after Gingrich's speech, one blogger lambasted the comparison between prosperity and the ghetto, calling Gingrich's remarks "bigotry" (Stickings, 2007, n.p.). Responding to critics, Gingrich issued an *apologia* on YouTube where he claimed his word choice was "poor," and he did not intend for his comments to be perceived as an attack on the Spanish language (Gingrich, 2007a, n.p.). To add *ethos* to his position, Gingrich delivered the apology entirely in Spanish, claiming that "I know that my Spanish is not perfect, but I am studying so it will be better" (Gingrich, 2007a, n.p.). To address the criticism directly, Gingrich pleaded that, "'But my point was simply this—in the United States, it is important to speak the English language well in order to advance and have success," and that his speech "is an expression of support for Latinos, not an attack on their language. I have never believed that Spanish is a language of people of low incomes, nor a language without beauty" (Gingrich, 2007a).

A few years later, during the early months of the most recent presidential campaign, former governor of Alaska and former vice presidential candidate Sarah Palin weighed in on the English Only debate, as well as the larger issue of immigration. During an interview with CNN's Jake Tapper, Palin commented, "We can send a message and say, 'You want to be in America, A, you'd better be here legally or you're out of here. B, when you're here, let's speak American. Let's speak English, and that's a kind of a unifying aspect of a nation is the language that is understood by all'" (cited in Feeney, 2015, n.p.). Clearly, there is no language called "American," but Palin's malapropism underscores the populist and nativist link between language and citizenship. Plus, to many conservatives and supporters of Palin's (Navarrette, 2008), referring to English as "American" resonates as accurate and patriotic.

Even Donald Trump entered the English Only debate during the 2016 presidential campaign. In September 2015, Trump reviled against Republican presidential opponent Jeb Bush's use of Spanish during Bush's campaign events. During an interview, Trump said, "I like Jeb. He's a nice man. But he should really set the example by speaking English while in the United States" (cited in McAfee, 2015, n.p.). One wonders whether Trump was jealous of Bush's Spanish-speaking abilities, or Trump was backlashing against Bush's statement in Miami that "*el hombre no es conservador*," claiming that Trump is not a conservative (McAfee, 2015, n.p.). While the federal government has not made English the official language, 31 states have ("Americans Overwhelmingly," 2014). Clearly the issue has salience with the American people. In fact, according to a Rasmussen poll, 83 percent of U.S. adults support English as the official language ("Americans Overwhelmingly," 2014). Given that the consensus of citizens believe English Only is a valued idea, the obloquy surrounding the issue is unlikely to abate anytime soon.

Birthright Citizenship

Another immigrant-related and controversial issue that Trump addressed during the campaign trail was the idea of "birthright citizenship" (Merolla et al., 2013). The Fourteenth Amendment to the U.S. Constitution stipulates that "all persons born or naturalized in the United States, and subject to the jurisdiction thereof, are citizens of the United States and of the state wherein they reside." This means, of course, that a child of undocumented immigrants, if born in the United States, automatically is considered a U.S. citizen. Despite the language of the Constitution, President Trump firmly believes that people born in the United States are not automatically citizens. One of the problems associated with birthright citizenship is that it "remains the biggest magnet for illegal immigration" (Kopan, 2015, n.p.). Additionally, Trump claims, "I don't think they have American citizenship and if you speak to some very, very good lawyers—and I know some will disagree—but many of them agree with me and you're going to find they do not have American citizenship. We have to start a process where we take back our country. Our country is going to hell" (cited in Diamond, 2015, n.p.). Thus, not only does Trump argue against the notion of birthright citizenship, but he also asserts that—somehow—birthright citizenship is causing the U.S. to go "to hell." This type of incendiary language certainly does not contribute to a temperate climate for conversation, and, now as president, he slants the discussion in a negative way and in the direction he wishes. Many conservatives argue that "having children become U.S. citizens is a motivating factor for immigrants to come into the country illegally, and that when the child reaches adulthood he or she can try to sponsor their parents for citizenship" (Kopan, 2015, n.p.). Thus, some sort of change should be made to the Fourteenth Amendment. In fact, during the 2016 presidential campaign, other Republicans echoed Trump's position—Rand Paul argued for 14th Amendment restrictions, Lindsey Graham said it is a "mistake," Marco Rubio advocated for a repeal of the 14th Amendment, and Louisiana Governor Bobby Jindal said it should be repealed (Kopan, 2015, n.p.). Only Jeb Bush said that birthright citizenship is a "constitutionally protected right," and, as such, should not be revoked (Kopan, 2015, n.p.).

Overall

I have tried to focus on the major argumentative threads concerning immigration. Undoubtedly, other themes exist, such as the argument that immigrants put a drain on energy usage (Garling, 2000) or that immigrants smuggle drugs, which is just a variant of the crime theme (Savage, 2010). These sorts of claims, even if they have some validity, occur infrequently and have relatively no impact on the larger discussion. Additionally, we must pay attention to the types of studies and methodologies used by partisans on this issue (Bean and Stevens, 2003). In the end, despite the separate argumentative themes and rhetorical tactics used, we should keep in mind how both sides of this issue frame the debate. When we do, the specific arguments and tactics emerge and are much easier to identify and follow.

CONCLUSION

Immigration is a timely and intense controversial topic. It strikes a nerve in many on both sides of the issue. Particularly during times of economic stress, the specter of non-citizens securing jobs, government services, and potentially promoting social ills, such as crime or terrorism, triggers alarms for many Americans. When popular media figures such as Michael Savage or Glenn Beck or groups such as FAIR or LULAC circulate exaggerations and innuendo, an already heated topic will naturally become even more contentious.

Because polarizing extremists disseminate their vitriol in various ways and in various contexts, but primarily in their own echo chambers, the issue of immigration spirals in intensity. The way the debate is articulated and framed undergirds the venom that is unleashed. We also know that the use of emotionally laden words can be very persuasive. As Corbett and Connors suggest,

> There's another method that speakers and writers use to stir emotions, which is not as dependable as methods we have been describing. This second method does not so much "earn" an emotional response as it "begs" for it. This is the method that relies for its effect mainly on the use of emotion-laden words. The author makes use of those honorific or pejorative terms, of those favorable or unfavorable connotations of words, that will touch an audience. (Corbett & Connors, 1999, p. 81)

When we combine the emotionally laden words, such as "illegal," with popular stereotypes, we encounter many fallacies, not the least of which is the fallacy of composition— the idea that a couple of parts create the sum, or a few bad apples create the idea that the entire group, in this case immigrants, are bad.

In the case of immigration, it is not enough to just say the issue is contested terrain, nor is it sufficient to say that there are pro-immigrant groups and anti-immigrant groups. The topic is much more complicated than that. For example, in Virginia, former

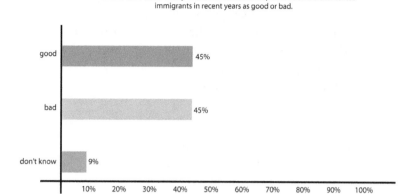

Americans were asked if they viewed the increased deportation of undocumented immigrants in recent years as good or bad.

good 45%

bad 45%

don't know 9%

10% 20% 30% 40% 50% 60% 70% 80% 90% 100%

Figure 6.9: Divided Views over Deportation.

Republican House minority leader Eric Cantor recently lost his primary election to a Tea Party candidate. Most political commentators speculate the reason for Cantor's loss was that the challenger characterized him as too closely aligned with Obama's policies of offering "amnesty and citizenship to illegal immigrants" (Lee, 2014, n.p.). Overall, this should not be too surprising to us since both the Republicans and the Democrats—and now the Tea Party—politicize immigration for their own electoral gains (Newell, 2014).

The polarizing nature of the immigration debate is succinctly stated by Jeb Bush and Clint Bolick:

> Even though immigration reform is one of the few major issues on which the potential for bipartisan consensus clearly exists, that consensus is constantly undermined, obviously by strident opposition at the extremes of both parties but also by a lack of political courage. All too often, elected officials who possess ample political capital to make comprehensive immigration reform a reality wither instead, in the face of hostile opposition from extreme elements of their respective partisan bases. … The combination of ideological rancor, demagoguery, and political cowardice is lethal, with the result that we remain saddled with an immigration regime that nearly everyone agrees is profoundly dysfunctional. (Bush and Bolick, 2013, pp. 5–6)

As a result, Americans appear to be divided on immigration (Maestas, 2014). Americans seem split: "Immigration legislation is stalled in the House, but the public continues to broadly support a path to legalization for undocumented immigrants. At the same time, however, Americans are evenly divided over the growing number of undocumented immigrants who have been deported from the U.S. in recent years, with as many viewing this as a good thing as a bad thing (45% each)" (Pew Research,

2014c, n.p.). Thus, immigration is an important, contemporary, and contentious issue that becomes polarizing when political pundits engage in their extremist and divisive discourse (Doherty and Suls, 2014). Nevertheless, ignoring the problems won't make them go away. And given the gridlock in Congress, Obama's procrastination on the issue and Trump's anti-immigrant positions, it seems like our politicians will continue with their inaction. This is extremely problematic, because if

> policy makers ignore this uncomfortable situation simply because it seems hard to change, or alternatively because it is easy to overlook during years when economic and job growth are strong, they risk a virulent and potentially harmful backlash against legal immigrants and immigration during years when circumstances become more difficult. (Bean & Stevens, 2003, p. 260)

IMAGE CREDITS

- Fig. 6.1: "Picture of Emma Lazarus," http://www.nps.gov/stli/historyculture/emma-lazarus.htm. Copyright in the Public Domain.
- Fig. 6.2: "Ceded Territory from Mexico, 1848," http://firedog520.tripod.com/. Copyright in the Public Domain.
- Fig. 6.3: Adapted from: "Honduras Leading Murder Capital," http://www.pewresearch.org/fact-tank/2014/07/01/dhs-violence-poverty-is-driving-children-to-flee-central-america-to-u-s/. Copyright © by Pew Research Center
- Fig. 6.4: "Unaccompanied Minors," www.cbp.gov/newsroom/stats/southwest-border-unaccompanied-children. Copyright in the Public Domain.
- Fig. 6.5: Data from Department of Homeland Security (2012).
- Fig. 6.6: "Mexicans in Their Homeland,"http://bunkerville.wordpress.com/2011/03/16/government-funded-la-raza-group-expands/.
- Fig. 6.7: Adapted from: "Federal Crimes," http://www.pewhispanic.org/2014/03/18/the-rise-of-federal-immigration-crimes/. Copyright © by Pew ResearchCenter.
- Fig. 6.8: Adapted from: "Divided View over Deportation," http://www.people-press.org/2014/02/27/public-divided-over-increased-deportation-of-unauthorized-immigrants/. Copyright © by Pew Research Center.

CHAPTER SEVEN

The Rhetoric of Race and Racism

On August 9, 2014, a young man named Michael Brown was shot and killed by a police officer for allegedly robbing a convenience store and then resisting arrest in the now famous small town of Ferguson, Missouri. The incident called attention to a number of other police shootings against unarmed black men. On one hand, the Michael Brown shooting bore witness to possible police brutality against racial subjects. However, many have argued that indictments regarding racialized police actions are unfounded. Regardless of one's position on this topic, the reality is that police shootings—particularly involving race—are highly controversial. The intensity summoned by the shooting of Michael Brown and others like him stirred massive protests, generated a new social movement (i.e., Black Lives Matter), prompted large-scale and highly visible investigations, and stimulated widespread conversations across the country. However, some argue that Black activism started even sooner, with the shooting of Trayvon Martin and the subsequent acquittal of George Zimmerman (Smith, 2014). Nevertheless, the two years since the first edition of this book have witnessed what the Pew Research Center (2016) calls "a series of flashpoints" that have "exposed deep racial divides" that have generated an explosion of a new discourse about race and race relations in the United States.

Of course, police-involved shootings are not the only contemporary issue surrounding race. Problems associated with poverty, crime, social status, the legal system, etc. complicate our discussions about race. In fact, according to a United Nations working

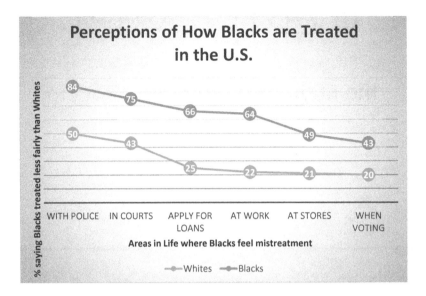

Figure 7.1: Black & White perceptions of how Blacks are treated in the U.S

group that visited major American cities in 2016, Blacks are "facing systemic racial discrimination" in areas such as the following:

> discriminatory voter ID laws; states' rejection of Medicaid expansion, which serves as just one way in which African Americans' realization of the right to health is thwarted; the existence of "food deserts" in many African American communities; schools' insufficient covering of the period of enslavement and the "root causes of racial inequality and injustice ... [thereby] contribut[ing] to the structural invisibility of African-Americans"; the housing crisis, high rates of homelessness and gentrification; the high unemployment rate of African Americans; and the environmental justice denied African Americans by highly polluting industries often disproportionately being placed in their communities (Germanos, 2016, n.p.).

And issues relating to racism do not solely involve black Americans. Racial challenges touch everyone, some more directly than others. Although clearly there is a wide chasm between how Blacks and Whites feel about race issues in this country (see Figure 7.1). As I will note in this chapter, issues of race affect Asians, Hispanics, Jews, Muslims, other minority groups, and Whites. While matters of race and certainly racism relate to other social issues and impact everyone in our society, I obviously cannot exhaust every connection between race and other variables. Combined with some of the other chapters in this book, I hope that some of the intersections between race and related issues can be noted and explored in the future.

CONTEXT OF U.S. RACE RELATIONS

As we will soon see, the United States has a long and troubled history involving race. Part of the complication when analyzing race also concerns the idea of "race" as a social and theoretical concept. Like most controversial issues, matters of race reside at the many intersections of culture, history, economics, expression, criminal justice, and of course politics. In order for us to discuss race in any meaningful way, we first need to recognize and understand some of these intersections. As is true with any matter of controversy, race relations are complex, and they deserve a careful and critical examination.

Notes on Language and Labels

Before I begin discussing an issue of this magnitude and complexity, I should first look at the meanings of some of the key terms, labels, and concepts. After all, the power of words and the power of naming helps create, shape, and sustain conceptions of reality. Uncovering the meanings of the symbols associated with race can help us in our exploration of it as a concept. Furthermore, as Ian Haney López (2014) examines, language is often coded in what he calls "dog whistles" so that race is discussed without explicit references or direct racial words. Dog whistles, then, function to insert race into political discussions in a way that avoids blatant signs of race and dodges overt racist appeals. Identifying dog whistle rhetoric not only helps us understand how race discursively operates, but it also reveals one troubling way that racism is perpetuated in public dialogue.

While this chapter concerns race and racial issues, the concept of race is often conflated to, and overlaps with, the notion of ethnicity. In terms of intercultural communication, race is typically associated with a person's biological ancestry, whereas ethnicity relates to the geographical location of origin of a person's family. Both concepts relate to a person's ancestry, both can be considered socially/culturally constructed, and both are arbitrary and illusory. But there are important differences as well. First, race is a category that is imposed upon a person and largely is static in that a person's race cannot change (at least not with a high degree of difficulty and personal cost). Ethnicity can more easily be modified or chosen. Second, racial groups have historically been targeted with higher levels of discrimination than ethnic groups. Ethnic groups, to be sure, have also experienced discrimination. However, during the historical moments when ethnic groups have endured discrimination, they were considered racial categories as well. Given this, some of the issues discussed in this chapter will involve both racial and ethnic categories. Additionally, racial and ethnic minority groups who experience controversial issues in the United States often are related to some of the issues discussed in the other chapters, such as immigration, crime (gun control), and religion (Muslims and Jews). To minimize repetition and maximize clarity, I will try to distinguish between these issues. But it is important to note that, as is true with life in general, these concepts and issues are complex, interrelate with each other, and can mutually reinforce each other.

I also should note how the use of epithets impact racial discourse in contemporary America. Each racial and ethnic group has slurs associated with it. Pejorative labels are often used to describe racial and ethnic groups in stereotypical and demeaning ways. These words are common in explicitly racist discourse. However, they are also seen in some historical documents and contexts, used when offenders claim to be joking, and when in-group members (those who identify or who are identified with the racial/ethnic group) use the specific words during artistic expression or political re-articulation. Many of these words exist, but some are more common than others. Additionally, some of the pejorative slurs can be extremely toxic, which can obviously intensify political discourse that is already polarizing.

For example, the *n-word* is often invoked to emphasize certain racist notions. It has been called the "epithet that generates epithets" (Kennedy, 2002, p. 22), the "cursed yet bonding epithet" (Benston, 1982, p. 3), the "nuclear bomb of racial epithets" (Chideya, 1999, p. 9), and a "malicious insult" (Grogan, 2011, n.p.). On the other hand, a variant of the word—the *n-word* ending with an "a" or an "uh"—frequently is uttered in hip-hop music (Rawson, 1989; Smitherman, 2000). The actual *n-word* itself has also been used for a variety of reasons, including "to lampoon slavery," to jab at the "grisly phenomenon of lynching," to highlight the "tragic reality of Jim Crow subjugation," and to "satirize 'legal' disenfranchisement" (Kennedy, 2002, p. 28). Many white people have found this use of the word, and occasionally the *n-word* itself, by members of the black community as a double standard, if not hypocritical. Some Whites are repelled (or repulsed) by the use of the term, and they become infuriated when it is deemed acceptable for Blacks (or in-group members) to deploy the word as opposed to its use by racist Whites. Squireso (2011) suggests this reaction is a form of racial "entitlement disorder," in that Whites with racist proclivities resent how black in-group members can use the word while out-group members have been censored from their "ability to intimidate Others indiscriminately" (p. 69).

Some scholars, however, counter that if the *n-word* is deplorable in its etymological reification of slaves as property, no iteration of it should be condoned, even a variant such as the "softer" ending of the *–a*. Additionally, some argue that any variant of the *n-word* gives the actual pejorative meaning of the *n-word* legitimacy (Kennedy, 2002). Of course, there is also the argument that previously pejorative slurs can be re-articulated, or reclaimed, by oppressed communities as a form of empowerment, such as the word *Chicano* for Mexican-Americans or the word *queer* for homosexuals (Grogan, 2011). In those instances, prior smears have been appropriated for politically liberating purposes, especially when there is a "sensibility that is aware of black history" (Major, 1970, p. 84). In any case, the debate rages about whether certain words should be used, who should use them, when they should be used, etc. For our purposes, an acknowledgement that these words have multiple purposes within the larger polarizing environment is important as we move forward in trying to understand the rhetoric of race in the United States. And since some groups are offended by the use of these words, we should probably avoid them altogether.

Last, I should note the use of certain labels when referring to or when identifying racial and ethnic groups. For ethnic groups who are American citizens, a commonly accepted form of addressing such groups is by hyphenating their identifying name. For example, part of my ancestral lineage hails from Rome and Abruzzi in Italy. The other part of my lineage can be traced to Ireland. A person may refer to me as an Italian-American or an Irish-American, or since I have multiple ethnic tracings, I might simply be called an "American." Some people argue that if we are referring to first-generation or newly arriving immigrants, we should hyphenate the name, provided they are considered American citizens (Byers, 2013). If my family was indigenous to northern America, I may be called a Native American, an Indian, or an indigenous person. Some who are part of that in-group may object to the name "Native American" in that it includes "American" when indigenous people should be able to claim their identity in a way that is separate from the colonization—and subsequent genocidal events—of the European settlers. Some may also object to the word "Indian," since it frustrates the same moniker for people who come from the country India. Others also problematize the word "American," since Canadians, Brazilians, Hondurans, etc. are also all "Americans," albeit North *American*, Central *American*, South *American*, and so on.

A similar complication might occur with the name Mexican-American. Since indigenous people from the current area known as the southern United States and northern Mexico have a history prior to European colonization, the hyphenated part of the name (i.e., -*American*) suggests a legitimization and reification of the colonial invasion by Americans. Hence, the previously pejorative word *Chicano* (which meant someone from the lowest class whose purpose in society was to perform the least preferable jobs) serves for many Mexican-Americans as not only a re-articulated empowering term, but it also functions as an alternative to the colonizing moniker of -*American*.

Racial identifying markers for Blacks can also be problematic. Like their ethnic counterparts, racial labels are couched in a history replete with oppression. For members of the black community, we know that the *n-word* was a name used to identify them as slaves (Kennedy, 2002, p. 4, 10). Prior to the Civil War and then during the post-Civil War era, a variant of the *n-word* was commonly used: *negro*. At the time, *negro* was so much more preferable to its derivative, that its use was embraced virtually without criticism. In fact, the United Negro College Fund began in 1944 and obviously utilized the word in its official name. However, it is virtually impossible to erase the historical trappings of the *n-word* since *negro* is its variant. As a result, the name "colored" became used during the Civil Rights era. We know that this name was embraced since the National Association for the Advancement of Colored People (NAACP), an organization that has been on the front lines fighting against the oppression of the black community, obviously incorporated "colored" in its official name. Over time, however, the word "colored" began to be used in a pejorative manner, so a new, less-offensive name had to be found. During the post-Civil Rights era, or the so-called "hippy" era, many in the black community attached part of their cultural identity to their African roots. The name "Afro" emerged as a moniker. Yet its use was rather informal, also referred to a hair style, and failed to adequately capture the connection with Africa. Thus, folks started to use the name "African-American." This identity label is still common today, but it too has been criticized on similar post-colonial grounds as the names Native American and Mexican-American. Plus, not all dark-skinned people in America originated from Africa, so the term may be inaccurate for some population groups.

Although the name "colored" people or "colored" person was rejected several decades ago, in our contemporary political climate, alternatives to the problematic terms used to identify African-Americans have become scant. As a result, some have been using the term "people of color" or "persons of color" as a form of re-articulated identity from the "colored" notions of the Civil Rights era. By emphasizing the human being in the name (i.e., by putting the words "people" or "person" first and before the adjective "color"), the moniker sheds much of its earlier pejorative baggage. In journalism, there seems to be a consensus that the word "black" should be used as an adjective, but "African American" should be used as a noun, and when "African-American" is used as an adjective, it should be hyphenated (Byers, 2013). Even among journalist organizations, however, deference and discretion are usually given to the writer. Another alternative is to use the label "Black." Some authors never capitalize it, but since I often use this name as a proper noun, I believe it should be capitalized, just like the label "White." However, when "black" or "white" are adjectives describing a noun, the word should appear without capitalization. For variance, I will use both "people/persons of color" and "Black" when referring to this racial group. My intention is not to offend, but rather in order to have a discussion about issues of controversy involving racial identities, some type of a label must be used, and hopefully this section of the chapter will prompt meaningful discussion, rather than cause offense.

The Rhetorical Situation

As we know, Bitzer (1968) describes how rhetoric is a product of its situation. In other words, the situational nature of relationships or of events drives the substance and style of the rhetoric occurring involving and during the situation. When discussing the rhetoric of race, understanding the situation—or context—is vital. The meaning of a single word or a single gesture may be dictated by the situation, or perhaps more importantly, by the audience of the particular situation. For Bitzer, the audience is a key component to the rhetorical situation. Exigencies, or opportunities, and constraints, or the limitations and challenges faced by a rhetor, are the other two key components to a rhetorical situation. Regarding race, all three components will be necessary for exploration into the polarizing nature of its rhetoric.

In this chapter, I will explore a variety of different rhetorical situations concerning the rhetoric of race. For each instance, I will note the different exigencies, constraints, and audiences involved in racial rhetorical exchanges. Some of these situations include police-involved racial shootings, anti-Semitism, Asian discrimination, and voter suppression laws, and others. An obvious area that could be included in this list is the recent surge in Islamophobia happening in the United States; after all, this chapter will discuss matters related to anti-Semitism. However, to be "Jewish" can encompass both cultural and religious elements, whereas Islamophobia is a reaction solely to the people who practice the Islamic faith. Hence, I will discuss the growing reaction to militant Muslims—and Muslims in general—in the chapter on religion. Similarly, racial/ethnic tensions involving Hispanics will be discussed in the immigration chapter. One noticeable area that is absent in our current discussion is the rhetoric involving Native Americans. The racial rhetoric of indigenous people should probably be its own chapter for the next edition of this book. But, for now, I point to a number of other scholars who have written on this subject, such as Black (2009), Endres (2015), Hegeman (1989), Kelly (2014), Lake (1983, 1991), McCue-Enser (2017), Morris and Wander (1990), Sanchez and Stuckey (2000).

Of course, people could argue that other groups should be included as well, such as Puerto Ricans, European Americans, other religious groups that face discrimination, and so on. I cannot possibly examine every oppressed group or exhaust every racial controversy that exists in modern America. It is my sincere hope, however, that by highlighting these major areas, we can better understand how race, ethnicity, and culture operate as a whole in this country. As such, what we learn here can hopefully help us in other similar situations and contexts.

For Bitzer, the rhetorical situation is a specific event, when exigencies, constraints, and audiences collide. The rhetor should map the terrain of these elements to produce the most persuasive message they can. While this notion is useful when examining a rhetorical snapshot, it largely ignores how historical forces and cultural traditions shape individual situations.

The Historical Context

If we include the rhetoric of indigenous peoples, the history of racial rhetoric in the land now known as the United States goes back for centuries. However, if we leave Native American rhetoric for a discussion for another time, we can begin tracing the history of American racial rhetoric with slavery. Of course, describing the history of slavery, people of color, and race relations as a whole could fill several books, and they are not the subject of this book nor this chapter. But, as we have learned, we cannot understand contemporary rhetoric without knowing about its historical development and context. And we certainly cannot understand contemporary racial rhetoric without considering some of the historical influences that helped create the current racial climate.

We know that some of the earliest settlers to the so-called "New World" brought slaves to help with crop production, especially tobacco. Dating back to the early 17th century, it appears that slaves existed in Jamestown, Virginia (Berry, 2014). It is important to note that during this point in history, slavery, especially slavery of Africans, was widespread in Europe, the Caribbean, and what is now known as Central and Southern America. I make this point not to excuse it, but rather to provide the context for why slavery became commonplace in early America. Thus, once slaves were brought to Jamestown, it established a precedent to continue the practice as the new colonies developed.

Over time, slavery proliferated, particularly in the South. Of course, not all Southerners owned slaves, but the affluent property owners, particularly the wealthy crop-growing Southerners, owned and used slaves to help with agriculture. The more slaves one had, the more crops they could grow. A professor at the University of Texas, Daina Berry (2014), claims that about 25% of Southerners owned slaves from around 1800 to 1850. Of course, slavery ended with the ratification of the 13th Amendment on December 6, 1865—that's 246 years of oppressive, dehumanizing, and shameful treatment of fellow human beings. As tragic as slavery was, it merely laid the groundwork for decades of future discrimination and mistreatment of Blacks.

What followed the dark period of slavery was only slightly brighter. While former African slaves were now considered "free," they experienced an American society that, in part, resented the fact that slaves were no longer permitted as cheap labor, a society that disliked the idea that white Americans would now need to support an entirely new class of people, and a society that begrudgingly accepted the notion that citizens who were previously not considered fully human were now perceived to have the same rights as traditional Americans. On top of these feelings of frustration by the society writ large, former slaves struggled to find jobs, housing, education, and other basic necessities of life. During the reconstruction period, attention was paid to rebuilding Southern cities and infrastructure (e.g., the city of Atlanta), but virtually nothing was done to help former slaves transition into normal society. While many in the North took a moral position against slavery, it was not until 1868 with the ratification of the Fourteenth Amendment that Blacks were legally granted "equal" rights. Then, in 1870, the Fifteenth Amendment was ratified, which granted black men suffrage rights.

The 13th, 14th, and 15th Amendments were intended to ease the pathway to regular citizenship for former slaves. One of the problems with the Amendments was that they required enforcement against individuals, businesses, and communities that did not abide by their precepts. In addition to inadequate implementation of Amendments' frameworks, the country experienced a major economic crash in 1890. Southerners, in particular, feared losing their jobs to former slaves who would work for less wages. These fears coupled with rampant racism led to the passage of laws all over the South that treated Whites and Blacks differently, mostly by characterizing Blacks as inferior and second-class citizens. These new laws stipulated things like separate schools, separate water fountains, separate housing areas, etc. Called "Jim Crow"– a pejorative term for black field workers—these new laws created a two-tiered, caste-like society.

Based on the principle of federalism, Jim Crow laws were enacted by individual Southern states. In the *Plessy v. Ferguson* decision, the Supreme Court in 1896 held that individual states had the right to pass legislation distinguishing between racial groups as long as such laws could be considered "separate but equal." Until a federal law, under the Constitution's Supremacy Clause, could trump state legislators and governors, the Jim Crow laws reigned absolute within the confines of state borders. Jim Crow laws permitted state-based racism against Blacks who had no recourse for any grievances. Essentially, the only option open for people of color during this time was to protest and march in the streets. The police, court system, and state governments stacked the deck in the favor of Whites and, of course, against Blacks.

In the 1940s, President Truman tried to abolish some racist laws, such as poll taxes that required people to pay a tax before voting, which negatively impacted poor people and people of color. Unsuccessful, Truman did manage to use his executive authority to integrate the armed forces. When Eisenhower became president, any hope for progressive racial policies at the federal level vanished. However, in 1950, the NAACP filed suit against the states of Virginia and South Carolina by arguing that their "separate but equal" premises were unconstitutional. There was a similar predicament in Delaware and in Topeka, Kansas. After several appeals, the Supreme Court agreed to hear the four cases as a single constitutional issue. Thus, in 1954, the Court ruled in *Brown v. Board of Education of Topeka* that "separate but equal" laws were unconstitutional since they violated the Equal Protection Clause of the Fourteenth Amendment. This landmark decision overturned the *Plessy* decision, thereby legally invalidating all Southern Jim Crow laws.

Of course, Southern states did not immediately comply with the Court's ruling. For example, in 1957, the governor of Arkansas, Orval Faubus, rejected the desegregation doctrine of *Brown v. Board*. In fact, Faubus used the Arkansas National Guard to prevent Blacks from enrolling in White schools. President Eisenhower was forced to act, and in order to stop full-scale riots after nine black children entered a white school, the President federalized the Arkansas National Guard, which then enforced desegregation (Lewis, 1957). Similarly, in 1963, the newly elected governor of Alabama, George Wallace, promised "Segregation now! Segregation tomorrow! Segregation forever!" and prevented Blacks from entering the University of Alabama at Tuscaloosa (Bell, 2013). In response, President John F. Kennedy federalized the Alabama National Guard. The threat of escalation worked, and Governor Wallace rescinded his blockade. However, later that year, Wallace attempted to keep his segregation promise by preventing black high school students from attending the white Tuskegee High School. Again, President Kennedy used the Alabama National Guard to pressure Wallace to comply with desegregation mandates, and Wallace eventually capitulated.

We also know that during the turbulent times of the late 1950s and 1960s, Blacks protested segregation laws, voter suppression, and other racist policies. In fact, many attribute the beginning of the civil rights movement to the 1955 bus boycott. When Rosa Parks refused to sit at the back of a Birmingham, Alabama, bus, members of the community, led in part by a charismatic local lawyer and preacher, Dr. Martin Luther King, Jr., engaged in an orchestrated boycott of the city's buses. The boycott caused a stir all across the segregated South because it was the first time an organized resistance occurred to segregated policies. Then, in August 1963, many Americans, but mostly black Americans, held a rally in Washington, D.C. Known as the "march on Washington," the rally drew tens of thousands to clamor for more freedom and jobs for people of color. That rally ended with Dr. Martin Luther King's famous "I Have a Dream" speech. Additionally, in 1965, the march on Selma was meant to draw attention to, and ultimately change, barriers to voter registration efforts for Blacks.

Meanwhile, during this period, organizations such as the Southern Christian Leadership Conference (SCLC) and the Student Non-Violent Coordinating Committee (SNCC) were formed to apply systematic and organized pressure against segregationist policies as well as to provide places where Blacks could come together and form advocacy groups. With King's message of non-violence, some members of the black community—such as Stokely Carmichael of the Black Panthers and Malcolm X of the Nation of Islam—began professing that non-violent and reformist efforts were failing, and, instead, they articulated more violent alternatives. Malcolm X's famous "The Ballot or the Bullet" (1964a) speech exemplifies the forced choice dilemma of reformist failures versus more effective radical solutions, according to Malcolm X and others. Additionally, after his pilgrimage to Africa, Malcolm X spoke at his Founding Rally of the Organization of Afro-American Unity in 1964. In this speech, Malcolm X trumpeted the value of Pan-African unity and famously declared: "That's our motto. We want freedom by any means necessary. We want justice by any means necessary. We want equality by any means necessary" (Malcolm X, 1964b, n.p.).

Due to mounting pressure from the civil rights movement, Supreme Court decisions and the slowly changing attitudes of many allied white Americans, the federal legislative landscape regarding race began to change. The U.S. House of Representatives History, Art & Archives website provides a valuable overview of the many civil rights-oriented acts of legislation. Beginning in 1957, Congress adopted the 1957 Civil Rights Act which established a federal civil rights commission to investigate civil rights complaints in conjunction with the Department of Justice, and the scope of this power was extended in the so-called "1960 Civil Rights Act." In 1964, Congress passed the Civil Rights Act that banned segregation in education and prohibited employment discrimination based on race and other factors. Four years later, Congress enacted the 1968 Civil Rights Act to address racial and other types of discrimination in housing. In 1965, Congress passed the Voting Rights Act that sought to eliminate barriers to Black voting rights, which essentially provided the enforcement and codified mechanisms for the Fifteenth Amendment. The Voting Rights Act has been extended several times—1970 to allow oversight of precincts with lower registration rates, 1975 to extend voter right protection to other minority groups like Native Americans, 1982 to reward jurisdictions with a 10-year clean record of protecting voters' rights as well as providing assistance to the disabled and non-native English speakers, and 2006 which extended the Voting Rights act for 25 more years as well as reinforced provisions to protect bilingual voters. There have also been other extensions to the Civil Rights Act, including the 1987 Restoration Act which covers anti-discrimination efforts to organizations receiving federal funds, and the 1991 Civil Rights Act which, despite previous Supreme Court decisions, raised the bar for workers to prove employment discrimination.

Despite all of the Supreme Court decisions, Congressional acts of legislation and Presidential actions to implement integration and reduce racial discrimination, we know that problems continued to occur and continue to persist today. For instance, Mychal Denzel Smith (2014) explains,

Despite its undeniable impact, the civil-rights movement didn't solve the issue of racial injustice. The world that young black people have inherited is one rife with race-based disparities. By the age of 23, almost half of the black men in this country have been arrested at least once, 30 percent by the age of 18. The unemployment rate for black 16-to-24-year-olds is around 25 percent. Twelve percent of black girls face out-of-school suspension, a higher rate than for all other girls and most boys. Black women are incarcerated at a rate nearly three times that of white women. While black people make up 14.6 percent of total regular drug users, they are 31.2 percent of those arrested on drug charges and are likely to receive longer sentences. According to a report issued by the Malcolm X Grassroots Movement, which used police data as well as newspaper reports, in 2012, a black person lost his or her life in an extrajudicial killing at the hands of a police officer, security guard or self-appointed vigilante like George Zimmerman every twenty-eight hours. (n.p.)

Although we have laws on the books to eliminate job, education, and housing discrimination, grievances and abuses in these areas still happen. In fact, some government actions, like the 1996 Crime Bill, incentivized states to convict more violent criminals in exchange for additional federal funding. Although the Crime Bill "put more cops on the beat, trained police and lawyers to investigate domestic violence, imposed tougher prison sentences and provided money for extra prisons," it had deleterious effects on people of color (Johnson, 2014, n.p.). Additionally, since 1994, violent crime has only increased, indicating that more punitive measures do not rehabilitate criminals, and they certainly do not deter them. According to Vega (2015), what may be worse is that incarcerating more people translated directly into putting more Blacks in jail and prisons. After the Crime Bill, young black males have a one in three chance of incarceration. When 33% of all young black males are likely to have jail and/or prison time, it has far-reaching and devastating consequences. When black men are in jail, they cannot hold a job, cannot be supportive husbands and fathers, cannot vote, and cannot be productive members of society. Once released, it is more challenging to find a job to replace the one they lost when arrested, and it is even more difficult for convicted felons. In fact, a "survey by the Ella Baker Center for Human Rights found that 76% of former inmates said finding work after being released was difficult or nearly impossible. Nearly two thirds of the respondents were unemployed or underemployed five years after being released from prison" (Vega, 2015, n.p.).

Racial disparity in the criminal justice system can also be seen in the way individuals are sentenced for their crimes. For instance, sentencing guidelines of mandatory minimums require that someone found with one gram of crack is equivalent to someone with 18 grams of cocaine, yet the substances are nearly identical—they just happen to be ingested differently and typically by different people. Despite the 18:1 ratio disparity, the sentencing guidelines used to be much worse. The Fair Sentencing Act of 2010 changed the sentencing ratio from 100:1 to 18:1. While that is a substantial improvement, the guidelines still unfairly target poor people, and particularly poor people of color who are more likely to smoke crack than they are to snort cocaine (Kulze, 2015).

Although racial issues have improved since the civil rights movement, people of color continue to face serious discrimination in other areas than the criminal justice system. In employment, housing and education, Blacks continue to suffer from oppressive and discriminatory practices. According to Settles, Buchanan and Yap (2011), "Despite Title VII of the Civil Rights Act (1964, 1991)—which mandated that organizations eliminate workplace discrimination based on an employee's sex, race, color, religion, or national origin—racial discrimination and harassment persists with significant costs to targets, co-workers, and the organization as a whole" (p. 150). Thus, workplace discrimination against Blacks continues, even though the Civil Rights Act was passed to eliminate such behavior.

Blacks also experience racially motivated frustrations in the sphere of housing. The Department of Housing and Urban Development (HUD) studies the degree to which people of color feel discriminated against in housing situations. In their 1977 study, HUD found that the majority of respondents experienced blatant discrimination, including "door-slamming" when applicants were outright rejected any possibility for housing appointments or applications based on the color of their skin. In their 2013 study, HUD reported that housing discrimination still occurs, but it is less overt. Today, Blacks can usually receive an appointment for housing, but they are frequently asked questions about their finances, and they were given fewer options than their White counterparts (Dewan, 2013). Even Trump's new HUD secretary, Ben Carson, who is himself Black, recently remarked to HUD employees, "That's what America is about, a land of dreams and opportunity. There were other immigrants who came here in the bottom of slave ships, worked even longer, even harder for less" (Estepa, 2017b, n.p.). Referring to slaves as immigrants to the people supposedly in charge of reducing racial discrimination in housing is disheartening. In addition, the racial disparity in housing between Blacks and Whites is highlighted by the situations in Milwaukee and St. Louis, two cities, incidentally, who have witnessed serious racial tensions in the past several years. According to a 2016 study conducted by the National Community Reinvestment Coalition, for Milwaukee, "Whites represent 70 percent of the population, yet received 81 percent of the loans. African Americans are 16 percent of the population yet only received four percent of the loans" (NCRC, 2016, n.p.). And St. Louis is tragically similar: "While white residents are 75 percent of the population, they received 83 percent of the mortgage loans. In contrast, African American residents are 18 percent of the population, but received only four percent of the loans" (NCRC, 2016, n.p.). Thus, while legislation exists aimed at protecting against racial discrimination in housing-related matters, racist practices and behaviors clearly continue to plague American communities.

Additionally, in education, people of color are victims of racial oppression. In higher education, affirmative action and racial preference programs have all but been eliminated. Since the 2003 Supreme Court *Gratz v. Bollinger* decision, when the

Court ruled that preferential status based on diversity is unconstitutional, universities and colleges around the country have eviscerated affirmative action-related admissions and scholarship programs, which have had serious negative consequences not just on Blacks but also the overall campuses and learning environments (Bollinger, 2002). With K–12 programs, racial problems are different, but they are nonetheless severe. According to the U.S. Department of Education, which conducts a Civil Rights study every two years, black students are suspended or expelled three times as often as their white counterparts. Additionally, black schools tend to have far fewer veteran teachers, including 7% of black students who attend schools where as many as 20% of their teachers lack proper licensing and certification (Resmovits, 2014). These are grave statistics, since this sort of "discrimination lowers academic performance for minority students and puts them at greater risk of dropping out of school" (Resmovits, 2014, n.p.). Plus, according to Daria Hall who works for a K–12 advocacy organization, since black students are suspended and expelled more often, they receive "less instructional time," and, consequently, they "get less access to high level courses" (Resmovits, 2014, n.p.).

The rhetoric surrounding race and crime helps frame how society imagines and represents black youth. In 1996, the First Lady at the time, Hillary Clinton, gave a speech in New Hampshire supporting her husband's 1994 Violent Crime Control and Law Enforcement Act (aka the 1994 Crime Bill). In her speech, Hillary did not specifically refer to black youth, but she did mention drug cartels, organized mobs, and gangs. In so doing, she stated, "They are often the kinds of kids that are called super-predators—no conscience, no empathy. We can talk about why they ended up that way, but first, we have to bring them to heel" (cited in Graves, 2016, n.p.). The day after the speech, Hillary apologized for using the term "super-predators," which suggests she knew that it had obvious racial implications. During the recent 2016 presidential race, Clinton's 20-year-old comment drew controversy when an activist at a South Carolina fundraiser asked the candidate to comment about the racial implications of such a statement. Clinton issued an apology and said, "We need to end the school-to-prison pipeline and replace it with a cradle-to-college pipeline" (cited in Gearan & Phillip, 2016, n.p.). Hence, racial comments in the political sphere can have enormous impact for many years, even if the rhetor's intention was not necessarily racist.

CONTEMPORARY RHETORICAL CLIMATE

In the last two years alone, we have witnessed racial tensions reach a boiling point. The summer of 2015, which was the summer following the Michael Brown shooting in Ferguson, Missouri, was a very hot summer indeed. Other race-related police shootings followed, and for the subsequent year and a half, the United States became a hotbed of racial frustrations and acrimony. On one hand, the presidential campaigns that began in the late summer/early fall of 2015 helped Americans take their minds off of Black/White racial issues. But, on the other hand, the extremist discourse that accompanied the presidential election generated other types of racial and ethnic discord, primarily against immigrant Hispanics, Muslims, and Jewish places of worship. However, all in all, the presidential campaign only deteriorated the discourse on race. Republican candidate Rick Santorum referred to President Obama as a "n****r," which was made into an issue during the 2016 race (Santorum, 2012); Hillary Clinton said that Trump was taking the "hate movement mainstream" (Lee, 2016); and Trump responded by calling Clinton a "bigot" (Schleifer & Diamond, 2016)—not much good can result from such discursive discord. Indeed, according to the Southern Poverty Law Center, over "300 incidents of harassment or intimidation have been reported" since Donald Trump won the election (Bailey, 2016, n.p.). As a result of this tumultuous contemporary rhetorical climate, I will explore some of these discursive areas by briefly analyzing their contexts, the core arguments, the fallacies, and the techniques used by polarizing rhetoricians.

Police-Involved Shootings and Altercations

Perhaps no other issue has highlighted the troubling nature of contemporary race relations in America more than police-involved shootings. From one perspective, many places around the country, particularly urban areas, seem like militarized war zones, occupied by unjust, power-hungry police officers. This sentiment is best expressed in this way:

> In the two years since Brown was fatally shot by Ferguson police officer Darren Wilson, there's been a pileup of other controversial police encounters that have resulted in the deaths of unarmed black men. During one harrowing week this July, two police-involved shootings happened within two days, only to be followed by a deadly attack targeting Dallas police officers. The country then mourned a second attack on police on July 17 in Baton Rouge. Meanwhile, the protests and calls for justice have only grown louder. (Hare, 2016, n.p.)

From another perspective, law enforcement officers feel they are under-appreciated and disrespected while they daily put their lives on the line, and some even perceive that there is a serious risk of attack from anti-police forces.

Additionally, the highly publicized police shootings draw attention to other layers of the racial divide. For instance,

> After each of these incidents, reports issued by government commissions seeking answers cited hauntingly identical findings. Police brutality, poor relations between the police and the community, a sense of hopelessness fueled by a lack of jobs, economic inequality, inadequate schools, discriminatory housing practices, an unresponsive political system many felt shut out of, along with policies that created segregated neighborhoods which further isolate communities of color were highlighted again and again. Again and

again the recommendations included expanding community policing strategies and social programs, making them more consistent with the extent of the problems. (Finney, 2014, n.p.)

Like most controversial social issues, racial turmoil is complex. While police shootings have drawn the most attention, some observers claim that deeper, more root causes of tension, like unemployment, the unjust criminal "justice" system and other forms of systemic oppression, go unnoticed (Kurtzleben, 2014; Reed, 2016). Despite other causal factors that exist for racial disparity, we also cannot ignore the real pain that recent police-involved altercations with the Black community have generated, as well as the fact that these Black-police encounters have largely framed the overall discussion about race in the United States.

Indeed, there have been far too many law enforcement-related shootings and confrontations with the black community in recent years (see Figures 7.2–7.5). Of course, there have been many more shootings and altercations than the ones presented here;

Figure 7.2: Timeline of Black-police altercations, 1999-2014

Figure 7.3: Timeline of Black-police altercations, 2014-2015.

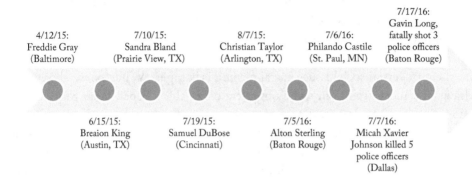

Figure 7.4: Timeline of Black-police altercations, 2015-2016.

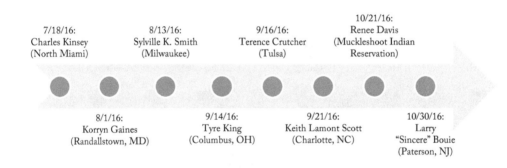

Figure 7.5: Timeline of Black-police altercations, 2016.

but these represent the events receiving the most media coverage and, by extension, some of the most contentious events between people of color and the law enforcement community.

I do not have the space to thoroughly detail and critique each of the listed incidents. However, examining a few of them should provide us with a snapshot of the key arguments and rhetoric techniques used—by both sides of the debate—regarding these altercations.

Before Michael Brown, there was Amadou Diallo, a 23-year-old immigrant American citizen from Guinea. Living in New York City, Diallo was shot and killed by four plain-clothed NYC police officers in February 1999. The officers were driving by shortly after midnight and saw Diallo standing outside of his apartment building as he was returning from an evening meal. The officers claimed he fit the general description of a serial rapist. As a result, the officers claimed they exited their vehicle, identified themselves as NYPD officers, and told him to put his hands in the air; Diallo walked toward his front door instead. A light was out on the porch, showing only a silhouette of Diallo, so when he reached in his pocket for his wallet, one officer saw the object in Diallo's hand and yelled "gun!" The officers discharged their weapons a total of 41 times, 19 of which hit Diallo. All four officers were charged with second-degree murder, but all were acquitted (Fritsch, 2000).

Seven years later, another suspicious shooting incident involving a black person and law enforcement occurred. This is not to say there were not suspicious incidents during those interim seven years, but this next case received considerable media coverage, especially due to the questionable facts of the case. On November 25, 2006, Sean Bell, a 23-year-old black male was shot and killed by NYPD officers. His two friends, Trent Benefield and Joseph Guzman, were also shot, but they survived the incident. All three were at a strip club for a Bachelor party. Allegedly Guzman had an altercation with another patron and told one of their friends to retrieve his gun. Believing a gun fight was immanent, a plain-clothed officer, Gescard Isnora, alerted his back-up team who were there investigating a possible prostitution ring. According to the officers, they identified themselves to Guzman, Bell, and Benefield who were now in their vehicle. Bell accelerated the vehicle which hit Isnora and then crashed into an unmarked police van. Isnora claimed he saw Bell reach for a gun and then yelled to his fellow officers that Bell had a weapon. Isnora and four other cops discharged their weapons for a total of 50 rounds into Bell's car. However, according to Guzman, the officers never identified themselves. Al Sharpton arrived afterward and represented the Bell family, but it is alleged that many of the eyewitnesses were paid by Sharpton's organization (Bennett, 2007). New York City Mayor Michael Bloomberg said "it sounds to me like excessive force was used," and then he called the shooting "inexplicable" and "unacceptable" (Cardwell & Chan, 2006, n.p.). Former New York Governor George Pataki concurred, calling it "excessive" (Healy, 2006). All of the officers were indicted and charged, and Isnora and one other officer were charged with homicide, but in the end, all officers were acquitted and all were either fired or resigned from the New York Police Department (Buckley & Rashbaum, 2006; Mac Donald, 2007).

One year later, on November 26, 2007, a young 16-year-old black kid from Detroit, named Brandon Moore, was shot in the back while running away from a security officer—an officer with a history of brutality and who had been fired from the police department for a fatal hit-and-run DUI (Younge, 2015).

Five years later, on February 2, 2012, Ramarley Graham, a young 18-year-old black man in New York City was spotted by officers of the NYPD Street Narcotics Enforcement Unit, who saw Graham leave a bodega as he was tugging and adjusting his waistband, leading the officers to believe Graham had a gun. They followed Graham into an apartment building, and they reported that they saw the butt of a gun on Graham's person, although later there was no evidence that this was true. The officers claimed they approached Graham and identified themselves as police officers. The officers initially claimed that Graham started running to his apartment, but later that was changed due to video surveillance that showed Graham walking, not running. Two officers were granted access to the building by a first-floor tenant, and they then went to Graham's apartment and kicked-in his front door. Upon seeing the police, Graham fled to his bathroom where he allegedly flushed drugs down his toilet. Officer Richard Haste yelled, "show me your hands," and "gun" before shooting Graham in the upper chest. Officer Haste claimed later that he thought Graham was going for a gun in his waistband. Officer Haste was immediately placed on modified duty, was then indicted for manslaughter, but then acquitted (Kemp, 2012; Lysiak et al., 2012; Savali, 2012).

A month later, on March 21, 2012, a young 22-year-old black woman named Rekia Boyd experienced a random encounter with a Chicago Police Department (CPD) officer, Dante Servin. Officer Servin entered Douglas Park after hearing of a noise complaint. He approached some individuals who were partying, and allegedly some form of verbal altercation occurred. It is unclear whether Servin's attitude was calm or aggressive, but one of the partyers claimed that Servin asked to buy drugs. When the group said, "No, get your crackhead ass" out of here (Tolentino, 2015, n.p.), Servin began shooting into the group, hitting Rekia Boyd in the head and Antonio Cross in the hand; initially, CPD claimed that Servin discharged his weapon after perceiving that Antonio Cross had a weapon, but it later turned out to be a cell phone. No charges or indictments were filed against the officer, and he resigned before he could be fired from the CPD (Tolentino, 2015).

Almost a year later, Ricardo Diaz-Zeferino, of Gardena, California, encountered the police on June 2, 2013. Diaz-Zeferino, a Hispanic, "was trying to help his brother find his stolen bike. Dashboard camera videos (which the police in Los Angeles tried to keep secret) later showed that he was shot when he was mistaken for the thief and did not keep his hands still in the air as instructed. The three officers involved were not charged" (Cave & Oliver, 2016, n.p.).

Another year later, on April 30, 2014, Donte Hamilton, from Milwaukee, Wisconsin, was sleeping in Red Arrow Park. Although Hamilton had been diagnosed with schizophrenia, officer Christopher Manney was unaware of Hamilton's mental illness. In fact, officer Manney had received a call to check on a subject who was sleeping in Red Arrow Park, but he did not check his voicemail. Since Manney failed to respond, two other officers were dispatched; they nudged Hamilton, who then woke up and provided ID. He said he was fine and was just taking a nap—it was 2:00 pm; they left, thinking Hamilton was fine and not a danger to anyone. At 3:30 pm, Manney finally checked his voicemail, then proceeded to the park; he asked Hamilton to wake up, and he complied. Manney began to pat Hamilton down, and Hamilton resisted. Manney then hit Hamilton several times with his baton; Hamilton somehow was able to obtain Manney's baton and threatened to hit the officer, which is when the officer grabbed his gun and shot Manney 14 times, which resulted in 15 gunshot wounds. According to Kertscher (2016), "So, Hamilton had no weapon when Manney approached him. He was armed, with Manney's baton, only after Manney struck him with the baton" (n.p.). The officer was never charged (Luthern, 2014).

Just two weeks later, on July 17, 2014, a major, highly publicized event occurred between police officers and an alleged perpetrator, Eric Garner. Garner, a 43-year-old black man hanging out on a street in Staten Island, New York, was approached by officers for allegedly selling illegal cigarettes. They wrestled him to the ground, and one officer used a chokehold to subdue him; Garner kept yelping, "I can't breathe." Garner died on the scene from a heart attack (Cave & Oliver, 2016).

After Garner's death, the New York Police Department became embittered over the nation's reactions against the police in general, and the reaction of Mayor Bill de Blasio in particular. The mayor convened a meeting with the police commissioner and Al Sharpton, which gave "greater prominence than police defenders thought he should have because Mr. Sharpton is a firebrand with an unsavory past," and the mayor "said after the Garner killing that he had told his biracial son, Dante, to 'take special care' in encounters with the police" (*The New York Times*, 2014, n.p.). As a result, many members of the NYPD refused to respond to "low-level offenses," such as the call that went out on Garner. Doing so, of course, would likely mean skyrocketing crime rates all over the city. As reported by *The New York Times* (2014), "many cops have latched on to the narrative that they are hated, with the mayor orchestrating the hate" (n.p.). To make matters worse, the U.S. attorney general, Eric Holder, announced that he would conduct a federal investigation in possible "civil rights violations" in the Eric Garner case (Lewis, 2014). These sorts of reactions by government officials simply inflamed the animosity and resentment that the police officers were feeling.

On the flip side, members of the community were outraged when the grand jury failed to indict the police officer who killed Garner with the chokehold. *Guardian* columnist Stephen Thrasher (2014) added to the polarizing rhetoric by saying, "Another grand jury failed to indict another police officer for killing another unarmed black man in America—this one a bona-fide [sic] homicide caught on camera" (n.p.). By phrasing his comment with "killing another unarmed black man," it implies that the police were on a rampage focused entirely on Blacks, which, even if true, the Garner case does not, by itself, support. Additionally, Thrasher called the incident a "*bona fide* homicide," which of course means a verifiably true murder. However, obviously the members of the grand jury—as well as many citizens all over the country—did not believe it was "*bona fide*," nor did anyone prove it was a murder, which requires malicious intent. Garner's death may have just been a tragic accident. By using this powerful rhetoric, Thrasher adds to the overall divisive discourse regarding police-involved shootings.

Not long after the Garner incident, on August 5, 2014, a 22-year-old young black man named John Crawford III was shot to death by officer Sean Williams in Beavercreek, Ohio. In a local Walmart, Crawford was holding a toy BB gun. He reportedly was waving the weapon around and perhaps even pointing it at people. Officers arrived at the pet supplies area and saw Crawford with the gun. The officers claimed he did not respond to verbal commands, and he appeared as if he was trying to escape. Not knowing that the weapon was a BB/air rifle, an officer shot two rounds at him, one hitting him in the arm and the other in the torso. Williams died shortly afterward. A bystander, Angela Williams, died while suffering a heart attack at the scene; both officers were not indicted (Chittal, 2014).

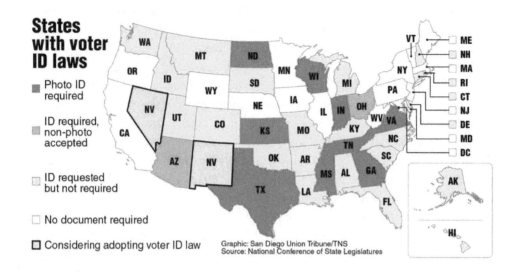

Figure 7.6: Current map of voter ID laws.

Just four days later, on August 9, a young 18-year-old named Michael Brown was shot and killed in Ferguson, Missouri. Brown was confronted by police after walking down the middle of the road. Brown allegedly scuffled with the officer and reached for officer Darren Wilson's gun, but was unable to obtain it. Brown reportedly moved away from the squad car, and officer Wilson shot and killed Brown. Later, the medical examiner's report indicated that Brown was not walking/running away from the car, but was instead lunging back toward the officer. After the shooting, the police left Brown's body in the street for hours claiming it was part of the investigation. Officer Wilson was not indicted (Cave & Oliver, 2016).

From the perspective of an outraged American Black, Patton (2014) emotionally responded to the Michael Brown shooting, even likening it to 19th-century lynchings:

> Black America has again been reminded that its children are not seen as worthy of being alive—in part because they are not seen as children at all, but as menacing threats to white lives. ... Black children are not afforded the same presumption of innocence as white children, especially in life-or-death situations. Note officer Darren Wilson's description of his confrontation with Michael Brown. ... In his grand jury testimony, Wilson described Brown as a "demon," "aggressive," and said that Brown had taunted him by saying, "You are too much of a p—-y to shoot me."... Wilson told the jury, "I felt like a 5-year-old holding onto Hulk Hogan .... That's how big he felt and how small I felt just from grasping his arm." Wilson claimed that Brown charged at him through a hail of bullets before he shot him in the head. The official history of that night paints Wilson as an innocent white child was so threatened by a big, black beast that his only option was to use lethal

force. … Such descriptions, so similar to 19th-century defenses of lynching, are invoked each time a black child is gunned down in America. (n.p.)

Katch (2015) and Taylor (2015) also called the shooting a modern-day lynching: "When the police killed Mike Brown and left his body lying in the street for four-and-a-half hours, it transformed this police killing into a lynching. … If a cop was willing to shoot an unarmed teenager with his hands raised in the air and leave his body in the street as a clear message, then they were willing to do anything to maintain their authority and control over the community" (Taylor, 2015, n.p.). The obviously leftist periodical the *Socialist Worker* (2014b) went even farther, saying that the "*legal murder* of Mike Brown has shown a spotlight on a country where African Americans are 21 times more likely to die at the hands of police than whites" (my emphasis, n.p.).

Michael Brown's stepfather was later investigated for his violent behavior during the Ferguson protests. Caught on video, Brown's stepfather was seen stomping up and down on the hood of a car, yelling, "Burn this bitch down!" The incident was investigated to see if he was partially responsible for, or at least contributed to, some of the violence that occurred during the so-called Ferguson "riots" (Riedel, 2014). When all was said and done, no charges were filed. According to Hare (2016), subsequent to the shooting of Michael Brown, two separate investigations of officer Wilson occurred—one was the criminal investigation, and the other was a civil rights investigation conducted by federal agents. However, when the Department of Justice investigated the Ferguson police department, their findings were alarming (Hernandez, 2015; Reilly & Stewart, 2015b). As Reilly and Stewart (2015b) explain, "The [DOJ] report found that city, police and court officials have worked in concert to maximize revenue at every stage of the enforcement process" for several years. "City and police leadership pressure officers to write citations, independent of any public safety need, and rely on citation productivity to fund the City budget," the report states (n.p.). And Hernandez (2015) summarizes that the DOJ report emphasizes how "Blacks make up 67 percent of the population in Ferguson. But they make up 85 percent of people subject to vehicle stops and 93 percent of those arrested. Blacks are twice as likely to be searched as whites, but less likely to have drugs or weapons. The report found that 88 percent of times in which Ferguson police used force it was against blacks and all 14 cases of police dog bites involved blacks" (n.p.). Furthermore, while the city and the county were identified as over-policing in Black areas seemingly to generate revenue (Reilly & Stewart, 2015a), they were not the only entities that engaged in racist and racially motivated discourse. After the Ferguson protests, documents revealed that the Missouri National Guard characterized the protesters as "enemy forces" and "adversaries" (Walters, 2015). Honestly, I cannot think of a better situation of someone engaging in "us vs. them" and vilifying rhetoric.

In March 2015, the Department of Justice revealed they were not criminally charging officer Wilson, but they were filing suit against the city of Ferguson for their misconduct (Hare, 2016). As a result, protests went on for months in Ferguson. The demonstrations, anger, and outcries became even more pronounced when it was announced that the grand jury decided to not indict officer Wilson (Hare, 2016). That decision not only caused an uproar in Ferguson; it also "touched a raw, national nerve" that triggered protests all over the country (Hare, 2016, n.p.). Some of the demonstrators engaged in violent behavior and other criminal acts, such as looting. While heavily criticized by many, including law enforcement officials, emotionally charged people of color described how such behavior was justified:

> Perhaps looting seems like a thing we can control. I refuse. I refuse to condemn the folks engaged in these acts, because I respect black rage. I respect black people's right to cry out, shout and be mad as hell that another one of our kids is dead at the hands of the police. Moreover I refuse the lie that the opportunism of a few in any way justifies or excuses the murderous opportunism undertaken by this as yet anonymous officer. The police mantra is "to serve and to protect." But with black folks, we know that's not the mantra. The mantra for many, many officers when dealing with black people is apparently "kill or be killed."... We are talking about justifiable outrage. Outrage over the unjust taking of the lives of people who look like us. How dare people preach and condescend to these people and tell them not to loot, not to riot? Yes, those are destructive forms of anger, but frankly I would rather these people take their anger out on property and products rather than on other people. ... We are tired of these people preaching a one-sided gospel of peace. "Turn the other cheek" now means "here are our collective asses to kiss." We are tired of forgiving people because they most assuredly do know what they do. ... Black people have every right to be angry as hell about being mistaken for predators when really we are prey. (Cooper, 2014, n.p.)

Given the intensity and raw emotion, I feel this quote deserves citing at length. Plus, Cooper's statement also reveals how, even in the face of contrasting evidence, she and others either refused to, or simply could not, believe that Michael Brown was charging at officer Wilson.

Yet that is precisely what the medical examiner's report found, along with some corroborating witness testimony. After the struggle of Wilson's gun, apparently Michael Brown did back away, but the angle and location of Wilson's bullets confirm that Brown must have turned around and lunged toward Wilson (Desiderio, 2014; Somashekhar & Kelly, 2014). In fact, Lowry (2014) explains this tragic reality:

> The bitter irony of the Michael Brown case is that if he had actually put his hands up and said don't shoot, he would almost certainly be alive today. His family would have been spared an unspeakable loss, and Ferguson, Missouri wouldn't have experienced multiple bouts of rioting, including the torching of at least a dozen businesses the night it was announced that Officer Darren Wilson wouldn't be charged with a crime. Instead, the credible evidence (i.e., the testimony that doesn't contradict itself or the physical evidence) suggests

that Michael Brown had no interest in surrendering. After committing an act of petty robbery at a local business, he attacked Officer Wilson when he stopped him on the street. Brown punched Wilson when the officer was still in his patrol car and attempted to take his gun from him. The first shots were fired within the car in the struggle over the gun. Then, Michael Brown ran. Even if he hadn't put his hands up, but merely kept running away, he would also almost certainly be alive today. Again, according to the credible evidence, he turned back and rushed Wilson. The officer shot several times, but Brown kept on coming until Wilson killed him. (n.p.)

Instead of accepting the grand jury's decision, Marcia Fudge, Democrat Representative from Ohio, exclaimed that their decision to not indict was a "slap in the face." She cried, "We waited to hear our country say loud and clear: There are consequences for taking the lives of others. ... It was a painful reminder that, just like with Trayvon Martin and Tamir Rice, and so many others, law enforcement officers kill our black and brown men and boys without repercussions" (cited in Dolan, 2014, n.p.).

Although reactions like Cooper's and Fudge's are understandable given the circumstances, the manner in which they articulated their frustrations most certainly added to the rhetorical powder keg. Tensions were high, people felt betrayed, both the Black community and law enforcement felt disrespected and maligned. And this type of discourse only fuels the fire of animosity, even hatred. To make matters worse, musician and NRA spokesman Ted Nugent had this to say about the protests in Ferguson: "Here's the lessons from Ferguson, America—don't let your kids grow up to be thugs who think they can steal, assault & attack cops as a way of life & badge of black (dis)honor. When a cop tells you to get out of the middle of the street, obey him & don't attack him as brainwashed by the gangsta assholes you hang with & look up to. It's that simple unless you have no brains, no soul, no sense of decency whatsoever" (cited in Foster, 2014, n.p.). The vilifying, us vs. them, and hyperbolic rhetorical fallacies exhibited by both sides were highly problematic and divisive. Of course, as is true with all controversial issues, the media threw gasoline on these rhetorical fires and certainly are culpable for much of the conflict (O'Kelly, 2014).

While the nation was in uproar over the shooting of Michael Brown, just three days later another shooting took place. In Los Angeles, a 25-year-old black male named Ezell Ford, who had previously been convicted of possession of marijuana and firearms and was later diagnosed with schizophrenia, bipolar disorder, and depression, was shot and killed. According to officers Wampler and Villegas, they approached Ford as part of a routine "investigative stop." The officers were equipped with a Taser, but they left it in their vehicle. When Ford saw the officers approaching, he appeared to be reaching for a weapon, so Villegas reached for his gun. Ford fled and went between some vehicles, which made the officers believe Ford was ditching his drugs; however, later no drugs were discovered. Officer Wampler claimed that Ford tackled him, and they wrestled. Villegas tried to handcuff Ford, but when doing so, Villegas sensed Ford was reaching for his gun. Ford allegedly continued to resist, so Wampler reached for his gun and shot Ford in the back. The officers handcuffed Ford after he was shot. However, other witnesses provided a different account; that is, Ford did not tackle Wampler, but, rather, it was the other way around; Ford had raised his hands in the air and did not resist, but when his hands were in the air, he was shot three times, after the officers beat him. Ultimately the investigation reported that both officers were justified in their measure of force against Ford, but their initial stop was unjustified because they had no reasonable suspicion to think Ford was in possession of drugs (Ferner, 2014; Larrubia & Keller, 2015; Moreno et al., 2014; Stoltze & McNary, 2015).

After the hot month of August, there was the shooting of Darrien Hunt in Saratoga Springs, Utah, on September 10, 2014. Hunt was a 22-year-old black male who we now know was playing with a sword at a local store. The police claimed that they were responding to a call of a man waving a samurai sword. When officers arrived, they claimed that Hunt lunged at them and swung his sword at them. The officers responded by shooting six shots at him. The fatal wound hit Hunt in the back, which made people suspicious that the officers shot him when he was away from them, not lunging toward them. In fact, as we learned later from the medical examiner's report, not a single shot hit Hunt from the front (Lee, 2014). Then, in October 2014, a 17-year-old black kid in Chicago was fatally shot. Laquan McDonald walked past the police after he had been running, and was shot because he "was fleeing" an officer (Cave & Oliver, 2016).

One month later, on November 22, 2014, a young 12-year-old black kid was fatally shot in Cleveland, Ohio. Young Tamir Rice was shot dead when officers saw him with a gun, even though the gun was a pellet gun. Officer Timothy Loehmann shot Rice twice at close range because he thought Rice had a weapon. After an investigation, the officer received no indictment (Cave & Oliver, 2016; Chirbas, Smith & Ortiz, 2016; Fantz & Shoichet, 2015). According to prosecuting attorney Tim McGinty, "Police are trained that it only takes a third of a second or less to draw and fire a weapon at them. Therefore, they must react quickly to any threat" (cited in Fantz & Shoichet, 2015, n.p.). However, allegedly Tamir Rice had his hands in his pockets at the time of the shooting (*The Plain Dealer*, 2015). Nonetheless, the Rice family attorney, who also is Black, said, "This is not a black and white issue. This is a right and wrong issue" (cited in CNN, 2014, n.p.).

In December 2014, a young 18-year-old black male named Antonio Martin was shot and killed in Berkeley, Missouri. According to the police, Martin pulled a gun on a white officer. Allegedly, Martin and one other subject fit the description of two suspects who had just shoplifted from a Mobil Oil convenience store. Although no shots were fired from Martin's gun, the officer claimed he saw the weapon and feared for his life and the lives of others, so the officer discharged his weapon three times, one of which fatally hit Martin. It took paramedics six minutes to arrive at the scene. Protesting erupted over the length of time it took for medical attention to arrive and for the perceived racial motivation of the officer's shooting (Lowery, 2014).

Beginning the so-called police "rampage" in 2015 was the February shooting of a 35-year-old Hispanic man named Antonio Zambrano-Montes. In Pasco, Washington, Zambrano-Montes apparently ran from police after being accused of throwing rocks at the officers and their squad cars while his hands were in the air. Two of the officers were White and one was Hispanic, but the event caught the attention of the media because it was yet another example of an apparently inexcusable shooting of a person of color (Cave & Oliver, 2016).

In March 2015, Tony Terrell Robinson, Jr., from Madison, Wisconsin, was killed during a police encounter. The 19-year-old was seemingly a suspect in a confrontation at a home in Madison. Responding to the call, an officer responded to a battery at a residence, whereby an altercation ensued between Robinson and officer Kenny. The officer shot Robinson seven times. According to the police report, the officer said due to "space and time considerations," non-lethal force was not an option. Additionally, a friend of Robinson's said he was "going crazy" and was "punching walls," but his mother described him as a "gentle giant" and a "good boy who did not deserve this" (Johnson, 2015a, n.p.).

There were two notable shootings in April 2015, both of which caused enormous media and public outcry. The first occurred on April 5, when a 50-year-old black man named Walter Scott was shot in the back eight times as he was running away from a police officer. The officer claimed he felt threatened after Scott tried to take his Taser (Campbell, 2015). The video of a passer-by showed the encounter, and the fact that Scott was shot in the back created a nationwide outcry. The officer in question claimed "he did not know at the time that Scott was unarmed," and he apparently felt "total fear" after Scott "grabbed his stun gun during a scuffle between the two men" (McLeod, 2016, n.p.). By virtually all accounts, officer Slager's actions seemed to be, what law enforcement officers call, a "bad shoot." In other words, Slager appeared to wrongfully shoot, and kill, Walter Scott. The video that captured the incident even showed what looks to be Slager "picking something up and then dropping it near Scott's body— perhaps the Taser" (Graham, 2015, n.p.). As such, it appears that the officer planted the evidence to corroborate his story. Officer Slager was charged with murder, and later convicted.

The incident drew national attention, in part because it was captured on video, but also in part because Reverend Al Sharpton traveled to Charlotte to highlight the ordeal. Although the Scott family did not want Sharpton's help or presence, Sharpton nevertheless spoke about the injustices black men continue to face in this country (Lysiak et al., 2015). Sharpton's politicizing of the event, however, was a lightning rod for conservatives who, like actor James Woods, called Sharpton a "race pimp" (Sustar, 2015, n.p.). Despite the negative attention brought by Sharpton, others tried to use the situation for some degree of positive racial justice. As Younge (2015) expressed:

> And so Scott's murder stands not simply as an outrageous and horrific inci-
> dent in its own right but as an emblem for all the Brandon Moores who have
> gone down in a hail of bullets to deafening silence; a proxy for a reign of racial
> terror that has not been removed since the civil rights era but merely refined;
> a harsh illustration of a system that both systemically criminalises working-
> class black communities and, on occasion, cavalierly condemns those who

live in them to summary execution. It lends a name and a moving image to those who have perished unnamed and unseen, and whose deaths could not move the nation's conscience. (n.p.)

While such outrage is justified, reactions to it further polarize the rhetoric of race and racial injustice. In a rather reasonable effort to describe how racial shootings like this occur, Coleman (2015) says, "In the 21st century, black men and women are framed by law enforcement. Evidence is planted. Arrests are made, convictions rendered and lives are ruined—if life is even preserved—because we also know that innocent black men and women are killed by law enforcement" (n.p.). But taking one incident like the Scott killing does not necessarily mean all racially motivated shootings have tampered evidence with innocent people that result in murder. These sorts of statements are generalizations that could, and often, do damage in our discussions about race.

A week later, in Baltimore, a young 25-year-old black male was arrested by police officers and cuffed inside of a van for transport. As a result, Freddie Gray suffered a spinal injury while being transported by Baltimore police. He died a week later (Cave & Oliver, 2016). As the *Socialist Worker* (2015) described it, "then the lid blew off in Baltimore after police chased and tackled Freddie Gray for a 21st century version of a Black Code violation: making eye contact with a cop and then running. Gray was 'folded up like origami,' in the gruesome words of one eyewitness, and by the time he emerged from a police van, he had a nearly severed spinal chord [sic] and crushed voice box" (n.p.). The black prosecutor, Marilyn Mosby, faced intense pressure to convict a police officer over this event. However, all charges were dropped against all of the officers, which triggered massive protests in Baltimore (Woods, 2016). Since Mosby could not convict the individual officers, she "pinned blame for the unsuccessful prosecution on 'systemic and inherent problems' with the police investigation," since "we all bore witness to an inherent bias that is a direct result of when police police themselves" (Woods, 2016, n.p.).

On June 15, 2015, Breaion King, a young black woman in Austin, Texas, was simply driving 15 mph over the speed limit. Upon being pulled over for speeding, King was thrown violently to the ground by a police officer, and told by another officer that "black people have 'violent tendencies' and whites are justifiably afraid" (Weber, 2016, n.p.). While not resulting in massive abuse or death, this incident exemplifies how racial prejudice can influence typical police behavior.

Less than a week later, on July 10, 2015, a young 28-year-old black woman named Sandra Bland from Naperville, Chicago, who was searching for a job in Texas, was pulled over for a traffic stop in Prairie View, Texas. After repeatedly being asked to extinguish her cigarette, Bland continued to refuse. The officer responded with, "I am giving you a lawful order." When she again refused, he threatened to use a Taser. According to the dash-cam video, the officer said "I will light you up" (Becerrill & St. Hill, 2015, n.p.). She then left her vehicle. The officer stated in his report that Bland was "combative and uncooperative." He also stated that, "Bland began swinging her elbows at me and then kicked my right leg in the shin. Force was used to subdue Bland to the ground, to which Bland continued to fight back" (Becerrill & St. Hill, 2015, n.p.). Officer Encinia's abuse of Bland was off-camera, but the camera recorded the audio of Bland saying, "You're a real man now. You just slammed me, knocked my head in the ground" (Becerrill & St. Hill, 2015, n.p.). The Bland family and their attorney also suggested that the final version of the dash-cam video was edited because the quality was "grainy," and there was no time stamp (Becerrill & St. Hill, 2015). She was arrested, and three days later, she hung herself in her cell (Becerrill & St. Hill, 2015; Cave & Oliver, 2016). A special inspection report from the Texas Commission on Jail Standards found that the "police did not follow proper procedures," especially since the officers should have had a "visual, face-to-face observation of all inmates by jailers no less than once every 60 minutes" (Hassan & Yan, 2016, n.p.). After the incident, officer Encinia was later convicted of perjury (because the video recordings conflicted with his statements), and he was subsequently fired (Becerill & St. Hill, 2015).

The Sandra Bland shooting generates a unique set of circumstances for the polarizing rhetoric of race. On one hand, we are dealing with two separate issues—the officer's alleged mistreatment of her along with her arrest, and then her suicide three days later. While the Texas Commission report reveals police misconduct since they failed to abide by certain protocols, evidently Bland's depression that caused her suicide was a result of her own family's failure to pay her bail (Ward, 2015). Additionally, the "day after the arrest, Bland called her sister and said she didn't understand why she had been arrested. She also stated that she believed her arm had been broken or fractured as a result of the abuse she sustained" (Becerrill & St. Hill, 2015, n.p.). After asking her sister to help remove her from jail, the sister and the rest of the family failed to post bail, which was set at $515. The jailers contend that her family's failure to act caused Bland to be severely depressed, which led to her suicide (Ward, 2015). Her death, then, does not necessarily follow from the actual arrest. Nevertheless, "Outrage over her arrest and the mystery surrounding her death appeared to be the last straw for advocates. ... Calls are growing to elevate the profiles of the black women and girls who suffer violence at the hands of police. A campaign dubbed 'Say Her Name' is organizing to make sure they are not left out of the movement, and that their names be remembered" (Sakuma, 2015, n.p.). And, according to Becerrill & St. Hill (2015), Sandra Bland "has become the latest person added to the ever-growing list of victims of racist police violence in the U.S. after her death in a Texas jail cell earlier this month" (n.p.).

On July 19, 2015, a 43-year-old black man named Samuel DuBose was pulled over for a routine traffic stop (due to no front license plate) by a University of Cincinnati police officer, Ray Tensing. When DuBose failed to produce a driver's license and refused to exit his vehicle and acted like he was going to drive off, the officer became frustrated. The situation escalated, and the officer fatally shot DuBose in the head (Cave & Oliver, 2016; *Harvard Law Review*, 2016; Horn & Sparling, 2015; Kaufman, 2015b; Pérez-Peña, 2015). The officer's body camera caught the incident on video, which apparently also revealed that DuBose "did not act aggressively or pose a threat" (Pérez-Peña, 2015). The prosecuting attorney, Joseph T. Deters, as he was responding to the murder indictment of the police officer, said, "It was a senseless, asinine shooting"

(Pérez-Peña, 2015, n.p.). The theory was that the officer may have lost his temper just because DuBose did not want to exit his vehicle (Pérez-Peña, 2015). In addition to the indictment, a separate University of Cincinnati report also concluded that the officer "used poor judgment and improper police tactics" (Horn & Sparling, 2015, n.p.).

In August 2015, Christian Taylor, a 15-year-old unarmed black student football player, was shot and killed in Arlington, Texas (Cave & Oliver, 2016). Almost a year later, on July 5, 2016, in Baton Rouge, Louisiana, a 37-year-old black man named Alton Sterling was shot several times at close range while held to the ground by two white police officers. Officers were dispatched to investigate a homeless man who allegedly was harassing a man by asking him for money. A 911 caller said they saw a man outside of a convenience store selling CDs who apparently had a gun (Heath, 2016). Although Louisiana is an open carry and a conceal state, which means that citizens are legally allowed to carry a gun, the police evidently thought a man selling CDs posed a threat (Heath, 2016). As the police were trying to apprehend Sterling, one officer yelled that he saw a gun, which prompted another officer to shoot Sterling in the chest several times. However, the convenience store owner, Muflahi, video recorded the incident on his phone, which later revealed that Sterling did not appear to be holding a gun, nor was he acting in a threatening manner (Heath, 2016).

Just one day later, on July 6, in St. Paul, Minnesota, Philando Castile, a 32-year-old black man, was pulled over by a police officer for a "routine traffic stop" (Heath, 2016). Castile told the officer he had a license to carry a weapon. However, the officer shot Castile while he was reaching for his license and registration. Castile's girlfriend, Diamond "Lavish" Reynolds, began video recording the incident on her phone immediately after Castile was shot. As Castile sat in the driver's seat, covered in blood, Reynolds can be heard crying and yelling,

> We got pulled over for a busted taillight in the back … and the police just … he, he's covered—they killed my boyfriend. He's licensed, he's licensed to carry. … He was trying to get out his ID in his wallet out of his pocket, and he let the officer know that he was … that he had a firearm and that he was reaching for his wallet. And the officer just shot him in his arm . …. Yes I will, I'll keep my hands where they are . …. Please don't tell me this, Lord. Please, Jesus, don't tell me that he's gone. Please don't tell me that he's gone. Please, officer, don't tell me that you just did this to him. You shot four bullets into him, Sir. He was just getting his licence [sic] and registration. (cited in Heath, 2016, n.p.)

Watching the video can be shocking, especially hearing Reynolds reacting to the situation. But, of course, we do not see what happened prior to the shooting. Nevertheless, Minnesota Governor Mark Dayton called the shooting racially motivated, saying, "Would this have happened if those passengers, the driver and the passengers, were white? I don't think it would have. So I'm forced to confront, and I think all of us in

Minnesota are forced to confront, that this kind of racism exists" (cited in Miller et al., 2016, n.p.).

On July 18, in North Miami, a black mental health caregiver named Charles Kinsey was shot, although not fatally. Kinsey went to the street to help a black autistic man who sat in the road, cross-legged, playing with a toy truck. Kinsey was shot by police who were answering a call of "an armed man threatening suicide" (Chappell, 2016, n.p.). One officer yelled to get on the ground, and Kinsey was pleading with the autistic man to lie down, but the man refused, continuing to play with his truck. As a consequence, the officer shot his weapon three times, one of which hit Kinsey in the leg. Kinsey lay on the ground with his hands up, yelling "please don't shoot; there's no need to fire your weapon, sir" (Chappell, 2016, n.p.). The officers approached and physically rolled Kinsey and the autistic man over, then handcuffed them. It appears that since the dispatched call concerned a man in the road (with a gun), the shot may have been intended for the autistic man, which was later confirmed when one of the officers said the shooter was trying to protect Kinsey from the man in the road (Alvarado et al., 2016). According to Rabin (2016), "The incident highlights how explosive a situation can get when cops already on edge are forced to confront someone with autism or a mental disability" (n.p.). And the incident arrived "as the country is still on edge over issues of race and law enforcement" (Alvarado et al., 2016, n.p.).

On August 1, 2016, Korryn Gaines, a 23-year-old black woman in Randallstown, Maryland (near Baltimore), was shot and killed by police officers. Officers went to her home to serve warrants for traffic violations. Gaines told the officers to leave because she had her five-year-old son in the house with her. The officers arrived later in the day with a key from the landlord, and Gaines exclaimed that she had a gun and would shoot anyone who entered. The police tactical team breached the home, killing Gaines and injuring her son (King, 2016b). This incident sparked a great deal of controversy, particularly in the Baltimore area. According to Shaun King (2016b), countless threatening white men are apprehended by police without dying. Yet "Korryn Gaines doesn't have a violent history. She was a cosmetologist and, according to her friends and family, a doting mother. She should've received the treatment that all of those armed white men received. Somehow, in each of those cases, police found in their hearts to overcome their fears without unloading their guns on those men. That's white privilege" (n.p.).

Sylville K. Smith was killed by a police officer in Milwaukee, Wisconsin on August 13, 2016. Smith, a 23-year-old black male, was stopped for a traffic violation. For some reason, Smith fled the scene on foot and had a stolen handgun. A video shows Smith facing officer Dominque Heaggan-Brown with the weapon. The officer shot first and hit Smith in the arm as he was tossing his gun over a fence, and he fell on his back. Officer Heaggan-Brown then shot a second time, fatally hitting Smith in the chest. Two nights of rioting in Milwaukee ensued. The officer was charged with homicide, and the case is still pending (Smith & Pérez-Peña, 2016).

Almost a month later, on September 14, in Columbus, Ohio, a young 13-year-old black male named Tyre King was shot and killed. The police were investigating reports of a suspect who committed an armed robbery. The police believed they saw King take a gun from his waistband, and an officer shot him multiple times. The gun later was determined to be a BB gun (Chirbas, Smith, & Ortiz, 2016).

Two days later, on September 16, in Tulsa, Oklahoma, a 40-year-old black male named Terence Crutcher was fatally shot by a police officer. Crutcher's back was turned, his hands went up, then the officer thought he reached into his SUV for a weapon—but there was no weapon and the window was all the way up. Crutcher "had his hands in the air when he was shot next to his car" (BBC, 2016a, n.p.). The police arrived because they received a call of a car blocking the road and reports that the driver was "smoking something" (BBC, 2016b, n.p.). The attorney for the Crutcher family, Benjamin L. Crump, argued, "Let us not be thrown a red herring and to say because something was found in the car that is justification to shoot him" (cited in BBC, 2016b, n.p.). There were two videos—one from a hovering helicopter and one from an officer body-cam, but both were obstructed (BBC 2016a, 2016b; Stack, 2016). However, one of the videos clearly shows "Crutcher walking to his vehicle with his hands raised and that Shelby had her gun pointed at his back" (McBride, 2016, n.p.). Crutcher's attorney, Benjamin L. Crump, noted that this "is not unique to Tulsa, Oklahoma. This is an issue that seems to be an epidemic happening all around America" (cited in Stack, 2016, n.p.). According to Shaun King (2016a), who is critical of police shootings, one eyewitness account claiming that Crutcher was calm and unthreatening cannot trump police accounts of incidents, because "the evidence must be outrageously overwhelming" (n.p.). Additionally, King (2016a) argues, the Crutcher shooting exemplifies "something that we've seen many, many times in shootings like this. After they shot Terence Crutcher … the police acted like they could care less. They provided no first aid or comfort. According to Goss, several minutes went by before they even really took a look to check on him" (n.p.). While King's discourse concerning police shootings is often polarizing, he is correct that it is alarming that when a citizen is shot, law enforcement waits for an inexcusable amount of time before calling for an ambulance. The same thing occurred in the Michael Brown shooting. Of course, law enforcement personnel retort with the notion that it is a crime scene, and the scene needs to be secured before EMTs can trample on it. Although there is some merit to this counter-argument, police are also well trained (or at least they should be) to secure these areas quickly to allow for emergency medical personnel to do their jobs. After all, lives are at stake, because not all of the victims of police shootings die instantly.

A week later, on September 21, in Charlotte, North Carolina, a 43-year-old black man was shot and killed after running from his vehicle. According to police, Keith Lamont Scott had a handgun and ran when the police tried to stop him. As he fled, Scott was shot in the back, but the police argued that Scott posed a safety risk to others. According to the police, they gave "loud, clear verbal commands," yet Scott allegedly still exited his "vehicle armed with a handgun as the officers continued to yell at him to drop it" (Wootson et al., 2016, n.p.). The incident was captured on a cell phone video by a passer-by, and it was immediately uploaded to social and mainstream media. Since Scott was shot in the back and ultimately died, protests in Charlotte ensued. The protests were so intense that Governor Pat McCrory declared a state of emergency (Barber, 2016; Wootson et al., 2016). Incidentally, not long after the Keith Lamont Scott shooting, the Massachusetts Supreme Court ruled that Blacks can legitimately run away from police; in essence, judges should evaluate fleeing on a case-by-case basis because Blacks are disproportionately stopped and searched, meaning their fleeing is not necessarily an admission of guilt (Mortimer, 2016).

A month later, on October 21, 2016, a young woman on the Muckleshoot Indian Reservation in the state of Washington was shot and killed. The police confronted Renee Davis as they responded to a call of a suicidal woman who was allegedly armed. The police could see two children running around in the house, but no one would answer the door. They entered her home and shot her multiple times, killing her at the scene. The children were unharmed. Davis was a teacher's aide and was described as a "kind and gentle person" (Waánatan, 2016, n.p.).

On October 30, 2016, a 41-year-old black male named Larry "Sincere" Bouie, from Paterson, New Jersey, was on the side of the road because the battery in his vehicle had died. Bouie called his brother for assistance, but his brother told him he was too busy at work to help him. When the police arrived, Bouie was "acting crazy" because he was seemingly upset about his brother's failure to help. A female officer exited her vehicle when Bouie was still "acting crazy." Perceiving Bouie to be a threat, she shot him. He was critically injured (Craven, 2016).

What do these police-involved altercations mean for our understanding of race relations? There are several components at work within all of these narratives. First, there is the tension between law enforcement accounts of incidents and the accounts from bystanders and those involved. Second, the communities of color and the police express their own "rhetorical spin" of the events, obviously aimed at trying to support and substantiate their subsequent version of the facts. And, of course, this discussion tells us about some of the tragedies faced by people of color when they have altercations with law enforcement. According to the latest statistics at the time of this writing, "Black males aged 15–34 were nine times more likely than other Americans to be killed by law enforcement officers last year, according to data collected for The Counted, an effort by the *Guardian* to record every such death. They were also killed at four times the rate of young white men" (Swaine & McCarthy, 2017, n.p.). Additionally, many individual police officers respond to incidents the way they are trained, or based on departmental regulations, or as a result of a larger departmental climate. This is not to say that individual officers are not responsible for their actions, but it does suggest that some of these issues may be deeper and/or caused by forces other than individual cops (Hudson, 2016).

One of the important issues about these police-involved shootings is that they received enormous media attention, and they stimulated nationwide conversations about the role of police in minority communities (de Laureal, 2015; *Socialist Worker*, 2014b, 2015). For some, there was, and continues to be, a real concern about the way police departments are trained and equipped. The mantra has been to "de-militarize" our police departments, with the idea being that they are too equipped like military forces, trained to invoke maximum damage on a battlefield, rather than to "serve and protect."

Attacks on the Police

Many of the police-involved shootings can be disputed, or at least some arguments can be made justifying the actions of the police. For example, it is not uncommon for an officer to arrest a driver who is caustic and disrespectful, so Sandra Bland was placed in jail in a manner that was, arguably, not racially motivated. The police department apparently failed to abide by certain protocols that should have—or may have—prevented her suicide, but equally responsible, one could argue, is the failure of her family to post her bond. In fact, Ward (2015) reports that Bland's suicide was triggered because she was not released on bail. In another example, some have argued that the chokehold used on Eric Garner is a common, typically non-lethal move that police use instead of Tasers (Garner & Maxwell, 2002). When Eric Garner said, "I can't breathe," some were suspicious, like New York Representative Peter King, about the actual severity of the chokehold, because if Garner could speak, he should have been able to breathe. King also noted that Garner's poor health, including obesity, asthma, and high blood pressure, were the main factors resulting in his death, demonstrating that the action was not racially motivated (Bobic, 2014).

However, despite the possible counter-arguments for each incident listed in Figures 7.2 through 7.5, the egregious nature of some of the incidents along with the frequency of these occurrences has created massive distrust and a plummeting level of confidence in the nation's police (Taibbi, 2014). While a growing number of citizens have become outraged by recent police actions, it is absolutely tragic when the outrage and frustration becomes violent.

On July 7, 2016, a horrific event happened in Dallas, Texas. During the day, there were non-violent Black Lives Matter demonstrations that were largely a response to the recent deaths of Alton Sterling and Philando Castile (Helsel, 2016). In the early evening, shots were fired. We later learned that the gunshots were unrelated to the Black Lives Matter protesters. After five police officers were killed and nine others were injured, the Dallas police located the shooter. After negotiations failed to have the shooter yield to surrender, the Dallas police used a robot to deliver an explosive device that killed the gunmen (Peterson, 2016). We now know that the shooter was a deranged Army Reserve veteran, Micah Xavier Johnson. Some were critical of the Dallas police for using the robot, as it signaled a growing militarization of the police force. However, as Peterson (2016) notes, "the way the robot was used in the Dallas case is likely legally no different from sending an officer in to shoot a hostile suspect, according to University of Washington law professor Ryan Calo" (n.p.). And, according to Dallas Police Chief David Brown, the suspect "has told our negotiators that the end is coming, and he is going to hurt and kill more of us, meaning law enforcement, and that there are bombs all over the place in this garage and downtown" (Helsel,

2016, n.p.). If that was indeed what the shooter said, police probably have a stronger justification for using the robot.

The Dallas shootings demonstrate the intensity of the debate regarding police-involved shootings of people of color. On one hand, we see the peaceful demonstrators who marched in solidarity with recent victims of police shootings, and, on the other hand, we witness the life-and-death reality of what it means to be a police officer. To make matters worse, some polarizing figures politicized the event and inflamed tensions even more. Joe Walsh was former congressman of 8th congressional district of Illinois, when he served from January 2011 through January 2013. When the Illinois districts were redrawn, he resided in the new 14th district and ran against Democrat Tammy Duckworth, who handedly beat him (Garcia & Eldeib, 2012). Immediately after the Dallas shootings, Joe Walsh tweeted, "3 Dallas Cops killed, 7 wounded. This is now war. Watch out Obama. Watch out black lives matter punks. Real America is coming after you" (Einenkel, 2016, n.p.). After a series of responses, Walsh quickly removed that tweet, but then added another: "10 Cops shot. You did this Obama. You did this liberals. You did this #BLM. Time to defend our Cops. Wake up" (Einenkel, 2016, n.p.). As Einenkel (2016) notes, this is the "definition of race-baiting" (n.p.). And not long after the Dallas shootings, conservative talking-head Tomi Lahren exclaimed that Black Lives Matter is the new KKK (Zurawik, 2016). Of course, we also have examples of calmer heads discussing the Dallas shootings. Texas Governor Greg Abbott said, "In times like this we must remember—and emphasize—the importance of uniting as Americans" (Helsel, 2016, n.p.).

A little over a week later, on July 17, 2016, a 29-year-old honorably discharged Marine named Gavin Long, from Kansas City, Missouri, shot and killed three police officers, critically injured another, and injured other bystanders in Baton Rouge, Louisiana (Ruder, 2016). After the shootings, President Obama said, "We as a nation have to be clear that nothing justifies violence against law enforcement. … Attacks on police are an attack on all of us, and the rule of law that makes society possible" (cited in Ruder, 2016, n.p.).

Another example of attacks against police officers occurred on October 1, 2016, in Palm Springs, California. Officers were responding to a domestic disturbance call, when two of the officers were fatally shot. In addition, a young mother, another officer, and a soon-to-be-retired veteran were injured. As a result of the "officer down" call, dozens of additional officers arrived on the scene to locate and apprehend the shooter. Apparently, during an exchange of gunfire, the shooter was injured. This allowed law enforcement to arrest the 26-year-old John Felix, as they took him to a nearby hospital. Felix had been arrested before for assault with a deadly weapon, and given his actions on October 1, he was charged with two counts of homicide (Workman & Bromwich, 2016).

Overall, some believe that law enforcement is being targeted. Other incidents have also been reported. In 2016, there was a San Antonio detective who was ambushed, then fatally shot. A sergeant on the St. Louis police force was shot twice in the face as he was sitting in his squad car. Other officers were shot during routine traffic stops in Sanibel, Florida, and Gladstone, Missouri. When a Wayne State University police officer was shot and killed during an off-campus altercation in Detroit, the Chief of Police for the Wayne State University police department said, "This is not unique to Detroit. This is going on everywhere" (Hicks et al., 2016, n.p.).

The "Ferguson Effect"

As a response to some of the attacks against police and the growing frustration emanating from mainly communities of color (because such communities could no longer believe or rely on police reports, some police officers have reduced their presence in certain neighborhoods and have lessened their level of commitment to some dispatched calls and neighborhood policing. Called the "Ferguson Effect," the decrease in attention paid to these communities seems to suggest that some law enforcement officers are hesitant to perform duties in areas where they are distrusted and even hated. According to Mac Donald (2015), "Cops are now routinely called racists and murderers at protests and as they go about their daily duties. Policing in urban areas has become dangerously fraught, with jeering, hostile crowds surrounding officers and interfering with their authority when they try to make an arrest or conduct an investigation" (n.p.).

The so-called Ferguson Effect even received the attention of now former-FBI director, James Comey. He has gone so far as to suggest that with a decrease in police presence in some communities, it has resulted in higher crime rates in those neighborhoods. According to Comey, "I do have a strong sense that some part of the explanation is a chill wind that has blown through American law enforcement over the last year" (Schmidt & Apuzzo, 2015, n.p.). While there is little data to substantiate Comey's claim that crime is increasing as a result of reduced police presence (Schmidt & Apuzzo, 2015), there does seem to be some merit to the argument that many police officers fear visiting some neighborhoods given the lack of trust and level of hostility shown to them.

However, others contest the entire theory behind the Ferguson Effect, not just Comey's claim that crime is increasing as a result. For instance, Samuel Sinyangwe (2015a) has thoroughly studied police-race relations, especially since the killing of Michael Brown. Sinyangwe argues that "we would expect police to be hesitant to use force, especially deadly force against unarmed black civilians," a scenario that is challenged by the facts of racially motivated police actions in the past two years (n.p.). Moreover, Sinyangwe reports that "police killed 665 people nationwide in 2014 before the Ferguson protests began on August 9th. In 2015, police killed 721 people over the same time period—an 8% increase. Moreover, police killed more black people including more unarmed black people during this period in 2015 compared to the same period in 2014" (2015a, n.p.). Again, these data suggest that police are actually more involved in communities of color, not less. Similarly, Balko (2015) uses FBI data to show how there is no war against law enforcement, since "assaults on cops are at their lowest point since 1996 and have been dropping consistently since 2008" (n.p.).

Militarized Police Forces

One of the consequences of the reactions to many of these police shootings, and the Black Lives Matter demonstrations in particular, has been the critique of modern police departments as militarized institutions. The debate over militarized police departments began during the Ferguson riots, after the death of Michael Brown. While some of the protestors were deemed "violent," the police entered the ordeal with combat-like force. As Taylor (2015) describes, "Meanwhile, young Black protesters in Ferguson were denounced as 'violent' even while the militarized local police force used tanks, tear gas and military-grade weaponry against unarmed men, women and children. The overwhelming response of the state and the heroic persistence of protesters in Ferguson made this an issue that wouldn't go away, and in so doing, it forced a larger public discussion about racial inequality, injustice, the police and the criminal justice system that would not have occurred otherwise" (n.p.). Apparently, according to some reports, the police used tear gas, even though the use of tear gas has been banned by the Chemical Weapons Convention (Dohrn, 2015; McCoy, 2014).

To many, the highly militarized Ferguson police force did not square with reality. In other words, why would a small town like Ferguson need war-like weapons, gear, and tactics? As Dohrn reports (2015),

> The young people of Ferguson did not back down in the face of a highly militarized small town police force armed with federally-funded Kevlar helmets, assault-friendly gas masks, combat gloves and knee pads, woodland Marine Pattern utility trousers, tactical body armor vests, some 120 to 180 rounds for each shooter, semiautomatic pistols attached to their thighs, disposable handcuff restraints hanging from their vests, close-quarter-battle receivers for their M4 carbine rifles and Advanced Combat Optical Gunsights. There are scattered reports of stun grenade use in Ferguson. ... They are designed to temporarily blind and deafen, thanks to a shrapnel-free casing that is only supposed to emit light and sound upon explosion. The grenade launchers used against unarmed youth in Ferguson included the ARWEN 37, which is capable of discharging 37mm tear gas canisters or wooden bullet projectiles. The police used tear gas unsparingly in Ferguson. (n.p.)

After Ferguson, complaints were levied against other cities concerning their use of highly militarized forms of law enforcement (*Socialist Worker*, 2015).

Another problem with militarized police departments is that with military-style weapons comes military-style training. Some have argued that when police officers become trained in military techniques, they cease their role of "protecting and serving," and instead become soldiers in neighborhoods, in what Stoughton (2015) calls the "warrior culture" (n.p.). Vitale (2014) even claims that such police techniques risk escalation when an officer confronts a citizen on the street, such as what happened in the Eric Garner incident in July 2014.

Not only are militarized police forces problematic in the sense that they typically provide responses not commensurate with the crime, but they are also highly racialized. As Vitale (2014) explains, "What underlies most of these militarized forms of policing is a cynical politics of race that has perverted criminal justice policies; they are no longer about crime or justice, but instead the management of poor and non-white populations through ever-more-punitive practices" (n.p.). Vitale goes on to explain that much of the militarization in law enforcement has been purposefully used to deter and repel protesters: "One of the uses of this new hardware has been specifically in the suppression of dissent. While many big-city departments have resisted this trend, many others, along with hundreds of medium-sized and smaller cities, have invested millions in body armor, riot shields and less lethal weaponry. Some of this technology was on display in several cities during the Occupy movement" (2014, n.p.).

The other side of the argument, however, claims that militarized police forces are necessary in this day and age of terrorist threats in the homeland. Should a terrorist incident occur, like the Boston marathon bombing on April 13, 2013, or when law enforcement has actionable intelligence to prevent a terror plot, then better trained officers with militarized equipment are necessary (Apuzzo, 2014). Of course, other high-impact and specialized criminal activities can also be confronted with more militarized agencies. For example, some argue that criminals have more advanced weapons than the police; therefore, the police should be militarized to equalize the playing field (MacGillis, 2014). Preparedness against terror threats was the main purpose behind the initial militarization of police forces, and, in fact, was why the Pentagon arranged for many police forces to have access to military-grade hardware and tactics (Vitale, 2014).

THE IMPACT OF RACE-RELATED SHOOTINGS

Overall, despite the polarizing rhetoric and the instances of unarmed Blacks being shot or harmed by white police officers, we know two things—the instances have been terrible tragedies, and the discourse surrounding the events has been divisive and troubling. The evidence should be evident:

> Communities of color react to killings of unarmed young black men, symbolically and iconographically, as they should, because even one unjust race-related event creates an atmosphere of race-related injustice. Each unpunished killing is treated as a symbol of overall social injustice to whole communities of people of color. Attempts to suppress nonviolent expressions of outrage are disturbing insofar as they fail to respect human sensibilities and encroach on First Amendment rights. (Zack, 2015, p. 99)

While these reactions are expected, hopefully we can all learn to engage in conversations about Black-police altercations in more productive and civil ways.

Regardless of where one finds themselves in this ongoing debate about police-related shootings with Blacks, the fact remains that black males are 21 times more likely to be fatally shot by police than are white males (Gabrielson et al., 2014). This figure comes from a study by *ProPublica*. Although there are some questions about the methodology of the study, "experts concur that the racial disparity in terms of police-induced gunshot fatalities is egregious and significantly slanted against black men" (Gabrielson et al., 2014, n.p.). Moreover, even if the fatalities are less, the actual number is still too high. Finally, it bears noting that while many people are critical of police officers, police departments, and public officials, it does not mean that they are necessarily generalizing everyone in those terms, or that they do not believe that some police officers, departments and officials are decent, selfless, and caring for their communities. Indeed, as Naomi Zack (2015) explains, "To criticize police practices is not the same thing as saying that all American police officers are bad people. ... Local police departments often create the impression of not distinguishing between being blame-worthy and accepting responsibility" (p. 97).

School Racial Tensions

While racial conflicts have perhaps been the most acute concerning confrontations with the police, they certainly persist in other areas of society as well. On October 13, 2016, at Stone County High School in Mississippi, a black sophomore football player was approached by at least four White students who put a noose around his neck and then yanked him around. While the school released a statement saying this "matter has been one that tears at the fabric of our schools and our community and the administration does not intend for it to be swept under the rug or otherwise ignored," they only disciplined one of the four students responsible for the incident (Tesfaye, 2016, n.p.).

In addition, since the presidential election in November 2016, there has been a wave of racially charged incidents reported at schools all over the country. As Yan et al. (2016) describe, the list of racial episodes is extensive, and these are, of course, just the ones that have been reported and the instances that have received significant media attention. A high school volleyball tournament in Northwest Texas, near El Paso, witnessed students chanting "build the wall." In Wellsville, New York, someone spray-painted a swastika with the words, "Make America White Again," in a softball dugout. At the State University of New York College at Genese, a swastika with the word "Trump" was spray-painted on a residence hall wall. In Ann Arbor, Michigan, a young female Muslim student at the University of Michigan was assaulted by a man; the man threatened to set the woman on fire unless she removed her hijab. The name "Trump!" was written on the door of a Muslim prayer room at New York University's Tandon School of Engineering. At Maple Grove High School in Minnesota, racist graffiti stating "Trump," "Whites Only," and "White America" was found inside a bathroom. And at Canisius College in New York, a black doll was found hanging from a residence hall curtain rod (Yan et al., 2016).

And there was the incident at the University of Oklahoma where fraternity members were caught on video singing "there will never be a N***** at SAE." The University of Oklahoma chapter of Sigma Alpha Epsilon was closed in response to the video. The SAE national office released a statement calling the actions "inappropriate." Apparently, the brief video reveals the fraternity members in formal attire clapping while they sing racist lyrics to the tune of "If You're Happy and You Know It" during a date function (Kingkade, 2015, n.p.).

Of course, other racially charged events have happened at schools and college campuses. For example, recently protests at the University of Missouri, including the football team's threat to boycott their games, forced the president and chancellor to resign due to the administration's inaction over racially involved turbulence on campus, including racial slurs that had been yelled at the student body president (Schulte, 2015). There have been racially charged ordeals at Yale and Princeton universities (Bonhomme, 2015). And at "Claremont McKenna College in California, demonstrations and a hunger strike forced the dean of students to resign. At Ithaca College in upstate New York, students walked out of classes in a call for the college president to resign over his mishandling of racism on campus. In Madison, Wisconsin, some 1,500 people marched from the University of Wisconsin to the state Capitol building, linking campus racism to police brutality in the city" (Schulte, 2015, n.p.).

Voter Suppression

The Declaration of Independence stresses how the new nation should rule based on the "consent of the governed" (Waldman, 2016, p. 5). This happens primarily by citizens voting. However, while the Declaration of Independence implied this notion of guaranteeing the "consent of the governed," the Constitution did not codify this principle. In fact, the Constitution might even appear to be relatively undemocratic, at least in terms of voting. As Waldman (2016) notes, citizens "could not vote for U.S. senators, who were chosen by state legislators, or for the president, to be chosen by the Electoral College. While representation in the House was proportional to population, slaves were counted as three-fifths of a person" (p. 29). And since the Constitution did not explicitly guarantee a right to vote, it "made it far easier to deny that right in later years" (Waldman, 2016, p. 31). Nevertheless, the Constitution did imply a right to vote, particularly when selecting the House of Representations.

Of course, black Americans had no such rights. They were not even considered to be a whole person (only three-fifths of a person, to be exact). But once the Civil War ended, Blacks were considered full, free citizens (hence the title, "Emancipation Proclamation"). Yet the *post-bellum* period was turbulent and contentious:

> But the right to vote carried such power, was such proof of full citizenship, that black suffrage was hard for most white Americans to swallow. First steps toward enfranchisement stumbled. The Thirteenth Amendment ended slavery in 1865; now the slaves were freed but could not vote. … In Louisiana in July

1866 the pro-Union governor called a convention to discuss voting rights; a white political militia known as "The Thugs" stormed the meeting, killing forty-seven black men and injuring 116 more. National outrage over the massacre helped produce the Fourteenth Amendment. (Waldman, 2016, p. 64)

The Fourteenth Amendment (1868) guaranteed equal protection under the law. Theoretically this amendment applies to all citizens equally; but, as we know, people of different races, religions, sexual orientations, abilities, etc., have been fighting for equality long after 1868. For instance, just two years later, in 1870, the Fifteenth Amendment was passed and adopted, giving black men the right to vote.

However, as we shall see, the Fifteenth Amendment was worded in such a way that Southern states could exploit the loophole that allowed restricting voting rights of Blacks (Waldman, 2016). Such loopholes included practices like requiring a tax be paid before voting, redistricting congressional areas to limit the influence of minority voters, mandating literacy tests, and so on. The loophole legislation that some states adopted after 1870 were part of what is known as "Jim Crow" laws. The period of Jim Crow was when states, typically in the South, would circumvent federal rules and laws so that discrimination, suppression, and restrictions against black Americans could continue. Largely articulated as policies of "federalism" (i.e., states' rights vis-à-vis the federal government), these Jim Crow laws permitted state-sanctioned discrimination. So much so, that "Jim Crow laws and disenfranchising constitutions of the 1890s and early twentieth century were devastatingly effective in suppressing black political participation in the South" (Waldman, 2016, p. 142).

With voting rights in particular, the issue of federalism took center stage. Especially since the Constitution originally framed voting rights as a state responsibility when electing members of the House of Representatives, individual states used voting rights as the lynchpin for their federalist arguments after the Civil War. Additionally, early debates regarding voting rights centered largely on the question of guaranteeing universal voting rights or securing limited voting rights to reduce the likelihood of fraud and manipulation. In other words, some advocated that in a democracy, everyone should have the right to vote, versus the counter-argument that expressed concern that poor people, minorities, immigrants, and folks who did not own property could easily have their votes purchased by political manipulators with the means to buy those votes. It was this latter logic that prevailed for decades, which privileged white property owners (Waldman, 2016).

Nevertheless, since the inception of the American experiment, multiple amendments have been passed to correct, improve, and fundamentally alter the original Constitution. In terms of voting rights, "five separate amendments in the next two centuries would address that right directly: for African American men (the Fifteenth Amendment), for women (Nineteenth), for the poor without a poll tax (Twenty-fourth), for the young (Twenty-sixth). The Fourteenth Amendment at least temporarily reduced congressional representation for states that block "the right to vote." And the

Seventeenth Amendment established the right to vote for U.S. senators" (Waldman, 2016, pp. 31–32).

Even with the amendments improving voting rights, states still had some recourse to what they viewed as encroachment into their constitutionally protected jurisdiction. Many states in the South used a loophole procedure known as the "white primary" to restrict further the voting rights of Blacks. The white primary was a primary election when a political party would choose its nominees for the general election, much like contemporary primaries. However, prior to 1944, only Whites were allowed to vote in the white primaries, thereby essentially gutting suffrage rights for people of color (Waldman, 2016). The Supreme Court decision in *Smith v. Allwright* struck down a Texas "white primary" law by ruling that all state primaries fall within the jurisdiction of the federal government and should not infringe on a person's right to vote based on race.

Other loopholes around the Fifteenth Amendment existed, such as the so-called "voucher rules" that required black voters to have a white person "vouch" for them before they were allowed to vote. In other states, they implemented literacy tests, which included "arcane questions," such as "if a person charged with treason denies his guilt, how many persons must testify against him before he is convicted?" (Waldman, 2016, p. 144). Other tests would ask the black voter to count the number of bubbles produced by a bar of soap, define legal terms from Latin, or recount the news of the day from a foreign newspaper (Waldman, 2016). Needless to say, questions like these are so obscure, that the majority of citizens would not know the answer, much less minorities who typically did not receive the best education.

As early as 1957, Dr. Martin Luther King, Jr. was advocating for equality in voting rights. During a prayer pilgrimage in Washington, D.C., King declared, "all types of conniving methods are still being used to prevent Negroes from becoming registered voters. The denial of this sacred right is a tragic betrayal of the highest mandates of our democratic tradition. And so our most urgent request to the president of the United States and every member of Congress is to give us the right to vote. Give us the ballot, and we will no longer have to worry the federal government about our basic rights" (King, 1957, n.p.).

In 1965, with the support of teachers and other citizens, King also organized a series of marches from Selma, Alabama, to the state capitol of Montgomery for fair voting rights (Waldman, 2016). During the first march, a fellow demonstrator, named Amelia Boynton, was beaten by police. A photograph of the incident immediately circulated internationally in newspapers, and commentators called the incident "Bloody Sunday." By all accounts, the marches from Selma to Montgomery helped persuade Congress to pass the Voting Rights Act later that year (Berman, 2015b; Waldman, 2016).

President Johnson unveiled the Voting Rights Act to the American people by presenting it with rhetorical flourish. He expressed that it is

> wrong—deadly wrong—to deny any of your fellow Americans the right to vote in this country. What happened in Selma is part of a far larger movement which reaches into every section and State of America. It is the effort

of American Negroes to secure for themselves the full blessings of American life. Their cause must be our cause too. Because it is not just Negroes, but really it is all of us, who must overcome the crippling legacy of bigotry and injustice. And—we—shall—overcome! (cited in Waldman, 2016, p. 155)

Immediately after the passage of the Voting Rights Act, massive voter registration drives took place in black communities. As a result, during the next election, the number of Blacks voting at the polls skyrocketed (Waldman, 2016).

In an effort to make voting easier and thereby increase voter turnout, the Clinton administration urged Congress to pass the National Voter Registration Act (NVRA) of 1993, also known as the "Motor Voter" law. The legislation requires state social welfare agencies and state motor vehicle departments to supply voter registration forms. The intent of the NVRA was to establish registration procedures designed, in part, to "increase the number of eligible citizens who register to vote in elections for Federal office … protect the integrity of the electoral process … [and] ensure that accurate and current voter registration rolls are maintained" (U.S. GAO, 2014, n.p.). While the law did not catapult the number of voters to the point that Clinton had hoped, it did significantly increase the number of citizens who registered to vote, since registering was now easier than ever (Waldman, 2016).

Given the hype about voter fraud, Arizona passed a voter identification law, requiring that voters show proof of citizenship before being eligible to vote (Brinkerhoff, 2013). By the time it reached the Supreme Court, it was too close to the election, so the Court decided not to order Arizona to change its law for fear of causing confusion. Despite this procedural rationale in *Purcell v. Gonzalez* (2006), the Court still took the opportunity to weigh in with its perspective on potential voter fraud. Justice Stevens, who wrote the *per curiam* decision, declared, "A State indisputably has a compelling interest in preserving the integrity of its election process. Confidence in the integrity of our electoral processes is essential to the functioning of our participatory democracy. Voter fraud drives honest citizens out of the democratic process and breeds distrust of our government. Voters who fear their legitimate votes will be outweighed by fraudulent ones will feel disenfranchised" (n.p.). In a related case two years later, the Supreme Court ruled in *Crawford v. Marion County Election Board* that there is a compelling state interest to check against voter impersonation; therefore, voter identification laws are justified (Atkeson et al., 2014).

Along with these Supreme Court cases, there is the core, foundational case that the Court decided in 2013. The *Shelby County v. Holder* decision became a landmark decision regarding voting rights. In *Shelby*, the Court reviewed the rationale and function of the 1965 Voting Rights Act (VRA). The Court struck down the requirement in the VRA that a bloc of states, mostly in the South, should have their voting laws cleared with the Justice Department. The Obama administration had been pushing for the restoration of a modified version of this provision (Bacon, 2016). One of the arguments considered was that conditions for African-American voting in the South have greatly improved, which was the premise behind the law in the first place. As such, if conditions have improved, Blacks no longer need the VRA to guarantee suffrage equality. Instead of striking down the law, the Court functionally removed enforcement procedures of Section 5 of the Act, which is the section used to ascertain fairness in state-based voting laws (Cohen, 2013; Waldman, 2016). This is why Justice Scalia has called the VRA a form of "racial entitlement," meaning that it grants special status simply due to a person's race (Davidson, 2013, n.p.).

However, the *Shelby* decision, by making Section 5 of the VRA essentially inoperable, gutted enforcement provisions of the VRA (The Leadership Conference Education Fund, 2016). In so doing, *Shelby* removes federal oversight of election procedures, thereby allowing states to change voting laws without notice or scrutiny. As a result, the *Shelby* decision permits widespread disenfranchisement by

> making voting more confusing and less accessible by engaging in massive reductions in the number of polling places. Polling place closures are a particularly common and pernicious tactic for disenfranchising voters of color. Decisions to shutter or reduce voting locations are often made quietly and at the last minute, making pre-election intervention or litigation virtually impossible. These changes can place an undue burden on minority voters, who may be less likely to have access to public transportation or vehicles, given continuing disparities in socioeconomic resources. Once an election is conducted, there is no judicial remedy for the loss of votes that were never cast because a voter's usual polling place has disappeared. (The Leadership Conference Education Fund, 2016, n.p.)

What is also problematic is that the *Shelby* decision gives states the latitude to alter polling locations without notifying the public in advance. According to The Leadership Conference Education Fund (2016), "voters have to rely on news reports and anecdotes from local advocates who attend city and county commission meetings or legislative sessions where these changes are contemplated to identify potentially discriminatory polling place location and precinct changes" (n.p.). Consequently, citizens will have "at least 868 fewer places to cast ballots in the 2016 presidential election than they did in past elections, a 16 percent reduction," and those cancelations were not publicly announced in advance (The Leadership Conference Education Fund, 2016, n.p.).

In terms of racial discrimination, the *Shelby* decision obviously grants states the ability to suppress voting rights, many of which will impact people of color (Cohen, 2013). To make matters worse, since Section 5 of the VRA was gutted by *Shelby*, there is no federal oversight or investigation process into the occasions when states change venues, cancel polling places, or otherwise alter the voting process. For minorities, this means that any state action that is racially motivated will not be identified as such, essentially allowing states to commit racial discrimination and disenfranchisement willy-nilly (The Leadership Conference Education Fund, 2016). Al Sharpton (2013a), the racial provocateur, called this action in *Shelby* a "slick maneuver" to cut against

Figure 7.7: An upset black woman.

previous gains made in the name of civil rights. According to Bazelon and Rutenberg (2016), "the gutting of Section 5 facilitated an onslaught of restrictive new laws that made voting disproportionately harder for minorities across the country, marking the biggest setback to minority voting rights in the half-century since President Johnson signed the Voting Rights Act" (n.p.). Despite the problems associated with the *Shelby* decision regarding what many would consider fundamental, constitutionally protected voting rights, Congress has refused to pass new legislation to protect voting rights (Hebert & Lang, 2016).

Another consequence of the *Shelby* decision is that states almost immediately adopted voter suppression laws, which include voter ID laws (Berman, 2015b; See Figure 7.6). Of course, this impacts people of color disproportionately. According to Berman (2015a), these laws "have disenfranchised thousands of voters, disproportionately those of color. In the past five years, 395 new voting restrictions have been introduced in 49 states, with half the states in the country adopting measures making it harder to vote. If anybody thinks there's not racial discrimination in voting today, they're not really paying attention" (n.p.).

According to the Pew Research Center, "one of every eight names on the voter rolls were no longer valid or were significantly inaccurate" (Waldman, 2016, p. 180). Trumpeted by Republicans, this data originates from a software program known as Crosscheck with the obvious purpose to point out possible voter fraud. Crosscheck examines voter rosters lists in multiple states—it has identified around 7 million names as possible people who vote in more than one state—the list disproportionately impacts people of color because the names most heavily weighted are common Asian, Black, and Hispanic names, such as "Jackson, Garcia, Patel and Kim—ones common among minorities, who vote overwhelmingly Democratic. Indeed, fully 1 in 7 African-Americans in those 27 states, plus the state of Washington ... are listed as under suspicion of having voted twice. This also applies to 1 in 8 Asian-Americans and 1 in 8 Hispanic voters" (Palast, 2014, n.p.). While the Crosscheck program has the capacity to check multiple criteria, voter fraud hatchet people just use a person's surname, and occasionally the first name. By only using this broad search parameter, the program yields a massive amount of false positives (Millhiser, 2014). Failure to check the other criteria is devastating—of the supposed seven million double-voters, virtually all of them are justified when middle names, suffixes, and "inactive" users are taken into consideration:

> Twenty-three percent of the names—nearly 1.6 million of them—lack matching middle names. "Jr." and "Sr." are ignored, potentially disenfranchising two generations in the same family. And, notably, of those who may have voted twice in the 2012 presidential election, 27 percent were listed as "inactive" voters, meaning that almost 1.9 million may not even have voted once in that race. (Palast, 2014, n.p.)

As a result, Joseph Lowery, who co-founded SCLC with Dr. Martin Luther King, Jr., says the process of Crosscheck is "Jim Crow all over again" (cited in Palast, 2014, n.p.). When the data were reviewed by the noted statistician, Mark Swedlund, he noted that "Crosscheck does have inherent bias to over-selecting for potential scrutiny and purging voters from Asian, Hispanic and Black ethnic groups. In fact, the matching methodology, which presumes people in other states with the same name are matches, will always over-select from groups of people with common surnames" (cited in Palast, 2014, n.p.). Equally troubling is that voters do not even know that political parties, election boards, and other involved entities are using Crosscheck to possibly purge them from voter registration lists (Millhiser, 2014; Palast, 2014). In other words, a voter can travel to a polling place and be rejected without ever knowing why.

In response to the Crosscheck data, Congress passed legislation in 2002 that requires universal adoption of electronic voting machines. However, since the inception of high-tech voting machines, there have been a number of complications, which challenge the assumption that the machines reduce fraud and voter inaccuracies: instances of hacking, machine breakdowns, too few machines at precincts (which produces long lines or, in some cases, turning citizens away who then become disenfranchised), and obsolete technology (Waldman, 2016).

Yet massive voter fraud is counter-intuitive and is, in fact, "exceedingly rare" (Waldman, 2016, p. 183). Candidates do not really benefit from one or two more votes, especially when weighed against the risks of being caught. According to Waldman (2016), a single case of fraud in the state of Wisconsin automatically yields a $10,000 fine and up to three years in prison. Similarly, the argument that waves of immigrants commit voter fraud is equally untenable. As Waldman (2016) describes, this argument "poses a logical problem; few individuals would trek from home, find their way across the border, evade capture, then march into a government office and declare their name and address" just to vote (p. 183). Election officials in Georgia also argue that voter fraud, impersonation, or double-voting does not make rational sense. They claim that in most cases, it is difficult to motivate people to vote once, much less more than once (Palast, 2014).

According to Lorraine Minnite, a professor of public policy at Rutgers, "federal prosecutors indicted far more people for violations of the nation's migratory-bird laws than for election fraud" (Eichenwald, 2016, n.p.). Minnite also claims "Voter fraud remains rare because it is irrational behavior. You're not likely to change the outcome of an election with your illegal fraudulent vote, and the chances of being caught are there and we have rules to prevent against it" (cited in Edge & Holstege, 2016, n.p.). And Justin Levitt (2008) of the Brennan Center for Justice at the New York University School of Law argues that "Every once in a great while, a report of in-person impersonation fraud, or a report of an attempt at in-person impersonation fraud, appears to be substantiated. It has been known to happen. What is notable, however, is how rarely it has been known to happen. Americans are struck and killed by lightning more often" (n.p.). Simply put, the statistics on voter fraud do not support the claims that fraud is a serious problem. In terms of double-voting, not a single conviction has ever occurred (Palast, 2014). As Waldman (2016) notes, "Nationwide from 2002 to 2005 only twenty-four people were convicted of illegal voting in federal elections and no one was charged with voter impersonation; by 2007 only 120 people had been charged and eighty-six convicted" (p. 187). Of those instanced discovered, the majority apparently were products of improperly completed registration forms and misunderstandings regarding voter eligibility.

In another study from 2012, 2,068 alleged election-related fraud incidents from all 50 states were analyzed. While "some fraud had occurred since 2000, the rate was infinitesimal compared with the 146 million registered voters in that 12-year span. The analysis found only 10 cases of voter impersonation, the only kind of fraud that could be prevented by voter ID at the polls" (Edge & Holstege, 2016, n.p.). Furthermore, political and public policy experts at Dartmouth College conducted a study. They argue that there was no "widespread" voter fraud in the 2016 presidential election, and "the voter fraud fears fomented and espoused by the Trump campaign are not grounded in any observable features of the election" (Cottrell et al., 2016, n.p.). Given the number of independent studies on this issue that point to the insignificance of voter fraud, the likely rationale for conservatives to perpetuate the voter fraud "myth" is to lay the groundwork for voter suppression. In fact, "Conservatives have used the specter of voter fraud, which a number of studies have shown is virtually non-existent in American elections, to pass laws that make it more difficult for people of color and college students to vote. Both of those groups tend to back Democratic candidates" (Bacon, 2016, n.p.). Of course, voter ID laws vary from state to state (U.S. GAO, 2014).

Some studies also measure the effectiveness of voter ID and voter suppression laws. One such study, highlighted by the U.S. GAO report (2014), finds that depending on the state and the state's laws, voter turnout could increase, or it could decrease; it depends on the state. There is also another source that validates the GAO report

(Wihbey, 2014). With Kansas and Tennessee, for example, voter turnout, particularly among minorities, decreased after the voter suppression laws were enacted.

Thus, there are still many political practitioners, mainly conservatives (Atkeson et al., 2014; Bacon, 2016), who believe voter fraud, election fraud, and voter impersonations are a real threat. One argument levied is that the instances of voter fraud that have been caught prove the system works—the people were caught and were not successful with their fraud (Haley, 2016). And Christopher Coates, the former chief of the voting section in the Department of Justice, claims that each instance of fraud undermines the integrity of the democratic, voting process (Edge & Holstege, 2016). Wisconsin Governor Scott Walker makes a similar claim (Edge & Holstege, 2016). Thus, even if there is just a single instance of voting fraud, impersonation, or manipulation, the overall process of democratic suffrage becomes illegitimate. At least in one state, voter fraud is considered "rampant." Governor Greg Abott of Texas and the Texas Office of the Attorney General demonstrates that "360 allegations of voter fraud were sent to the attorney general since 2012. Fifteen of those cases were successfully prosecuted" (Edge & Holstege, 2016, n.p.).

Despite the overwhelming evidence to the contrary (Edge & Holstege, 2016), many right-wing pundits use the myth of voter fraud as a fear appeal tactic for larger issues, such as opposition to immigration, undercutting support for Democrats, and stereotypical depictions of Blacks. For instance,

> Panic over improper voting became a recurring riff on the right. Fox News, the conservative-leaning cable network, set up a "Voter Fraud Watch." Former House majority leader Dick Armey, head of the organization Freedom Works, declared preposterously that 3 percent of all ballots were fraudulent votes cast by Democrats. Using coded language he told Fox News that the problem "is pinpointed to the major urban areas, to the inner cities." (Waldman, 2016, p. 189)

Additionally, these fear appeals are apparently effective. A study from the University of Delaware asked white voters if they believed voter identification should be required in order to cast a ballot. "When a photo of a black man voting accompanied the question, support for voter ID jumped by 6 percent over responses to the question illustrated by a photo of a white voter" (Waldman, 2016, p. 190). What is interesting, however, is that voter ID laws, at best, could only reduce voter impersonation—it would do nothing for double-voting, dead people voting, or other types of fraud (Edge & Holstege, 2016).

Part of the appeal to voter identification laws is the sense that they are not too cumbersome. After all, every citizen should have some form of identification, and if a person wants to purchase alcohol, for instance, they should be able to provide proper ID to prove their age. And in many cases, the types of identification that can be used for voting are not unreasonable. However, even something simple like a simple driver's license can be problematic, particularly for a poor person of color. Waldman (2016) reports that Blacks are three times as likely as White voters to lack a proper photo ID, including a driver's license. What is more, in order to secure a photo ID, such as a passport, driver's license or other identification, a person needs to produce proper identity documentation, like a birth certificate, marriage certificate, etc. To obtain those documents—and in many cases a person will need two, three, or more for a state-sanctioned photo ID—requires inconvenient, if not challenging, transportation to the government office that houses such documents, and these documents can be costly, especially if a person needs multiple forms of documentation, and then the costs accumulate when they also need to pay for a driver's license or state ID (Edge & Holstege, 2016). In other words, securing recognized identification is not as easy or inexpensive as many people might think (U.S. GAO Report, 2014). Furthermore, while there are virtually no instances of voter fraud or impersonations, nearly five million citizens are negatively impacted by voter ID laws, making it "significantly harder" for them to vote (Waldman, 2016, p. 205).

To compensate for the high cost of securing a proper identification, some states have adopted measures for so-called "free" IDs (U. S. GAO, 2014). After all, to impose a cost on a requirement before voting sounds very similar to a poll tax. However, even if state-based photo IDs are free, there are still other costs associated, like what is known as "underlying documents," or those documents that are used to validate state-based photo IDs. Such documents can include birth certificates, marriage certificates, passports, etc. Thus, even if the actual photo ID is "free," the underlying documents necessary to prove or justify the state-based ID still cost money and time and energy (Earls, 2015; U.S. GAO, 2014).

Now, some form of identification is already necessary in order to vote. The federal government requires minimum ID standards for all states when they register people to vote (Atkeson et al., 2014). It establishes a "floor," or a minimum requirement in which states can use, or the states may impose stricter requirements. But, of course, states can never be more lenient than what the federal government stipulates.

Finally, there is the issue of the voter ID law in North Carolina. North Carolina imposed rather strict guidelines for what should constitute as proper identification for voter. As a result, the burden placed on voters in order to actually vote was high. As I have been discussing, this burden was especially onerous for people of color. The North Carolina law was especially problematic since North Carolina is considered a so-called "battleground" state, especially in presidential elections. In part because Republicans were worried that minority voters would sway to the Democrats, voter suppression laws were enacted to curtail fringe voting. The measures were so severe and problematic that they were considered a new era of Jim Crow, ushered in by right-wing extremism (Pilkington, 2014). However, conservative Republicans argue that the North Carolina law does not result in voter suppression. In fact, according to empirical evidence, the law actually resulted in more Black voters turning out during the elections, not less, which is what supposed "suppression" laws should do (Lucas, 2014). As a result, conservatives argue that the North Carolina law is race-neutral (Pilkington, 2014), and opponents to such laws, like the Obama administration, are engaging in what is known as "race-baiting," or the forced pressure to have others "talk about racism and how it impacts black people in America" (King, 2013). Of course, such conservatives also claim that the North Carolina law, as well as similar measures, are race-neutral (Pilkington, 2014).

Although the Supreme Court has consistently validated the constitutionality of voter identification laws, the polarizing and fear-based rhetoric emanating from the far right has not abated. A conservative pundit, Matthew Vadum (2011), claims that "registering the poor to vote ... is like handing out burglary tools to criminals," and registering them is fundamentally "un-American" (n.p.). These sentiments perpetuate classism, but they are also "dog whistles" in that urban poor people tend to be disproportionately people of color, or, as López (2014) points out, "Racial demagoguery and culture-war politics ... is also evident in efforts to suppress the votes of the poor and of nonwhites" (p. 159). Steve King, a U.S. representative from Iowa, says there "was a time in American history when you had to be a male property owner in order to vote. The reason for that was, because [the founders] wanted the people who voted ... to have some skin in the game" (cited in Beinart, 2014, n.p.). The president of the Tea Party Nation, Judson Phillips, echoes this sentiment: "If you're a property owner you actually have a vested stake in the community. If you're not a property owner, you know, I'm sorry but property owners have a little bit more of a vested interest in the community than non-property owners" (cited in Glink, 2010, n.p.). The important thing to realize here is that voter fraud has the potential to seriously impact elections (Atkeson et al., 2014)

The black community makes a similar testament. The ever-present and opportunity-seeking Al Sharpton (2013a) remarks,

> When creative schemes threaten to disenfranchise the rights of Americans, we need a Justice Department and an Attorney General that are not afraid to stand up for the liberties afforded to all of us despite our socio-economic background, race, color or creed. This summer we watched renewed attacks on our freedoms, but we also witnessed a revival of nonviolent demonstrations, mobilization and action. Now we must carry that same fighting spirit into the new season. Those attempting to destroy progress will not win, plain and simple. (n.p.)

As Kang (2015) notes, "Despite the long history of black voter suppression, in the Court's view the increase in black voter registration and the prominence of black elected officials in current American politics erases that history. The precipitous erasure of that history then obscures the present and continuing reality of black subordination in the political system because of their underrepresentation, their limited opportunities for creating meaningful policy, and their disenfranchisement due to structural barriers" (p. 1396). And, according to Sharpton, actions speak louder than words, meaning that he advocates active social change against forces of oppression as opposed to a reality where Blacks are continually subjugated. As Sharpton explains,

> In August, some 180,000 to 200,000 people gathered in Washington, D.C. to join National Action Network and Martin Luther King III as we paid

homage to the 50th anniversary of Dr. Martin Luther King Jr.'s historic "March on Washington for Jobs and Freedom."…The numbers, though great, aren't enough. We must sustain a commitment to tackle the issues we raised because words must be matched by visible action. (2013a, n.p.)

And it seems that most Americans agree with Rev. Al Sharpton. A study conducted by Atkeson, Alvarez, Hall and Sinclair (2014) points out that "respondents can see both the advantages and disadvantages of identification laws. They tend to believe the laws work to prevent fraud. The majority does not believe the laws prevent legitimate voting. Nevertheless, most tend to think that ensuring participation trumps preventing fraud as well" (p. 1387). While "voters generally agree that ID laws prevent fraud (70 percent) … a majority preferred ensuring access (54 percent) to preventing fraud (46 percent). Interestingly, this suggests that, when the debate is framed as a conflict between two competing policy positions, voters appear less supportive of policies that might reduce turnout" (p. 1388, 1391). Thus, when debating about voter ID laws, as well as voter fraud in general, there appears to be two competing argumentative frames—either suppress voter fraud or secure access to voting for everyone (Atkeson et al., 2014).

But, as we have seen, the arguments in favor of voter ID laws are generally used as racial tools in the fight for democracy. Indeed, Lorraine Minnite (2015) makes this claim powerfully: "The myth of voter fraud persists because it is a racialized weapon in a power struggle over the soul of American democracy." And voter suppression is equally troubling for our democracy, as Anita Earls argues: "What's at stake is how we define our democracy—who can participate and who will be kept out of the electorate" (n.p.).

Suffrage rights are vital, and not just because our constitutional amendments have declared them as such. Democracies, by definition, are based on free and fair elections (Franck, 1992). And as Waldman (2016) professes, "hashtag campaigns and the profusion of creative new ways to press for change will fall short if they do not translate, soon, into real political activity expressed at the ballot box. When we fail to vote, we leave political power on the table" (pp. 263–264). Thus, it is severely troubling when political officials, pundits, commentators, and the like use vitriol when discussing voting rights.

We can begin by seeing the way our new president, Donald Trump, discussed the issue of voting rights. According to Trump, "In addition to winning the Electoral College in a landslide, I won the popular vote if you deduct the millions of people who voted illegally" (cited in Milbank, 2016, n.p.). He also said, "There's a lot of dirty pool played at the election. If you don't have voter ID, you can just keep voting and voting and voting" (cited in Edge & Holstege, 2016, n.p.). He went so far as calling the entire process "rigged" (Gillman, 2017, n.p.). Trump's anguish over potential fraud was not objective; he had a personal interest in the matter. Trump's ego cannot handle the fact that Clinton won the popular vote, so he is peddling the voter fraud myth to claim he won both the Electoral College and the popular vote (Kessler, 2016). Despite evidence to the contrary, Trump claimed that 3 to 5 million popular votes in the 2016 presidential election were fraudulent (Gillman, 2017). Along with these claims, Trump argued that "illegal" immigrants were supposedly voting in waves. This assertion has also been discounted:

> Among other things, he falsely asserted that illegal immigrants were tipping the results in elections, based on a misinterpretation of disputed data. Even the researcher who produced the data said Trump was taking his findings out of context: "Our results suggest that almost all elections in the U.S. are not determined by non-citizen participation, with occasional and very rare potential exceptions." (Kessler, 2016, n.p.)

And if immigrants are not the problem, Trump has even blamed dead people—or voters claiming the identity of deceased individuals—for voting in the election: "I will be asking for a major investigation into VOTER FRAUD, including those registered to vote in two states," as well as "those registered to vote who are dead (and many for a long time). Depending on results, we will strengthen up voting procedures!" (emphasis in original, Jackson & Johnson, 2017, n.p.). The idea that dead people are voting, especially during the presidential election, is unfounded. The examples that some people, like Trump, cite have been clerical errors, not dead people voting (Jackson & Johnson, 2017). Not only has President Trump not provided support for his conjectures; we now know that the baseless claims are also flat-out false (Phillip & DeBonis, 2017). The Civil Rights division of the Justice Department had over 500 people in 28 states monitor the presidential election—no cases of fraud were reported (Jackson & Johnson, 2017).

But this type of divisive rhetoric has not just emanated from Trump. Senator Ted Cruz has added to the discourse. When asked by Sean Hannity about voting rights and voter laws, the conversation turned to Obama and that Black voting was clearly responsible for his presidential victories. Cruz said, "If the slaves were never freed in the Civil War, you have to wonder, where would Obama be today? Certainly not the White House, not in the capacity he's in. And you have some in America that think that might not be a bad thing" (cited in Rock, 2014, n.p.). For some reason, Cruz's comments barely made a blip on the media radar screen, and no one seemed to follow up to figure out what he really meant. Nevertheless, to imply that perhaps we should still have slavery is extremely inflammatory. In a similar statement, extreme conservative instigator Ann Coulter added to the conversation. Not only did Coulter agree that voter suppression—or voter ID laws—are justifiable; she also went so far as to advocate for a return to Jim Crow laws. When asked on a *Fox News* segment about "literacy tests," Coulter responded, "I just think it should be, well for one thing, a little more difficult to vote. There's nothing unconstitutional about literacy tests. Instead, we have ballots being given in 124 different languages. And I'm pretty sure Senate debates will not be taking place in Urdu. So, what are they voting on?" (cited in Edwards, 2015, n.p.). In typical Coulter-fashion, she uses sarcasm to temper her blatantly racist remark. Her position appears to be so outlandish to most reasonable thinkers that she has to use sarcasm as a form of rhetorical spin to soften the blow.

We have not heard much in the media about voter fraud, despite some of the headlines from Trump's rhetoric. However, online media has exploded regarding this issue. Although virtually every study that has been conducted points to no or very insignificant instances of voter fraud, conservative online media outlets continue to perpetuate the myth that voter fraud is rampant and gravely serious. From several accounts, the so-called voter fraud "myth" began with a few unsubstantiated tweets by Gregg Phillips, "a self-described conservative voter fraud specialist, who started making claims even before data on voter history was actually available in most jurisdictions" (Kessler, 2016, n.p.). Then, the conservative, and extremist, online source *Infowars* led the charge about voter fraud by using the tweets from Phillips as their source (Milbank, 2016). And, as we know, the way echo chambers operate, other conservative online sources re-post and cite the original reporting from *Infowars*, making the arguments about voter fraud not only appear legitimate, but they also make it seem like there is a consensus of news sources that support such claims.

As is true with most controversial issues, right-wing conservatives are not the only ones contributing to polarizing rhetoric. Liberal Democrats, like Shripal Shah, who is a vice president at American Bridge, which is a liberal think tank that specializes in oppositional research, calls Trump a "conspiracy theorist," and then Shah uses a childish rhetorical maneuver that we might hear on a playground: "Donald Trump would rather investigate baseless conspiracy theories about Americans exercising their right to vote, than the confirmed role his Russian handler Vladimir Putin had in hacking our election" (cited in Gillman, 2017, n.p.). In other words, Shah on one hand bashed Trump for baseless claims about voter fraud, but then on the other hand asserts that Putin is Trump's "handler." The twisted, below-the-belt, argument is tantamount to claiming "my daddy can beat up your daddy." Instead of sticking to the facts, which do not support Trump's position, Shah engages in *ad hominem* attacks. The always outspoken Elijah Cummings, the Democrat Representative from Maryland, also contributes to the polarization of this issue by presuming that Trump's arguments about voter fraud are just ways to justify additional voter suppression (Jackson & Johnson, 2017). Again, instead of focusing on the facts, Cummings associates an intent to Trump's position, which just clouds the issue and does not advance civil dialogue. Finally, Walt Dismay (2015), who reports for *Left Wing Nation*, says this about Fox News and Ann Coulter:

> Fox News and their right-wing lunatic guests are inching ever closer to finally saying what they actually believe: We don't want non-whites to vote. If you think I'm race-baiting or being unfair, how do you explain their desire to bring back the explicitly racist idea of "literacy tests"? … it would keep almost every person that watches Fox News from voting and that would immeasurably improve the IQ of the electorate. (n.p.)

Using *ad hominem* attacks by calling conservatives "lunatics" with "low IQs" who engage in "explicitly racist" arguments demonstrates that some liberals participate in polarizing discourse just like some conservatives. The overall discussion about voter ID laws and voter suppression is not helped when political officials and pundits talk in these ways.

ASIAN DISCRIMINATION

Asian-Americans occupy a unique place in our conversations about race. Race is too often considered White or Black, a bifurcated sense of reality that is neither helpful nor accurate. Other so-called minority groups besides Asian-Americans also complicate our typically bimodal understanding of race. Such a logic either lumps minorities, like Asian-Americans, into the category of White or the category of Black—depending on one's perspective, the situation, or the argument. Or, it is possible to just ignore Asian-Americans altogether, rendering them invisible and silenced during our discussions about race. Yet as Mao and Young (2008) explain in their excellent collection on Asian American rhetoric, "Asian American rhetoric is intimately tied to, and indeed constituted by, particularizing speech settings, specific communicative purposes, and situated discursive acts" (p. 3).

Speaking from his own experiences, Howard University law professor, Frank Wu, explains his perspective on how Asian-Americans are both generalized as minorities writ-large or invisible altogether: "As a member of a minority group everywhere in my country except among family or through the self-conscious effort to find other Asian Americans, I alternate between being conspicuous and vanishing, being stared at or looked through. Although the conditions may seem contradictory, they have in common the loss of control. In most instances, I am who others perceive me to be rather than how I perceive myself to be" (Wu, 2002, pp. 7–8). The lack of control to which Wu refers is a powerful testament to how society can govern our perceptions of reality. As Wu continues to argue, the "stereotype of Asian Americans has become all the more powerful because Asian Americans are at once highly visible in popular culture and virtually invisible in serious discourse, allowing popular culture to define serious discourse" (Wu, 2002, p. 26).

If our identities—or, rather, in this context, the identities of Asian-Americans—are products of social construction, we may wonder how a racial group can alter the way society views them, and ultimately how society treats them. For our purposes, it is worth noting how the construction of identity occurs discursively. As Wu (2002) explains, "In race matters, words matter too. Asian Americans have been excluded by the very terms used to conceptualize race." Of course, in our bimodal logic of race, Asian-Americans do not easily fit into the category of White or Black. Wu continues, "People speak of 'American' as if it means 'white' and 'minority' as if it means 'black.' In that semantic formula, Asian Americans, neither black nor white, consequently are neither American nor minority" (p. 20). This limitation as a consequence of our racial logic not only excludes groups like Asian-Americans, but it also necessarily provides an incomplete and inaccurate framework for understanding race as a whole.

Asian American injustice and discrimination typically occurs in one of two ways—either through stereotypes (like most racial groups), or through direct oppression and violence, most notably from other minority groups. For the first—stereotypes—we should not be surprised by the ignorance displayed by many Americans, nor should we excuse it. I have often experienced hearing Americans comment about Asian tourists, joking about how they always take pictures, eat chop suey, and are responsible for World War II. Of course, lumping all Asians together is part of the problem. I have traveled to many different Asian countries, and the diversity of customs, food, spiritual beliefs, history, etc. always impress me. However, to the average American, all Asians are Chinese or Japanese or Korean. A Wu (2002) describes,

> Although they rarely mention their personal lives, people will always make it a point to tell me about the hit movie they saw last night or the museum exhibit they toured over the weekend if it had a vaguely Asian theme, whether Chinese, Japanese, Korean, Vietnamese, or whatever, because, "It reminded me of you." They tell me I resemble the cellist Yo-Yo Ma or their five-year-old son's friend in school. Or in a passing instant, a white boy or a black boy, whom I would credit with childhood innocence, can rekindle my memory of the ordinary intolerance of days past. (p. 8)

As an Italian/Irish-American, I cannot imagine if groups of people just lumped me into the category of "European," as if my family heritage shares something in common with folks from Germany, Portugal, or Finland. Not only do they speak different languages, they have enormous differences in foods, histories, religious beliefs, and so on. The same is true for Asians.

One specific area where Asian American injustice occurs is voter identification laws. As I have discussed previously in this chapter, Crosscheck is a program that seeks to locate instances of voter fraud. However, if the program uses only a narrow search routine, such as surnames, it discriminately targets racial groups. Asian-Americans are notably impacted by the Crosscheck program for two reasons—the number of common surnames in Asian cultures exceeds that of other communities, and first names tend to be more unique than surnames, meaning that if Crosscheck fails to consider other criteria and merely focuses on surnames, Asian-Americans will be disproportionately affected (Palast, 2014). Considering the common surnames of Chung, Park, Kim, Hashimoto, etc., this is not too hard to believe. "In fact, a sixth of all Asian-Americans share just 30 surnames and 50 percent of minorities share common last names, versus 30 percent of whites" (Palast, 2014, n.p.).

Of course, it does not help when historical legacies of racism linger in our culture unapologetically. Much like how Blacks still hear jokes about slavery or still see so-called comedy in black-face, Asian Americans still observe and experience offensive discourse from yesteryear. By way of example, Wu says, "I am disgusted that Idaho officials refuse to rename the landmark 'Chink's Peak' and Houston officials desire to keep 'Jap Road'" (Wu, 2002, p. 23). Just the other day I heard someone refer to an Asian (who happened to be a Korean) as a "chink." When I tell people I have visited Nagasaki, I have heard some people describe how "those Japs had it coming." Of course, these semantic markers are deeply outrageous and offensive, but they also should remind us of the power of language. When there is a lack of knowledge and critical thinking, some people resort to what they have heard others say or what they think people want them to say. In either case, the power of racial rhetoric resonates, particularly with the aggrieved party.

Another type of injustice faced by Asian Americans is similar to the inexcusable events faced by Blacks, Jews, and other racial minority groups—violence. There are many instances when Asian Americans have been attacked, threatened, and pressured by means of violence. What makes matters even worse is that such violent episodes have more often than not been perpetuated by other racial minority groups. Wu (2002) again helps explain the historical and cultural dynamics here:

> African American clergy such as the Reverend Al Sharpton led the 1990 boycotts of Asian-owned stores as he tried to shut down the Red Apple store in New York City following a dubious claim that the owners had assaulted a customer. African American activists called for Asian immigrants to surrender their stores to African Americans. Rappers such as Ice Cube san of brutalizing Asian entrepreneurs with lyrics such as, "Pay respect to the black fist, or we'll burn your store right down to a crisp," on his Death Certificate album. (Wu, 2002, p. 30).

To help quantify the problem, Wu continues:

> In 1992, nine Asian American small business owners were shot to death in Washington, D. C.; in 1993, fifteen were killed in Los Angeles, many by African Americans (although whether there were racial motivations in the cases is unclear). ... In San Francisco ... African American children pick on Asian American children, just as whites have done. But Asian Americans who can fight back do so without remorse. Whether African American on Asian American violence and Asian American on African American violence can be appropriately juxtaposed, and if the effect is productive, requires meditation. (Wu, 2002, p. 31).

Yet Wu correctly identifies how none of us are morally neutral on this front. All racial groups, at least during certain historical moments, have engaged in these types of behaviors and have embraced stereotypical descriptions of other racial groups. As he explains, "Race relations, like bad relationships of any type, can become fixed and unchanging. ... One side becomes the villain, the other the victim. As crude caricatures, both give up free will and neither can claim moral responsibility" (Wu, 2002, p. 28).

Wu (2002) spends considerable time discussing the importance of building alliances and coalitions. Despite past examples of how minority racial groups have conflicted with each other, Wu sincerely believes that a way forward is to put aside differences and focus on the strengths of coming together. To his credit, while one group's oppression may not be equivalent to another's, the fact that both groups—as well as others—have experienced similar oppressive conditions can be a place from which different racial groups can coalesce.

To conclude, Wu (2002) frames the discriminatory experiences of Asian Americans in perspective with the whole of society—a refreshing perspective that is not often given or acknowledged by many:

> The general absence of Asian Americans and the stereotyping of Asians were not to the detriment of Asian Americans and Asians alone. They affect our society and are related to other problems. My white classmates failed to learn about the people around them, and I was not introduced to African Americans, Latino/as, American Jews, Arab Americans, and others. We knew one another as nothing but shadows, without substance. (p. 309–310)

WELFARE

In his 1976 presidential campaign speech in New Hampshire, Ronald Reagan famously said, "She has 80 names, 30 addresses, 12 Social Security cards and is collecting veterans' benefits on four non-existing deceased husbands. … She's collecting Social Security on her cards. She's got Medicaid, getting food stamps and she is collecting welfare under each of her names. Her tax-free cash alone is over $150,000" (Reagan, 1976; *The Washington Star*, 1976, n.p.). Since then, the topic of welfare has entered American conversations with someone almost certainly uttering some version of Reagan's anecdote. We have probably all heard the variations—a black person picks up their welfare check in their Cadillac, they spend their food stamps on rib-eyes and soda, they sell their food stamps so they can use the money to buy alcohol or drugs, they are lazy and will not secure a job, they have more children to obtain even more welfare money each month, etc., etc. Despite evidence to the contrary, this welfare myth—the legend of Reagan's "welfare queen"—has a prominent place in contemporary racial rhetoric.

Representations of welfare recipients serve a special discursive function in public policy debates, conversations about the national debt, and, of course, race relations. A particularly troubling example of this type of rhetoric can be seen in the remarks by Republican Mississippi state representative, Gene Alday, who is on record saying he opposes increased funding for education because "from a town where all the blacks are getting food stamps and what I call 'welfare crazy checks.' They don't work." Later, Alday scoffed, "I liked to died. I laid in there for hours because they (black people) were in there being treated for gunshots" (cited in Delaney & Scheller, 2015, n.p.). Schram and Soss (2015) carefully sort through some of the conservative rhetorical portrayals and explain how they have ideological implications:

> When economic anxieties spread, political entrepreneurs start peddling the same old stories and slanders, polishing them up as newly discovered social problems that demand get-tough solutions. Conjuring images of lavish and irresponsible lifestyles, critics in media and government deride the folly of public aid programs, ridiculing them as counterproductive and costly drains on the nation. ... Now as in the past, such images serve powerful ideological functions. As the richest Americans have mobilized to hoard wealth and power in recent decades, the middle and working classes have fallen into an extended era of precarity and anxiety. Now as in the past, elites have rolled out tales of a parasitic and undeserving poor to deflect public anger from themselves. Lazy and criminal "takers" who abuse the goodwill of hardworking taxpayers are offered up as a handy scapegoat for the new hard times and a ready explanation for fiscal shortfalls. Deeply racialized stories of a threatening underclass captivate the public imagination, while on the periphery lobbyists and public officials rewrite policies and administrative procedures to redistribute wealth upward. (n.p.)

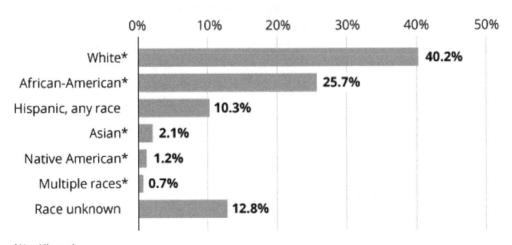

A Large Share Of SNAP Recipients Are White

Participating households by race and ethnicity of the household head, 2013

*Not Hispanic

Note: Seven percent of households had no household head and no adult listed on the file.

Source: U.S. Department of Agriculture   THE HUFFINGTON POST

Figure 7.8

Later in their article, Schram and Soss (2015) explain how these welfare characterizations exude racist inclinations:

> The repetitive ritual of getting tough on the poor is, as many critics point out, a form of "dog-whistle politics," successfully mobilizing racial resentments in a society where explicitly racist appeals are usually condemned. The "welfare queen" and the "criminal thug"—infamous, gender-stereotyped paragons of a deviant and threatening blackness—do the symbolic lifting for a politics that dares not reveal its own racism. Together, they evoke a potent stew of class, gender, and racial biases, deepening divisions among potential allies as they smooth the way for an ugly assortment of partisan and policy goals. (n.p.)

As an example of liberal divisive discourse, the Schram and Soss (2015) article points out the fallacies and problems of some conservative portrayals of welfare recipients, but Schram and Soss also use hyperbole and sweeping generalizations.

Those on the right, however, engage in their own polarizing posturing. A popular conservative website, *Freedom Daily* (2017), shows a picture of an apparently screaming and angry black woman, with the title of the article saying, "Welfare Queen Goes Crazy after She Sees this Sign at Grocery Store" (see Figure 7.7). The sign placed throughout the store says they no longer take EBT cards, which function like food stamps. In addition to this obviously outrageous representation of black women, the article also blames Obama for the apparently severe problem of welfare in this country: "Obama's administration has done nothing but contribute to the "welfare state," growing it to 41% or more than $193 billion since he took office. We're officially spending more on welfare on a country than we are on securing the nation. Now, many grocery stores throughout the nation are taking a stand where Obama has refused to" (*Freedom Daily*, 2017, n.p.). Other common stereotypes about welfare recipients—typically pictured as Black (Johnson, 2015b; Williams, 2013)—are that they are all drug addicts, they intend to stay on welfare forever, and they keep having kids so they can obtain more welfare benefits.

Each one of these stereotypical portrayals are easily debunked. Of course there are probably some examples somewhere that could validate these images, but these characterizations are sweeping generalizations with deep racial animus. For example, regarding the claim that welfare recipients are lazy and do not work, most family benefit programs require proof of work in order to receive the benefits (Johnson, 2015b). In terms of the Temporary Assistance for Needy Families (TANF, and formerly known as Aid to Families with Dependent Children), recipients are obligated to work at least 30 hours per week. Failure to work, if caught, can cause all benefits to be terminated, along with possible charges of fraud (Williams, 2013). Simply put, "Most people on welfare are hardworking, taxpaying citizens, just like the rest of us. Or they are impoverished children, elders, or folks with disabilities" (Johnson, 2015b, n.p.). Of course, people with disabilities may not work, and for that they must undergo a complicated and rigorous vetting process with the Supplemental Security Income (SSI) (Williams, 2013).

The claim that welfare recipients are all drug users is also not based on reliable evidence. According to Johnson (2015b),

> Federal government research tells us that the population of welfare receivers on drugs is basically the same as that of the American population in general—in some cases, even lower. Recent drug testing results from individual states also prove the falseness of this widely accepted myth. In July 2014, Tennessee began testing their welfare applicants, resulting in a whopping 1-in-800 people testing positive for illegal drugs. That's less than 1%. In Florida, four months of drug testing revealed that only 2.6% of applicants tested positive (in contrast, 8% of Florida's non-welfare receiving population regularly test positive for drugs). (n.p.)

Wes Williams (2013) also confirms these results.

Regarding the assertions that recipients want to be on welfare forever and they keep having children to receive more benefits, proponents simply lack sufficient evidence for these claims. According to Williams (2013), the overwhelming majority of recipients (80.4%) receive benefits for five years or less. And the stereotype of children for money is also false. Again, Williams (2013) explains this myth:

> According to a 2010 report released by the federal Department of Health and Human Services (HHS), the average family receiving TANF benefits has 1.8 children, which is about the same as the national average. Half of the families receiving TANF benefits only have one child. In fact, the average size of families receiving welfare benefits has declined from 4.0 in 1969 to 2.4 in 2010. Also, some states, such as Delaware and Georgia, make it clear to those who sign up for TANF benefits that their benefits will not increase if they have additional children. (n.p.)

We know that occasionally some people abuse the system, but to generalize to the entire group is clearly fallacious.

What is also troubling is that with each of these welfare myths, the image of the recipient to whom the myths refer is almost always going to be Black. The racial implications of these representations are enormous. If the stereotypes of lazy, cheating, fraudulent "takers" is attached to the signifier of "Black," then the generalization being made that "all" welfare recipients act in these ways is extended to then imply that "all" Blacks must also behave in these ways (see Figure 7.9). The fallacious logic just becomes perpetuated. This malicious (mis)representation is also alarming when we consider that most welfare recipients are actually White! According to Delaney and Scheller (2015):

> Nationally, most of the people who receive benefits from the Supplemental Nutrition Assistance Program are white. According to 2013 data from the

U.S. Department of Agriculture, which administers the program, 40.2 percent of SNAP recipients are white, 25.7 percent are black, 10.3 percent are Hispanic, 2.1 percent are Asian and 1.2 percent are Native American. (n.p.)

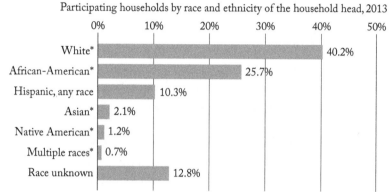

A Large Share of SNAP Recipients are White
Participating households by race and ethnicity of the household head, 2013

*Not Hispanic
Note: Seven percent of households had no household head and no adult listed on the file.

Source: U.S Department of Agriculture   **The Huffington Post**

Figure 7.9

Additionally, if we are to discuss the pros and cons of welfare, one recipient group is often ignored or overlooked in such conversations. According to John Avlon (2009), the main recipients of welfare, by a difference of several billion dollars, are not poor Blacks, Whites, or Hispanics, but rather corporate America, who receives tens of billions a dollars per year in the form of subsidies, special contracts, tax breaks, etc.

MICROAGGRESSIONS

As overt and blatant acts of racism have become less common, more subtle versions of racism have erupted. According to Schoulte et al. (2011), "While overt acts of racism as well as institutional and systemic perpetuation of racist processes exist in our society, even individuals who consider themselves nonracist—in addition to individuals who are racist—may be performing acts of discrimination called *microaggressions*" (p. 291). Nearly 45 years ago, Charles Pierce (1970) discussed the concept of subtle racist messages as "microaggressions." Since then, a number of scholars have researched how it develops, its consequences, and possible solutions. Defining microaggressions, however, can be a bit tricky. As Sue et al. (2007) suggest, *microaggressions* are "brief and commonplace daily verbal, behavioral, and environmental indignities, whether intentional or unintentional, that communicate hostile, derogatory, or negative racial slights and insults to the target person or group" (p. 273). And as Alabi (2015) notes, microaggressions are "subtle, derogatory messages conveyed to people of color" (p. 179). Furthermore, O'Keefe et al. (2015) claim that microaggressions "refer to prejudicial messages expressed through seemingly meaningless and unharmful actions. These messages may be delivered through the form of snubs and dismissive looks and are automatic to the point of being dismissed and deemed innocent. Although these communications externally appear harmless, the intention is to deliver hidden denigrating, hostile, or negative messages about a person or group" (p. 567). Of course, what one considers derogatory may not be shared with others in a discourse community, especially if such messages are unintentional. The question of intent, as challenging as that is to determine, is why many of these scholars argue that we move away from the premise of racial *intent* to a focus on racial *impact* (Fleras, 2016).

O'Keefe et al. (2015) define microaggressions in terms of the experiences of racial groups, since "more subtle and pervasive forms of racial discrimination exist and are experienced by individuals who belong to various racial minority groups, including racial microaggressions" (p. 567). This is important to note for two reasons. First, microaggressions are not limited to just racial groups. Wheeler (2016), for example, examines the impact of microaggressions on the LGBTQ+ community. But, for our purposes here, I shall discuss microaggressions in their racial context. The second item worth noting about the definition from O'Keefe et al. is that they view microaggressions as relating to all racial groups, not just Blacks. This is significant because most of the discussions about microaggressions in popular media, and even some scholarly circles, solely focus on the impact on Blacks. Instead, microaggressions can occur with any racial groups, and some studies have looked at their impact not only on Blacks, but also Hispanics and Asian-Americans (Malott et al., 2015; O'Keefe et al., 2015; Ong et al., 2013).

Related to the idea of microaggressions is the concept known as "dog whistling." Dating back to at least 1988 (Safire, 2008, p. 190), the notion of a "dog whistle" means "coded talk centered on race; while the term could encompass clandestine solicitations on any number of bases, here it refers to racial appeals ... racial dog whistle politics diverges from the more general practice because the hidden message it seeks to transmit violates a strong moral consensus" (López, 2014, p. 4). According to López, the rhetorical strategy of a dog whistle involves three stages, "(1) punch racism into the conversation through references to culture, behavior, and class; (2) parry claims of race-baiting by insisting that absent a direct reference to biology or the use of a racial epithet, there can be no racism; (3) kick up the racial attack by calling any critics the real racists for mentioning race and thereby 'playing the race card'" (p. 130). One of the reasons that understanding dog whistle politics is so important is because it operates on an unconscious level, much like how microaggressions can occur without intent. López calls this "commonsense racism" because it "evokes the overwhelming ordinariness, pervasiveness, and legitimacy of much social knowledge; it expresses the intuitive certainty that many things are just what they are, widely known, widely recognized, and not needing any further explanation" (p. 181). This means that for most of us, our "racial beliefs operate in this fashion. For many, it simply seems "true," an unquestioned matter of commonsense, that blacks prefer welfare to work, that undocumented immigrants breed crime, and that Islam spawns violence" (p. 181). Our ideas, feelings, and beliefs about race are predicated and constituted by shared cultural understandings that cohere with others whom we share linguistic commonalities, such as our friends, families, co-workers, media echo chambers, etc. Stereotypes form based on our limited personal experiences and the anecdotes we hear from our linguistic communities. As a result, because "race infiltrates our minds so thoroughly, even persons deeply and genuinely committed to humane engagement with others often nevertheless draw upon pernicious racial stereotypes. In turn, racism gains a large degree of social power from the actions of good people enthrall to racist beliefs" (López, 2014, p. 45).

Furthermore, dog whistle politics shapes our linguistic behavior, especially the way we receive and process the messages of others. When Ronald Reagan, for example, described the "welfare queen" in 1976, most of the audience members—as well as most of the audience members targeted by such messages today—conjure in their minds an image of a black woman. This is why dog whistle appeals are known as "code words" because they subtly convey a racial meaning, even though Reagan never actually stated the race of the person he was describing. This is also why López (2014) says that audiences of these appeals "are themselves victims of manipulation, rather than covert racists. It intimates that rather than being committed to racial politics, most whites resoundingly reject it when it's brought into the light" (p. 178). Of course, the real victims of dog whistle politics are the people for whom the coded words are depicting, much like microaggressions.

Microaggressions frequently occur by innocent, well-meaning individuals. Any racist implications are unintentional, as Malott et al. (2015) describe: "Such racism is often enacted by well-meaning Whites who may be unconsciously expressing dominant, normative beliefs absorbed from societal Whiteness messages" (p. 386). Of course, whether the verbal or nonverbal message is intentional or not, the receiving party may still perceive the discursive episode as racist and harmful. Since microaggressions are subtle and often unintentional, understanding the context of the discursive event is absolutely crucial (Sue et al., 2007). For instance, if a person has a history of displaying genuine care and sincere sensitivity, a perceived microaggression from them may not necessarily be as offensive as if the comment were made by a flippant, ignorant individual. In this way, the identification and the impact of the microaggression might fall in a sort of range that can only be determined by context. This is especially important since "victims and perpetrators alike may have difficulty identifying an incident as a transgression. Microaggressions are usually subtle, so that confronted perpetrators may be unaware of their motivation and may deny having committed an act considered by the victim to be hostile" (Schoulte et al., 2011, p. 292).

What is also absolutely vital, and crucial for our purposes, is understanding that while racism can be examined from cultural, sociological, historical and other perspectives, microaggressions are uniquely discursive and rhetorical in nature. As Fleras (2016) describes, microaggressions "consist of those words and interactions perceived as racist by racialized targets that rarely reflect vindictive intent yet inadvertently inflict insult or injury." And by analyzing them as a "discursive framework," we are able to situate the "definitional locus of racism within the lived-experiences of the micro-aggressed" (p. 1). In other words, since microaggressions occur as either verbal or nonverbal messages of intentional or unintentional racism, viewing them as acts of rhetoric helps us understand how they are formed as well as how they are received by those claiming to be harmed by them.

But what are some examples of microaggressions? Constantine and Sue (2007) offer a variety of examples, but they include when someone is "driving while Black" and is stopped not because of a traffic violation, but rather because of the color of their skin, and "shopping while Black," when shoppers are closely followed and surveilled due to their skin color and the concomitant stereotype that they might be shoplifters. According to Sue et al. (2007), there are three main types of microaggressions, along with a number of specific ways these types of microaggressions operate. The first type of microaggression is known as a "microassaults." They suggest that instances of "Referring to someone as 'colored' or 'Oriental,' using racial epithets, discouraging interracial interactions, deliberately serving a White patron before someone of color, and displaying a swastika are examples. Microassaults are most similar to what has been called "old fashioned" racism conducted on an individual level" (p. 274). In other words, microassaults are what we would typically consider to be overt forms of racism, but can still occur in subtle ways, such as when so-called jokes use these rhetorical devices.

The second type of microaggression is called "microinsults." Microinsults may be the most common form of what we think of when we discuss microaggressions. They are "behaviors that are insensitive, rude, or inconsiderate of a person's identity. Microinsults are especially difficult for people to understand because they tend to be subtle in nature and may be unconscious and unintentional, but [they] nonetheless demean the target or their group" (Wheeler, 2016, p. 324). Wheeler (2016) offers the example of when his colleagues would be introduced with a proper handshake, but for him someone might perform what he calls an "unorthodox hand-shaking ritual involving twisting out of a traditional handshake and into what I presume was considered a black handshake" (p. 324). Wheeler then adds, "The person committing the microaggression probably thought he was building a relationship with me; however, the message I received was that I am not as professional as my white colleagues. Often, when a microaggression occurs, the person who commits the act does not realize she is actually being offensive—in fact, she may think she is giving a compliment or building a relationship. Though the intent was not to hurt my feelings, the impact was that I felt stereotyped, misunderstood, and marginalized" (p. 325). It is important to note that microinsults also happen with nonverbal gestures, such as "when a White teacher fails to acknowledge students of color in the classroom or when a White supervisor seems distracted during a conversation with a Black employee by avoiding eye contact or turning away" (Sue et al., 2007, p. 274). Another example might be when a teacher tells a student of color that "You're *so* smart and well spoken" (Malott et al., 2015, p. 388). Personally, I know this is a challenge for me as an educator. When I grade student performance, I regularly tell students that they are "articulate" or they "write extremely well" or they "raise excellent points" in class. While I say these things to all of my students, and I sincerely mean them, a student of color may consider them to be microaggressions. In those instances, I can only hope that context will dictate the meaning of such comments, and that my students will defer to seeing them as my genuine praise, rather than a subtle racist jab.

The final type of microaggressions is termed "microinvalidations." These "are characterized by behavior that minimizes the psychological thoughts, feelings, or experiences of targets. Like microinsults, microinvalidations are subtle and often unintentional" (Wheeler, 2016, p. 325). A good example of microinvalidation is the concept of colorblindness. As Malott et al. (2015) describe, a person might say "'I don't see color, I just see human beings,' which implies that all persons are treated equally or have equal opportunities, regardless of race. Such comments negate the reality of racism and its impacts for people of color" (p. 388). Another example is when Hispanics are praised for how well they speak English or even when they are frequently asked where they are from, or if they are citizens, all of which "negate their U.S. American heritage and to convey that they are perpetual foreigners" (Sue et al., 2007, p. 274).

In addition to these three types of microaggressions, Sue et al. (2007) map out particular ways these types of microaggressions occur in discourse. Each one of these instances can fall under any one of the three types. Also known as the "categories of and relationships among racial microaggression" (see Figure 7.10), the specific instances they notice are:

- Ascription of Intelligence—Assigning a degree of intelligence to a person of color based on their race.
- Second-Class Citizen—Treated as a lesser person or group.

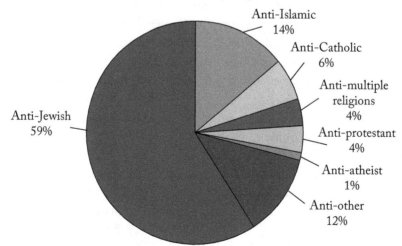

Figure 7.10: 2014 Religious hate crimes.

- Pathologizing Cultural Values/Communication Styles—Notion that the values and communication styles of people of color are abnormal.
- Assumption of Criminal status—Presumed to be a criminal, dangerous, or deviant based on race.
- Environmental Microaggressions (Macro-level)—Racial assaults, insults, and invalidations that are manifested on systemic and environmental levels.
- Alien in Own Land—Belief that visible racial/ethnic minority citizens are foreigners.
- Color Blindness—Denial or pretense that a White person does not see color or race.
- Myth of Meritocracy—Statements that assert that race plays a minor role in life success.
- Denial of Individual Racism—Denial of personal racism or one's role in its perpetuation. (p. 278)

Thus, by viewing this schema of microaggressions, we can see how the three types of microaggressions can happen in specific exchanges.

While this type of discourse is called *micro*-aggression, for many individuals, the impact of them is anything but "micro." Of course, individuals experience microaggressions differently, and the way the microaggressions affect them may differ as well (Wheeler, 2016). However, based on a number of studies, we know that microaggressions can have very serious repercussions. First, we know that racial stress occurs in individuals as they "are exposed to negative life events related to a stigmatizing and discriminating environment, and that it is the totality of these experiences within the dominant society in which they live that contributes to stress" (O'Keefe et al., 2015, p. 567). The cumulative effect of stress from racial experiences can "result in diminished mortality, augmented morbidity and flattened confidence" (Sue et al., p. 279). According to Schoulte et al. (2011), the long-term consequences that build up from instances of things like microaggressions can "foster inequalities, impair relationships, create emotional turmoil, and decrease mental and physical health. Clearly, microaggressions potentially have a deleterious impact on the victim" (pp. 291–292).

Second, microaggressions can create an uncomfortable and serious reaction during the actual discursive episode. According to one study, many of the participants who identified and experienced a microaggression "reported similar levels of distress to individuals in the larger sample who had experienced transgressions such as betrayal, sexual abuse, and physical abuse" (Schoulte et al., 2011, pp. 296–297). Schoulte et al. (2011) also note that participants felt "self-doubt, frustration, and isolation on the part of victims" (pp. 279). In a different study, subjects reported that experiencing a microaggression "thwarts a person's sense of belonging and acceptance, potentially rendering them more vulnerable to suicide" (O'Keefe et al., 2015, p. 573). In the study conducted by Sue et al. (2007), they describe how the participants' "experience with microaggressions resulted in a negative racial climate and emotions of self-doubt, frustration, and isolation on the part of victims" (p. 279). Additionally, Philomena Essed (1991, 2002) reports that participants felt humiliated, degraded, and undermined when they experienced microaggressions. Following up on Essed's work, Fleras (2016) notes that many of these discursive episodes are "perceived by the majority to be normal and neutral, yet these putdowns and demotions are negatively experienced by minority women and men as a violation of their dignity and humanity" (p. 4).

While microaggressions can have very grave consequences, not every discursive episode may actually be a microaggressions. We need to remind ourselves that context is important. Certainly many individuals—usually the ones committing the microaggression—fail to see how their messages and actions are racist. If the instance is questionable, or if it might be a stretch to actually consider it a microaggression, labeling it as such might do more harm than good. In 2013, an education professor teaching a graduate class at UCLA was called a racist by a couple dozen students because he graded the grammar of their work very strictly (Jacobson, 2013). Despite dozens of other students hailing him as an excellent professor who was gentle and kind, the aggrieved students, who were taking their next step into academia as Ph.D. students, continued their portrayal of the professor's grading as microaggressions. Ultimately, the professor was suspended for a year, and the university formed a committee to investigate other possible microaggressions on campus. The incident created a nationwide outrage, particularly among academics, who claimed the professor's academic freedom was violated, not to mention that by all other reports, the professor acted professionally and cared for his students deeply. As this example shows, calling strict grading a "microaggression" did the students a disservice as they were about to try to find scholarly jobs, and it practically destroyed a professor's career who was trying to make his students better students.

Of course, another reason why microaggressions can be considered divisive discourse is the way some people reacted to this UCLA incident. Heather Mac Donald (2014), who is a contributor to *City Journal*, calls the students "unmoored from reality," engaged in "victim ideologies." She writes, the "very idea of taking 'this' 'extremely seriously' presupposes that there was something to be taken seriously and solved, as opposed to a mere outburst of narcissistic victimhood" (2014, n.p.). Mac Donald is clearly engaging in *ad hominem* attacks, as well as demeaning the feelings of the students involved. Similarly, Katherine Timpf (2015) characterizes the situation at UCLA as "based on questionable assumptions," especially since now there is "a tendency to assume that almost anything is racist rather than the prevalence of racism itself" (n.p.). In these sections of Timpf's article, she, like Mac Donald, dismisses, if not demeans, the feelings and experiences of the students. However, in a more reasonable manner, Timpf concludes by saying, "No doubt, racism and sexism exist. But it's important to carefully examine problems before jumping to do something to try and solve them just so you can say that you're trying—especially when some of the ideas run the risk of making things worse" (2015, n.p.).

Undoubtedly, some folks will consider microaggressions as "racializing all snubs (from offhand comments to derogatory putdowns); inflating specious charges of racism by playing the 'race' card; fostering a hyper-sensitized victimhood culture; pushing political correctness to risible extremes; or politicizing every criticism of racialized minorities" (Fleras, 2016, n.p.). Perhaps some discursive moments do not quite rise to the level of a microaggression; but dismissing them *carte blanche* is also problematic and dangerous. Rhetorically speaking, "the perpetrator usually believes that the victim has overreacted and is being overly sensitive and/or petty. After all, even if it was an innocent racial blunder, microaggressions are believed to have minimal negative impact" (Sue et al., 2007, p. 278). We should also underscore that even if the perpetrator believes the victim is acting silly or is overreacting, the victim may find difficulty in continuing in the conversation, trusting the microaggressor, or "building empathy for the offender" (Schoulte et al., 2011, p. 293).

Additionally, Tom Slater (2015), who writes for an online news magazine, is concerned about the direction microaggressions are taking us regarding our rhetoric of race. He writes that we are in a dangerous place in society "where merely saying the wrong thing, even unintentionally, is enough to mark you out as a moral leper" (n.p.). I think labeling the microaggressor a "leper" overstates his point, but Slater remarks that it is difficult to have an honest conversation about race when merely being in the same room with another racial group or when every word that is said is held to an unreasonable standard can be considered racist. He continues, "More often than not, what amounts to a microaggression is little more than clumsy curiosity—from asking where someone is 'from' [sic] to asking to touch their hair. It's not cool, but it can hardly be called racist. And the idea that a few grating comments amount to a form of structural oppression only belittles minority students' ability to navigate the public sphere" (2015, n.p.).

Overall, I think Slater's argument is worth noting. If we come to a place where we cannot engage in a conversation for fear of offending someone, or if we cannot have a discussion because we believe everything the other party is doing is offensive and racist, we may, in fact, be doomed. It is difficult to imagine being able to move forward when such a scenario occurs or is considered. John McWhorter (2014) echoes this sentiment when he calls microaggressions a form of "bullying," by which he means calling a discursive episode a microaggression bullies interlocutors into sterile speech. Like Slater's use of the word "leper," I think McWhorter is using the rhetorical trope of hyperbole to emphasize his point.

Fortunately, not everyone considers every rhetorical act a microaggression, and not everyone who is called out for (unintentionally) engaging in a microaggression goes on a rampage. Most people are reasonable people. Like most controversial issues, people can, and do, come together and have meaningful conversations. We obviously need to educate ourselves about what constitutes a microaggression, why they are damaging, and how we might avoid them. Additionally, as Wheeler (2016) suggests, we should avoid making assumptions about anyone's race, sexual orientation, or gender identity" (p. 328).

ANTI-SEMITISM

Discussing the rhetoric of race regarding Jews is interesting for a couple of reasons. First, Jews can be considered a racial as well as an ethnic group. As I mentioned at the beginning of this chapter, there is already considerable overlap between the two concepts. But for Jewish people, there are identifiable biological markers that constitute a racial group, and, of course, Jewish people are identifiable ethnically in terms of their Hebrew language, religious beliefs, customs, etc. Of course, Jews are not just a racial/ ethnic group. They are also considered a religious group. However, not all Jews practice Judaism, so it is inaccurate to call discrimination against Jews automatically a form of religious discrimination (like Islamophobia is only directed at Muslim believers). Yet discrimination against a Jew could be considered to be a form of racial oppression. These distinctions are why Saunders (2009) states, "Jewish identity is multi-faceted" (n.p.).

Another reason that it is interesting to examine Jewish racial rhetoric is because of the concept "anti-Semitism." Some people consider any degrading, derogatory or hate-filled discourse directed at Jews to be anti-Semitic. This is especially true if the offender is an Arab, as in the tumultuous discourse between Jews and Arabs regarding Middle East peace efforts. However, technically, an Arab cannot be "anti-Semitic." A Semite is a person who belongs to a particular linguistic group. Etymologically, Semites speak languages related to Aramaic, Arabic, and Hebrew (Bernard, 2003). Specifically, Semitism "was invented to refer to a language type and a type of human being: a race and what we would now call a culture. It referred above all to the Jews and their biblical Hebrew-speaking ancestors, and to the Arabs" (Kalmar, 2009, p. 136). Obviously, Arabs speak Arabic, and Jews speak Hebrew. Thus, according to this historical and linguistic perspective, both Jews and Arabs are Semitic peoples.

Of course, the contemporary usage of the term "anti-Semitism" takes a slightly different and particular form. Beginning in 19th-century Europe, the unique way Jews were characterized as being a burden and causing social turmoil justified its own name. Since Jews are Semites, it made sense to call such stereotypes "anti-Semitic." The Anti-Defamation League, which is an organization that monitors and fights Jewish injustice, clarifies how the term anti-Semitism developed specifically to refer to the hatred directed at Jewish people:

> Despite the linguistic etymology of the word "Semite," the word "anti-Semite" was "formulated to refer specifically to the hatred of Jews. The term has never been used to refer to hatred against Arabs. Claims to the contrary are an effort to diminish the term's potency or to seize ownership of it. … Quite simply, anti-Semitism refers to the hatred of Jews, whatever the nationality, race, color or creed of the perpetrator. Attempting to dismiss the term anti-Semitism because of semantics does not erase the fact of its existence or its history. (Anti-Defamation League, n.d., n.p.)

In this way, most people today consider anti-Semitism to mean specifically anti-Jewish sentiment and behavior. With this interpretation, it certainly makes sense that any non-Jewish person engaging in this behavior or rhetoric could be considered an anti-Semite. While even more nuanced and complex, theoretically even Jewish people could be called anti-Semitic if they participate in this type of discourse. An anti-Semitic Jew might also be deemed a so-called "self-hating" or "self-loathing" Jew, since the concept of "Jewish self-hatred" is more common now in "mainstream culture, particularly in recent years, when disputes over Zionism and Israel among Jews have given the term a fresh lease of life" (Cohen, 2012, n.p.).

So, we might wonder what actually constitutes anti-Semitism during contemporary conversations. According to numerous sources, one common answer is the use of stereotypes, particularly stereotypes that refer to Jews as having too much political and economic power, too much control in the media, too much influence in Hollywood, etc. (Bitran, 2016; Robbins, 2016; Rudee, 2014; Saunders, 2009). Of course, anti-Semitism can involve much more, including violence (Rudee, 2014). According to Saunders (2009), there are two main types of anti-Semitism: (1) replacement theology, or "the belief that one religion has replaced all others," typically associated with rhetoric calling for Jews to "convert or die," or "lying about Judaism to discredit it," and (2) the "new anti-Semitism"—although "related to Jewish national identity," it is difficult to define precisely (Saunders, 2009, n.p.). Saunders lists a series of "symptoms" of the new anti-Semitism, but notes that some of the symptoms by themselves may not be anti-Semitic; however, "the more of them a person exhibits, the more likely it is that he or she is antisemitic, even if that person has no racial or religious prejudices against Jews" (2009, n.p.). The symptoms include "denying Jewish national/ethnic identity" (claiming Jewish identity is religious or cultural, but not both), "denying the Jewish right to national self-determination" (arguing that Jews are inferior and do not deserve self-determination), "denying that the land of Israel is the only legitimate place for Jewish self-determination" (arguing in various ways the state of Israel should not exist), "stating that Israel exists on sufferance" (stating "that the world could withdraw Israel's 'right to exist' if it does not behave"), "telling lies or misleading half-truths about the State of Israel" (claiming Israel is not a democracy, that it is theocratic, that it denies civil rights to Arabs, etc.), "abusing the public's lack of knowledge" (using the credibility and "trustworthiness" of scholars, journalists and politicians as facts instead of actual documents, agreements, and historical events), "engaging in "moral flexibility" (using moral arguments against Israeli actions, such as their use of cluster bombs, but not holding the enemies of Israel to the same standards), advocating "fair-weather humanitarianism" (believing in humanitarian treatment for Palestinians, but not being consistent when it comes to other racial/ethnic groups around the world), deploying "traditional antisemitic rhetoric" (using common conspiracy theories about Jews), deploying "other inappropriate rhetoric" (using, for example, Apartheid or Holocaust imagery to suggest a comparison between the historical Holocaust and what Israel is doing to the Palestinians; this is also known as "Holocaust trivialization"), "redefining Zionism" (claiming that Zionism is a theocratic malevolent ideology, instead of a liberation movement), "acting oppressed" (suggesting that being critical of Israel or Jews in general will result in condemnation, politically correct censorship, or even oppressive counter-attacks), and "doubting the rise of antisemitism" (claiming that "real" anti-Semitism only involves neo-Nazi-style violence, thereby negating other types of hatred, including subtle attempts at demeaning and oppressing Jews).

Simply put, anti-Semitism is when "Jews are scapegoated for global problems" (Rudee, 2014). What has become clear, especially in recent years is that it is difficult to separate anti-Semitism from hostility, even hatred, to the state of Israel. When Saunders (2009) mentions a symptom of anti-Semitism involving particular types of rhetoric, this is one way that being anti-Semitic and being anti-Israel conjoin:

> It has been seen in the form of blood libels; allegations that Jews are a fifth column who look after themselves and hate non-Jews (far right, militant secularist and Islamic fundamentalist rhetoric all overlap here); conspiracy theories that Jews/Zionists control business and finance, the media, political parties and governments (an allegation made at a fringe meeting at the Liberal Democrat conference last year); assertions that the War on Terror or the invasion of Iraq are 'Jewish/Zionist wars' (despite the fact that Israel advised against the invasion of Iraq , and that al-Qaeda was formed primarily to remove US bases from Saudi Arabia), whether by arguing that Israel's existence or actions have given legitimate grounds for Islamic terrorism or through conspiracy theories alleging that Jews or Zionists control western governments or even that terrorist attacks in the west, including the September 11 attacks, were staged by Israel and/or Jews/Zionists in the Bush administration. (n.p.)

Interestingly, many of the stereotypes used in anti-Semitism can be rooted in one way or another with the actions and origins of Israel. While anti-Semitism is technically not the same as being anti-Israel, too often criticisms of Israel are used as a way of masking anti-Semitism, even to the point of displaying representations of Holocaust images (Rudee, 2014). Indeed, according to Bitran (2016), "'Anti-Israel' has become a camouflage platform for expressing anti-Semitism under a more socially acceptable umbrella. … Anti-Israel is no longer a distinct concept from anti-Semitism, because the two concepts are so intertwined that they have fused into the same monster" (n.p.). In the current era of toxic talk, social media benefits the anti-Semite. Bitran (2016) argues about how "anti-Semitic rumors … spiral out of control quickly. On social media, anything can spread at lightning speed, be deemed credible, and incite violence" (n.p.).

Some, of course, make the argument that there is a difference between a critique of Israel, especially Israeli policy, and anti-Semitism. One can, after all, be critical of Israel, but still love Jews and Jewish culture. For Rudee (2014), criticism of Israel becomes anti-Semitism when it is infused with, and has its origins in, hatred. She argues, "if you accuse Israel of mistreating Palestinians without denouncing the horror of their living conditions under Hamas rule as well as their third-class status in Lebanon, Syria and most of the Arab world, this not only crosses the line, it makes you a hypocrite—a bigot—not an activist. These recurring instances of crossing the line are not random; they are systemic and evidence of a greater trend of neo-anti-Semitism, where hatred of Israel is used to mask hatred of Jews" (n.p.). However, Wildman (2012) reminds us that "We should know by now that supporting the State of Israel does not mean uncritical support by all, that Jewish identity is not always under attack when a government of Israel faces criticism" (n.p.).

In terms of divisive discourse, we should also keep in mind some of the dangers of using the label "anti-Semitism." First, many legitimate claims against the country of Israel are often quickly branded as anti-Semitic. But we know that no country in the world is 100% correct 100% of the time. Many critics of Israel occasionally feel they do not have the freedom to openly speak against Israeli policy for fear of being called an anti-Semite (Robbins, 2016). Second, disagreeing with Israel or having an honest disagreement with a Jew also does not (and probably should not) automatically count as "anti-Semitism." Labeling something anti-Semitic when it really is not trivializes the real, ugly hatred of the anti-Semitism that does occur (Wildman, 2012). In fact, as Wildman (2012) explains,

> That is why when anti-Semitism is falsely applied, we must also stand up and decry it as defamation, as character assault, as unjust. That is why when we debase the term by using it as a rhetorical conceit against those with whom we disagree on policy matters, we have sullied our own promises to our grandparents. For if we dilute the term, if we render the label meaningless, defanged, we have failed ourselves, our legacy, our ancestors, our children. (n.p.)

Furthermore, Wildman (2012) warns us that a single instance that is called anti-Semitic can quickly reverberate in echo chambers, thereby charactering the instance as more horrific than it actually was. This is particularly problematic, obviously, when the single instance does not rise to the level of actual anti-Semitism. Thus, Wildman urges all of us, but particularly Jewish writers, journalists, and political pundits, to be extra-vigilant before using the term "anti-Semitism."

Now that we have an idea of what constitutes anti-Semitism, we should briefly explore some of the ways animus such as anti-Semitism are utilized in discursive practices. Like elsewhere in this chapter, I am broadly defining what I mean by "discursive practices" to include anything, verbal or nonverbal, that carries a message or has meaning. This, of course, includes violent acts, especially if such violence is motivated by hate.

Unfortunately, we have seen an upsurge of anti-Semitic language and violence in recent years. Alarmingly, the Anti-Defamation League released its report on anti-Semitism, and the figures are disturbing: American incidents of anti-Semitism, including "a wave of more than 150 bomb threats" (Zoll, 2017, n.p.), "skyrocketed by 86% in the first three months of the year," which represents 541 incidents, and anti-Semitic assaults, vandalism and harassment were up 34% last year as well (Kaleem, 2017, n.p.). Rudee (2014) says that the sudden proliferation of anti-Semitism began in 2014, primarily associated with Israeli acts against Palestinians in Gaza and the West Bank. Yet, even in 2009, Daniel Saunders argued that anti-Semitism in the United States was tied to the policies of Israel. However, since the end of 2015, and especially in the early months of 2017, anti-Semitic acts have skyrocketed. Mark Potok, a senior fellow at the Southern Poverty Law Center, who closely monitors acts of extremism like anti-Semitism, blames the campaign and election of Donald Trump to be culpable, at least in part. There is not much direct evidence linking the president to acts of anti-Semitism (especially since his Jewish son-in-law, Jared Kushner, married his daughter Ivanka, who converted to Judaism), except that his trusted advisor, Steve Bannon, condoned, if not encouraged, anti-Semitic rhetoric when he oversaw *Breitbart*, so such a statement in itself is polarizing. But one thing is for sure—something has created quite a stir of anti-Semitic sentiment.

According to Robbins (2016), "we heard anecdotes from Jewish racial justice advocates that they were called 'kikes' or targeted with other anti-Jewish slurs. When they tried to address the epithets, they were told they need to understand that 'it's because of Israel.' Here's the thing, though. It's not. It's anti-Semitism" (n.p.). Of course, such slurs might very well be tied to Israel, but it would be a hatred toward Israel, which also makes them anti-Semitic. But even more troubling, and recent, is the almost daily instances of what the *Associated Press* (2017a) calls a "scourge" of anti-Semitism in this country. Just part of this national scourge, as Bacon (2017) explains, occurs around Jewish cemeteries and community centers: "Desecration of grave sites at cemeteries in Philadelphia and outside St. Louis. Swastikas etched on cars in Miami Beach. Bomb threats forcing evacuation of Jewish community centers. Another wave of intimidation targeting Jewish communities swept across the nation Monday, and community leaders and law enforcement struggled to stop it" (n.p.). Indeed, according to the same *Associated Press* (2017a) report, "Jewish centers and schools in Alabama, Delaware, Florida, Indiana, Maryland, Michigan, New York, North Carolina, Rhode Island and Virginia also were threatened, according to the JCC Association of North America. Since January, the group has tracked a total of 89 incidents in 30 states and Canada" (n.p.).

Moreover, the language of anti-Semitism spreads like wildfire on social media. Bitran (2016) offers a couple of examples of extremist anti-Semitic rhetoric that have occurred on social media. In Austria, "a Facebook user posted, 'I could have annihilated all the Jews in the world, but I left some of them alive so you will know why I was killing them,' yet an Austrian prosecutor ruled that this anti-Semitic post was merely a legitimate way to criticize Israel" (n.p.). In another instance, "An anti-Israel post sparked this anti-Semitic comment: 'Jews are born to create problems, just like they tried to create in Germany. But Hitler cleared all that trash. Likewise same is needed to be done by Palestinians. Eradicate and operate out this Jewish cancer'" (n.p.). Of course, these are just two examples, but they are representative of the spiteful and noxious hatred that is promulgated on social media.

On college campuses, too, Jewish students experience anti-Semitism almost on a daily basis. Emily Shire (2015) calls the anti-Semitism in American colleges and universities "pernicious." As she explains,

At schools where students strive to protect the rights of ethnic and racial minorities, stomp out sexual and gender discrimination, and regularly remind people to "check their privilege," hate speech against the Jewish community has become a pernicious problem. "We still find anti-Semitic slogans written on bathrooms. We see swastikas on doors still, but they're kind of dismissed. They're painted over because there are just so many things that happened," says Ori Herschmann, a senior at UC Berkeley who serves in the student government. (n.p.)

Rudee (2014) shares a similar assessment: "Degenerates at Emory University spray painted swastikas on a Jewish fraternity house following Yom Kippur, the holiest day on the Jewish calendar. A Temple University student was called a 'kike' and was sent to the hospital after being physically assaulted. Students for Justice in Palestine created such a hostile climate at DePaul University that Jewish female students felt intimidated and 'no longer safe on campus'" (n.p.). Robbins (2016) provides an example of a situation when a Jewish student was called a "pariah" simply because they defended Israel and refused to denounce Israeli actions against the Palestinians. Shire (2015) says the problem of anti-Semitism on campuses is even worse than we think, as frequently instances are under-reported. Shire claims that many university administrations do not take charges of anti-Semitism seriously, thus many students do not feel safe or supported in coming forward. Even so, Shire shares a 2014 survey from the Louis D. Brandeis Center for Human Rights Under Law and Trinity College, which reports that a "majority of Jewish college students, 54 percent, reported being subjected to or witness to anti-Semitism on campus during a six-month period" (n.p.). That is extremely significant, especially if many other instances are not being reported at all.

Speaking of Jewish and anti-Jewish divisive discourse on campuses, a recent movement has developed in the United States and all over the world that exists primarily at colleges and universities. Called the Boycott, Divestment and Sanctions (BDS) movement, its followers primarily direct their attacks at the policies and actions of the Israeli government. According to Aked (2017), BDS has three main goals—end the Israeli occupation of Palestinian territories, achieve full equality for Palestinian citizens of Israel, and uphold the rights of Palestinian refugees. As a result, BDS has created a global movement to apply pressure on the Israeli government to stop its "settler-colonialism, ethnic cleansing and apartheid practices" (Aked, 2017, n.p.). Aked claims that BDS models its movement after the anti-Apartheid movement of the late 1980s and early 1990s, arguing that Israel's occupation of Gaza and the West Bank, and corollary policies toward the Palestinians, mimic, at least to a degree, the policies of South African Apartheid. Like the activists who protested against Apartheid, BDS claims that boycotting, divesting, and sanctioning Israel can break the stranglehold Israel has on the Palestinians. Indeed, such a strategy was very effective at pressuring South Africa to eventually dismantle Apartheid (Knight, 2004).

Of course, BDS attracts much criticism, which I will discuss below. To help buffer against those notions, BDS claims and cites testimonials from various Jews and Jewish groups who support the overall goals of BDS (Aked, 2017). Additionally, since BDS overtly campaigns against the Israeli government, many people argue that they are anti-Semitic. As we just learned, many people believe that criticizing the state of Israel is an example of anti-Semitism. However, as we might expect, BDS vehemently denies being anti-Semitic or racist. They argue that they target institutions, not individuals, and their entire project is aimed at promoting human rights, not degrading human beings (Aked, 2017). Nevertheless, their critique of Israeli policies attracts much attention.

This chapter is not the place to discuss the very complex problem known as the Israeli-Palestinian conflict since Israel's independence in 1948. But to better understand the arguments of BDS, we should know a little about why they claim the Israeli government is illegitimate. To begin, according to BDS, Israeli democracy is a myth; they more accurately should be called an "ethnocracy," according to Winstanley (2015), since all laws and policies in Israel serve the Jewish people. The Palestinians who live in Israel, despite Israeli claims otherwise, do not receive the same rights or treatment as Israeli Jews. According to Winstanley (2015), "The state officially discriminates against the indigenous population of historic Palestine—who awoke one day in 1948 to find that they were suddenly defined as 'Israeli Arabs' by a state that, at best, regards them with suspicion" (n.p.). Just like knowing history is important to understand Jewish discrimination, so too is knowing a bit about Palestinian history. As Winstanley (2015) explains:

> From 1948 until 1966, the Palestinian citizens of Israel were subjected to a military regime, under which they were barred [sic] from free movement, and were in thrall to a strict regime of permits. In 1967, Israel invaded and illegally occupied the West Bank, the Gaza Strip and the section of south-west Syria known as the Golan Heights. The Palestinians in the newly-occupied territories were subjected to a brutal military rule, one that (although its forms have shifted since the Oslo accord) has continued until the present day. ... Palestinians living the same territory, where they and their ancestors have lived since time immemorial, are tried under Israeli military law—a system of kangaroo courts in which military officers rubber stamp the decisions of their colleagues. The conviction rate of these "courts" is 99.7 percent—a figure to make even the most brutal regional dictator blush. (n.p.)

Similarly, Hagai El-Ad (2015), the executive director of B'Tselem, the Israeli Information Center for Human Rights in the Occupied Territories, explains how Israel is not a true democracy, especially since millions of so-called citizens are forbidden to vote:

> If you look at all the land Israel controls between the Jordan and the Mediterranean, that area contains some 8.3 million Israelis and Palestinians

of voting age. Roughly 30 percent—about 2.5 million—are Palestinians living outside Israel under varying degrees of Israeli control—in East Jerusalem, the West Bank and the Gaza Strip. They have some ability to elect Palestinian bodies with limited functions. But they are powerless to choose Israeli officials, who make the weightiest decisions affecting them. International humanitarian law does not grant a people living under temporary military occupation the right to vote for the institutions of the occupying power. But "temporary" is the operative word. Military occupations are meant to have an end. And common sense says half a century is not "temporary." Nevertheless, that is the basis for denying Palestinians their political rights: Their status is temporary, we are told, until a political agreement with Israel allows them to vote for sovereign Palestinian institutions. (n.p.)

In fact, El-Ad calls the democracy in Israel a "charade, "especially since "the Palestinian Authority remains subject to the whims of the occupying power—as was demonstrated most recently when Israel froze (and then unfroze) the transfer of Palestinian tax revenues to it" (n.p.). And when Israeli supporters claim that Israel is the only democracy in the Middle East it (a) presumes that Israel is actually a democracy, and (b) ignores how other countries in the region can also be considered democracies, like Turkey and Jordan. Many Israelis and Israeli supporters will counter that Israel has given the Palestinians many chances for peace and for territorial deals, but others, such as Aked (2017), argue those efforts, too, are merely a façade to maintain international support.

However, as I have mentioned, BDS has drawn a tremendous amount of attention not only to the issues in Israel, but also to their campaign as a whole. First, Bitran (2016) explains that

> Building on the media's distortions, anti-Israel events which frequently call for BDS boycotts of Israel spread hateful accusations against Israel, falsely claiming that Israel is guilty of apartheid, ethnic cleansing, genocide, and a number of other war crimes in an effort to demonize Israel by portraying it as the embodiment of the world's true evils. Additionally, these claims are rarely, if ever, balanced with an acknowledgement of Palestinian terrorism against Israeli civilians, [and] Israel's continual efforts to make peace with the Palestinians. (n.p.)

Plus, critics of BDS emphatically state that they engage in venomous anti-Semitism by perpetuating lies about Israel (Milstein, 2016). Like most controversial issues, opposing sides claim their opponents distort facts and manipulate people's fears. To be fair, both sides on this question engage in these tactics. But there are (at least) two sides of every story. While BDS claims Israel is not a democracy, obviously supporters of Israel refute that. Adelman (2016) notes that while "Israel is hardly perfect, it is a democratic, First World, high-tech, modern state governed by the rule of law that applies to Jews and Arabs, men and women" (n.p.). Adelman continues by saying that in the post-independence era of former colonized nations, Israel was one of the few that "remained democratic from the start. Hebrew and Arabic were the official languages and all Jews and Arabs could vote. An Arab party existed from the start and today an Arab party has the third largest number of delegates (16) in the Knesset" (n.p.). Others echo how Arabs are treated equally and fairly (Bitran, 2016; Saunders, 2009). Additionally, these advocates for Israel remind us that Israel has made generous offers to the Palestinians (Adelman, 2016), they are not anywhere close to being like Apartheid (Adelman, 2016; Bitran, 2016), they participated in full-faith negotiations (Adelman, 2016), and they continue to be the only democracy in the Middle East (Milstein, 2016).

Thus far, I have outlined a few of the core arguments on both sides of this debate, including some potentially anti-Semitic discourse from BDS advocates. Unfortunately, the toxic talk does not end there. Although Israeli supporters could rely on historical and factual evidence to support their positions, they nevertheless also engage in divisive, polarizing rhetoric. For example, Bitran (2016) and Milstein (2016) both argue that BDS ultimately wants to destroy the existence of Israel. Bitran even calls the BDS "sinister," while Milstein says they "demonize the State of Israel, with the eventual goal of destroying it" (n.p.). And the Prime Minister of Israel, Benjamin Netanyahu, says the BDS acronym means "bigotry, dishonesty and shame" (Aked, 2017, n.p.), which might be rhetorically clever, but it also is a form of an *ad hominem* fallacy as well as a blatant attempt at framing the BDS as a villain. All of these statements clearly vilify the opponent and intensify the "us versus them" dynamic of this discourse.

Milstein (2016), in particular, enters into the polarizing fray by claiming to use the "actual" words of BDS advocates to reveal how they have ulterior motives. For example, Milstein says BDS hates America and America's "way of life," but then quotes a Purdue professor who says the boycott will deal a "permanent blow against American empire" (n.p.). The notion of "American empire" is a description of how the United States dominates global military and economic issues. To criticize that type of dominance is not the same thing as "hating" America. Next, Milstein claims that BDS supporters hate America's democracy, then quotes a Berkeley professor who tries to motivate followers to take action, like the Palestinians did during the *Intifada*. Milstein incorrectly defines *Intifada* as "armed struggle," which is his only link to how BDS might be anti-democratic. However, *Intifada* literally means "tremor," or "shock (to the system)," which does not necessarily need to be violent. In fact, the underlying motivation and purpose of the Palestinian intifada from 1987 through 1991 was to promote civil disobedience through non-violent struggle, such as boycotts, protest marches, and media events to sway international opinion. But Milstein ignores those facts to intensify his polarizing message. Milstein's next point is that BDS leaders "hate our justice system and disparage the work of our police officers" (2016, n.p.). Yet, for evidence, he simply uses quotes from a Berkeley professor who was critical of the Michael Brown shooting in Ferguson. As we know, criticizing the criminal justice system and certain police behavior happens with many people, and it certainly is not the same thing as "hating." Finally, Milstein says we must reject BDS since they are a threat to "every American who values democratic freedoms" (2016, n.p.). This is a blatant fear appeal, as well as hyperbole, if not an outright half-truth. He also engages in a slippery slope argument by saying that currently BDS is focused against Israel, but they will soon be "coming for the entire Western world and our way of life" (Milstein, 2016, n.p.).

Anti-Semitic rhetoric and anti-BDS rhetoric exemplify very well how divisive discourse operates in contemporary politics. Many different types of fallacies and rhetorical techniques are present in this discourse, such as *ad hominem* attacks, fear appeals, us vs. them rhetoric, slippery slope arguments, hasty and over-generalizations, etc. While I have pointed out how Bitran (2016) contributes to some of this polarizing discourse, she does suggest that "education can curb the frequency that people actually believe and spread anti-Semitic lies." I also would add that such education can also curb the toxic discourse that emanates from certain Jewish groups as well.

IMPLICATIONS FOR THE RHETORIC OF RACE

This chapter has really only scratched the surface about racial rhetoric. There are quite literally examples of divisive racial rhetoric happening every day in our coffee shops, town halls, family get-togethers, and press reports. Of course, our politicians often serve as negative role models for us as well. For example, on the topic of immigration, the U.S. Republican Representative from Alabama, Mo Brooks, said, "This is a part of the war on whites that's being launched by the Democratic Party. And the way in which they're launching this war is by claiming that whites hate everybody else . ... It's part of the strategy that Barack Obama implemented in 2008, continued in 2012, where he divides us all on race, on sex, greed, envy, class warfare, all those kinds of things" (cited in Isquith, 2014a, n.p.). While obviously over-simplifying and mischaracterizing the issue, Brooks intensifies the wedge between many Americans who already feel divided about the immigration debate. Similarly, during the 2016 presidential campaign, Bernie Sanders reportedly said, "There was an effort to delegitimize the president ... do I think in some parts of that Republican base there's racism involved? Absolutely. ... Nobody has asked for my birth certificate. Maybe it's the color of my skin" (cited in Howley, 2016, n.p.). Clearly Sanders was not saying that the entire Republican party was racist, but he did imply that many Republicans were, and the discourse about Obama's birth certificate certainly represented a racially motivated strategy.

On the flip side, most of us are very sensitive to labels of "racism" and being called a "racist." Wu (2002) explains how this sentiment relates to our self-perceptions and individual ways of seeing the world:

> People nowadays concur that racism is wrong. Almost all of us swear that we do not practice it. We have fooled ourselves into believing that if we vow we aren't doing it then it cannot persist. ... People who have committed offenses—and it is more than that they are offensive—may well wish to

be colorblind. They probably would be shocked if they were told they had treated people differently based on race even though thinking of themselves as polite. (pp. 14–16)

But this is not a new phenomenon. When discussing social welfare programs and the riots of the 1960s, Ann Coulter (2012) professes:

All Americans walked on eggshells for fear of being called a racist and having their reputations ruined. The elites' ceaseless defense of behavior that would never have been tolerated from a white person destroyed lives and got people killed—and most of them black. ... Honest discussion about the effects of these policies, such as exploding black crime rates, racial discrimination against white college applicants, and the black illegitimacy crisis was "taxed" by the penalty of being called a racist and possibly losing one's job. Meanwhile, the black crime rate, dropout and illegitimacy rates continued their ever-upward spiral. Black college students were expected to major in "Being Black," instead of subjects that might get them jobs outside of a university or a government agency. (p. 13)

Coulter's objections to charges of racism, or being labeled a racist, are not surprising. She did, after all, write an entire book on the subject, called *Mugged* (2012). In the book, she castigates Democrats for using Blacks and race as a political weapon. She goes so far as to declare that "Liberals pioneered the method of calling anyone who disagrees with them on politics a racist" (2012, p. 108). And later, she charges that "Liberals are incapable of formulating an argument without accusing someone of racism" (p. 247).

While pundits like Coulter oversimplify and use scare tactics to portray a world where people cannot express themselves freely in discussions about race, they do nonetheless depict what many Americans feel, at least to some degree. Many Americans shudder at the thought of having a conversation about race. This is very disheartening, as Wu (2002) remarks:

Many Americans react so vehemently to the charge of "racism," often countering it with the claim of "political correctness," that we lose the shades that distinguish types of racial thinking. Many assumptions and attitudes can be racial without necessarily being racist. There are gradations, intellectual and social, from the unrepentant white supremacist who agitates to remove people of color from the country, to the respectful segregationist who counsels that everyone is better off among their own, to the unwitting racialist, who without malice relies on generalizations about strangers. (pp. 28–29)

Maybe Americans do not want to offend, or perhaps they are fearful of being offended, or they may not want to be attacked, or perhaps they feel uncomfortable. Whatever the reason, the controversy of race has virtually silenced many of us. Yet, for others, they do not appear to ever shut up when it comes to racial issues.

For example, political commentators like Ann Coulter, despite her objections that liberals too often use the charge of racism to gain political points, talk about race all of the time. Similarly, we can point to Rush Limbaugh, who

> regularly replays videos of excerpts of speeches by prominent African Americans. But Limbaugh chooses the replays for their bombast and grandiloquence for a point or two that he might later challenge, and especially for their stammers, mispronunciations, or grammatical shakiness. ... He wordlessly and continually comments on the speech and on the very idea of black expertise with a panoply of rolled eyes, raised brows, nods, snickers, and chortles. ... Limbaugh is seldom without words but is perhaps never more dangerous than when he is. The performance enables Limbaugh to walk the border between the unspoken and the (until recently) unspeakable. He both participates in the refurbishment of an openly racist discourse à la The Bell Curve and its mainstream press attention and retains the possibility of defending his performance not only as a joke and a neutral attack on liberals but also on the grounds that he didn't say a word. (Roediger, 1997, pp. 41, 43)

In part because Limbaugh helps constitute a conservative echo chamber, working-class people "tune in to venomous talk-radio hosts who translate economic anguish, psychological distress, and political confusion into blind rage" (Kimmel, 2013, p. 4). Used as a wedge issue and as a form of divide and conquer, race typifies the strategy of dividing, rather than united, Americans. Kimmel calls this "aggrieved entitlement," which is the "sense that those benefits to which you believed yourself entitled have been snatched away from you by unseen forces larger and more powerful" (p. 18). Aggrieved entitlement utilizes blaming, "blaming others for your plight is the essence of scapegoating. ... Scapegoating—whether of Jews, minorities, immigrants, women, whomever—directs the blame for your predicament away from the actual institutional sources of our problem and onto other groups who are less powerful" (Kimmel, 2013, p. 24).

Of course, the other side of the political spectrum has its representatives who seem like they incessantly talk about race. From the liberal perspective, Al Sharpton prominently speaks about issues regarding race. Sharpton suddenly appears wherever race emerges as a controversial topic. For instance, when Tawana Brawley, a fifteen-year-old black girl, accused six white men of raping her in November 1987,

> Al Sharpton became her adviser, championing her cause in the media and using her allegations as a way to discuss racism among police and city officials. ... But in October 1988, the New York grand jury released an extensive and daunting report indicating that Brawley's story was fabricated and that she was personally responsible for the abhorrent condition in which she was found. (Harris-Perry, 2011, pp. 165–166).

Melissa Harris-Perry (2011) continues by arguing that Sharpton's grandstanding helped bring "shame and silence to black women," since the situation "evoked shaming anxieties" of abused black women in the popular press (pp. 165–166). From a different point of view, at least politically, Ann Coulter (2012) says this about Sharpton's involvement with the Brawley event:

> In addition to libeling innocent men in the Tawana Brawley hoax and whipping up mobs in Brooklyn's Crown Heights where a rabbinical student was stabbed to death, Sharpton famously incited an anti-Semitic pogrom against a Jewish-owned clothing store in Harlem, saying, "We will not stand by and allow them to move this brother so that some white interloper can expand his business." A deranged black man who was listening to Sharpton later decided to storm the store and start shooting, wounding several employees and setting a fire that killed seven people. (p. 64)

Since Sharpton was criticized from various perspectives, especially back in the late 1980s and early 1990s, he responded with "the one case that seems to take more precedence over every good I have done in my career." And he says, "I stood up for her. ... And with Brawley and everything they threw at us, I never in my own mind wavered—even knowing that it would be politically expedient to do so. And if that girl lied, that's on her. But I wasn't going to lie about my belief in her" (2002, pp. 229, 239).

Another moment when Sharpton jumped into the political and racial fray was when Michael Brown was shot. Almost immediately after he arrived in Ferguson, Missouri, Sharpton gave the first of many speeches during his stay. In that first speech, according to Taylor (2016), Sharpton

> blamed protesters for the violence that had been the central theme of the mainstream media. He told the group, "I know you are angry. ... I know this is outrageous. When I saw that picture [of Brown lifeless on the ground], it rose up in me in outrage. But we cannot be more outraged than his mom and dad. If they can hold their heads in dignity, then we can hold our heads up in dignity." He added, "To become violent in Michael Brown's name is to betray the gentle giant that he was. Don't be a traitor to Michael Brown." Even though Sharpton had just arrived in town, he was describing Mike Brown's character and personality to his friends and peers. It was condescending and presumptuous. Sharpton's words also lent legitimacy to Ferguson officials' accounts, which blamed violence on protesters even as police blatantly violated their rights to assemble. ... Sharpton not only condemned the young people of Ferguson but invoked stereotypes to do so. It confirmed a sense among the new activists that Sharpton and those like him were out of step. (pp. 159–160).

Taylor (2016) argues that Sharpton used the situation to not only grandstand in the spotlight of the national media, but also to craft a distinction between his traditional, albeit old, style of civil rights activism with the new generation's reaction to racial violence. In a later speech, Sharpton said, "And now we get to the 21st century, we get to where we've got some positions of power. And you decide it ain't Black no more to be successful. Now, you want to be a 'nigger' and call your woman a 'ho.' You've lost where you're coming from" (cited in Taylor, 2015, n.p.). By using this type of language, Sharpton is clearly differentiating himself from the new hip-hop-influenced genera- tion of black activists. Solidifying his point, Taylor (2015) concludes, "Sharpton's vitriol directed at the young protesters in Ferguson wasn't simply a disagreement about the strategy and tactics needed to take the movement forward. This public attack was his attempt to reassert control over the direction of the struggle" (n.p.).

Sharpton's characterization of the younger generation of black activists touches on another subject in the rhetoric of race—the debate over institutional (or systemic) racism versus individual responsibility. In other words, much of the debate about race in America resides on the premise of the underlying cause of discrimination and in- justice. According to many conservatives, if individuals are largely culpable for their own condition, it provides support for the claim that they should also be responsible for improving themselves. On the other hand, as many Blacks and liberals argue, if the problem is based on institutional or structural conditions, like slavery, the criminal justice system, housing rules, school admissions policies, employment regulations, and so on—virtually any external, societal force that constructs a framework of oppres- sion—individuals are not responsible for their own social location. As Taylor (2016) explains,

> Institutional racism, or structural racism, can be defined as the policies, pro- grams, and practices of public and private institutions that result in greater rates of poverty, dispossession, criminalization, illness, and ultimately mortal- ity of African Americans. Most importantly, it is the outcome that matters, not the intentions of the individuals involved. Institutional racism remains the best way to understand how Black deprivation continues in a country as rich and resource-filled as the United States. (p. 8)

What is interesting, however, is that Taylor reports that "53 percent of African Americans say that Blacks who do not get ahead are mainly responsible for their situ- ation, while only 30 percent say that discrimination is to blame" (p. 9). Undoubtedly, many Blacks have fallen prey to the cultural messages about racism, such as they are to blame for their own predicament. Taylor also reports that "Black poverty, imprison- ment, and premature death are widely seen as the products of Black insolence and lapsed personal responsibility" (p. 6).

On the other hand, as we have already glimpsed, Al Sharpton articulates a dif- ferent perspective. At the end of his book, Sharpton tries to call readers to action by urging that "Black folks must begin to pick ourselves up by our bootstraps and take responsibility for ourselves" (2002, p. 263). However, Sharpton's message is not as clear cut as most of the conservative racial discourse in America. Sharpton does not pull any punches when he emphasizes the need for personal responsibility. But he has also framed his entire career fighting racial oppression, which is mainly systemic and institutional. Thus, Sharpton's overall message is twofold—fight oppression, but take responsibility for fighting it:

> We will not be worthy until we pick up our mats and walk, as Jesus told the crippled man in Luke 5. The first thing black America must do is stop making excuses for why we aren't where we need to be and find a way to get where we must go. Those people who built our legacy didn't make excuses. They made a way out of no way. They didn't just sit around complaining about the white man; they fought the system that oppressed us. … If I come from behind this podium and knock you onto the floor, that's on me. If I come back a week later and you're still on the floor, that's on you. Yes, racism in America may have knocked us down, but we are responsible for making sure we get back up. Racism is an overused excuse. (2002, pp. 261–262)

In this way, Sharpton articulates a sort of permutation between the two polarities. People should confront injustice and oppression, but they should not wait for, nor should they expect, others to address the injustice for them.

Finally, the media definitely share some responsibility for the tensions spurred by the rhetoric of race. I have already mentioned in a few places the role social media have played with some events. A vast array of studies exist detailing how news media report racial issues, especially regarding how the media use racial identity and frames to portray certain ideological messages (Feagin, 2013; Foreman et al., 2016; Hall et al., 2016; Obasogie & Newman, 2016; Sonnett et al., 2015; Stone & Socia, 2017; Valentino &

Figure 7.11: Example of racial images of Katrina news coverage.

Figure 7.12: Racial images of Katrina news coverage.

Neuner, 2017). But when we want to discuss the role media play in discussions about race, we really only need to say two words: Hurricane Katrina.

On August 29, 2005, a cyclone that originated off the coast of the Bahamas swept through the Gulf of Mexico and hit the coast of Louisiana. Called "Hurricane Katrina," the massive storm broke the outdated and dilapidated levees of New Orleans on August 30. As a result, 80% of the entire city of New Orleans was flooded (*CNN Library*, 2016). Citing the Federal Emergency Management Agency (FEMA), *CNN* lists Katrina as "the single most catastrophic natural disaster in US history," and with the total estimated damage of the hurricane hovering over the $100 billion level, it was also the "costliest hurricane in US history" (*CNN Library*, 2016, n.p.).

As devastating as the hurricane was, it was the aftermath that sent a shockwave through America. With over 60% of New Orleans populated by Blacks, the wreckage and ruin caused by Katrina disproportionately impacted people of color (U.S. Census Bureau, 2010). A number of scholarly studies document the racial discourse surrounding news coverage of Katrina's effect (Fahmy et al., 2007; Johnson et al., 2011; Voorhees et al., 2007). However, we only have to look at the juxtaposition of two racialized images of news coverage that circulated on social media (see Figure 7.12). One image portrays Blacks as looting stores, depicting them as criminals who take advantage of the crisis. The other image shows Whites searching for food and supplies. When juxtaposed together, both images frame a narrative that says "Blacks are criminals, even in times of crisis, while Whites are concerned about survival." When paired together, these images show a bifurcated America where one group is criminalized and the other are innocent victims. These two images have now become iconic representations for how the media—and others—use racial imagery to perpetuate racist, or at least racialized, attitudes and beliefs. In reality, as Heldman (2010) so accurately observes, both images reveal everyday people scavenging for survival. The news media, of course, by using a popular racialized stereotype of criminalization, frame Blacks much differently than Whites. Kanye West famously captured this sentiment on a live television broadcast on September 2, 2005, when he said, "I hate the way they portray us in the media. You see a black family, it says, 'They're looting.' You see a white family, it says, 'They're looking for food'" (cited in Harris-Perry, 2011, p. 10).

The story, however, does not end there. FEMA, the federal government's entity responsible for domestic disaster relief, slowly responded to the victims of Katrina. When they did, their efforts were slipshod, disorganized, and inadequate. To make matters worse, post-crisis analysis reveals massive corruption consumed the agency (Baker, 2015; Lipton, 2006; Zeleny, 2013). Of course, the government's mishandling of the situation negatively impacted Blacks the most. This is why Melissa Harris-Perry (2011) suggests that "the explanation of why whites and blacks feel so differently about Katrina lies in racialized beliefs about the failure of government to respond to the needs of African Americans" (p. 147). Melissa Harris-Perry (2011), herself a native of New Orleans, describes the racial imagery of reporting as follows:

> Television news reported roving, armed gangs of young black males opportunistically profiting from the tragedy. Reports suggested these men were stealing from electronics stores, raping women trapped in the evacuation centers, and trying to assassinate relief workers. Later evidence showed that most of these young black men were organizing to assist other survivors who were unable to find supplies: the elderly, the sick, and women with children. These men were portrayed as rabid criminals, but their "madness" resulted from trying to save and care for their companions and fellow survivors. ... That desperate survivors were portrayed as dangerous criminals was largely a result of the racialized nature of the Katrina disaster. (p. 13)

Indeed, news coverage of the relief efforts showed a shift in racial imagery. The shift noticeably depicted not only black men as criminalized thugs, but also black women as hopeless jezebels in need of saving. Again, Harris-Perry puts this into perspective: "Within five days of the storm, national media reports began to shift away from black men represented as looters, rapists, and snipers and to focus instead on black women and children trapped in the city's evacuation centers. These women became the sympathetic victims of the storm" (p. 15).

While countless examples exist revealing how mainstream news coverage perpetuates racial bias, imagery, and framing, the tragic circumstances during and after hurricane Katrina amply demonstrate how news media contribute to our divisive racialized discourse. Furthermore, we could easily examine news coverage of every other instance mentioned in this chapter to locate additional examples of racialized reporting. We must digest our news exposure carefully, especially since racial stereotypes and images easily reside in our subconscious and can then unintentionally creep into our own communication styles.

So far in this chapter, I have explored many discursive facets of racism in modern America. Especially given the events of the past two years, the rhetoric regarding police shootings and altercations takes up most of our examination concerning the rhetoric of race. The next major issue, particularly given the recent presidential election, was voter ID laws and voter suppression. I then touched on the racial rhetoric concerning anti-Semitism, Asian-Americans, microaggressions, and welfare. As we have seen, each discursive aspect of race has its own audience groups along with its own exigencies and constraints (Bitzer, 1968). The rhetorical situations of race help frame our understanding of exactly how discourse about race occurs, how it escalates, and how it divides Americans.

We have also seen just how complex and diverse the issue of race really is in the United States. Not only do we have a variety of different racial groups, but our laws, history, traditions, and language complicate the different dynamics of race. When we add the fact that our conversations about race also involve persuasive components, the rhetorical fallacies and techniques used often inflame our polarizing positions.

Having said that, I also know that this chapter does not nearly cover all of the racial rhetoric in the United States. As I said at the outset, this chapter does not address Native American rhetoric, nor does it include Islamophobia, which is discussed in the religion chapter. Other racial areas include the racial discourse and imagery of reparations (see Coates, 2014; Horowitz, 2001; Sharpton, 2002), the Black Lives Matter movement (see Lowery, 2016; Taylor, 2016), affirmative action (see Cahn, 1995; Eastland, 1997; Greenwalt, 1983), racial profiling (see Alexander, 2011; Zack, 2015), the criminal justice system (see Alexander, 2011), the impact of hip hop music (see Jacobson, 2015; Rose, 1994; Watts, 1997), and the rhetoric involving black women (see Collins, 2008; Harris-Perry, 2011). Nevertheless, hopefully this chapter improves our understanding of race in American in general, and our understanding of the rhetoric of race in particular.

CONCLUSION

As we have seen, the topic of race can be very heated, and personal, and it can quickly devolve into a toxic exchange of insults, misunderstandings, and over-simplified characterizations. Indeed, it is extremely challenging to engage in a meaningful conversation about race with people who share dissimilar views. Unfortunately, some of the vitriol turns to anger, which turns to hate, which turns to hate crimes. This logic is not fallacious, nor is it mythical. In December 2016, a young, troubled. and hate-filled Dylann Roof stormed into the Emmanuel African Methodist Episcopal Church in Charleston, South Carolina, where he shot and killed nine innocent, unarmed, God-worshipping people of color. After the tragic Charleston shooting, at least four other black churches were burned in the American South. According to the FBI and ATF, at least three of those fires were determined to be arson and race-related (Prager, 2015). But even this senseless tragedy did not escape divisive discourse, as many conservatives characterized the shooting as being anti-Christian, not anti-Black (Hock, 2015).

The polarizing rhetoric of race uses many tools. It frequently deploys fallacies, such as *ad hominem* attacks, hasty generalizations (and stereotypes), faulty equivocation, *argumentum ad baculum* (fear appeals), red herrings, and slippery slope fallacies. It also uses other rhetorical techniques, such framing issues in an "us vs. them" manner, vilifying the opposition, and misdirection. Each of these can be found in the examples found in this chapter. There are undoubtedly more at work.

Part of the way forward is to be able to recognize these polarizing linguistic techniques. Once we can identify them, we will be better suited to deal with them. Furthermore, we must also be self-reflective; we must look internally into ourselves and critically examine our own experiences, perspectives, and belief systems. Typically, when we enter conversations that are controversial, we approach the topic based on what we know and how we feel—our own unique set of glasses which we use to see the world. But others in the conversation are seeing the world from their own unique sets of glasses. When we do not see the same thing, or have not experienced the same situations, we will not be seeing reality the same way. This is why Wu (2002) adamantly urges us to carefully take an internal inventory:

> Much of what we as individuals and as a society need to figure out, we can know only if we critique ourselves and what we believe we know. If any of us, however thoughtful, looks at race through the lens of our own lives without additional perspectives, we will distort our understanding and impair our vision, the minority no less than the majority. We are all of us unreliable narrators of our own lives, in which our egos have the better of the facts. As individuals we confuse our meager experience with a supreme truth, extrapolating from a story to a stereotype. We also impose a fictional order on the contingencies and the messiness of ordinary life, which further misleads us. (p. 313)

As we engage in these conversations, we must also remember that context is vital. The context shapes an event, it shapes our perceptions of the event, and it shapes how we communicate about it. Here, Wu again is helpful:

> Words also show us the paramount importance of context. Race is meaningless in the abstract; it acquires its meanings as it operates on its surroundings. With race, the truism is all the more apt that the same words can take on different meanings depending on the speaker, the audience, the tone, the intention, and the usage. (p. 22)

Finally, through continued education and learning about the experiences of others, we can better gauge right from wrong, facts from lies, the real from the unreal. Although she was speaking specifically about anti-Semitism, Bitran (2016) argues that overcoming ignorance helps with overcoming insensitivity, discrimination, and hatred. Obviously, more knowledge will not be a panacea. But it is certainly a start. And by "becoming more conscious of our own perceptions, as a society we will be able to neutralize racial prejudice. The necessary but not sufficient threshold is acknowledging that race operates in our lives, relentlessly and pervasively" (Wu, 2002, p. 325).

IMAGE CREDITS

- Fig. 7.1: Source: http://www.pewsocialtrends.org/2016/06/27/on-views-of-race-and-inequality-blacks-and-whites-are-worlds-apart/?utm_source=adaptivemailer&utm_medium=email&utm_campaign=16-6-27%20race%20press%20release&org=982&lvl=100&ite=148&lea=9344
- Fig. 7.6: Source: http://www.sunherald.com/news/politics-government/article60535351.html.
- Fig. 7.7: Source: http://freedomdaily.com/welfare-queen-goes-crazy-after-she-sees-this-sign-at-grocery-store/
- Fig. 7.8: Source: http://www.huffingtonpost.com/2015/02/28/food-stamp-demographics_n_6771938.html?ncid=fcbklnkushpmg00000013.
- Fig. 7.9: Source: Derald Wing Sue, et al., "Categories of and Relationships among Racial Microaggression from 'Racial Microaggressions in Everyday Life.'"
- Fig. 7.10: Source: http://forward.com/news/325988/jews-are-still-the-biggest-target-of-hate-crimes/?shareimg=326038
- Fig. 7.11: Source: http://www.salon.com/2005/09/02/photo_controversy/
- Fig. 7.12: Source: http://www.americusumterobserver.com/hurricane-katrina-the-ethnic-cleansing-black-new-orleans/

CHAPTER EIGHT

Foreign Policy Rhetoric

I f Americans know little about domestic politics, they know even less about global politics and geography (Camera, 2015; Little, 2016; Ungar, 2015). Most K–12 programs are pressed for time to cover U.S. history, much less world history. And only 17 states require a geography class in middle or high school (Camera, 2015). Moreover, a perception exists, rightly or wrongly, that Americans generally do not care about international news (Colorito, 2000). It is no surprise, then, that most American news sources fail to extensively cover global issues and specific international events. In fact, in an age when budget cuts are practically an everyday occurrence, news agencies typically cut their international news first (Colorito, 2000).

However, it is rather simplistic to say that Americans, in general, are ignorant about foreign affairs. Indeed, most of our knowledge about international issues comes from media coverage. That most of our understanding of global events stems from the media can be troubling, especially since "recent research has found that American media are uncritical of American government policies, especially when compared with their European and Asian counterparts" (Groshek, 2008, p. 53; See also Media Tenor, 2003a, 2003b, 2004; Rendall & Broughel, 2003). While our news media are relatively uncritical of U.S. foreign policy on the one hand, on the other hand the media play a significant role in telling us how to think and what to think about. In fact, "At this point in agenda-setting research, it is widely accepted that the news media are incredibly successful in telling their audiences both *what* to think about and *how important* these issues are, relative to one another. In fact, years of subsequent research have shown the media agenda to be a strong, highly correlated predictor of the public agenda" (emphasis in original, Groshek, 2008, p. 56). Thus, most scholars tend to agree that our news media "significantly influence their audience's picture of the world" (McCombs, 2004, p. 19). As a result, it is not surprising that "many American viewers are only interested in international news when it involves Americans" (Flournoy & Stewart, 1997, p. 200), otherwise Americans will simply not pay attention (Groshek, 2008).

When the media know that most Americans do not care about international issues and when the media are faced with budget cutbacks, a newsworthy story about foreign policy must be salient, sensational, and consonant with other values. After all, media outlets are businesses and are ultimately concerned with generating ratings and revenue. What this means for us is that the majority of news stories concerning U.S. foreign policy probably involve polarizing rhetoric since it will capture the attention of the audience, inflate the issue's importance, and ultimately generate controversy.

Therefore, in this chapter, I will discuss some areas of American foreign policy that are highly divisive, not just because the issues themselves are hyper-partisan in nature, but also because the discourse surrounding them is often inflammatory and contentious. Obviously we cannot examine every contemporary foreign policy issue, and even analyzing a single topic could warrant its own book. As such, I will highlight the divisive discourse of three—and in some ways interrelated—foreign policy areas: the Iran Nuclear Deal, Trump's so-called "Muslim ban" in conjunction with the Syrian refugee crisis, and the terrorist threat from ISIS. I will also describe other key foreign policy areas, but for the interest of time and space, that discussion will be very brief.

CONTEXT OF U.S. FOREIGN POLICY

While the subject of this book concerns the polarizing rhetoric that occurs in American political discussions, we simply cannot understand why some statements and arguments about global issues are made without knowing a little about the larger historical and contextual nature of U.S. foreign policy. Obviously we cannot explore in depth the historical nature of each foreign policy issue, nor can we fully know everything about the context of a global issue. Nevertheless, a cursory review of an issue's history and context can allow us to locate the type of rhetorical techniques used for a given foreign policy topic as well as help us to understand how those techniques might possibly be divisive in nature.

The Rhetorical Situation

In previous chapters, I have used Bitzer's (1968) concept of the rhetorical situation, which examines a situation's exigency, constraints, and audience as they shape and guide the function and purpose of rhetoric for that particular situation. These components of a rhetorical situation can be useful when analyzing the polarizing rhetoric of foreign policy, especially since each international event is governed by its unique situation. Because a rhetor intends to persuade a specific audience group during a moment that has particular

opportunities and challenges, Bitzer's notion of the rhetorical situation can help us identify the type of rhetorical appeals and techniques employed for foreign policy issues.

Additionally, like other political events, foreign policy issues can emerge suddenly
in the context of a whirlwind of multiple actors, cultures, ideologies, and challenges.
While Bitzer's rhetorical situation views time as a linear concept (persuade audience
"x," when opportunity "y" occurs, all the while noting constraints "z"), or the Greek
concept of *chronos*, not all foreign policy issues happen precisely in this manner. Instead,
occasionally an issue emerges in the moment that cannot be predicted, or it takes an
unexpected turn, such that the rhetor must either rise to the occasion or fail miserably
in the crafting of their message. This notion of time, as we have discussed elsewhere,
is known as *kairos*. The Greeks, then, had at least two different ideas about time—one
is a natural, linear progression of time (*chronos*), and the other is the unanticipated
moment that ruptures *chronos*, which can be an opportunity or an impediment to effective rhetoric (*kairos*). Contemporary foreign policy can fit into this framework because
"Political time arises from different combinations of two primary temporalities: *chronos*,
understood as homogeneous, predictable and deterministic flow; and *kairos*, a moment
of opportunity for transformative action" (Hom, 2016, p. 168).

Thus, in this chapter, I will explore the polarizing rhetoric of different foreign policy
issues. Depending on the context, we may want to view the discourse as shaped by the
rhetorical situation, since, as Bitzer (1968) describes, rhetoric is driven by the situation.
At other times, a *kairotic* perspective may be more useful, as the unfolding events may
produce a sudden moment when a rhetor seizes the opportunity or becomes a victim
to the unpredictable rhetorical storm. Or, as Fretheim (2012) explains, *kairos* "denotes
the character of a given moment in time, or a moment with special characteristics. In
the field of rhetoric, *kairos* thus refers to the right moment to act or to speak" (p. 136).
For example, on Tuesday, April 4, 2017, Bashar al-Assad dropped sarin gas onto his
own population, killing innocent civilians, including children (McKirdy, 2017). No one
expected Assad's brutal behavior, in part because he was supposed to have eliminated all
of his chemical weapons by 2014 (Lister, 2016). Nonetheless, in the midst of a turbulent
week—hosting the heads of state from Egypt, Jordan, and China; recovering from the
defeat of his healthcare legislation; trying to secure his Supreme Court nominee's appointment; and responding to multiple investigations about possible illegal surveillance
and possible collusion with Russia during the 2016 presidential election—President
Trump had a *kairotic* opportunity to address the atrocity in Syria. Just two days after
the Assad attack, Trump announced that such heinous acts will not go unpunished, as
nearly 60 tomahawk ballistic missiles were ordered by the Commander-in-Chief to
hit the airbase where Assad launched his ghastly attack (Lamothe et al., 2017). Time
will tell if Trump's military and rhetorical response to the Syrian crisis is effective; but
what we do know is that during an unanticipated moment, while his plate was already
full, Trump the rhetor could have sat on the sidelines, or he could have taken the
opportunity to persuade the American people—and the world—that his presidency
stands for a set of principles. In this example of *kairos*, Trump performed the latter.

The Historical Context

American foreign policy arguably can be traced back to the origins of the country, when George Washington solicited French assistance in fighting the British during the Revolutionary War in 1778. Most of the 1800s were spent building the nation, until 1898 when the *USS Maine* exploded off the coast of Cuba, thereby triggering U.S. military confrontation with Spain, which ultimately involved the U.S. in Cuban independence (that resulted in American occupation of Guantanamo Bay) and the Filipino resistance movement against Spain that made the Philippines a *de facto* colony of the United States for nearly 50 years (1898–1946).

At the turn of the twentieth century, a vibrant debate occurred between isolationists versus those who advocated for global engagement. Except for the Spanish-American War, the United States largely kept to itself in global affairs (Kaufman, 2017). Even when World War I consumed Europe and Russia, the United States maintained a policy of "non-intervention," which President Woodrow Wilson used as his campaign platform that locked his re-election. However, in 1917, the British intercepted a communique from Germany to Mexico, asking Mexico's alliance to fight against the United States. Feeling that American involvement was inevitable, the memo became the *casus belli* for America's involvement in World War I. President Wilson wanted to prevent another global war, so he helped form the League of Nations in 1920 that established an international forum for countries to resolve their differences diplomatically. However, the League of Nations could not prevent German aggression and the subsequent fomenting of World War II. Of course, the United States did not want to enter World War II either, except the Japanese forced our participation with the bombing of Pearl Harbor on December 7, 1941.

By most accounts, American involvement in World War II shifted the course of the war, allowing the allies to be victorious over the axis powers (Kaufman, 2017). As a result, America received a high degree of prestige and respect all over the world. American reconstruction efforts for the war-torn areas in Europe and Japan also strengthened the image of the United States as a moral and humanitarian leader. Although the League of Nations failed and as a result withered away, the prominent powers at the end of World War II (Britain, France, the Soviet Union, and the United States) strongly felt a similar institution was needed to prevent a third global war, especially given America's development of the atomic bomb that would almost certainly guarantee the next world war would be even more devastating than the Second World War. The thinking was that the world could learn from the mistakes of the League of Nations so that a new organization could be more effective. Thus, in 1945, the United Nations was formed while Franklin D. Roosevelt was president.

Despite being allies during World War II, the United States and the Soviet Union (USSR) quickly became rivals, as they jockeyed for global hegemony. No longer would the United States occupy itself with the notion of "non-intervention," for the post-World War era required the United States to check against Soviet influence all over the planet. The two sides became locked against each other diplomatically, economically, militarily, and ideologically. While the two countries occasionally would butt heads in a third-party state (e.g., Angola, Afghanistan, etc.), known as proxy battles, the U.S. and the USSR never actually fought each other in a "hot war," although they were perilously close in 1962 during the 13-day stand-off known as the Cuban Missile Crisis, when U.S. satellites discovered Soviet nuclear missiles in Cuba. Thus, the period between 1945 and 1989 was called the "Cold War," since the two nations engaged in every type of confrontation except an actual shooting war. The Cold War largely determined the course of American foreign policy during that era (Kaufman, 2017). U.S. foreign policy was guided by resisting communism at every juncture (e.g., Vietnam, Korea, Nicaragua), including the formation of key alliances with the North Atlantic Treaty Organization (NATO), the Australia, New Zealand and U.S. alliance (ANZUS), the U.S.-Japan Treaty of Mutual Cooperation and Security, and the Republic of Korea (ROK)-U.S. Mutual Security Agreement. Of course, the United States had other alliance partnerships as well, such as the close ties with Israel, but many of those, while important, were tangentially related to America's Cold War doctrine.

Of course, no discussion of U.S. foreign policy would be complete without mentioning Vietnam (Kaufman, 2017). The communist Viet Minh developed to fight against French colonialism. Then, during World War II, the Viet Minh fought against Japanese occupation. After the war, the French returned, ultimately fighting the Indochina War that they lost in 1955, but end of the war brought about the partitioning of the country into North and South. The Viet Minh and the North Vietnamese Army ruled the North, and the South became the Republic of Vietnam, supported by the United States, although Viet Minh agents and another communist group—the Viet Cong—were prevalent in the South. After 1960, the Viet Minh dissipated and the Viet Cong took over in the North and maintained a heavy presence in the South (Pennybaker, 2017). From 1955 until 1975, the United States was engaged, in various ways, to prevent, resist and combat the perceived threat of communism in Vietnam. As classic proxy "pawns," the Vietnamese paid a heavy price for the larger war that the Soviets and Americans were fighting. Ultimately, of course, the "north" Vietnamese, led by the militant communist party, the Viet Cong, prevailed, but Vietnam eventually became a representative democracy with a budding capitalist economy.

After different Soviet premiers directed the USSR's foreign policy doctrine of communist expansion, Mikhail Gorbachev became the general secretary of the communist party (aka, the "premier") in 1985. Almost immediately, Gorbachev introduced two new policy platforms for all of Soviet society—*perestroika* (restructuring) and *glasnost* (openness). The idea was that in order for the USSR to function in a more globalized world, it needed to adopt more flexible economic policies, and it needed more transparency in the press and governmental affairs. By 1989, Soviet changes had become so significant that, under the principle of *glasnost*, the Berlin Wall was torn down. By 1991, the USSR fell apart, breaking up into 15 different nation-states. Also in 1991, Gorbachev resigned.

The United States, under the presidency of Ronald Reagan, claimed much credit for the Soviet Union collapse, even though Reagan's presidency ended in 1989. In part, the Soviet economy simply could not keep-up with the massive conventional and nuclear arms race it had entered with the United States. The economic pressure that Reagan imposed on the USSR undoubtedly put their economy on the brink of disaster. Relatedly, the USSR simply could not maintain its empire-like status in the Caucuses, the Baltics, and Central Asia, which precipitated the decompression into 15 different countries (Kaufman, 2017).

Between 1991 through 2001, the United States enjoyed unfettered global hegemony. With its economy on the upswing and no other superpower to challenge American foreign policy, the United States secured its control over various economic, military and diplomatic efforts around the world. However, on September 11, 2001, all of that changed (Kaufman, 2017). A new era of U.S. foreign policy was about to emerge. With the 9/11 terrorists attacks on the U.S. homeland, America had to rethink its *modus operandi* with global events, as well as its relationships with countries and other entities around the world.

While during the Cold War American foreign policy centered on fears and policies involving the communist Soviet Union, in a post-9/11 world, U.S. foreign policy focused on fears and policies surrounding radical Islam and terrorism. Meanwhile, as the United States grappled with its military incursions in Iraq and Afghanistan, other global threats emerged, such as a resurgent Russia, a bellicose North Korea, a potentially nuclear Iran, an economically challenging China, a troubling civil war in Syria, and other hotspots. Thus, after 9/11, the United States had to reorient itself vis-à-vis other nation-states as well as non-state actors (such as al-Qaeda and ISIS) in a radically different way than it approached the Cold War. Even today, almost twenty years after 9/11, the United States is still struggling to formulate a cohesive and comprehensive foreign policy, especially as America's new president, Donald Trump, has not articulated an overarching foreign policy strategy or doctrine (Larison, 2017). Additionally, this new foreign policy era poses multiple opportunities and challenges, such as growing nationalism throughout the world, such as the UK's withdrawal from the EU, known as "Brexit" (Lowry, 2016); rising global authoritarianism, like the recent referendum in Turkey (Stevens, 2017), President Duterte's control in the Philippines (Santos, 2016), and Putin in Russia (Kramer, 2016); threatening corruption that cripples nations, such as in Brazil (C. Long, 2017) and South Korea (Kim, 2017); mounting radicalism along with struggling pro-democracy groups in the Maghreb (Reinares, 2015; Yerkes, 2015); and countless other issues in over 200 countries. With a new president who has zero foreign policy experience and who is new to Washington politics, the divisive discourse concerning contemporary U.S. foreign policy is extremely interesting to study.

CONTEMPORARY RHETORICAL CLIMATE

Of the many different, contemporary foreign policy crises, we cannot examine the rhetoric of all of them. In this section, I will focus on the discourse of three distinct, yet interrelated foreign policy issues—the Iran Nuclear Deal, the fight against Al-Qaeda and ISIS, and the Syrian refugee crisis. In addition, because of their salience and prominence at the time of this writing, I will also briefly examine the rhetoric concerning American foreign policy toward China, North Korea, and U.S. allies.

The Iran Nuclear Deal

Long before the current saber-rattling between the U.S. and Iran, the two countries were at one time close friends. Between 1953 and 1979, the United States and Israel supported the Shah, Mohammad Reza Pahlavi. In fact, the U.S. "bankrolled" the Shah's military to a total sum of $9 billion, including the massacre of hundreds of dissident groups in 1978, which marked the beginning of the Islamic revolution. In 1979, the Shah fled to Egypt, as the Grand Ayatollah at that time—the highest spiritual leader in Shia Islam—seized power over the country (Shima, 2014). Incidentally, it was during the period of U.S.-Iranian partnership, in 1967, that the U.S. gave Iran its first nuclear power reactor—a five-megawatt reactor that was fueled by uranium that the U.S. also supplied (Davenport, 2016). Of course, all nuclear projects affiliated with the United States were halted after the 1979 revolution.

In the 1980s and 1990s, the United States identified Iran's culpability in a number of terrorist incidents, the support of insurgent groups in Lebanon and Israel, and affiliations with other rogue regimes. As a result, the American State Department placed Iran on its official list of state-sponsored terrorism, which concomitantly ushered in sweeping sanctions (Davenport, 2016). Between 2002 and 2005, Iran underwent a series of nuclear inspections by the International Atomic Energy Agency (IAEA), which is an affiliated agency to the United Nations responsible for verifying compliance with international nuclear agreements, such as the Nuclear Non-Proliferation Treaty, of which Iran became a signatory party in 1970.

In April 2006, Iran admitted to enriching uranium for its Natanz nuclear power plant, which was supported by Russia. Given the relative ease with which enriched uranium for peaceful energy can be re-purposed for weapons-grade capabilities, the international community became concerned. In September, the outspoken conservative pundit, Glenn Beck, declared, "The Middle East is being overrun by 10th-century barbarians. That's what I thought at 5 o'clock this morning, and I thought, 'Oh, geez, what—what is this?' If they take over—the barbarians storm the gate and take over the Middle East (this is what I'm thinking at 5 o'clock in the morning)—we're going to have to nuke the whole place" (cited in *Media Matters*, 2016, n.p.). And in November, the boisterous Rush Limbaugh announced, "Fine, just blow the place up" (cited in *Media Matters*, 2016, n.p.). The permanent members of the UN Security Council (Russia, China, Britain, France, and the U.S.) plus Germany adopted a resolution requiring Iran to suspend all uranium enrichment activities (Davenport, 2016). Called the P5+1 proposal (the five members plus Germany), the proclamation functionally was ordering Iran to cease any and all nuclear endeavors, even for peaceful purposes, such as nuclear energy and cancer research. Iran immediately rejected the proposal, but said it could provide elements for a framework for future constructive talks. Iran's refusal to abide by the Security Council resolution resulted in additional sanctions.

In 2007, a U.S. National Intelligence Report claimed that Iran was moving forward with its nuclear program, including potential weaponization (Davenport, 2016). As a result, the UN Security Council in 2008 adopted additional sanctions on Iran to prohibit any material that could be used for nuclear activities. In 2008, the P5+1 group proposed another agreement, termed a "freeze-for-freeze" approach—the Security Council would suspend all sanctions in exchange for Iran ceasing all current enrichment activities (Davenport, 2016). The proposal failed to gain traction, however, after Mahmoud Ahmadinejad won re-election for the Iranian presidency. Ahmadinejad, a loyalist to the Ayatollah who frequently spouted rhetoric like "Israel should be wiped off the map," perceived the Security Council proposals as Western bullying (Charbonneau, 2012, n.p.). In 2009, IAEA and U.S. intelligence reports documented how "Iran has been constructing a secret, second uranium-enrichment facility, Fordow, in the mountains near the holy city of Qom" (Davenport, 2016, n.p.). Consequently, the work of the P5+1 became even more urgent. Later in 2009, the P5+1 and Iran tentatively agreed to suspend some sanctions if Iran exported its enriched uranium. Additionally, the agreement allowed Iran to receive 20 percent enriched uranium for its peaceful energy purposes. By mid-2010, the UN Security Council expanded the sanctions on Iran for Iran's failure to comply with the agreement. Additionally, the U.S. Congress passed the Comprehensive Iran Sanctions, Accountability and Divestment Act, which added targeted sanctions on companies investing in Iran's energy sector, including businesses that sold refined petroleum to Iran (Davenport, 2016). The EU decided to support the American sanctions. Up to this point, all sanctions levied against Iran were related to its nuclear programs. Thus, the new U.S. sanctions broadened the scope of penalties on Iran with the hopes that heightened pressure would cause Iranian capitulation.

Between 2010 and 2013, the U.S., the EU, the UN, and Iran went round and round with various negotiations concerning Iran's nuclear program. According to some reports, the crippling economic impact from the sanctions created internal domestic pressure in Iran, leading to the election of the moderate, Hasan Rouhani, for president (Remnick, 2014). Others argue that it was the Israeli threat of a unilateral military strike on Iran's facilities that pressured the regime to the negotiating table (Porter, 2014). Regardless, with a new leader who was more receptive to international cooperation, the P5+1 had an opportunity to revisit serious considerations about Iran's nuclear weapons program. From September through November, Iran and the P5+1 engaged in high-level talks, culminating in the Joint Plan of Action (JPOA) agreement on November 24 (Davenport, 2016).

The JPOA and its subsequent, longer-term agreement culminated into what we now call the "Iran Nuclear Deal." While the agreement is complicated, especially the various enforcement and verification measures, the deal can be summarized as follows:

> Iran and the six powers agreed to a "Joint Plan of Action" that specified the steps each side would take during a six-month interim period and the

"elements" of a longer-term "comprehensive solution." Iran agreed to a long list of "voluntary" limits on its nuclear program for the six-month interim period, including halting enrichment of uranium to 20 percent, the dilution or fabrication into fuel rods of its existing stockpile of 20 percent enriched uranium, and no "further advances" of its activities at the Arak heavy water reactor. In addition, Iran agreed to much more intrusive IAEA inspections, including daily visits by inspectors to enrichment facilities. In return for these concessions, the United States and the other five powers agreed to allow a very limited easing of sanctions during the interim period, but no change in the most damaging sanctions of all—those that had cut Iranian foreign exchange earnings from oil exports in half. Both sides promised that within a year they would "conclude negotiating and commence implementing" a longer-term comprehensive solution that would include a "mutually defined enrichment programme." (Porter, 2014, p. 301)

Additionally, under the agreement:

Iran agreed to restrict its nuclear activities and open itself up to intrusive U.N. inspections; in exchange, all U.S. and Iranian nuclear sanctions were lifted on January 16, and Iran was to begin re-entering the world economy. … Officially known as the Joint Comprehensive Plan of Action or JCPOA, the 159-page accord Iran signed with the U.S., the European Union, Britain, France, Germany, China and Russia, Iran accepted verified limits on its nuclear program in exchange for relief from an array of sanctions that had slashed its oil exports by more than half and crippled its banking and trade across nearly every sector of the economy, triggering runaway inflation and a plunging currency. Critics complain that the deal didn't address Iran's other bad behavior and that most of the nuclear restrictions expire over time . … Deal defenders … point out that other arms control agreements, like the 1991 accord to eliminate excess Soviet nuclear and chemical weapons, didn't change Russian bad behavior either. That deal faced many of the same criticisms from lawmakers worried Russia could now spend more on newer weapons. (Lakshmanan, 2016, n.p.)

The point to the Iran Nuclear Deal, of course, was to stop Iran's march toward nuclear proliferation. As such, the deal forecloses two possible ways Iran could proliferate—by capping the amount of centrifuges for both uranium and plutonium, requiring that any centrifuges are the older models that cannot convert to weaponization, and that all stocks of radioactive material must be constantly monitored (Menon, 2017). Additionally, while opponents to the deal correctly argue that Iran will still be allowed to possess enriched uranium under the agreement after the so-called ten-year "sunset clause," they ignore how the enrichment levels permitted under the accord do not come anywhere near weaponization levels; and the enriched uranium that Iran is allowed to

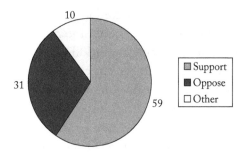

Figure 8.1: Percentage of Americans supporting the Iran Nuclear Deal.

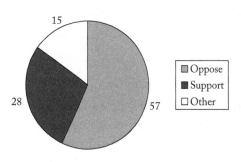

Figure 8.2: Percentage of Americans supporting the Iran Nuclear Deal.

have can only be used for energy, research, and medical purposes (Menon, 2017).

The road to the Iran Nuclear Deal was anything but smooth. Not only did the U.S.—and the international community—need to reach an agreement with Iran; the Obama administration also had serious challenges persuading the U.S. Congress and the American people on the merits of the deal. President Obama and key members of his foreign policy staff held countless meetings with members of Congress, engaged in a number of press conferences, and granted several media interviews to lobby support for the agreement (Hirschfield, 2015).

Similarly, those opposed to the Iran Nuclear Deal employed a full-court press to dissuade lawmakers from approving it. The American Jewish lobby, the American Israel Public Affairs Committee (AIPAC), engaged in one of its most expensive and concerted campaigns in opposition to the deal (Rosenberg, 2015). Likewise, Israel's Prime Minister, Benjamin Netanyahu, did virtually everything he could possibly do to kill the deal, including video conferences with Jewish leaders in the United States, multiple phone calls to U.S. lawmakers, and even an address to a joint session of Congress after being invited by then-Speaker of the House John Boehner (Brekhus, 2015; Hirschfield, 2015; Labatt et al., 2015; Liptak & Krieger, 2015; Nir, 2015). In a highly dismissive move, many Democrat members of Congress boycotted Netanyahu's speech. To escalate matters, the extremist, conservative radio talk show host Andrea Shea King suggested that those who boycotted the speech should not only "pay with their jobs … but also with their lives." She continued her rant:

> I would like to think that these guys could pay with their lives, hanging from a noose in front of the U.S. Capitol Building. What they are doing is they are putting their own interests above that of America, and to me that is criminal. … [The Congressional Black Caucus members'] districts are all dumb clucks because these dumb clucks wouldn't be electing these people if they knew better. How do people like this get to represent us in Congress? Because there are stupid people out there in those congressional districts who are so ignorant it's dangerous. … Stupid, stupid people. Our lives are on the

line and all they can think of is skin color. All of us will turn black if we end up in a cage on fire. (cited in Tashman, 2015, n.p.)

On the flip side, California Democratic Representative and House minority leader Nancy Pelosi characterized Netanyahu's address as "condescending" (cited in Kershner, 2015). And Netanyahu's language in the address did not do much to de-escalate the overall divisive rhetoric. Despite Netanyahu (2015) claiming his speech was not intended to be "political," he continued to portray Iran as horrific, if not evil:

Today the Jewish people face another attempt by yet another Persian potentate to destroy us. Iran's Supreme Leader Ayatollah Khamenei spews the oldest hatred, the oldest hatred of anti-Semitism with the newest technology. He tweets that Israel must be annihilated—he tweets. You know, in Iran, there isn't exactly free Internet. But he tweets in English that Israel must be destroyed. (n.p.)

He also labeled the Iranian leadership "religious zealots," who target Jews, but like Nazi Germany, threaten "the peace of the entire world." And without providing evidence, Netanyahu claimed that the current Iranian regime still "cries 'Death to America,'" and calls America the "Great Satan," meaning that "Iran's regime is as radical as ever." And in a different speech, Netanyahu called the Iranian government a "messianic apocalyptic cult" (Goldberg, 2009, n.p.). Of course, one can locate such statements in previous Iranian history, but to label and characterize the current Iranian government in these ways is unfounded and extremely divisive. He also, of course, names Iran as a terrorist state. Basic negotiating 101 should tell us that calling the party on the other side of the table "anti-Semitic terrorists," who threaten the planet like Nazi Germany will not bode well for negotiations. After all, if we were called such things, we probably would not stand for such rhetoric, nor would we believe the other side was negotiating in good faith. At the end of his speech, he presented the audience with a forced choice/false dichotomy:

History has placed us at a fateful crossroads. We must now choose between two paths. One path leads to a bad deal that will at best curtail Iran's nuclear ambitions for a while, but it will inexorably lead to a nuclear-armed Iran whose unbridled aggression will inevitably lead to war. The second path, however difficult, could lead to a much better deal that would prevent a nuclear-armed Iran, a nuclearized Middle East and the horrific consequences of both to all of humanity. You don't have to read Robert Frost to know. You have to live life to know that the difficult path is usually the one less traveled, but it will make all the difference for the future of my country, the security of the Middle East and the peace of the world, the peace, we all desire. (n.p.)

As we will explore in a moment, Netanyahu's false dichotomy is problematic and does not assess the Iran Nuclear Deal from an objective point of view. Thus, Netanyahu made it clear in his address that he was not only opposed to the Iran Nuclear Deal; he also was actively seeking its demise. Of course, I also need to point out that the rhetoric from the Iranian side was not absolved of culpability in the divisive discourse. A prominent Iranian Shia cleric, Imam Hassan Qazwini, used an *ad hominem* attack by calling Netanyahu "poison," saying that Netanyahu was intent on having a war with Iran ("Iran Nuclear Deal's Islamist Supporters," 2015, n.p.). Qazwini also labeled Israel and Saudi Arabia "illegitimate" "pariah regimes" ("Iran Nuclear Deal's Islamist Supporters," 2015, n.p.). Again, like Netanyahu's rhetoric, these comments only exacerbate the already very heated discourse.

In addition, in an unprecedented move, 47 Republican senators signed a letter that they sent to Ayatollah Khamenei, urging him to reconsider the deal because it would not be ratified by the Senate, so it would functionally be an executive order (not a treaty), which could easily be rescinded by future administrations (Terkel, 2015; United States Institute of Peace, 2015a). The Senate was clearly upset that Obama dodged their objections and their ability to block the agreement (Larison, 2015). Given their obvious desperate ploy to frustrate the negotiations, the Republican senators instead brought embarrassment upon themselves (Easley, 2015). Since the P5+1 and Iran eventually agreed to the deal, the letter obviously was ineffective. In fact, Iran essentially sloughed it off, claiming that such a tactic was a typical propaganda ruse (United States Institute of Peace, 2015b). The letter was clearly meant to be divisive by purposefully trying to undermine the president's foreign policy. However, the divisive discourse did not just happen on the side of the Republicans. Noted liberal pundit Michael Luciano (2015) called the 47 senators "a troupe of treacherous clowns hellbent on circus-ifying" the negotiations (n.p.). He even went so far as to label the letter unlawful. Other liberal commentators accused the author of the letter, Arkansas Republican Senator Tom Cotton, of actually wanting to initiate a war with Iran, since he met with defense contractors the day after submitting the letter (L. Fang, 2015; Longfellow, 2015). Thus, while the now infamous letter exemplifies how turbulent the lobbying was both for and against the deal, it also demonstrates how polarizing the rhetoric surrounding the deal became.

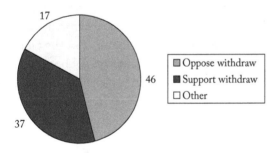

Figure 8.3: Public opinion concerning the possibility of U.S. withdrawal from the Iran Nuclear Deal. From March to August in 2015, the numbers of Americans who support the Iran Nuclear Deal swap. In March, nearly 60% supported the deal (Clement & Craighill, 2015). By August, virtually the same number opposed it. However, that was in 2015 (Clement, 2015). After the 2016 presidential election, in January 2017, more Americans than not disagreed with the idea of withdrawing from the deal (The Washington Post, 2017).

The massive lobbying efforts by both sides of the debate could be politely described as "bitter." For Israel and its supporters, the Iran Nuclear Deal suffered from a number of major flaws, not the least of which was permitting an enormous influx of cash—when sanctions were lifted—that Iran could use to fund terrorism, as well as providing legitimacy to Iran's nuclear program, both by permitting its small-scale use of uranium for peaceful purposes and its potential to "break out" with nuclear weapons after the 10-year sunset clause expires. Those in opposition also had other concerns. Since the mounting economic sanctions were decimating Iran's economy, many did not understand why continuing, or even intensifying, sanctions would be the better option. Additionally, many doubts were raised concerning the inspections and other verification protocols of the agreement. A staunch opponent to the deal, renowned constitutional scholar Alan Dershowitz (2015), characterized the accord in no uncertain and polarizing terms:

> The deal that has been offered to Iran … does not serve the interest of peace … a bad deal is worse than no deal. This is a very bad deal for America, its allies, and peace. Diplomacy is better than war, but bad diplomacy can cause bad wars … virtually everyone agrees that a nuclear armed Iran would pose unacceptably grave dangers to the United States and its allies … the Iranian leadership is playing for time—that they want to make insignificant concessions in exchange for significant reductions in the sanctions that are crippling their economy . … These leaders, and many experienced nuclear and diplomatic experts, fear that a bad deal … would allow the Iranians to inch closer to nuclear weapons capacity while strengthening their faltering economy. The net result would be a more powerful Iran with the ability to deploy a nuclear arsenal quickly and surreptitiously. (pp. 138–139)

Stating that we "were playing checkers against the people who invented chess, and their ayatollah checkmated our president," Dershowitz paints a dismal picture of how the Obama administration—and, indeed, the rest of the world—were hoodwinked by the Iranians to concede virtually everything while receiving virtually nothing in return (2015, p. 194).

On the other side, however, the Iran Nuclear Deal appeared to be the best option in a very troubling conundrum. After decades of wrestling with Iran over its nuclear program, the international community finally had a diplomatic opportunity to stave off future weaponization risks. As President Obama characterized it, if the global community did not move forward with the deal, the only way to guarantee Iran's cessation of nuclear activities would be war (Boot, 2015). Of course, Obama's argument of "the deal, or war" is a false dichotomy, or forced choice, much like Netanyahu's rhetorical tactic from the other perspective. Obama later denied actually calling opponents "warmongers," but insisted that without the deal, Iran would continue enriching uranium, which would leave the world no choice but to use military force (Richter, 2015). Some opponents to the deal advocated tougher sanctions, not war, and still others argued that Obama should have supported the pro-democratic dissident forces in Iran to heighten domestic pressure on the hard-liners in the government (Pierce, 2016). Although elsewhere the conservative ideologue Anne Pierce claims that "words matter," especially extremist ones (Pierce, 2015), she does not pull any punches when she lashes out at the way Obama (mis)handled the Iran nuclear crisis: "*His words and actions implied that respect for Iran as a whole meant respect for Iran's most repressive leaders. …* President Obama didn't just reach out to the new President Ahmadinejad. He catered to him, flattered him, and handed him the words he needed to succeed" (2016, pp. 121–122). Additionally, many Jewish groups were concerned that Obama's characterization of their arguments as "war-monger" arguments could "end up "fueling and legitimizing anti-Semitic stereotypes out there that Jews are warmongers" (Liptak & Krieger, 2015, n.p.). The sensitivity of these groups was reinforced when Obama also said the opposition to the Iran Nuclear Deal was well financed, thereby linking Jewish concerns with money and financial influence (Liptak & Krieger, 2015). Interestingly, however, according to one poll, 53% of American Jews supported the agreement (Liptak & Krieger, 2015).

Another concern about the Iran Nuclear Deal was Iran's access to large sums of money that it could use for malevolent purposes. When the sanctions are lifted, Iran "will be flush with cash," as right-wing commentator Charles Krauthammer puts it (2015b, n.p.). As Israeli Prime Minister Netanyahu characterizes the deal, Iran will "get a jackpot, a cash bonanza of hundreds of billions of dollars, which will enable it to continue to pursue its aggression and terror in the region and in the world. This is a bad mistake of historic proportions" (cited in Pengelly, 2015, n.p.). In another interview, Netanyahu claimed that "far-reaching concessions were made in areas that were supposed to prevent Iran from acquiring nuclear weapons. … Iran will receive hundreds of billions of dollars, with which it can fuel its terror machine, and pursue its aggression and terror in the region and the world" (cited in Ravid, 2015, n.p.). And Jewish lawyer and foreign policy pundit Alan Dershowitz echoes Netanyahu's concerns when he writes, "The deal will enhance Iran's economic capacity to export terrorism and threaten its neighbors" (2015, p. 10). In response, many deal defenders claim benefits to Iran's economy will translate into improved social services, infrastructure, and peaceful development, not military or nuclear expansion (Guttman, 2015; Richter, 2015; Ross, 2016; Qiu, 2016). Additionally, some supporters argue that opponents overstate the amount of money Iran will receive, pointing out that most of the assets will necessarily be used to offset much of Iran's outstanding debts (Guttman, 2015; Richter, 2015). Nevertheless, Nathan Guttman (2015) also concedes that "while opponents of the deal clearly overstated the magnitude of the sanctions relief and neglected to mention that these are funds that belong to Iran and are not a bonus from the West, they still are correct to point out the potential damaging effect of even a few billion dollars becoming available for nefarious activity" (n.p.).

People who disagree with the Iran Nuclear Deal also argue that it simply does not work at preventing an Iranian nuclear weapons program. First, apparently transitioning from the enriched uranium needed for an energy reactor to weapons-grade material is not too difficult. Thus, even if the IAEA notices something awry in Iran's activities, it could either be a false positive (it could register as a violation when, in fact, it is within the confines of the agreement), or Iran could cheat "under the radar" (Unger,

2016, n.p.). This becomes even more complicated and troubling when we consider that inspectors are only allowed to investigate areas that have been disclosed by the Iranians. In other words, a suspected venue must undergo a separate process before inspectors can actually visit the site, meaning that during the process of approval, the target country can move, dismantle, or destroy its activities (Kershner, 2015). Another factor of the agreement that has opponents concerned is the apparently standard procedure of the IAEA crafting so-called "side deals" with the target country. In other words, the inspections agency negotiates separately, and in secret, with the country to reach an agreement about the specific implementation of inspection protocols. Theoretically, these side deals are common in arms agreements because they help ensure compliance—the target country feels they have some degree of control and autonomy, making them more likely to follow the details of the accord (Richter, 2015). Skeptics worry that the side deals might include a provision stating that "inspectors don't need to enter the top-secret Parchin base, but can rely on Iranian officials to take environmental samples that the IAEA would then test to determine whether Iran conducted illicit weapons research. Lawmakers have expressed outrage over this purported agreement" (Richter, 2015, n.p.). According to New Jersey Democrat Senator, Bob Menendez, this idea is "the equivalent of the fox guarding the chicken coop" (cited in Richter, 2015, n.p.). Some of this concern might be hyperbolic, since evidently all negotiating partners know the *substance* of the side deals, just not the *details* of their implementation. But, at the very least, critics argue that the IAEA side deals guarantee international inspectors will oversee the logistics, blocking out American inspectors (Guttman, 2015).

While not perfect, the agreement did establish a number of verification procedures that helped ensure Iran's compliance, such as constant, everyday monitoring of all uranium facilities, electronic seals on uranium containers, online and physical monitoring, unannounced on-site inspections, and "'anytime, anywhere' access to all known nuclear facilities. The 24-day process will apply only to suspected undeclared sites, and even they will be monitored from outside during the process" (Guttman, 2015, n.p.; see also Clapper, 2016; Menon, 2017). Plus, many of the verification measures are overlapping, which means if one should fall short, other procedures are likely to compensate (Kopan, 2015). The agreement also calls for what is known as "snapback" sanctions, meaning that if Iran is held in violation, the previous sanctions—both in quality and quantity—would be immediately re-invoked (Menon, 2017). However, critics of the deal point out that even if the United States were to resurrect the sanctions, it is highly unlikely that the other P5+1 countries would follow, after all, once the sanctions are lifted, our partners benefit (as well as Iran) by allowing their companies to profit from new economic relationships with Iran (Lorber, 2016). On the flip side, if we did not secure the Iran Nuclear Deal and left the sanctions regime in place, it is very unlikely the sanctions alone would have produced a peaceful outcome. Most of the European countries wanted an incremental lifting of the sanctions anyway, and short of military confrontation, there simply was not an effective way to absolutely prohibit Iran from accessing the necessary materials to develop a nuclear weapon (Gelb, 2015).

The main argument, of course, that skeptics make against the deal is that not only does it not stop Iran from acquiring nuclear weapons; it actually makes it easier for weapons to proliferate, or even ensures that this will happen. There are a couple of different variations to this argument. First, by negotiating with Iran and then capitulating to many of Iran's demands, the United States and the Western powers are legitimizing Iran's nuclear ambitions. Since Iran keeps its nuclear infrastructure under the deal and it can pursue more sophisticated enrichment techniques after the 10-year sunset clause, critics argue that the deal itself validates an aspirant Iran. To support this claim, opponents point to President Obama's remark in 2009, when he said that "any nation—including Iran—should have the 'right' to access peaceful nuclear power if it complies with its responsibilities under the Nuclear Non-Proliferation Treaty" (cited in Pierce 2016, n.p.). Immediately after the president's comment, President Ahmadinejad would use Iran's "right to peaceful nuclear technology" as a justification for all of Iran's nuclear activities (Pierce, 2016, n.p.). This confirms that, especially in the realm of foreign affairs, words have consequences. And a simple sentence can provide a rationale for extremely dangerous foreign policies.

In addition, opponents to the deal worry that the sunset provision in the Iran Nuclear Deal simply means that Iran's proliferation will be delayed, but not eliminated. As Lorber (2016) succinctly states, "the front-loaded nature of the sanctions relief means that Iran has enjoyed many of the benefits before fully living up to its obligations for the duration of the agreement. Similarly, the deal's sunset provisions mean that the agreement at best delays Iran's program and, in many ways, provides them with a patient pathway to the bomb" (n.p.). The hardcore conservative pundit and Fox News commentator Charles Krauthammer (2015a) explains the perils of the sunset provision this way:

> Then it got worse: News leaked Monday of the elements of a "sunset clause." President Obama had accepted the Iranian demand that any restrictions on its program be time-limited. After which, the mullahs can crank up their nuclear program at will and produce as much enriched uranium as they want. Sanctions lifted. Restrictions gone. Nuclear development legitimized. Iran would reenter the international community, as Obama suggested in an interview in December, as "a very successful regional power." A few years—probably around 10—of good behavior and Iran would be home free. (n.p.)

Now, of course, what right-wing extremists fail to mention is that sunset provisions are common, if not expected, in arms control agreements (Nephew, 2015). In fact, under the presidency of George W. Bush, the 2002 United States and Russian Federation on Strategic Offensive Reductions stipulated a sunset clause, as did the START I (the Strategic Arms Reduction Treaty of 1991, which was proposed by President Reagan and signed by President George H. W. Bush), START II (1993, signed by President George H. W. Bush), the Strategic Offensive Reductions Treaty (SORT, signed by President George W. Bush in 2003), and the New START (2010) agreement between the U.S.

and Russia, signed by President Obama (Fahrenthold, 2012). Additionally, in terms of Iran, the language of a sunset provision originated with the P5+1 framework that was initially proposed by the Bush presidency of 2008 (Fahrenthold, 2012). Finally, Iran has consistently demanded that a sunset clause be a part of any negotiated agreement, meaning that if a deal was to be reached, and if it was important enough to the West, a sunset provision was a *fait accompli* (Nephew, 2015). Nevertheless, Krauthammer and others vociferously claimed that the sunset clause only delays Iranian proliferation: "The most astonishing thing is…they are not closing a single nuclear facility. Their entire nuclear infrastructure is intact. … So, they are going to have the entire infrastructure in place either for a breakout after the agreement expires or when they have enough sanctions relief and they want to cheat and to break out on their own" (cited in Miller, 2015, n.p.).

In response, supporters of the Iran Nuclear Deal claim it is the only way to prevent a nuclear Iran. Notably, Iran was on the path to proliferating before the P5+1 Joint Plan of Action. Even the skeptic of the deal, Alan Dershowtiz, admits that Iran was developing an inter-continental ballistic missile (ICBM) capable of not only reaching the United States, but also of carrying a nuclear payload (2015, p. 4). Other outspoken anti-Iranian critics argue that Iran was already trying to develop and "to acquire nuclear weapons and has spent years continuously violating nuclear non-proliferation laws" (Bayefsky, 2015, n.p.; see also Goldberg, 2009; Mirengoff, 2015; Pierce, 2016). Simply put, sanctions alone were not solving the problem (Khajehpour et al., 2016). To the charge that the Iran Nuclear Deal makes it easier for Iran to proliferate, defenders of the deal remind us of the comprehensive inspections and verification measures. An arms control expert at the Brookings Institution, Robert Einhorn, says, "It's not as though they are free to develop nuclear weapons. … It's not as though it's a free pass to nuclear weapons after expiration" (cited in Mufson & Zezima, 2015, n.p.). Einhorn's point is that since IAEA inspectors will have already thoroughly examined all of Iran's facilities, and all electronic and online monitoring will be in place, even after the sunset provision has elapsed, Iran will still be constrained, and will have incentives, to not proliferate since they must abide by the Nuclear Non-Proliferation Treaty (NPT) (Guttman, 2015). Simply put, if the status quo was unable to curtail Iran's nuclear ambitions, the deal, even if not 100% perfect, is a step in the right direction. Indeed, Ross (2016) reports that under the Iran Nuclear Deal, Iran will have to "destroy 97 percent of its enriched uranium," and the remaining uranium will not be weapons-grade (n.p.). Additionally, Iran is dismantling or handing over thousands of its centrifuges, so even if it somehow keeps or acquires weapons-grade uranium, it will not be able to process it—and of the remaining centrifuges that are purposed for research and energy, the deal's inspections and verification protocols should keep Iranian activity above-board (Qiu, 2016).

Other notable examples of divisive discourse concerning the Iran Nuclear Deal involve primarily conservative figures, which is not surprising since the deal was being championed by Obama. Perhaps the most famous statements on this issue came from former Arkansas governor and presidential candidate Mike Huckabee. On a *Breitbart* news program, Huckabee announced:

> This president's foreign policy is the most feckless in American history. It is so naive that he would trust the Iranians. By doing so, he will take the Israelis and march them to the door of the oven. This is the most idiotic thing, this Iran deal. It should be rejected by both Democrats and Republicans in Congress and by the American people. I read the whole deal. We gave away the whole store. It's got to be stopped. (emphasis added, cited in Wilde, 2015, n.p.)

President Obama reacted to Huckabee by saying his outrageous comments are "part of a general pattern that would be considered ridiculous if it weren't so sad" (cited in Brand, 2015, n.p.). In response, Huckabee doubled-down on his position:

> What's ridiculous and sad is that President Obama does not take the Iran threats seriously. For decades, Iranian leaders have pledged to "destroy," "annihilate," and "wipe Israel off the map" with a "big Holocaust."... "Never again" will be the policy of my administration and I will stand with our ally Israel to prevent the terrorists in Tehran from achieving their own stated goal of another Holocaust. (cited in Brand, 2015, n.p.)

He reinforced his position in another statement as well: "What's 'unacceptable' is a mushroom cloud over Israel. If we don't take seriously the threats of Iran, then God help us all. What's 'ridiculous and sad' is that @POTUS does not take Iran's repeated threats seriously" (cited in Bayefsky, 2015, n.p.). Obviously, Huckabee is using fear appeals and historical allusions to buttress his claims. However, even many Jewish groups were shockingly appalled at Huckabee's comments. The National Jewish Democratic Council noted, "To state that President Obama is leading Israelis 'to the door of the oven' is not only disgustingly offensive to the president and the White House, but shows utter, callous disregard for the millions of lives lost in the *Shoah* and to the pain still felt by their descendants today" (cited in Pangelly, 2015, n.p.). Others also noted how Huckabee was trivializing the Holocaust with his comparison (Mirengoff, 2015). Interestingly, Israeli Prime Minister Benjamin Netanyahu has also compared the "Islamic republic of Iran to the Nazi regime and the recently signed accords with Iran (the P5+ 1 agreement) to the Munich pact of 1938;" yet his remarks have not received the same scrutiny or criticism as Huckabee's (Goldman, 2015, n.p.).

For another notorious example of polarizing rhetoric on this issue, we can look at the comments made by former Republican Representative from Minnesota and former presidential candidate, Michele Bachmann. On a Protestant evangelical radio program, Bachmann preached:

> All the nations of the world signed an agreement that slams the door against Israel and opened it up to enriching and empowering the leading state sponsor of terrorism in the world, whose ultimate goal is the annihilation of the Jewish State. That is Zechariah 12:3, folks. ... We live in this world. ... We

know how this is going to turnout. As the prophets foretold, the prophets longed to live in this day. (cited in Edelman, 2015, n.p.)

Calling the Iran Nuclear Deal the trigger for the "End of Days" and "World War III" (Hensch, 2015, n.p.), Bachmann was trying to persuade her audience that Obama embodied evil, and that he wanted a nuclear Iran to usher-in a nuclear Armageddon:

> We need to realize how close this clock is getting to the midnight hour. We in our lifetimes potentially could see Jesus Christ returning to earth and the rapture of the church. We see the destruction, but this was a destruction that was foretold. ... We are literally watching, month by month, the speed move up to a level we've never seen before with these events. ... Barack Obama is intent. It is his number one goal to ensure that Iran has a nuclear weapon. ... If you look at the president's rhetoric, and if you look at his actions, everything he has done has been to cut the legs out of Israel and lift up the agenda of radical Islam. ... We will suffer the consequences as a result. (cited in M. Fang, 2015, n.p.)

In another interview, Bachmann called the Iran Nuclear Deal "literally the worst part" of Obama's presidency (Garcia, 2015). She went on to frame her position by means of a fear appeal: "This puts Iran in a position where they would have the firepower to be able to take out not only Israel, but they would have the firepower to use intercontinental ballistic missiles against the United States with nuclear-tipped warheads" (cited in Garcia, 2015, n.p.).

Even the generally reasonable and brilliant Alan Dershowitz falls prey to rhetorical spin, fallacies, and other manipulative techniques. In his book *The Case against the Iran Deal*, Dershowitz (2009) employs several of these divisive tactics. Throughout the book, he labels Iran in pejorative terms, using *ad hominem* attacks by naming them "terrorists," "tyrannical," "aggressive," and other negative qualities (p. 35). He also frequently compares contemporary Iran to Nazi Germany (p. 4, 50, 139). Moreover, when describing Iran in these ways, he often exaggerates their previous actions and potential threats without substantiating evidence. This is particularly interesting since he claims in the beginning of the book that his manuscript is well-researched; and for the most part, it is, except in places where it really counts. While he demonizes Iran, he also paints Israel as a pure and innocent victim (p. 82). In so doing, he magnifies the negative characteristics of one side while simultaneously amplifying virtuous qualities of another, the result of which is a hyperbolic framing of good vs. evil (p. 14, 27, 39, 96). The book is also riddled with inaccuracies. Frequently Dershowitz will say that Obama should not have precluded military options during negotiations—but Obama did not do that (p. 107, 117). Similarly, Dershowitz claims the Iran Nuclear Deal is "unconditional," but as we have seen, the snapback provisions alone prove that the deal is not unconditional (p. 176). He also uses condescending language, such as supporters of the deal must be "unreasonable," and "any reasonable" and "thinking" individual would oppose the deal (p. 37, 141). A final fallacy worth noting is what I call "argument decompression." In other words, when we take a step back and look at the big picture, are a person's arguments consistent or not? In Dershowitz's book, he claims in several places that Obama should have negotiated a stronger deal, or that he should have threatened military action to increase the pressure on Iran (p. 120). However, Dershowitz also makes it clear that Iran is a regime with whom we cannot reason (p. 38). An irrational entity, by definition, cannot be deterred or cannot be persuaded by reasonable, rational arguments. Thus, by continuously characterizing Iran as irrational, terroristic zealots, Dershowitz undermines—or decompresses—his overarching position.

Of course, like most things, the proof is in the pudding. Now that the Iran Nuclear Deal has been in effect for over a year and a half (at the time of this writing), we should be able to examine if Iran is upholding its part of the deal. Simply put, we should have some indication if it is working or not. Also like most contentious issues, we can find opinions on both sides of this question. Generally, conservative sources claim that Iran has already violated the agreement, while liberal sources, typically, will posit the opposite. For example, Joseph Puder (2016) states that IAEA inspectors have caught Iran violating the "130 metric ton threshold for heavy water" that is used to cool its nuclear energy reactors (n.p.). In other words, Iran should only need 130 metric tons (or less) of water if the reactor is only generating nuclear power. If, on the other hand, the reactor is operating at a much higher temperature that needs more water for cooling down, it might be an indication that the reactor centrifuges are being used for something other than the purposes outlined in the JPOA agreement. However, Iran only exceeded the allotment by 0.9 tons—130.9 vs. 130. Although Puder mentions this, he does not emphasize how insignificant the excess was, nor does he explain that a 0.9 overage is not sufficient for a centrifuge used for weaponization. Perhaps more alarming is Puder's (2016) report that Iran has also violated a ballistic missile ban that was extended under the JPOA. If Iran continues to test ballistic missiles, we might wonder their purpose, especially since Iran theoretically will not (or should not) have nuclear payload capabilities. This question of the purpose behind testing missiles supports Lorber's (2016) concern that Iran "has become more aggressive since agreeing to the nuclear deal" (n.p.). While Lorber does not specify as to how Iran has been aggressive, we can surmise that Iran has not ceased its support for Hezbollah, the Assad regime in Syria, or the Palestinians in Gaza.

On the other side of the debate, we can look at the reports from more liberal sources that are generally more favorable toward the Iran Nuclear Deal. First, while Lorber (2016) states that Iran has been more aggressive since the signing of the JPOA, we should remember that the Iran Nuclear Deal was not intended for anything other than curtailing Iran's nuclear weapons program. Moreover, the JPOA does not dismantle all sanctions—just the sanctions relating to Iran's nuclear program. Thus, sanctions relating to terrorism, Iran's ballistic missile program, human rights abuses, and other issues are unaffected by the Iran Nuclear Deal (Ross, 2016; Toosi, 2016). More significantly, IAEA inspectors declared in January 2016 that Iran was complying with the JPOA (Qui, 2016). Based on that report, the P5+1 began lifting all nuclear-related sanctions, including oil and petroleum sanctions (since those related to energy concerns). At the one-year anniversary of the deal's signing, in July 2016, IAEA inspectors again reported that Iran was in compliance with the accord (Beauchamp, 2016). Indeed, arms control expert and director of the East Asia Nonproliferation Program at the Middlebury Institute of International Studies in Monterey, Jeffrey Lewis, believes the effectiveness of the Iran Nuclear Deal "has gone very well," according to the way the agreement was written. He states that "Iran is basically complying with the core parts of the agreement—such as limiting the number of centrifuges it has and eliminating its stockpile of highly enriched uranium that could quickly be converted to weapons-grade material—that make it harder for the country to make a nuclear weapon" (cited in Beauchamp, 2016, n.p.). And the United Nations confirms reports by the IAEA that Iran is in compliance, and the "deal is working" (Lakshmanan, 2016, n.p.).

Since the Iran Nuclear Deal was a foreign policy victory for the Obama administration, many Republicans naturally opposed it. During the 2016 presidential campaign, Donald Trump noted his displeasure with the deal, calling it "the worst deal in history" (cited in Menon, 2017, n.p.). Trump also said that he had "never seen something so incompetently negotiated—and I mean never" (cited in Bash et al., 2015, n.p.), because the deal is "catastrophic for America, for Israel, and for the whole of the Middle East" (cited in Menon, 2017, n.p.). As a result, on the campaign trail, Trump claimed his "number-one priority is to dismantle the disastrous deal with Iran" (cited in Menon, 2017, n.p.). However, although Trump ridiculed Obama's foreign policy skills and said the deal is "horrible," he also promised that he would "police that contract so tough that they (the Iranians) don't have a chance" (cited in Puder, 2016, n.p.). So, on one hand Trump said his number-one priority was to scrap the deal, but on the other hand he said he would personally and vigorously enforce the agreement. Of course, during Trump's first 100 days in office, he did not revoke the accord. His polarizing language about Obama and the nature of the deal may have been campaign banter, but given that the agreement was already highly contentious, Trump's remarks further perpetuated its divisiveness. President Trump's maneuver from criticizing the Iran Nuclear Deal during the campaign to pragmatically working with it now that he is in office could be a strategic result of what we know as "double-speak"—the "incongruity between what is said, or left unsaid, and what really is. It's the incongruity between the word and the referent, between seem and be, between the essential function of language (communication) and what doublespeak does" (Lutz, 1999, p. x).

Despite the many objections to the deal, "this agreement extends the time for an Iranian nuclear breakout to a bomb and enhances our knowledge of what's going on with nuclear programs inside Iran through greater inspections. It's surely not heaven, and the Iranians surely can't be trusted, but it's surely better than the idiotic alternatives. These would be forgoing the agreement and letting Iran simply get to a bomb quickly, as the severest critics fear they will, or going to war with Iran to delay that day" (Gelb, 2015, n.p.). Of course, even if Iran maintains its compliance with the JPOA, its other activities in terrorism, human rights abuses, etc., are likely to pose continued foreign policy challenges for the United States (Clapper, 2016).

The Iran Nuclear Deal provides a useful and significant case study for how polarizing rhetoric operates with U.S. foreign policy discussions. Not surprisingly, most of the divisive discourse occurred during the negotiations and leading up to the actual agreement. Both sides of the issue—those favoring the deal and those opposing it—engaged in polarizing rhetorical tactics in order to characterize the positions of the opposition as weak, scary, misinformed, and ultimately damaging to U.S. foreign policy as well as to the stability of the planet. President Obama said his opponents engaged in "war-mongering" (thereby functionally calling them "war-mongers"), Republican senators sought to unravel Obama's foreign policy with their letter to the Ayatollah, Israel's Netanyahu used divisive rhetorical techniques in general but in his address to Congress in particular, and pundits on both sides can be seen in various media formats utilizing different fallacies and tactics of rhetorical spin to amplify their position while weakening the position of their opponents. Finally, this type of discourse continues. As I write this, Secretary of State Rex Tillerson just announced that Iran is complying with the deal, but they continue to support terrorism. As a result, the Trump administration is reviewing the various ways the U.S. government is involved with the Iran Nuclear Deal, suggesting the possibility that President Trump may withdraw American participation in the deal (Labott & Gaouette, 2017).

Fighting al-Qaeda and ISIS

While Iran has had ties with various terrorist groups in the Middle East, new terrorist threats have emerged in the past decade that are largely unrelated to Iran. For example, the terrorist group responsible for the 9/11 attacks was al-Qaeda. Arabic for "the base," al-Qaeda was formed by Osama bin Laden in 1988 (Bajoria & Bruno, 2012). Bin Laden's radicalism started long before then, however. When the Soviet Union invaded and tried to take control of Afghanistan between 1979 and 1989, many Muslims perceived the USSR's actions as a Western "cultural attack on the Muslim world" (Shavit, 2006, n.p.). Although the United States funded and supported bin Laden and the mujahedeen to counter the Soviets in Afghanistan, bin Laden and his followers saw the USSR as the invading, Western force. Then, in 1990, Iraq invaded Kuwait, and in response, President George H. W. Bush militarily engaged Iraq to push them back out of Kuwait. For Muslims like bin Laden, the U.S. now became the invading Western force into the Muslim world. To make matters worse, the United States allied with Saudi Arabia—who feared that Iraq's president, Saddam Hussein, would invade them after Kuwait—which allowed the U.S. to establish a military base in the Saudi city of Riyadh, not far from the Kuwaiti border. The U.S. military subsequently established two other military bases in Saudi Arabia, one in Khamis Mushayt, and the other in Dammam ("Riyadh Air Force Base," n.d.). We should also note that Saudi Arabia houses two of the three most important Muslim religious cities in the world—Mecca and Medina, with the third being Jerusalem, which of course is in Israel. Thus, for the United States to now have a military base in the Muslim holy land, bin Laden and others feared that the "Western cultural penetration of the kingdom was just a precursor to a Western military reconquest of the Middle East" (Shivat, 2006, n.p.).

Interestingly, Osama bin Laden was born in Saudi Arabia and came from a very wealthy and influential Saudi family, and his al-Qaeda, jihadist teachings were financed and supported by Saudi Arabia for years (Bajoria & Bruno, 2012; Shivat, 2006). Later, we also know that 15 of the 19 terrorists responsible for 9/11 were Saudi citizens and members of al-Qaeda, and allegedly Saudi Arabia granted sanctuary for the terrorists to train before the dreadful attacks (Taylor, 2016). Hence, it was peculiar to see Saudi Arabia welcoming U.S. military forces onto its soil to deter Saddam Hussein when ideologically the Saudis represent anti-American interests. In fact, even while the U.S. was stationed in Riyadh, the Saudi king "promoted the idea of a clash of civilizations between an aggressive, materialistic, hegemony-seeking Western civilization and a spiritual Muslim civilization led by Saudi Arabia" in many of his public addresses (Shivat, 2006, n.p.). The United States largely ignored the proclamations emanating from the Saudi royal family by writing them off as domestic political maneuvering.

The first Iraq war (known as the "Gulf War" and "Operation Desert Shield," and then "Operation Desert Storm") lasted just about six months. The U.S. military bases, however, still remain in Saudi Arabia ("Riyadh Air Force Base," n.d.). Since the American military presence did not leave after the Gulf War, extremists like bin Laden strengthened their resolve and radicalism. As a result, bin Laden formed a coalition between al-Qaeda and groups from Egypt, Pakistan, and Bangladesh, called "The World Islamic Front for the Jihad against the Jews and the Crusaders" (Shivat, 2006, n.p.). One of the outcomes to the formation of this coalition was bin Laden's *pièce de résistance*—the multiple, coordinated attacks against the United States on September 11, 2001.

Immediately after 9/11, President George W. Bush initiated the so-called "war on terror" when he said during his address to the nation "Our *war on terror* begins with Al Qaeda, but it does not end there" (emphasis added, Bush, 2001, n.p.). The war on terror obviously sought to prevent and counter terrorism around the world, but it also included confronting countries that harbored and/or supported terrorist organizations. The Bush administration knew that Osama bin Laden and al-Qaeda were responsible for the 9/11 attacks, and they knew that bin Laden was taking refuge in Afghanistan. President Bush initially asked the Taliban government in Afghanistan to extradite bin Laden to the United States. They refused, saying that until the U.S. could provide concrete evidence of bin Laden's involvement in the attacks, they would not extradite. As a result, President Bush ordered the U.S. military incursion into Afghanistan on October 7, 2001 (Council on Foreign Relations, 2014). Then, in 2003, despite never offering evidence linking Saddam Hussein to 9/11 or evidence proving the existence of weapons of mass destruction (WMD), Bush ordered the military invasion of Iraq (Stein & Dickinson, 2006). After 2001 and 2003, respectively, the United States fought the war on terror on two primary fronts, along with other tactical attacks periodically happening in other parts of the world, like Libya. While President Obama's policy was to officially dismantle the war on terror, our engagements in Afghanistan and Iraq continued, although Obama did reduce the number of U.S. military personnel in both countries by 2014. What was most notable during the Obama presidency, however, was his order to dispatch Seal Team Six into a compound in northern Pakistan on May 2, 2011, where U.S. military forces located and killed Osama bin Laden (Mahler, 2015).

Although severely weakened after their leader's death, al-Qaeda still exists. Once thought to be the "supreme council" of the world Islamic front, al-Qaeda no longer poses the threat to global stability it once did when bin Laden was orchestrating its activities, but it still "remains deadly with its networks all over the world" (Bajoria & Bruno, 2012, n.p.). Killing bin Laden was a major triumph for the U.S. military and for Obama's foreign policy. However, the two wars in Iraq and Afghanistan produced serious negative consequences as well. First, the incessant portrayals of Muslims *as* terrorists by our government leaders and the popular media triggered widespread hysteria associating Islam with violence and terrorism. For example, a post on the extremely conservative online news source, *Breitbart*, declares, as if fact, that "I don't mean a 'radical Islam' problem or an 'extremist Islam problem.' Violence is not the extreme in Islam any more: it's the norm" (Yiannopoulos, 2016, n.p.). Acts of Islamophobia swept across the nation by means of stereotyping, attacks against Mosques and Muslim cultural centers, brutal assaults against innocent Muslims, and so on, despite the fact that since 9/11, "twice as many people have been killed by white supremacists and non-Muslim extremists as by radical Muslims" (Schuchter, 2015, p. 231). Second, while every city liberated, every terrorist killed, and every objective met can be, and have been, framed as a foreign policy victory, we also know that one of the key motivating factors behind terrorist groups like al-Qaeda—as well as one of their core recruiting tools—is the presence and military action of the United States in the Middle East. Thus, each "new intervention and action in the Middle East that aims to solve or ameliorate terrorism threats seems to lead to new ones and new vulnerabilities to the advance" of terrorist groups (Schuchter, 2015, p. ix). Or, as Shah (2013) puts it, U.S. military action created "a self-fulfilling prophecy; creating more anger and resentment against the US, more potential terrorists" (n.p.). Finally, American military engagements in Iraq and Afghanistan have resulted in over 6,000 deaths of U.S. military personnel along with countless numbers of injured soldiers. Additionally, although no one knows for certain, experts estimate that at least 600,000 civilians have been killed, and surely many more have suffered injuries (Shah, 2013). Of course, on the other hand, we do not know how many lives have been saved as a result of confronting terrorist groups like al-Qaeda.

With the waning strength of al-Qaeda, the incremental draw-down of U.S. forces under the Obama presidency, and the growing economic despair throughout the region, another radical, extremist, jihadist group emerged. During the American incursion in Iraq, a terrorist group called al-Qaeda in Iraq (AQI), started by Abu Musab al-Zarqawi, became more radical as the United States continued its military campaign. Part of the U.S. strategy was to train Iraqi forces—including soldiers and ex-police officers—and supply them with American weapons, equipment, vehicles, etc. In 2006, the U.S. killed al-Zarqawi, and a couple of years later, under Obama, the U.S. presence began to decrease with the idea that the now-trained Iraqi forces could protect themselves (Erickson, 2015; Gerges, 2016). However, the poor economy and the growing radicalization of jihadist groups attracted many of the Iraqi soldiers, who then shifted allegiance to AQI, now called the Islamic State in the Levant (ISIL), which promised economic benefits and refuge from what they perceived as American imperialism. When many of the Iraqis changed sides, they took with them all of the American military supplies and weapons (Clapper, 2016).

While Iraq plunged into civil war, with multiple sectarian factions dividing the country into different ethnic, racial and ideological groups, a vacuum was created as the U.S. presence weakened (Incidentally, a major cause for the U.S. draw-down in Iraq was at the Iraqi government's behest, as they did not extend the status of forces agreement, or SOFA, meaning that American forces no longer had an official, legal basis for its military presence (Karon, 2011). Seeing an opportunity to exert influence, Iran supported Shia groups and aided resistance to the fragmented Iraqi government. It is important to recall that between 1980 and 1988, Iran and Iraq—as they share a border and exemplify the internal turmoil within Islam, as Iran represents Shia Islam and Iraq is largely composed of Sunni Muslims—were at war with each other, and at that time, the United States supported the Iraqi regime led by Saddam Hussein. Therefore, when Iraq imploded, Iran was able to assert control that they were unable to do during their eight-year war with Iraq. The Sunnis, of course, resented not only the American military intrusion, but also the growing encroachment of Iranian-backed Shia groups. As a consequence, the AQI offshoot, led by extremist Abu Bakr al-Baghdadi, became more radicalized. They changed their name to the Islamic State of the Levant (ISIL), and they changed their tactics. ISIL took advantage of similar turmoil occurring in Syria—disgruntled Sunnis who were discriminated against by the fringe Muslim sect, the Alawites, who ruled the Syrian government, frustrated Arabs who disliked American action in the region, and a brewing civil war that began in 2011, just as the U.S. was beginning to leave Iraq—and used the American-trained troops and supplies from the Iraq war and began conquering cities and territory in Syria. Since they were now operating in Iraq *and* Syria, the group changed its name once again, but now to the Islamic State in Iraq and Syria, or ISIS. Sometimes simply called "the Islamic State," ISIS

> became notorious for its brutality, including mass killings, abductions and beheadings. ISIS demanded that Muslims across the world swear allegiance to its leader, Abu Bakr al-Baghdādi. On 29 June 2014, ISIS announced the establishment of a worldwide caliphate with Al-Baghdādi as Caliph. ... ISIS forces grew to include about 30,000 foreign fighters from as many as 80 countries. ... In roughly a dozen years, ISIS/ISIL has surpassed Al-Qaeda as an international jihadist movement, but still is only one among many terrorist groups that threaten the US and the international community. (Schuchter, 2015, pp. 4–5)

By controlling over 350 oil wells, recruiting followers in the tens of thousands, and acquiring over $2 billion in assets, ISIS rather quickly surfaced as a global menace and, as the self-declared path to a new caliphate, they became the mouthpiece of radical jihadists all over the world (Schuchter, 2015). In 2014, after ISIS captured the Iraqi city of Mosul, they declared that they were instigating a "holy war" against minority Muslim sects, apostates, American "crusaders," and America's "Zionist" ally, Israel (Schucter, 2015, p. 3).

By now it is clear that ISIS opposes U.S. action and influence in the Middle East. Viewed as imposing its corrupt, Western values into Islamic communities, America symbolizes virtually everything that ISIS detests. Additionally, U.S. influence is at odds with ISIS's goal of establishing a caliphate. Western culture and the idea of a pure, Islamic caliphate operate as a zero-sum game, especially since ISIS "disdains arbitration or compromise" (Gerges, 2016, p. 112). To put this in context, Sekulow (2014) describes the ISIS caliphate in these terms:

> The last Sunni Caliphate was ruled by Ottoman sultans for five hundred years, during the Ottoman Empire. When the Ottoman Empire collapsed following World War I … the titles of sultan and caliph were rendered mere names with no real power. … Reestablishment of the Caliphate has been a long-standing goal of Sunni Muslims. … Al-Qaeda, ISIS, and other jihadist groups also seek to reestablish a new Caliphate. ISIS has gone further than any other to make that radical dream a present reality. (p. 19)

This vision of a new Muslim world fuels the overall mission of ISIS. They harness social media in very savvy ways to recruit followers from over 80 countries, "doubling the number of its volunteers in just the past 12 months" (Schuchter, 2015, p. 120). ISIS also utilizes a propaganda machine based on nine key tactics:

> 1) Winner's message: Projecting an image of strength and concealing weaknesses. 2) Discrediting the competition: Undercutting the legitimacy of rival jihadist groups, including al-Qaeda and the Taliban. 3) The illegitimacy of political Islamists: Accusing political Islamist groups, such as the Muslim Brotherhood, of possessing a deviant methodology. 4) Sowing discord within enemy ranks: Spreading misinformation in an effort to highlight, exacerbate, or create fissures within the ranks of rival groups. 5) Exploiting sectarian tensions: Fueling conflict between Sunni and Shia, often with the intent of forcing Sunnis to seek IS' protection. 6) The caliphate as an Islamic utopia: Presenting the caliphate as a pious, harmonious, and thriving Islamic state. 7) Jihadist adventure and camaraderie: Glorifying jihad as an opportunity for brotherhood and excitement. 8) Driving a wedge between Muslims and the West: Inflaming tensions between Muslims living in the West and their societies in order to galvanise Muslims to support the caliphate. 9) Religious obligation to join the caliphate: Invoking religious doctrine to pressure Muslims to be aligned with the caliphate. (Gartenstein-Ross et al., 2016, pp. 5–6)

In short, the concept of the caliphate not only separates ISIS from previous terrorist organizations, but the "group's legitimacy" also "hinge[s] on the caliphate's continued viability" (Gartenstein-Ross et al., 2016, p. 12).

The notion that ISIS will bring forth a unified caliphate means a couple of things in terms of its terrorist inclinations. First, it suggests that ISIS is intent on global domination—not just governing over all Muslims, Sunni and Shia alike, but also over all other belief systems. To implement such a worldview, people will either have to convert to ISIS's brand of Islam, or they will need to be eliminated. ISIS's terror campaign initially seeks to gather followers to their cause by demonstrating the hypocrisy, aggression, and morally bankrupt Western culture. In terms of divisive discourse, some may argue that depictions of ISIS are couched in fear appeals, inaccuracies, vilification, and *ad hominem* attacks. For instance, while some commentators label ISIS a bunch of "psychopaths" (Sekulow, 2014, p. 27), Zack Beauchamp (2015) notes that, "in the aggregate ISIS acts as a rational strategic enterprise" (n.p.). However, Beauchamp is not condoning ISIS or apologizing for their behavior. Facts are facts (unless we believe Kellyanne Conway who has noted the significance of "alternative facts" [Bradner, 2017b]). Beauchamp goes on to say, "[t]his isn't to minimize ISIS' barbarity. They've launched genocidal campaigns against Iraq's Yazidis and Christians. They've slaughtered thousands of innocents, Shia and Sunni alike. But they pursue these horrible ends deliberately and strategically. And that's what really makes them scary" (n.p.). As such, part of ISIS's strategic use of terror has included "massacres, beheadings, and other atrocities. It has engaged in religious and ethnic cleansing against Yazidis and Kurds as well as Shia" (Gerges, 2016, p. 112). To be sure, the world has encountered terrorism before, "but what makes ISIS *especially* dangerous is its possession of both the means and will to carry out its threats. It's the best-equipped, richest terrorist force in the world" (emphasis in original, Sekulow, 2014, p. 40). And to make matters worse, Sekulow (2014) claims that "ISIS also possesses radiological material that could make dirty bombs," and they could be developing even more advanced techniques for WMD capabilities (p. 41).

Part of the divisive nature of the discourse surrounding ISIS concerns the way its genesis has been characterized. For many, especially conservative Republicans, the cause of ISIS and its subsequent acts of brutality lies solely on the shoulders of former president Obama. Calling Obama's policy in Syria a "disaster" and a "failure," journalist Fred Hiatt (2014) reports that Obama's continued resistance to fund and support the Syrian opposition groups to president Bashar al-Assad have allowed ISIS to prosper. Additionally, Cohen, Acosta and Liptak (2014) reported how Congressional Republicans criticized Obama's "passive approach" to ISIS, like Senator John McCain, who said Obama's reckless ISIS policy all but guaranteed "we will pay a heavy price in years to come" (Cohen et al., 2014, n.p.). Even the Democratic Senator from California, Dianne Feinstein, lamented that Obama was being "too cautious" when dealing with ISIS (Hart, 2014, n.p.). Of course, it did not help matters when Obama practically admitted foreign policy failure regarding ISIL: "The options that I'm asking for from the Joint Chiefs focuses primarily on making sure that ISIL is not overrunning Iraq .... We don't have a strategy yet. We're seeing some news reports suggesting we are further ahead than we are" (cited in Gillespie, 2014, n.p; see also Miller, 2014). Essentially, at the time, Obama was more concerned about addressing the budding civil war in Iraq than he was tackling ISIS in Syria (Rogin & Lake, 2014). Nevertheless, Obama tried to reassure Americans that he was taking ISIS seriously:

> Rooting out a cancer like ISIL won't be easy and it won't be quick. But tyrants and murderers before them should recognize that kind of hateful vision ultimately is no match for the strength and hopes of people who stand together for the security and dignity and freedom that is the birthright of every human being. … America does not forget. Our reach is long. We are patient. Justice will be done. (cited in Epstein, 2014, n.p.)

But even when Obama finally ordered airstrikes against ISIL, the purpose was not to carve out a "cancer," but rather to protect Iraqi troops. As the President announced, "The limited strikes we're conducting have been necessary to protect our people and have helped Iraqi forces begin to push back these terrorists" (cited in Epstein, 2014, n.p.).

Around the same time that Obama's ISIS policy was being heavily scrutinized, ISIS circulated a video on YouTube that captured the brutal essence of its ideology—base, animalistic cruelty meant to attract more and more followers. ISIS beheaded American journalist James Foley on camera for the world to see. Because Obama ordered air-strikes against the Islamic State in Iraq, ISIS politicized the situation by taking an innocent victim and putting him to death in a barbaric, almost medieval manner. ISIS also threatened to kill another American reporter whom they held captive if Obama continued the air campaign (Dickey, 2014). There were no more airstrikes at the time, and we do not know if Obama's decision was a capitulation to the terrorists' demands, or if there were other justifying reasons.

A few months later, another horrific video surfaced. Perhaps even more haunting than the Foley beheading, the new video showed ISIS soldiers immolating a Jordanian fighter pilot. Produced like an MTV video with high-tech videographics and mood music, the video shows the pilot, Moaz al-Kasasbeh, burning alive while in a cage, like a trapped animal. Evidently, ISIS claims they drugged al-Kasasbeh before the immola-tion to add to the cinematic effect (Gayle, 2015). Parenthetically, to be fair (if there is such a thing in the brutal war of terrorism), Fox News on an episode of *Fox & Friends* recently showed the Trump-authorized Tomahawk missile strike on Syria with similar macabre appreciation of the hyperreal simulacra (Baudrillard, 1995) of war:

> Ainsley Earhardt (co-host): Geraldo, that video's black and white.
> Geraldo Rivera: Good morning.
> Earhardt: But that is what freedom looks like. That's the red, white and blue.
> Rivera: Well one of my favorite things in the 16 years I've been here at Fox News is watching bombs drop on bad guys. (Rivera, 2017, n.p.)

But at the end of the ISIS pilot video, ISIS listed other Arab troops who fought in collusion with the evil West, and then the video announced that ISIS calls on all Muslims to embrace their holy cause and kill those who actively support the American military. Unlike Obama, the Jordanians unleashed 56 more airstrikes, along with executing two ISIS-related prisoners in response to the pilot video (Botelho & Ford, 2015; Gayle, 2015). Always known to give a good speech, Obama said in response to the Jordanian pilot execution that it was "just one more indication of the viciousness and barbarity of this organization. … It, I think, will redouble the vigilance and determination on the part of a global coalition to make sure that they are degraded and ultimately defeated. … It also just indicates the degree to which whatever ideology they're operating off of, it's bankrupt" (cited in Botelho & Ford, 2015, n.p.). Supporting his boss, Defense Secretary Chuck Hagel declared, "This horrific, savage killing is yet another example of ISIL's contempt for life itself. … The United States and its military stand steadfast alongside our Jordanian friends and partners; Jordan remains a pillar of our global coalition to degrade and ultimately destroy ISIL, and this act of despicable barbarity only strengthens our shared resolve" (cited in Botelho & Ford, 2015, n.p.). In conjunction with Obama's reaction, most Arab and Middle Eastern leaders condemned the ISIS video. The foreign minister of the United Arab Emirates, for example, said, "This heinous and obscene act represents a brutal escalation by the terrorist group, whose evil objectives have become apparent" (Associated Press, 2015, n.p.).

When ISIS says they want to establish a caliphate with global reach, the true scope of their ambitions are difficult to fathom, especially from an American perspective. To put it in some context:

> Islamic civilization is huge, extending to more than thirty-two countries of majority Muslim population from Africa's Atlantic coast to the Middle East and Far East and incorporating most of the northern part of Africa, Zanzibar and Mauritania, part of the Caucasus and much of Central Asia, and including parts of Albania, Bosnia, Bulgaria, and Macedonia in Europe. There are an estimated one and a half billion Muslims in the world, with Indonesia, the fourth most populous country on earth, possessing the largest Muslim population. (Pfaff, 2010, p. 107)

Many Americans are unaware of Muslim demographics and the multi-faceted dynamics that constitute a Muslim identity. For instance, despite the stereotypes that are often perpetuated, not all Muslims are Arab, just like not all Arabs are Muslim—for instance, many Palestinians are Christian (Seidel, 2006). Thus, it is important to note that of "the Muslim world's billion and a half people, fewer than one fifth are Arabs. The rest are Europeans, Africans, Indonesians (87 percent Muslim), Iranians, Chinese, Turks, Afghans, Indians, Pakistanis, and other Asians in the Malay peninsula and Southwestern and Central Asia. Most of these people are ignorant of or indifferent to Arabs, Israelis, and Americans and their allies" (Pfaff, 2010, p. 108).

During the 2016 presidential election campaign, Donald Trump bombastically announced he would "knock the hell out of" ISIS if elected. He also claimed, "I know more about ISIS than the generals do . . . . Believe me" (cited in Miller, 2017, n.p.). The polarizing rhetoric between the presidential candidates did not end there, however. Beginning a cascade of tit-for-tat jabs, Trump accused Obama of being "the Founder of ISIS," along with Hillary Clinton as the "co-founder" (cited in Fernandez, 2016, n.p.). Nick Fernandez, contributor for *Media Matters for America*, notes how Trump boasted about creating those names: "No, it's no mistake. Everyone's liking it. I think they're liking it" (Fernandez, 2016, n.p.). In her own *ad hominem* response, Hillary Clinton called Trump the "ISIS recruiter" (cited in Fernandez, 2016, n.p.). Trump's blows against Obama and Clinton received quite a bit of mainstream media coverage, but not much was said about what Clinton said about Trump. Conservatives on Fox News, namely Steve Doocy, Ainsley Earhardt, and Clayton Morris, pointed out the hypocrisy and the apparent double standard in media reporting. During one of their *Fox & Friends* episodes, their guest, Tony Sayegh, who is a Republican campaign strategist and political analyst, argued that "reality is, there is as double standard. Donald Trump is the first candidate on the Republican side who has effectively confronted this double standard and will call the media out and will say it was a sarcastic statement, it was a figure of speech" (cited in Fernandez, 2016, n.p.). Double standard or not, a terrorism expert on Chris Matthew's *Hardball*, Malcolm Vance, reported, "We have already seen ISIS use Donald Trump in their propaganda directly. I will go so far as to say Donald Trump is the ISIS candidate. He inflames the passions of people in the West to perform Islamophobia, to draw recruits to them, to make them say 'this is what America is. They're willing to compromise all of their values in an effort to come and kill us'" (cited in Fernandez, 2016, n.p.). And political analyst David Ignatius agrees, stating that "inflammatory, xenophobic statements about Muslims reinforce the jihadists' claims that they are Muslim knights fighting against an intolerant West. Trump unwittingly gives them precisely the role they dream about" (Ignatius, 2016, n.p.). Thus, while both the Trump and Clinton campaigns participated in polarizing discourse, there apparently was some factual basis to Clinton's remarks.

Meanwhile, ISIL experiences serious setbacks in Iraq because Iraqi Security Forces now once again occupy the greater Ramadi region, and continued airstrikes are severely damaging ISIL's resources (Clapper, 2016). In Syria, American and coalitional forces are constrained by the influence of Russia. Since the Syrian dictator, Bashar al-Assad, has cozied up to Putin, Russia now views Syria as a key sphere of influence (Schuchter, 2015). Now that Trump is president, his tone has changed. He recently signed an executive order commanding his relevant cabinet members and the joint chiefs of staff to develop a comprehensive foreign policy strategy to fight ISIS. By all accounts, Trump wants to intensify American pressure against the terror organization (Miller, 2017). And at the very least, Trump is maintaining the same level of military force as Obama, as U.S. "forces have carried out more than 200 airstrikes in Iraq and Syria since Trump's inauguration, roughly the same pace as during the waning days of the Obama administration" (Miller, 2017, n.p.). That said, just two days after I originally wrote this paragraph, President Trump authorized the U.S. military command in Afghanistan to drop the GBU-43/B Massive Ordnance Air Blast (MOAB), or the "mother of all conventional bombs," which causes a massive blast one mile in every direction (Cooper & Mashal, 2017, n.p.). Part of Trump's new policy of yielding on-the-ground military decisions to military commanders in the field, the GBU bomb was used to strike a nerve center of ISIS tunnels and caves, leading General John W. Nicholson, Jr., the United States commander in Afghanistan, to say, "This is the right munition to reduce these obstacles and maintain the momentum of our offensive" (Cooper & Mashal, 2017, n.p.). Preliminary battle assessment reports from the Afghanistan government claim that over 90 ISIS extremists were killed during the bombing (Ackerman & Rasmussen, 2017; Faiez, 2017). Other consequences to the attack remain to be seen.

Moreover, what we do know is that ISIS did not come into being overnight, nor will its demise be rapid. When we consider the history of the Soviet occupation of Afghanistan, the Iran-Iraq war, the U.S. incursions into Iraq, Syria, and Afghanistan, and the internal economic and political realities in these countries, it should be evident that "ISIS is a creature of accumulated grievances, of ideological and social polarization and mobilization a decade in the making" (Gerges, 2016, p. 115). As this foreign policy challenge continues, we should also pause to note the type of rhetoric that is being used to characterize Muslims, American foreign policy, and the way terrorists are portrayed. Indeed, the use of fear appeals, demonization, *ad hominem* attacks, vilification, fallacies of causation, and generalizations are all prominent in the discourse of terrorism (see Joseph, 2016; Hodges & Nilep, 2007; Redfield, 2009; Stocchetti, 2007; Tuman, 2010).

Syrian Refugee Crisis

In the past couple of years, much attention has been directed toward the humanitarian crisis in Syria. In fact, many foreign policy issues happen to converge in Syria. Syrians have been embroiled in a civil war, which has precipitated a massive humanitarian crisis. Part of the humanitarian calamity involves the millions of Syrians who are internally displaced and who have fled the country as refugees. Since Iran and Russia support the Syrian government, U.S. foreign policy toward Syria must be delicately determined with a balance in mind of opposing the actions of Syria that we dislike compared to the potential consequences that such actions may cause with Russia and Iran, who are important to U.S. foreign policy for other reasons than Syria. Finally, most Americans are concerned about potential terrorist attacks both in the U.S. and abroad. Given the massive amounts of Syrians fleeing their civil war, some are worried that Muslim terrorists could use the camouflage that refugee status provides in order to infiltrate the United States and/or our European allies. In other words, although Syria is on the other side of the planet and most Americans cannot locate it on a map, the problems in Syria impact the United States in many different ways. However, to be fair, most Americans (67%) know that the U.S. bombs ISIS in Syria, as opposed to bombing them in Egypt, Pakistan, or Kuwait, but only "38% could identify Benjamin Netanyahu as the current prime minister of Israel" (Doherty et al., 2014, n.p.).

Since 2011, when the Syrian civil war began, there have been over seven million internally displaced persons (IDPs) and over four million refugees, not to mention hundreds of thousands who have been killed and injured (Zorthian, 2015). The civil strife essentially involves two main parties—the government, led by President Bashar al-Assad, and rebels who fight against the government. Of course, the conflict is much more complicated. For one thing, Bashar al-Assad's father, Hafaz al-Assad, was an Alawite Muslim—a particular sect of Islam that has Shia tendencies and is often considered heretical due to its belief in a divine triad in the form of one god, Allah (Mouzahem, 2016). This is important to know because Bashar al-Assad continues the Alawite traditions of his father, while the majority of Syria's Muslims are Sunni. Assad's close relationship with Shia-led Iran exacerbates this dynamic. Second, Assad rules Syria much like his father—with a draconian iron fist (Anderson, 2011). It is not an exaggeration to label Assad as a dictator, since he prevents freedom of assembly, prohibits any semblance of democratic governance, and limits civil rights. He also uses torture and summary executions to keep his citizenry in line, as well as commits brutal atrocities against his own citizens, such as gassing them with chemical weapons, as I will discuss later.

As the old saying goes, the more Assad tightens his fist of power, the easier it is for opposition forces to slip through the cracks. Assad's brutal form of rule not surprisingly has fostered a great deal of resistance, especially as pro-democracy movements gained momentum during the so-called "Arab Spring" in 2011 (Zorthian, 2015). After resemblances of Arab Spring activity happened in Damascus (called the "Damascus Spring"), Assad immediately cracked down on protesters and shut down the Internet (Anderson, 2011; Thompson, 2015). According to the BBC, there are over one thousand armed rebel groups in Syria ("Guide to the Syrian Rebels," 2013). While many of the rebel groups are pro-democracy groups, such as the Free Syrian Army (which Senator John McCain believes the U.S. should support), some are also enemies of the United States, such as the terrorist groups al-Nusra and ISIS. One of the rebel groups are Kurdish people who, because Turkey would rather have them in Syria than in Turkey, is supported by the Turkish government. To make matters even more complicated, Russia and Iran have both pledged support for the Assad regime, making the geopolitical nature of the Syrian civil war a global quagmire (Anderson, 2011).

While Assad and his father have been committing human rights abuses and funding terrorist groups for decades, the recent controversies have their origins in the pro-democracy uprisings in 2011. When Assad moved against the Damascus Spring movement, the Obama administration swiftly moved to impose economic sanctions on Syria for committing human rights abuses (Pierce, 2016). The opposition groups did not go quietly away, even under the threat of more force by Assad. They demanded comprehensive regime change, including the removal of Assad.

[By] January 2012, the government began to use large-scale artillery against insurgents destroying many civilians' homes. From this point on, the protests were decreasing in intensity, and the armed conflicts expanded rapidly. In mid-2012, the United Nations officially declared Syria in a state of civil war, and the conflict moved to the largest cities of Syria, Damascus and Aleppo. (emphasis in original, Thompson, 2015, p. 5)

As such, the civil war intensified, including suspicions that Assad was using chemical weapons on his own people. In March 2012, U.S. Defense Secretary Leon Panetta announced the U.S. would not use airstrikes against the Syrian regime, in part because President Obama wanted to gather a coalition of support for any military action. One month later, Secretary of State Hillary Clinton threatened to ask the United Nations to impose sanctions on Syria, which would then allow the UN Security Council the option to authorize military force. Before any votes were taken on the possible use of force against Assad, however, former Secretary-General of the United Nations, Kofi Annan, in April 2012, proposed a peace agreement that essentially required all involved parties in the Syrian civil war to cease fighting and withdraw military forces from cities ("Kofi Annan's Six-Point Plan," 2012). All parties, including Russia, agreed to the precepts of the plan, and early signs indicated it would be successful. But once the deadline to stop all fighting happened, neither the Syrian government nor the opposition would comply with the ceasefire (Barnard & Gladstone, 2012). Once the ceasefire terms were violated, President Obama imposed additional sanctions on Syria (Pierce, 2016). Those did not work, either. On July 19, 2012, Assad commanded a full-scale military onslaught against various rebel groups into the largest city of Aleppo—a city of nearly six million people in 2011 and less than four million by 2016, which exemplifies the significance of the volume of people who have fled or perished in just one city ("Monthly Statistical Report," 2017).

The "Battle of Aleppo" became the iconic moment of the Syrian civil war, since Assad snubbed virtually all international pressure to limit additional military force, and since Aleppo became a humanitarian nightmare. Assad's use of barrel bombs, chlorine bombs, and cluster munitions, coupled with wave after wave of artillery bombardment, practically decimated the entire city. The UN High Commissioner for Human Rights, Zeid Ra'ad Al Hussein, called Aleppo a "slaughterhouse" ("Crimes of Historic Proportion," 2016). Additionally, in just one aerial campaign, the "Syrian Observatory for Human Rights, a Syrian monitoring group, said that aerial attacks killed 457 civilians, including 85 children" ("War Crimes in Month of Bombing Aleppo," 2016, n.p.). Overall, after a long, four-year siege, reporters estimate that the "Battle of Aleppo" killed over 31,000 people, many of whom were innocent civilians (Hauslohner & Ramadan, 2013, n.p.; "Monthly Statistical Report," 2017; "Syrian Death Toll," 2016). It was a key victory for the Assad regime.

After speculative reports surfaced in the fall of 2012 that Assad was using chemical weapons in Aleppo, President Obama declared the infamous "red line," stipulating that if Assad was caught using chemical weapons again, the United States would unilaterally initiate massive airstrikes on the Syrian government (Merica et al., 2017; Pierce, 2016). The reports that Assad was using chemical weapons continued, particularly in an August 2013 battle in the outskirts of Damascus, where 1,400 people were gassed with sarin (Dickey, 2017). On August 30, 2013, Obama sought congressional approval to order airstrikes. Before authorization was given, Russia stepped in with a proposal—Assad would agree to dismantle, destroy, or hand over all chemical weapons by the end of 2014 with full inspections if Obama agreed to forestall airstrikes (Calamur, 2017). All parties agreed, and it was thought that Assad was in full compliance with the agreement (Dickey, 2017). As we now know, Assad still had some chemical weapons.

The civil war still continues. Although the statistics are a little outdated, they nevertheless portray a haunting and horrific picture of the crisis' magnitude:

> The number of deaths, given the dimension of the conflict, reached extremely high numbers. In January 2015, the death toll was above 220,000 and in April 2015 was estimated to be 310,000. Almost 8 million Syrians have been internally displaced, more than 5 million fled to other countries in the region (Turkey, Lebanon, Jordan, Iraq, Egypt, Kuwait) and a few hundred thousand went to other foreign countries (Germany, Sweden, Greece) becoming refugees. (emphasis in original, Thompson, 2015, p. 6)

The most recent estimates echo this assessment: "More than 400,000 Syrians have been killed during more than six years of war in the country and roughly 5 million have fled Syria as refugees. Many more Syrians have been internally displaced" (Albarazi, 2017, n.p.). Throughout the course of the civil war, many groups, like the United Nations, have tried different peace proposals. For example, in 2016, Russia and the United States developed a ceasefire for all involved parties that would permit a "political transition over five years" ("Syria Ceasefire Deal Explained," 2016, n.p.). Despite everyone tentatively and initially agreeing to the proposal, it ultimately failed, like all plans before it, before it was even implemented.

While everyone believed Assad was complying with the 2013 Russian-proposed chemical weapons agreement, he obviously did not eliminate the entirety of his chemical and biological weapons (CBWs) stockpile. On April 4, 2017, the Syrian air force dropped sarin nerve gas bombs on the town of Khan Sheikhoun in the northwestern province of Idlib, killing at least 70 people (McKirdy, 2017), twenty of whom were children (Chulov & Shaheen, 2017). What made this attack particularly horrifying was the video footage showing innocent civilians—and toddlers and infants—piled up as dead victims from the chemical weapons. President Trump called the attack a "disgrace on humanity" (Baldo, 2017, n.p.). As Trump spoke from the Rose Garden the day after Assad's attack, he displayed noticeable nonverbal cues of sadness and contempt. Although just days earlier the Trump administration announced a shift in their Syria policy—moving from regime change to focusing on ISIS—the April 4 CBW attack evidently gave Trump a pause, at least long enough to address Assad's brutal and inexcusable act of barbarism (DeBonis et al., 2017). Just two days later, on April 6, Trump authorized the launching of 59 Tomahawk cruise missiles from U.S. naval war ships targeting the Syrian airbase of Al Shayrat, which U.S. intelligence confirmed was the base where Assad launched his CBW offensive 48 hours prior (Baldo, 2017; Lamothe et al., 2017; Starr & Diamond, 2017).

One of the first things out of Trump's mouth, which was repeated by the White House Press Secretary, Sean Spicer, was that Obama's failed Syrian policy has been responsible for Assad's chemical attacks (Merica et al., 2017). Since Obama did not follow through with his "red line" ultimatum, Assad still retained some CBWs. Obviously, then, Assad violated the 2013 agreement because he still had CBWs. And since he used those weapons, he crossed the "red line" that Obama previously drew. President Trump, consequently, endorsed and fulfilled Obama's promise to respond if Assad crossed that red line. Syria and Russia both called Trump's attack an "act of aggression" (Baldo, 2017, n.p.), and they claimed that the nerve gas did not come from their bombs, but rather that their airstrikes on April 4 hit a terrorist compound that was storing such weapons (McKirdy, 2017; Weaver et al., 2017). However, not only did U.S. intelligence reliably confirm Assad's culpability in the attack; the Russian account simply does not make sense. For instance, if Russia's claims are true, and Syrian bombs fell onto a terrorist warehouse storing the CBWs, the chemicals would have been stored separately, which would not have yielded the mixture necessary to produce a lethal dose, or they would have already been mixed, and the detonation of the bombs would have instantly caused the chemicals to burn up (Graham-Harrison, 2017; Marcus, 2017). In either case, people would not have died from the actual nerve gas. Nevertheless, naysayers still exist who argue that Trump did not have reliable intelligence confirming Assad's culpability, or that the evidence was supplied by the Israeli intelligence agency, the Mossad, who have historically been known to distort evidence to fit the larger policy goals of Israel (Nelson, 2017; Walberg, 2017).

As we know, matters involving Syria are complex. And, as we learned earlier in this chapter, ISIS is intent on ousting Assad from power. Interestingly, then, Trump's recent missile strikes against Assad indirectly support one of the main goals of ISIS. Of course, for Trump and his administration, responding to Assad's brutality and fighting ISIS are not necessarily mutually exclusive. Indeed, the administration continues to declare that their number-one priority in Syria is to eliminate ISIS—and any regime change can happen later and would be an added benefit (Albarazi, 2017; Merica et al., 2017; Sommerfeldt, 2017).

Another key foreign policy issue concerning Syria is the number of internally displaced persons (IDPs) and refugees who flee from the civil war. In most cases, IDPs and refugees are trying to leave Syria, if only briefly, for their own survival (as we have already noted how Assad attacks civilians), with the hopes of returning to Syria once it becomes more stable (Barnard, 2017). The sheer amount of refugees and IDPs from Syria is mind-boggling:

One of the most drastic consequence and with long-term effect is, neverthe-less, the refugees' crisis, as the civil war caused millions to leave their homes. In March 2015, 10.9 million Syrians (almost half the population) was dis-placed, of which 3.8 million were made refugees. In 2013, 1 in 3 of Syrian refugees (about 667,000 people) sought safety in Lebanon (normally 4.8 mil-lion population). Others went to Jordan, Turkey, and Iraq. Turkey accepted more than 1.700.000 Syrians [sic] refugees (until 2015), spread around cities and in camps placed under the direct authority of the Turkish Government. (Thompson, 2015, p. 9)

A few pages later, Thompson continues to detail how the problem is not improving:

Statistics show an increasing number of refugees in 2015. In July, the UN refugee agency reported over 4,000,000 Syrian refugees, most of them resid-ing in Turkey, Lebanon, Jordan and Iraq. During this year, in its first half, large numbers of Syrian refugees also crossed the borders into European Union states, reaching 313,000 UNHCR applications across Europe by early August 2015. The largest numbers were recorded in Germany with over 89,000 and Sweden with over 62,000 in early August. More than 100,000 refugees crossed the European Union's borders in July alone. Syrians formed the largest group of refugees to Europe. (Thompson, 2015, p. 12).

Overall, Thompson reports that nearly "12 million Syrians have been forced from their homes by the fighting; half are children," another "7.6 million have been displaced within Syria," and more "than 240,000 people have been killed" (Thompson, 2015, p. 26). While this is happening, Syrians who desperately fear for their lives need to find a temporary home somewhere. This is no small undertaking. Millions of Syrians flee on foot, carrying only what they can on their persons, until they can find a place to relocate, often several thousand miles away from home. At first, they went to neighboring Jordan and Turkey. When those countries reached capacity and could not receive any more, the refugees went to Greece, the Balkan countries (Macedonia, Croatia, Serbia, Kosovo, Bulgaria, Slovenia), Hungary, and Austria. When those countries' infrastructures and social ser-vices were overstretched, the Syrians went north to Scandinavia, particularly Sweden, or they went further west to Germany, France, and even the UK. If they could secure air or sea travel, some Syrian refugees sought to enter the United States or Australia, and many of them did. But during the 2016 presidential election, Donald Trump emphatically announced he would prohibit Syrian refugees from coming to the U.S.

But the way Trump articulated his plans became very important, and for our purposes, it illustrates how a single word can be extremely polarizing. While at campaign rallies, Trump would say that once in office he would impose a "Muslim ban," which would prevent Muslims from entering the country. In so doing, Trump used fear appeals to persuade his audience that Muslims pose a terrorist risk when they are allowed to freely move about in the U.S. To make matters worse, on November 13, 2015, an orchestrated terrorist attack occurred in two different parts of Paris—one at the *Stade de France*, where three terrorists ignited suicide bombs, and one in a Paris suburb, where mass shootings took place on the streets and in cafés. According to French police, one of the suspects had a Syrian refugee passport. Once news of the terrorist's affiliation with the refugee status became known, conservative Americans, like Trump, argued that the Paris attacks provided proof that Muslim refugees can enter the U.S. and commit terrorism (Amanpour & Patterson, 2015; Lifson, 2015; McManus, 2015). For example, Vice President-elect Mike Pence said, "two Syrian refugees were involved in the attack of Paris" (Oreskes, 2016, n.p.). However, Pence's statement, like the accusations of his running mate, was inaccurate. While the terrorist had a refugee passport, it was later revealed to be a fabricated passport made by the terrorist organization to enter the country under the camouflage of the refugee crisis (Oreskes, 2015).

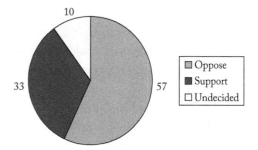

Figure 8.4: Percentage of Americans supporting Trump's Muslim ban. One poll shows the majority of Americans support Trump's Muslim ban.

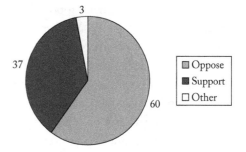

Figure 8.5: Percentage of Americans supporting the admitting of Muslim refugees. Phrased slightly differently, another poll shows that a clear majority of Americans oppose admitting Muslim refugees into the U.S.

Nevertheless, once in office, Donald Trump signed an executive order on January 27, 2017, banning travelers from seven majority-Muslim countries (Iran, Iraq, Libya, Somalia, Sudan, Syria, and Yemen) from entering the United States for 120 days, even if they had a valid visa or a green card (Mansfield, 2017; Shear & Cooper, 2017). Additionally, refugees from Syria would be blocked indefinitely (Shear & Cooper, 2017). Trump and the order's supporters argued that the so-called "Muslim ban" would be temporary, until the U.S. State Department could properly and accurately vet refugees to ensure that they would pose no national security risks (Hayward, 2017). It did not take long, however, before a federal appeals judge invoked a stay on the executive order, meaning that the judge hit the "pause" button—the order could not be implemented until the constitutionality of it was determined (Thrush, 2017). By stating that refugees were prohibited from countries that are largely Muslim, the order relied on religious discrimination as its premise. Some supporters of the executive order correctly point out that the order never referred to a religion (Buncombe, 2017; Hayward, 2017). However, when Trump praised his own actions, he explicitly stated that his plan was intended "to keep out radical

Islamic terrorists" (Shear & Cooper, 2017, n.p.). And when the same debate occurred later involving Trump's second executive order, the Hawaii federal judge said "a reasonable, objective observer...would conclude that the Executive Order was issued with a purpose to disfavour a particular religion" (cited in Buncombe, 2017, n.p.).

After a few days of *ad hominem* attacks against the "so-called" judge (Landler, 2017), Trump and his staff decided to re-word the ban by signing a second executive order that removed Iraq from the list, changed the 120 day wait to 90 days, permitted travelers with a valid visa or green card as of January 27, 2017, and no longer made the ban on Syrian refugees indefinite (Germanos, 2017; Thrush, 2017). Yet a different federal judge ruled that the second executive order's intent still relied on the religious identification of the refugee. The judge made that determination based on the single word—"Muslim"—that Trump used during the campaign and during his signing of the first executive order. The second executive order was seen as a watered-down replica of the first (Kelleher, 2017; Prupis, 2017; Thrush, 2017). In other words, while Trump was attempting to galvanize support from certain, albeit Islamophobic, audiences when he labeled the refugees as "Muslims," he also doomed his ability to actually prevent their entry into the country. Hence, a single word—a single rhetorical utterance—can have massive consequences in the field of politics and can be considered polarizing by its very nature (Byman, 2017; Miller & Ryan, 2017).

The federal judges who blocked Trump's executive orders ruled that not only did the actions unfairly target a religious group; they also harmed the economics of states and municipalities (since those travelers would not be coming to America to work or spend money). With these disadvantages emanating from the ban, the government also never proved a compelling state interest—i.e., the government never offered sufficient evidence that refugees pose a substantial national security risk large enough to curtail their civil liberties (Kelleher, 2017; Landler, 2017). Yet Trump and his legal team at the Department of Justice maintained that the executive orders should be considered lawful and constitutional, since the president has the constitutional authority to limit freedom of movement in his national security judgment (Landler, 2017). As such, the Trump administration and supporters of the executive orders continued to emphasize the serious terrorism risks posed by allowing refugees from the listed countries into the United States.

Ruud Koopmans, a professor of sociology and migration research at the Humboldt University of Berlin and the director of integration research at the WZB Berlin Social Science Centre, posits that half of the 1 billion Muslims in the world are believers in "an arch-conservative Islam which places little worth on the rights of women, homosexuals, and people of other faiths" (cited in Hohmann, 2017, n.p.). Of those 500 million, 10 percent—or 50 million—approve or support the use of violence or jihad to defend their faith (Hohmann, 2017). Koopmans states that not all of the 50 million conservative Muslims would necessarily commit violent acts themselves, but they will condone or support the use of violence by other extremists. Koopmans claims these numbers are on the low end and could quite conceivably be much higher (Hohmann, 2017). While not refugees, two Muslim extremists went on a shooting spree in San Bernardino, California, killing 14 people and injuring more than 20 others. On December 2, 2015, Syed Rizwan Farook and Tashfeen Malik, both from Pakistan and who were betrothed, open fired on a Department of Public Health training and holiday party. According to the FBI, the two had been radicalized for some time, long before ISIS claimed to represent a global caliphate, but ISIS nevertheless praised the attack (Karimi et al., 2015). A year and a half later, on June 2, 2016, a young man named Omar Mateen inflicted the deadliest mass shooting in U.S. history (Daly et al., 2016). At a night club in Orlando, Florida, Mateen opened fire to avenge the death of Iraqi ISIL leader Abu Waheeb. Just prior to the massacre in Orlando, Mateen swore allegiance to the ISIL caliphate, and he later told a negotiator during the three-hour standoff that he was fighting in response to the thousands who have been killed by American bombings in Iraq and Syria. Mateen was an American citizen who wanted a career in Florida law enforcement, but later became radicalized after multiple rejections from various law enforcement agencies. We also know, of course, that at least one of the terrorist shooters in the 2015 Paris attack had documents indicating he was a Syrian refugee. Additionally, according to conservative pundit David French, "We know that terrorists are trying to infiltrate the ranks of refugees and other visitors. We know that immigrants from Somalia, for example, have launched jihadist attacks here at home and have sought to leave the U.S. to join ISIS" (French, 2017, n.p.). Finally, the autocratic leader of Syria, Bashar al-Assad, claims that of the nearly five million Syrian refugees, some are undoubtedly members of terrorist groups (S. Lee, 2017). According to Assad, "You can find it on the [Internet]. ... Those terrorists in Syria, holding the machine gun or killing people, they [appear as] peaceful refugees in Europe or in the West" (cited in Lee, 2017, n.p.), and they are "definitely," at least some of them, "aligned with terrorists" (cited in Isikoff, 2017, n.p.).

Yet despite arguments like these, the federal appeals judges (four in total) all ruled that the U.S. government did not make its case; they all said that there was no risk of terrorism from the refugees or travelers coming from the countries listed in Trump's executive orders. Even according to the government's own studies, namely from the Department of Homeland Security, measures to restrict terrorists from a particular country are not necessarily the most efficient way of tackling the problem (McCauley, 2017). For one thing, most terrorists, at least the ones in America, became radicalized *after* they entered the country, meaning that a heightened vetting process or a ban will not solve the issue (McCauley, 2017). Another component to this argument offers that the countries listed in Trump's executive orders are not the key areas of threat, since none of the countries on the list were responsible for 9/11—those who have empirically posed a terrorism risk come from Egypt, Lebanon, Saudi Arabia, and the UAE, none of whom are in Trump's executive orders (Byman, 2017). Trump supporters respond, however, by claiming that the countries listed in the executive orders were named sponsors of terrorism under Obama's Terrorist Prevention Act of 2015, which identified "countries that have a history of training, harboring, [and] exporting terrorists" (Hayward, 2017, n.p.). But even if that is the case, refugees, particularly Syrian refugees, have been linked to zero terrorist incidents in the U.S. (Byman, 2017). Even when defenders of the Trump orders point to examples like the Orlando shooting (Elliott,

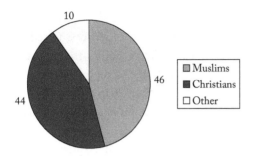

Figure 8.6: Percentage of migrants admitted into the U.S. by religion, 2016.

2016), such evidence does not really support their argument. In other words, a stricter vetting process would not have prevented the Orlando shooting, unless, of course, the United States banned all Muslims from all countries in perpetuity on the off chance that someday there would be a radical Muslim who would become a terrorist (Benjamin, 2017; Saletan, 2016). Such logic is nonsense, and a fallacy of causation, because the same reasoning could be applied to any ideology or religion. Additionally, the facts simply do not support the government's contention that refugees pose a terrorism risk. Here I am revealing my own political bias, but it is supported by the facts: simply put, immigrants and Muslims pose an infinitesimal risk to terrorism in America:

> Immigrants as a group commit crimes at a lower rate than the native born, and in the U.S. that is true of second generation immigrants as well. What's more, more than a third of terrorist crimes are committed by converts, and, in many years, more terrorist deaths are caused by native-born right wingers than jihadists … only one-third of one percent of all murders in the U.S. were attributable to terrorist violence by Muslim Americans. Since September 12, 2001, the total is about one two-hundredth of one percent. (Benjamin, 2017, n.p.)

Additionally, what is often overlooked by measures like Trump's executive orders are more realistic and verifiable threats. In other words, most reputable studies—including those conducted by the U.S. government—make clear that the most pressing and dangerous threats from terrorism emanate internally from home-grown American-based radicals; many of them are white supremacists, not Muslims (Benjamin, 2017; Bergen, 2017; Boehlert, 2017; Bruer, 2015; Frostenson, 2016).

Indeed, one could make the case that Trump's so-called "traveler ban"—which, of course, singles out Muslims—could have an adverse effect on dealing with terrorism. In other words, it is possible that actions like Trump's refugee/traveler ban and other restrictions might invite more terrorism and lead to "an increase in terrorist attacks against Americans," instead of the intended goal of reducing it (Byman, 2017, n.p.). The so-called "Muslim ban" could trigger more terrorism in a couple of different ways. First, many Muslim groups and communities help the U.S. fight against radical Islamist terrorism. Since Trump's executive orders ban all people from the listed countries, it means that moderate Muslims and those sympathetic to the U.S. will be isolated, alienated, and will fear cooperating with the U.S. as they might be targets of harassment (Benjamin, 2017; Byman, 2017). As such, the ban will make it very difficult for our

Muslim allies and friends to support America in its efforts against ISIS (Byman, 2017). Simply put, since the executive orders do not trust even moderate Muslims, they in turn will probably not trust the U.S. government, including law enforcement, which means that those who have the closest pulse on potential terror activities will be reluctant to provide such information (Benjamin, 2017; Miller & Ryan, 2017). Additionally, and perhaps more important, the Trump bans also provide evidence for what terror groups like ISIS have been spewing, namely that America and the West hate Muslims (Miller & Ryan, 2017). Thus, groups like ISIS benefit by enhancing their recruiting efforts, claiming that the West is targeting the Islamic faith (Sultan & Omar, 2016). Simply put, Trump's "Muslim" ban offers iron-clad proof that the West abhors Islam, which provides a very usable recruiting tool for groups like ISIS (Benjamin, 2017; Fernandez, 2016; Sultan & Omar, 2016; Tierney, 2015). In response to this last argument, Simon Cottee offers a very interesting rebuttal:

> But the argument that it will aid ISIS recruitment just doesn't stand up to scrutiny. First, it contains a contemptible implication about Muslims: namely, that they're not thinking, reasoning individuals capable of agency, but mere vessels of feeling in a larger geopolitical game between America and the jihadists. From within this dehumanizing perspective, your average Muslim doesn't do anything, and he or she certainly doesn't make things happen. Rather, things are done or happen to them; they are "pushed" or "driven" to extremes by forces beyond their control. They are "inflamed," "provoked," "humiliated" … it posits an overly simplistic understanding of jihadist radicalization, linking this exclusively to grievances over domestic and foreign policy. But everything we know about radicalization and terrorism suggests that it is far more complex than this and cannot be reduced to secular political grievances. (Cottee, 2017, n.p.)

Of course, even if Cottee is correct, it means that large groups of people are rationally and decisively amenable to large-scale violent attacks that harm innocent civilians, such as terrorist attacks.

In terms of Muslim refugees, both sides of the debate—those who feel that refugees pose a terrorism risk and those who believe that the "refugees are the victims of terrorism, not the perpetrators of terrorism" (Bergen, 2017, n.p.)—can contribute to the overall divisive nature of the discourse. The anti-Muslim refugee rhetoric began in the early moments of the 2016 American presidential campaign. For example, in response to the Paris shootings, presidential candidate Ben Carson said that "the U.S. simply cannot, should not and must not accept any Syrian refugees"—of course he failed to confirm that the perpetrators were from Syria or that they were, in fact, refugees (cited in McManus, 2015, n.p.). Reinforcing the stereotype that Muslims are terrorists, presidential candidate and U.S. Senator from Texas Ted Cruz said, "[The] idea that we should bring tens of thousands of Syrian Muslim refugees to America? It is nothing less than lunacy. … On the other hand, Christians who are being targeted … we should be providing safe haven to them" (cited in McManus, 2015, n.p.). According to Cruz, Christian refugees deserve special status over other refugees. And then, during the election, Republican candidate Chris Christie so humanely declared, "I don't think orphans under 5 … should be admitted into the United States at this point" (cited in McManus, 2015, n.p.). While those Republican presidential candidates sound insensitive to the plight of Syrian refugees, they also were trying to be pragmatic, given the potential national security implications of the global refugee crisis. Other conservative politicians were not so pragmatic, as their language was unquestionably racist. For instance, Republican Iowa State Senator Jason Schultz made these remarks:

> We already have problems with concentrations of Middle Eastern refugees or migrants coming in and taking over communities. … They don't want to assimilate. They do not want to become Americans. They only want the free stuff from America. … [They] practice a religion that orders them to dominate and they want to live under Sharia law which they will not subordinate under our law while they live here and enjoy our protections and our goodies. (cited in Keyes, 2015, n.p.)

Notably, these characterizations of Syrian refugees by politicians have occurred in a context generally constructed by the previous Democratic administration of President Obama, who largely did nothing for Syrian refugees.

Both liberals and conservatives participated in divisive discourse concerning these so-called "Muslim bans." For instance, without addressing the details of the executive orders, the Senate Democrat leader from New York, Chuck Schumer, labeled Trump's policies as "mean-spirited and un-American" (Thrush, 2017, n.p.). Obviously, Schumer is incorporating name-calling into his objection to the bans, but he is also amplifying the "us vs. them" tactic by portraying Trump and his orders as "un-American." Additionally, in response to Trump's traveler ban, Schumer said, "Tears are running down the cheeks of the Statue of Liberty tonight" (cited in French, 2017, n.p.). Obviously the use of *pathos* and imagery from the iconic Statue of Liberty were used by Schumer to persuade potential followers. In another example, the photo of the young Syrian boy who washed ashore, dead, was widely circulated by mainstream media and politicized for rhetorical effect by liberals (see Figure 8.7). This photograph, which went viral worldwide, portrayed the heartless policies of Western nations—particularly the United States—who declared they would limit or prohibit altogether the number of Syrian refugees entering their countries. Along with his older brother and mother, three-year-old Alan Kurdi washed up along the

Figure 8.7: Syrian refugee boy on the beach

beach shore in Bodrum, Turkey, after the family's small refugee boat capsized as it headed for Greece. Despite several pleas for refugee status, the Canadian government denied the Kurdis entrance; nevertheless, the family of three, along with a boat full of other Syrian refugees, were fleeing to Europe, Canada, and America to escape the horrific plight they were facing in Syria. The still image of the lifeless Alan lying on the beach purposefully communicated an extreme shock to anyone following the story. Given its intent to provoke sympathetic, even angry, reactions, liberal pro-refugee groups and the mainstream media disseminated this image to sway public opinion. In response to Trump's anti-refugee executive orders, California Democrat Representative Barbara Lee called them "heartless" and "xenophobic" (Germanos, 2017, n.p.). Since many liberals believe Trump's policy helps the recruitment efforts of ISIS, they have even resorted to calling him an ISIS "stooge" (Saletan, 2016, n.p.). And progressive "socialist" Bernie Sanders said the traveler bans were "racist" and "anti-Islamic," adding, "This isn't about keeping America safe. A president responsible for keeping our citizens safe would not hand over ideological ammunition to terrorists seeking new recruits to kill Americans" (cited in Germanos, 2017, n.p.).

In response, many conservatives cried for people to be "reasonable" and to "separate fact from hysteria" (French, 2017, n.p.), especially since, in their view, venues like *The Washington Post* published a "dossier of hysteria" such that any "clear-eyed adults" (meaning readers of the *Post* are crying children) should examine the "plain facts" of the ban (Hayward, 2017, n.p.). This sentiment was encouraged by conservative leaders, like Speaker of the House Paul Ryan, who yelped that the Muslim ban "advances our shared goal of protecting the homeland," reinforcing the fear appeal that restricting Muslims was key to our national security (Thrush, 2017, n.p.). Consequently, when the federal judges ruled against the executive orders, White House Press Secretary Sean Spicer called their reactions "outrageous," and later, President Trump tweeted that they were "terrible decisions" that will allow "many very bad and dangerous people" to enter the U.S. (Landler, 2017, n.p.).

As we know from the chapter on immigration, many Americans already have fears about foreigners entering the United States. When those fears are linked to stereo-typical images (perpetuated most often by political figures and media portrayals) of Muslim terrorists, concerns and anxiety become acute. On the campaign trail, Trump would frequently lump Syrian refugees with other immigration problems, thereby reinforcing the fear appeal that immigrants (and refugees) pose a national security risk (Sultan & Omar, 2016). A key factor in the refugee debate is the degree to which refugees are "vetted" by U.S. agencies prior to being admitted into the country. Clearly, if the U.S. has sufficient vetting, the risk of terrorists infiltrating under the guise of refugees is not as high as it might be with other countries whose admittance policies are not as sophisticated. The problem, however, is that it is difficult to fully understand the U.S. vetting process, and depending on whom we use as our source for information, the answers we receive will be quite different. In other words, most liberals—who generally favor admitting more rather than less Muslim refugees—claim that the U.S. uses a vigorous and safe vetting procedure (Lifson, 2015; McManus, 2015). For example,

Daniel Benjamin from *Politico* writes, "Over the past decade and a half, U.S. immigration enforcement has improved vastly to the point where it bears scant resemblance to the system whose vulnerabilities were exposed on 9/11. Travelers from all over the world are screened three or more times, with their names run through databases that draw on staggering amounts of intelligence and law enforcement information. The process flags all manner of misdeeds or suspicious information" (Benjamin, 2017, n.p.). And liberal CNN commentator Peter Bergen argues that the Syrian refugees must be screened by multiple federal agencies, and they "must also give up their biometric data—scans of their retinas, for instance—[and] submit their detailed biographic histories and submit to lengthy interviews. These refugees are also queried against a number of government databases to see if they might pose a threat—and the whole process takes two years, sometimes more" (Bergen, 2017, n.p.). Most conservatives, on the other hand, who generally feel that Muslim refugees pose a national security threat, argue that American vetting procedures are inadequate and cause an unnecessary risk. For instance, former FBI Director James Comey testified before Congress that the "only thing we can query is information that we have. So, if we have no information on someone, they've never crossed our radar screen, they've never been a ripple in the pond, there will be no record of them there and so it will be challenging." Comey later said that obtaining intelligence on the refugees we screen is a particularly tough challenge for Syrian refugees who are coming from "a failed state that does not have any infrastructure, so to speak. So all of the dataset, the police, the intel services that normally you would go to seek information doesn't exist" (cited in Lifson, 2015, n.p.). What we do know, however, is that refugees entering Europe received virtually no screening, so comparing their levels of terrorist risks and incidents to the United States is a faulty analogy (Bergen, 2017).

To add another layer to the already complex discussion concerning Syrian refugees in the U.S., some liberal commentators postulate that Trump's recent missile strikes against Assad for "humanitarian" reasons smack of hypocrisy. If Trump was so moved by the image of babies being killed (Lamothe et al., 2017; Parker, 2017), he should be equally moved by the tens of thousands of babies and children who are with their parents, fleeing the Syrian civil war (Filipovic, 2017; Nadeau, 2017; Snowdon, 2017). Of course, conservatives say there is a double standard here—Trump should not invoke religion to ban Muslims, but it was acceptable for Obama to put Christian refugees at the back of the line (Hayward, 2017). In either case, people have been—and are—suffering, yet politicians use divisive discourse to advance their own agenda instead of dealing with the problem.

Other Foreign Policy Concerns

So far, I have tried to outline the divisive discourse encompassing the current foreign policy issues of the Iran Nuclear Deal, dealing with ISIS and global terrorism, and managing Syrian refugees. These three areas are the main spheres of divisive discourse I wanted to examine in this chapter. However, in the last two years, several other areas have emerged that require mentioning. These include North Korea, China, and the way the new U.S. president, Donald Trump, has dealt with allies. This section will be brief—providing only a snapshot of the polarizing rhetoric surrounding these controversial issues. But it is my hope that this cursory glance at these issues will produce fruitful discussion.

North Korea

North Korea has been a serious foreign policy problem for the United States ever since the Korea war (1950–1953) when the North invaded the South. As we have already discussed, the Cold War between the U.S. and the USSR was treacherous, and frequently disagreements between the two super-powers would occur in proxy states. The Korea War was no exception. The North, funded by the Soviets, invaded the South to regain important territory and to demonstrate strength. The resistance in the South quickly became friends of the United States as a way to counter-balance the incursions from the North. Since their defeat in 1953, the North Koreans have been subservient to the Soviet Union, and later to the Russians and the communist Chinese. During that time, the authoritarian regime in North Korea positioned itself as divinely inspired and situated, much like feudal kings used to do. The Kim family rose to power, not only as the leaders of North Korea, but also as the earth-bound conduits of God.

During the Clinton, Bush, and Obama years, North Korea exhibited serious foreign policy threats by inching toward a nuclear weapons program. During those years, the American administrations imposed tough sanctions on North Korea with the intent that economic pressure would force Pyongyang to abandon its nuclear weapons program; however, more often than not, the North Korean regime would simply move forward with its military ambitions while its people would starve. Obviously, American allies in the region, namely South Korea and Japan, have been concerned for decades about the true ambitions of North Korea.

Yet during the Obama-Trump transition period, North Korea, now led by Kim Jung-un, has seemed to be ratcheting up its bellicose intentions. Kim Jung-un has been

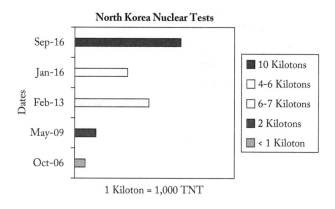

Figure 8.8: North Korea Nuclear Tests

accelerating North Korea's ballistic missile tests, with the eventual goal of reaching countries like the United States (Griffiths, 2017; Hancocks et al., 2017; Watkins, 2017; see Figure 8.8). Moreover, North Korea has been continuing its tests for nuclear weapons, essentially examining whether its enrichment programs are capable of yielding weapons-grade uranium for a missile payload. In response to North Korea's latest missile tests, Senator John McCain called Kim Jung-un the "crazy fat kid" (Smith, 2017, n.p.). Reacting to the American statesman's remarks, the *Korean Central News Agency* said it was "a grave provocation" and was short of "a declaration of war" (Smith, 2017, n.p.). They also apparently reported that "the service personnel and people of the DPRK are regarding the dignity of their supreme leadership as their life and soul," and that the U.S. "will have to bitterly experience the disastrous consequences to be entailed by their reckless tongue-lashing and then any regret for it will come too late. They will have to be entirely responsible for their foolhardy tongue-lashing" (Embury-Dennis, 2017, n.p.). In a separate announcement, the *Korean Central News Agency* threatened a possible nuclear response, saying, "The revolutionary forces of the DPRK with its nuclear force as its pivot will fulfill its sacred mission of devotedly defending its supreme leadership representing the destiny and life of its people by dealing a merciless sledge-hammer blow at those daring [to] hurt the dignity of the supreme leadership" (Moore, 2017a, n.p.). Adding to the toxic discourse, McCain doubled-down on his initial comment on Greta van Susteren's show on MSNBC, and said the "crazy fat kid that's running North Korea. ... He's not rational. ... We're not dealing even with someone like Joseph Stalin, who had a certain rationality to his barbarity" (cited in Smith, 2017, n.p.). When asked about provoking the North Koreans, McCain responded, "What, did they want me to call him a crazy skinny kid?" (cited in Smith, 2017, n.p.). But what McCain and others like him failed to consider is that the North Koreans view their supreme leader as a deity, a divine spirit on earth. Thus, ridiculing their leader is viewed with high suspicion and, yes, as a provocation to war.

The current crisis, at the time of this writing, is Kim Jung-un's reaction to Trump's bombings of the facilities in Syria. When Trump announced he had no patience for "killing babies" and then unleashed nearly 60 Tomahawk missiles at Syria's airfield, places like North Korea took notice. In response, Kim Jung-un has been recalcitrant and even threatened to accelerate his nuclear tests. Of course, Trump has said that he is willing to place nuclear weapons in South Korea to deter the North (Arkin, McFadden, Monahan, & Windrem, 2017). Moreover, President Trump ordered an "armada" of naval ships, led by the USS *Carl Vinson*, to position themselves off the coast of North Korea (Osborne, 2017); we later learned that Trump was being dishonest, as the carrier battle group actually never left the sea between Australia and Indonesia (Landler & Schmitt, 2017). By most accounts, China is the linchpin for any resolution with North Korea, in part because they are a neighbor to North Korea, and "China is the North's only major ally. It also gives a lot of aid to the country" ("China Warns North Korea," 2017, n.p.). Fortunately for the United States, and perhaps as a result of the summit between President Trump and President Xi Jinping of China just a week prior, China has consulted with North Korea to stand down. As of this writing, we can only hope

North Korea backs down, because Trump has signaled he is ready to launch a full-scale military attack on North Korea if they appear to go nuclear (Arkin, McFadden, & Abou-Sabe, 2017).

China

President Donald Trump said he would "get tough" on China on day one—that did not happen, fortunately (Long, 2017). Trump said many things during the presidential campaign and in his first weeks in office that could have ruptured relations with China. For instance, Trump said China was committing "rape" against America, and they were "killing" our economy with their trade practices (Collinson, 2017). President Trump and Chinese President Xi Jingpin were scheduled to meet, but Trump forecasted a "difficult meeting" with Xi before it even happened—not exactly a wise diplomatic move. As Trump tweeted, "The meeting next week with China will be a very difficult one in that we can no longer have massive trade deficits...and job losses. American companies must be prepared to look at other alternatives" (Collinson, 2017, n.p.). Although we do not know much about the recent meeting between President Trump and President Xi, we do know that it was not as "difficult" as Trump predicted. Nevertheless, whether it was China's incursion into the South China Sea (Hunt, 2017), its alleged currency manipulation, its policy regarding Taiwan, or the overall Sino-U.S. relationship, the Trump administration has lambasted China on many different fronts.

The significance of the South China Sea cannot be understated. This area of water is home to hundreds of islands, many of which are underwater for parts of the year, meaning that most are uninhabitable. But the importance of the South China Sea does not lie so much on the islands that can sustain human populations. Instead, this territory houses enormous deposits of natural gas, nearly 11 billion estimated barrels of oil, and "lucrative fishing grounds" (Economy et al., 2017, n.p.). The South China Sea is also a vital Sea Lines of Communication (SLOCs), like the Strait of Hormuz in the Persian Gulf, such that the South China Sea is responsible for over five trillion dollars in trade every year (Economy et al., 2017). As a result, since the first mineral resources were discovered in the 1970s, the surrounding countries express territorial possession to various parts of the South China Sea, causing conflicts over overlapping claims and providing a real potential for armed conflict (Economy et al., 2017). The disputing nations are China, Malaysia, Vietnam, Brunei, Taiwan, Indonesia, and the Philippines. Plus, tensions that arise in the South China Sea have become even more likely since 2010, when China began building "artificial islands on 3,200 acres of landfill," making the islands that are partially submerged by water viable for strategic purposes (Jennings, 2017, n.p.). And to make matters worse, China has built three airstrips (Economy et al., 2017) and "significant point-defense capabilities, in the form of large anti-aircraft guns and probable close-in weapons systems" on the Spratly Islands ("China's New Spratly Island Defenses," 2016, n.p.).

In terms of U.S. foreign policy, the United States is occasionally pulled into some of these disputes since America has a defense agreement with Taiwan and the Philippines.

Of course, when China flexes its military muscles in the South China Sea, the United States perceives that as a national security concern, especially given the possible damage China could cause in the SLOCs, which are important to the U.S. economy in particular, and the larger global economy in general. As an area with American national security concerns, the new Trump administration has not been silent regarding China's aggressive behavior in the South China Sea. Early in December, for example, President-elect Trump took to Twitter (as he so often does) to accuse China for erecting a "massive military complex" in the South China Sea (Collinson, 2016). And President Trump's Secretary of State, Rex Tillerson, recently warned that "building islands and then putting military assets on those islands is akin to Russia's taking of Crimea. Its taking of territory that others lay claim to. … We're going to have to send China a clear signal that first, the island-building stops, and second, your access to those islands also not going to be allowed" (cited in Hunt, 2017, n.p.).

Tillerson's warnings about China's intentions are not without evidence. As we know, China has constructed military-related facilities in the Spratly Islands, and according to U.S. military intelligence and satellite imagery, China has recently made islands in the South China Sea venues for weapons systems (Hunt, 2016). Of course, China rejects such evidence and denies that they are in any way responsible for violating international law regarding the islands (Brunnstrom & Martina, 2015).

Regarding currency manipulation and trade, Trump was, for a time at least, on a collision course with China. Before he took the oath of office, President-elect Trump—on Twitter, of course—accused China of devaluing its currency (Collinson, 2016). This was consistent with what Trump had been saying for years. For example, in a 2015 *Wall Street Journal* op-ed, Trump wrote that if elected president, he would designate China as a currency manipulator "on day one of office" (Long, 2017). And a couple of weeks into Trump's presidency, he announced China the "grand champions" of currency manipulation (Holland & Lawder, 2017, n.p.). Trump's divisive rhetoric may not seem all that alarming; after all, most countries technically "manipulate" their currencies, especially to maximize trading opportunities. However, the label of "currency manipulator" would be a "verbal slap to hurt China's pride" that would frustrate future trade negotiations and possibly other areas of U.S.-Chinese relations (Long, 2017, n.p.). If the countries cannot reconcile their differences over the currency value, the U.S. may resort to "punitive" actions, such as levying tariffs, scaling back trade, and other forms of economic and diplomatic pressure (Holland & Lawder, 2017, n.p.).

According to Fred Bergsten and Joseph Gagnon of the Peterson Institute for International Economics, currency manipulation occurs when a country maintains a level of undervaluing of its currency, typically by intervening in foreign exchange markets, so that their trade position is improved (Bergsten & Gagnon, 2012). An undervalued currency allows a country to strengthen its international competitiveness and secure positive trade surpluses with those with whom they trade (Bergsten & Gagnon, 2012). Bergsten and Gagnon (2012) estimate the impact of this type of economic subterfuge on the United States to be between $200 and $500 billion a year in trade deficits that translate to the loss of 1 to 5 million jobs. Thus, for the United States, currency manipulation is a serious issue. As of 2017, however, China's economy has slowed slightly, as the Chinese administration is concerned about the amount of money that is fleeing the country (Long, 2017). America must also keep in mind a number of other financial issues regarding China, such as intellectual property protections, the economic implications of climate change, and so on (Long, 2017). While Trump's discourse on this issue has been direct and confrontational, his Treasury Secretary, Stephen Mnuchin, has fortunately dialed back the polarizing verbiage, saying that there is "a process of addressing currency devaluation, and the U.S. is not making any judgments until we go [sic] continue that process" (Holland & Lawder, 2017, n.p.).

Another potential hot-button issue between President Trump and President Xi is the role of Taiwan in American foreign policy. Shortly after taking the oath of office, Trump placed a phone call to the president of the Republic of China (ROC), also known as Taiwan, to reaffirm the U.S.-Taiwanese relationship. During the conversation, Trump reportedly told President Tsai that he was considering establishing formal relations that would recognize Taiwan as its own sovereign country. In a radio interview shortly after the two presidents' phone discussion, Trump declared, "Taiwan is our ally. ... That is a country that we have backed because they believe in freedom. We ought to back our ally, and if China doesn't like it, screw 'em" (cited in Collinson, 2016, n.p.). This type of language is potentially very toxic, as CNN commentator Stephen Collinson (2016) notes: "But the diplomatic balance over Taiwan is so delicate that some analysts fear Trump could be starting a confrontation that could easily spin out of control, endanger other crucial areas of the US-China relationship and even so hike tensions that a military clash is possible in the Pacific" (n.p.).

If Trump were to formally recognize Taiwan as a sovereign nation-state, he would be unraveling what is known as the "One-China Policy." The U.S.-China-Taiwan relationship is complex, but a brief history is crucial to understand the contemporary fragility of that relationship. In the early twentieth century, China was a divided land mass that was governed by various warlords. A revolution in 1911 allowed one group in particular, known as the Kuomintang (KMT), to emerge with significant strength. The KMT was able to muster substantial governing power over much of China until 1949, when the Communist Party of China took over and united the entire country. The KMT, led by Chiang Kai-shek, fled to the large island, known as Formosa, off the coast of China. For several decades, the KMT ruled Taiwan in an authoritarian fashion, until becoming democratic in the 1990s. With Formosa having once been a part of the fractured "China," before Chinese unification, and since the KMT came from mainland China, the PRC has always considered Taiwan a part of the PRC. Additionally, the constitution of the PRC has an anti-secession clause which makes the actions of the KMT illegal, and the PRC has always maintained its sovereignty over the island since it views the formation of the ROC as an illegal act. The United States, however, viewed Taiwan as its own country, as did the Taiwanese, of course, until 1978, when, as a consequence of President Richard Nixon's recognition of the PRC as a sovereign country in 1972, the U.S. altered its view on the status of Taiwan to maintain its newly established diplomatic relationship with the PRC. As a result, in 1978, the

U.S. abandoned all official diplomatic relations with Taiwan, declaring that there is only "One China," and, as such, Taiwan is a part of the PRC. This "One-China Policy" has determined U.S. foreign policy toward both the PRC and the ROC ever since. The One-China Policy, however, did not mean that the U.S. completely abandoned Taiwan. In 1979, America established a "non-diplomatic relationship" with the ROC by, in addition to other things, formalizing the Taiwan Relations Act (TRA), which established low-level diplomatic ties, economic trade protocols, and a security arrangement that falls just short of an actual military alliance (Kan & Morrison, 2014). Therefore, if President Trump decides to establish formal diplomatic relations with Taiwan, it would almost guarantee the disruption of all diplomatic and trade relations with the PRC.

Fortunately, President Trump softened his earlier polarizing rhetoric on the Taiwan issue. President Xi of the PRC agreed to a phone conversation with President Trump in early February, but only if Trump would confirm the long-standing One-China Policy. That President Xi would demand Trump's acknowledgment of the One-China Policy before even speaking on the phone demonstrates the severity of this issue with the PRC. After the two presidents spoke, Trump reiterated his commitment to the One-China Policy (Landler & Forsythe, 2017). Changing Trump's toxic tone was fortunate and effective, since Trump noted that the talk was "extremely cordial," and the two presidents agreed to meet in person (Landler & Forsythe, 2017, n.p.). The state news agency in the PRC agreed, reporting that Trump "stressed that he fully understood the great importance for the U.S. government to respect the One China policy," and the "U.S. government adheres to the One China policy" (Landler & Forsythe, 2017, n.p.). Given that both presidents agreed to a face-to-face meeting (which they have done) provided an enormous sigh of relief for those worried about the destruction of U.S.-China relations. Evan S. Medeiros, who was the senior director for Asian issues on Obama's National Security Council, optimistically points out that the "The U.S.-China relationship only works if the two leaders have a serious relationship and use their contact to do real business. … Given the rigidity of the Chinese system, leader-level contact provides essential stability, direction and momentum to U.S.-China ties" (cited in Landler & Forsythe, 2017, n.p.).

While not much of a risk to U.S.-Sino relations, North Korea does point to one of the reasons why strong U.S.-Beijing relations are important. Recently, as I have detailed earlier in this chapter, North Korea has become a serious threat to the United States and to the East Asian region. President Trump continued his typical knee-jerk comments early in April 2017 when he said, "If China is not going to solve North Korea, we will" (cited in Collinson, 2017, n.p.). Since China is North Korea's main trading partner and shares a border with the rogue regime, it is intuitive to expect or hope China to pressure North Korea to scale back its pugnacious rhetoric. However, President Trump, as he often does, took such a position too far by shaming the Chinese and causing them to lose face. Fortunately, China appears to have thick skin. China has reportedly amassed 150,000 troops, artillery, and lines of tanks on their border with North Korea (McDonald, 2017). At the same time, China is also stressing the importance of a diplomatic resolution. China's Foreign Minister, Wang Yi, reminded all involved parties, "Once a war really happens, the result will be nothing but multiple loss," emphasizing that dialogue, whether "official or unofficial, through one channel or dual channels, bilateral or multilateral" should be prioritized and that "China is willing to give support to all of them" (cited in Meyers, 2017, n.p.).

As should be clear, given China's status as a world power, our overlapping mutual interests, and our various policies with each other, relations between the U.S. and China are of the utmost importance. CNN reporter Stephen Collinson (2017) notes, "No global relationship is more important than the one between China and the United States. Beijing has never been more powerful in the modern era" (n.p.). American policy with China runs the gambit—economic, military, and diplomatic issues. And, of course, I have just scratched the surface of the wide range of issues that influence the U.S.-China relationship. Other key areas include human rights, Tibet, climate change, and sphere of influence issues in Africa and Latin America.

Relations with Allies

In addition to President Trump's potentially risky rhetoric toward countries like North Korea and China, he has also made several discursive gaffes toward important American allies, all in the first weeks of office. As Collinson (2017) notes, "Trump has taken some shaky first steps on the global stage. His most important visitor so far, German Chancellor Angela Merkel, appeared baffled by the President's decision to make a joke about the former US practice of tapping her phone—as he stuck by his baseless allegations that he was wiretapped by former President Barack Obama" (n.p.). Merkel's entire visit can be summarized by a single word—"awkward" (Estepa, 2017a, n.p.). Both leaders seemed tense, especially since they differ on many issues, like how to deal with Russia, the Syrian refugee crisis, etc. Despite those differences, however, Germany is an important U.S. ally, especially as it has the strongest European economy. Their face-to-face meeting, while necessary and important, risked undermining our entire relationship. According to Mason and Rinke (2017), "Merkel appeared relaxed, the body language between them was not especially warm," and although Trump and Merkel shook hands when she arrived at the White House, they "did not do so in the Oval Office where she frequently leaned towards him while he stared straight ahead, sitting with his legs apart and hands together" (n.p.). Politely, at the end of the meeting, both leaders said their discussion was "very good" (Mason & Rinke, 2017, n.p.). One of Germany's priorities is to preserve a strong NATO alliance, in large part to counter-balance the rising power of Putin's Russia. During the campaign, Trump consistently slammed NATO, claiming that the U.S. pays for Europe's security without receiving anything in return, and even suggesting that the U.S. might withdraw from the alliance. When Trump and Merkel met, he reassured her that he will remain committed to NATO. However, the day after her visit, Trump wrote two tweets, the first saying, "Despite what you have heard from the FAKE NEWS, I had a GREAT meeting with German Chancellor Angela Merkel. Nevertheless, Germany owes …" and the second finishing the thought: " … vast sums of money to NATO & the United States must be paid more for the powerful, and very expensive, defense it provides to Germany!" (cited in Raymond, 2017, n.p.). Thus far, despite Trump's tweets and although their meeting seemed rocky, nothing negative has emerged as a consequence.

And then there is Britain, America's oldest ally. President Trump's first visitor to the White House was British Prime Minister Theresa May. At the same time, Trump signed his first executive order banning refugees, which put Theresa May "in an awkward political position back home after announcing the first iteration of his travel ban hours after she left the White House" (Collinson, 2017, n.p.). In response to Trump's executive order, the Speaker of the House of Commons of the British Parliament, John Bercow, announced that Trump "will not be welcome to address Parliament on his state visit to the UK because of its opposition to racism," indicating that the migrant ban was racist in its targeting of Muslims (Stone, 2017, n.p.). Minister Bercow noted that an invitation to address Parliament is "not an automatic right," but is instead "an earned honour" (cited in Stone, 2017, n.p.). Reportedly, members of Parliament erupted with applause when they heard of Bercow's statement (Stone, 2017). Additionally, "Labour leader Jeremy Corbyn" and other members are urging that Trump's visit should be canceled altogether until he withdraws his "Muslim ban" (Stone, 2017, n.p.).

Trump's lack of foreign policy experience and diplomacy jeopardized relations with another long-standing ally—Australia. In a phone call scheduled to last 45 minutes between Trump and Australia's Prime Minister Malcolm Turnbull, Trump abruptly terminated the conversation after about 25 minutes (Miller & Rucker, 2017; Thrush & Innis, 2017). According to Miller and Rucker (2017), Trump "blasted" Turnbull "over a refugee agreement," and then told the prime minister that of the four phone conversations Trump had with foreign leaders that day, including one with Putin, "this was the worst call by far" (n.p.). The so-called "refugee agreement" was a deal struck between Australia and President Obama in which the United States would accept 1,250 refugees from an Australian detention center, mainly from Iran, Sudan, Somalia, Syria, and Iraq, so long as the refugees passed rigorous security screenings (Tapper et al., 2017). Reluctantly, Trump has said he would honor the agreement, although he yelped, "This is the worst deal ever" (Miller & Rucker, 2017, n.p.). Trump also told Turnbull that the prime minister would "get killed" politically, and then claimed Australia was going to export to the U.S. the "next Boston bombers" (Miller & Rucker, 2017, n.p.). Of course, not only does Trump dislike the agreement that was leftover by the Obama administration; he also knows that this refugee agreement is contrary to his executive orders banning refugees directly from entering the United States. Trump's tirade over this agreement seemed to never stop, as he professed, "I don't want these people" (cited in Miller & Rucker, 2017, n.p.). According to Thrush and Innis (2017), "The flare-up—and conflicting characterizations of the call from Mr. Trump and Mr. Turnbull—threatened to do lasting damage to relations between the two countries and could drive Canberra closer to China, which has a robust trading relationship with Australia and is competing with Washington to become the dominant force in the Asia-Pacific region" (n.p.).

Of course, President Trump has notoriously frustrated U.S. relations with Mexico. One of Trump's rallying cries during the presidential campaign was that America will build a wall along our southern border and that, somehow, Mexico will pay for it. Mexico's President, Peña Nieto, refused a face-to-face visit with Trump as a result of this divisive language, and, of course, has refused to pay for a wall (Salama, 2017; Tapper et al., 2017). Instead, Nieto agreed to have a phone conversation with Trump. Reportedly, based on a transcript obtained by CNN, Trump told Nieto, "You have some pretty tough *hombres* in Mexico that you may need help with. We are willing to help with that big-league, but they have [to] be knocked out and you have not done a good job knocking them out" (cited in Tapper et al., 2017, n.p.). Evidently, Trump offered to help Nieto with Mexico's drug cartel problem, which has been interpreted by some as suggesting, or threatening, to send American troops into Mexico unless Nieto enhances efforts at tackling the problem (Salama, 2017). In fact, according to the Associated Press, Trump said, "You have a bunch of bad *hombres* down there. ... You aren't doing enough to stop them. I think your military is scared. Our military isn't, so I just might send them down to take care of it" (cited in Salama, 2017, n.p.). Although Trump's language was insulting, if not racist, a Mexican spokesman for Nieto "denied the tone of the conversation was hostile or humiliating, saying it was respectful" (Salama, 2017, n.p.). And, in his typical rhetorical spin, White House Press Secretary Sean Spicer called the phone conversation "productive," and said Trump's comments were "made in jest" and "reflected Mr. Trump's standing offer to help Mexico battle drug gangs and control border crossings" (Thrush & Innis, 2017, n.p.). The two leaders also bickered over trade because Trump announced he was considering imposing a 20 percent tax on all Mexican imports, which obviously would impact the nearly $1.6 billion daily cross-border trade (Salama, 2017).

While Trump's rhetoric with some U.S. allies has been prickly thus far, not all communication with friendly leaders has been problematic. When Japan's prime minister, Shinzō Abe, visited the White House in February 2016, he and President Trump had a positive, productive meeting (Collinson, 2017). Additionally, in early April, Trump met with King Abdullah II of Jordan to discuss ways of improving relations, along with possible measures to fight ISIS (Collinson, 2017). In that same week, Trump met with the president of Egypt, Abdel Fattah Saeed Hussein Khalil el-Sisi, when the two leaders confirmed their commitment to one another, especially in fighting terrorism (Collinson, 2017).

Other Foreign Policy Issues

A host of other international issues challenge America, and our foreign policy with individual countries try to address them. In Israel, the U.S. continues to support its strong ally (Karni, 2017). President Trump is also pursuing the possibility of a new round of Israeli-Palestinian peace accords, as so many previous presidents have attempted before him (Harel, 2017).

There is also the continuous tension with Russia. While President Obama was in office, Vladimir Putin, the President of Russia, intervened into the Crimea, the easternmost part of the Ukraine, where the majority of inhabitants are Russian (Roberts,

2014). While Obama condemned Russia's invasion, he essentially did nothing to counter Putin's actions, nor did Obama do anything to prevent future Russian incursions (Curl, 2014; Krauthammer, 2014; Miller, 2014; Pollak, 2014). Violating the sovereign territory of the Ukraine, however, signals to other parts of the region, like Belarus and Moldova, that Putin may not stop with just Crimea. Inching ever closer to Europe, America's NATO allies are becoming increasingly worried, suggesting that Russia's behavior in the Ukraine threatens global stability (Charap, 2016). Russia poses challenges in a wide array of other issues as well, including its support for Syria's Assad, nuclear weapons reductions, climate change, trade, sex trafficking, energy production, and so on (Clapper, 2016).

Trump must also eventually deal with Cuba. President Obama put into place several measures to improve relations with Cuba (Gratius, 2015; López-Levy, 2014/2015; Rampersad, 2015). However, friendly relations with the communist regime are still very unpopular among conservatives, which means Trump will most likely be pressured into either eroding Obama's policies or creating new initiatives that frustrate the budding relationship. Cuba will have presidential elections in 2018, so it will be a telling year (Clapper, 2016). Additionally, President Trump will face challenges regarding U.S. foreign policy with Honduras (Frank, 2015), Afghanistan (Cohen et al., 2014; Clapper, 2016), and Yemen (Clapper, 2016; Lackner, 2017; Watkins, 2015), just to name a few.

IMPLICATIONS FOR FOREIGN POLICY RHETORIC

Although not really an issue today, Hillary Clinton's involvement with the Benghazi catastrophe generated considerable polarizing rhetoric during the presidential campaign. In 2012, while Hillary Clinton was Secretary of State, a U.S. compound in Benghazi, Libya, was attacked by terrorists, resulting in the murder of U.S. Ambassador to Libya, Christopher Stevens, and an information management officer, Sean Smith (Feinstein et al., 2014). The initial events, the causes, and the impact of the attacks were hazy in the beginning. The Obama administration was criticized for not calling, at first, the attacks an act of terrorism. There was also a dispute about the cause, whether it was a spontaneous gathering of violent hoodlums or the result of an orchestrated terrorist plot spawned by an anti-American video shown in Egypt (Feinstein et al., 2014). Since it was under Clinton's watch and the ambassador was a State Department employee, many criticized Hillary Clinton's handling of the issue. Specifically, conservatives engaged in a barrage of divisive discourse about Clinton in 2012, when the attacks occurred, in 2014, when the Senate held an investigation into the issue, and during the 2016 presidential campaign. (For more on the Benghazi incident and the subsequent rhetoric, readers should see Adams, 2013; Benen, 2014a; Cohen, 2014; Corn, 2014; Korb, 2013; Kurtz, 2014; McCalmont, 2014; Tesfaye, 2014; Jones, 2015.)

As we have seen, the rhetoric surrounding contemporary foreign policy is ripe with peril and opportunities. International incidents can occur without notice, meaning that viewing how rhetors address them through the framework of *kairos* is important. In each moment discussed in this chapter, we can see how the context helped create a rhetorical situation when a rhetor was challenged to address their audience on the fly. If the rhetor has experience and up-to-date knowledge about the issues and actors involved, the rhetor has a greater chance of success—of seizing that *kairotic* moment for an effective rhetorical message. On the other hand, as we have seen, when a rhetor lacks experience and knowledge, they may be unable to capitalize on the *kairotic* moment. When President Trump had phone conversations with the president of Mexico and the prime minister of Australia, and when he met with German Chancellor Angela Merkel, for example, Trump was unable to convert those *kairotic* moments into positive and effective rhetorical messages. As a result, his rhetoric can be perceived to be divisive, as it complicated our relations with important allies. But for President Trump, there is hope, as he was able to maximize his position as a rhetor during the *kairotic* moments when he met with King Abudullah from Jordan, President Sisi of Egypt, and Prime Minister Abe from Japan.

Since many Americans lack foreign policy knowledge, they do not often engage in polarizing discourse except when they parrot the headlines and talking points they hear and see from the media, pundits, and politicians. But the polarizing discourse we see and hear from those sources can be quite extreme. Whether it is the way Muslims are characterized, the manner in which Mexicans are portrayed, the sentiment expressed about refugees and migrants, or the language used when addressing our allies, divisive rhetoric can have serious consequences. To the point, a single word can be interpreted or perceived to be highly polarizing. We only need to look at the way President Trump and his administration described his executive orders regarding the ban of refugees and migrants. By characterizing it as a "Muslim" ban during his presidential campaign and even after he took the oath of office, Trump needlessly complicated his initiative.

CONCLUSION

Foreign policy discourse, like the rhetoric used in all of the issues we have examined in this book, is a product of timing, the rhetors involved (*ethos*), the type of information being communicated (*logos*), and certain rhetorical appeals that tend to be emotional in nature (*pathos*). Framing perspectives often involves the use of rhetorical spin. Many types of fallacies are also present, such as *ad hominem* attacks, fear appeals, slippery slope arguments, hasty generalizations, and so on. In the end, foreign policy rhetoric can be as polarizing as domestic politics, but often involving much more grave implications.

Although most Americans do not have the ability to directly influence foreign policy, they do have the capability of contacting representatives, senators, lobbying organizations, and even the president. Identifying the tactics and strategies used in foreign policy rhetoric is not only important for understanding the issues and gaining information, but also crucial in our ongoing process of being better critical thinkers and engaged citizens. Indeed, as Robert Kagan (2016) notes,

Today, however, because many Americans no longer recall what the world "as it is" really looks like, they cannot imagine it. They bemoan the burdens and failures inherent in the grand strategy but take for granted all the remarkable benefits. Nor do they realize, perhaps, how quickly it can all unravel. The international system is an elaborate web of power relationships, in which every nation, from the biggest to the smallest, is constantly feeling for shifts or disturbances. (pp. 32–33)

While Kagan is a bit sullen and perhaps even a little condescending, his overall point is worth considering. Global events can occur in the blink of an eye, and a citizenry, uninformed about history and current events, will be forced to play catch-up when addressing emergent issues. And putting our head in the sand is not a reasonable or responsible option, either.

IMAGE CREDIT

- Fig. 8.7: Source: http://www.msnbc.com/msnbc/aylan-kurdi-the-syrian-toddler-drowned-bodrum-beach.

CHAPTER NINE

Concluding Comments on Divisive Discourse

———————————————————————————

This has been a book about important things: language and politics. On some level, one could argue that all language is political and all politics require language. But such a perspective is as unwieldy as it is broad. My purpose in writing this book looks at language and politics in a much more specific context. Some political commentators and public officials use language in very polarizing ways. When these individuals command tremendous media attention and garner groups of followers, their extreme talk contributes to the decay of democracy, and it encourages heated disagreement and division in our communities.

In this final chapter, I want to accomplish a few things. First, I would like to suggest some limitations and areas for potential future research on this subject. Second, I want to connect the dots between the diverse threads that exist in the previous chapters. And finally, I hope to offer some options for improving our current conundrum of polarized political discourse.

CONSTRAINTS AND OPPORTUNITIES

Every book has its limitations. This one is no exception. There are a number of contemporary issues that I have not discussed, but perhaps I will be able to address some of them in future editions. I chose the chapters for this edition mainly for three reasons: (1) they are all contemporary issues, (2) they are all issues in which I am interested, and (3) they all provided examples for some of the larger arguments I wanted to make, which I will discuss in the next section on "connecting the dots."

Although I could not possibly examine every contemporary political issue in this book, I was able to concentrate on a select few. I hope my readers will appreciate the depth and time it took for each chapter. Certainly, more could have been written on each topic, but I tried to balance complexity of coverage with readability, and of course some areas had a degree of overlap, such as discussing Trump's foreign policy with Mexico while also examining Mexican immigrants in Chapter Six. If some of the chapters appear too long, I encourage folks to tackle the chapters by section rather than reading the entire chapter all at once.

Another potential limitation to this book is my own political biases. Some of them may emerge as people read the chapters. I tried to balance my coverage of right-wing and left-wing extremism. Some of the topics are inherently tilted toward one over the other. For example, conservatives tend to levy more arguments about religious freedom than do liberals, so the chapter on religion may have more examples of extremism from the right. My aim is not to bash one side over the other—my aim is to bash all of them. I had students ask me last semester what my political ideology is. I told them that my ideology is to be pro-democracy. I have other biases and inclinations, of course, but I genuinely have hope in democracy. That is the underlying premise of this book.

My other goal is to invite more people to the conversation about American politics. Our polarizing discourse tends to alienate and silence, which I believe is fundamentally at odds with a professed democracy. We need more people expressing their views, opinions, and beliefs, not fewer. And, with that, we need to listen to them. Occasionally, even the extremist has something valuable to say. Too often, our political pundits and politicians have meaningful content, but the manner in which they deliver their points is highly problematic. Hopefully, after people read this book, they will feel more comfortable in discussing their political perspectives. We should not let the media and political professionals bully us into submission.

CONNECTING THE DOTS

As my students will probably tell you, I am fond of saying a few things. When my students travel to their home towns (or other places) on the weekend, I genuinely want them to have fun, but I also worry about them, so I typically say, "Have a good weekend, but be careful … it's a crazy world out there." My cautionary, if not paternalistic, tale is, of course, not without its merits. I attempt to remind my students that the world is not what it appears to be. We must always question the way the world is framed, and if we don't, we may pay the consequences.

When I teach my political communication courses, many of my students initially find the material boring or uninteresting. I try to portray the subject matter as something vital to their well-being—after all, democracy is crucial to our individual liberties and our sense of justice and fairness. However, I find it a hard sell. Most of my students believe my classes are "required" or part of some scheme to hoodwink them into being more engaged politically. Of course, they are not far from the truth when it comes to the latter—I desperately want them to be more engaged. However, I absolutely wish that they do not become active in their version of politics if they have no idea what that means. In other words, ignorance should not be the basis for political action.

I say these things to illustrate one of my primary motivations for writing this book. I am concerned about the state of our democracy, and, as a result, I am concerned for our future. When my students ask me why I am a professor, I jokingly respond that it is because of the salary and vacation days. The reality, however, is that I teach because I cannot think of a better opportunity or occupation to try to invoke change and "give back." I know it is a trite cliché, but the reality is that our students of today are our leaders of tomorrow. And if my students do not understand the problematic nature of our contemporary politics, we are indeed doomed.

So, after writing and reading this book, what have we learned? I believe there are a few things that stand out regarding the intersection of rhetoric and polarizing political perspectives. I believe there are many things to be learned from this book, but I want to highlight some of the most important: the primary rhetorical tactics used by polarizing extremists, the role of digital and social media, the power behind the echo chamber, and the significance of political disinterest and apathy among the populace.

The Primary Rhetorical Tactics

Throughout this book, I have examined the many different types of rhetorical tactics used by extremists in their divisive discourse. Here, I want to highlight some of the most used and most significant. These are in no particular order, but they all demonstrate some of the ways political pundits manipulate language to further their political perspectives. The main rhetorical tactics include deductive reasoning, fear appeals, other *pathos* appeals, us/them dichotomies, the fallacy of composition (part-to-the-whole thinking, aka "stereotypes"), *ad hominem* attacks, labeling, naming, and framing.

- Deductive reasoning—As we saw in several contexts, but most notably the immigration debate, commentators will structure their arguments in a deductive manner. As any basic argumentation or formal logic class will attest, deductive arguments are interesting, very prominent, and extremely sneaky. They consist of at least two premises that build off each other to form a "structurally certain" conclusion. This means that the conclusion follows directly from the premises—it is structurally certain. The conclusion does not need to be "truthful," just certain. A standard example is this:

    Socrates is a man.
    All men are mortal.
    Ergo, Socrates is mortal.

However, we can change this to demonstrate the structural certainty of a conclusion, even though one of the premises might be false:

> Socrates is a man.
> All men are immortal.
> Ergo, Socrates is immortal.

We need to note two things from this example. First, deductive arguments are extremely problematic, since anyone can position what they want their audience to believe by working backward. In other words, if I want you to believe that same-sex marriage is a good thing, I would start with that conclusion, then phrase my premises accordingly to support that conclusion. Second, as consumers of information, deductive arguments highlight the need for us to be very, very vigilant about what we consume as information. If a source is telling us that "x" is true, or that "y" is preferred, or that "z" is key to the preservation of a value we all hold dear, we absolutely should look carefully (and critically) at the rest of the argument to ensure that everything is above board. If not, the rhetor may be using deductive reasoning in a way that is less than ethical.

- Fear appeals—As John Avlon says, "When you pull the curtain back on Wingnut politics, behind the all-or-nothing demands, the apocalyptic warnings, and the addiction to self-righteous anger, you'll see that fear is the motivating factor: fear of the other, fear wrapped up in the American flag, fear calling itself freedom" (Avlon, 2014, p. 261). As one of my students so succinctly put it, "fear sells." Virtually every polarizing issue by any extremist pundit involves fear. Fear is the currency that pays dividends on any issue and for any opinion. For guns, fear mobilizes a need for protection. For religion, fear frames threats to what we believe. For healthcare, fear embodies our most banal instincts for our own survival. For LGBTQ+ issues, fear lodges a wedge into what we think should be versus what is. And for immigration, fear manifests itself into xenophobia— "fear," literally, of the other. Fear is an extremely motivating emotion. Ask just about anyone—if they are in fear, they will believe or do just about anything. When fear seems real, we react accordingly. This is why—out of all of the emotions—Aristotle says fear (along with love) is the most universal (Aristotle, 350 BCE/1997). Additionally, to take a pop culture reference, "fear is the mind killer" (Herbert, 1965). This means, of course, that fear numbs our senses. We do not think rationally in the face of fear. And, as a result, fear is a very valuable tool for the political manipulator.
- *Pathos* appeals—In addition to fear appeals, many political extremists will use other emotional appeals. Appeals to pity, love, patriotism, anger, hatred, etc. all fit within this category. I will not examine here what I have already analyzed elsewhere in the book, but we should note that appeals to emotion are very powerful, and they are frequently used by manipulators of language to sway us in a particular direction.

- Us/them dichotomy—If our intent is to characterize our position *vis-à-vis* an opponent, thereby clearly differentiating our perspective from his or her perspective, we may want to portray the situation as an us-versus-them relationship. To be sure, if we need an indicator to reveal whether individuals are engaging in polarizing political discourse, we could use this simple test: Do they portray their viewpoint as correct and all others—who, by chance, oppose theirs—as incorrect? Does the rhetor position the debate in a "we *versus* them" manner? A very famous example of this occurred when former president George W. Bush, after 9/11, said, "Either you are with us, or you are with the terrorists" (Voice of America, 2009). In this way, President Bush drew a bright line between his version of truth, reality, and principle against other versions. Anyone attempting to characterize his or her political position as "truthful" may resort to a similar tactic.
- Part-to-the-whole—When people use arguments that utilize a "part-to-the-whole" technique, what they are essentially doing is using a particular example and representing it as a key reference to the whole. We often paint a broad stroke to larger elements based upon singular instances. When we travel to Europe, we might characterize all of Europe based upon our single visit to France. A member of an organization is sometimes considered a "representative" of his or her organization along similar lines of thought. While this type of thinking may be helpful because it provides a shortcut (i.e., we do not need to know every member of an organization if we can look to its figureheads), it can also be quite problematic. We use stereotypes in a similar vein. If we target or isolate a single instance to represent a larger whole, we are clearly overlooking the intricacies of other people or isolated factors. The part-to-the-whole technique can be manipulated to pronounce a certain perspective. If we can identify it, though, we should be careful to make such generalizing claims or conclusions.
- *Ad hominem* attacks—Attacking a person instead of addressing the substance of an issue, and calling people names can be very powerful tactics. While labeling an individual or group something outrageous might seem obvious, we nevertheless can notice how *ad hominem* attacks happen without a moment's notice. For instance, when some folks characterize others as "free riders" or "moochers" or "leeches" (as in the case of the healthcare or immigration debate), some might not think twice about these names. However, what we can witness from afar is the power of name-calling—labeling or characterizing individuals or entire groups of people as a particular entity, which reduces their entire identity into a particular frame. We often do not realize it, but "language constitutes consciousness. Use different language and you deploy a different perception or conception of the world" (Del Gandio, 2008, pp. 102–103).
- Labeling and naming—In a related way, not only do some political pundits call their opposition "names"; they also label and create names in such a way as to manipulate the discursive terrain in their favor. This also happens when a group labels or names themselves in a particular light. Pro-choice and pro-life folks, for instance, use the rhetorical tactic of labeling and naming very purposefully. After

all, such advocacy groups probably do not want to be known as pro-abortion (or "pro-death") or pro-religion, respectively. The power of naming/labeling is an extremely important power, indeed. If we can portray ourselves—and others—in a certain light, we can in many ways control the debate.

- Framing—As we learned in the immigration chapter, framing is the process of literally placing a frame around a concept to target our audience's attention to a certain idea. In other words, "Framing is another way to understand the relationship between language and consciousness … [the] frame creates a particular window of understanding; it creates a lens by which we see and understand the issue" (Del Gandio, 2008, pp. 103–104). Many people underestimate the power of framing, but I hope we can see its significance in the examples illustrated in this book. If we can focus our audience's attention on a particular problem, group, or issue, we can—quite literally—misdirect its attention. Much like how a magician misdirects our attention when he or she is palming a card by focusing our attention elsewhere, a polarizing political pundit directs our focus in very particular ways in a manner he or she desires. Framing is, I submit, perhaps the most powerful and probably the least studied way of tactically shifting people's attention and, by extension, their knowledge and beliefs.

Again, these are some of the most important and most frequently employed rhetorical tactics used by extremist politicians and political pundits. Of course, other tactics exist, as I have intimated in this book. But if we can at least identify some of the more common tactics, we are well on our way to improving our political conversations and our democracy.

Digital and Social Media

Many of my students rave about social media. They are Facebook and Twitter experts. I, however, am not. I gleefully acknowledge my inability to articulate the benefits of social media, but I will try. Digital and social media undoubtedly allow us to communicate with people over long distances with speed. The ability to transfer files, articles, and video with the push of a button is tantalizing as well as extremely helpful. Additionally, the wealth of information that is accessible because of digital and social media should make our conversations about American democracy more meaningful. But just because the information is available does not mean that people will take advantage of the opportunity. Since digital and social media also serve entertainment purposes (Carr, 2011), most of us, when given the choice, use the media for entertainment rather than for news or valuable information (Lovink, 2011), which is why researchers use the name "shallowing hypothesis" to describe the phenomenon where we primarily receive our news from social media (Logan & Lafreniere, 2016; Shah et al., 2001).

I understand the political potential of digital and social media, but I also have my reservations. Many, of course, point to the Arab Spring events in Tunisia, Libya, and Egypt as proof of the power of social media to enact social change, even calling the movement a "Twitter Revolution" (Howard and Hussain, 2011; Lotan et al., 2011). I was in Tunisia two months after the vendor immolated himself, and I can certify that social media was not the "cause" or the "reason" for an uprising—those sentiments had already been brewing, and face-to-face interaction was the principal means of communicating unrest. I can also attest, having visited Myanmar before some of their political liberalization efforts in 2010, that the Burmese government used digital media to frustrate activists, mainly by submitting misinformation. And, of course, when a country, such as Egypt, can turn off the Internet and place blocks on cell phone towers, activists are forced to resort to face-to-face and old-school communication techniques. In fact, much of the Arab revolutionary activities in 2011 were not new and did not utilize digital or social media. Many of the activists utilized cultural traditions, public gatherings in town squares, and planning in people's homes as a way of communicating and spreading their revolutionary impulse (Khatib & Lust, 2014, pp. 9–10). I do not mean to suggest that social media played no role in the Arab Spring, but I also do not want us to think that the actions of protestors was conducted solely via social media.

Moreover, I find it difficult to believe that when we need richer and more sophisticated conversations about politics and American democracy, somehow such discussions can occur in the 140-character-or-less Twitter generation. Our current president, Donald Trump, enjoys circumventing the mainstream media by tweeting his thoughts and comments about current issues (Ott, 2016). His "role modeling," or "nocturnal submissions" of tweeting, may or may not be detrimental to our overall democratic discourse (McGill, 2017, n.p.). Donald Trump's "impetuous and aggressive tweeting has been a habit of Mr. Trump's for years," and now that he is president, he has nearly 20 million followers (Hess, 2017, n.p.). Trump's tweeting is extremely problematic because "Twitter promotes public discourse that is simple, impetuous, and frequently denigrating and dehumanizing" (Ott, 2016, p. 60), which means that "by demanding simplicity, Twitter undermines our capacity to discuss and, subsequently, to think about issues and events in more complex ways" (Ott, 2016, p. 61). Scientists argue that Twitter reduces our attention spans, causes us to think more superficially, and can even "harm young people's emotional development" ("Scientists Warn," 2009, n.p.). In terms of our political discourse, relying too heavily on social media, especially Twitter, can exacerbate the vitriol since its truncated messages almost guarantee invective. As Brian Ott argues, "Twitter ultimately trains us to devalue others, thereby, cultivating mean and malicious discourse" (2016, p. 60). With over 500 million subscribers who generate over 400 million tweets per day, we must be conscientious about how Twitter impacts our political discussions (Zubiaga, 2015). Moreover, we should be extra vigilant when we use social media to be careful in our own messaging and to guard against being sucked into the widespread vituperation.

There are also some very serious negative implications to our reliance on digital and social media, such as a reduced capacity for compassion, lessened ability to make emotional connections, hampered reflective thinking, attention deficit syndromes, and so on (Carr, 2011; Turkle, 2011). Despite the problematic nature of digital and social media, such media still hold some sort of romantic and novel appeal to scholars and political consumers alike. Howard Rheingold (2002), for instance, points to the "Battle for Seattle" as a testament to how activists used social media to organize effective "smart mobs" that protested global capitalism.

Echo Chambers

Relating to some of the troubles associated with media, we can identify one problem in particular—the echo chamber. An echo chamber is, essentially, occurs when we see "angry people from the same party inciting each other to extremes on television or online, demonizing a phantom opposition, and engaging in a partisan pile-on" (Avlon, 2014, p. 110). An echo chamber also occurs when "several people" repeat and reproduce "the opinions of a few," of course, in a politically polarized way (Papacharissi, 2010, p. 154). Another name for an echo chamber is a "silo." Like a missile or grain silo, our exposure to media can be limited and contained. In either case, the idea is that people surround themselves with like-minded believers. This creates what is known as "homophily," which means knowledge emanating from a single source or similar venues (McPherson et al., 2001). This notion is also very similar to the concept of "confirmation bias," which is our proclivity to be attracted to, and to actively seek out, people who will confirm and legitimize our belief systems (Nickerson, 1998). When this occurs, we encounter a reverb effect. This by itself is not a problem, but when it becomes all we experience—the same sort of news over and over again—then our ideological beliefs become hardened and reinforced. As Sanger suggests, the silo effect can be "fun and compelling for a lot of us. They make us feel like we belong. They reinforce our core assumptions, and give us easily digestible talking points, obviating the necessity of difficult individual thought. They appeal to our epistemic vanity and laziness" (Sanger, 2013, n.p.).

Part of the problem with our fascination with digital and social media is that we become reliant on them for our information. This is becoming more and more pertinent with each subsequent generation (Shah et al., 2001). My theory is that technology is becoming sort of like candy—the more it is unique and available, the more people will gravitate toward it. Of course, the technology itself is not a problem, but using the medium for nefarious reasons can be. Thus, when an unsubstantiated story is placed on a blog, then is repeated on another website, then is tweeted and hyperlinked, etc., the initial half-truth becomes truth (DiFonzo, 2011). And unfortunately, whatever appears online now is considered, at least in some form, to be truth. How do we know what is true from not true? Obviously, we cannot know with any certainty unless we absolutely trust the source (*ethos*), but we can ascertain "truth" if we acknowledge multiple sources. Particularly with the amount of inaccurate, misleading, and distorted information disseminated during the course of the 2016 presidential campaign, we now have, unfortunately, an entire genre of media known as "fake news," which ranges from fabricated websites that appear like legitimate news sources, to information gleaned from blogs and social media, to statements from public officials and their surrogates that attempt to camouflage, dodge, or otherwise manipulate "real" facts (Sharockman, 2016). Thus, exposing ourselves to multiple sources of information, not being satisfied with just noticing a single headline, consulting fact-checking sites like Snopes and PolitiFact, diversifying the types of media we digest, and challenging our own inclination to reside in an echo chamber can help minimize the influence of fake news on us. We obviously cannot do much for our friends and family, except to be good role models and encourage them to practice similar behaviors.

More to the point, echo chambers reinforce partisan politics (see Figure 9.1). They limit our exposure to other ways of thinking by entrenching political perspectives (Thomas, 2014). On one hand, we enjoy choices, and the ability to select our news sources is part of having choices. On the other hand, we tend to self-select our information sources based on our political predispositions. When this happens, people "primarily hear an echo of their own beliefs and consequently also avoid dissonant information that cuts against their political opinions" (Levendusky, 2013, p. 4). This is how echo chambers function (Yusuf et al., 2014). Another way of stating this is that the "echo chamber isolates and intensifies grassroots politics, breeding groupthink in tiny platoons that can have disproportionate influence on political debates … it can create a Tower of Babel, condemning us to mutual incomprehensibility. It's easier to demonize people who disagree with you if you don't know them" (Avlon, 2014, p. 140). In this way, polarizing politics is perpetuated. When we do pay attention to political news, we typically are exposed to certain beliefs that fail to acknowledge other points

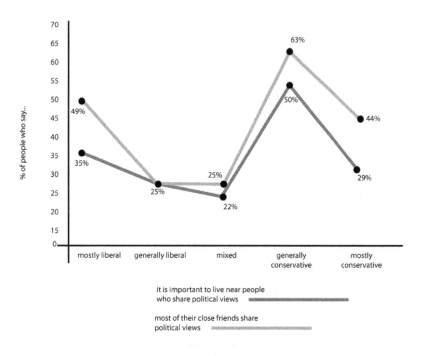

Figure 9.1: Ideological Echo Chambers.

of view. When political debates are lopsided, they cease to be debates at all, and we silo ourselves into one-way types of thinking.

Political Disinterest and Apathy

As I discussed in the Introduction and in Chapter One, most Americans appear to be dissatisfied, even angry, toward politics. Shockingly, according to Gallup (2016), only 39 percent of Americans follow politics closely. It is difficult to put into a single word the current state of political malaise—many individuals are disinterested, apathetic, frustrated, dissatisfied, angry, bored, and troubled with politics. There are a number of causes for this range of feelings. Politics can seem complicated and overwhelming. Politicians can appear distant and untrustworthy. Many Americans do not believe they will be taken seriously or that their actions will have any impact on politics as a whole (a sense that they lack political efficacy). Entire books have been written on this subject, so I am only scratching the surface (see Bauerlein, 2009; Lawless & Fox, 2015; Lupia, 2015).

However, one thing that is directly pertinent for our discussion is how many Americans are disinterested or apathetic to politics. On one hand, I just described how people who pay attention to political news are often trapped in echo chambers. On the other, however, the majority of Americans simply do not pay notice to the news at all. Politics just does not seem sexy or entertaining. I honestly do not know why. As I tell my students, who almost unanimously enjoy watching sports, American politics has all of the features as sporting events—there are our favorite teams, there are statistical data on certain types of "plays," there are winners and losers, there is strategy, and it is a spectator event. Most of my students roll their eyes at my analogy! However, during the 2016 presidential campaign, Chuck Todd of MSNBC, who calls himself the "referee of political rules" (Fondacaro, 2017, n.p.), narrated an advertisement for the network in which he said:

> Politics is a sport. Except it happens to be a sport that affects your life. It happens to be a sport that really matters. It happens to be a sport that the outcome will decide whether you feel as if your life's gonna get better or your life's gonna get worse. While the game is a lot of fun to follow sometimes, the outcome really matters.

So, there it is—even Chuck Todd agrees with me!

I am deeply troubled by the ambivalent and dismissive reaction to American politics, which is, in part, why I wrote this book. I also feel strongly that it is not the fault of most Americans that they feel this way. We do not explain the importance of politics in our K–12 education. Most of our university politics and history classes are as boring as the evening news. We are told to not discuss politics at the dinner table—or, for some, their families avoid talking about it altogether. And other issues in our society—such as reality television, sporting events, and leisure activities—take precedence. I am not much of a conspiracy theorist, but the Senate in ancient Rome employed a strategy known as *panem et circenses*, which means "bread and circuses." The idea was that if the masses were concerned about putting food on the table, or if they were distracted by large spectacles, like a circus or gladiators in the arena, they would not pay attention to political issues. We suffer from our own *panem et circenses*—tabloids line the check-out line (not political treatises), reality TV shows and last night's football game are the topics of water cooler conversations (not the president's latest speech), and we are constantly concerned about how to pay our bills rather than discuss how we can vote for politicians who could improve our economy or raise our wages.

Final Thoughts in Our Contemporary Climate

I want to make a final comment about divisive discourse in the era of a Trump presidency. While I have not identified hypocrisy or double standards as a specific rhetorical tactic, largely because a rhetor usually does not purposefully intend on being hypocritical, there is, nevertheless, a rhetoric of hypocrisy that has emanated from Trump, as both a candidate and as president. This is important to note because, as I mentioned earlier in the book, Americans generally do not appreciate hypocrisy. Therefore, when a politician's discourse reveals a double standard, it impacts the overall nature of polarization.

One area of hypocrisy in the rhetoric of Donald Trump is his criticism of Obama's use of executive orders (CNN Wire, 2017; "Hypocrisy on Executive Orders," 2017). Although Trump "lambasted" President Obama's use of executive orders during the last months of his presidency, Trump has signed more executive orders than "any president in their first 100 days since World War II" (*Associated Press*, 2017b). Another area of hypocrisy concerns, in my opinion, the most boring sport in the world—golf. For years, Donald Trump ridiculed and criticized President Obama for golfing while he was in office. For example, Trump tweeted in 2014: "Can you believe that, with all of the problems and difficulties facing the U.S., President Obama spent the day playing golf. Worse than Carter" (cited in Carroll, 2017). Despite saying on the campaign trail, "I'm going to be working for you, I'm not going to have time to go play golf" (cited in Dawsey, 2017, n.p.), Trump has frequented his residence in Palm Beach, Florida, to play golf, including with President Xi of China, for whom it is considered an insult as golf is often perceived in China as a classist sport (Jiang, 2017). In a related matter, Trump obviously uses Air Force One every time he flies to Florida or New York. Yet he was highly critical of Obama: "Taxpayers are paying a fortune for the use of Air Force One on the campaign trail by President Obama and Crooked Hillary. A total disgrace!" and "Looking at Air Force One @ MIA. Why is he campaigning instead of creating jobs & fixing Obamacare?" (cited in Dawsey, 2017, n.p.).

Additionally, on yet another related matter, Trump spent nearly $20 million in travel costs back and forth to Florida in just 80 days, which already approaches Obama's personal travel expenditures for his entire eight years (Merica, 2017). This, of course, is contrary to "Trump's calls for belt tightening across the federal government and the fact that he regularly criticized Obama for costing the American taxpayer money every time he took a trip" (Merica, 2017). Plus, it is hypocritical when we consider that Trump was highly accusatory of Obama—"The habitual vacationer, @BarackObama, is now in Hawaii. This vacation is costing taxpayers $4 million +++ while there is 20% unemployment," which Trump tweeted in 2011. And then there is Trump's tweet: "President @BarackObama's vacation is costing taxpayers millions of dollars——Unbelievable!" (cited in Merica, 2017, n.p.). Additionally, there is the added cost of Secret Service protection. While Melania Trump continued to live in Trump Tower in New York City, it cost taxpayers between $127,000 to $146,000 per day for protection (Merica, 2017). And, each time Trump goes to Mar-a-lago in Florida it costs additional money. Plus, for each officer or agent that is used for protection, it means one less officer or agent securing us from criminal and terrorist threats (Merica, 2017).

In summary, when we discuss divisive discourse in contemporary America, we cannot help but include the current president, Donald Trump. He may be oblivious to how his actions have fermented feelings of polarization. As Douglas Brinkley, a presidential historian, explains, "Donald Trump has zero worry about contradicting himself, because he does it all day long. … He figures he can get away with it because he does it all the time. There is no worry about it. He says one thing and then does another, and his supporters don't hold it against him" (cited in Dawsey, 2017, n.p.). Of course, it is well known that Trump engages in impulsive behavior. And I am not suggesting that Obama was guilt-free from hypocritical rhetoric. In fact, Obama claimed in 2009, "I did not run for office to be helping out a bunch of fat cat bankers on Wall Street," yet as soon as he left office, he accepted a speaking gig on Wall Street for $400,000 (cited in Tate, 2017, n.p.). But we now live in the age of Trump, and divisive discourse is rampant. As president, Trump and others have a responsibility for how political discussions occur in the United States. And I want to be clear about this: conservatives are not the only ones engaging in this divisive discourse. For instance, Trump barely entered the White House when Congresswoman Maxine Waters, a Democrat from California, yelped, "Donald Trump is someone that found his way to the presidency of the United States of America—I still don't know how. … But he's someone that I'm committed to getting impeached!… He's a liar! He's a cheat! He's a con man! We've got to stop his ass!" (cited in Williams, 2017, n.p.). Clearly, this type of extreme, outrageous rhetoric is highly polarizing and has no place in a democracy.

MOVING FORWARD

We obviously cannot silence every political extremist, nor should we. Not only do we enjoy freedom of speech in this country, we should welcome diverse views, regardless of how toxic some of them may seem. Democracy, after all, requires diversity of perspectives. But the point should be to have a conversation about the many viewpoints, respecting them and attempting to understand them. The goal should not be to silence them. Unfortunately, polarizing political discourse tends to silence others.

Self-righteous pundits tend to believe their opinions are the only ones worth discussing, and if such opinions are the only opinions to which we are exposed, we lose the opportunity to entertain other ideas.

Of course, if extremist, polarizing perspectives are reinforced and perpetuated in mediated echo chambers certain divisive pundits slowly obtain a monopoly on political ideas (Thomas, 2014). Not only do we lose the ability to hear other perspectives; we also find that power becomes more solidified in the hands of the few. Political ideas of extremist elites dictate how we think about politics as a whole and how policies—and which ones—are implemented. In this way, democracy is imperiled. Our government ceases to be by and for the people; instead, it is by and for the select few who hold the megaphone or microphone.

So, as Lenin famously asked, "What is to be done?" I want to offer here a number of concrete, common-sense suggestions for improving the climate and tenor of our political conversations. There is no panacea, and I do not expect that our democracy will change for the better overnight. However, I have hopes that we can all play our own, individual part in making our world a better place. Here are some ideas:

- **Let's join hands in stomping out ignorance.** Too often, no knowledge is as problematic and painful as distorted or partisan knowledge. One scholar notes, "Today's young adults are less politically interested and informed than any cohort of young people on record" (Rimmerman, 2011, p. 50). It is tempting for me to blame my students when they do not know who the Speaker of the House is, or if they cannot name more than five countries in Africa. For example, in a recent survey, "64 percent [of those surveyed] knew the name of the latest 'American Idol,' [but] only 10 percent could identify the speaker of the U.S. House of Representatives" (Bauerlein, 2009, p. 19). Yet the problem is much more complex than this. As I discussed above, as a society, we simply do not consider political knowledge as important. But we can change this. We should abandon the anti-democratic and just plain nonsensical notion that we should not discuss politics (or religion) at family gatherings. We should encourage our families to watch and read the news. We should discuss political issues in the workplace. The problem is not always the content, but rather *how* we discuss these things. In that vein, educators (and families) should stress civility and respect when conversing with others about controversial issues. Therefore, in both substance and form, we can reduce ignorance about contemporary political issues. Simply put, "Democracy is a practice. It is important for colleges and universities to be intentional about identifying the democratic skills they would like students to learn" (Thomas & Hartley, 2010, p. 101).
- **We must diversify our news and information sources.** Once we urge folks to pay attention to the news, we then need to encourage them to seek information from a variety of sources. As I mention above, it is natural for us to seek out others, including news sources, who are aligned with our thinking. However, echo chambers do not produce a healthy democracy. We must expose ourselves to

diverse perspectives. At the end of the day, we may (and probably will) still believe what we believe, but at least we can know about opposing viewpoints, and we can appreciate them.

- **Let's become more involved and engaged.** Receiving news is a necessary first step, but then we must do something with that knowledge. We can be more critical voters. Or, if voting is not to a person's liking, they can join a social movement. Or, better still, they can begin a social movement. We have political liberties that not only allow us to engage in political action; they demand it. It is the only way a democracy can survive. I have had the benefit of traveling to politically repressive regimes (i.e., Myanmar, Sri Lanka, the Dominican Republic, and Honduras). It is a shame that Americans do not take advantage of the political freedoms that others around the world are struggling, even dying, to acquire. Our society truly is a synergy—the sum of all of us is greater than our individual parts. But it only works if we are involved. One simple thing we can do is reflect upon what interests us and matters to us—maybe it is sports, food, music, education, or career planning. All of these are highly political realms. Issues of race and economics, for example, are woven into athletics and music, such as the amount athletes and celebrities earn as compared to everyday working people, or the portrayals of and discrimination against racial minorities. Our food is integrally connected to environmental, and by extension economic, concerns. Education policy is extremely contentious, and it impacts us at the national and local levels. And if we are concerned about our jobs or potential career areas, obviously political and economic decisions made by our elected officials have relevance. By choosing an area that interests us, we are much more likely to pay attention to the news and become involved.
- **As I discussed in the Introduction, we must be mindful of so-called "fake" news.** This, of course, relates to the suggestion that we should diversify our news sources, but it also means we should be vigilant in how we digest such news sources. We must be critical and question the news we digest, and in so doing, we must realize how our own perspectives may differ from the facts offered from reality.
- **We should reward good behavior.** At least where I live, when people vote, they are given a little sticker that says, "I voted!" While I personally think the stickers are a bit obnoxious (and they reinforce the idea that voting is sufficient by itself), their intent is good. Not only do they make the voters feel good about what they are doing; they also signify to others that perhaps they should go vote as well. Similarly, we should support our peers when they become politically engaged in whatever way that suits their fancy. Some will consider running for public office. Others may protest in the streets. Our political freedoms are protected by law—within reason—and should be encouraged and rewarded. After all, if we know people who intend on improving our society, we should support and reward their efforts, particularly if we benefit from their hard work.
- **Let's be mindful of the pros and cons of technology.** Digital and social media can be useful tools for democratic pursuits, but they can also be distracting and

looked upon as panaceas. Utilizing social media to spread the word and to do some of the other things I am suggesting can be vital, but we must be cautious. Clicking "like" on Facebook or adding our name to an online petition may exemplify our good intentions, but they also may be nothing more than what is now considered "slacktivism" (Albers, 2014; Goldsborough, 2011; Savidge, 2008), or "clicktivism" (Schradie, 2014). Slacktivism really "only changes how active people think they are" (Savidge, 2008, n.p.). In other words, slacktivism gives a false sense of engagement. We feel good about what we are doing, but we are doing very little. If, however, online "slacktivism" can yield offline engagement, online activism may have some real, beneficial impacts (Ingram, 2011; Kristofferson et al., 2014; Rotman et al., 2011). Thus, digital and social media are merely tools, but we must be vigilant in our use of such tools, and we should be cautious in how they can be distracting and addicting. We also need to be reminded that social media, in particular, shortens our attention spans, encourages vituperative speech, and "prizes emotionalism over reason," such that we are "only as relevant as" our "last tweet" (Carr, 2015).

- **We should spread the word.** Politics is a game of language, and we should use language to emphasize the political. I once had a student who took my political communication course who was very honest f\rom the first day of class. She said she hated politics and saw no value in it but took my class because it fulfilled a requirement. I said, "Fair enough"; after all, I appreciate honesty from my students. I then asked her what she did value and what she cared about. She said she was a mother of two, and her children meant the world to her. I used that as an opportunity to discuss how politics intersects with education policy, and even how her PTA meetings had political implications. I cannot say that she became an instant convert, but she slowly began to see how politics was relevant to her life. We have the opportunity to capitalize on these sorts of "learning moments" all of the time, but we often do not take advantage of them. Allowing folks to see the forest instead of staring at the tree in front of them is an extremely important component to sustaining democracy. It is, in part, a way of combating the *panem et circenses* that are occurring around us, and all it takes is for us to talk.

- **Finally, we need to play offense** (Avlon, 2010, p. 242). As Avlon reminds us, we must be aware of how elite politicians structure the political game in their favor. One way they do this is by gerrymandering. Gerrymandering is the structural way of ensuring that a person's constituents are supportive of that person. It redistricts House seats so that Republicans or Democrats can rig the game in their favor. What does this mean for us? We should first be knowledgeable of procedural impediments to democracy, such as gerrymandering, the *Citizens United v. Federal Election Commission* Supreme Court decision, and filibusters. Of course, many of the steps I have suggested are cumulative. Most Americans may not know about filibusters or the impact of the *Citizens United* decision. If we educate people and spread the word, just possibly, we can enhance our democracy by playing "offense" in a way that suits *our* interests, not the interests of the elites.

FINALLY

There is no real conclusion to a book like this. The whole point of this project is to point to a particular claim. In a sense, this entire project is a syllogism—here are my many premises (i.e., the chapters), and now you, the reader, should naturally follow to a specific conclusion. The conclusion, of course, is that **democracy matters**. At least, it *should* matter. As I have clearly and not so clearly intimated throughout this book, the way we *talk* about politics is the way we *think* of politics. As such, we really need to talk about politics in a way that is pertinent and enticing to the average citizen. When we disagree, and we will, we should learn how to communicate in a civil manner so that everyone's voice is heard.

Q.E.D.

REFERENCES

Abcarian, Robin (2014, May 5). After Supreme Court Prayer Decision, Satanist Offers His Own Prayer. *Los Angeles Times*. Available, http://www.latimes.com/local/abcarian/la-me-ra-abcarian-scotus-20140505-column.html

Abington School District v. Schempp. 374 U.S. 203 (1963).

Aborn, Richard M. (1995). The Battle over the Brady Bill and the Future of Gun Control Advocacy. *Fordham University Law Journal* 22, 417–439.

Abramowitz, Alan I. (2010). *The Disappearing Center: Engaged Citizens, Polarization, & American Democracy*. New Haven, CT: Yale University Press.

Abramowitz, Alan I. (2014, January 20). How Race and Religion Have Polarized American Voters. *The Washington Post*. Available, http://www.washingtonpost.com/blogs/monkey-cage/wp/2014/01/20/how-race-and-religion-have-polarized-american-voters/

Abramowitz, Alan I. and Morris P. Fiorina (2013, March 11). Polarized or Sorted? Just What's Wrong with Our Politics, Anyway? *The American Interest*. Available, http://www.the-american-interest.com/articles/2013/03/11/polarized-or-sorted-just-whats-wrong-with-our-politics-anyway/

Abramowitz, Alan I. and Kyle L. Saunders (1998). Ideological Realignment in the U.S. Electorate. *The Journal of Politics* 60(3), 634–652.

Abramowitz, Alan I. and Kyle L. Saunders (2005). Why Can't We All Just Get Along? The Reality of a Polarized America. *The Forum* 1076, 1–22.

Ackerman, Spencer, and Sune Engel Rasmussen (2017, April 14). 36 ISIS Militants Killed in US 'Mother of All Bombs' Attack, Afghan Ministry Says. *The Guardian*. Available, https://www.theguardian.com/world/2017/apr/13/us-military-drops-non-nuclear-bomb-afghanistan-islamic-state

Acton, John (2013, October 6). The Problem with Pro-Choice Rhetoric. *Harvard Political Review*. Available, http://harvardpolitics.com/united-states/the-problem-with-pro-choice-rhetoric/

Adams, Becket (2013, December 9). Watch what Happens when a Democrat Rep. Decides She Doesn't want to Answer Questions about Benghazi. *The Blaze*. Available, http://www.theblaze.com/stories/2013/12/09/watch-what-happens-when-a-democratic-rep-decides-she-doesnt-want-to-answer-questions-about-benghazi/

Adams, John (1856/1819, March 31). Letter to J.H. Tiffany. *The Works of John Adams, Second President of the United States* (Vol.10). Boston: Little, Brown & Co.

Adelman, Jonathan (2016, November 15). Israel as an Apartheid, Repressive, Militarist State? Hardly. *The Huffington Post*. Available, http://www.huffingtonpost.com/jonathan-adelman/israel-as-an-apartheid-re_b_12962346.html

Adomanis, Mark (2013, September 25). Think Obamacare Is Socialized Medicine? 5 Things You Should Know about Soviet Healthcare. *Forbes*. Available, http://www.forbes.com/sites/markadomanis/2013/09/25/think-obamacare-is-socialized-medicine-5-things-you-should-know-about-soviet-healthcare/

Agee, B. Christopher (2014, July 8). Eric Holder just Sued another State, and the Reason Why will Blow Your Mind. *Western Journalism*. Available, http://www.westernjournalism.com/eric-holder-just-sued-another-state-reason-will-blow-mind/

Aizenman, Nurith (2016, September 22). There's a "Glaring" Gap in the War against Poverty and Disease. *NPR: All Things Considered*. Available, http://www.npr.org/sections/goatsandsoda/2016/09/22/495051955/theres-a-glaring-gap-in-the-war-against-poverty-and-disease

Aked, Hilary (2017, January 11). Boycott, Divestment, Sanctions: What Is BDS? *Al Jazeera*. Available, http://www.aljazeera.com/indepth/features/2017/01/boycott-divestment-sanctions-bds-170110165203991.html

Alabi, Jaena (2015). "This Actually Happened": An Analysis of Librarians' Responses to a Survey about Racial Microaggressions. *Journal of Library Administration*, 55(3), 179–191.

Albarazi, Hannah (2017, March 31). Trump Administration Position on Syria's Assad Decried by Lawmakers. *CBS San Francisco*. Available, http://sanfrancisco.cbslocal.com/2017/03/31/trump-administration-position-on-syrias-assad-decried-by-lawmakers/

Albers, Sarah (2014, August 12). Place and the Politics of Slacktivism. *The American Conservative*. Available, http://www.theamericanconservative.com/place-and-the-politics-of-slacktivism/

Alexander, Michelle (2011). *The New Jim Crow: Mass Incarceration in the Age of Colorblindness*. New York: The New Press.

Allegheny County v. ACLU. 492 U.S. 573 (1989).

Allegheny College (2016, October 17). *Allegheny Survey: 2016 Presidential Campaign Reveals Chilling Trend Lines for Civility in U.S. Politics*. Available, http://sites.allegheny.edu/news/2016/10/17/allegheny-survey-2016-presidential-campaign-reveals-chilling-trend-lines-for-civility-in-u-s-politics/

Alter, Charlotte (2014, July 17). Todd Akin Still Doesn't Get What's Wrong with Saying 'Legitimate Rape.' *Time*. Available, http://time.com/3001785/todd-akin-legitimate-rape-msnbc-child-of-rape/

Altman, Stuart and David Shactman (2011). *Power, Politics, and Universal Health Care: The Inside Story of a Century-Long Battle*. Amherst, NY: Prometheus Books.

Alvarado, Francisco, Michael E. Miller, and Mark Berman (2016, July 21). Florida Cop Shot Black Man with His Hands Up. *The Washington Post*. Available, https://www.washingtonpost.com/news/morningmix/wp/2016/07/21/flapoliceshootblackmanwithhishandsupashetriestohelpautisticpatient/

Amanpour, Christiane, and Thom Patterson (2015, November 15). Passport Linked to Terrorist Complicates Syrian Refugee Crisis. *CNN*. Available, http://www.cnn.com/2015/11/15/europe/paris-attacks-passports/

Amato, John and David Neiwert (2010). *Over the Cliff: How Obama's Election Drove the American Right Insane*. Sausalito, CA: PoliPoint Press.

The American Health Care Act: A Summary of the New Bill (2017, March 9). *Health Markets*. Available, https://www.healthmarkets.com/resources/health-insurance/american-health-care-act-summary/

American Immigration Law Foundation (2007). Illegal Immigration Solutions. *ProCon.org*. Available, http://immigration.procon.org/view.answers.php?questionID=000786

American Public Health Association (2012, August). *Affordable Care Act Overview*. Available, http://www.apha.org/NR/rdonlyres/26831F24-882A-4FF7-A0A9-6F49DFBF6D3F/0/ACAOverview_Aug2012.pdf

Americans Overwhelmingly Put English First (2014, August 13). *Rasmussen Reports*. Available, http://www.rasmussenreports.com/public_content/lifestyle/general_lifestyle/august_2014/americans_overwhelmingly_put_english_first

Anderson, Claudia (2017, February 7). Civility and the Long View. *NM Politics*. Available, http://nmpolitics.net/index/2017/02/civility-and-the-long-view/

Anderson, James H. (2011). Spoiler Alert: What Syria's President Really Wants. *World Affairs, 173*(5), 83–91.

Angster, Daniel and Salvatore Colleluori (2015, March 23). New York City Television Stations Continue Disproportionate Coverage of Black Crime. *Media Matters for America*. Available, http://mediamatters.org/research/2015/03/23/report-new-york-city-television-stations-contin/202553

Annear, Steve (2015, January 15). Activists Shut Down Highway During 'Black Lives Matter' Protest. *Boston Magazine*. Available, http://www.bostonmagazine.com/news/blog/2015/01/15/highway-protests-93-black-lives-matter/

Ansolabehere, Stephen and Shanto Iyengar (1995). *Going Negative: How Attack Ads Shrink and Polarize the Electorate*. New York: Free Press.

Ansolabehere, Stephen, Jonathan Rodden, and James M. Snyder, Jr. (2006). Purple America. *Journal of Economic Perspectives 20*(2), 97–118.

Anti-Defamation League (ADL) (n.d.). Arabs Cannot be Anti-Semitic. *ADL: Response to Common Inaccuracy*. Available, https://www.adl.org/education/resources/fact-sheets/response-to-common-inaccuracy-arabs-cannot-be-anti-semitic

Anti-Defamation League (ADL) (2012a, September 4). *Anti-Abortion Violence: America's Forgotten Terrorism*. Available, http://www.adl.org/combating-hate/domestic-extremism-terrorism/c/anti-abortion-violence-americas-forgotten-terrorism-1.html

Anti-Defamation League (ADL) (2012b). *Hate Crime Laws*. Available, http://www.adl.org/assets/pdf/combating-hate/Hate-Crimes-Law.pdf

Anti-Illegal Immigration/Stop Supporting, Start Deporting Facebook page (2014, August 16). Available, https://www.facebook.com/StopSupportingStartDeporting.

Apuzzo, Matt (2014, September 9). After Ferguson Unrest, Senate Reviews Use of Military-Style Gear by Police. *The New York Times*. Available, http://www.nytimes.com/2014/09/10/us/ferguson-unrest-senate-police-weapons-hearing.html?action=click&contentCollection=Politics&module=RelatedCoverage&region=Marginalia&pgtype=article

Araujo, Derek C. (2010). Brief of *Amicus Curiae*: Center for Inquiry in Support of Appellees. *Center for Inquiry*. Available, http://www.centerforinquiry.net/uploads/attachments/10-1973_Brief_of_Amicus_Curiae_Center_for_Inquiry_in_Support_of_Appellees-4.pdf

Areshidze, Giorgi (2013, July 8). Tolerating the Intolerant: A Review of the New Religious Intolerance. *The Claremont Institute Review 13*(2). Available, http://www.claremont.org/index.php?act=crbArticle&id=173#.U7Cu-Pm-2dk

Aristotle (1926). *The Art of Rhetoric* (J. H. Freese, trans.). Loeb Classical Library. Cambridge, MA: Harvard University Press.

Aristotle (1997). *Poetics* (Malcolm Heath, trans.). New York: Penguin.

Arizona v. United States. 567 U.S. ___ (2012). Available, http://www.supremecourt.gov/opinions/11pdf/11-182b5e1.pdf.

Arizona Republic (2014, July 2). GOP, Stop Obama! Pass Immigration Reform. *Arizona Central*. Available, http://www.azcentral.com/story/opinion/editorial/2014/06/30/gop-stop-obama-pass-immigration-reform/11812683/

Arkin, William M., Cynthia McFadden, and Kenzi Abou-Sabe (2017, April 13). U.S. May Launch Strike If North Korea Reaches For Nuclear Trigger. *NBC News*. Available, http://www.nbcnews.com/news/world/u-s-may-launch-strike-if-north-korea-reaches-nuclear-n746366

Arkin, William M., Cynthia McFadden, Kevin Monahan, and Robert Windrem (2017, April 7). Trump's Options for North Korea Include Placing Nukes in South Korea. *NBC News*. Available, http://www.nbcnews.com/news/us-news/trump-s-options-north-korea-include-placing-nukes-south-korea-n743571

Artz, Lee (2011). The New Rhetoric of the Global War on Terrorism. In Gerald Sussman (Ed.), *The Propaganda Society: Promotional Culture and Politics in Global Context*. New York: Peter Land.

Ashtari, Shadee (2014, March 21). KKK Leader Disputes Hate Group Label: 'We're a Christian Organization.' *The Huffington Post*. Available, http://www.huffingtonpost.com/2014/03/21/virginia-kkk-fliers_n_5008647.html

Associated Press (2006, June 5). Activists Say Immigration Debate Shows Signs of Racism. *Fox News*. Available, http://www.foxnews.com/story/2006/06/05/activists-say-immigration-debate-shows-signs-racis-1391179528/

Associated Press (2007, April 1). Newt Gingrich Decries 'Ghetto' Nature of Bilingual Education. *Fox News*. Available, http://www.foxnews.com/story/2007/04/01/newt-gingrich-decries-ghetto-nature-bilingual-education.html

Associated Press (2015, February 4). Mideast Outraged over ISIS Burning of Jordanian Hostage. *New York Post*. Available, http://nypost.com/2015/02/04/mideast-outraged-over-isis-burning-of-jordanian-hostage/

Associated Press (2017a, February 27). Jewish Centers Targeted with Bomb Threats Day after Cemetery Vandalized. *Fox News*. Available, http://www.foxnews.com/us/2017/02/27/jewish-centers-targeted-with-bomb-threats-day-after-cemetery-vandalized.html

Associated Press (2017b, April 25). Trump Touts Executive Orders He Once Lambasted. *CNBC*. Available, http://www.cnbc.com/2017/04/25/trump-touts-executive-orders-he-once-lambasted.html

Atkeson, Lonna Rae, R. Michael Alvarez, Thad E. Hall, and J. Andrew Sinclair (2014). Balancing Fraud Prevention and Electoral Participation: Attitudes toward Voter Identification. *Social Science Quarterly*, 95(5), 1381–1398.

Avidor, Ken, Karl Bremer, and Eva Young (2012). *The Madness of Michele Bachmann: A Broad-Minded Survey of a Small-Minded Candidate*. Hoboken, NJ: Wiley & Sons.

Avlon, John (2004). *Independent Nation: How Centrists Can Change American Politics*. New York: Three Rivers Press.

Avlon, John (2009, March 21). The New Welfare Queens. *The Daily Beast*. Available, http://www.thedailybeast.com/articles/2009/03/21/the-new-welfare-queens.html

Avlon, John (2010). *Wingnuts: How the Lunatic Fringe Is Highjacking America*. New York: Beast Books.

Avlon, John (2014). *Wingnuts: How the Lunatic Fringe Is Highjacking America* (2nd ed.). New York: Beast Books.

Azzimonti, Marina (2013, September). *The Political Polarization Index. Working Paper No. 13–41*. Philadelphia, PA: Federal Reserve Bank of Philadelphia Research Department.

Bailey, J. Michael and Pillard, Richard C. (1991). A Genetic Study of Male Sexual Orientation. *Archives of General Psychiatry 48*(12), 1089–1096.

Bacon, John (2017, February 27). Jewish Sites Reported 31 Threats Monday; More than 100 in '17. *USA Today*. Available, http://www.usatoday.com/story/news/nation/2017/02/27/latest-wave-threats-vandalism-rocks-jewish-community/98477568/

Bacon, Perry, Jr. (2016, November 29). Will Trump Join GOP's Voter ID Push from the White House? *NBC News*. Available, http://www.nbcnews.com/politics/white-house/will-trump-join-gop-s-voter-id-push-white-house-n689176

Bailey, Chelsea (2016, November 14). Hundreds of Hate Crimes Reported Since Election: SPLC. *NBC News*. Available, http://www.nbcnews.com/news/us-news/hundreds-hate-crimes-reported-election-splc-n683761

Bajoria, Jayshree, and Greg Bruno (2012, June 6). *Backgrounder: al-Qaeda (a.k.a. al-Qaida, al-Qa'ida)*. Council on Foreign Relations. Available, http://www.cfr.org/terrorist-organizations-and-networks/al-qaeda-k-al-qaida-al-qaida/p9126

Baker, Jeremy E. (2008, July 31). Defining Them and Us: The Dynamics of Framing Contests that Occur During Union Organizing Drives. *Paper Presented at the American Sociological Association Annual Meeting, Boston, MA*. Available, http://citation.allacademic.com/meta/p237614_index.html

Baker, Russ (2015, August 24). Corruption and Contempt: The Hidden Story of Hurricane Katrina. *Who What Why*. Available, http://whowhatwhy.org/2015/08/24/corruption-and-contempt-the-hidden-story-of-hurricane-katrina/

Baldassarri, Delia and Peter Bearman (2007). Dynamics of Political Polarization. *American Sociological Review 72*(5), 784–811.

Baldo, Lolita C. (2017, April 6). U.S. Attacks Syrian Air Base with Dozens of Missiles in Response to Chemical Attack. *Chicago Tribune*. Available, http://www.chicagotribune.com/news/nationworld/ct-us-syria-airstrikes-20170406-story.html

Balko, Radley (2015, October 29). FBI Data Show Assaults on Police Officers Dropped Sharply in 2014. *The Washington Post*. Available, https://www.washingtonpost.com/news/the-watch/wp/2015/10/29/fbi-data-show-assaults-on-police-officers-dropped-sharply-in-2014/?postshare=9111446210367630&utm_term=.8114f81a4e71

Ball, Molly (2013, February 7). How the Gun-Control Movement Got Smart. *The Atlantic*. Available, http://www.theatlantic.com/politics/archive/2013/02/how-the-gun-control-movement-got-smart/272934/

Balluck, Kyle (2015, May 24). Cleveland Police: 71 Arrested as Protests Turn Violent. *The Hill*. Available, http://thehill.com/blogs/blog-briefing-room/news/243034-cleveland-police-71-arrested-in-night-of-protests

Balogun, Dele (2014, December 3). Anger in the Streets of Portland. *Socialist Worker*. Available, http://socialistworker.org/2014/12/03/anger-in-the-streets-of-portland

Balz, Dan (2011, January 11). Cross Hairs: Crossroads for Palin? *The Washington Post*. Available, http://businessmobilenews.blogspot.com/2011/01/cross-hairs-crossroads-for-palin.html

Balz, Dan (2016, July 8). Killings and Racial Tensions Commingle with Divided and Divisive Politics. *The Washington Post*. Available, https://www.washingtonpost.com/politics/killings-and-racial-tensions-commingle-with-divided-and-divisive-politics/2016/07/08/5a422e08-451e-11e6-88d0-6adee48be8bc_story.html?utm_term=.e49a37af542f

Banks, Ralph Richard (2014). Rights and Meanings: How Same Sex Marriage Will Change Marriage for Everyone. *The Journal of Gender, Race & Justice 17*, 1–8.

Barber, Benjamin R. (1998). *A Place for Us: How to Make Society Civil and Democracy Strong*. New York: Hill and Wang.

Barber, William (2016, September 23). Why We Are Protesting in Charlotte. *The New York Times*. Available, http://www.nytimes.com/2016/09/24/opinion/whyweareprotestingincharlotte.html

Barnard, Anne (2017, February 23). For Syrian Refugees, There Is No Going Home. *The New York Times*. Available, https://www.nytimes.com/2017/02/23/world/middleeast/lebanon-syria-refugees-geneva.html

Barnard, Anne, and Rick Gladstone (2012, April 3). Syrian Leader Accused of Escalating Attacks. *The New York Times*. Available, http://www.nytimes.com/2012/04/04/world/middleeast/syria-cease-fire.html

Barnett, Brooke (2017, March 19). Encouraging Difficult Classroom Discussions in Complicated Times. *Insight into Diversity*. Available, http://www.insightintodiversity.com/encouraging-difficult-classroom-discussions-in-complicated-times/

Baron, Miron (1993, August 7). Genetic Linkage and Male Homosexual Orientation. *British Medical Journal 307*(6900), 337–338.

Barrett, Ted and Tom Cohen (2013, April 18). Senate Rejects Expanded Gun Background Checks. Available, http://www.cnn.com/2013/04/17/politics/senate-guns-vote/index.html

Barron, Laura G. (2009). Promoting the Underlying Principle of Acceptance: The Effectiveness of Sexual Orientation Employment Antidiscrimination Legislation. *Journal of Workplace Rights 14*(2), 251–268.

Barry, Jaime Yaya, and Dionne Searcey (2017, January 18). President's Term Running Out, Gambia Shudders as He Refuses to Quit. *The New York Times*. Available, https://www.nytimes.com/2017/01/18/world/africa/gambia-yahya-jammeh-adama-barrow.html

Bartels, Larry M. (2002). Beyond the Running Tally: Partisan Bias in Political Perceptions. *Political Behavior 24*(2), 117–150.

Barthes, Roland (1987). *Mythologies*. New York: Hill & Wang.

Bash, Dana, Eugene Scott and Jeremy Diamond (2015, September 9). Trump, Cruz Thump Iran Nuclear Deal at Capitol Hill Rally. *CNN Politics*. Available, http://www.cnn.com/2015/09/09/politics/donald-trump-ted-cruz-iran-nuclear-deal-rally-capitol-hill/index.html

Bassett, Laura (2014a, April 3). The Return of the Back-Alley Abortion. *The Huffington Post*. Available, http://www.huffingtonpost.com/2014/04/03/back-alley-abortions_n_5065301.html

Bassett, Laura (2014b, February 24). Virginia Republican Says a Pregnant Woman Is Just a 'Host,' Though 'Some Refer to Them as Mothers.' *The Huffington Post*. Available, http://www.huffingtonpost.com/2014/02/24/steve-martin-virginia_n_4847959.html

Bauder, David (2011, January 22). Keith Olbermann Fired? MSNBC Relationship Was 'Failing for a Long Time.' *The Huffington Post*. Available, http://www.huffingtonpost.com/2011/01/22/keith-olbermann-fired-msn_n_812637.html

Baudrillard, Jean (1995). *The Gulf War Did Not Take Place* (Paul Patton, Trans. & Intro.). Bloomington, IN: Indiana University Press.

Bauer, Lisa J. (2004). Comment, The Effect of Post-9/11 Border Security Provisions on Mexicans Working in the United States: An End to Free Trade? *Emory International Law Review 18*(2), 725–761.

Bauer, Scott (2011, April 14). National Day of Prayer Lawsuit Thrown Out by Federal Appeals Court. *The Huffington Post*. Available, http://www.huffingtonpost.com/2011/04/14/national-day-of-prayer-_n_849295.html

Bauerlein, Mark (2009). *The Dumbest Generation: How the Digital Age Stupefies Young Americans and Jeopardizes Our Future*. New York: Tarcher/Penguin.

Bayefsky, Anne (2015, July 31). Huckabee Is Right: Iran Nuclear Deal Brings Us Closer to Catastrophe of Holocaust Proportions. *Breitbart*. Available, http://www.breitbart.com/national-security/2015/07/31/huckabee-iran-deal/

Bazelon, Emily and Jim Rutenberg (2016, January 3). The Next Big Voting-Rights Fight. *The New York Times*. Available, http://portside.org/2016-01-04/next-big-voting-rights-fight

BBC (2016a, September 19). Terence Crutcher, Black Man Shot by Tulsa Police, Was Unarmed. Available, http://www.ghanaclass.com/bbc-black-man-shot-by-tulsa-police-unarmed/

BBC (2016b, September 23). Tulsa Shooting: The Unanswered Questions. Available, http://www.bbc.com/news/world-us-canada-37435445

Beamon, Todd (2013, July 20). Rhetoric Heats Up over State 'Stand Your Ground' Laws. *Newsmax*. Available, http://www.newsmax.com/Headline/stand-your-ground-/2013/07/19/id/516089/

Bean, Frank D. and Gillian Stevens (2003). *America's Newcomers and the Dynamics of Diversity*. New York: Russell Sage Foundation.

Beauchamp, Zack (2015, November 15). 7 Biggest Myths about ISIS. *Vox*. Available, http://www.vox.com/cards/isis-myths-iraq/crazy-irrational

Beauchamp, Zack (2016, July 14). It's been a Year Since the Iran Deal was Signed. So Far, It's Worked. *Vox*. Available, http://www.vox.com/2016/7/14/12187790/iran-deal-one-year

Becerrill, Crystal Stella and Todd St. Hill (2015, July 23). What Did They Do to Sandra Bland? *Socialist Worker*. Available, http://socialistworker.org/2015/07/23/what-did-they-do-to-sandra-bland /

Beck, Glenn (2007). *An Inconvenient Book: Real Solutions to the World's Biggest Problems*. New York: Threshold Editions.

Beck, Glenn (2010a). *Arguing with Idiots: How to Stop Small Minds and Big Government*. New York: Threshold Editions.

Beck, Glenn (2010b, September 24). Glenn Beck: Truth about Church and State. *Fox News*. Available, http://www.foxnews.com/story/2010/09/27/glenn-beck-truth-about-church-and-state/

Beck, Paul Allen, Dalton, Russell J., Greene, Steven, and Huckfeldt, Robert (2002). The Social Calculus of Voting: Interpersonal, Media, and Organizational Influences on Presidential Choices. *The American Political Science Review 96*(1), 57–73.

Beinart, Peter (2014, October 22). Should the Poor Be Allowed to Vote? *The Atlantic*. Available, https://www.theatlantic.com/politics/archive/2014/10/the-new-poll-tax/381791/

Beirich, Heidi (2014). The Anti-Immigrant Movement. *Southern Poverty Law Center*. Available, http://www.splcenter.org/get-informed/intelligence-files/ideology/anti-immigrant/the-anti-immigrant-movement

Bell, Debra (2013, June 11). George Wallace Stood in a Doorway at the University of Alabama 50 Years Ago Today. *U.S. News & World Report*. Available, https://www.usnews.com/news/blogs/press-past/2013/06/11/george-wallace-stood-in-a-doorway-at-the-university-of-alabama-50-years-ago-today

Benen, Steve (2014a, May 2). Benghazi Conspiracy Theorists Come Unglued. *The Rachel Maddow Show*. Available, http://www.msnbc.com/rachel-maddow-show/benghazi-conspiracy-theorists-come-unglued

Benen, Steve (2014b, April 23). Georgia's 'Guns Everywhere Bill.' *The Rachel Maddow Show*. Available, http://www.msnbc.com/rachel-maddow-show/georgias-guns-everywhere-bill

Benjamin, Daniel (2017, January 27). The Disastrous Consequences of Trump's New Immigration Rules. *Politico*. Available, http://www.politico.com/magazine/story/2017/01/trump-immigration-refugee-vetting-consequences-executive-order-214702

Bennett, Brian, and Noah Bierman (2017, January 25). Trump Orders Moves on Border Wall and 'Sanctuary Cities' and Is Considering a Refugee Ban. *Los Angeles Times*. Available, http://www.latimes.com/politics/la-na-pol-trump-immigration-20170125-story.html

Bennett, Chuck (2007, October 2). Rev. Al in Tax Deal. *New York Post*. Available, http://nypost.com/2007/10/02/rev-al-in-tax-deal/

Bennett, David H. (2001). Immigration and Immigrants: Anti-Immigrant Sentiment. *Encyclopedia of the United States in the Nineteenth Century* (3 vols.). Charles Scribner's Sons. Available, http://www.gale.cengage.com/pdf/whitepapers/gdc/Immigration_whtppr.pdf

Bennett, Stephen Earl (2009). Who Listens to Rush Limbaugh's Radio Program and the Relationship between Listening to Limbaugh and Knowledge of Public Affairs, 1994–2006. *Journal of Radio & Audio Media 16*(1), 66–82.

Benston, Kimberly W. (1982). I Yam What I Am: Naming and Unnaming in Afro-American Literature. Black *American Literature Forum, 16*(1), 3–11.

Berg, Rebecca (2017, March 16). Health Care Push Tests Trump's Sway on Capitol Hill. *Real Clear Politics*. Available, http://www.realclearpolitics.com/articles/2017/03/16/health_care_push_tests_trumps_sway_on_capitol_hill.html

Bergen, Peter (2017, January 28). Trump's Big Mistake on Syria Refugees. *CNN*. Available, http://www.cnn.com/2017/01/28/opinions/trumps-big-mistake-on-syrian-refugees-bergen/index.html

Bergsten, C. Fred, and Joseph E. Gagnon (2012, December). *Currency Manipulation, the US Economy, and the Global Economic Order*. Peterson Institute for International Economics. Available, https://piie.com/publications/policy-briefs/currency-manipulation-us-economy-and-global-economic-order

Berman, Ari (2015a, June 24). Congressional Democrats Introduce Ambitious New Bill to Restore the Voting Rights Act. *The Nation*. Available, http://www.thenation.com/article/congressional-democrats-introduce-ambitious-new-bill-to-restore-the-voting-rights-act/

Berman, Ari (2015b, March 5). 50 Years after Bloody Sunday, Voting Rights are under Attack. *The Nation*. Available, http://www.thenation.com/blog/200193/50-years-after-bloody-sunday-voting-rights-are-under-attack

Berman, Ari (2016, August 1). 6 Major GOP Voting Restrictions Have Been Blocked in 2 Weeks. *The Nation*. Available, https://www.thenation.com/article/5-major-gop-voting-restrictions-were-blocked-in-10-days/

Berman, Mark (2015, July 13). Boy Scouts Executive Committee Endorses Ending Ban on Gay Leaders. *The Washington Post*. Available, https://www.washingtonpost.com/news/post-nation/wp/2015/07/13/boy-scouts-executive-committee-endorses-ending-ban-on-gay-leaders/

Bernard, Steven (2012, May 10). *Freedom from Religion Foundation v. John Hickenlooper*, Colorado Court of Appeals, No. 10CA2559. Colorado Court of Appeals of District VI. Available, http://ffrf.org/uploads/legal/CAOpinion.pdf

Berry, Daina Ramey (2014, October 21). Four Myths about Slavery in the US. *Raw Story*. Available, http://www.rawstory.com/2014/10/four-myths-about-slavery-in-the-us/

Berry, Jeffrey M. and Sarah Sobieraj (2008). *The Outrage Industry*. Paper prepared for the Conference on Going to Extremes: The Fate of the Political Center in American Politics, Rockefeller Center for Public Policy and the Social Sciences, Dartmouth College, June 19–21, 2008.

Bersani, Bianca E. (2014). An Examination of First and Second Generation Immigrant Offending Trajectories. *Justice Quarterly, 31*(2), 315–343.

Beusman, Callie (2013, December 12). 'Slut-Shaming' has been Tossed around so much, It's Lost All Meaning. *Jezebel*. Available, http://jezebel.com/slut-shaming-has-been-tossed-around-so-much-its-los-1478093672

Beutler, Brian (2010, October 19). Limbaugh Defends O'Donnell: Separation of Church and State Not in the Constitution. *Talking Points Memo*. Available, http://talkingpointsmemo.com/dc/limbaugh-defends-o-donnell-separation-of-church-and-state-not-in-the-constitution

Bhatta, Basudeb (2010). *Analysis of Urban Growth and Sprawl from Remote Sensing Data*. Heidelberg: Springer.

Binder, John (2016, November 10). 'Die Whites Die': Anti-Trump Rioters Vandalize NOLA Monuments. *Breitbart*. Available, http://www.breitbart.com/texas/2016/11/10/die-whites-die-anti-trump-rioters-vandalize-nola-monuments/

Binder, Sarah (2014, January 13). How Political Polarization Creates Stalemate and Undermines Lawmaking. *The Washington Post*. Available, http://www.washingtonpost.com/blogs/monkey-cage/wp/2014/01/13/how-political-polarization-creates-stalemate-and-undermines-lawmaking/

Bishop, Bill (2009). *The Big Sort: Why the Clustering of Like-Minded America Is Tearing Us Apart*. Boston: Houghton Mifflin Harcourt.

Birnie, Billie F. (2016). Promoting Civil Discourse in the Classroom. *Kappa Delta Pi Record, 52*, 53-55.

Bitran, Deedee (2016, April 26). "Anti-Israel," a Camouflage Platform for Anti-Semitism. *FIU Law Review*, Student News. Available, https://law.fiu.edu/anti-israel-camouflage-platform-anti-semitism/

Bitzer, Lloyd (1968). The Rhetorical Situation. *Philosophy & Rhetoric 1*(1), 1–14.

Black, Jason E. (2009). Native Resistive Rhetoric and the Decolonization of American Indian Removal Discourse. *Quarterly Journal of Speech*, *95*(1), 66–88.

Bobbitt, Philip (1982). *Constitutional Fate: Theory of the Constitution*. New York: Oxford University Press.

Bobic, Igor (2014, December 4). Peter King Says There Are 'No Elements of Racism' in Eric Garner Case. *The Huffington Post*. Available, http://www.huffingtonpost.com/2014/12/04/peter-king-eric-garner-racism_n_6269152.html

Boehlert, Eric (2017, February 3). Exciting the Right Wing, Trump Downplays Threat of Right-Wing Terror. *Media Matters for America*. Available, https://mediamatters.org/blog/2017/02/03/exciting-right-wing-trump-downplays-threat-right-wing-terror/215226

Boggioni, Tom (2014, April 28). Citing Religious Freedom, NC Clergymen Sue State for Right to Perform Same-Sex Marriages. *Raw Story*. Available, http://www.rawstory.com/rs/2014/04/28/citing-religious-freedom-nc-clergymen-sue-state-for-right-to-perform-same-sex-marriages/#.U16A-S-0LPM.facebook

Boggioni, Tom (2016, July 10). Rudy Giuliani: Black Parents Should Teach Their Children to Fear Other Black Kids—Not Cops. *Raw Story*. Available, https://www.rawstory.com/2016/07/rudy-giuliani-black-parents-should-teach-their-children-to-fear-other-black-kids-not-cops/

Bohon, Dave (2014, May 2). National Day of Prayer Includes Call to Repentance, Challenge to "Abortion President." *The New American*. Available, http://www.thenewamerican.com/culture/faith-and-morals/item/18179-national-day-of-prayer-includes-call-to-repentance-challenge-to-abortion-president

Bollinger, Lee C. (2002). Seven Myths about Affirmative Action in Universities. *Willamette Law Review*, *38*(4), 535–548.

Bonhomme, Edna (2015, December 3). What the Fight Is about at Princeton. *Socialist Worker*. Available, http://socialistworker.org/2015/12/03/what-princetons-fight-is-about

Boot, Max (2015, August 10). Obama's Intentionally Divisive Iran Nuclear Deal Rhetoric. *Commentary Magazine*. Available, https://www.commentarymagazine.com/2015/08/10/obama-iran-deal-rhetoric/

Borchers, Callum (2015, November 23). Conservative Media Offer a VERY Different Take on What Trump Supporters Did to that Black Lives Matter Activist. *The Washington Post*. Available, https://www.washingtonpost.com/news/the-fix/wp/2015/11/23/conservative-media-offer-a-very-different-take-on-what-trump-supporters-did-to-that-black-lives-matter-activist/?postshare=1891448298071772&tid=ss_tw

Bornschein, John (2012). What Is Prayer? *National Day of Prayer Task Force*. Available, http://nationaldayofprayer.org/what-is-prayer/ (accessed 7/3/14).

Boston, Rob (2013, April). Marriage Equality: Conservative Religious Interests Want to Control Civil Marriage Law. Will The Supreme Court Let Them? *Church & State*, 7–10.

Botelho, Greg, and Dana Ford (2015, February 4). Jordan Executes Prisoners after ISIS Hostage Burned Alive. *CNN*. Available, http://www.cnn.com/2015/02/03/world/isis-captive/

Bowers, John W., Donovan J. Ochs, Richard J. Jensen, and David P. Schulz (2010). *The Rhetoric of Agitation and Control* (3rd ed.). Long Grove, IL: Waveland Press.

Bowers v. Hardwick. 478 U.S. 186 (1986).

Bradner, Eric (2017a, January 13). Ryan: GOP Will Repeal, Replace Obamacare at Same Time. *CNN Politics*. Available, http://www.cnn.com/2017/01/12/politics/paul-ryan-town-hall/

Bradner, Eric (2017b, January 23). Conway: Trump White House Offered 'Alternative Facts' on Crowd Size. *CNN Politics*. Available, http://edition.cnn.com/2017/01/22/politics/kellyanne-conway-alternative-facts/index.html

Brady Center to Prevent Gun Violence (2006). *The NRA: A Criminal's Best Friend: How the National Rifle Association Has Handcuffed Federal Gun Law Enforcement*. Available, http://www.bradycampaign.org/sites/default/files/criminals-best-friend.pdf

Brekhus, Keith (2015, September 8). GOP's Epic Failure to Stop Iran Deal Started with Netanyahu Stunt in March. *Politicus USA*. Available, http://www.politicususa.com/2015/09/08/gops-epic-failure-stop-iran-deal-started-netanyahu-stunt-march.html

Brewer, Paul R. (2003). The Shifting Foundations of Public Opinion about Gay Rights. *The Journal of Politics 65*(4), 1208–1220.

Brewer, Paul R. and Clyde Wilcox (2005). Trends: Same-Sex Marriage and Civil Unions. *Public Opinion Quarterly 69*(4), 599–616.

Breyer, Stephen (2014, May 5). Dissenting Opinion. *Town of Greece v. Galloway.* No. 12-696, 572 U.S. ___ (2014).

Brinker, Eric (2017, January 23). Conway: Trump White House Offered 'Alternative Facts' on Crowd Size. *CNN Politics.* Available, http://www.cnn.com/2017/01/22/politics/kellyanne-conway-alternative-facts/

Brinker, Luke (2014a, May 12). "*God Less America*": An Ugly Look at what *Still* Motivates the Right's Culture Warriors. *Media Matters.* Available, http://mediamatters.org/mobile/blog/2014/05/12/god-less-america-an-ugly-look-at-what-still-mot/199268

Brinker, Luke (2014b, April 29). The One Religious Liberty Case Anti-Gay Conservatives Want to Ignore. *Equality Matters* blog. Available, http://equalitymatters.org/blog/201404290001

Brinkerhoff, Noel (2013, June 19). Arizona Voter ID Law Overturned by the U.S. Supreme Court. *AllGov.* Available, http://www.allgov.com/news/top-stories/arizona-voter-id-law-overturned-by-the-us-supreme-court-130619?news=850337

Bronars, Stephen (2013, July 15). Do Stand Your Ground Laws Deter Violent Crime? *Bronars Economics.* Available, http://sbronars.wordpress.com/2013/07/15/do-stand-your-ground-laws-deter-violent-crime/

Bronner, Stephen Eric (2014). *The Bigot: Why Prejudice Persists.* New Haven, CT: Yale University Press.

Broockman, David and Joshua Kalla (2016). Durably Reducing Transphobia: A Field Experiment on Door-to-Door Canvassing. *Science, 352*(6282), 220–224.

Brown v. Board of Education of Topeka (1954). 347 U.S. 483. Available, https://www.law.cornell.edu/supremecourt/text/347/483

Brown, Chris (2011, October 3). Rachel Maddow Highlights NRA and Fox Extremism. *Media Matters for America.* Available, http://mediamatters.org/blog/2011/10/03/rachel-maddow-highlights-nra-and-fox-extremism/181779

Brownstein, Ronald (2007). *The Second Civil War: How Extreme Partisanship Has Paralyzed Washington and Polarized America.* New York: Penguin.

Bruer, Wes (2015, February 20). DHS Intelligence Report Warns of Domestic Right-Wing Terror Threat. *CNN Politics.* Available, http://www.cnn.com/2015/02/19/politics/terror-threat-homeland-security/

Brunnstrom, David, and Michael Martina (2015, September 25). Xi Denies China Turning Artificial Islands into Military Bases. *Reuters.* Available, http://www.reuters.com/article/us-usa-china-pacific-idUSKCN0RP1ZH20150925

Buckley, Cara and William K. Rashbaum (2006, November 27). A Day after a Fatal Shooting, Questions, Mourning and Protest. *The New York Times.* Available, http://www.nytimes.com/2006/11/27/nyregion/27shot.html

Bui, Quoctrung and Amanda Cox (2016, July 11). Surprising New Evidence Shows Bias in Police Use of Force but Not in Shootings. *The New York Times.* Available, https://www.nytimes.com/2016/07/12/upshot/surprising-new-evidence-shows-bias-in-police-use-of-force-but-not-in-shootings.html

Bump, Philip (2015, July 2). Surprise! Donald Trump Is Wrong about Immigrants and Crime. *The Washington Post.* Available, http://www.washingtonpost.com/blogs/the-fix/wp/2015/07/02/surprise-donald-trump-is-wrong-about-immigrants-and-crime/

Bunch, Will (2011). *The Backlash: Right-Wing Radicals, Hi-Def Hucksters, and Paranoid Politics in the Age of Obama.* New York: Harper.

Buncombe, Andrew (2017, March 15). Donald Trump's New Travel Ban Blocked Nationwide by Hawaii Federal Judge Hours before It Was Due to Begin. *The Independent.* Available, http://www.independent.co.uk/news/world/americas/us-politics/hawaii-judge-donald-trump-travel-ban-muslim-countries-a7632366.html

Burger, Warren E. (1970). *Walz v. Tax Commission of the City of New York.* 397 U.S. 664 (1970), pp. 666–680.

Burke, Daniel (2014, May 5). After Supreme Court Ruling, Do Religious Minorities Have a Prayer? *CNN.* Available, http://religion.blogs.cnn.com/2014/05/05/supreme-court-religious-minorities-dont-have-a-prayer/

Burke, Kenneth (1969). *A Rhetoric of Motives.* Berkeley, CA: University of California Press.

Burke, Kenneth (1984). *Permanence and Change: An Anatomy of Purpose* (3rd ed.). Berkeley, CA: University of California Press.

Burns, Alexander (2015, July 31). Donald Trump's Instinct for Racially Charged Rhetoric, before His Presidential Bid. *The New York Times.* Available, http://www.nytimes.com/2015/08/01/nyregion/trumps-instinct-for-racially-charged-rhetoric-before-his-presidential-bid.html?smid=tw-share&_r=0

Burstyn v. Wilson (1952). 72 S. Ct. 777.

Burwell v. Hobby Lobby Stores (2014). 573 US ___ . Available, https://www.oyez.org/cases/2013/13-354

Bush, George W. (2001, September 20). Transcript of President Bush's Address. *CNN.com.* Available, http://edition.cnn.com/2001/US/09/20/gen.bush.transcript/

Bush, Jeb and Bolick, Clint (2013). *Immigration Wars: Forging an American Solution.* New York: Threshold Editions.

Butler, Sim, Richard Mocarski, and Betsy Emmons (2012). Cocoon Minorities: Understanding Rush Limbaugh's Co-Option of the Rhetorical Strategies of the Disenfranchised Position through Homological Analysis. *Journal of Radio & Audio Media 19*(2), 239–256.

Butterfield, Fox (1995, May 8). Terror in Oklahoma: Echoes of the N.R.A.; Rifle Association Has Long Practice in Railing against Federal Agents. *The New York Times.* Available, http://www.nytimes.com/1995/05/08/us/terror-oklahoma-echoes-nra-rifle-association-has-long-practice-railing-against.html

Butterfield, Jeanne A. (2005). Broken Fences: Legal and Practical Realities of Immigration Reform in the Post-9/11 Age: Restoring the Rule of Law: Reflections on Fixing the Immigration System and Exploring Failed Policy Choices. *University of Maryland Law Journal of Race, Religion, Gender and Class 5*(Fall), 187–200.

Byers, Dylan (2013, April 3). 'An African American', or 'a Black'? *Politico*. Available, http://www.politico.com/blogs/media/2013/04/an-african-american-or-a-black-160773

Byman, Daniel L. (2017, January 30). Why Trump's Policies Will Increase Terrorism—and Why Trump Might Benefit as a Result. *The Brookings Institution*. Available, https://www.brookings.edu/blog/markaz/2017/01/30/why-trumps-policies-will-increase-terrorism-and-why-trump-might-benefit-as-a-result/

Byne, William and Bruce Parsons (1993). Human Sexual Orientation: The Biologic Theories Reappraised. *Archives of General Psychiatry 50*(3), 228–241.

Byrne, Sahara and Philip Sol Hart (2009). The Boomerang Effect: A Synthesis of Findings and a Preliminary Theoretical Framework. *Communication Yearbook 33*, 3–38.

Cahill, Sean (2004). *Same-Sex Marriage in the United States: Focus on the Facts*. Oxford, UK: Lexington.

Cahn, Steven M. (Ed) (1995). *The Affirmative Action Debate*. New York: Routledge.

Calamur, Krishnadev (2017, April 4). How Is Syria Still Using Chemical Weapons? *The Atlantic*. Available, https://www.theatlantic.com/international/archive/2017/04/syria-chemical-weapons-attack/521883/

Callahan, Jane Dunlap (2014, January 31). Church Tax-Exempt Status Enhances Society. *The Orlando Sentinel*. Available, http://articles.orlandosentinel.com/2014-01-31/news/os-ed-church-tax-exemption-pro-20140130_1_churches-exemption-property-tax

Camarota, Steven A. (2002, September). How the Terrorists Get In. *Center for Immigration Studies*. Available, http://cis.org/HowTerroristsGetIn

Camarota, Steven A. and Karen Zeigler (2009). Jobs Americans Won't Do? A Detailed Look at Immigrant Employment by Occupation. *Center for Immigration Studies*. Available, http://www.cis.org/illegalImmigration-employment

Camera, Lauren (2015, October 16). U.S. Students Are Really Bad at Geography. *U.S. News & World Report*. Available, https://www.usnews.com/news/articles/2015/10/16/us-students-are-terrible-at-geography

Cameron, Paul and Kirk Cameron (1996). Homosexual Parents. *Adolescence 31*(124), 757–776.

Campbell, Andy (2015, April 7). Video Shows Officer Michael Slager Shooting Unarmed Black Man in the Back in South Carolina. *The Huffington Post*. Available, http://www.huffingtonpost.com/2015/04/07/officer-michael-slager-shoots-man-in-back-video_n_7021134.html

Campbell, Karlyn Khors, Susan Schultz Huxman, and Thomas A. Burkholder (2014). *The Rhetorical Act: Thinking, Speaking, and Writing Critically* (5th ed.). Stamford, CT: Cengage Learning.

Cannon, Michael F. (2014, July 21). Halbig v. Burwell Would Free more than 57 Million Americans from the ACA's Individual & Employer Mandates. *Forbes*. Available, http://www.forbes.com/sites/michaelcannon/2014/07/21/halbig-v-burwell-would-free-more-than-57-million-americans-from-the-acas-individual-employer-mandates/

Cardwell, Diane and Sewell Chan (2006, November 27). Mayor Says Shooting Was 'Excessive.' *The New York Times*. Available, http://www.nytimes.com/2006/11/27/nyregion/28shootcnd.html

Carmines, Edward G., Michael J. Ensley, and Michael W. Wagner (2012). Who Fits the Left-Right Divide? Partisan Polarization in the American Electorate. *American Behavioral Scientist 56*(12), 1631–1653.

Carmines, Edward G. and James A. Stimson (1981). Issue Evolution, Population Replacement, and Normal Partisan Change. *The American Political Science Review 75*(1), 107–118.

Carpenter, Elizabeth (2014, July 17). Upcoming Federal Court Decision Could Mean Premium Increases for Nearly 5 Million Americans. *Avalere blog*. Available, http://avalere.com/expertise/managed-care/insights/upcoming-federal-court-decision-could-mean-premium-increases-for-nearly-5-m

Carr, Nicholas (2011). *The Shallows: What the Internet Is Doing to Our Brains*. New York: Norton.

Carr, Nicholas (2015, September 2). How Social Media Is Ruining Politics. *Politco*. Available, http://www.politico.com/magazine/story/2015/09/2016-election-social-media-ruining-politics-213104

Carroll, Conn (2009, August 7). Another Study Shows Obamacare Would Dump Americans into Government-Run Health Care. *The Daily Signal*. Available, http://dailysignal.com/2009/08/07/another-study-shows-obamacare-would-dump-americans-into-government-run-health-care/.

Carroll, John M. (1980). Naming and Describing in Social Communication. Language and Speech 23(4), 309–322.

Carroll, Lauren (2017, April 17). Who Plays More Golf: Donald Trump or Barack Obama? *PolitiFact*. Available, http://www.politifact.com/truth-o-meter/article/2017/apr/17/who-plays-more-golf-donald-trump-or-barack-obama/

Carroll, Rory (2013, November 4). California Police Use of Body Cameras Cuts Violence and Complaints. *The Guardian*. Available, http://www.theguardian.com/world/2013/nov/04/california-police-body-cameras-cuts-violence-complaints-rialto

Carsey, Thomas M. and Geoffrey C. Layman (2006). Changing Sides or Changing Minds? Party Identification and Policy Preferences in the American Electorate. *American Journal of Political Science 50*(2), 464–477.

Carter, Gregg Lee (2012). *Guns in American Society: An Encyclopedia of History, Politics, Culture, and the Law* (Vol. 1). Santa Barbara, CA: ABC-CLIO.

Carter, Sara A. (2007, November 26). Islamic Terrorists Target Army Base—in Arizona. *Espresso Pundit*. Available, http://www.espressopundit.com/2007/11/terroists-targe.html

Caulfield, Mike (2017). *Web Literacy for Student Fact-Checkers*. Available, https://webliteracy.pressbooks.com/

Cave, Damien and Rochelle Oliver (2016, September 19). The Raw Videos that have Sparked Outrage over Police Treatment of Blacks. *The New York Times*. Available, https://www.nytimes.com/interactive/2015/07/30/us/police-videos-race.html

Center for Policing Equity (2016, July). *The Science of Justice: Race, Arrests, and Use of Force.* Available, http://policingequity.org/research/1687-2/

Chacón, Justin Akers (2014, July 9). Children Forced on a Dangerous Journey. *Socialist Worker.* Available, http://socialistworker.org/2014/07/09/forced-on-a-dangerous-journey

Chafets, Zev (2008, July 6). Late-Period Limbaugh. *New York Times Magazine.* Available, http://www.nytimes.com/2008/07/06/magazine/06Limbaugh-t.html?pagewanted=all&_r=0

Chait, Jonathan (2007). *The Big Con: The True Story of How Washington Got Hoodwinked and Hijacked by Crackpot Economics.* New York: Houghton Mifflin.

Chaitin, Daniel (2015, November 15). O'Malley Calls Trump an 'Immigrant-Bashing Carnival Barker.' *The Washington Examiner.* Available, http://www.washingtonexaminer.com/omalley-calls-trump-an-immigrant-bashing-carnival-barker/article/2576396

Chamber of Commerce of the United States of America et al. v. Whiting et al. 563 U.S. ___ (2011). Available, http://www.supremecourt.gov/opinions/10pdf/09-115.pdf.

Chappell, Bill (2016, July 21). Black Man Says He Was Shot by North Miami Police while Lying on the Ground. *NPR: The Two-Way.* Available, http://www.npr.org/sections/thetwo-way/2016/07/21/486869035/north-miami-police-shoot-black-man-who-was-reportedly-lying-on-the-ground

Charap, Samuel, and Jeremy Shapiro (2016). How to Avoid a New Cold War. In Glenn P. Hastedt (Ed.), *Readings in American Foreign Policy* (pp. 77–85). Lanham, MD: Rowman & Littlefield.

Charbonneau, Louis (2012, September 24). In New York, Defiant Ahmadinejad Says Israel Will Be "Eliminated." *Reuters.* Available, http://www.reuters.com/article/us-un-assembly-ahmadinejad-idUSBRE88N0HF20120924

Chauncey, George (2004). *Why Marriage? The History of Shaping Today's Debate over Gay Equality.* Cambridge, MA: Basic Books.

Chavez, Leo R. (2013). *The Latino Threat: Constructing Immigrants, Citizens, and the Nation.* Stanford, CA: Stanford University Press.

Chemerinsky, Erwin (2004). Keynote Address: Putting the Gun Control Debate in Social Perspective. *Fordham Law Review 73*(2), 477–485.

Chideya, Farai (1999). *The Color of Our Future: Race in the 21st Century.* New York: Harper Perennial.

China's New Spratly Island Defenses (2016, December 13). *Asia Maritime Transparency Initiative.* Available, https://amti.csis.org/chinas-new-spratly-island-defenses/

China Warns North Korea, Tries to Ease Korea Tensions (2017, April 13). *Voice of America News.* Available, http://learningenglish.voanews.com/a/china-warns-north-korea-and-tries-to-ease-korea-tensions/3808852.html

Chirbas, Kurt, Alexander Smith, and Erik Ortiz (2016, September 15). Tyre King, 13, Fatally Shot by Police in Columbus, Ohio. *NBC News.* Available, http://www.nbcnews.com/news/us-news/tyre-king-13-fatally-shot-police-columbus-ohio-n648671

Chittal, Nisha (2014, August 9). Cops Shoot and Kill Man Holding Toy Gun in Wal-Mart. *MSNBC News.* Available, http://www.msnbc.com/msnbc/cops-shoot-and-kill-man-holding-toy-gun-walmart

Chomsky, Aviva (2007). *"They Take Our Jobs!" and 20 Other Myths about Immigration.* Boston: Beacon Press.

Christianity Today (2008, April 13). Obama: 'They Cling to Guns or Religion.' *Christianity Today.* Available, http://www.christianitytoday.com/gleanings/2008/april/obama-they-cling-to-guns-or-religion.html?paging=off

Chulov, Martin, and Kareem Shaheen (2017, April 5). Syria: Suspected Chemical Attack Kills Dozens in Idlib Province. *The Guardian.* Available, https://www.theguardian.com/world/2017/apr/04/syria-chemical-attack-idlib-province

Chumley, Cheryl K. (2013, August 21). Atheists Incensed after IRS Grants Them Tax Exemption as Religious Group. *The Washington Times.* Available, http://www.washingtontimes.com/news/2013/aug/21/atheists-incensed-after-irs-grants-them-tax-exempt/

Church of Lukumi Babalu Aye., Inc. v. Hialeah. 113 S. Ct. 2217 (1993).

Cicero, Marcus Tullius (1949). *De Inventione.* Loeb Classical Library. Cambridge, MA: Harvard University Press.

Cisneros, Josue David (2012). Looking "Illegal": Affect, Rhetoric, and Performativity in Arizona's Senate Bill 1070. In D. Robert DeChaine (Ed.), *Border Rhetorics: Citizenship and Identity on the US–Mexico Frontier* (pp. 133–150). Tuscaloosa, AL: University of Alabama Press.

Citizens United v. Federal Election Commission. 558 U.S. ___ (2010).

Clapper, James R. (2016, February 9). *Statement for the Record: Worldwide Threat Assessment of the US Intelligence Community.* Available, https://www.dni.gov/files/documents/SASC_Unclassified_2016_ATA_SFR_FINAL.pdf

Clemmitt, Marcia (2014). Assessing the New Health Care Law. In CQ Researcher's *Issues for Debate in American Public Policy* (14th ed.; pp. 301–324). Washington, D.C.: Congressional Quarterly Press.

Clifton, Allen (2014, March 11). In One Sentence, Michele Bachmann Proves How Ignorant Republicans Are about the Constitution. *Forward Progressives.* Available, http://www.forwardprogressives.com/one-sentence-michele-bachmann-proves-ignorance-republicans-constitution/

CNN (2010, September 11). Build Islamic Center on Ground Zero, Says Moore. *Political Ticker Blog.* Available, http://politicalticker.blogs.cnn.com/2010/09/11/moore-build-islamic-center-on-ground-zero/

CNN (2014, November 24). 12-Year-Old with Air Gun Dies in Cleveland Police Shooting. *Fox4KC.* Available, http://fox4kc.com/2014/11/24/12-year-old-with-air-gun-dies-in-cleveland-police-shooting/

CNN (2016, November 12). Reports of Racist Graffiti, Hate Crimes Post-Election. *Cleveland News.* Available, http://www.newsbreakapp.com/n/0590isQ4?s=i0

CNN Library (2016, August 23). Hurricane Katrina Statistics Fast Facts. *CNN*. Available, http://www.cnn.com/2013/08/23/us/hurricane-katrina-statistics-fast-facts/

CNN Wire (2017). Once Critical of Executive Orders, Trump Signs Most in First 100 Days Since Truman Presidency. *KTLA 5*. Available, http://ktla.com/2017/04/27/once-critical-of-executive-orders-trump-signs-most-in-first-100-days-since-truman-presidency/

Coates, Ta-Nehisi (2014, June). The Case for Reparations. *The Atlantic*. Available, https://www.theatlantic.com/magazine/archive/2014/06/the-case-for-reparations/361631/

Cohen, Andrew (2013, June 25). On Voting Rights, a Decision as Lamentable as Plessy or Dred Scott. *The Atlantic*. Available, http://www.theatlantic.com/national/archive/2013/06/on-voting-rights-a-decision-as-lamentable-as-plessy-or-dred-scott/276455/

Cohen, Ben (2012, November 15). Self-Hatred of Self-Help? *Jewish Ideas Daily*. Available, http://www.jewishideasdaily.com/5370/features/self-hatred-or-self-help/

Cohen, Tom (2014, May 2). Benghazi—Government Cover-up or Right-wing Conspiracy Theory? *CNN Politics*. Available, http://www.cnn.com/2014/05/01/politics/benghazi-controversy-questions/

Cohen, Tom, Jim Acosta, and Kevin Liptak (2014, May 28). Obama Outlines Foreign Policy Vision of 'Might and Right.' *CNN Politics*. Available, http://www.cnn.com/2014/05/28/politics/obama-west-point-foreign-policy/

Coker, Jason (2016, July 11). Whiteness and Racial Identity. *Baptist News Global*. Available, https://baptistnews.com/article/whiteness-and-racial-identity/#.WLu_F28rLIU

Cole, David (2012, July 16–23). United States 1, Arizona 0. *The Nation*. Available, http://www.thenation.com/article/168630/immigration-united-states-1-arizona-0

Coleman, Charles F., Jr. (2015, April 8). Walter Scott's Death and the Cycle of Contempt for Black Lives. *Portside*. Available, http://portside.org/2015-04-08/walter-scott%E2%80%99s-death-and-cycle-contempt-black-lives

Collins, Patricia Hill (2008). *Black Feminist Thought: Knowledge, Consciousness, and the Politics of Empowerment*. New York: Routledge.

Collinson, Stephen (2016, December 6). Trump and China on Collision Course. *CNN Politics*. Available, http://edition.cnn.com/2016/12/05/politics/donald-trump-china-taiwan-clash/

Collinson, Stephen (2017, April 3). Trump Prepares for Critical Week of Diplomacy. *CNN Politics*. Available, http://www.cnn.com/2017/04/03/politics/trump-foreign-policy/

Colorito, Rita (2000, May). Ignoring Foreign News. *World & I*, *15*(5). Available, EbscoHost.

Commieblaster (2014, July 31). Obamacare Socialism. *Commieblaster.com*. Available, http://commieblaster.com/healthcare/

Condit, Celeste Michelle (1990). *Decoding Abortion Rhetoric: Communicating Social Change*. Urbana, IL: University of Illinois Press.

Connor, Jackson (2015, April 10). 'Hannity' Guest Storms Off During Walter Scott Debate: 'I'm Not Going to Listen to this Hate!' *The Huffington Post*. Available, http://www.huffingtonpost.com/2015/04/10/hannity-walter-scott-guest-storms-off-camera_n_7040586.html?ncid=fcbklnkushpmg00000018

Conservative Tribune (2014a, November 30). Limbaugh, Levin, Beck Reveal What the Media Doesn't Want You to Know about Ferguson. *Conservative Tribune: In Defense of Western Civilization*. Available, http://conservativetribune.com/limbaugh-levin-beck-reveal-what-the-media-doesnt-want-you-to-know-about-ferguson/

Conservative Tribune (2014b, November 28). The Stupidity of Ferguson Rioters Summed Up in One Picture. *Conservative Tribune: In Defense of Western Civilization*. Available, http://conservativetribune.com/ferguson-rioters-are-literally-stupid/

Constantine, Madonna G., and Derald Wing Sue (2007). Perceptions of Racial Microaggressions among Black Supervisees in Cross-Racial Dyads. *Journal of Counseling Psychology*, *54*(2), 142–153.

Conway, Mike, Maria Elizabeth Grabe, and Kevin Grieves (2007). Villains, Victims, and the Virtuous in Bill O'Reilly's "No-Spin Zone." *Journalism Studies* 8(2), 197–223.

Cooper, Brittney (2014, August 12). In Defense of Black Rage: Michael Brown, Police and the American Dream. *Salon*. Available, http://www.salon.com/2014/08/12/in_defense_of_black_rage_michael_brown_police_and_the_american_dream/?utm_source=facebook&utm_medium=socialflow

Cooper, Helene, and Mujib Mashal (2017, April 13). U.S. Drops 'Mother of All Bombs' on ISIS Caves in Afghanistan. *The New York Times*. Available, https://www.nytimes.com/2017/04/13/world/asia/moab-mother-of-all-bombs-afghanistan.html?_r=0

Corbett, Edward P. J., and Robert J. Connors (1999). *Classical Rhetoric for the Modern Student* (4th ed.). New York: Oxford University Press.

Corn, David (2014, May 2). Why There is No Cure for the GOP's Benghazi Fever. *Mother Jones*. Available, http://www.motherjones.com/politics/2014/05/gop-benghazi-fever-issa-boehner-ben-rhodes

Cornell, Saul and Nathan DeDino (2004). Historical Perspectives: A Well Regulated Right: The Early American Origins of Gun Control. *Fordham Law Review* 73(2), 487–528.

Corvino, John (2005). Homosexuality and the PIB Argument. *Ethics 115*(3), 501–534.

Cottee, Simon (2017, February 1). Trump's Travel Ban Will Not 'Help' ISIS Recruitment. *The Atlantic*. Available, https://www.theatlantic.com/international/archive/2017/02/isis-travel-ban-propaganda-trump/515283/

Cottrell, David, Michael C. Herron, and Sean J. Westwood (2016, December 2). Dartmouth Study Finds No Evidence of Voter Fraud. Dartmouth Press Release. Available, http://www.dartmouth.edu/press-releases/no_evidence_voter_fraud.html

Coulter, Ann (2007). *If Democrats Had Any Brains, They'd be Republicans*. New York: Three Rivers Press.

Coulter, Ann (2012). *Mugged: Racial Demagoguery from the Seventies to Obama*. New York: Sentinel.

Council on Foreign Relations (2014). *U.S. War in Afghanistan*. Available, http://www.cfr.org/afghanistan/us-war-afghanistan/p20018

Covey, Stephen (2004). *The 7 Habits of Highly Effective People*. New York: Free Press.

Cowan, Richard, and Susan Cornwell (2017, January 14). House Votes to Begin Repealing Obamacare. *Reuters*. Available, http://www.reuters.com/article/us-usa-obamacare-idUSKBN14X1SK

Craven, Julia (2016, November 1). New Jersey Police Shot, Injured Unarmed Black Man in Front of His Two Sons. *The Huffington Post*. Available, http://www.huffingtonpost.com/entry/larry-bouie-police-shooting_us_5818bab9e4b064e1b4b4e34f

Cravens, Annalisa (2013). "This Is Not the System Congress Created": Rethinking Louisiana's Immigration Law after Arizona v. United States. *Tulane Law Review 88*, 161–191.

Crawford v. Marion County Election Board (2008). 553 U.S. 181. Available, https://supreme.justia.com/cases/federal/us/553/181/

Crimes of Historic Proportions being Committed in Aleppo, UN Rights Chief Warns (2016, October 21). *UN News Center*. Available, http://www.un.org/apps/news/story.asp?NewsID=55364#.WOs7LPkrLIV

Crowley, Sharon (2006). *Toward a Civil Discourse: Rhetoric and Fundamentalism*. Pittsburgh: University of Pittsburgh Press.

Crummy, Karen E. and Jordan Steffen (2012, July 21). Aurora Police Chief: Gunman Acted with "Calculation and Deliberation." *The Denver Post*. Available, http://www.denverpost.com/theatershooting/ci_21130020/aurora-police-chief-gunman-acted-calculation-and-deliberation

Culbertson, Tucker (2007). Arguments against Marriage Equality: Commemorating & Reconstructing Loving v. Virginia. *Washington University Law Review 85*, 575–609.

Cummins, Joseph (2016, February 17). This Is the Dirtiest Presidential Race Since '72. *Politico*. Available, http://www.politico.com/magazine/story/2016/02/2016-elections-nastiest-presidential-election-since-1972-213644

Curl, Joseph (2014, August 31). With Islamic State, 9/11 Anniversary, Obama's Incompetence Is Truly Dangerous. *The Washington Times*. Available, http://www.washingtontimes.com/news/2014/aug/31/curl-with-islamic-state-911-anniversary-obamas-inc/

Daly, Michael, Justin Miller, Katie Zavadski, and Shane Harris (2016, June 12). Omar Mateen, Terrorist Who Attacked Orlando Gay Club, Had Been Investigated by FBI. *The Daily Beast*. Available, http://www.thedailybeast.com/articles/2016/06/12/omar-mateen-id-d-as-orlando-killer.html

Dara, Khurram (2014, May 28). Muslim is the New Catholic. *The Huffington Post*. Available, http://www.huffingtonpost.com/khurram-dara/muslim-is-the-new-catholi_b_5399801.html

Darsey, James (2001). From "Gay Is Good" to the Scourge of AIDS: The Evolution of Gay Liberation Rhetoric, 1977–1990. In Charles E. Morris III & Stephen Howard Browne (Eds.), *Readings on the Rhetoric of Social Protest* (pp. 301–325). State College, PA: Strata.

Davenport, Kelsey (2016, August). Timeline of Nuclear Diplomacy with Iran. *Arms Control Association*. Available, https://www.armscontrol.org/factsheet/Timeline-of-Nuclear-Diplomacy-With-Iran

Davidson, Amy (2013, February 28). In Voting Rights, Scalia Sees a "Racial Entitlement." *The New Yorker*. Available, http://www.newyorker.com/news/amy-davidson/in-voting-rights-scalia-sees-a-racial-entitlement

Davidson, Lee, Elaine Jarvik, Lois M. Collins, and Chuck Gates (2010, June 28). Fact or Fiction? The Myths and Realities of Illegal Immigration. *Deseret News*. Available, http://www.deseretnews.com/article/700043538/Fact-or-fiction-The-myths-and-realities-of-illegal-immigration.html?pg=all

Davidson, Osha Gray (1993). *Under Fire: The NRA & the Battle for Gun Control*. New York: Henry Holt and Company.

Davies, Garth, and Jeffrey Fagan (2012, May). Crime and Enforcement in Immigrant Neighborhoods: Evidence from New York City. *The Annals of the American Academy of Political and Social Science, 641*, 99–124.

Davis, Julie Hirschfeld (2017, January 25). Trump Orders Mexican Border Wall to Be Built and Plans to Block Syrian Refugees. *The New York Times*. Available, https://www.nytimes.com/2017/01/25/us/politics/refugees-immigrants-wall-trump.html

Davis, Julie Hirschfeld, David E. Sanger, and Maggie Haberman (2017, January 24). Trump to Order Mexican Border Wall and Curtail Immigration. *The New York Times*. Available, https://www.nytimes.com/2017/01/24/us/politics/wall-border-trump.html?_r=0

Davis, Zac (2015, September 23). Vice President Biden's Comments about Abortion in America Interview Kick Off New Conversations. *America Magazine*. Available, http://www.americamagazine.org/content/all-things/biden-interview-starts-new-conversations-abortion-debate

Dawsey, Josh (2017, February 21). Trump Forgets His Obama Criticisms. *Politico*. Available, http://www.politico.com/story/2017/02/trump-obama-golf-235217

DeBonis, Mike, Adam Entous, Greg Jaffe, and Abby Phillip (2017, April 7). 'Awful' Images of Suffering in Syria Moved Trump to Strike, Advisers Say. *Chicago Tribune*. Available, http://www.chicagotribune.com/news/nationworld/politics/ct-trump-syria-airstrikes-20170407-story.html

DeBrabander, Firmin (2015). *Do Guns Make Us Free?: Democracy and the Armed Society*. New Haven, CT: Yale University Press.

de Certeau, Michel (1988). *The Practice of Everyday Life*. Berkeley: University of California Press.

de Gastyne, Joshua (2014, May 8). Medicaid: Half of Doctors Won't Accept New Patients. *The Daily Signal*. Available, http://dailysignal.com/2014/05/08/medicaid-half-doctors-wont-accept-new-patients/

Delaney, Arthur and Alissa Scheller (2015, February 28). Who Gets Food Stamps? White People, Mostly. *The Huffington Post*. Available, http://www.huffingtonpost.com/2015/02/28/food-stamp-demographics_n_6771938.html?ncid=fcbklnkushpmg00000013

de Laureal, Ryan (2015, January 13). The Media's One-Trick Pony. *Socialist Worker*. Available, http://socialistworker.org/2015/01/13/the-medias-one-trick-pony

deLespinasse, Paul F. (2003, May 15). Illegal Immigration Solutions. *ProCon.org*. Available, http://immigration.procon.org/view.answers.php?questionID=000786

Del Gandio, Jason (2008). *Rhetoric for Radicals: A Handbook for 21st Century Activists*. Gabriola Island, British Columbia: New Society Publishers.

Delmore, Erin (2014, April 28). Palin: Gun Free Zones Are Stupid on Steroids. *All In with Chris Hayes*. Available, http://www.msnbc.com/all/sarah-palin-gun-free-zones-stupid-steroids

D'Emilio, John (2007). Will the Courts Set Us Free? Reflections on the Campaign for Same-Sex Marriage. In Craig A. Rimmerman & Clyde Wilcox (Eds.), *The Politics of Same-Sex Marriage* (pp. 39–64). London: University of Chicago Press.

D'Emilio, John (2009, May–June). LGBT Liberation: Build a Broad Movement (John D'Emilio interview by Sherry Wolf). *International Socialist Review 65*, 21–22.

Department of Health & Human Services (2014, July). *About the Law*. Available, http://www.hhs.gov/healthcare/rights/

Derrida, Jacques (1994). *The Politics of Friendship* (George Collins, Trans.). London: Verso.

Dershowitz, Alan (2015). *The Case against the Iran Deal: How Can We Now Stop Iran from Getting Nukes?* New York: Rosetta Press.

Desiderio, Andrew (2014, November 25). Megyn Kelly: Sharpton 'Stoked the Fires,' Gave 'Misinformation' to Ferguson Protestors. *Mediaite*. Available, http://www.mediaite.com/tv/megyn-kelly-sharpton-stoked-the-fires-gave-misinformation-to-ferguson-protestors/

Detrow, Scott (2017, March 9). Paul Ryan Sells Health Care Bill as a 'Once-In-A-Lifetime Opportunity.' *NPR*. Available, http://www.npr.org/2017/03/09/519484050/paul-ryan-sells-health-care-bill-as-a-once-in-a-lifetime-opportunity

DeVega, Chauncey (2016, July 14). Sorry Conservatives, New Research from Harvard Shows a Profound Amount of Racism by Police … Not Less of It. *Salon*. Available, http://www.salon.com/2016/07/14/sorry_conservatives_new_research_from_harvard_shows_a_profound_amount_of_racism_by_policenot_less_of_it/

de Vogue, Ariane (2016, December 6). Supreme Court Tackles Racial Gerrymander Cases. *CNN Politics*. Available, http://www.cnn.com/2016/12/05/politics/supreme-court-gerrymandered-districts/

Dewan, Shaila (2013, June 11). Discrimination in Housing Against Nonwhites Persists Quietly, U.S. Study Finds. *The New York Times*. Available, http://www.nytimes.com/2013/06/12/business/economy/discrimination-in-housing-against-nonwhites-persists-quietly-us-study-finds.html

DeWeese, Tom (2014, February 18). ObamaCare: The Terrifying Consequences to Healthcare. *The New American*. Available, http://www.thenewamerican.com/reviews/opinion/item/17656-obamacare-the-terrifying-consequences-to-healthcare

Diamond, Jeremy (2015, August 19). Donald Trump: Birthright Babies Not Citizens. *CNN Politics*. Available, http://www.cnn.com/2015/08/19/politics/donald-trump-birthright-american-citizenship/

Diaz, Tom (2013). *The Last Gun: How Changes in the Gun Industry Are Killing Americans and What It Will Take to Stop It*. New York: The New Press.

Dickey, Christopher (2014, August 19). Medieval Cruelty in Modern Times: ISIS Thugs Behead American Journalist. *The Daily Beast*. Available, http://www.thedailybeast.com/articles/2014/08/19/medieval-cruelty-in-modern-times-isis-beheads-american-journalist.html

Dickey, Christopher (2017, April 5). Obama Was Right to Abandon 'Red Line' on Syria's Chemical Weapons. *The Daily Beast*. Available, http://www.thedailybeast.com/articles/2017/04/05/obama-was-right-to-abandon-red-line-on-syria-s-chemical-weapons.html

DiFonzo, Nicholas (2011, April 21). The Echo-Chamber Effect. *The New York Times*. Available, http://www.nytimes.com/roomfordebate/2011/04/21/barack-obama-and-the-psychology-of-the-birther-myth/the-echo-chamber-effect

Dimaggio, Paul, John Evans, and Bethany Bryson (1996). Have Americans' Social Attitudes Become More Polarized? *American Journal of Sociology 102*(3), 690–755.

Dimock, Michael, Carroll Doherty, Jocelyn Kiley, and Vidya Krishnamurthy (2014, June 26). Beyond Red vs. Blue: The Political Typology. *Pew Research Center*. Available, http://www.people-press.org/files/2014/06/6-26-14-Political-Typology-release.pdf

Dimock, Michael, Carroll Doherty, Jocelyn Kiley, and Russ Oates (2014, June 12). Political Polarization in the American Public: How Increasing Ideological Uniformity and Partisan Antipathy Affect Politics, Compromise and Everyday Life. *Pew Research Center*. Available, http://www.people-press.org/files/2014/06/6-12-2014-Political-Polarization-Release.pdf

Dinan, Stephen (2015, October 30). Feds Say 179,027 Criminal Illegals Are Loose on U.S. Streets. *The Washington Times*. Available, http://www.washingtontimes.com/news/2015/oct/30/feds-say-179027-criminal-illegals-are-loose-on-us-/

Dismay, Walt (2015, April 15). Fox News Wants Return of Racist 'Literacy Tests' because Why should THOSE People get to Vote? *Left Wing Nation*. Available, http://www.addictinginfo.org/2015/04/15/fox-news-wants-return-of-racist-literacy-tests-because-why-should-those-people-get-to-vote/

District of Columbia v. Heller. 554 U.S. 570 (2008).

Dizard, Jan E., Robert Merrill Muth, and Stephen P. Andrews, Jr., (Eds.) (1999). The Rise of Gun Culture in America: Introduction: Guns Made Us Free—Now What? *Guns in America: A Reader* (pp. 1–13). New York: New York University Press.

Dobbs, Lou (2014). *Upheaval*. New York: Threshold Editions.

Doc Vega (2013, January 12). The Leftist Assault on American Gun Owner Rights. *Politisite.com*. Available, http://www.politisite.com/2013/01/12/the-leftist-assault-on-american-gun-owner-rights/?relatedposts_exclude=73939

Doherty, Carroll and Rob Suls (2014, February 27). Public Divided over Increased Deportation of Unauthorized Immigrants. *Pew Research Center for the People & the Press*. Available, http://www.people-press.org/2014/02/27/public-divided-over-increased-deportation-of-unauthorized-immigrants/

Doherty, Carroll, Alec Tyson, and Rachel Weisel (2014). From ISIS to Unemployment: What Do Americans Know? *Pew Research Center*. Available, http://www.people-press.org/2014/10/02/from-isis-to-unemployment-what-do-americans-know/

Dohrn, Bernardine (2015, March 4). Youth Resistance Unleashed. *Portside*. Available, http://portside.org/2015-03-18/youth-resistance-unleashed

Dolan, Eric W. (2014, December 2). Black Congresswoman: Decision not to Indict Darren Wilson Was a 'Slap in Our Face.' *Raw Story*. Available, http://www.rawstory.com/rs/2014/12/black-congresswoman-decision-not-to-indict-darren-wilson-was-a-slap-in-our-face/

Dolan, Peter (2013). An Uneasy Union: Same-Sex Marriage and Religious Exemption in Washington State. *Washington Law Review* 88, 1119–1152.

Donohue, John J. (2004). Guns, Crime, and the Impact of State Right-To-Carry Laws. *Fordham Law Review* 73(2), 623–652.

Donovan, Chuck (2011, May 5). An Especially Timely National Day of Prayer. *The National Review*. Available, http://www.nationalreview.com/corner/266458/especially-timely-national-day-prayer-chuck-donovan

Douglas, William O. (1970). *Walz v. Tax Commission of the City of New York*. 397 U.S. 664 (1970). (pp. 700–728).

DPCC (2009, November 19). The Patient Protection and Affordable Care Act Detailed Summary. *Responsible Reform for the Middle Class*. Available, http://www.dpc.senate.gov/healthreformbill/healthbill04.pdf

DPCC (2011, March 16). Republicans' Reckless Plans Would Drive Up Drug Prices for Seniors, Put Sick Kids at Risk and Explode Our Deficit. *The Democratic Policy & Communications Center*. Available, http://www.dpcc.senate.gov/?p=issue&id=57

Dreier, Peter (2013). Massacres and Movements: Challenging the Gun Industrial Complex. *New Labor Forum* 22(2), 92–95.

Duberman, Martin (1993). *Stonewall*. New York: Plume.

Dunn, Geoffrey (2011). *The Lies of Sarah Palin: The Untold Story Behind Her Relentless Quest for Power*. New York: St. Martin's Press.

Dvorsky, George (2016, November 9). Donald Trump Is about to Declare War on Women's Bodies. *Gizmodo*. Available, http://gizmodo.com/donald-trump-is-about-to-declare-war-on-women-s-bodies-1788774127

Earls, Anita (2015, March 6). New Strict Voter ID Laws Challenged in Court. *Bill Moyers & Company*. Available, http://billmoyers.com/2015/03/06/challenges-voter-id-laws-national-perspective/

Easley, Jason (2015, March 13). President Obama Tears Apart Senate Republicans for Sending Treasonous Iran Letter. *Politicus USA*. Available, http://www.politicususa.com/2015/03/13/president-obama-tears-senate-republicans-sending-treasonous-iran-letter.html

Easterbrook, Frank H. (2011, April 14). *Freedom from Religion Foundation, Inc., v. Obama*, No. 10–973. Chief Judge, United States Court of Appeals for the Seventh Circuit. Available, http://ffrf.org/uploads/legal/A1180676.PDF

Eastland, Terry (1997). *Ending Affirmative Action: The Case for Colorblind Justice*. New York: Basic Books.

Economy, Elizabeth C., Joshua Kurlantzick, and Robert D. Blackwill (2017, April 14). *Territorial Disputes in the South China Sea*. Council on Foreign Relations. Available, http://www.cfr.org/global/global-conflict-tracker/p32137#!/conflict/territorial-disputes-in-the-south-china-sea

Edelman, Adam (2015, August 10). President Obama's Iran Nuclear Deal Is Proof that We Are Living in Bible's 'End of Days,' Former Rep. Michele Bachmann Claims. *New York Daily News*. Available, http://www.nydailynews.com/news/politics/iran-nuke-deal-proff-biblical-times-bachmann-article-1.2320818

Edge, Sami and Sean Holstege (2016, August 20). Voter Fraud Is Not a Persistent Problem. *Voting Wars*. Available, https://votingwars.news21.com/voter-fraud-is-not-a-persistent-problem/

Edwards v. Aquillard. 107 S. Ct. 2573 (1987).

Edwards, David (2013, January 15). Coulter: 'Not a Gun Problem,' U.S. Has 'Demographic Problem' with Non-Whites. *Raw Story*. Available, http://www.rawstory.com/rs/2013/01/15/coulter-not-a-gun-problem-u-s-has-demographic-problem-with-non-whites/

Edwards, David (2015, April 15). Fox and Ann Coulter Prep for 2016: Brink Back 'Literacy Tests' so Voting is "a Little More Difficult.' *Raw Story*. Available, http://www.rawstory.com/rs/2015/04/fox-and-ann-coulter-prep-for-2016-bring-back-literacy-tests-so-voting-is-a-little-more-difficult/

Edwards, Jane (2007). 'Marriage Is Sacred': The Religious Right's Arguments against 'Gay Marriage' in Australia. *Culture, Health & Sexuality* 9(3), 247–261.

Egberto Willies (2014, May 25). Michael Moore on UC Santa Barbara Shootings: "Guns Don't Kill People—Americans Kill People. Available, http://egbertowillies.com/2014/05/25/michael-moore-elliot-rodger-killing-guns/

Eichenwald, Kurt (2016, May 3). Don't Blame Trump: American Democracy Was Broken before He Muscled In. *Newsweek*. Available, http://www.newsweek.com/2016/05/13/american-democracy-electorate-voters-election-2016-donald-trump-454655.html

Einenkel, Walter (2016, July 7). Former Congressman Calls for Revenge against Obama and Black Lives Matter for Dallas Shooting. *The Daily Kos*. Available, http://www.dailykos.com/story/2016/7/7/1546262/-Ex-Congressman-calls-for-revenge-against-President-Obama-and-Black-Lives-Matter-for-Dallas-shooting

Eisenstadt v. Baird. 405 U.S. 438 (1972).

El-Ad, Hagai (2015, May 31). Israel's Charade of Democracy. *The New York Times*. Available, https://www.nytimes.com/2015/06/01/opinion/israels-charade-of-democracy.html

Elder, Larry (2014, November 28). Ferguson Obscures Much Bigger Problems in the 'Black Community.' *Washington Examiner*. Available, http://www.washingtonexaminer.com/ferguson-obscures-much-bigger-problems-in-the-black-community/article/2556738

Elder, Larry (2016, July 14). Ignorance of Facts Fuels the Anti-Cop 'Movement.' *Creators*. Available, https://www.creators.com/read/larry-elder/07/16/ignorance-of-facts-fuels-the-anti-cop-movement

Elliott, Philip (2016, June 13). What Caused Orlando? Hillary Clinton Blames Guns. Donald Trump Blames Immigration. *Time*. Available, http://time.com/4367193/orlando-shooting-hillary-clinton-donald-trump-speeches/

Ellis, Christopher and James A. Stimson (2012). *Ideology in America*. Boston: Cambridge University Press.

Embury-Dennis, Tom (2017, March 31). North Korea Threatens War with US after John McCain Brands Kim Jong-un a 'Crazy Fat Kid.' *The Independent*. Available, http://www.independent.co.uk/news/world/asia/north-korea-john-mccain-kim-jong-un-crazy-fat-kid-war-us-threat-a7658616.html

Employment Division, Department of Human Resources of Oregon vs. Smith. 494 U.S. 872 (1990).

Endres, Danielle (2015). American Indian Permission for Mascots: Resistance or Complicity within Rhetorical Colonialism? *Rhetoric & Public Affairs*, *18*(4), 649–689.

Engel v. Vitale. 82 S. Ct. 1261 (1962).

Engles, Jeremy (2012). The Rhetoric of Violence: Sarah Palin's Response to the Tucson Shooting. *Symplokē 20*(1–2), 121–138.

Enwemeka, Zeninjor (2016, September 24). Mass. High Court Says Black Men May Have Legitimate Reason to Flee Police. *WBUR News*. Available, http://www.wbur.org/news/2016/09/20/mass-high-court-black-men-may-have-legitimate-reason-to-flee-police

Epperson v. Arkansas. 89 S. Ct. 266 (1968).

Epps, Garrett (2014, May 5). With the Supreme Court's Help, Religion Creeps toward the State. *The Atlantic*. Available, http://www.theatlantic.com/politics/archive/2014/05/with-the-supreme-courts-help-religion-creeps-toward-the-state-town-of-greece/361754/.

Epstein, Jennifer (2014, August 26). Obama Vows to Remove ISIL 'Cancer.' *Politico*. Available, http://www.politico.com/story/2014/08/obama-isil-james-foley-110352

Erickson, Erick (2015, September 4). That Drowned Syrian Boy on the Beach Is Obama's Fault. *Fox News*. Available, http://www.foxnews.com/opinion/2015/09/04/that-drowned-syrian-boy-is-obamas-fault.html

Esbeck, Carl E. (2014, May 5). Why I'm Not Cheering Today's Supreme Court Prayer Decision. *Christianity Today*. Available, http://www.christianitytoday.com/ct/2014/may-web-only/carl-esbeck-supreme-court-prayer-greece-galloway.html

Eskridge, Jr., William N. (1996). *The Case for Same-Sex Marriage: From Sexual Liberty to Civilized Commitment*. New York: The Free Press.

Eskridge, Jr., William N. (2004). Yale Law School and the Overruling of *Bowers v. Hardwick*. *Yale Law Review*, winter, 36–39.

Essed, Philomena (1991). *Understanding Everyday Racism: An Interdisciplinary Theory*. Newbury Park, CA: Sage.

Essed, Philomena (2002). Everyday Racism: A New Approach to the Study of Racism. In David Theo Goldberg and John Solomos (Eds.), *A Companion to Racism and Ethnic Studies* (pp. 202–216). Oxford, UK: Blackwell.

Estepa, Jessica (2017a, March 17). Awkward: Merkel Asks for a Handshake, Trump Doesn't Respond. *USA Today*. Available, https://www.usatoday.com/story/news/politics/onpolitics/2017/03/17/angela-merkel-donald-trump-handshake/99310398/

Estepa, Jessica (2017b, March 6). Ben Carson Refers to Slaves as Immigrants. *MSN News*. Available, http://www.msn.com/en-us/news/politics/ben-carson-refers-to-slaves-as-immigrants/ar-AAnUe9i

Estrich, Susan (2006). *Soulless: Ann Coulter and the Right-Wing Church of Hate*. New York: Harper Collins.

Ettelbrick, Paula L. (1989). Since When Is Marriage a Path to Liberation? *OUT/LOOK, National Gay and Lesbian Quarterly*, fall, issue 6.

Evans, John H. (2003). Have Americans' Attitudes become More Polarized? An Update. *Social Science Quarterly 84*(1), 71–90.

Everson v. Board of Education. 330 U.S. 1 (1947).

Fahmy, Shahira, James D. Kelly, and Yung Soo Kim (2007). What Katrina Revealed: A Visual Analysis of the Hurricane Coverage by News Wires and U.S. Newspapers. *Journalism & Mass Communication Quarterly*, *84*(3), 546–561.

Fahrenthold, David A. (2012, December 15). Sunset Clauses Are Commonly Passed but Rarely Followed Through. *The Washington Post*. Available, https://www.washingtonpost.com/politics/in-congress-sunset-clauses-are-commonly-passed-but-rarely-followed-through/2012/12/15/9d8e3ee0-43b5-11e2-8e70-e1993528222d_story.html?utm_term=.e4b1af44342e

Faiez, Rahim (2017, April 15). Afghan Official: Massive US Bomb Death Toll Rises to 94 Militants. *ABC News*. Available, http://abcnews.go.com/International/wireStory/afghan-official-massive-us-bomb-dead-toll-rise-46813354

FAIR (2013). Illegal Aliens Taking U.S. Jobs. *Federation for American Immigration Reform*. Available, http://www.fairus.org/issue/illegal-aliens-taking-u-s-jobs

Family Research Institute (2009, February 3). Getting the Facts: Same-Sex Marriage. *Family Research Report*. Available, http://www.familyresearchinst.org/category/pamphlets/

Family Research Institute (2013a, April). Attention Boy Scouts! Evidence Links Molestation to Homosexuality. *Family Research Report*. Available, http://www.familyresearchinst.org/2014/01/frr-apr-2013-evidence-links-molestation-to-homosexuality/

Family Research Institute (2013b, February). Does Protecting Homosexuals = Protecting Pedophiles? *Family Research Report*. Available, http://www.familyresearchinst.org/2014/01/frr-feb-2013-protecting-homosexuals-protecting-pedophiles/

Family Research Institute (2013c, November). Homosexual Interests and 'Fixation.' *Family Research Report*. Available, http://www.familyresearchinst.org/2014/01/frr-nov-2013-homosexual-interests-and-fixation/

Family Research Institute (2013d, November). Pakistan—Steeped in Homosexuality and Violence. *Family Research Report*. Available, http://www.familyresearchinst.org/2014/01/frr-nov-2013-homosexual-interests-and-fixation/

Family Research Institute (2014, March). Are Gay Parents more Apt to Commit Incest? *Family Research Report*. Available, http://www.familyresearchinst.org/2014/04/frr-mar-2014-are-gay-parents-more-apt-to-commit-incest/#more-1180

Fanelli, Carlo (2014). Climate Change: 'The Greatest Challenge of Our Time.' *Alternate Routes 25*(1), 15–31.

Fang, Lee (2015, March 9). Immediately after Launching Effort to Scuttle Iran Deal, Senator Tom Cotton to Meet with Defense Contractors. *The Intercept*. Available, https://firstlook.org/theintercept/2015/03/09/upon-launching-effort-scuttle-iran-deal-senator-tom-cotton-meets-defense-contractors/

Fang, Marina (2015, April 21). Michele Bachmann: The Rapture Is Coming and It's Obama's Fault. *The Huffington Post*. Available, http://www.huffingtonpost.com/2015/04/20/michele-bachmann-obama-rapture_n_7104136.html

Fantz, Ashley and Catherine E. Shoichet (2015, December 28). Tamir Rice Shooting: No Charges for Officers. *CNN*. Available, http://www.cnn.com/2015/12/28/us/tamir-rice-shooting/

Feagin, Joe, R. (2013). *The White Racial Frame: Centuries of Racial Framing and Counter-Framing*. New York: Routledge.

Fearnside, W. Ward and William B. Holther (1959). *Fallacy: The Counterfeit of Argument*. Englewood Cliffs, NJ: Spectrum/Prentice Hall.

Feeney, Nolan (2015, September 7). Sarah Palin Wants Immigrants to 'Speak American.' *Time*. Available, http://time.com/4024396/sarah-palin-speak-american-energy-department/

Feinstein, Dianne et al. (2014, January 15). *Review of the Terrorist Attacks on U.S. Facilities in Benghazi, Libya, September 11–12, 2012*. U.S. Senate Select Committee on Intelligence. Available, https://www.intelligence.senate.gov/sites/default/files/publications/113134.pdf

Ferdman, Roberto A. (2014, September 4). One Reason Democrats Are so scared of Obama's Promise to Act on Immigration. *The Washington Post*. Available, http://www.washingtonpost.com/blogs/wonkblog/wp/2014/09/04/one-reason-democrats-are-so-scared-of-obamas-promise-to-act-on-immigration/

Fernandez, Nick (2016, August 12). Fox News Is Wrong: Trump Is a Terrorist Recruiting Tool. *Media Matters for America*. Available, https://mediamatters.org/research/2016/08/12/fox-news-wrong-trump-terrorist-recruiting-tool/212366

Ferner, Matt (2014, August 14). LAPD Shouted 'Shoot Him' before Killing Unarmed, Mentally Ill Black Man. *The Huffington Post*. Available, http://www.huffingtonpost.com/2014/08/13/lapd-suggests-mentally-il_0_n_5675782.html

Filipovic, Jill (2017, April 7). Hey, Trump: If You Really Cared, You'd Welcome Syrian Refugees. *Cosmopolitan*. Available, http://www.cosmopolitan.com/politics/a9246512/syria-missile-strikes-donald-trump-refugees/

Finlayson, Alan (2012). Rhetoric and the Political Theory of Ideologies. *Political Studies 60*(4), 751–767.

Finney, Karen (2014, December 3). Conservative Media Still Denying How Racism and History Fueled Ferguson. *Media Matters for America*. Available, http://mediamatters.org/blog/2014/12/03/conservative-media-still-denying-how-racism-and/201751

Fiorina, Morris (2011). *Culture War? The Myth of a Polarized America* (3rd ed.). New York: Longman.

Fisher v. University of Texas (2013). 570 U.S. ___. Available, https://supreme.justia.com/cases/federal/us/570/11-345/

Fleras, Augie (2016). Theorizing Micro-aggressions as Racism 3.0: Shifting the Discourse. *Canadian Ethnic Studies, 48*(2), 1–19.

Flournoy, Don M., and Robert K. Stewart (1997). *CNN: Making News in the Global Market*. London: University of Luton Press.

Foley, Elise (2014, August 22). Civil Rights Groups Sue over Treatment of Mothers in Deportation Proceedings. *The Huffington Post*. Available, http://www.huffingtonpost.com/2014/08/22/aclu-lawsuit-detention_n_5701044.html?ncid=fcbklnkushpmg00000013

Follman, Mark and Williams, Lauren (2013, July 19). Actually, Stand Your Ground Played a Major Role in the Trayvon Martin Case. *Mother Jones*. Available, http://www.motherjones.com/politics/2013/07/stand-your-ground-george-zimmerman-trayvon-martin

Fondacaro, Nicholas (2017, March 12). NBC's Politics 'Referee' Mocks GOP Criticisms of ObamaCare, Compares to Sports Talk. *News Busters*. Available, http://www.newsbusters.org/blogs/nb/nicholas-fondacaro/2017/03/12/nbcs-referee-mocks-gop-criticisms-obamacare-compares-sports

Forbes, Stefan (Producer) (2008). Boogie Man: The Lee Atwater Story. *PBS Frontline*. Available, http://www.pbs.org/wgbh/pages/frontline/atwater/

Foreman, Kelsey, Cecilia Arteaga, and Aushawna Collins (2016). The Role of Media Framing in Crime Reports: How Different Types of News Frames and Racial Identity Affect Viewers' Perceptions of Race. *Pepperdine Journal of Communication Research, 4*(12), Available, http://digitalcommons.pepperdine.edu/cgi/viewcontent.cgi?article=1039&context=pjcr

Foster, Stephen D., Jr. (2014, November 28). Ted Nugent Goes Full Racist about Ferguson Protesters and the Black Community. *Addicting Info*. Available, http://www.addictinginfo.org/2014/11/28/ted-nugent-goes-full-racist-on-social-media-about-ferguson-protesters-and-the-black-community-images/

Foucault, Michel (1982). *The Archaeology of Knowledge*. New York: Vintage.

Franck, Thomas M. (1992). The Emerging Right to Democratic Governance. *The American Journal of International Law, 86*(1), 46–91.

Frank, Dana (2015, June 1). US Underwrites Corruption and Violence in Honduras. *Al Jazeera America*. Available, http://america.
aljazeera.com/opinions/2015/6/us-underwrites-corruption-and-violence-in-honduras.html#sthash.dAnwNYxb.dpuf

Frea, Rick (2010, July 3). The True Meaning of the Statue of Liberty. *Freedom Nation*. Available, http://freadomnation.blogspot.
com/2010/07/true-meaning-of-statue-of-liberty.html

Freedom Daily (2017, February 24). Welfare Queen goes Crazy after She Sees this Sign at Grocery Store. *Freedom Daily*. Available,
http://freedomdaily.com/welfare-queen-goes-crazy-after-she-sees-this-sign-at-grocery-store/

Freedom from Religion Foundation v. John Hickenlooper (2012, May 10). Colorado Court of Appeals, No. 10CA2559. Available, http://
ffrf.org/uploads/legal/CAOpinion.pdf

Freedom from Religion Foundation, Inc., v. Obama, No. 10-973. (2011, April 14). 7th Circuit of Appeals, Wisconsin. Available, http://
ffrf.org/uploads/legal/A1180676.PDF

Freeman, Antiphon (2015, September 21). White House Releases Official Statement, Calls the Entire
Republican Party Racist. *Addicting Info*. Available, http://www.addictinginfo.org/2015/09/21/
white-house-releases-official-statement-calls-the-entire-republican-party-racist-video/

Free Thought Today (2013, June/July). Politicking Churches Get Free Pass. *The Free Thought Today*. Available, http://ffrf.org/
publications/freethought-today/item/18457-politicking-churches-get-free-pass

French, David (2017, January 20). Can America's Divides Be Healed? *National Review*. Available, http://www.nationalreview.com/
article/444064/donald-trump-political-polarization-problem-too-big-one-man-fix

French, David (2017, January 28). Trump's Executive Order on Refugees—Separating Fact
from Hysteria. *National Review*. Available, http://www.nationalreview.com/article/444370/
donald-trump-refugee-executive-order-no-muslim-ban-separating-fact-hysteria

Fretheim, Kjetil (2012). The Power of Invitation: The Moral Discourse of Kairos Palestine. *Dialog: A Journal of Theology*, 51(2),
135–144.

Fridell, Lorie (2015, May 26). Why Do US Police Keep Killing Unarmed Black Men? *BBC News*. Available, http://www.bbc.com/
news/world-us-canada-32740523

Fritsch, Jane (2000, February 26). The Diallo Verdict: The Overview; 4 Officers in Diallo Shooting Are Acquitted of All Charges. *The
New York Times*. Available, http://www.nytimes.com/2000/02/26/nyregion/diallo-verdict-overview-4-officers-diallo-shooting-
are-acquitted-all-charges.html

Frostenson, Sarah (2016, September 9). Most Terrorist Attacks in the US are Committed by Americans—Not Foreigners. *Vox*.
Available, http://www.vox.com/2015/11/23/9765718/domestic-terrorism-threat

Fryer, Roland G., Jr. (2016, July). An Empirical Analysis of Racial Differences in Police Use of Force. The National Bureau of
Economic Research (NBER). *NBER Working Paper No. 22399*. Available, http://www.nber.org/papers/w22399

Gabriel, Brigitte (2008). *Because They Hate: A Survivor of Islamic Terror Warns America*. New York: St. Martin's Griffin.

Gabrielson, Ryan, Ryann Grochowski Jones & Eric Sagara (2014, October 10). Deadly Force, in Black and White. *The Huffington Post*.
Available, http://www.huffingtonpost.com/2014/10/10/racial-disparity-police-killings_n_5965706.html?ncid=fcbklnkushpmg00
000013&ir=Politics

Galinsky, Adam D., Cynthia S. Wang, Jennifer A. Whitson, Eric M. Anicich, Kurt Hugenberg, and Galen V. Bodenhausen (2013).
The Reappropriation of Stigmatizing Labels: The Reciprocal Relationship between Power and Self-Labeling. *Psychological Science*
24(10), 2020–2029.

Gallagher, Maggie (2010, May 5). Sarah Palin's Girl Power. *Real Clear Politics*. Available, http://www.realclearpolitics.com/
articles/2010/05/20/sarah_palins_girl_power_105650.htmlU

Gallup (2016, September 22). Number of Americans Closely Following Politics Spikes. Available, http://www.gallup.com/poll/195749/
number-americans-closely-following-politics-spikes.aspx

Galston, William and Nivola, Pietro S. (2006). Delineating the Problem. In Pietro S. Nivola & David W. Brady (Eds.), *Red and Blue
Nation? Volume 1* (pp. 1–47). Washington, D.C.: Brookings Institution.

Gao, George (2014, August 11). 5 Facts about Honduras and Immigration. *Pew Research Fact Tank*. Available, http://www.
pewresearch.org/fact-tank/2014/08/11/5-facts-about-honduras-and-immigration/

Garcia, Arturo (2015, April 8). Michele Bachmann: Obama's Deal with Iran 'Virtually Guarantees' World War III. *Raw Story*.
Available, http://www.rawstory.com/2015/04/michele-bachmann-obamas-deal-with-iran-virtually-guarantees-world-war-iii/

Garcia, Monique, and Duaa Eldeib (2012, November 7). Duckworth Defeats Walsh in Congressional Contest. *Chicago Tribune*.
Available, http://articles.chicagotribune.com/2012-11-07/news/chi-duckworth-walsh-election-results-illinois-8th-
district-20121106_1_kaitlin-fahey-duckworth-campaign-manager-democrat-tammy-duckworth

Garcia, Tamyra Carroll, Amy B. Bernstein, and Mary Ann Bush (2010, May). *Emergency Department Visitors and Visits: Who Used the
Emergency Room in 2007?* NCHS Data Brief, no. 38. Available, http://www.cdc.gov/nchs/data/databriefs/db38.pdf

Garland, Sarah (2012, December 5). Was 'Brown v. Board' a Failure? *The Atlantic*. Available, https://www.theatlantic.com/national/
archive/2012/12/was-brown-v-board-a-failure/265939/

Garling, Scipio (2000). Immigration 101: A Primer on Immigration and the Need for Reform. *Federation for American Immigration
Reform*. Available, http://www.fairus.org/DocServer/immigration101.pdf

Garner, Joel H., and Christopher D. Maxwell (2002). *Understanding the Prevalence and Severity of Force Used By and Against the Police,
Executive Summary*. National Criminal Justice. Washington, DC: United States Department of Justice, National Institute of
Justice. Available, https://www.ncjrs.gov/pdffiles1/nij/grants/196693.pdf

Gartenstein-Ross, Daveed, Nathaniel Barr, and Bridget Moreng (2016, March). *The Islamic State's Global Propaganda Strategy*. International Centre for Counter-Terrorism—The Hague. Available, https://www.icct.nl/wp-content/uploads/2016/03/ICCT-Gartenstein-Ross-IS-Global-Propaganda-Strategy-March2016.pdf

Gauchet, Marcel (1996). Right and Left. In Pierre Nora (Ed.) & Arthur Goldhammer (Trans.), *Realms of Memory: Rethinking the French Past. Volume 1: Conflicts and Divisions* (pp. 241–299). New York. Columbia University Press.

Gayle, Damien (2015, February 9). Jordanian Pilot Who Was Burned to Death in Sickening ISIS Video 'Was so Heavily Sedated He Had No Idea What Was about to Happen to Him.' *Daily Mail*. Available, http://www.dailymail.co.uk/news/article-2946587/Jordanian-pilot-burned-death-sickening-ISIS-video-heavily-sedated-unaware-happen-him.html

Gearan, Anne, and Abby Phillip (2016, February 25). Clinton Regrets 1996 Remark on 'Super-Predators' after Encounter with Activist. *The Washington Post*. Available, https://www.washingtonpost.com/news/post-politics/wp/2016/02/25/clinton-heckled-by-black-lives-matter-activist/?utm_term=.a2fddd0273f1

Gelb, Leslie H. (2015, March 10). GOP Hates Obama more than a Nuclear Iran. *The Daily Beast*. Available, http://www.thedailybeast.com/articles/2015/03/10/open-letter-to-iran-shows-gop-senators-hate-obama-more-than-they-love-america.html?source=TDB&via=FB_Page

Gerber, Alan S., Gregory A. Huber, David Doherty, Conor M. Dowling, and Seth J. Hill (2013). Who Wants to Discuss Vote Choices with Others? Polarization in Preferences for Deliberation. *Public Opinion Quarterly* 77(2), 474–496.

Gerges, Fawaz A. (2016). ISIS and the Third Wave of Jihadism. In Glenn P. Hastedt (Ed.), *Readings in American Foreign Policy* (pp. 110–116). Lanham, MD: Rowman & Littlefield.

Germanos, Andrea (2016, January 30). UN Experts Catalog Seemingly Endless List of Racial Discrimination in US. *Common Dreams*. Available, https://portside.org/print/2016-01-30/un-experts-catalog-seemingly-endless-list-racial-discrimination-us

Germanos, Andrea (2017, March 6). "Still Unconstitutional": Critics Lambast Trump's Muslim Ban 2.0. *Common Dreams*. Available, http://www.commondreams.org/news/2017/03/06/still-unconstitutional-critics-lambast-trumps-muslim-ban-20

Gerney, Arkadi and Chelsea Parsons (2013, December 13). The Gun Debate 1 year after Newtown: Assessing Six Key Claims about Gun Background Checks. *The Center for American Progress*. Available, http://americanprogress.org/issues/guns-crime/report/2013/12/13/80795/the-gun-debate-1-year-after-newtown/

Gerney, Arkadi, Chelsea Parsons, and Charles Posner (2013, April). America under the Gun: A 50-State Analysis of Gun Violence and Its Link to Weak State Gun Laws. *The Center for American Progress*. Available, http://americanprogress.org/issues/civil-liberties/report/2013/04/02/58382/america-under-the-gun/

Giffords, Gabrielle, and Mark Kelly (2014). *Enough: Our Fight to Keep America Safe from Gun Violence*. New York: Simon & Schuster.

Gilchrist, Jim (2014a, August 26). Obama Executive Amnesty: 'Get Prepared.' *The Minuteman Project*. Available, http://minuteman-project.com/obama-executive-amnesty-get-prepared-5938

Gilchrist, Jim (2014b, August 11). Refugee Status for Illegal Alien Children Is a Myth. *The Minuteman Project*. Available, http://minutemanproject.com/refugee-status-for-illegal-alien-children-is-a-myth-5836

Giles v. Harris (1903). 189 U.S. 475. Available, https://supreme.justia.com/cases/federal/us/189/475/

Gill v. Office of Personnel Management. 1:09-cv-10309-JLT, U.S. Dist. Ct., Mass (2010, July 8).

Gill, Emily R. (2012). *An Argument for Same-Sex Marriage: Religious Freedom, Sexual Freedom, and Public Expressions of Civic Equality*. Washington, D.C.: Georgetown University Press.

Gillespie, Nick (2014, August 29). The Deep Roots of Obama's "We Don't Have a Strategy Yet" Problem—and What To Do Next. *Reason*. Available, http://reason.com/blog/2014/08/29/the-deep-roots-of-obamas-we-dont-have-a

Gillman, Todd J. (2017, January 25). Trump, Mocked for Debunked Claim of Massive Voter Fraud, Vows 'Major Investigation.' *Dallas Morning News*. Available, Lexis-Nexis.

Gingrich, Newt (2007a, April 5). Gingrich on English Language Newt Gingrich released an apology on YouTube.com for remarks he made about bilingual classes and ballots. *C-SPAN*. Available, https://www.c-span.org/video/?197505-1/gingrich-english-language

Gingrich, Newt (2007b, March 31). Newt Gingrich: Spanish Is Language of the Ghetto. *YouTube*. Uploaded 1/25/12. Available, https://www.youtube.com/watch?v=_rF694NzjPU

Gingrich, Newt (2013). Breakout: Pioneers of the Future, Prison Guards of the Past, and the Epic Battle That Will Decide America's Fate. New York: Regnery.

Glendon, Mary Ann (1991). *Rights Talk: The Impoverishment of Political Discourse*. New York: The Free Press.

Glink, Ilyce (2010, December 1). Tea Party: Don't Let Renters Vote. *CBS News*. Available, http://www.cbsnews.com/news/tea-party-dont-let-renters-vote/

Goldberg, Jeffrey (2009, March). Netanyahu to Obama: Stop Iran—Or I Will. *The Atlantic*. Available, https://www.theatlantic.com/magazine/archive/2009/03/netanyahu-to-obama-stop-iran-or-i-will/307390/

Golden, Karris (2013, March 8). Religious Groups' Tax Exemptions Cause Divisions. *WCF Courier*. Available, http://wcfcourier.com/lifestyles/faith-and-values/religious-groups-tax-exemptions-cause-division/article_1efb0c46-8741-11e2-9974-0019bb2963f4.html

Goldman, Dana P., James P. Smith, and Neeraj Sood (2006). Immigrants and the Cost of Medical Care. *Health Affairs*, 25(6), 1700-1711.

Goldman, Shalom (2015, July 30). The Iran Deal and the Power of Rhetoric. *IslamiCommentary*. Available, http://islamicommentary. org/2015/07/the-iran-deal-and-the-power-of-rhetoric-by-shalom-goldman/

Goldsborough, Reid (2011, January 10). 'Slacktivism' Is Becoming the New Activism. *Technology Today*, p. 13.

Gomez, Alan (2014 May 14). Government Released Hundreds of Immigrant Felons. *USA Today*. Available, http://www.usatoday.com/ story/news/nation/2014/05/14/immigration-releases-convicted-felons/9090557/

Gonshorowski, Drew (2014, May 14). What Happens If There Is No Employer Mandate for Obamacare? *The Daily Signal*. Available, http://dailysignal.com/2014/05/14/yes-employer-mandate-distorts-labor-markets/

Gonzalez-Barrera, Ana, Jens Manuel Krogstad, and Mark Hugo Lopez (2014, July 1). DHS: Violence, Poverty, Is Driving Children to Flee Central America to U.S. *Pew Research Center*. Available, http://www.pewresearch.org/fact-tank/2014/07/01/ dhs-violence-poverty-is-driving-children-to-flee-central-america-to-u-s/

Goodale, Gloria (2012, April 4). Keith Olbermann: The Cautionary Tale of Why He Was Fired, Again. *Christian Science Monitor*. Available, http://www.csmonitor.com/USA/Elections/Vox-News/2012/0404/ Keith-Olbermann-the-cautionary-tale-of-why-he-was-fired-again

Goodnough, Abby (2005, April 27). Florida Expands Right to Use Deadly Force in Self-Defense. *The New York Times*. Available, http://www.nytimes.com/2005/04/27/national/27shoot.html

Gooren, Louis (1990). Biomedical Theories of Sexual Orientation: A Critical Examination. In David P. McWhirter, Stephanie A. Sanders & June Machover Reinisch (Eds.), *Homosexuality/Heterosexuality: Concepts of Sexual Orientation* (pp. 71–87). New York: Oxford University Press.

Govtrack.us (2014). H.R. 972 (109th): Trafficking Victims Protection Reauthorization Act of 2005. Available, https://www.govtrack. us/congress/bills/109/hr972

Graham, David A. (2015, April 8). The Shockingly Familiar Killing of Walter Scott. *The Atlantic*. Available, https://www.theatlantic. com/national/archive/2015/04/the-shockingly-familiar-killing-of-walter-scott/390006/

Graham-Harrison, Emma (2017, April 5). Syria Chemical Weapons Attack: What We Know about Deadly Air Raid. *The Guardian*. Available, https://www.theguardian.com/world/2017/apr/05/syria-chemical-weapons-attack-what-we-know-khan-sheikhun

Gramsci, Antonio (1975). *History, Philosophy and Culture in the Young Gramsci* (P. Cavalcanti, & P. Piccone, Eds.). St. Louis: Telos Press.

Gratius, Susanne (2015, April 16). Cuban-US Relations 'Game Changer.' *The Parliament Magazine*. Available, https://www. theparliamentmagazine.eu/blog/cuban-us-relations-game-changer

Gratz v. Bollinger (2002). 539 U.S. 244. Available, https://www.law.cornell.edu/supct/html/02-516.ZO.html

Graves, Allison (2016, August 28). Did Hillary Clinton Call African-American Youth 'Superpredators?' *Politifact*. Available, http://www. politifact.com/truth-o-meter/statements/2016/aug/28/reince-priebus/did-hillary-clinton-call-african-american-youth-su/

Great Quail (2008, April 11). Obama's "Cling to Guns or Religion" Comment Is Being Misread! *Daily Kos*. Available, http://www. dailykos.com/story/2008/04/11/493923/-Obama-s-cling-to-guns-or-religion-comment-is-being-misread

Greenawalt, Kent (1983). *Discrimination and Reverse Discrimination*. New York: Borzoi Books.

Griffiths, James (2017, March 21). North Korea Rocket Engine Test: What Did We Learn? *CNN*. Available, http://www.cnn. com/2017/03/20/asia/north-korea-rocket-engine/

Grim, Ryan and Jeffrey Young (2014, July 22). Two Republican Judges Gut Obamacare, Threatening Health Care for Millions. *The Huffington Post*. Available, http://www.huffingtonpost.com/2014/07/22/republican-judges-obamacare-ruling-gutted_n_5609795. html?ncid=webmail1

Groer, Annie (2012, October 24). Indiana GOP Senate Hopeful Richard Mourdock Says God 'Intended' Rape Pregnancies. *The Washington Post*. Available, https://www.washingtonpost.com/blogs/she-the-people/wp/2012/10/24/ indiana-gop-senate-hopeful-richard-mourdock-says-god-intended-rape-pregnancies/?utm_term=.64abe94b38b9

Grogan, Stephanie C. (2011). The "N-Word:" The Use and Development of the Term "Nigger" in African-American Culture, as Depicted in the Plays of August Wilson. *Inquiries Journal: Social Sciences, Arts, & Humanities*, *3*(1). Available, http://www. inquiriesjournal.com/articles/357/the-n-word-the-use-and-development-of-the-term-nigger-in-african-american-culture-as-depicted-in-the-plays-of-august-wilson

Groshek, Jacob (2008). Homogenous Agendas, Disparate Frames: CNN and CNN International Coverage Online. *Journal of Broadcasting & Electronic Media*, *52*(1), 52–68.

Grutter v. Bollinger (2003). 539 U.S. 306. Available, https://supreme.justia.com/cases/federal/us/539/306/

Guerrero, Julian (2014, December 3). Hands Up, Walk Out! *Socialist Worker*. Available, http://socialistworker.org/2014/12/03/ hands-up-walk-out

Guide to the Syrian Rebels (2013, December 13). *BBC News*. Available, http://www.bbc.com/news/world-middle-east-24403003

Gutmann, Amy (2007). The Lure & Dangers of Extremist Rhetoric. *Daedalus 136*(4), 70–78.

Guttman, Nathan (2015, August 13). Fact-Checking the Flame Throwers on Both Sides of Iran Deal. *Forward*. Available, http:// forward.com/news/319072/fact-checking-the-flame-throwers-on-both-sides-of-iran-deal/

Hafner, Josh (2016, July 27). Why Black Lives Matter Doesn't Focus on 'Black-on-Black' Crime. *USA Today*. Available, http://www.usatoday.com/story/news/nation-now/2016/07/27/ why-doesnt-black-lives-matter-doesnt-focus-talk-about-black-black-crime/87609692/

Haider-Markel, Donald P. and Joslyn, Mark R. (2005). Attributions and the Regulation of Marriage: Considering the Parallels between Race and Homosexuality. *PS: Political Science and Politics 38*(2), 233–239.

Halbrook, Stephen P. (2000). Nazi Firearms Law and the Disarming of the German Jews. *Arizona Journal of International and Comparative Law 17*(3), 483–532.

Haley, Charly (2016, October 28). Voter Fraud Suspect Arrested in Des Moines. *The Des Moines Register.* Available, http://www. desmoinesregister.com/story/news/crime-and-courts/2016/10/28/voter-fraud-suspect-arrested-des-moines/92892042/

Hall, Alison V., Erika V. Hall, and Jamie L. Perry (2016). Black and Blue: Exploring Racial Bias and Law Enforcement in the Killings of Unarmed Black Male Civilians. *American Psychologist, 71*(3), 175–186.

Hall, Stuart (1986). Gramsci's Relevance to the Study of Race and Ethnicity. *Journal of Communication Inquiry 10*(2), 5–27.

Halley, Janet E. (1994). Sexual Orientation and the Politics of Biology: A Critique of the Argument from Immutability. *Stanford Law Review 46*, 503–568.

Hamer, Dean H., Stella Hu, Victoria L. Magnuson, Nan Hu, and Angela M. L. Pattatucci (1993). A Linkage between DNA Markers on the X Chromosome and Male Sexual Orientation. *Science 261*(5119), 321–327.

Hancocks, Paula, Barbara Starr, and Joshua Berlinger (2017, April 5). North Korea Fires Ballistic Missile, US State Department Says. *CNN.* Available, http://www.cnn.com/2017/04/04/asia/north-korea-projectile/

Hansen, Ronald J. (2013, November 2). Arizona Employer-Sanctions Law Seldom Used. *The Arizona Republic.* Available, http://archive.azcentral.com/business/news/articles/20131102arizona-employer-sanctions-law-seldom-used.html

Harcourt, Bernard E. (2004). On Gun Registration, the NRA, Adolf Hitler, and Nazi Gun Laws: Exploding the Gun Culture Wars. *Fordham Law Review 73*(1), 653–680.

Harden, Nathan (2014, March 24). Feminist Professor Who Attacked Pro-Life Student Charged with Criminal Battery. *The College Fix.* Available, http://www.thecollegefix.com/post/16817/

Hare, Breeanna (2016, August 9). How Did We get Here from Ferguson? *CNN.* Available, http://www.cnn.com/2016/08/09/us/ferguson-michael-brown-timeline/

Harp, Dustin, Jaime Loke, and Ingrid Bachmann (2010). First Impressions of Sarah Palin: Pit Bulls, Politics, Gender Performance, and a Discursive Media (Re)Contextualization. *Communication, Culture & Critique 3*(3), 291–309.

Hart, Andrew (2014, August 30). Sen. Dianne Feinstein: Obama 'Too Cautious' on ISIS. *The Huffington Post.* Available, http://www.huffingtonpost.com/2014/08/30/feinstein-obama-cautious-isis_n_5742552.html?ncid=fcbklnkushpmg00000013

Hart, Roderick P., Jay P. Childers, and Colene J. Lind (2013). *Political Tone: How Leaders Talk & Why.* Chicago: University of Chicago Press.

Harvard Law Review (2014). Developments in the Law: Sexual Orientation & Gender Identity. *Harvard Law Review, 127*(6), 1680–1814.

Harvard Law Review (2016, February 10). The Shooting of Samuel DuBose: University Police Officer Shoots and Kills Non-University-Affiliated Motorist During Off-Campus Traffic Stop. *Harvard Law Review, 129.* Available, http://harvardlawreview.org/2016/02/the-shooting-of-samuel-dubose/

Harvey, Linda (2014, June 4). 12 Ways Homosexual Adults Endanger Children. *Barbwire.com.* Available, http://barbwire.com/2014/06/04/twelve-ways-homosexual-adults-endanger-children/

Hassan, Carma and Holly Yan (2016, September 15). Sandra Bland's Family Settles for $1.9M in Wrongful Death Suit. *CNN.* Available, http://www.cnn.com/2016/09/15/us/sandra-bland-wrongful-death-settlement/

Hatt, Kyle (2011). Gun-shy originalism: The Second Amendment's Original Purpose in *District of Columbia v. Heller. Suffolk University Law Review 44*, 505–523.

Hattem, Julian (2014, April 26). NRA's LaPierre: 'We're the Good Guys.' *The Hill.* Available, http://thehill.com/blogs/blog-briefing-room/news/204461-nras-lapierre-were-the-good-guys

Hauslohner, Abigail, and Ahmed Ramadan (2013, December 24). In Syria, 'Barrel Bombs' Bring more Terror and Death to Aleppo. *The Washington Post.* Available, https://www.washingtonpost.com/world/middle_east/in-syria-barrel-bombs-bring-a-new-form-of-terror-and-death-to-aleppo/2013/12/23/6f8a7f0c-6bed-11e3-aecc-85cb037b7236_story.html?utm_term=.6ac03890f5b7

Hawkes, David (2003). *Ideology: The New Critical Idiom* (2nd ed.). London: Routledge.

Hawkins, Awr (2014, July 7). 80 Percent Drop in Deportation of Minors from Bust to Obama. *Breitbart.* Available, http://www.breitbart.com/Breitbart-California/2014/07/07/80-Percent-Drop-In-Deportation-of-Minors-From-Bush-To-Obama

Hayden, Sara (2009). Revitalizing the Debate between <Life> and <Choice>: The 2004 March for Women's Lives. *Communication and Critical/Cultural Studies 6*(2), 111–131.

Hayes, Danny (2005). Candidate Qualities through a Partisan Lens: A Theory of Trait Ownership. *American Journal of Political Science 49*(4), 908–923.

Hayward, John (2017, January 29). Seven Inconvenient Facts about Trump's Refugee Actions. *Breitbart.* Available, http://www.breitbart.com/big-government/2017/01/29/trumps-immigration-pause-sober-defenses-vs-hysterical-criticism/

Headlee, Celeste (2015, May) 10 Ways to Have a Better Conversation. *TED Talk.* Available, https://www.ted.com/talks/celeste_headlee_10_ways_to_have_a_better_conversation

Healy, Patrick (2006, November 30). Police Commissioner Looks Ahead, and Back. *The New York Times.* Available, http://www.nytimes.com/2006/11/30/nyregion/30kelly.html

Heath, Terrance (2015, June 19). Call It What It Is, or Be Complicit. *Portside.* Available, http://portside.org/2015-06-20/call-it-what-it-or-be-complicit

Heath, Terrance (2016, July 7). When Black Lives Don't Matter: Police Kill 136 Blacks Since January. *Our Future.* Available, https://ourfuture.org/20160707/when-black-lives-dont-matter-police-kill-136-blacks-since-january

Heatherington, Marc J. (2001). Resurgent Mass Partisanship: The Role of Elite Polarization. *The American Political Science Review* 95(3), 619–631.

Heatherington, Marc J. and Jonathan D. Weiler (2009). *Authoritarianism and Polarization in American Politics*. New York: Cambridge University Press.

Hebert, J. Gerald and Danielle Lang (2016, August 3). Courts Are Finally Pointing Out the Racism Behind Voter ID Laws. *The Washington Post*. Available, Lexis-Nexis.

Hedges, Chris (2006). *American Fascists: The Christian Right and the War on America*. New York: Free Press.

Hegeman, Susan (1989). Native American Texts' and the Problem of Authenticity. *American Quarterly*, 41(2), 265–83.

Heldman, Caroline (2010, August 25). The Truths of Katrina. *Pop Politics*. Available, https://carolineheldman.me/2010/08/25/the-truths-of-katrina/

Helsel, Phil (2016, July 8). 11 Dallas Officers Shot, 4 Dead in Shooting as Protest Ended. *Signs of the Times*. Available, https://www.sott.net/article/321696-11-Dallas-officers-shot-4-dead-in-shooting-as-protest-ended

Henigan, Dennis A. (2009). *Lethal Logic: Exploding the Myths that Paralyze American Gun Policy*. Dulles, VA: Potomac Books.

Hensch, Mark (2015, April 9). Bachmann: Obama's Foreign Policy 'Virtually Guarantees' World War III. *The Hill*. Available, http://thehill.com/blogs/blog-briefing-room/238366-bachmann-obamas-foreign-policy-virtually-guarantees-wwiii

Herbert, Frank (1965). *Dune*. Philadelphia: Chilton Books.

Herbst, Susan (2010). *Rude Democracy: Civility and Incivility in American Politics*. Philadelphia: Temple University Press.

Herek, Gregory (2006, October 18). Penguins, Pedophiles and Paul Cameron. *Beyond Homophobia* blog. Available, http://www.beyondhomophobia.com/blog/category/myths-stereotypes/

Herek, Gregory (2007a, June 26). Hate Crimes Hit 1 in 5 Sexual Minorities. *Beyond Homophobia* blog. Available, http://www.beyondhomophobia.com/blog/category/hate-crimes/

Herek, Gregory (2007b, September 13). Overkill in Alabama: All the Rage. *Beyond Homophobia* blog. Available, http://www.beyondhomophobia.com/blog/category/hate-crimes/

Herek, Gregory (2008, June 11). The Lawrence King Murder: Arraignment on Thursday. *Beyond Homophobia* blog. Available, http://www.beyondhomophobia.com/blog/category/hate-crimes/

Herek, Gregory (2009a, June 26). Public Opinion Supports Repealing "Don't Ask, Don't Tell." *Beyond Homophobia* blog. Available, http://www.beyondhomophobia.com/blog/category/polling-public-opinion/

Herek, Gregory M. (2009b). Sexual Stigma and Sexual Prejudice in the United States: A Conceptual Framework. In D.A. Hope (Ed.), *Contemporary Perspectives on Lesbian, Gay and Bisexual Identities: The 54th Nebraska Symposium on Motivation* (pp. 65–111). New York: Springer.

Heritage Center for Health Policy Studies (2013, October 31). After Repeal of Obamacare: Moving to Patient-Centered, Market-Based Health Care. *The Heritage Foundation Backgrounder*, no. 2847. Available, http://thf_media.s3.amazonaws.com/2013/pdf/BG2847.pdf

Herman, Didi (1997). *The Antigay Agenda: Orthodox Vision and the Christian Right*. Chicago: University of Chicago Press.

Hernandez, Rigoberto (2015, March 4). A Few Reactions to the DOJ's 'Scathing' Report on Ferguson Cops and Racial Bias. *NPR*. Available, http://www.npr.org/blogs/codeswitch/2015/03/04/390487872/a-few-reactions-to-the-dojs-scathing-report-on-ferguson-cops-and-racial-bias

Herreras, Mari (2010, September 5). Why Becoming a Legal Immigrant Is Next to Impossible. *Alternet*. Available, http://www.alternet.org/story/148088/why_becoming_a_legal_immigrant_is_next_to_impossible

Hess, Amanda (2017, January 15). Trump, Twitter and the Art of His Deal. *The New York Times*. Available, https://www.nytimes.com/2017/01/15/arts/trump-twitter-and-the-art-of-his-deal.html?_r=0

Heston, Charlton (1999, May). NRA Keynote Speech. *Varmint Al's Gun Rights & Politics*. Available, http://www.varmintal.com/heston4.htm

Hiatt, Fred (2014, June 1). Obama's Values-Free Foreign Policy. *The Washington Post*. Available, http://www.washingtonpost.com/opinions/fred-hiatt-obamas-values-free-foreign-policy/2014/06/01/45338556-e824-11e3-afc6-a1dd9407abcf_story.html

Hicks, Mark, Candice Williams and James David Dickson (2016, November 22). Charges Reviewed in Shooting Death of WSU Officer. *The Detroit News*. Available, http://www.detroitnews.com/story/news/local/detroit-city/2016/11/22/wayne-state-police-report-officer-shot/94308368/

Hillcox, Jack (2013, April 24). Ann Coulter Claims the Hijab Is Worthy of Imprisonment. *Jack Hillcox Blog*. Available, http://jackhillcox.wordpress.com/2013/04/24/ann-coulter-claims-the-hijab-is-worthy-of-imprisonment/

Himmelstein, David U., Deborah Thorne, Elizabeth Warren, and Steffie Woolhandler (2009). Medical Bankruptcy in the United States, 2007: Results of a National Study. *The American Journal of Medicine* 122(8), 741–746.

Hing, Julianne (2016, September 1). Trump, in a Major Immigration Speech, Is Back in Fearmongering. *The Nation*. Available, https://www.thenation.com/article/trump-in-major-immigration-speech-is-back-in-fear-mongering-form/

Hirschfield Davis, Julie (2015, August 4). Obama begins Campaign in Congress for Iran Nuclear Deal. *The New York Times*. Available, http://www.nytimes.com/2015/08/05/us/politics/netanyahu-appeals-to-american-jews-to-oppose-iran-nuclear-deal.html?_r=0

History, Art & Archives of the United States House of Representatives (n.d.). *Constitutional Amendments and Major Civil Rights Acts of Congress*. Referenced in Black Americans in Congress. Available, http://history.house.gov/Exhibitions-and-Publications/BAIC/Historical-Data/Constitutional-Amendments-and-Legislation/

Hock, Dylan (2015, June 18). White Fox Hosts Spin Charleston Shooting as Hate Crime against Christians, Push Arming Churches. *Addicting Info*. Available, http://www.addictinginfo.org/2015/06/18/white-fox-hosts-spin-charleston-shooting-as-hate-crime-against-christians-push-arming-churches-video/

Hodges, Adam, and Chad Nilep (2007). Introduction: Discourse, War and Terrorism. In Adam Hodges & Chad Nilep (Eds.), *Discourse, War and Terrorism* (pp. 1–18). Amsterdam: John Benjamins Publishing.

Hodges, Dave (2014, July 12). The U.S. Is Being Infiltrated by Paramilitary Forces and Terrorists Armed with WMD's. *The Common Sense Show*. Available, http://www.thecommonsenseshow.com/2014/07/12/the-u-s-is-being-infiltrated-by-paramilitary-forces-and-terrorists-armed-with-wmds/

Hoffmann, Bill and Joe Concha (2013, November 11). Sarah Palin: 'Angry Atheists' Wage War against Christmas. *Newsmax*. Available, http://www.newsmax.com/Newsfront/christmas-war-atheists-sarah-palin/2013/11/11/id/536041/

Hoffman, Sharona (2011). DOMA, ENDA, and Sexual Orientation as an Immutable Characteristic. *The Faculty Lounge: Conversations about Law, Culture, and Academia*. Available, http://www.thefacultylounge.org/2011/02/doma-enda-and-sexual-orientation-as-an-immutable-characteristic.html

Hohmann, Leo (2017, February 13). 50 Million Reasons to Support Trump's Travel Ban. *World Net Daily*. Available, http://www.wnd.com/2017/02/50-million-reasons-to-support-trumps-travel-ban/

Holland, Steve, and David Lawder (2017, February 24). Trump Calls Chinese 'Grand Champions' of Currency Manipulation. *Reuters*. Available, http://www.reuters.com/article/us-usa-trump-china-currency-exclusive-idUSKBN1622PJ

Hollihan, Thomas A. (2009). *Uncivil Wars: Political Campaigns in a Media Age* (2nd ed.). Boston: Bedford/St. Martin's.

Holmberg, Eric (2014, March 6). Making Gay OK: Cognitive Dissonance, Confirmation Bias and the Normalization of Homosexuality. *The Apologetics Group*. Available, http://theapologeticsgroup.com/science/making-gay-ok-cognitive-dissonance-confirmation-bias-and-the-normalization-of-homosexuality/

Hom, Andrew R. (2016). Angst Springs Eternal: Dangerous Times and the Dangers of Timing the 'Arab Spring.' *Security & Dialogue*, *47*(2), 165–183.

Homsher, Deborah (2004). Response to Bernard E. Harcourt's on Gun Registration, the NRA, Adolf Hitler, and Nazi Gun Laws: Exploding the Gun Culture Wars (a Call to Historians). *Fordham Law Review 73*(2), 715–719.

Horn, Dan, and Hannah Sparling (2015, September 14). UC Report: Sam DuBose Shooting 'Entirely Preventable.' *Cincinnati.com*. Available, http://www.cincinnati.com/story/news/2015/09/11/uc-release-new-dubose-shooting-report/72058718/

Howard, Philip N., and Muzammil M. Hussain (2011). The Role of Digital Media. *Journal of Democracy 22*(3), 35–48.

Howley, Patrick (2016, February 23). Bernie Sanders: Republican Base Is 'Absolutely' Racist. *Breitbart*. Available, http://www.breitbart.com/big-government/2016/02/23/bernie-sanders-republican-base-is-absolutely-racist/

Huang, Zhihuan Jennifer, Stella M. Yu, and Rebecca Ledsky (2006). Health Status and Health Service Access and Use among Children in U.S. Immigrant Families. *American Journal of Public Health, 96*(4), 634–640.

Huber, Lindsay Pérez (2009). Challenging Racist Nativist Framing: Acknowledging the Community Cultural Wealth of Undocumented Chicana College Students to Reframe the Immigration Debate. *Harvard Educational Review 79*(4), 704–729.

Huckfeldt, Robert (2001). The Social Communication of Political Expertise. *American Journal of Political Science 45*(2), 425–438.

Hudson, Redditt (2016, July 7). I'm a Black Ex-Cop, and This Is the Real Truth about Race and Policing. *Vox*. Available, http://www.vox.com/2015/5/28/8661977/race-police-officer

Huffington, Arianna (2008). *Right is Wrong: How the Lunatic Fringe Hijacked America, Shredded the Constitution, and Made Us All Less Safe*. New York: Alfred A. Knopf Publishing.

The Huffington Post (2010, May 10). Sarah Palin: American Law Should Be 'Based on the God of the Bible and the Ten Commandments.' Available, http://www.huffingtonpost.com/2010/05/10/sarah-palin-american-law_n_569922.html

The Huffington Post (2013, May 7). Lawrence O'Donnell Lambastes Wayne LaPierre for 'Exploiting' Boston Bombing. Available, http://www.huffingtonpost.com/2013/05/07/lawrence-odonnell-wayne-lapierre-nra-boston-bombing-comments_n_3228843.html

HuffPost Politics (2013, August 5). Westboro Baptist Church Counter-Protested at Soldier's Funeral. *The Huffington Post*. Available, http://www.huffingtonpost.com/2013/08/05/westboro-baptist-church-counter-protest_n_3707180.html

Hunt, Katie (2016, December 15). China Instills Weapons on Contested South China Sea Islands, Report Says. *CNN*. Available, http://www.cnn.com/2016/12/14/asia/south-china-sea-artificial-islands-spratlys-weapon-systems/

Hunt, Katie (2017, January 12). Tillerson Sets Stage for Showdown with Beijing over South China Sea. *CNN Politics*. Available, http://www.cnn.com/2017/01/12/politics/china-tillerson/index.html

Hutson, James H. (Ed.) (1998). America as a Religious Refuge: The Seventeenth Century. *Religion and the New Republic: Faith in the Founding of America*. The Library of Congress. Available, http://www.loc.gov/exhibits/religion/rel01.html

Hypocrisy on Executive Orders: Our View (2017, February 1). *USA Today*. Available, https://www.usatoday.com/story/opinion/2017/02/01/executive-orders-president-trump-obama-editorials-debates/97347492/

Ibbetson, Paul A. (2011). *The Good Fight: Why Conservatives Must Take Back America*. North Charleston, NC: CreateSpace Publishing.

Ignatius, David (2016, June 13). Trump's Reckless, Dangerous Islamophobia Helps the Islamic State. *The Washington Post*. Available, https://www.washingtonpost.com/blogs/post-partisan/wp/2016/06/13/trumps-islamophobia-helps-to-motivate-the-islamic-state/?utm_term=.7349042244b1

Immigration Policy Center (2014, March 1). *How the United States Immigration System Works: A Fact Sheet.* Available, http://www.immigrationpolicy.org/just-facts/how-united-states-immigration-system-works-fact-sheet

Ingraham, Laura (2010). *The Obama Diaries.* New York: Threshold Editions.

Ingram, Mathew (2011, January 18). The Internet Makes It More Likely You Will Be Social, Not Less. *Gigaom.* Available, https://gigaom.com/2011/01/18/pew-research-internet-social/

The Inquisitr (2014, July 11). Minuteman Project Urges Thousands to Go to Border to Stop 'Invasion' of Illegal Immigrants. *Inquisitr.* Available, http://www.inquisitr.com/1347063/minuteman-project-urges-thousands-to-go-to-border-to-stop-invasion-of-illegal-immigrants/

Institute on Taxation and Economic Policy (2017, March 1). Undocumented Immigrants' State & Local Tax Contributions. *ITEP.* Available, http://itep.org/itep_reports/2017/03/undocumented-immigrants-state-local-tax-contributions-2.php#.WQPkEBMrLIU

The Iran Nuclear Deal's Islamist Supporters (2015, September 11). *The Investigative Project on Terrorism.* Available, http://www.investigativeproject.org/4975/the-iran-nuclear-deal-islamist-supporters

Isikoff, Michael (2017, February 9). Syria's Assad Tells Yahoo News Some Refugees Are 'Definitely' Terrorists. *Yahoo News.* Available, https://www.yahoo.com/news/exclusive-syrias-assad-tells-yahoo-news-some-refugees-are-definitely-terrorists-182401926.html

Isquith, Elias (2014a, August 4). GOP Rep. Mo Brooks: Dems are Waging a "War on Whites." *Salon.* Available, http://www.salon.com/2014/08/04/gop_rep_mo_brooks_dems_are_waging_a_war_on_whites/?utm_source=facebook&utm_medium=socialflow

Isquith, Elias (2014b, April 16). Paul Krugman Slams "Obamacare Truther" Joe Scarborough for "Vile" Accusations. *Salon.* Available, http://www.salon.com/2014/04/16/paul_krugman_slams_obamacare_truther_joe_scarborough_for_vile_accusations/

Israel, Josh (2012, December 21). Everything You Need To Know about NRA's Wayne LaPierre. *Think Progress.* Available, http://thinkprogress.org/politics/2012/12/21/1368881/everything-you-need-to-know-about-the-nras-wayne-lapierre/

Istook, Ernest (2014, August 31). America's Poor and Minorities Are Victims of Illegal Immigration. *Tea Party News Network.* Available, http://www.tpnn.com/2014/08/31/americas-poor-and-minorities-are-victims-of-illegal-immigration/#sthash.q52VI1Ht.dpuf

Izadi, Elahe (2015, November 9). The Incidents that Led to the University of Missouri President's Resignation. *The Washington Post.* Available, https://www.washingtonpost.com/news/grade-point/wp/2015/11/09/the-incidents-that-led-to-the-university-of-missouri-presidents-resignation/?utm_term=.b00814c44e35

Jacobs, Lawrence R. and Theda Skocpol (2012). *Health Care Reform and American Politics: What Everyone Needs To Know.* New York: Oxford.

Jackson, Brooks and Kathleen Hall Jamieson (2007). *Un-Spun: Finding Facts in a World of [Disinformation].* New York: Random House.

Jackson, David, and Keving Johnson (2017, January 26). Trump Seeks Investigation into Alleged Voter Fraud. *USA Today.* Available, Lexis-Nexis.

Jacobson, William A. (2013, November 22). UCLA Prof Accused of Racist "Micro-aggression" for Correcting Student Grammar. *College Insurrection.* Available, http://collegeinsurrection.com/2013/11/ucla-prof-accused-of-racist-micro-aggression-for-correcting-student-grammar/

Jacobson, Ginger (2015). Racial Formation Theory and Systemic Racism in Hip-Hop Fans' Perceptions. *Sociological Forum, 30*(3), 832–851.

Jefferson, Thomas (1802, January 1). *Wall of Separation Letter* (Letter from Jefferson to Messrs. Nehemiah Dodge, Ephraim Robbins, and Stephen S. Nelson, a committee of the Danbury Baptist association in the state of Connecticut). The Library of Congress. Available, http://www.constitution.org/tj/sep_church_state.htm

Jeffreys-Jones, Rhodri (2010). Changes in the Nomenclature of the American Left. *Journal of American Studies 44*(1), 83–100.

Jelen, Ted G. (1998). The Electoral Politics of Gun Ownership. In John M. Bruce & Clyde Wilcox (Eds.), *The Changing Politics of Gun Control* (pp. 224–245). Lanham, MD: Rowman & Littlefield.

Jennings, Ralph (2017, January 16). Beijing Strengthens Control over the South China Sea as Its Last Rival goes Soft. *Forbes.* Available, https://www.forbes.com/sites/ralphjennings/2017/01/16/china-strenghtens-control-over-disputed-sea-as-its-last-enemy-vietnam-fades/#1ed26ac93f38

Jiang, Steven (2017, April 3). Why Trump's Golf Diplomacy Won't Work with China's Xi Jinping. *CNN Politics.* Available, http://www.cnn.com/2017/04/02/politics/trump-xi-jinping-golf-diplomacy-wont-work/

Jimenez, Stephen (2013). *The Book of Matt: Hidden Truths about the Murder of Matthew Shepard.* Hanover, NH: Steerforth.

Johnson, Alex (2015a, May 12). Tony Robinson Shooting: No Charges for Wisconsin Police Officer. *NBC News.* Available, http://www.nbcnews.com/news/us-news/tony-robinson-shooting-no-charges-lawful-use-force-n357876

Johnson, Bob (2009). *Deism: A Revolution in Religion, a Revolution in You.* Escondido, CA: World Union of Deists.

Johnson, Carrie (2014, September 12). 20 Years Later, Parts of Major Crime Bill Viewed as Terrible Mistake. *NPR: Morning Edition.* Available, http://www.npr.org/2014/09/12/347736999/20-years-later-major-crime-bill-viewed-as-terrible-mistake

Johnson, Danica (2015b, March 30). 7 Lies about Welfare that Many People Believe Are Fact. *Groundswell.* Available, https://groundswell.org/7-lies-about-welfare-that-many-people-believe-are-fact/

Johnson, Jeff (2008, July 7). Website Labels Illegal Immigration Opponents 'Racists.' *CNS News*. Available, http://cnsnews.com/news/article/website-labels-illegal-immigration-opponents-racists

Johnson, Kevin R. (1996–1997). "Aliens" and the U.S. Immigration Laws: The Social and Legal Construction of Nonpersons. *Inter-American Law Review 28*(2), 263–292.

Johnson, Kirk A., Mark K. Dolan, and John Sonnett (2011). Speaking of Looting: An Analysis of Racial Propaganda in National Television Coverage of Hurricane Katrina. *Howard Journal of Communications, 22*(3), 302–318.

Jones, Sarah (2015, May 4). Hillary Clinton Gives the Republican Benghazi Conspiracy Theory the Finger. *Politicus USA*. Available, http://www.politicususa.com/2015/05/04/hillary-clinton-republican-conspiracy-theory-finger-testify-benghazi.html

Joseph, Jonathan (2016). Reading Documents in Their Wider Context: Foucauldian and Realist Approaches to Terrorism Discourse. In Priya Dixit & Jacob L. Stump (Eds.), *Critical Methods in Terrorism Studies* (pp. 19–32). New York: Routledge.

Joslyn, Mark R. and Donald P. Haider-Markel (2013). The Politics of Causes: Mass Shootings and the Cases of the Virginia Tech and Tucson Tragedies. *Social Science Quarterly 94*(2), 410–423.

Jost, Kenneth (2014). Gay Marriage Showdowns. In CQ Researcher's *Issues for Debate in American Public Policy* (14th ed.) (pp. 273–300). Washington, D.C.: Congressional Quarterly Press.

Kabbany, Jennifer (2014, March 12). Feminist Studies Professor Accused of Assaulting Teenage Profile Demonstrator. *The College Fix*. Available, http://www.thecollegefix.com/post/16673/

Kaduce, Lonn Lanza and Andrea Davis (2013, March 20). License to Kill: A Theoretical Critique of "Stand Your Ground." *University of Florida Law School Spring Lecture Panel Sessions*. Available, http://scholarship.law.ufl.edu/csrrr_events/10thspringlecture/panels/2/

Kagan, Robert (2016). Allure of Normalcy: What America Still Owes the World. In Glenn P. Hastedt (Ed.), *Readings in American Foreign Policy* (pp. 11–34). Lanham, MD: Rowman & Littlefield.

Kahn, Chris (2017, January 31). More Americans Support Donald Trump's Travel Ban than Oppose It, Poll Shows. *The Independent*. Available, http://www.independent.co.uk/news/world/americas/donald-trump-muslim-ban-travel-immigration-refugees-iran-iraq-syria-a7556186.html

Kaiser Family Foundation (2013, April 25). Summary of Affordable Care Act. *The Henry J. Kaiser Family Foundation*. Available, http://kff.org/health-reform/fact-sheet/summary-of-new-health-reform-law/

Kaleem, Jaweed (2013, May 7). Link between Islam and Violence Rejected by Many Americans after Boston Bombings: Pew Survey. *The Huffington Post*. Available, http://www.huffingtonpost.com/2013/05/07/islam-violence-muslims-survey_n_3231987.html

Kalmar, Ivan Davidson (2009). Anti-Semitism and Islamophobia: The Formation of a Secret. *Human Architecture: Journal of the Sociology of Self-Knowledge, 7*(2), 135–144.

Kan, Shirley A., and Wayne M. Morrison (2014, December 11). U.S.-Taiwan Relationship: Overview of Policy Issues. *Congressional Research Service*. Available, https://fas.org/sgp/crs/row/R41952.pdf

Kane, Tim, and Kirk A. Johnson (2006, March 1). The Real Problem with Immigration … and the Real Solution. *The Heritage Foundation Backgrounder #1913*. Available, http://www.heritage.org/research/reports/2006/03/the-real-problem-with-immigration-and-the-real-solution

Kang, Stephanie N. (2015). Restoring the Fifteenth Amendment: The Constitutional Right to an Undiluted Vote. *UCLA Law Review, 62*, 1392–1423.

Kapur, Sahil (2014, July 22). Federal Appeals Courts Clash over Obamacare Subsidies. *Talking Points Memo*. Available, http://talkingpointsmemo.com/dc/4th-circuit-court-obamacare-subsidies-halbig

Karimi, Faith, Catherine E. Shoichet, and Dana Ford (2015, December 7). San Bernardino Shooters Were Radicalized 'for Quite Some Time,' FBI Says. *CNN*. Available, http://www.cnn.com/2015/12/07/us/san-bernardino-shooting/

Karon, Tony (2011, October 21). Iraq's Government, Not Obama, Called Time on the U.S. Troop Presence. *Time*. Available, http://world.time.com/2011/10/21/iraq-not-obama-called-time-on-the-u-s-troop-presence/

Katch, Danny (2015, February 4). #BlackLivesMatter Looks to the Future. *Socialist Worker*. Available, http://socialistworker.org/2015/02/04/blacklivesmatter-looks-ahead

Kates, Jr., Don B. (1992). Bigotry, Symbolism and Ideology in the Battle over Gun Control. *Public Interest Law Review 31*, 31–46.

Kates, Don B., Henry E. Schaffer, John K. Lattimer, George B. Murray, and Edwin H. Cassem (1994). Guns and Public Health: Epidemic of Violence or Pandemic of Propaganda? *Tennessee Law Review 62*, 513–596.

Kato, Takao and Chad Sparber (2013). Quotas and Quality: The Effect of H-1B Visa Restrictions on the Pool of Prospective Undergraduate Students from Abroad. *The Review of Economics and Statistics 95*(1), 109–126.

Kaufman, Joyce P. (2017). *A Concise History of U.S. Foreign Policy* (4th ed.). Lanham, MD: Rowman & Littlefield.

Kaufman, Scott Eric (2015a, June 16). Donald Trump Refers to Immigrants as "Rapists" in Presidential Campaign Launch. *Salon*. Available, http://www.salon.com/2015/06/16/donald_trump_refers_to_immigrants_as_rapists_in_presidential_campaign_launch/

Kaufman, Scott Eric (2015b, July 29). This Is, Without Question, a Murder": Prosecutor Indicts "Asinine" White Cop in Shooting Death of Unarmed Black Motorist. *Salon*. Available, http://salon.com/2015/07/29/this_is_without_question_a_murder

Keating, Joshua (2014, August 25). "El Qaida": The Persistent, Baseless Claim that Terrorists Will Swarm the U.S. from Mexico. *Slate*. Available, http://www.slate.com/blogs/the_world_/2014/08/25/rick_perry_says_isis_could_sneak_into_the_u_s_from_mexico_the_el_qaida_meme.html

Keen, Lisa Melinda and Suzanne Beth Goldberg (2000). *Strangers to the Law: Gay People on Trial.* Ann Arbor, MI: University of Michigan Press.

Kelleher, Jennifer Sinco (2017, March 30). Donald Trump's 'Muslim Travel Ban': Judge Extends Order Blocking President's Restrictions. *The Independent.* Available, http://www.independent.co.uk/news/world/americas/donald-muslim-trump-travel-ban-hawaiian-judge-derrick-watson-extends-douglas-chin-blocking-order-a7657186.html

Kelly, Casey Ryan (2014). "We Are Not Free": The Meaning of <Freedom> in American Indian Resistance to President Johnson's War on Poverty. *Communication Quarterly, 62*(4), 455–473.

Kemp, Joe (2012, February 3). NYPD Cops Involved in Shooting of Unarmed Man Placed on Modified Duty. *New York Daily News.* Available, http://www.nydailynews.com/new-york/nypd-cops-involved-shooting-unarmed-man-modified-duty-article-1.1016643

Kenber, Billy (2013, August 28). Nidal Hasan Sentenced to Death for Fort Hood Shooting Rampage. *The Washington Post.* Available, http://www.washingtonpost.com/world/national-security/nidal-hasan-sentenced-to-death-for-fort-hood-shooting-rampage/2013/08/28/aad28de2-0ffa-11e3-bdf6-e4fc677d94a1_story.html

Kennedy, Anthony (2014, May 5). Majority Opinion. *Town of Greece v. Galloway.* No. 12-696, 572 U.S. ___ (2014).

Kennedy, James and Jerry Newcombe (2004). *What's Wrong with Same-Sex Marriage.* Wheaton, IL: Crossway Books.

Kennedy, Randall (2002). *Nigger: The Strange Career of a Troublesome Word.* New York: Vintage.

Kentish, Ben (2017, January 26). President Donald Trump to Publish Weekly List of Crimes Committed by Immigrants. *Independent.* Available, http://www.independent.co.uk/news/world/americas/donald-trump-publish-weekly-list-crimes-immigrants-commit-refugees-aliens-executive-order-us-a7546826.html

Kepner, Jim (2004). Why Can't We All Get Together, and What Do We Have in Common? In Robert B. Ridinger (Ed.), *Historic Speeches and Rhetoric for Gay and Lesbian Rights (1892–2000)* (pp. 700–720). New York: Harrington Park Press.

Kershner, Isabel (2015, July 14). Iran Deal Denounced by Netanyahu as 'Historic Mistake.' *The New York Times.* Available, https://www.nytimes.com/2015/07/15/world/middleeast/iran-nuclear-deal-israel.html?_r=0

Kertscher, Tom (2016, February 18). Black Man Shot Dead by White Milwaukee Police Officer Was 'Unarmed,' Hillary Clinton Says. *Politifact.* Available, http://www.politifact.com/wisconsin/statements/2016/feb/18/hillary-clinton/black-man-was-unarmed-when-shot-dead-white-milwauk/

Kessler, Glenn (2013a, July 16). Harry Reid's Claim that House GOP Efforts to Repeal 'Obamacare' All Ended in Failure. *The Washington Post.* Available, http://www.washingtonpost.com/blogs/fact-checker/post/harry-reids-claim-that-house-gop-efforts-to-repeal-obamacare-all-ended-in-failure/2013/07/15/403e0330-ed95-11e2-9008-61e94a7ea20d_blog.html

Kessler, Glenn (2013b, May 15). How Many Pages of Regulations for 'Obamacare'? *The Washington Post.* Available, http://www.washingtonpost.com/blogs/fact-checker/post/how-many-pages-of-regulations-for-obamacare/2013/05/14/61eec914-bcf9-11e2-9b09-1638acc3942e_blog.html

Kessler, Glenn (2015, June 16). The Stale Statistic that One in Three Black Males 'Born Today' Will End Up in Jail. *The Washington Post.* Available, https://www.washingtonpost.com/news/fact-checker/wp/2015/06/16/the-stale-statistic-that-one-in-three-black-males-has-a-chance-of-ending-up-in-jail/?utm_term=.f82c6a340671

Kessler, Glenn (2016, November 27). Donald Trump's bogus claim that millions of people voted illegally for Hillary Clinton; Trump makes a bold tweet—based on no evidence. *The Washington Post.* Available, Lexis-Nexis.

Keyes, Scott (2015, September 11). Lawmaker Rants against Accepting Refugees: 'They Only Want the Free Stuff from America.' *Think Progress.* Available, https://thinkprogress.org/lawmaker-rants-against-accepting-refugees-they-only-want-the-free-stuff-from-america-3b8028f939e2

Khajehpour, Bijan, Reza Marashi, and Trita Parsi (2016). The Trouble with Sanctions. In Glenn P. Hastedt (Ed.), *Readings in American Foreign Policy* (pp. 236–250). Lanham, MD: Rowman & Littlefield.

Khalek, Rania (2014, June 23). Cities Fight Obama's Deportation Machine. *Truth-out.org.* Available, http://www.truth-out.org/news/item/24508-cities-fight-obamas-deportation-machine

Khan, Surina (1998). *Calculated Compassion: How the Ex-Gay Movement Serves the Right's Attack on Democracy.* A report from Political Research Associates, the Policy Institute of the National Gay and Lesbian Task Force, and Equal Partners in Faith. Available, http://www.politicalresearch.org/wp-content/uploads/downloads/2012/11/CalculatedCompassion.pdf

Kiefer, Francine (2014, July 15). Why Some Democrats Are Blasting Bipartisan Border Crisis Bill. *Christian Science Monitor.* Available, EbscoHost.

Kienpointer, Manfred (2013). Strategic Maneuvering in the Political Rhetoric of Barack Obama. *Journal of Language and Politics, 12*(3), 357–377.

Kim, Stella (2017, April 17). South Korea's Ex-President Park Geun-hye Indicted on Corruption Charges. *NBC News.* Available, http://www.nbcnews.com/news/world/south-korea-s-ex-president-park-geun-hye-indicted-corruption-n747261

Kim, Suzanne A. (2011). Skeptical Marriage Equality. *Harvard Journal of Law & Gender 34*, 37–80.

Kimberley, Margaret (2015, September 16). Hurricane Katrina: The Ethnic Cleansing Black New Orleans. *AmericUSumter Observer.* Available, http://www.americusumterobserver.com/hurricane-katrina-the-ethnic-cleansing-black-new-orleans/

Kindy, Kimberly, Wesley Lowery, and Julie Tate (2016, July 7). Fatal Shootings by Police Are Up Over 2015. *The Washington Post.* Available, https://www.washingtonpost.com/national/fatalshootingsbypolicesurpass2015srate/2016/07/07/81b708f23d4211e684e81580c7db5275_story.html?hpid=hp_hptoptablemain_sixmonths306pm%3Ahomepage%2Fstory

King, C. (2013, July 22). What Race Baiting Really Means. *Social Political Commentary*. Available, http://www.socialpoliticalcommentary.com/what-race-baiting-really-means/

King, Eden B., Eric M. Dunleavy, Whitney Botsford Morgan, Dana G. Dunleavy, Salman Jaffer, and Katie Elder (2011). Discrimination in the 21st Century: Are Science and the Law Aligned? Psychology, *Public Policy & Law*, *17*(1), 54–75.

King, Martin Luther, Jr. (1957, May 17). "Give Us the Ballot" Address at the Prayer Pilgrimage for Freedom. *The Stanford King Encyclopedia*. Available, http://kingencyclopedia.stanford.edu/encyclopedia/documentsentry/doc_give_us_the_ballot_address_at_the_prayer_pilgrimage_for_freedom/

King, Shaun (2016a, September 19). Arrest the Tulsa Officer Who Killed Terence Crutcher. *New York Daily News*. Available, http://www.nydailynews.com/news/national/king-arrest-tulsa-officer-killed-terence-crutcher-article-1.2798021

King, Shaun (2016b, August 2). Cynicism Toward Korryn Gaines, Baltimore Mom Killed by Cops, Illustrates Power of White Privilege. *New York Daily News*. Available, http://www.nydailynews.com/news/national/king-cynicism-mom-slain-cops-illustrates-white-privilege-article-1.2735539

Kingkade, Tyler (2015, March 8). Oklahoma Frat Boys caught Singing 'There will Never be a N***** in SAE.' *The Huffington Post*. Available, http://www.huffingtonpost.com/2015/03/08/frat-racist-sae-oklahoma_n_6828212.html

Kingwell, Mark (2012). *Unruly Voices: Essays on Democracy, Civility and the Human Imagination*. Ontario: Biblioasis.

Kinney, Aaron (2005, September 1). "Looting" or "Finding"? *Salon*. Available, http://www.salon.com/2005/09/02/photo_controversy/

Kleck, Gary, and Marc Gertz (1995). Armed Resistance to Crime: The Prevalence and Naturs of Self-Defense with a Gun. *Journal of Law and Criminology*, *86*(1), 150–187.

Klein, Rebecca (2013, July 30). Kentucky School Prayer Petition Links Prayer Ban with AIDS Epidemic. *The Huffington Post*. Available, http://www.huffingtonpost.com/2013/07/30/kentucky-school-prayer-petition_n_3676932.html

Klofstad, Casey A., Anand Edward Sokhey, and Scott D. McClurg (2013). Disagreeing about Disagreement: How Conflict in Social Networks Affects Political Behavior. *American Journal of Political Science* 57(1), 120–134.

Knight, Richard (2004, October). *Documenting the U.S. Solidarity Movement—With Reflections on the Sanctions and Divestment Campaigns*. A report to the conference, "A Decade of Freedom: Celebrating the Role of the International Anti-Apartheid Movement in South Africa's Freedom of Struggle," at Durban, South Africa. Available, http://richardknight.homestead.com/files/aaapdurban2004.htm

Knight, Robert H. (2004, April 5). Born or Bred? Science Does Not Support the Claim that Homosexuality Is Genetic. *Newsweek*. Available, http://www.cwfa.org/born-or-bredscience-does-not-support-the-claim-that-homosexuality-is-genetic/

Knoll, Stefanie and Leighton Walter Kille (2014, December 10). Undocumented Migration to the United States and the Wages of Mexican Immigrants. *Journalist's Resource*. Available, http://journalistsresource.org/studies/government/immigration/undocumented-migration-mexico-united-states-wages?utm_source=JR-email&utm_medium=email&utm_campaign=JR-email

Koed, Elizabeth (2005). A Symbol Transformed. *The Social Contract Press 15*(4). Available, http://www.thesocialcontract.com/artman2/publish/tsc1504/article_1332.shtml

Kofi Annan's Six-Point Plan for Syria (2012, March 27). *Al Jazeera*. Available, http://www.aljazeera.com/news/middleeast/2012/03/2012327153111767387.html/

Kopan, Tal (2015, August 18). Birthright Citizenship: Can Donald Trump Change the Constitution? *CNN Politics*. Available, http://www.cnn.com/2015/08/18/politics/birthright-citizenship-trump-constitution/index.html

Koppelman, Andrew (2005). The Rule of Lawrence. In H. N. Hirsch (Ed.), *The Future of Gay Rights in America* (pp. 151–168). New York: Routledge.

Korb, Lawrence J. (2013, May 24). On Benghazi, Congress Could Take a Lesson From Beirut. *The Atlantic*. Available, http://www.theatlantic.com/politics/archive/2013/05/on-benghazi-congress-could-take-a-lesson-from-beirut/276189/

Kramer, David J. (2016, August 18). Russia Is Now a Threat. The U.S. Should Treat It Like One. *The Washington Post*. Available, https://www.washingtonpost.com/news/in-theory/wp/2016/08/18/russia-is-now-a-threat-the-u-s-should-treat-it-like-one/?utm_term=.5ea3f7ec14f6

Krauthammer, Charles (2013). *Things that Matter: Three Decades of Passions, Pastimes and Politics*. New York: Crown Forum.

Krauthammer, Charles (2014, June 2). Obama's Empty Foreign Policy Speech at West Point. *Chicago Tribune*. Available, http://www.chicagotribune.com/news/opinion/commentary/ct-obama-west-point-commencement-oped-0602-20140602-16,0,1530542.column

Krauthammer, Charles (2015a, February 26). The Fatal Flaw in the Iran Deal. *The Washington Post*. Available, https://www.washingtonpost.com/opinions/the-fatal-flaw-in-the-iran-deal/2015/02/26/9186c70e-bde1-11e4-8668-4e7ba8439ca6_story.html?utm_term=.95ee8b9a845e

Krauthammer, Charles (2015b, July 16). Worse than We Could Have Imagined. *The Washington Post*. Available, https://www.washingtonpost.com/opinions/worse-than-we-could-have-imagined/2015/07/16/aa320b42-2bf0-11e5-bd33-395c05608059_story.html?utm_term=.ce5cb879ea91

Kravis, Andrew (2012/2013). Is the Inability to Marry a Marital Status? Levin v. Yeshiva University and the Intersection of Sexual Orientation and Marital Status in Housing Discrimination. *Columbia Journal of Gender and Law 24*(1), 1–28.

Kristofferson, Kirk, Katherine White, and John Peloza (2014). The Nature of Slacktivism: How the Social Observability of an Initial Act of Token Support Affects Subsequent Prosocial Action. *Journal of Consumer Research*, *40*. Available via JSTOR.

Kromm, Chris (2016, November 4). Will Barriers to Black Voting Tip the Critical Battlegrond State of North Carolina? *Facing South*. Available, https://www.facingsouth.org/2016/11/will-barriers-black-voting-tip-critical-battleground-state-north-carolina

Krouse, William (2002). Gun Control. *Congressional Research Service Report*. Available, http://www.policyalmanac.org/crime/archive/crs_gun_control.shtml

Ku, Leighton (2009). Health Insurance Coverage and Medical Expenditures of Immigrants and Native-Born Citizens in the United States. *American Journal of Public Health*, 99(7), 1322–1328.

Kulze, Elizabeth (2015, February 22). How Crack vs. Coke Sentencing Unfairly Targets Poor People. *Vocativ*. Available, http://www.vocativ.com/underworld/drugs/crack-vs-coke-sentencing/

Kurtz, Howard (2014, May 2). Benghazi Emails: Despite Spin, Not Just a Fox Story Any More. *Fox News*. Available, http://www.foxnews.com/politics/2014/05/02/benghazi-emails-despite-spin-not-just-fox-story-any-more/

Kurtzleben, Danielle (2014, December 13). The Median Wealth for Whites in the US is Nearly $142,000. For Blacks, It's $11,000. *Vox*. Available, http://www.vox.com/2014/12/13/7383033/the-median-wealth-for-whites-in-the-us-is-nearly-142000-for-blacks

Labott, Elise, Deirdre Walsh and Sunlen Serfaty (2015, August 3). Washington Battle Rages over Iran Nuclear Deal's Fate. *CNN Politics*. Available, http://www.cnn.com/2015/08/03/politics/aipac-iran-nuclear-deal-congress/

Lachman, Samantha (2014, March 19). Susanne Atanus Who Blames Gay Rights for Tornadoes, Wins GOP Nomination for Congress. *The Huffington Post*. Available, http://www.huffingtonpost.com/2014/03/19/susanne-atanus-congress-_n_4993555.html

Lackner, Helen (2017, March 26). The War in Yemen: Two Years Old and Maturing? *Open Democracy*. Available, https://www.opendemocracy.net/arab-awakening/helen-lackner/war-in-yemen-two-years-old-and-maturing

LaHaye, Tim (1978). *The Unhappy Gays: What Everyone Should Know about Homosexuality*. Cambridge, UK: Tyndale House.

Laird, Lorelei (2014, May 1). Courts Are Hearing New Challenges to Tax Exemptions for Religion. *ABA Journal: Law News Now*. Available, http://www.abajournal.com/magazine/article/courts_are_hearing_new_challenges_to_tax_exemptions_for_religion/

Lake, Randall (1983). Enacting Red Power: The Consummatory Function in Native American Protest Rhetoric. *Quarterly Journal of Speech*, 69(2), 127–142.

Lake, Randall (1991). Between Myth and History: Enacting Time in Native American Protest Rhetoric. *Quarterly Journal of Speech*, 77(2), 123–151.

Lakoff, George and Sam Ferguson (2006). The Framing of Immigration. *The Rockridge Institute*. Available, https://web.archive.org/web/20081021045141/http://www.rockridgeinstitute.org/research/rockridge/immigration.html

Lakshmanan, Indira A. R. (2016, July 15). Inside the Plan to Undo the Iran Nuclear Deal. *Politico*. Available, http://www.politico.com/magazine/story/2016/07/iran-nuclear-deal-foreign-policy-barack-obama-hassan-rouhani-javad-zarif-israel-john-kerry-214052

Lam, Charles and Phil Helsel (2017, March 4). Seattle-Area Sikh Man Shot in Possible Hate Crime. *NBC News*. Available, http://www.nbcnews.com/news/asian-america/police-investigate-possible-hate-crime-after-sikh-man-shot-n729161

Lamothe, Dan, Missy Ryan, and Thomas Gibbons-Neff (2017, April 6). U.S. Strikes Syrian Military Airfield in First Direct Assault on Bahar al-Assad's Government. *The Washington Post*. Available, https://www.washingtonpost.com/world/national-security/trump-weighing-military-options-following-chemical-weapons-attack-in-syria/2017/04/06/0c59603a-1ae8-11e7-9887-1a5314b56a08_story.html?utm_term=.70e06831183f

Langerak, Edward (2014). *Civil Disagreement: Personal Integrity in a Pluralistic Society*. Washington, D.C.: Georgetown University Press.

Landler, Mark (2017, February 4). Appeals Court Rejects Request to Immediately Restore Travel Ban. *The New York Times*. Available, https://www.nytimes.com/2017/02/04/us/politics/visa-ban-trump-judge-james-robart.html

Landler, Mark, and Michael Forsythe (2017, February 9). Trump Tells Xi Jinpoing U.S. will Honor 'One China Policy.' *The New York Times*. Available, https://www.nytimes.com/2017/02/09/world/asia/donald-trump-china-xi-jinping-letter.html?_r=0

Landler, Mark, and Eric Schmitt (2017, April 18). Aircraft Carrier Wasn't Sailing to Deter North Korea, as U.S. Suggested. *The New York Times*. Available, https://www.nytimes.com/2017/04/18/world/asia/aircraft-carrier-north-korea-carl-vinson.html

LaPierre, Wayne (1994). *Guns, Crime, and Freedom*. Washington, D.C.: Regnery Publishing.

Larison, Daniel (2015, March 9). The Senate GOP's Obnoxious Iran Letter. *The American Conservative*. Available, http://www.theamericanconservative.com/larison/the-senate-gops-obnoxious-iran-letter/

Larison, Daniel (2017, April 12). Trump's Woeful Lack of Preparedness on Foreign Policy. *The American Conservative*. Available, https://www.theamericanconservative.com/larison/trumps-woeful-lack-of-preparedness-on-foreign-policy/

Larrubia, Evelyn, and Chris Keller (2015, June 11). 13 Seconds from Stop to Shots: The Events that Led to Ezell Ford's Death. *KPCC*. Available, http://www.scpr.org/news/2015/06/10/52338/13-seconds-from-stop-to-shots-the-events-that-led/

Larson, Magali Sarfatti and Douglas Porpora (2011). The Resistible Rise of Sarah Palin: Continuity and Paradox in the American Right Wing. *Sociological Forum* 26(4), 754–778.

LaTour, Michael S. and Herbert J. Rotfeld (1997). There Are Threats and (Maybe) Fear-Caused Arousal: Theory and Confusions of Appeals to Fear and Fear Arousal Itself. *Journal of Advertising* 26(3), 45–59.

Lauderdale, Benjamin E. (2013). Does Inattention to Political Debate Explain the Polarization Gap between the U.S. Congress and Public? *Public Opinion Quarterly* 77(S1), 2–23.

Lave, Tamara Rice (2013). Shoot to Kill: A Critical Look at Stand Your Ground Laws. *University of Miami Law Review 67*, 827–860.

Lawless, Jennifer L., and Richard L. Fox (2015). *Running from Office: Why Young Americans Are Turned Off to Politics.* New York: Oxford University Press.

Layman, Geoffrey C., Thomas M. Carsey, John C. Green, Richard Herrera, and Rosalyn Cooperman (2010). Activists and Conflict Extension in American Party Politics. *American Political Science Review 104*(2), 324–346.

Lazare, Sarah (2016, July 24). Police Incitement against Black Lives Matter Is Putting Protesters in Danger. *Alternet.* Available, http://www.alternet.org/grayzone-project/police-incitement-against-black-lives-matter-putting-protesters-danger

The Leadership Conference Education Fund (2016, November). *The Great Poll Closure.* Available, http://civilrightsdocs.info/pdf/reports/2016/poll-closure-report-web.pdf

Lee v. Weisman. 112 S. Ct. 2649 (1992).

Lee, Esther Yu-His (2014, July 17). This Bill Is Dubbed the HUMANE Act, But It Actually Hurts the Migrant Kids It Claims to Protect. *Think Progress.* Available, http://thinkprogress.org/immigration/2014/07/17/3460325/corynyn-cuellar-border-bill/

Lee, Kurtis (2016, August 24). Hillary Clinton Says Trump 'Taking a Hate Movement Mainstream.' *Los Angeles Times.* Available, http://www.latimes.com/nation/politics/trailguide/la-na-trailguide-updates-1472092317-htmlstory.html

Lee, Sarah (2017, February 11). Bahsar Assad: There Are 'Definitely' Terrorists among Syrian Refugees. *The Blaze.* Available, http://www.theblaze.com/news/2017/02/11/bashar-assad-there-are-definitely-terrorists-among-syrian-refugees/

Lee, Tony (2014, June 10). Eric Cantor Primary Loss a Referendum against Amnesty. *Breitbart.* Available, http://www.breitbart.com/Big-Government/2014/06/10/SHOCK-House-Majority-Leader-Eric-Cantor-Loses-Primary

Lee, Trymaine (2014, September 16). Autopsy Report Shows Police Shot Darrien Hunt in the Back, Lawyer Says. *MSNBC.* Available, http://www.msnbc.com/msnbc/darrien-hunt-carrying-toy-sword-shot-and-killed-utah-police

Left Coast Lucy (2013, November 23). Secular Victory: Religious Income Tax Exemption Ruled Unconstitutional. *The Examiner.* Available, http://www.examiner.com/article/secular-victory-religious-income-tax-exemption-ruled-unconstitutional

Legge, Nancy J., James R. DiSanza, John Gribas, and Aubrey Shiffler (2012). "He Sounded Like a Vile, Disgusting Pervert ... " An Analysis of Persuasive Attacks on Rush Limbaugh During the Sandra Fluke Controversy. *Journal of Radio & Audio Media 19*(2), 173–205.

Lehmann, Evan (2013, May 16). Researchers, Hunting for Climate Consensus, Find It among Scientists. *ClimateWire.* Available, https://www.eenews.net/climatewire/stories/1059981277/

Lemon v. Kurtzman. 91 S. Ct. 2105 (1971).

Lemuel, Joel M. (2010). *The Radical Voice in the Rhetoric of the Tea Party Movement.* Communication Theses, paper 63, Georgia State University. Available, http://digitalarchive.gsu.edu/communication_theses/63

Lencioni, Patrick (2006). *Silos, Politics and Turf Wars: A Leadership Fable about Destroying the Barriers that Turn Colleagues into Competitors.* San Francisco: Jossey-Bass.

Lepore, Jill (2012, April 19). The Lost Amendment. *The New Yorker.* Available, http://www.newyorker.com/online/blogs/newsdesk/2012/04/the-second-amendment.html

LeVay, Simon (1991). A Difference in Hypothalamic Structure between Heterosexual and Homosexual Men. *Science, 253*(5023), 1034–1037.

Levendusky, Matthew (2013). *How Partisan Media Polarize America.* Chicago: University of Chicago Press.

Levitt, Justin (2008, March 12). *In-Person Voter Fraud: Myth and Trigger for Disenfranchisement?* Testimony before the United States Senate Committee on Rules and Administration. Available, http://www.brennancenter.org/analysis/person-voter-fraud-myth-justin-levitt-senate-committee#_edn33

Lewis, Anthony (1957, September 24). President Sends Troops to Little Rock, Federalizes Arkansas National Guard; Tells Nation He Acted to Avoid an Anarchy. *The New York Times.* Available, http://www.nytimes.com/learning/general/onthisday/big/0925.html#article

Lewis, Bernard E. (2003, September 25). Who Are the Semites? *My Jewish Learning.* Available, http://www.myjewishlearning.com/article/who-are-the-semites/

Lewis, Paul (2014, December 3). US Department of Justice Opens Investigation into Eric Garner's Death. *The Guardian.* Available, http://www.theguardian.com/us-news/2014/dec/03/justice-department-eric-holder-eric-garner-investigation

Lewis, Paul and Tom Silverstone (2016, September 22). Ohio Trump Campaign Chair Kathy Miller Says There Was 'No Racism' before Obama. *The Guardian.* Available, https://www.theguardian.com/us-news/2016/sep/22/trump-ohio-campaign-chair-no-racism-before-obama

Lewis, Tyler (2009, April 29). House Passes Hate Crimes Bill. *Civil Rights Leadership Conference.* Available, http://www.civilrights.org/archives/2009/04/297-llechpa-house.html

Lewis, Gregory B., and Seong Soo Oh (2008). Public Opinion and State Action on Same-Sex Marriage. *State & Local Government Review 40*(1), 42–53.

Liberty Counsel (2007). *Flawed Immigration Policy Threatens America's Future.* Available, http://www.lc.org/attachments/immigration_white_paper.pdf

Life Insight (2007, March–April). Gonzalez v. Carhart: Cause for Renewed Hope. *USCCB Secretariat for Pro-Life Activities.* Available, http://www.usccb.org/upload/life-insights-lifeinsight042507.pdf

Lifson, Thomas (2015, November 16). Democrats going to the Mat over Taking in Tens of Thousands of Syrian Refugees. *American Thinker*. Available, http://www.americanthinker.com/blog/2015/11/democrats_going_to_the_mats_over_taking_in_tens_of_thousands_of_syrian_refugees.html

Lim, Julian (2013). Immigration, Asylum, and Citizenship: A More Holistic Approach. *California Law Review 101*(4), 1013–1077.

Limbaugh Apologizes for "Slut" Comment. (2012, March 3). *CNN Politics*. Available, http://politicalticker.blogs.cnn.com/2012/03/03/limbaugh-apologizes-for-slut-comment/

Limbaugh, Rush (1992). *The Way Things Ought To Be*. New York: Pocket Books.

Limbaugh, Rush (2012a, March 3). A Statement from Rush. *RushLimbaugh.com*. Available, http://www.rushlimbaugh.com/daily/2012/03/03/a_statement_from_rush

Limbaugh, Rush (2012b, March 5). Why I Apologized to Sandra Fluke. *RushLimbaugh.com*. Available, http://www.rushlimbaugh.com/daily/2012/03/05/why_i_apologized_to_sandra_fluke

Lind, Dara (2017, January 25). The Wall Is the Least Aggressive Part of Trump's Executive Actions on Immigration. *Vox*. Available, http://www.vox.com/2017/1/25/14378474/trump-immigration-order-wall-deport-sanctuary

Lipp, Murray (2013, May 12). 'Gay Marriage' and 'Marriage Equality'—Both Terms Matter. *The Huffington Post*. Available, http://www.huffingtonpost.com/murray-lipp/gay-marriage_b_3249733.html

Liptak, Kevin and Hilary Krieger (2015, August 10). Obama's Iran Nuclear Deal Rhetoric Troubles American Jews. *CNN Politics*. Available, http://www.cnn.com/2015/08/10/politics/jewish-concern-obama-rhetoric-iran-nuclear-deal/

Lipton, Eric (2006, June 27). 'Breathtaking' Waste and Fraud in Hurricane Aid. *The New York Times*. Available, http://www.nytimes.com/2006/06/27/washington/27katrina.html

Lister, Tim (2016, September 7). Analysis: Why Use Chlorine Bombs in Syria? *CNN*. Available, http://www.cnn.com/2016/09/07/middleeast/syria-chemical-weapons-analysis/index.html

Little, Becky (2016, September 13). Most Young Americans Can't Pass a Test on Global Affairs—Can You? *National Geographic*. Available, http://news.nationalgeographic.com/2016/09/survey-geography-foreign-relations-americans-students/

Liu, Frederick and Stephen Macedo (2005). The Federal Marriage Amendment and the Strange Evolution of the Conservative Case against Gay Marriage. *PS: Political Science and Politics 38*(2), 211–215.

Loesch, Dana (2014). *Hands Off My Gun: Defeating the Plot to Disarm America*. New York: Center Street.

Lofgren, Mike (2013). *The Party Is Over: How Republicans Went Crazy, Democrats Became Useless, and the Middle Class Got Shafted*. New York: Penguin.

Logan, Annisette E., and Kathryn D. Lafreniere (2016). Social Media, Texting, and Personality: A Test of the Shallowing Hypothesis. *Personality and Individual Differences*. Available, https://media.8ch.net/pdfs/src/1456655455863.pdf

Log Cabin Republicans (2014). About Us. Available, http://www.logcabin.org/about-us/

Loker, Thomas W. (2012). *The History and Evolution of Healthcare in America: The Untold Backstory of Where We've Been, Where We Are, and Why Healthcare Needs Reform*. Bloomington, IN: iUniverse.

Long, Chrissie (2013a, May 23). Crime in Immigrant Neighborhoods: Evidence from New York City. *Journalist's Resource*. Available, http://journalistsresource.org/studies/government/immigration/crime-enforcement-immigrant-neighborhoods-evidence-new-york-city

Long, Chrissie (2013b, October 28). "Illegal," "Undocumented," "Unauthorized": The Impact of Issue Frames on Perceptions of Immigrants. *Journalist's Resource*. Available, http://journalistsresource.org/studies/government/immigration/illegal-undocumented-unauthorized-equivalency-frames-issue-frames-public-opinion-immigration

Long, Ciara (2017, April 16). High-Level Corruption Scandal Threatens Brazil's Political Stability. *CBC News*. Available, http://www.cbc.ca/news/world/brazil-corruption-scandal-operation-car-wash-temer-1.4072010

Long, Heather (2017, January 23). Trump Didn't go after China on Day One. *CNN Money*. Available, http://money.cnn.com/2017/01/23/news/economy/donald-trump-china-currency/

Longfellow, S. (2015, March 10). GOP Senator Writes Letter to Iranian Leader to Stop Deal, then Meets with Defense Companies. *Addicting Info*. Available, http://www.addictinginfo.org/2015/03/10/gop-senator-writes-letter-to-iranian-leader-to-stop-deal-then-meets-with-defense-companies/

Lopez, German (2015, July 9). A Century of Research Says Donald Trump Is Wrong about Immigrants and Crime. *Vox*. Available, http://www.vox.com/2015/7/9/8922783/immigrants-crime-donald-trump

Lopez, German (2016, July 18). US Rep. Steve King Preaches Literal White Supremacy on National Television. *Vox*. Available, http://www.vox.com/2016/7/18/12218672/steve-king-racist-ignorant

López, Ian Haney (2014). *Dog Whistle Politics: How Coded Racial Appeals Have Reinvented Racism & Wrecked the Middle Class*. Oxford: Oxford University Press.

López-Levy, Arturo (2014/2015, winter). What Obama's New Cuba Policy Means for the Rest of the Americas. *NACLA—Report on the Americas, 47*(4), 4–6.

Lorber, Eric B. (2016, November 16). President Trump and the Iran Nuclear Deal. *Foreign Policy*. Available, http://foreignpolicy.com/2016/11/16/president-trump-and-the-iran-nuclear-deal/

Lotan, Gilad, Erhardt Graeff, Mike Ananny, Devin Gaffney, Ian Pearce, and Danah Boyd (2011). The Revolutions Were Tweeted: Information Flows During the 2011 Tunisian and Egyptian Revolutions. *International Journal of Communication 5*, 1375–1405.

Lott, John R., Jr. (2003). *The Bias against Guns: Why Almost Everything You've Heard about Gun Control Is Wrong*. Washington, D.C.: Regnery Publishing.

Lott, John R., Jr. (2010). *More Guns, Less Crime: Understanding Crime and Gun Control Laws* (3rd ed.). Chicago: University of Chicago Press.

Loving v. Virginia. 388 U.S. 1 (1967).

Lovink, Geert (2011). *Networks Without a Cause: A Critique of Social Media*. Cambridge, UK: Polity.

Lowen, Linda (2012, March 6). Sandra Fluke/Rush Limbaugh—Transcript of Her Testimony—His Slutshaming Comments. *About.com*. Available, http://womensissues.about.com/b/2012/03/06/sandra-fluke-rush-limbaugh-transcripts-of-her-testimony-his-slut-shaming-comments.htm

Lowery, Wesley (2014, December 30). Police: Multiple Witnesses Say Antonio Martin Pulled Gun on Officer. *The Washington Post*. Available, https://www.washingtonpost.com/news/post-nation/wp/2014/12/30/police-multiple-witnesses-say-antonio-martin-pulled-gun-on-officer/?utm_term=.e25120663656

Lowery, Wesley (2016). *They Can't Kill Us All: Ferguson, Baltimore, and a New Era in America's Racial Justice Movement*. New York: Little Brown and Company.

Lowry, Rich (2014, November 25). The Ferguson Fraud. *Politico*. Available, http://www.politico.com/magazine/story/2014/11/ferguson-fraud-113178.html#ixzz3K8r9DnAG

Lowry, Rich (2016, June 22). Brexit and the Case for Modern Nationalism. *Politico*. Available, http://www.politico.com/magazine/story/2016/06/yes-to-brexit-213984

Lucas, Fred (2014, July 1). Critics Who Claim Voter ID Laws are Racist won't Like the Results of this Study. *The Blaze*. Available, http://www.theblaze.com/stories/2014/07/01/critics-who-claim-voter-id-laws-are-racist-wont-like-the-results-of-this-study/

Lukensmeyer, Carolyn (2016, May 21). A Return to Civil Discourse. *Las Vegas Review-Journal*. Available, https://www.reviewjournal.com/opinion/a-return-to-civil-discourse/

Lunceford, Brett (2012). Rhetoric and Religion in Contemporary Politics. *Journal of Contemporary Rhetoric 2*(2), 19–29.

Lunsford, Andrea A., and John J. Ruszkiewicz (2007). *Everything's an Argument* (4th ed.). Boston: Bedford/St. Martin's.

Lupia, Arthur (2015). *Uninformed: Why People Seem to Know So Little about Politics and What We Can Do about It*. New York: Oxford University Press.

Lupu, Ira C., David Masci, and Robert W. Tuttle (2007). Religious Displays and the Courts. *The Pew Forum on Religion & Public Life*. Available, http://www.pewforum.org/files/2007/06/religious-displays.pdf

Lusero, Indra (2009, May 11). New study: Obama Can Halt Gay Discharges with Executive Order. *Palm Center*. Available, http://www.palmcenter.org/press/dadt/releases/New+Study+Says+Obama+Can+Halt+Gay+Discharges+With+Executive+Order

Luthern, Ashley (2014, December 22). Ex-Milwaukee Officer Won't Be Charged in Dontre Hamilton Shooting. *Milwaukee Journal Sentinel*. Available, http://archive.jsonline.com/news/milwaukee/former-officer-wont-be-charged-in-fatal-shooting-of-dontre-hamilton-b99398655z1-286559211.html

Lutz, William (1999). *Doublespeak Defined: Cut Through the Bull**** and Get the Point!* New York: Harper Collins.

Lutzer, Erwin W. (2010). *The Truth about Same-Sex Marriage*. Chicago: Moody Publishers.

Lynch, Matthew P. (2008). "Don't Ask, Don't Tell" Revisited: Debunking the Unit-Cohesion Rationale for the Continuing Exclusion of Gays from the Military. *University of Louisville Law Review, 47*(2), 391–408.

Lynn, Barry W. (2008, September 23). Why Don't Churches Pay Taxes? *The Los Angeles Times*. Available, http://www.latimes.com/la-oew-lynn-stanley23-2008sep23-story.html#page=1

Lysiak, Matthew, Daniel Beekman, and Larry McShane (2012, June 14). Cops Cheer NYPD Officer Richard Haste, Charged in Death of Teen Ramarley Graham. *New York Daily News*. Available, http://www.nydailynews.com/news/crime/nypd-officer-richard-haste-surrenders-face-charges-on-duty-killing-ramarley-graham-article-1.1094739

Lysiak, Matthew, Ginger Adams Otis, and Corky Siemasko (2015, April 10). Family of Walter Scott Tells Rev. Al Sharpton to Keep Away. *New York Daily News*. Available, http://www.nydailynews.com/news/crime/family-walter-scott-shot-dead-preparing-lawsuit-article-1.2179020

Mac Donald, Heather (2007, April 2). Time for the Truth about Black Crime Rates. *City Journal*. Available, https://www.city-journal.org/html/time-truth-about-black-crime-rates-10233.html

Mac Donald, Heather (2014, Autumn). The Microaggression Farce. *City Journal*. Available, https://www.city-journal.org/html/microaggression-farce-13679.html

Mac Donald, Heather (2015, November 17). Written Testimony before the United States Senate Committee on the Judiciary. *Hearing on "The War on Police: How the Federal Government Undermines State and Local Law Enforcement."* Available, https://www.judiciary.senate.gov/imo/media/doc/11-17-15%20Mac%20Donald%20Testimony.pdf

MacGillis, Alec (2014, August 21). Libertarians Who Oppose a Militarized Police Should Support Gun Control—But They Don't, of Course. *New Republic*. Available, https://newrepublic.com/article/119170/libertarians-oppose-militarized-police-not-gun-control-make-sense

Maddow, Rachel (2013, April 3). Next Stage in the Culture War: Official State Religions. *MSNBC*. Available, http://www.msnbc.com/rachel-maddow-show/next-stage-the-culture-war-official

Maestas, Adriana (2014, February 27). Americans Divided over Deportations, But Majority Still Supports a Path to Legal Status. *Politics365.com*. Available, http://politic365.com/2014/02/27/americans-divided-over-deportations-but-majority-still-supports-a-path-to-legal-status/

Mahler, Jonathan (2015, October 15). What do We Really Know about Osama bin Laden's Death? *The New York Times*. Available, https://www.nytimes.com/2015/10/18/magazine/what-do-we-really-know-about-osama-bin-ladens-death.html

Major, Clarence (1970). *Dictionary of Afro-American Slang*. New York: New World Paperbacks.

Malcolm X (1964a, April 3). The Ballot or the Bullet Speech. Available, http://www.edchange.org/multicultural/speeches/malcolm_x_ballot.html

Malcolm X (1964b, June 28). Speech at the Founding Rally of the Organization of Afro-American Unity. Available, http://www.blackpast.org/1964-malcolm-x-s-speech-founding-rally-organization-afro-american-unity

Mallicote, Ben (2017, February 9). How to Reason with a Trump Voter. *CNN*. Available, http://www.cnn.com/2017/02/07/opinions/reasoning-with-trump-voters-mallicote/index.html

Malott, Krista M., Tina R. Paone, Scott Schaefle, and Jiabao Gao (2015). Is it Racist? Addressing Racial Microaggressions in Counselor Training. *Journal of Creativity in Mental Health*, 10(3), 386–398.

Man, Caroline (2015, June 30). Coulter: 'I'm Offended' Is Not an Argument against Trump. Facts Back Him Up. *Breitbart*. Available, http://www.breitbart.com/big-government/2015/06/30/coulter-im-offended-is-not-an-argument-against-trump-facts-back-him-up/

Mansfield, Katie (2017, January 30). Shock Poll: More than Half of Americans Support Trump's Controversial Border Controls. *Express*. Available, http://www.express.co.uk/news/world/760914/donald-trump-poll-half-americans-support-refugee-travel-ban-united-states

Mantel, Barbara (2014). Gun Control. In Congressional Quarterly's *Issues for Debate in American Public Policy* (pp. 225–248). Thousand Oaks, CA: Congressional Quarterly Press.

Mantilla, Camilo Cristancho (2013). *Political Disagreement in Contentious Politics*. Doctoral Dissertation at the Universitat Autònoma de Barcelona.

Mantyla, Kyle (2010, July 22). Newt Gingrich's First Amendment Hypocrisy. *Right Wing Watch*. Available, http://www.rightwing-watch.org/content/newt-gingrichs-first-amendment-hypocrisy

Mao, LuMing, and Morris Young (2008). Introduction: Performing Asian American Rhetoric into the American Imgainary. In LuMing Mao & Morris Young (Eds.), *Representations: Doing Asian American Rhetoric* (pp. 1–22). Logan, UT: Utah State University Press.

Marans, Daniel (2015, November 21). Trump Supporters Reportedly Beat Black Lives Matter Protester at Campaign Rally. *The Huffington Post*. Available, http://www.huffingtonpost.com/entry/trump-supporters-black-lives-matter_5650e463e4b0258edb31c94b?dx869a4i

Marcotte, Amanda (2012, March 4). Who Me? Limbaugh Regrets Not Slurring American Women with a Better Euphemism for Slut. *RH Reality Check*. Available, http://rhrealitycheck.org/article/2012/03/04/limbaugh-promises-better-euphemisms-when-slurring-99-american-women/

Marcus, Jeffrey (2017, April 5). The Holes in Russia's Account of the Syria Chemical Attack. *The New York Times*. Available, https://www.nytimes.com/2017/04/05/world/middleeast/russia-account-syria-chemical-attack.html

Markind, Johanna (2015, December 5). Jews are Still the Biggest Target of Religious Hate Crimes. *Forward*. Available, http://forward.com/news/325988/jews-are-still-the-biggest-target-of-hate-crimes/?shareimg=326038

Markoe, Lauren (2013, November 7). Supreme Court Tackles Legislative Prayer at Public Meetings. *The Huffington Post*. Available, http://www.huffingtonpost.com/2013/11/07/supreme-court-prayer_n_4228715.html

Marsh v. Chambers. 463 U.S. 783 (1983).

Marshall, Josh (2016, July 13). A Propagator of Race Hatred and Violence. *Talking Points Memo*. Available, http://talkingpointsmemo.com/edblog/a-propagator-of-race-hatred-and-violence

Martin, Philip (2003). Does the U.S. Need a New Bracero Program? *U.C. Davis Journal of International Law & Policy 9*(2), 127–142.

Mason, Jeff, and Andreas Rinke (2017, March 17). In First Trump-Merkel Meeting, Awkward Body Language and a Quip. *Reuters*. Available, http://www.reuters.com/article/us-usa-trump-germany-idUSKBN16O0FM

Mast, Nina (2016, July 27). Bill O'Reilly Lambasted for Claiming that Slaves Who Built White House Were "Well-Fed and Had Decent Lodgings." *Media Matters for America*. Available, http://mediamatters.org/research/2016/07/27/bill-o-reilly-lambasted-claiming-slaves-who-built-white-house-were-well-fed-and-had-decent-lodgings/211935

Mazza, Ed (2015, February 17). Mississippi Lawmaker: Blacks don't Work and get 'Crazy Welfare Checks.' *The Huffington Post*. Available, http://www.msn.com/en-us/news/politics/mississippi-lawmaker-blacks-dont-work-and-get-crazy-welfare-checks/ar-BBhEOQI

McAfee, Tierney (2015, September 3). Donald Trump Slams Jeb Bush for Speaking Spanish on the Campaign Trail. *People*. Available, http://people.com/celebrity/donald-trump-slams-jeb-bush-for-speaking-spanish-on-the-campaign-trail/

McBride, Bailey Elise (2014, April 25). Oklahoma High School's Bible Curriculum: Sinners Must 'Suffer.' *The Huffington Post*. Available, http://www.huffingtonpost.com/2014/04/25/oklahoma-hobbly-lobby-bible-curriculum-_n_5215118.html?utm_hp_ref=politics

McBride, Jessica (2016, September 20). Terence Crutcher Family: 5 Fast Facts You Need to Know. *Heavy*. Available, http://heavy. com/news/2016/09/terence-terrence-crutcher-family-sister-tiffany-twin-wife-children-father-married-shot-video-watch-tulsa-oklahoma-betty-shelby/

McCalmont, Lucy (2014, May 2). Rush Limbaugh: Why Media Ignores Benghazi. *Politico*. Available, http://www.politico.com/ story/2014/05/rush-limbaugh-media-benghazi-106292.html

McCarty, Nolan, Keith T. Poole, and Howard Rosenthal (2008). *Polarized America: The Dance of Ideology and Unequal Riches*. Cambridge, MA: MIT Press.

McCauley, Lauren (2015, June 1). Highlighting Government Failure, News Agencies Tally Killings by Police. *Common Dreams*. Available, http://www.commondreams.org/news/2015/06/01/highlighting-government-failure-news-agencies-tally-killings-police#sthash.D18eK83Q.dpuf

McCauley, Lauren (2017, March 3). Leaked Doc Puts "Stake in the Heart" of Trump's Travel Ban Rationale. *Common Dreams*. Available, http://www.commondreams.org/news/2017/03/03/leaked-doc-puts-stake-heart-trumps-travel-ban-rationale

McCollum v. Board of Education Dist. 71. 333 U.S. 203 (1948).

McCombs, Maxwell (2004). *Setting the Agenda: The Mass Media and Public Opinion*. Malden, MA: Blackwell Publishing.

McCoy, Terrence (2014, August 14). Tear Gas is a Chemical Weapon Banned in War. But Ferguson Police Shoot it at Protestors. *The Washington Post*. Available, http://www.washingtonpost.com/news/morning-mix/wp/2014/08/14/tear-gas-is-a-chemical-weapon-banned-in-war-but-ferguson-police-shoot-it-at-protesters/

McCreary County v. ACLU of Kentucky. 545 U.S. 844 (2005).

McCue-Enser, Margret (2017). Ada Deer and the Menominee Restoration: Rethinking Native American Protest Rhetoric. *Argumentation & Advocacy, 53*(1), 59–76.

McDonald, Andrew (2017, April 15). Video Shows Chinese Missile Tanks Rolling Towards North Korea as World Waits in Fear. *Daily Star*. Available, http://www.dailystar.co.uk/news/latest-news/605562/China-war-North-Korea-US-Russia-tanks-military-video

McFadden, Robert D. (2009, April 3). 13 Shot Dead During a Class on Citizenship. *The New York Times*. Available, http://www.nytimes.com/2009/04/04/nyregion/04hostage.html?pagewanted=all&_r=0

McGill, Andrew (2016, October 7). What Trump Tweets While America Sleeps. *The Atlantic*. Available, https://www.theatlantic.com/politics/archive/2016/10/what-trump-tweets-while-america-sleeps/503141/

McGough, Michael (2014, May 5). Opinion in Prayer Case, Supreme Court Justice Clarence Thomas Proves Critics Wrong. *The Los Angeles Times*. Available, http://www.latimes.com/opinion/opinion-la/la-ol-supreme-court-prayer-thomas-20140505-story.html

McKirdy, Euan (2017, April 5). Russia Says Deadly Syrian Airstrike Targeted Chemical Weapons Factory. *CNN*. Available, http://www.cnn.com/2017/04/05/middleeast/idlib-syria-attack/

McLaughlin, Michael (2015, July 1). Donald Trump Goes After Immigrants Again, Claiming to Have Facts. *The Huffington Post*. Available, http://www.huffingtonpost.com/2015/07/01/donald-trump-immigrants_n_7709798.html

McLeod, Harriot (2016, December 2). Trial over Walter Scott Killing by South Carolina Police Deadlocks over Holdout Juror. *The Huffington Post*. Available, http://www.huffingtonpost.com/entry/jury-deadlocked-over-police-shooting-of-unarmed-black-man_us_5841ecffe4b0c68e0480d6e4

McManus, Doyle (2015, November 18). Overheated Rhetoric Won't Solve the Syrian Refugee Issue. *Los Angeles Times*. Available, http://www.latimes.com/opinion/op-ed/la-oe-1118-mcmanus-syria-refugees-20151118-column.html

McNamara, Melissa (2005, October 14). America the Rude. *CBS News*. Available, https://www.cbsnews.com/news/america-the-rude/

McPherson, Miller, Lynn Smith-Lovin, and James M. Cook (2001). Birds of a Feather: Homophily in Social Networks. *Annual Review of Sociology, 27*, 415–444.

McWhorter, John (2014, March 21). 'Microaggression' is the New Racism on Campus. *Time*. Available, http://time.com/32618/microaggression-isthe-new-racism-on-campus/

Mears, Bill (2014, August 20). Supreme Court: No Same-Sex marriage in Virginia, Yet. *CNN Politics*. Available, http://www.cnn.com/2014/08/20/politics/virginia-same-sex-marriage/index.html

Meckler, Laura (2014, June 20). U.S. to Speed up Deportation of Migrants. *Wall Street Journal*. Available, http://online.wsj.com/articles/u-s-to-speed-up-deportation-of-migrants-1403291138

Media Matters (2006, December 22). Most Outrageous Statements of 2006. *Media Matters for America*. Available, http://mediamatters.org/research/2006/12/22/most-outrageous-comments-of-2006/137592

Media Tenor (2003a). Reality: Bush's PR Fiasco or Success Story? *Media Tenor Quarterly Journal, 2*, 46–47.

Media Tenor (2003b). The War on TV: "Better" Is Not Good Enough. *Media Tenor Quarterly Journal, 2*, 39–43.

Media Tenor (2004). No Global Media? *Media Tenor Quarterly Journal, 2*, 58–59.

Mehta, Hemant (2012, June 16). The Yearly Cost of Religious Tax Exemptions. *Patheos*. Available, http://www.patheos.com/blogs/friendlyatheist/2012/06/16/the-yearly-cost-of-religious-tax-exemptions-71000000000/

Mejia, Paula (2014, September 6). Obama Will Delay Action on Immigration Until after November. *Newsweek*. Available, http://www.newsweek.com/obama-will-delay-immigration-act-until-after-november-elections-268811

Menon, Rajan (2017, January 12). Will Trump Shred the Iran Nuclear Deal? *The Huffington Post*. Available, http://www.huffingtonpost.com/rajan-menon/will-trump-shred-the-iran-nuclear-deal_b_14134630.html

Merica, Dan (2017, April 11). Trump on Pace to Surpass 8 Years of Obama's Travel Spending in 1 Year. *CNN Politics*. Available, http://www.cnn.com/2017/04/10/politics/donald-trump-obama-travel-costs/

Merica, Dan, Eugene Scott, and Barbara Starr (2017, April 4). US Officials: Early Belief Is that Syrian Attack Used Sarin Gas. *CNN Politics*. Available, http://www.cnn.com/2017/04/04/politics/syria-chemical-attack-donald-trump-obama/index.html

Merolla, Jennifer, S. Karthick Ramakrishnan, and Chris Haynes (2013). "Illegal," "Undocumented," or "Unauthorized": Equivalency Frames, Issue Frames, and Public Opinion on Immigration. *Perspectives on Politics*, *11*(3), 789–807.

Meyers, Jessica (2017, April 14). China Urges Calm after North Korea Pledges to 'Ruthlessly Ravage' the U.S. in the Event of a Military Strike. *Los Angeles Times*. Available, http://www.latimes.com/politics/washington/la-na-essential-washington-updates-china-urges-all-parties-to-stop-1492220172-htmlstory.html

Migration Policy Institute (2013a, March). *Key Immigration Laws and Policy Developments Since 1986*. Available, file:///C:/Users/zompetti/Downloads/CIR-1986Timeline.pdf.

Migration Policy Institute (2013b, March). *Major US Immigration Laws, 1790–present*. Available, file:///C:/Users/zompetti/Downloads/CIR-1790Timeline.pdf.

Milbank, Dana (2010). *Tears of a Clown: Glenn Beck and the Tea Bagging of America*. New York: Doubleday.

Milbank, Dana (2016, November 29). Trump's 'News' Source: Voter Fraud! Also, Space Lizards! *The Washington Post*. Available, Lexis-Nexis.

Miller, Brian and Laud Humphreys (1980). Lifestyles and Violence: Homosexual Victims of Assault and Murder. *Qualitative Sociology* *3*(3), 169–185.

Miller, Greg, and Philip Rucker (2017, February 2). 'This was the Worst Call by Far': Trump Badgered, Bragged and Abruptly Ended Phone Call with Australian Leader. *The Washington Post*. Available, https://www.washingtonpost.com/world/national-security/no-gday-mate-on-call-with-australian-pm-trump-badgers-and-brags/2017/02/01/88a3bfb0-e8bf-11e6-80c2-30e57e57e05d_story.html?utm_term=.60017600dc15

Miller, Greg, and Missy Ryan (2017, January 29). Officials Worry that U.S. Counterterrorism Defenses Will Be Weakened by Trump Actions. *The Washington Post*. Available, https://www.washingtonpost.com/world/national-security/officials-worry-that-us-counterterrorism-defenses-will-be-weakened-by-trump-actions/2017/01/29/1f045074-e644-11e6-b82f-687d6e6a3e7c_story.html?utm_term=.bc1da289d6a3

Miller, Matthew, Deborah Azrael, and Davide Hemenway (2013). In Daniel W. Webster & Jon S. Vernick (Eds.), *Reducing Gun Violence in America: Informing Policy with Evidence and Analysis* (pp. 3–20). Baltimore: Johns Hopkins University Press.

Miller, Michael E., Wesley Lowery, and Lindsey Bever (2016, July 8). Minn. Governor Says Race Played Role in Fatal Police Shooting During Traffic Stop. *MSN News*. Available, http://www.msn.com/en-us/news/us/minn-governor-says-race-played-role-in-fatal-police-shooting-during-traffic-stop/ar-BBu22Up

Miller, Mike (2015, April). Charles Krauthammer Explains the 'Most Astonishing Thing' about Obama's Nuclear Deal with Iran. *Independent Journal Review*. Available, http://ijr.com/2015/04/287604-krauthammer-explains-astonishing-thing-obamas-nuclear-deal-iran/

Miller, Tom (2013, Fall). Conservative health-care reform: A reality check. *National Affairs*. Available, http://www.nationalaffairs.com/publications/detail/conservative-health-care-reform-a-reality-check

Miller, Zeke J. (2014, August 28). Obama Says 'We don't have a Strategy Yet' for Fighting ISIS. *Time*. Available, http://time.com/3211132/isis-iraq-syria-barack-obama-strategy/

Miller, Zeke J. (2017, January 28). President Trump Orders 30-Day Review of Strategy to Fight ISIS. *Time*. Available, http://time.com/4652696/president-trump-isis-review/

Millhiser, Ian (2012, August 7). NRA Sent Paranoid Fundraising Letter Three Days after Aurora Shooting. *Think Progress*. Available, http://thinkprogress.org/justice/2012/08/07/649891/nra-sent-paranoid-fundraising-letter-three-days-after-aurora-shooting/

Millhiser, Ian (2014, October 31). The Enormous, Secretive Effort to Purge Thousands of Minorities from 27 States' Voter Rolls. *Think Progress*. Available, http://thinkprogress.org/justice/2014/10/31/3587074/the-enormous-secretive-effort-to-purge-thousands-of-minorities-from-27-states-voter-rolls/

Milstein, Adam (2016, May 5). Boycott, Divestment and Sanctions (BDS) Leaders Hate America: Listen to Their Own Words! *The Huffington Post*. Available, http://www.huffingtonpost.com/adam-milstein/boycott-divestment-and-sa_b_9527960.html

Min Kim, Seung (2017, January 25). Trump Signs Orders on Border Wall, Immigration Crackdown. *Politico*. Available, http://www.politico.com/story/2017/01/donald-trump-immigration-234142

Minnite, Lorraine C. (2015, March 9). The Myth of Voter Fraud. *Portside*. Available, http://portside.org/2015-03-15/myth-voter-fraud

Mirengoff, Paul (2015, July 28). Mike Huckabee's Overblown Rhetoric on the Iran Deal. *Powerline*. Available, http://www.powerlineblog.com/archives/2015/07/mike-huckabees-overblown-rhetoric-on-the-iran-deal.php

Mirkinson, Jack (2012, March 30). Keith Olbermann Fired by Current TV; Replaced by Eliot Spitzer. *The Huffington Post*. Available, http://www.huffingtonpost.com/2012/03/30/keith-olbermann-out-current-eliot-spitzer_n_1392513.html

Mirkinson, Jack (2015, November 21). Trump Supporters Hit, Kick Black Protester at Alabama Rally. *Fusion*. Available, http://fusion.net/story/236868/trump-black-protester-kicked-punched-alabama/?utm_source=twitter&utm_medium=social&utm_campaign=socialshare&utm_content=desktop+top

Mohanty, Sarita A., Steffie Woolhandler, David U. Himmelstein, Susmita Pati, Olveen Carrasquillo, and David H. Bor (2005). Health Care Expenditures of Immigrants in the United States: A Nationally Representative Analysis. *American Journal of Public Health*, *95*(8), 1431–1438.

Molyneux, John (2003). *The Future Socialist Society*. Chicago: Haymarket Books.

Montgomery, Krista (2014, April 21). 'Jesus Is a Myth': Laura Ingraham Flips Out over Atheist Sign. *Americans Against the Tea Party*. Available, http://aattp.org/jesus-is-a-myth-laura-ingraham-flips-out-over-atheist-sign-video/

Monthly Statistical Report on Victims (2017, March). *Violations Documentation Center in Syria*. Available, http://vdc-sy.net/march-2017-monthly-statistical-report-on-victims/

Moore, Mark (2017a, March 30). Kim Threatens to Nuke US after McCain Calls Him 'Crazy Fat Kid.' *New York Post*. Available, http://nypost.com/2017/03/30/kim-threatens-to-nuke-us-after-mccain-calls-him-fat/

Moore, Mark (2017b, March 26). Schumer Blames Failed Healthcare Bill on Trump's Bullying. *New York Post*. Available, http://nypost.com/2017/03/26/schumer-blames-failed-healthcare-bill-on-trumps-bullying/

Moore, Michael (2007). *Sicko*. Dog Eat Dog Films.

Moorhead, Molly (2012, March 6). In Context: Sandra Fluke on Contraceptives and Women's Health. *Politifact.com*. Available, http://www.politifact.com/truth-o-meter/article/2012/mar/06/context-sandra-fluke-contraceptives-and-womens-hea/

Morales, Lymari (2009, May 29). Knowing Someone Gay/Lesbian Affects Views of Gay Issues. *Gallup*. Available, http://www.gallup.com/poll/118931/Knowing-Someone-Gay-Lesbian-Affects-Views-Gay-Issues.aspx

Moreno, John A., Melissa Palmer, and Nerissa Knight (2014, August 14). Police Fatally Shoot Man in South L.A.; Family Members Say He Was Lying Down When Shot. *KTLA*. Available, http://ktla.com/2014/08/12/man-hospitalized-after-being-shot-by-police-in-south-l-a/

Morris, Henry (2000). Evil-ution. *Acts & Facts* 29(8). Available, http://www.icr.org/article/evil-ution/

Morris, Richard B. (1973). *Seven Who Shaped Our Destiny: The Founding Fathers as Revolutionaries*. New York: Harper & Row.

Morris, Richard, and Philip Wander (1990). Native American Rhetoric: Dancing in the Shadows of the Ghost Dance. *Quarterly Journal of Speech*, 76(2), 164–191.

Morrison, Sara (2014, April 28). NRA's 2014 Convention Theme: FEAR. *The Wire*. Available, http://www.thewire.com/national/2014/04/nras-2014-convention-theme-fear/361285/

Mortimer, Caroline (2016, September 22). Black Men Have Legitimate Reason to Run from Police, Supreme Court Rules. *Independent*. Available, http://www.independent.co.uk/news/world/americas/black-men-have-legitimate-reason-to-run-from-police-us-court-ruling-charlotte-keith-lamont-scott-a7322151.html

Mouzahem, Haytham (2016, May 12). Who Are Syria's Alawites? *Al Monitor*. Available, http://www.al-monitor.com/pulse/originals/2016/05/alawite-sect-muslim-misconceptions.html

Mueller, Dennis C. (2003). *Public choice III*. Cambridge, UK: Cambridge University Press.

Mufson, Steven, and Katie Zezima (2015, March 3). Netanyahu Says U.S. Is on Verge of 'Bad Deal' with Iran over Nuclear Program. *The Washington Post*. Available, https://www.washingtonpost.com/business/economy/netanyahu-says-us-is-on-verge-of-bad-deal-with-iran-over-nuclear-program/2015/03/03/8dbb2774-c1c8-11e4-ad5c-3b8ce89f1b89_story.html?utm_term=.33d33988c380

Murguía, Janet (2014, July 21). Remarks at the 2014 NCLR annual conference. *National Council of La Raza*. Available, http://www.nclr.org/images/uploads/pages/Janet_Murguia_Monday%20NCLR_Conference_Speech_Final.pdf.

Muthusamy, Nithya, Timothy R. Levine, and Rene Weber (2009). Scaring the Already Scared: Some Problems with HIV/AIDS Fear Appeals in Namibia. *Journal of Communication* 59(2), 317–344.

Mutz, Diana C. (2006). How the Mass Media Divide Us. In Pietro S. Nivola & David W. Brady (Eds.), *Red and Blue Nation?: Characteristics and Causes of America's Polarized Politics*, Volume 1 (pp. 223–248). Washington, D.C.: Hoover Institution and Brookings Institution.

Nadeau, Barbie Latza (2017, April 7). Trump just Discovered the Slaughter of Syria's 'Beautiful Babies'? *The Daily Beast*. Available, http://www.thedailybeast.com/articles/2017/04/07/trump-just-discovered-the-slaughter-of-syria-s-beautiful-babies.html

NARAL (2011). 2011: The War on Women. *NARAL: Pro-Choice America*. Available, http://www.prochoiceamerica.org/get-involved/2011-the-war-on-women.html

National Community Reinvestment Coalition (NCRC) (2016, July 18). NCRC Report on Lending in St. Louis, Milwaukee and Minneapolis Shows Clear Racial Disparities. *NCRC*. Available, http://www.ncrc.org/media-center/press-releases/item/1160-new-report-on-lending-in-st-louis-milwaukee-and-minneapolis-shows-clear-racial-disparities

National Conference of State Legislatures (2016, September 26). *Voter Identification Requirements/Voter ID Laws*. Available, http://www.ncsl.org/research/elections-and-campaigns/voter-id.aspx

National Park Service (2014, August 18). *Emma Lazarus*. Available, http://www.nps.gov/stli/historyculture/emma-lazarus.htm

Navarrette, Ruben, Jr. (2008, December 24). Commentary: Sarah Palin Understands Small-Town America. *CNN Politics*. Available, http://www.cnn.com/2008/POLITICS/12/24/navarrette.palin.smalltown/index.html?_s=PM:POLITICS

NeJaime, Douglas (2012). Marriage Inequality: Same-Sex Relationships, Religious Exemptions, and the Production of Sexual Orientation Discrimination. *California Law Review 100*, 1169–1238.

Nelson, Steven (2017, April 7). Lawmakers Say Proof Lacking before Trump Bombed Syria. *U.S. News & World Report*. Available, https://www.usnews.com/news/articles/2017-04-07/lawmakers-say-proof-lacking-before-trump-bombed-syria

Netanyahu, Benjamin (2015, March 3). The Complete Transcript of Netanyahu's Address to Congress. *The Washington Post*. Available, https://www.washingtonpost.com/news/post-politics/wp/2015/03/03/full-text-netanyahus-address-to-congress/?utm_term=.69f090eff4ed

Newell, Jim (2014, August 28). GOP's Steve King problem: How Action on Immigration Could Become a Republican Nightmare. *Salon.* Available, http://www.salon.com/2014/08/28/gops_steve_king_problem_how_action_on_immigration_could_become_a_republican_nightmare/?utm_source=facebook&utm_medium=socialflow

Newton, Caleb R. (2016, July 23). Florida Judge goes on Insanely Racist Tirade: 'Get on a Ship & Go Back to Africa.' *Bipartisan Report.* Available, http://bipartisanreport.com/2016/07/23/florida-judge-goes-on-insanely-racist-tirade-get-on-a-ship-go-back-to-africa-video/

The New York Times (2014, December 30). When New York City Police Walk Off the Job. *The New York Times.* Available, http://www.nytimes.com/2014/12/31/opinion/when-new-york-city-police-walk-off-the-job.html?hp&action=click&pgtype=Homepage&module=c-column-top-span-region&region=c-column-top-span-region&WT.nav=c-column-top-span-region&_r=1

Nicola, Nassira (2010. Black Face, White Voice: Rush Limbaugh and the "Message" of Race. *Journal of Language and Politics, 9*(2), 281–309.

Nichols, James (2013, September 12). Matthew Shepard Murdered by Bisexual Lover and Drug Dealer, Stephen Jimenez Claims in New Book. *The Huffington Post.* Available, http://www.huffingtonpost.com/2013/09/12/stephen-jimenez-matthew-shepard_n_3914707.html

Nickerson, Raymond S. (1998). Confirmation Bias: A Ubiquitous Phenomenon in Many Guises. *Review of General Psychology 2*(2), 175–220.

Nimmo, Kurt (2012, December 17). Ed Schultz: Confiscate Guns and Kill the Second Amendment. *InfoWars.* Available, http://www.infowars.com/ed-schultz-confiscate-guns-and-kill-the-second-amendment/

Nimmo, Kurt (2014, March 31). Support for Obamacare Keeps Falling. *InfoWars.* Available, http://www.infowars.com/support-for-obamacare-keeps-falling/

Nir, Arad (2015, August 20). Netanyahu Playing Chess, not Checkers on Iran Deal. *Al Monitor.* Available, http://www.al-monitor.com/pulse/originals/2015/08/benjamin-netanyahu-congress-vote-iran-agreement-majority.html#

Nix, Jusint, Bradley A. Campbell, Edward H. Byers, and Geoffrey P. Alpert (2017). A Bird's Eye View of Civilians Killed by Police in 2015: Further Evidence of Implicit Bias. *Criminology & Public Policy, 16*(1), 309–340.

Notte, Jason (2013, August 26). Maybe Churches Shouldn't Be Tax-Exempt. *MSN Money.* Available, http://money.msn.com/now/post—maybe-churches-shouldnt-be-tax-exempt

Nuckols, Mark (2013, January 31). Why the 'Citizen Militia' Theory Is the Worst Pro-Gun Argument Ever. *The Atlantic.* Available, http://www.theatlantic.com/national/archive/2013/01/why-the-citizen-militia-theory-is-the-worst-pro-gun-argument-ever/272734/

Núñez, D. Carolina (2013). War of the Words: Aliens, Immigrants, Citizens, and the Language of Exclusion. *Brigham Young University Law Review 2013*(6), 1517–1562.

Nunez, Peter (2004, February). Preventing the Entry of Terrorists into the United States. Testimony before the U.S. House of Representatives, Committee on International Relations, Subcommittee on International Terrorism, Nonproliferation and Human Rights. *Center for Immigration Studies.* Available, http://cis.org/node/534

Nussbaum, Martha C. (2012). *The New Religious Intolerance: Overcoming the Politics of Fear in an Anxious Age.* Cambridge, MA: The Belknap Press.

Oakeshott, Michael (1965). Rationalism in Politics: A Reply to Professor Raphael. *Political Studies 13*(1), 89–92.

Obama, Barack (2008, April 11). Barack Obama's Small Town Guns and Religion Comments. *YouTube*, posted by potus08blog. Available, https://www.youtube.com/watch?v=DTxXUufI3jA

Obama, Barack (2015, June 22). President Barack Obama. *WTF with Marc Maron.* Available, http://www.wtfpod.com/podcast/episodes/episode_613_-_president_barack_obama?rq=obama

ObamaCareFacts (2014). *Obamacare Facts: Dispelling the Myths.* Available, http://obamacarefacts.com/affordablecareact-summary.php

Obasogie, Osagie K., and Zachary Newman (2016). Black Lives Matter and Respectability Politics in Local News Accounts of Officer-Involved Civilian Deaths: An Early Empirical Assessment. *Wisconsin Law Review, 2016*(3), 541–574.

Ohio Len (2005, July 1). Ann Coulter, Free Speech and Religion. *The Daily Kos.* Available, http://www.dailykos.com/story/2005/07/01/127263/-Ann-Coulter-Free-Speech-and-Religion

O'Keefe, Victoria, M., Laricka R. Wingate, Ashley B. Cole, David W. Hollingsworth, and Raymond P. Tucker (2015). Seemingly Harmless Racial Communications Are Not So Harmless: Racial Microaggressions Lead to Suicidal Ideation by Way of Depression Symptoms. *Suicide and Life-Threatening Behavior, 45*(5), 567–576.

O'Kelly, Morris W. (2014, November 13). Stop the Media's Reckless Provocation of Violence in Ferguson. *The Huffington Post.* Available, http://www.huffingtonpost.com/morris-w-okelly/stop-the-medias-reckless-_b_6148052.html

Olbermann, Keith (2011). *Pitchforks and Torches: The Worst of the Worst, from Beck, Bill, and Bush to Palin and Other Posturing Republicans.* Hoboken, NJ: Wiley.

Olsen, Ted (2014, May 5). Why We Pray before Public Meetings. *Christianity Today.* Available, http://www.christianitytoday.com/ct/2014/may-web-only/supreme-court-prayer-decision-editorial-greece-galloway.html

Omero, Margie, Michael Bocian, Bob Carpenter, Linda DiVall, Diane T. Feldman, Celinda Lake, Douglas E. Schoen, Al Quinlan, Joshua Ulibarri, and Arkadi Gerney (2013, March 27). What the Public Really Thinks about Guns. *The Center for American Progress.* Available, http://americanprogress.org/issues/civil-liberties/report/2013/03/27/58092/what-the-public-really-thinks-about-guns/

Ommundsen, Reidar, Kees van der Veer, S. Knud Larsen, and Dag-Erik Eilertsen (2014). Framing Unauthorized Immigrants: The Effects of Labels on Evaluations. *Psychological Reports: Sociocultural Issues in Psychology 114*(2), 461–478.

Ong, Anthony D., Anthony Burrow, Thomas E. Fuller-Rowell, Nicole M. Ja, Derald Wing Sue (2013). Racial Microaggressions and Daily Well-Being among Asian Americans. *Journal of Counseling Psychology, 60*(2), 188–199.

O'Reilly, Bill (2014, July 23). Bill O'Reilly: ObamaCare and Socialism. *The O'Reilly Factor*. Available, http://www.foxnews.com/on-air/oreilly/2014/07/24/bill-oreilly-obamacare-and-socialism

Oreskes, Benjamin (2016, October 4). Pence Is Wrong: Syrian Refugees Didn't Commit the Paris Attacks. *Politico*. Available, http://www.politico.com/blogs/2016-presidential-debate-fact-check/2016/10/pence-is-wrong-syrian-refugees-didnt-commit-the-paris-attacks-229150

Ortega, Alexander N., Hai Fang, Victor H. Perez, John A. Rizzo, Olivia Carter-Pokras, Steven P. Wallace, and Lillian Gelberg (2007). Health Care Use among Undocumented Latino Immigrants. *Health Affairs, 19*(4), 51–64.

Osborne, Samuel (2017, April 11). Donald Trump's 'Armada' Steams on as North Korea Warns of Nuclear Strike on US. *The Independent*. Available, http://www.independent.co.uk/news/world/asia/donald-trump-north-korea-armada-nuclear-strike-us-navy-strike-group-fleet-aircraft-carrier-china-a7679586.html

Oswald, Dana M. (2004). Learning to Be Civil: Citizen *Judith* and Old English Culture. In Gerard A. Hauser & Amy Grim (Eds.), *Rhetorical Democracy: Discursive Practices of Civic Engagement* (pp. 269–275). Mahwah, NJ: Lawrence Erlbaum Associates.

Ott, Brian L. (2016). The Age of Twitter: Donald J. Trump and the Politics of Debasement. *Critical Studies in Media Communication, 34*(1), 59–68.

Ottaviano, Gianmarco I. P., and Giovanni Peri (2005, August). *Rethinking the Gains from Immigration: Theory and Evidence from the U.S. Immigration Law Worldwide* (unpublished working paper). Available, http://www.ilw.com/articles/2005,1216-peri.pdf

Otto, Joe (2013, October 13). Obamacare's End Game: Socialism. *Conservative-Daily*. Available, http://conservative-daily.com/2013/10/13/obamacares-end-game-socialism/

Page, Clarence (2017, April 27). Trump Faces a Legal Wall Around 'Sanctuary Cities.' *Detroit Free Press*. Available, http://www.freep.com/story/opinion/contributors/2017/04/27/trump-sanctuary-cities/100970832/

Palast, Greg (2014, October 29). Jim Crow Returns: Millions of Minority Voters Threatened by Electoral Purge. *Al Jazeera America*. Available, http://projects.aljazeera.com/2014/double-voters/

Palin, Sarah (2009, August 7). Statement on the Current Health Care Debate. *Facebook*. Available, https://www.facebook.com/note.php?note_id=113851103434&ref=mf

Papacharissi, Zizi A. (2010). *A Private Sphere: Democracy in a Digital Age*. New York: Polity.

Park, Edwin and Robert Greenstein (2006, January 30). Latest Enrollment Data Still Fail to Dispel Concerns about Health Savings Accounts. *Center on Budget and Policy Priorities*. Available, http://www.cbpp.org/cms/?fa=view&id=775

Parker, Ashley, David Nakamura, and Dan Lamothe (2017, April 7). 'Horrible' Pictures of Suffering Moved Trump to Action on Syria. *The Washington Post*. Available, https://www.washingtonpost.com/politics/horrible-pictures-of-suffering-moved-trump-to-action-on-syria/2017/04/07/9aa9fcc8-1bce-11e7-8003-f55b4c1cfae2_story.html?utm_term=.38979109ac77

Parker, Jennifer (2007, June 19). Gingrich Rewrites 9/11 History in Immigration Ad. *ABC News*. Available, http://abcnews.go.com/blogs/politics/2007/06/gingrich_rewrit/

Parker, Walter C. (2003). *Teaching Democracy: Unity and Diversity in Public Life*. New York: Teachers College Press.

Parsons, Chelsea and Anne Johnson (2014, February). Guns: How Gun Violence Is Devastating the Millennial Generation. *The Center for American Progress*. Available, http://americanprogress.org/issues/guns-crime/report/2014/02/21/84491/young-guns-how-gun-violence-is-devastating-the-millennial-generation/

Parsons, Christi, Brian Bennett, and Lisa Mascaro (2014, July 25). White House Pursuing Plans to Expand Immigrant Rights. *The Los Angeles Times*. Available, http://www.latimes.com/nation/la-na-obama-immigration-20140726-story.html#page=1

Parton, Heather Digby (2014, June 26). Rise of a Right-Wing Quack: Faux-Historian David Barton's Shocking New Influence. *Salon*. Available, http://www.salon.com/2014/06/26/rise_of_a_right_wing_quack_faux_historian_david_bartons_shocking_new_influence/?utm_source=facebook&utm_medium=socialflow

Patel, Eboo (2011, May 12). Newt Gingrich: A Catholic Running against Islam? *The Huffington Post*. Available, http://www.huffingtonpost.com/eboo-patel/newt-gingrich-catholic_b_860995.html

Patel, Neil (2016a). 10 Things We Can Learn about Social Media from the 2016 Presidential Election. *The Daily Egg*. Available, https://www.crazyegg.com/blog/2016-presidential-social-media/

Patterson, Charlotte J., and Richard E. Redding (1996). Lesbian and Gay Families with Children: Implications of Social Science Research for Policy. *Journal of Social Issues 52*(3), 29–50.

Patton, Stacey (2014, November 26). In America, Black Children Don't get to be Children. *The Washington Post*. Available, http://www.washingtonpost.com/opinions/in-america-black-children-dont-get-to-be-children/2014/11/26/a9e24756-74ee-11e4-a755-e32227229e7b_story.html

Paul, Richard, and Linda Elder (2004). *The Thinker's Guide to Fallacies: The Art of Mental Trickery and Manipulation*. Dillon Beach, CA: The Foundation for Critical Thinking.

Pear, Robert, Thomas Kaplan, and Maggie Haberman (2017, March 24). In Major Defeat for Trump, Push to Repeal Health Law Fails. *The New York Times*. Available, https://www.nytimes.com/2017/03/24/us/politics/health-care-affordable-care-act.html?_r=0

Pearson, Mark (2009, September 30). Written Statement to Senate Special Committee on Aging. Disparities in Health Expenditure across OECD Countries: Why Does the United States Spend So Much More than Other Countries? *OECD*. Available, http://www.oecd.org/unitedstates/43800977.pdf

Pearson, Michael, Saeed Ahmed, and Kevin Conlon (2014, June 10). Sheriff's office: Las Vegas Couple Saw Police as Oppressors. *CNN*. Available, http://www.cnn.com/2014/06/09/justice/las-vegas-shooting/

Pengelly, Martin (2015, July 26). Huckabee Defends Claim that Iran Deal Will 'March Israelis to Oven Door.' *The Guardian*. Available, https://www.theguardian.com/world/2015/jul/26/huckabee-iran-nuclear-deal-obama-marching-israelis-to-door-of-the-oven

Pennacchia, Robyn (2014, April 23). Georgia's 'Guns Everywhere Bill' Violates the Freedom of People Who Wish Not To Be Killed by Angry Drunks. *Death and Taxes Magazine*. Available, http://www.deathandtaxesmag.com/219505/georgias-guns-everywhere-bill-violates-the-freedom-of-people-who-wish-not-to-be-killed-by-angry-drunks/

Pennybaker, Harrison (2017). Difference between Viet Cong and Viet Minh. *People of Our Everyday Life*. Available, http://peopleof.oureverydaylife.com/difference-viet-cong-viet-minh-9418.html

Pérez-Peña, Richard (2015, July 29). University of Cincinnati Officer Indicted in Shooting Death of Samuel Dubose. *The New York Times*. Available, https://www.nytimes.com/2015/07/30/us/university-of-cincinnati-officer-indicted-in-shooting-death-of-motorist.html

Perrin, Ellen C., Benjamin S. Siegel, and the Committee on Psychological Aspects of Child and Family Health (2013, March 20). Promoting the Well-Being of Children Whose Parents Are Gay or Lesbian. *Journal of Pediatrics*. Available, http://pediatrics.aappublications.org/content/early/2013/03/18/peds.2013-0377

Persily, Nathaniel (2006, April 29). Gay Marriage, Public Opinion and the Courts. *Penn Law Faculty Scholarship*, Paper 91. Available, http://scholarship.law.upenn.edu/cgi/viewcontent.cgi?article=1090&context=faculty_scholarship

Peterson, Andrea (2016, July 8). In an Apparent First, Dallas Police Used a Robot to Deliver Bomb that Killed Shooting Suspect. *The Washington Post*. Available, https://www.washingtonpost.com/news/the-switch/wp/2016/07/08/dallas-police-used-a-robot-to-deliver-bomb-that-killed-shooting-suspect/?utm_term=.7ad943fd8098

Petrovic, John E., and Aaron M. Kuntz (2013). Strategies of Reframing Language Policy in the Liberal State. *Journal of Language & Politics*, *12*(1), 126–146.

Petrow, Steven (2014, May 23). Civilities: What Does the Acronym "LGBTQ" Stand For? *The Washington Post*. Available, http://www.washingtonpost.com/blogs/style-blog/wp/2014/05/23/civilities-what-does-the-acronym-lgbtq-stand-for/

Pew Research Center (2014a, March 10). Changing Attitudes on Gay Marriage. *Pew Research Forum*. Available, http://www.pewforum.org/2014/03/10/graphics-slideshow-changing-attitudes-on-gay-marriage/

Pew Research Center (2014b, June 12). Political Polarization in the American Public: How Increasing Ideological Uniformity and Partisan Antipathy Affect Politics, Compromise and Everyday Life. *Pew Foundation Reports*. Available, http://www.people-press.org/files/2014/06/6-12-2014-Political-Polarization-Release.pdf

Pew Research Center (2014c, February 27). Public Divided Over Increased Deportation of Unauthorized Immigrants. *Pew Research Center for the People & the Press*. Available, http://www.people-press.org/2014/02/27/public-divided-over-increased-deportation-of-unauthorized-immigrants/

Pew Research Center (2016, June 27). *On Views of Race and Inequality, Blacks and Whites are Worlds Apart*. Available, http://www.pewsocialtrends.org/2016/06/27/on-views-of-race-and-inequality-blacks-and-whites-are-worlds-apart/?utm_source=adaptivemailer&utm_medium=email&utm_campaign=16-6-27%20race%20press%20release&org=982&lvl=100&ite=148&lea=9344&ctr=0&par=1&trk

Pew Research Center (2017, February 15). Americans Express Increasingly Warm Feelings toward Religious Groups. Available, http://www.pewforum.org/2017/02/15/americans-express-increasingly-warm-feelings-toward-religious-groups/

Pfaff, William (2010). *The Irony of Manifest Destiny: The Tragedy of America's Foreign Policy*. New York: Walker Publishing.

Phillip, Abby, and Mike DeBonis (2017, January 23). Without Evidence, Trump Tells Lawmakers 3 Million to 5 Million Illegal Ballots Cost Him the Popular Vote. *The Washington Post*. Available, https://www.washingtonpost.com/news/post-politics/wp/2017/01/23/at-white-house-trump-tells-congressional-leaders-3-5-million-illegal-ballots-cost-him-the-popular-vote/?utm_term=.7c22e9a53a50

Phillips, Camellia (2002). Immigrant Rights: Striving for Racial Justice, Economic Equality and Human Dignity. *Political Research Associates*. Available, http://www.publiceye.org/ark/immigrants/StrivingNNIRR.html

Picket, Kerry (2016, September 22). Charlotte Rioters Mercilessly Beat, Kick Innocent Man. *Daily Caller*. Available, http://dailycaller.com/2016/09/22/charlotte-rioters-mercilessly-beat-kick-innocent-man-video/

Pierce, Anne R. (2015, May 17). Rediscovering America's Voice. *The Washington Times*. Available, http://www.washingtontimes.com/news/2015/may/17/anne-pierce-america-must-speak-out-against-propaga/

Pierce, Anne R. (2016). *A Perilous Path: The Misguided Foreign Policy of Barack Obama, Hillary Clinton & John Kerry*. New York: Post Hill Press.

Pierce, Chester M. (1970). Offensive Mechanisms. In Floyd B. Barbour (Ed.), *The Black Seventies: Leading Black Authors Look at the Present and Reach into the Future* (pp. 265–282). Boston, MA: Porter Sargent.

Pildes, Richard H. (2011). Why the Center Does Not Hold: The Causes of Hyperpolarized Democracy in America. *California Law Review 99*(2), 273–333.

Pilkington, Ed (2014, July 6). North Carolina Voter Law Challenged: 'The Worst Suppression Since Jim Crow.' *The Guardian*. Available, http://www.theguardian.com/world/2014/jul/06/north-carolina-voter-id-jim-crow-challenge

Pitts, Sally (2012). Health Care from a Conservative Viewpoint. *Search for Clarity and Truth*. Available, http://www.search4clarity.com/health-care/perspective/conservative

The Plain Dealer (2015, December 5). Expert Says Tamir Rice Had Hands in Pockets When Shot by Cleveland Police. *Cleveland.com*. Available, http://www.cleveland.com/metro/index.ssf/2015/12/expert_says_tamir_rice_had_han.html

Planas, Rogue (2014, August 28). Watch Fox News Blow Several Facts on Major Immigration Story in Just Two Sentences. *The Huffington Post*. Available, http://www.huffingtonpost.com/2014/08/28/brian-kilmeade-immigration_n_5729456.html?ncid=fcbk lnkushpmg00000013&ir=Politics

Plessy v. Ferguson (1896). 163 US 537. Available, https://www.law.cornell.edu/supremecourt/text/163/537

PolitiFact (2009, August 10). Sarah Palin Falsely Claims Barack Obama Runs a 'Death Panel.' *Tampa Bay Times*. Available, http://www.politifact.com/truth-o-meter/statements/2009/aug/10/sarah-palin/sarah-palin-barack-obama-death-panel/

PolitiFact (2014, April 26). Sarah Palin: Eric Holder Wants Gun Owners to Wear ID Bracelets. *Tampa Bay Times*. Available, http://www.politifact.com/punditfact/statements/2014/may/01/sarah-palin/sarah-palin-eric-holder-wants-gun-owners-wear-id-b/.

Pollak, Joel B. (2014, May 26). Obama, Kerry Committed to Weak Posture on Ukraine. *Breitbart*. Available, http://www.breitbart.com/Big-Peace/2014/05/26/Obama-Kerry-Committed-to-Weak-Posture-on-Ukraine

Porter, Gareth (2014). *Manufactured Crisis: The Untold Story of the Iran Nuclear Scare*. Charlottesville, VA: Just World Books.

Posner, Sarah (2011, July 12). God's Law Is the Only Law: The Genesis of Michele Bachmann. *Religion Dispatches*. Available, http://religiondispatches.org/gods-law-is-the-only-law-the-genesis-of-michele-bachmann/

Postrel, Virginia (2005, November 3). Yes, Immigration May Lift Wages. *The New York Times*. C2. Available, http://www.nytimes.com/2005/11/03/business/03scene.html?_r=0

Potter, Wendell (2015, May 11). Court Case Shows how Health Insurers Rip Off You and Your Employer. *Public Integrity*. Available, http://www.publicintegrity.org/2015/05/11/17317/court-case-shows-how-health-insurers-rip-you-and-your-employer

Poulakos, John (1983). Toward a Sophistic Definition of Rhetoric. *Philosophy & Rhetoric* 16(1), 35–48.

Prager, John (2015, June 26). Three Black Churches have Burned since Dylann Roof's Brutal Terrorist Attack. *Addicting Info*. Available, http://www.addictinginfo.org/2015/06/26/three-black-churches-have-burned-since-dylann-roofs-brutal-terrorist-attack/

Prentice, Julia C., Anne R. Pebley, and Narayan Sastry (2005). Immigration Status and Health Insurance Coverage: Who Gains? Who Loses? *American Journal of Public Health*, 95(1), 109–116.

Press, Bill (2010). *Toxic Talk: How the Radical Right Has Poisoned America's Airwaves*. New York: Thomas Dunne/St. Martin's Press.

Press, Bill (2012). *The Obama Hate Machine: The Lies, Distortions, and Personal Attacks on the President—and Who Is Behind Them*. New York: Thomas Dunne Books.

Prupis, Nadia (2017, March 9). More States Sue to Block Trump's "Muslim Ban by Another Name." *Common Dreams*. Available, http://www.commondreams.org/news/2017/03/09/more-states-sue-block-trumps-muslim-ban-another-name

Puder, Joseph (2016, November 23). President Trump and the Iran Nuclear Deal. *Frontpage Magazine*. Available, http://www.frontpagemag.com/fpm/264896/president-trump-and-iran-nuclear-deal-joseph-puder

Purcell v. Gonzalez (2006). 549 U.S. 1. Available, https://supreme.justia.com/cases/federal/us/549/1/

Qiu, Linda (2016, March 17). No, Donald Trump, We are not Giving Iran $150 Billion for 'Nothing.' *Politifact*. Available, http://www.politifact.com/truth-o-meter/statements/2016/mar/17/donald-trump/no-donald-trump-we-are-not-giving-iran-150-billion/

Rabin, Charles (2016, July 20). Cop Shoots Caretaker of Autistic Man Playing in the Street with Toy Truck. *Miami Herald*. Available, http://www.miamiherald.com/news/local/crime/article90905442.html

Rachel (2013, April 10). The Dangers to Gun Control Efforts (and Civil Discourse) of Heightened Rhetoric. *Daily Kos*. Available, http://www.dailykos.com/story/2013/04/10/1200774/-The-dangers-to-gun-control-efforts-and-civil-discourse-of-heightened-rhetoric#

Rampersad, Indira (2015, April 17). That Obama-Castro Summit. *Trinidad Express*. Available, http://www.trinidadexpress.com/commentaries/-That-Obama-Castro-summit-300397251.html

Ramsey, Charles (2015, May 26). Why Do US Police Keep Killing Unarmed Black Men? *BBC News*. Available, http://www.bbc.com/news/world-us-canada-32740523

Rauch, Jonathan (2008, June 21). Gay Marriage Is Good for America. *The Wall Street Journal*. Available, http://www.jonathanrauch.com/jrauch_articles/2008/06/gay-marriage-is-good-for-america.html

Ravid, Barak (2015, July 14). Netanyahu: Iran Nuclear Deal Makes World much more Dangerous, Israel not Bound by It. *Haaretz*. Available, http://www.haaretz.com/israel-news/1.665821

Rawson, Hugh (1989). *Wicked Words: A Treasury of Curses, Insults, Put-Downs, and Other Formerly Unprintable Terms from Anglo-Saxon Times to the Present*. New York: Three Rivers Press.

Ray, Shalini Bhargava (2013). Optimal Asylum. *Vanderbilt Journal of Transnational Law* 46(5), 1215–1265.

Raymond, Laurel (2017, March 26). Trump's Awkward Meeting with Angela Merkel just got more Cringeworthy. *Think Progress*. Available, https://thinkprogress.org/trumps-awkward-meeting-with-angela-merkel-just-got-more-cringeworthy-853ca0b84ca4

Reagan, Ronald (1976, January). Ronald Reagan campaign speech, January 1976. *SoundCloud*. Available, https://soundcloud.com/slate-articles/ronald-reagan-campaign-speech

Real Clear Politics (2014, July 9). Obama Not Visiting the Border: "I'm Not Interested in Photo Ops." *Realclearpolitics.com*. Available, http://www.realclearpolitics.com/video/2014/07/09/obama_on_not_visiting_the_border_im_not_interested_in_photo_ops.html

Redfield, Marc (2009). *The Rhetoric of Terror: Reflections on 9/11 and the War on Terror*. New York: Fordham University Press.

Redmond, Helen (2014). The Affordable Care Act: The Reality behind the Rhetoric. *International Socialist Review*, issue 94, 41–62.

Reed, Adolph, Jr. (2016, October 17). How Racial Disparity Does Not Help Make Sense of Patterns of Police Violence. *New Labor Forum*. Available, http://newlaborforum.cuny.edu/2016/10/17/how-racial-disparity-does-not-help-make-sense-of-patterns-of-police-violence/

Reilly, Mollie (2013, September 30). Michele Bachmann: Obama Getting Americans Hooked on 'Crack Cocaine' of Health Care Dependency. *The Huffington Post*. Available, http://www.huffingtonpost.com/2013/09/30/michele-bachmann-obama_n_4017567.html

Reilly, Mollie (2014, April 27). Sarah Palin: 'Waterboarding Is How We'd Baptize Terrorists' If I Were in Charge. *The Huffington Post*. Available, http://www.huffingtonpost.com/2014/04/27/sarah-palin-waterboarding_n_5222665.html?ncid=fcbklnkushpmg00000013

Reilly, Ryan J. and Mariah Stewart (2015a, March 26). Fleece Force: How Police and Courts around Ferguson Bully Residents and Collect Millions. *The Huffington Post*. Available, http://www.huffingtonpost.com/2015/03/26/st-louis-county-municipal-courts_n_6896550.html?ncid=fcbklnkushpmg00000013

Reilly, Ryan J., and Mariah Stewart (2015b, March 4). DOJ Issues Damning Report on Ferguson Police, Courts. *The Huffington Post*. Available, http://www.huffingtonpost.com/2015/03/04/ferguson-police-report_n_6800440.html

Reinares, Fernando (2015, October 11). Recent Evolution of Terrorism in the Maghreb. *Elcano Real Instituto*. Available, http://www.realinstitutoelcano.org/wps/portal/rielcano_en/contenido?WCM_GLOBAL_CONTEXT=/elcano/elcano_in/zonas_in/ari62-2015-reinares-recent-evolution-terrorism-maghreb

Remnick, David (2014, January 27). Going the Distance: On and Off the Road with Barack Obama. *The New Yorker*. Available, http://www.newyorker.com/magazine/2014/01/27/going-the-distance-2

Rendall, Steve, and Tara Broughel (2003, May/June). Amplifying Officials, Squelching Dissent. *Fairness & Accuracy in Reporting*. Available, http://fair.org/extra/amplifying-officials-squelching-dissent/

Rendeiro, Joseph (2014, August 15). NCLR Marks Anniversary of DACA While Urging President to Take Additional Action. *National Council of La Raza*. Available, http://www.nclr.org/index.php/about_us/news/news_releases/nclr_marks_anniversary_of_daca_while_urging_president_to_take_additional_action/

Resmovits, Joy (2014, March 21). American Schools Are Still Racist, Government Report Finds. *The Huffington Post*. Available, http://www.huffingtonpost.com/2014/03/21/schools-discrimination_n_5002954.html

Reuters (2014, July 23). Latest Obamacare Legal Know Won't Be Easy to Untangle. *Raw Story*. Available, http://www.rawstory.com/rs/2014/07/23/latest-obamacare-legal-knot-wont-be-easy-to-untangle/

Reynolds v. Sims (1964). 377 U.S. 533. Available, https://supreme.justia.com/cases/federal/us/377/533/case.html

Reynolds v. United States. 98 U.S. 145 (1879).

Reynolds, Glenn Harlan (2012, December 14). Column: Gun-Free Zones Provide False Sense of Security. *USA Today*. Available, https://www.usatoday.com/story/opinion/2012/12/14/connecticut-school-shooting-gun-control/1770345/

Rheingold, Howard (2002). *Smart Mobs: The Next Social Revolution*. Cambridge, MA: Basic Books.

Rho, Hye Jin, and Schmitt, John (2010, March). *Health-Insurance Coverage Rates for US Workers, 1979–2008*. Washington, D.C.: Center for Economic and Policy Research.

Richter, Paul (2015, August 28). Rhetorical Abuse over Iran Deal Is Troubling, Obama Tells Jewish Groups. *Los Angeles Times*. Available, http://www.latimes.com/world/middleeast/la-fg-obama-iran-20150829-story.html

Riedel, Charlie (2014, December 2). Michael Brown's Stepfather Investigated for Comments after Grand Jury. *CBS News*. Available, http://www.cbsnews.com/news/ferguson-michael-brown-stepfather-investigated-for-comments-after-grand-jury-decision/

Riehl, Dan (2012, March 7). Dems Incite Death Threats against Limbaugh. *Breitbart*. Available, http://www.breitbart.com/Big-Government/2012/03/07/exclusive-dems-incite-death-threats-against-limbaugh

Riggs, Damien W. (2010). On Accountability: Towards a White Middle-Class Queer 'Post Identity Politics Identity Politics.' *Ethnicities 10*(3), 344–357.

Rimmerman, Craig A. (2002). *From Identity to Politics: The Lesbian and Gay Movements in the United States*. Philadelphia: Temple University Press.

Rimmerman, Craig A. (2011). *The New Citizenship: Unconventional Politics, Activism, and Service* (4th ed.). Boulder, CO: Westview Press.

Rivera, Geraldo "One of My Favorite Things" at Fox News "Is Watching Bombs Drop on Bad Guys" (2017, April 14). *Media Matters for America*. Available, https://mediamatters.org/video/2017/04/14/geraldo-rivera-one-my-favorite-things-fox-news-watching-bombs-drop-bad-guys/216032

Rivlin, Alice M. (2013, September/October). Health reform: What next? *Public Administration Review 73*(1), S15–S20.

Riyadh Air Force Base in Riyadh, Saudi Arabia (n.d.). *Military Bases*. Available, https://militarybases.com/riyadh-air-base-air-force-base-in-riyadh-saudi-arabia/

Robbins, David (2016, January 28). Crossing the Line: When Criticism of Israel becomes Anti-Semitic. *Anti-Defamation League* (ADL). Available, https://www.adl.org/blog/crossing-the-line-when-criticism-of-israel-becomes-anti-semitic-0

Roberts, Christine (2011, June 1). Michele Bachmann: "God Calling on Me to Run." *New York Daily News*. Available, http://readersupportednews.org/news-section2/318-66/6119-michele-bachmann-qgod-calling-on-me-to-runq

Roberts, Paul Craig (2014, April 26). Moving Closer to War. *Oped News*. Available, http://www.opednews.com/articles/Moving-Closer-To-War-by-Paul-Craig-Roberts-Confrontation_Crimea_NATO_Obama-140426-177.html

Rock, Matt (2014, April 18). Ted Cruz Interview Scrubbed by Website after Racist Comments. *National Report*. Available, http://nationalreport.net/ted-cruz-interview-scrubbed-website-racist-comments/

Roe v. Wade. 410 U.S. 113, (1973).

Roediger, David R. (1997). White Looks: Hairy Apes, True Stories, and Limbaugh's Laughs. In Mike Hill (Ed.), *Whiteness: A Critical Reader* (pp. 35–46). New York: New York University Press.

Rogers, Karl (2011). *Debunking Glenn Beck: How to Save America from Media Pundits and Propagandists*. Santa Barbara, CA: Praeger.

Rogin, Josh, and Eli Lake (2014, August 28). Why Obama Backed Off more ISIS Strikes: His Own Team couldn't Agree on a Syria Strategy. *The Daily Beast*. Available, http://www.thedailybeast.com/articles/2014/08/28/why-obama-backed-off-more-isis-strikes-his-own-team-couldn-t-agree-on-a-syria-strategy.html

Rohy, Valerie (2012). On Homosexual Reproduction. *Differences: A Journal of Feminist Cultural Studies* 25(1), 101–130.

Rom, Mark Carl (2007). Introduction: The Politics of Same-Sex Marriage. In Craig A. Rimmerman & Clyde Wilcox (Eds.), *The Politics of Same-Sex Marriage* (pp. 1–38). London: University of Chicago Press.

Romer v. Evans. (94–1039), 517 U.S. 620 (Colorado, 1996).

Rood, Craig (2014). "Moves" Toward Rhetorical Civility. *Pedagogy: Critical Approaches to Teaching Literature, Language, Composition, and Culture, 14*(3), 395-415.

Rose, Tricia (1994). *Black Noise: Rap Music and Black Culture in Contemporary America*. Middletown, CT: Wesleyan University Press.

Rosen, Christopher (2017, July 1). Donald Trump Calls Mika Brzezinski 'Dumb as a Rock' in New Tweet. *Entertainment Weekly*. Available, http://ew.com/tv/2017/07/01/donald-trump-mika-brzezinski-dumb-as-a-rock/

Rosenberg, Jeremy (2012, May 21). When This Law Ended, What Happened to Mexican Immigration? *KCET*. Available, https://www.kcet.org/history-society/when-this-law-ended-what-happened-to-mexican-immigration

Rosenberg, M. J. (2015, September 11). AIPAC Spent Millions of Dollars to Defeat the Iran Deal. Instead, It May Have Destroyed Itself. *The Nation*. Available, https://www.thenation.com/article/aipac-spent-millions-of-dollars-to-defeat-the-iran-deal-instead-it-may-have-destroyed-itself/

Ross, Casey (2016, July 21). Donald Trump Repeats False Claim that Nuclear Arms Deal Gives $150 Billion Back to Iran. *The Plain Dealer*. Available, http://www.cleveland.com/rnc-2016/index.ssf/2016/07/trump_repeats_false_claim_that.html

Ross, Chuck (2014, August 7). Texas Border Rancher Says Illegal Immigrant Surge 'Overwhelming.' *The Daily Caller*. Available, http://dailycaller.com/2014/08/07/texas-border-rancher-says-illegal-immigrant-surge-overwhelming/

Ross, Cody T. (2015, November 5). A Multi-Level Bayesian Analysis of Racial Bias in Police Shootings at the County-Level in the United States, 2011–2014. *Plos One*. Available, http://journals.plos.org/plosone/article?id=10.1371/journal.pone.0141854

Ross, Janell (2016, September 21). What Happened after Don King Used the N-Word while Stumping for Trump. *The Washington Post*. Available, https://www.washingtonpost.com/news/the-fix/wp/2016/09/21/what-happened-after-don-king-used-the-n-word-while-stumping-for-trump/?utm_term=.3cc895beb45c

Rotman, Dana, Jenny Preece, Sarah Vieweg, Ben Shneiderman, Sarita Yarida, Peter Pirolli, Ed H. Chi, and Tom Glaisyer (2011). From Slacktivism to Activism: Participatory Culture in the Age of Social Media. *Proceedings of the 2011 annual conference extended abstracts on Human Factors in Computing Systems*. Available, http://yardi.people.si.umich.edu/pubs/Yardi_CHI11_SIG.pdf

Rountree, Clarke (2013). Afterword: Reconstituting the Commonweal and Civil Society. In Clarke Rountree (Ed.), *Venomous Speech: Problems with American Political Discourse on the Right and Left*, Volume 2. Santa Barbara, CA: ABC-CLIO/Praeger.

Rubin, Barry (2014). *Silent Revolution: How the Left Rose to Political Power and Cultural Dominance*. New York: Broadside Books.

Rudee, Eliana (2014, October 17). Blurred Lines: Anti-Semitism vs. Anti-Israel. *The Observer*. Available, http://observer.com/2014/10/blurred-lines-anti-semitism-vs-anti-israel/

Ruder, Eric (2016, July 18). What's Hidden Behind Obama's Call for "Unity"? *Socialist Worker*. Available, https://socialistworker.org/2016/07/18/hidden-behind-obamas-call-for-unity

Ryan, Paul (2017, March 7). Our Health Care Plan for America: Paul Ryan. *USA Today*. Available, https://www.usatoday.com/story/opinion/2017/03/07/health-care-obamacare-replacement-paul-ryan-column/98858696/

Safire, William (2008). *Safire's Political Dictionary* (Rev. ed.). New York: Oxford University Press.

Saint Louis, Catherine (2013, March 21). Pediatrics Group Backs Gay Marriage, Saying It Helps Children. *The New York Times*. Available, http://www.nytimes.com/2013/03/21/health/american-academy-of-pediatrics-backs-gay-marriage.html?_r=0

Sakuma, Amanda (2014, April 12). Fewer Republicans Think Obamacare Will Ruin Their Lives. *MSNBC*. Available, http://www.msnbc.com/msnbc/republicans-obamacare-approval-gallup-poll.

Sakuma, Amanda (2015, August 5). The Time Has Come to 'Say Her Name.' *MSNBC*. Available, http://www.msnbc.com/msnbc/the-time-has-come-say-her-name

Sakuma, Amanda (2016, November 9). Trump Did Better with Blacks, Hispanics than Romney in '12: Exit Polls. *NBC News*. Available, http://www.nbcnews.com/storyline/2016-election-day/trump-did-better-blacks-hispanics-romney-12-exit-polls-n681386

Salama, Vivian (2017, February 2). Trump to Mexico: Take Care of 'Bad Hombres' or US Might. *Associated Press*. Available, http://bigstory.ap.org/article/trump-mexico-take-care-bad-hombres-or-us-might

Saletan, William (2016, June 13). Trump's Response to Orlando Is Exactly What ISIS Wants. *Slate*. Available, http://www.slate.com/articles/news_and_politics/politics/2016/06/trump_s_response_to_orlando_is_exactly_what_isis_wants.html

Salzillo, Leslie (2014, April 18). Rush Limbaugh Is in Ruins—Bad News Coming from Every Direction—Including the Right. *Daily Kos*. Available, http://www.dailykos.com/story/2014/04/18/1293043/-Rush-Limbaugh-Is-In-Ruins-Bad-News-Coming-From-Every-Direction-Including-The-Right#

Samuels, Jocelyn (2013, October 28). Commemorating the Fourth Anniversary of the Shepard-Byrd Hate Crime Prevention Act. *WhiteHouse.gov*. Available, http://www.whitehouse.gov/blog/2013/10/28/commemorating-fourth-anniversary-shepard-byrd-hate-crime-prevention-act

Sanchez, John, and Mary E. Stuckey (2000). The Rhetoric of American Indian Activism in the 1960s and 1970s. *Communication Quarterly*, *48*(2), 120–136.

Sanger, Larry (2013). What *Should* We Be Worried About? *The Edge*. Available, http://edge.org/response-detail/23777

Santa Fe Independent School District v. Doe. 530 U.S. 290 (2000). Available, http://www.law.cornell.edu/supct/html/99-62.ZS.html

Santinover, Jeffrey (1996). *Homosexuality and the Politics of Truth*. Grand Rapids, MI: Hamewith Books.

Santorum, Rick (2012, March 30). Rick Santorum Calls President Obama a "Nig." *YouTube*. Available, https://www.youtube.com/watch?v=IgrhJSAaYIc

Santos, Vergel O. (2016, November 15). Duterte's Descent into Authoritarianism. *The New York Times*. Available, https://www.nytimes.com/2016/11/16/opinion/dutertes-descent-into-authoritarianism.html

Sappenfield, Mark (2014, June 8). Seattle Campus Shooting: How Often Do Bystanders Stop Mass Killings? *The Christian Science Monitor*. Available, http://www.csmonitor.com/USA/2014/0608/Seattle-campus-shooting-How-often-do-bystanders-stop-mass-killings-video

Sargent, Greg (2014, March 11). Poll: Only Republicans and Conservatives Say Obamacare Is 'Too Liberal.' *The Washington Post*. Available, http://www.washingtonpost.com/blogs/plum-line/wp/2014/03/11/poll-only-republicans-and-conservatives-say-obamacare-is-too-liberal/

Saunders, Daniel (2009, January 26). Notes on the "New Anti-Semitism." *Jewcy*. Available, http://jewcy.com/jewish-religion-and-beliefs/notes_new_antisemitism

Savage, David G. (2014, May 5). Supreme Court Ruling Tilts Law to the Right on Public Prayer. *Los Angeles Times*. Available, http://www.latimes.com/nation/la-na-court-prayer-20140506-story.html

Savage, Michael (2010). *Trickle Up Poverty: Stopping Obama's Attack on Our Borders, Economy, and Security*. New York: William Morrow.

Savage, Michael (2012). *Trickle Down Tyranny: Crushing Obama's Dream of the Socialist States of America*. New York: William Morrow.

Savali, Kirsten West (2012, June 11). Ramarley Graham: NYPD Officer Indicted on Manslaughter Charges for Shooting Death of Unarmed Teen. *News One*. Available, https://newsone.com/2020234/ramarley-graham-richard-haste/

Savidge, Nico (2008, September 11). Slaktivists Are the New Activists. *National Public Radio*. Available, http://www.npr.org/templates/story/story.php?storyId=94509892

Schackner, Bill (2016, December 4). Learning the Art of Civil Argument in an Uncivil Time. *Pittsburgh Post-Gazette*. Available, http://www.post-gazette.com/news/education/2016/12/04/Learning-the-art-of-civil-argument-in-an-uncivil-time/stories/201612040113

Schempp v. School District of Abington Township, PA. 374 U.S. 203 (1963). Available, http://www.law.cornell.edu/supremecourt/text/374/203#writing-USSC_CR_0374_0203_ZD

Schlafly, Phyllis (2001, October). The Threat of Terrorism Is from Illegal Aliens. *The Phyllis Schlafly Report 35*(3). Available, http://www.eagleforum.org/psr/2001/oct01/psroct01.shtml

Schleifer, Theodore and Jeremy Diamond (2016, August 25). Clinton Says Trump Leading 'Hate Movement'; He Calls Her a 'Bigot.' *CNN Politics*. Available, http://www.cnn.com/2016/08/24/politics/donald-trump-hillary-clinton-bigot/

Schmidt, Michael S., and Matt Apuzzo (2015, October 23). F.B.I. Chief Links Scrutiny of Police with Rise in Violent Crime. *The New York Times*. Available, http://www.nytimes.com/2015/10/24/us/politics/fbi-chief-links-scrutiny-of-police-with-rise-in-violent-crime.html?_r=0

Schoulte, Joleen, Jessica M. Schultz, and Elizabeth M. Altmaier (2011). Forgiveness in Response to Cultural Microaggressions. *Counselling Psychology Quarterly*, *24*(4), 291–300.

Schram, Sanford and Joe Soss (2015, September 8). Brownback and the Myth of the "Welfare Queen." *Salon*. Available, http://www.salon.com/2015/09/08/how_welfare_restrictions_demonize_the_poor_partner/

Schreckhise, William D., and Todd G. Shields (2003). Ideological Realignment in the Contemporary U.S. Electorate Revisited. *Social Science Quarterly 84*(3), 596–612.

Schuchter, Arnold (2015). *ISIS Containment & Defeat: Next Generation Counterinsurgency—NexGen COIN*. Bloomington, IN: iUniverse.

Schulte, Elizabeth (2015, December 1). How Anger at Campus Racism Boiled Over. *Socialist Worker*. Available, http://socialistworker.org/2015/12/01/how-anger-at-campus-racism-boiled-over

Schultz, Ed (2010). *Killer Politics: How Big Money and Bad Politics Are Destroying the Great American Middle Class*. New York: Hyperion.

Schwartz, Carly and Christopher Mathias (2014, November 25). Protesters Shut Down Three New York City Bridges in Reaction to Ferguson Decision. *The Huffington Post*. Available, http://www.huffingtonpost.com/2014/11/25/nyc-ferguson-protests_n_6216528.html

Scientists Warn of Twitter Dangers (2009, April 14). *CNN*. Available, http://www.cnn.com/2009/TECH/ptech/04/14/twitter.study/

Sebelius, Kathleen (2013, September/October). Implementing the Affordable Care Act: A Historic Opportunity for Public Administrators. *Public Administration Review 73*(1), S13–S14.

Sedgwick, Eve Kosofsky (2007). *Epistemology of the Closet*. Berkeley, CA: University of California Press.

Seeman, Evan and Merriam, Dwight (2014, May 5). U.S. Supreme Court: Religious Prayer at Board Meetings Does Not Violate First Amendment. *Rlupia Defense*. Available, http://rluipa-defense.com/article.cfm?ID=323

Segan, Sascha (2014, July 14). What is Excessive Force? *ABC News*. Available, http://abcnews.go.com/US/story?id=96509

Seidel, Timothy (2006, August 2). Christianity in Palestine: Misrepresentation and Dispossession. *The Electronic Intifada*. Available, https://electronicintifada.net/content/christianity-palestine-misrepresentation-and-dispossession/6280

Sekulow, Jay (2011, May 5). Celebrating National Day of Prayer. *The American Center for Law and Justice*. Available, http://aclj.org/national-day-of-prayer/celebrating-national-day-of-prayer.

Sekulow, Jay (2014). *Rise of ISIS: A Threat We Can't Ignore*. New York: Howard Books.

Senti, Steve (2013, October 19). Bill O'Reilly Is Lying to You about Obamacare. *O'ReillySucks.com*. Available, http://www.oreilly-sucks.com/mainpage2012/obamacarelies.html

Settles, Isis H., NiCole T. Buchanan, & Stevie C. Y. Yap (2011). Race/Color Discrimination. In Michele A. Paludi, Carmen A. Paludi, Jr., & Eros DeSouza (Eds.), *Praeger Handbook on Understanding and Preventing Workplace Discrimination* (pp. 133–156). Westport, CT: Praeger.

Shah, Anup (2013, October 7). War on Terror. *Global Issues*. Available, http://www.globalissues.org/issue/245/war-on-terror

Shah, Dhavan V., Nojin Kwak, and Lance R. Holbert (2001). "Connecting" and "Disconnecting" with Civic Life: Patterns of Internet Use and the Production of Social Capital. *Political Communication 18*(2), 141–162.

Shaiko, Ronald G. (2007). Same-Sex Marriage, GLBT Organizations, and the Lack of Spirited Political Engagement. In Craig A. Rimmerman & Clyde Wilcox (Eds.), *The Politics of Same-Sex Marriage* (pp. 85–103). London: University of Chicago Press.

Shane, Scott (2011, December 21). In Islamic Law, Gingrich Sees a Mortal Threat to U.S. *The New York Times*. Available, http://www.nytimes.com/2011/12/22/us/politics/in-shariah-gingrich-sees-mortal-threat-to-us.html?pagewanted=all&_r=0

Shapiro, Ben (2013). *Bullies: How the Left's Culture of Fear and Intimidation Silences America*. New York: Threshold Editions.

Sharockman, Aaron (2016, November 16). Let's Fight Back against Fake News. *Politifact*. Available, http://www.politifact.com/truth-o-meter/article/2016/nov/16/lets-fight-back-against-fake-news/

Sharpton, Al (2002). *Al on America*. New York: Kensington Publishing.

Sharpton, Al (2013a, September 30). Can't Stop Now. *The Huffington Post*. Available, http://www.huffingtonpost.com/rev-al-sharpton/cant-stop-now_b_4018160.html

Sharpton, Al (2013b, September 23). 'Moral Man and Immoral Society.' *The Huffington Post*. Available, http://www.huffingtonpost.com/rev-al-sharpton/moral-man-and-immoral-soc_b_3976173.html

Shavit, Uriya (2006, Fall). Al-Qaeda's Saudi Origins. *Middle East Quarterly*, p. 3–13. Available, http://www.meforum.org/999/al-qaedas-saudi-origins

Shear, Michael D., and Helene Cooper (2017, January 27). Trump Bars Refugees and Citizens of 7 Muslim Countries. *The New York Times*. Available, https://www.nytimes.com/2017/01/27/us/politics/trump-syrian-refugees.html

Shelby County v. Holder (2013). 570 U.S. ___. Available, https://supreme.justia.com/cases/federal/us/570/12-96/

Sherfinski, David. (2014, April 25). NRA's LaPierre: Country 'Slipping Away,' Gun Owners 'Willing to Fight' for Control. *The Washington Times*. Available, http://www.washingtontimes.com/news/2014/apr/25/lapierre-us-slipping-away-gun-owners-should-fight/

Shirazi, Nima (2014, February 14). The Forgotten History of American Support for the Shah. *Muftah*. Available, http://muftah.org/forgotten-history-american-support-shah/#.WOdVAvkrLIU

Shire, Emily (2015, March 19). Berkeley's Swastika Problem: Are America's Liberal Colleges Breeding Anti-Semitism? *The Daily Beast*. Available, http://www.thedailybeast.com/articles/2015/03/19/berkeley-s-swastika-problem-are-america-s-liberal-colleges-breeding-anti-semitism.html

Siebold, Steve (2014, May 7). Supreme Court Wrong to Give Blessing on Public Prayer. *The Huffington Post*. Available, http://www.huffingtonpost.com/steve-siebold/supreme-court-wrong-prayer-ruling_b_5275509.html

Signorile, Michelangelo (2016, November 12). The Mike Pence (Donald Trump) Assault on LGBTQ Equality Is Already Underway. Available, http://www.huffingtonpost.com/entry/mike-pence-assault-lgbtq-equality_us_58275a17e4b02d21bbc8ff9b

Simpson, Dan (2014, June 10). Oklahoma Tea Party Candidate Calls for Homosexuals to be Stoned to Death! *Fire Brand Progressives*. Available, http://firebrandprogressives.org/oklahoma-tea-party-candidate-calls-for-homosexuals-to-be-stoned-to-death/

Singham, Mano (2013, April 16). The Mess Over Tax Exemptions for Churches. *Free Thought Blogs*. Available, http://freethoughtblogs.com/singham/2013/04/16/the-mess-over-tax-exemptions-for-churches/

Sinyangwe, Samuel (2015a, October 27). Stop Pretending the "Ferguson Effect" Is Real. *Medium*. Available, https://medium.com/@samswey/stop-pretending-the-ferguson-effect-is-real-40e3684fae3d#.x1oyc1gd4

Sinyangwe, Samuel (2015b, May 26). Why Do US Police Keep Killing Unarmed Black Men? *BBC News*. Available, http://www.bbc.com/news/world-us-canada-32740523

Sinyangwe, Samuel (2016, July 14). Stop Using that One Study to Pretend Racism Doesn't Exist in Police Shootings. *Medium*. Available, https://medium.com/@samswey/stop-using-that-one-study-to-pretend-racism-doesnt-exist-in-police-shootings-17a9e47a7117#.57xcn3q34

Skelding, Conor and Azi Paybarah (2014, December 24). Protesters March Uptown, Defy de Blasio. *The Capital New York*. Available, http://www.capitalnewyork.com/article/city-hall/2014/12/8559183/protesters-march-uptown-defy-de-blasio

Slater, Tom (2015, July 28). How Egalitarianism Became a Micro-Aggression. *Spiked-Online*. Available, http://www.spiked-online.com/newsite/article/how-egalitarianism-became-a-microaggression/17235#.WMnOsG8rLIU

Sleeper, Jim (1993, January 25). A Man of Too Many Parts. *The New Yorker*, 57–67.

Smith v. Allwright (1944). 321 U.S. 649. Available, https://supreme.justia.com/cases/federal/us/321/649/case.html

Smith, Alison M., and Cassandra L. Foley (2010, September 28). State Statutes Governing Hate Crimes. *Congressional Research Service*. Available, http://assets.opencrs.com/rpts/RL33099_20100928.pdf.

Smith, Ben (2008, April 11). Obama on Small-Town Pa.: Clinging to Religion, Guns, Xenophobia. *Politico*. Available, http://www.politico.com/blogs/bensmith/0408/Obama_on_smalltown_PA_Clinging_religion_guns_xenophobia.html

Smith, Craig R., and David M. Hunsaker (2004). *The Four Freedoms of the First Amendment*. Long Grove, IL: Waveland Press.

Smith, Mary Lynn and Claude Peck (2015, November 24). Five People Shot Near Black Lives Matter Protest in Minneapolis. *Star Tribune*. Available, http://www.startribune.com/several-people-were-shot-near-black-lives-matter-protest-site/353121881/

Smith, Mitch and Richard Pérez-Peña (2016, December 15). Milwaukee Officer Charged in Shooting that Set Off Riots. *The New York Times*. Available, https://www.nytimes.com/2016/12/15/us/sylville-smith-milwaukee-police-shooting-dominique-heaggan-brown.html

Smith, Mychal Denzel (2014, August 27). How Trayvon Martin's Death Launched a New Generation of Black Activism. *The Nation*. Available, http://m.thenation.com/article/181404-how-trayvon-martins-death-launched-new-generation-black-activism

Smith, Mychal Denzel (2015, November 1). The Movement against Police Violence Isn't Ignoring 'Black-on-Black Crime.' *The Nation*. Available, http://portside.org/2015-11-02/movement-against-police-violence-isn%E2%80%99t-ignoring-%E2%80%98black-black-crime%E2%80%99

Smith, Nicola (2017, March 30). North Korea Accuses John McCain of 'Blasphemy' for Calling Kim Jong-un 'that Crazy Fat Kid.' *The Telegraph*. Available, http://www.telegraph.co.uk/news/2017/03/30/john-mccain-sparks-war-words-north-korea-calling-kim-jong-un/

Smith, Peter J. (2010, September 28). Ann Coulter Rocks Homocon, Blasts Same-Sex "Marriage." *Life Site*. Available, http://www.lifesitenews.com/news/ann-coulter-rocks-homocon-blasts-same-sex-marriage

Smith, Rogers M. (2007). Church, State, and Society: Constitutional Consequences of the Rise of Christian Conservatism. *The Christian Conservative Movement & American Democracy conference*. Available, http://rsfconference.ucr.edu/papers/Smith2007.pdf

Smitherman, Geneva (2000). *Black Talk: Words and Phrases from 'Hood to the Amen Corner*. Wilmington, MA: Mariner.

Snowdon, Kathryn (2017, April 7). Donald Trump's Syria Airstrike Prompts Calls of Hypocrisy as Refugee Ban Remains in Place. *The Huffington Post*. Available, http://www.huffingtonpost.co.uk/entry/donlad-trump-syria-airstrike-hypocrisy-refugee-ban_uk_58e73267e4b05413bfe191fe

Sobieraj, Sarah, and Jeffrey M. Berry (2011). From Incivility to Outrage: Political Discourse in Blogs, Talk Radio, and Cable News. *Political Communication 28*(1), 19–41.

Socialist Worker (2014a, December 11). The Fight against Racism Returns to the Streets. SocialistWorker.org. Available, http://socialistworker.org/2014/12/11/the-fight-against-racism-in-the-streets

Socialist Worker (2014b, December 3). They Don't Give a Damn if Black America Burns. Socialistworker.org. Available, http://socialistworker.org/2014/12/03/they-dont-give-a-damn-if-black-america-burns

Socialist Worker (2015, April 29). The Baltimore Rebellion. Available, https://socialistworker.org/2015/04/29/the-baltimore-rebellion

Somashekhar, Sandhya and Kimbriell Kelly (2014, November 29). Was Michael Brown Surrendering or Advancing to Attack Officer Darren Wilson? *The Washington Post*. Available, http://www.washingtonpost.com/politics/2014/11/29/b99ef7a8-75d3-11e4-a755-e32227229e7b_story.html

Somin, Ilya (2004, September 22). When Ignorance Isn't Bliss: How Political Ignorance Threatens Democracy. *Policy Analysis* (CATO Institute), 535, 1–27.

Sommerfeldt, Chris (2017, March 30). Trump Administration Reverses U.S. Policy on Syria, No Longer Focused on 'Getting Assad Out.' *New York Daily News*. Available, http://www.nydailynews.com/news/politics/trump-admin-no-longer-focused-assad-article-1.3014690

Sonnett, John, Kirk A. Johnson, Kirk A., and Mark K. Dolan (2015). Priming Implicit Racism in Television News: Visual and Verbal Limitations on Diversity. *Sociological Forum, 30*(2), 328–347.

Soergel, Andrew (2016, July 19). Divided We Stand. *US News*. Available, https://www.usnews.com/news/articles/2016-07-19/political-polarization-drives-presidential-race-to-the-bottom

Squireso, Catherine R. (2011). N-word vs. F-word, Black vs. Gay: Uncovering Pendejo Games to Recover Intersections. In Michael G. Lacy & Kent A. Ono (Eds.), *Critical Rhetorics of Race* (pp. 65–78). New York: New York University Press.

Southern Poverty Law Center (2014). *Westboro Baptist Church*. Available, http://www.splcenter.org/get-informed/intelligence-files/groups/westboro-baptist-church.

Spenkuch, Jörg L. (2013, July). *Understanding the Impact of Immigration on Crime*. Available, http://www.kellogg.northwestern.edu/faculty/spenkuch/research/immigration_crime.pdf

Spitzer, Robert J. (2008). *The Politics of Gun Control*. Washington, D.C.: Congressional Quarterly Press.

Stack, Liam (2016, September 19). Video Released in Terence Crutcher's Killing by Tulsa Police. *The New York Times*. Available, https://www.nytimes.com/2016/09/20/us/video-released-in-terence-crutchers-killing-by-tulsa-police.html?_r=0

Stafford, Zach (2015, June 24). Racism is Alive in the US North too—Just Without Southern Accents and Flags. *The Guardian*. Available, http://www.theguardian.com/world/2015/jun/24/racism-us-north-south-confederate-flag?CMP=fb_us

Stanley, Erik (2008, September 23). Why Don't Churches Pay Taxes? *The Los Angeles Times*. Available, http://www.latimes.com/la-oew-lynn-stanley23-2008sep23-story.html#page=1

Starr, Barbara, and Jeremy Diamond (2017, April 7). Trump Launches Military Strike against Syria. *CNN Politics*. Available, http://www.cnn.com/2017/04/06/politics/donald-trump-syria-military/

Stein, Dan (2007, May 8). Case Closed: Illegal Immigration Is a Threat to Homeland Security. *PR Newswire*. Available, http://www.prnewswire.com/news-releases/case-closed-illegal-immigration-is-a-threat-to-homeland-security-58047497.html

Stein, Edward (2014). Immutability and Innateness Arguments about Lesbian, Gay, and Bisexual Rights. *Chicago Kent Law Review* 89, 597–640.

Stein, Jonathan, and Tim Dickinson (2006, September/October). Lie by Lie: A Timeline of How We Got into Iraq. *Mother Jones*. Available, http://www.motherjones.com/politics/2011/12/leadup-iraq-war-timeline

Stein, Sam (2014, August 5). The Case for Allowing the Blind to Buy Guns, from an NRA News Contributor. *The Huffington Post*. Available, http://www.huffingtonpost.com/2014/08/05/guns-blind-people_n_5651251.html?ncid=fcbklnkushpmg00000013

Stephenson, D. L. (2011, January). Health Insurance Reform Rhetoric's Two-Valued Orientation. *ETC: A Review of General Semantics* 68(1), 21–32.

Stern, Mark Joseph (2014a, July 29). Are Anti-Gay Activists Bigots? A Brilliant, Disturbing New Book Says Yes. *Slate.com*. Available, http://www.slate.com/blogs/outward/2014/07/29/stephen_eric_bronner_s_the_bigot_why_prejudice_persists_reviewed.html?wpisrc=obnetwork

Stern, Mark Joseph (2014b, July 10). Religious Exemption Laws: Explained in One Chart. *Slate.com*. Available, http://www.slate.com/blogs/outward/2014/07/10/one_chart_that_explains_religious_exemptions_controversy.html

Stevens, David (2017, April 17). The Referendum that just Brought Turkey Closer to One-Man Rule, Explained. *Vox*. Available, http://www.vox.com/world/2017/4/17/15320350/turkey-referendum-vote-erdogan-explained

Stevenson, Michael R. (2000). Public Policy, Homosexuality and the Sexual Coercion of Children. *Journal of Psychology & Human Sexuality* 12(4), 1–19.

Stewart, Potter (1963). The Dissent. *Schempp v. School District of Abington Township, PA*. 374 U.S. 203. Available, http://www.law.cornell.edu/supremecourt/text/374/203#writing-USSC_CR_0374_0203_ZD

Stickings, Michael J. W. (2007, April 4). Gingrich and the Ghetto. *The Reaction*. Available, http://the-reaction.blogspot.com/2007/04/gingrich-and-ghetto.html?m=0

Stimpson, Jim P., Fernando A. Wilson, and Dejun Su (2013). Unauthorized Immigrants Spend Less than Other Immigrants and US Natives on Health Care. *Health Affairs*, 32(7), 1313–1318.

Stocchetti, Matteo (2007). The Politics of Fear: A Critical Inquiry into the Role of Violence in 21st Century Politics. In Adam Hodges & Chad Nilep (Eds.), *Discourse, War and Terrorism* (pp. 223–241). Amsterdam: John Benjamins Publishing.

Stockdill, Brett C. (2003). *Activism against AIDS: At the Intersections of Sexuality, Race, Gender, and Class*. Boulder, CO: Lynne Rienner Publishers, Inc.

Stoltze, Frank and Sharon McNary (2015, June 10). Ezell Ford Family: Time for DA to 'Sep Up.' *KPCC*. Available, http://www.scpr.org/news/2015/06/10/52318/ezell-ford-family-time-for-da-to-step-up/

Stone v. Graham. 449 U.S. 39 (1980).

Stone, Jon (2017, February 6). Donald Trump Will Not be Allowed to Address Parliament on UK State Visit, Says Speaker John Bercow. *Independent*. Available, http://www.independent.co.uk/news/uk/politics/donald-trump-uk-state-visit-speaker-address-parliament-a7565651.html

Stone, Michael (2014, May 7). Constitutional Horror: Clarence Thomas Argues States Can Establish Official Religion. *Patheos*. Available, http://www.patheos.com/blogs/progressivesecularhumanist/2014/05/constitutional-horror-clarence-thomas-argues-states-can-establish-official-religion/.

Stone, Rebecca, and Kelly M. Socia (2017, January 29). Boy with Toy or Black Male with Gun: An Analysis of Online News Articles Covering the Shooting of Tamir Rice. *Race and Justice*. Available, http://journals.sagepub.com/doi/abs/10.1177/2153368716689594

Stop Patriarchy (2014). *Abortion on Demand and Without Apology!* Available, http://www.stoppatriarchy.org/abortionondemandstatement.html

Stoughton, Seth (2015, May 26). Why Do US Police Keep Killing Unarmed Black Men? *BBC News*. Available, http://www.bbc.com/news/world-us-canada-32740523

Stross, Randall (2013, April 6). Wearing a Badge, and a Video Camera. *The New York Times*. Available, http://www.nytimes.com/2013/04/07/business/wearable-video-cameras-for-police-officers.html?pagewanted=all&_r=0

Stryker, Robin (2011). Political Polarization. *National Institute for Civil Discourse*, Research Brief #6. Available, http://nicd.arizona.edu/sites/default/files/research_briefs/NICD_research_brief6.pdf

Sue, Derald Wing, Christina M. Capodilupo, Gina C. Torino, Jennifer M. Bucceri, Aisha M. Holder, Kevin L. Nadal, and Marta Esquilin (2007). Racial Microaggressions in Everyday Life: Implications for Clinical Practice. *American Psychologist*, 62(4), 271–286.

Suicide Attack Hits Nigeria's University of Maiduguri (2017, January 16). *Al Jazeera*. Available, http://www.aljazeera.com/news/2017/01/suicide-attack-hits-nigeria-university-maiduguri-170116112753904.html

Sultan, Ahmad, and Fahmy Omar (2016, November 14). Militant Islamist Groups Believe Trump's Rhetoric Will Help Recruitment. *CBC News*. Available, http://www.cbc.ca/news/world/trump-militant-groups-isis-al-qaeda-1.3849486

Sustar, Lee (2015, January 7). The Contradictions of Al Sharpton. *Socialist Worker*. Available, http://socialistworker.org/2015/01/07/the-contradictions-of-al-sharpton

Swaine, Jon and Ciara McCarthy (2017, January 16). Young Black Men again Faced Highest Rate of US Police Killings in 2016. *The Guardian*. Available, https://www.theguardian.com/usnews/2017/jan/08/thecountedpolicekillings2016youngblackmen

Syria Ceasefire Deal Explained (2016, September 10). *Al Jazeera*. Available, http://www.aljazeera.com/news/2016/09/syria-ceasefire-deal-explained-160910111132967.html

Syria Death Toll: UN Envoy Estimates 400,000 Killed (2016, April 23). *Al Jazeera*. Available, http://www.aljazeera.com/news/2016/04/staffan-de-mistura-400000-killed-syria-civil-war-160423055735629.html

Syvret, Paul (2011, August 16). Michele Bachmann's Elevation in Republican Party Signals Dangerous New Extremism in US Politics. *The Courier Mail*. Available, http://www.couriermail.com.au/news/michele-bachmanns-elevation-in-republican-party-signals-dangerous-new-extremism-in-us-politics/story-e6frerdf-1226115420761

Taibbi, Mat (2014, December 5). The Police in America Are Becoming Illegitimate. *Rolling Stone*. Available, http://www.rollingstone.com/politics/news/the-police-in-america-are-becoming-illegitimate-20141205

Talent, Jim (2004, July 13). Federal Marriage Amendment—Motion to Proceed. *Congressional Record*. Available, http://thomas.loc.gov/cgi-bin/query/C?r108:./temp/~r108T5ogUg

Tallman, Tisha R. (2005). Liberty, Justice, and Equality: An Examination of Past, Present, and Proposed Immigration Policy Reform Legislation. *North Carolina Journal of International Law & Commercial Regulation 30*(4), 869–894.

Tapper, Jake, Eli Watkins, Jim Acosta, and Euan McKirdy (2017, February 2). Trump had Heated Exchange with Australian PM, Talked 'Tough Hombres' with Mexican Leader. *CNN Politics*. Available, http://www.cnn.com/2017/02/01/politics/malcolm-turnbull-donald-trump-pena-nieto/

Tarraf, Wassim, Patricia Y. Miranda, and Hector M. González (2012). Medical Expenditures among Immigrant and Non-Immigrant Groups in the U.S.: Findings from the Medical Expenditures Panel Survey. *Medical Care*, 50(3), 233–242.

Tashman, Brian (2013, April 25). Robertson: Planned Parenthood Inspired Adolf Hitler, Behind 'Genocide' of Black Community. *Right Wing Watch*. Available, http://www.rightwingwatch.org/content/robertson-planned-parenthood-inspired-adolf-hitler-behind-genocide-black-community

Tashman, Brian (2014a, August 22). FRC: 'People Need to be Alarmed' about 'Very Dangerous' Gay Marriage. *Right Wing Watch*. Available, http://www.rightwingwatch.org/content/frc-people-need-be-alarmed-about-very-dangerous-gay-marriage

Tashman, Brian (2014b, July 23). Richard Land Links Gay Rights to Nazi Germany. *Right Wing Watch*. Available, http://www.rightwingwatch.org/content/richard-land-links-gay-rights-nazi-germany

Tashman, Brian (2015, March 2). Far-Right Pundit: Hang Officials Who Skip Netanyahu's Speech to Congress. *Right Wing Watch*. Available, http://www.rightwingwatch.org/content/far-right-pundit-hang-officials-who-skip-netanyahus-speech-congress

Tate, Kristin (2017, April 27). Obama's Speech Proves Hypocrisy of Democrat's Anti-Wall Street Rhetoric. *The Hill*. Available, http://thehill.com/blogs/pundits-blog/national-party-news/330806-obama-proves-democrats-anti-wall-street-rhetoric-a

Taylor, Adam (2016, April 19). How Allegations of Saudi Arabia's Ties to 9/11 Plotters became a Problem for Obama, Again. *The Washington Post*. Available, Lexis-Nexis.

Taylor, Keeanga-Yamahtta (2014, November 26). When Racism Wears a Badge. *Socialist Worker*. Available, http://socialistworker.org/2014/11/26/when-racism-wears-a-badge

Taylor, Keeanga-Yamahtta (2015, January 13). The Rise of the #BlackLivesMatter Movement. *Socialist Worker*. Available, http://socialistworker.org/2015/01/13/the-rise-of-blacklivesmatter

Taylor, Keeanga-Yamahtta (2016). *From #BlackLivesMatter to Black Liberation*. Chicago: Haymarket Books.

Telford, Marguerite (2014, July 17). HUMANE Act: Flawed Bill Offers More Lenient Process for Illegal Minors. *PR Newswire*. Available, EbscoHost.

Ten Tenets of Civility (2017, March 30). Be Civil Be Heard. Available, https://becivilbeheard.org/ten-tenets/

Terkel, Amanda (2015, March 10). Hawkish Republican Congressman Uneasy with GOP Senators' Letter to Iran. *The Huffington Post*. Available, http://www.huffingtonpost.com/2015/03/10/peter-king-iran_n_6839324.html?ncid=fcbklnkushpmg00000013

Tesfaye, Sophia (2014, May 21). Fox Puts Words in Pelosi's Mouth about Benghazi Select Committee. *Media Matters for America*. Available, http://mediamatters.org/blog/2014/05/21/fox-puts-words-in-pelosis-mouth-about-benghazi/199418

Tesfaye, Sophia (2016, October 26). NAACP Calls for Federal Probe after Noose Placed on Black High School Football Player in Mississippi. *Salon*. Available, http://www.salon.com/2016/10/26/naacp-calls-for-federal-probe-after-noose-placed-on-black-high-school-football-player-in-mississippi/

Therborn, Göran (1980). *The Ideology of Power and the Power of Ideology*. London: Verso.

Thistle, Scott (2013, April 2). Bill Would Broaden Church Property Tax Exemption. *Bangor Daily News*. Available, http://bangordailynews.com/2013/04/02/politics/bill-would-broaden-church-property-tax-exemption/

Thistle, Scott (2016, December 6). Gov. LePage Stands by Racially Charged Statements about Drug Dealers Coming to Maine. *Portland Press Herald*. Available, http://www.pressherald.com/2016/08/25/aclu-of-maine-asks-lepage-to-produce-binder-of-recent-maine-drug-arrests/

Thomas, Cal and Beckel, Bob (2008). *Common Ground: How to Stop the Partisan War that Is Destroying America*. New York: Harper.

Thomas, Jim (2014). Beware Bubbles and Echo Chambers. *The Hastings Center Report, 44*(55), 543–545.

Thomas, Lauren (2017, March 25). The 'Biggest Loser' after Obamacare Reform's Death May Be Trump's Whole Agenda, Analysts Say. *CNBC*. Available, http://www.cnbc.com/2017/03/25/the-biggest-loser-after-obamacare-reforms-death-may-be-trumps-whole-agenda-analysts-say.html

Thomas, Nancy L., and Matthew Hartley (2010). Higher Education's Democratic Imperative. *New Directions for Higher Education 152*, 99–107.

Thompson, Derek (2017, January 25). Everybody's in a Bubble, and That's a Problem. *The Atlantic*. Available, https://www.theatlantic.com/business/archive/2017/01/america-bubbles/514385/

Thompson, Thomas (2015, November 6). *Syrian Refugees: What-When-Why-How*. Lexington, KY: Lulu.

Thrasher, Steven W. (2014, December 3). The Eric Garner Decision Confirms a Holiday of Horrors. *The Guardian*. Available, http://www.theguardian.com/commentisfree/2014/dec/03/eric-garner-decision-more-protest-not-less?CMP=share_btn_fb

Thrush, Glenn (2017, March 6). Trump's New Travel Ban Blocks Migrants from Six Nations, Sparing Iraq. *The New York Times*. Available, https://www.nytimes.com/2017/03/06/us/politics/travel-ban-muslim-trump.html

Thrush, Glenn, and Michelle Innis (2017, February 2). U.S.-Australia Rift Is Possible after Trump Ends Call with Prime Minister. *The New York Times*. Available, https://www.nytimes.com/2017/02/02/us/politics/us-australia-trump-turnbull.html

Tierney, Dominic (2015, December 18). How Trump and ISIS Help Each Other. *MSN News*. Available, http://www.msn.com/en-au/news/world/how-trump-and-isis-help-each-other/ar-BBnGSsn

Timpf, Katherine (2015, May 12). Apparently, Just Being in the Same Room Is a Microaggression. *National Review*. Available, http://www.nationalreview.com/article/418273/university-study-certain-rooms-are-microaggressions-themselves-katherine-timpf

Tolchin, Susan (1996). *The Angry American: How Voter Rage Is Changing the Nation*. Boulder, CO: Westview Press.

Tolentino, Jia (2015, April 21). Cop Who Killed Rekia Boyd Out of 'Fear' Found Not Guilty on All Counts. *Jezebel*. Available, http://jezebel.com/cop-who-killed-rekia-boyd-out-of-fear-found-not-guilty-1699164997

Tomlinson, Simon (2014, June 1). Heartbroken Father of Man Killed During 'Virgin Killer's' Shooting Rampage Meets Privately with the Shooter's Father. *Daily Mail*. Available, http://www.dailymail.co.uk/news/article-2645707/Heartbroken-father-man-killed-Virgin-Killers-shooting-rampage-meets-privately-grieving-father-man-murdered-son-taking-life.html

Toosi, Nahal (2016, November 16). Iran Deal Critics to Trump: Please Don't Rip It Up. *Politico*. Available, http://www.politico.com/story/2016/11/donald-trump-iran-nuclear-deal-231419

TomP (2015, November 22). American Fascism: Trump Praises Crowd for Beating Up Protester—the New Brownshirts. *The Daily Kos*. Available, http://www.dailykos.com/story/2015/11/22/1453171/-American-Fascism-Trump-Praises-Crowd-for-Beating-Up-Protester-the-new-Brownshirts

Topaz, Jonathan (2014, June 16). Rick Perry: Leave Gay Question to Shrinks. *Politico*. Available, http://www.politico.com/story/2014/06/rick-perry-gay-comments-107891.html

Torcaso v. Watkins. 367 U.S. 488 (1961).

Torres, Alec (2014, March 24). UCSB Smears Pro-Lifers after Professor's Attack on Pro-Life Student. *The National Review*. Available, http://www.nationalreview.com/article/373957/ucsb-smears-pro-lifers-after-professors-attack-pro-life-student-alec-torres

Toulmin, Stephen E. (2003). *The uses of argument* (2nd ed.). New York: Cambridge University Press.

Town of Greece v. Galloway. No. 12-696, 572 U.S. ___ (2014).

Trobee, Kim (2014, May 1). Secular Group Wants to Silence National Day of Prayer. *Citizen Link*. Available, http://www.citizenlink.com/2014/05/01/secular-group-wants-to-silence-national-day-of-prayer/

Tuman, Joseph S. (2010). *Communicating Terror: The Rhetorical Dimensions of Terrorism* (2nd ed.). Thousand Oaks, CA: Sage.

Tumulty, Karen (2013, February 3). Why Immigration Reform Fell Short. *The Washington Post*. Available, http://www.washingtonpost.com/politics/why-immigration-reform-fell-short/2013/02/03/fbb643aa-6be7-11e2-8740-9b58f43c191a_story.html

Turkle, Sherry (2011). *Alone Together: Why We Expect More from Technology and Less from Each Other*. New York: Basic Books.

Turner v. Safley. 482 U.S. 78 (1987).

Ungar, Rick (2013, April 7). North Carolina Religion Bill Killed—But One Third of Americans Want Christianity as Official Religion of USA. *Forbes*. Available, http://www.forbes.com/sites/rickungar/2013/04/07/north-carolina-religion-bill-killed-but-one-third-of-americans-want-christianity-as-official-religion-of-usa/

Ungar, Sanford J. (2015, March 23). American Ignorance. *Inside Higher Ed*. Available, https://www.insidehighered.com/views/2015/03/23/essay-problems-american-ignorance-world

Unger, David C. (2016). A Better Internationalism. In Glenn P. Hastedt (Ed.), *Readings in American Foreign Policy* (pp. 35–44). Lanham, MD: Rowman & Littlefield.

United States v. Miller. 307 U.S. 174 (1939).

United States v. Windsor. 570 U.S. 12 (2013).

United States Census Bureau (2010). *2010 Census Briefs: The Black Population.* Available, https://www.census.gov/prod/cen2010/briefs/c2010br-06.pdf

United States Department of Justice (2016, August 10). *Investigation of the Baltimore City Police Department.* Available, https://www.justice.gov/opa/file/883366/download

United States Government Accountability Office (2014, September). *Elections: Issues Related to State Voter Identification Laws.* Available, http://www.gao.gov/assets/670/665966.pdf

United States Institute of Peace (2015a, March 9). *Part I: GOP Letter on Iran.* The Iran Primer. Available, http://iranprimer.usip.org/blog (accessed 3/9/15).

United States Institute of Peace (2015b, March 9). *Part II: Iran Responds to GOP Letter.* The Iran Primer. Available, http://iranprimer.usip.org/blog/2015/mar/09/part-ii-iran-responds-gop-letter

Urken, Ross Kenneth (2010, October 25). GOFG Exclusive with Rachel Maddow. *Guest of a Guest.* Available, http://guestofaguest.com/new-york/interview/gofg-exclusive-with-rachel-maddow-hear-her-dish-on-religion-broadcast-anchor-snafus-and-her-favorite-cocktail

Vadum, Matthew (2011, September 1). Registering the Poor to Vote Is Un-American. *American Thinker.* Available, http://www.americanthinker.com/articles/2011/09/registering_the_poor_to_vote_is_un-american.html

Valentino, Nicholas A., and Fabian G. Neuner (2017). Why the Sky Didn't Fall: Mobilizing Anger in Reaction to Voter ID Laws. *Political Psychology, 38*(2), 331–350.

Vaid, Urvashi (1995). *Virtual Equality: The Mainstreaming of Gay & Lesbian Liberation.* New York: Anchor.

Van Orden v. Perry. 545 U.S. 677 (2005).

Vaughns, Katherine L. (2005). Broken Fences: Legal and Practical Realities of Immigration Reform in the Post-9/11 Age: Restoring the Rule of Law: Reflections on Fixing the Immigration System and Exploring Failed Policy Choices. *University of Maryland Law Journal of Race, Religion, Gender and Class 5*(Fall), 151–186.

Veasey et al. v. Rick Perry (2014). 574 U.S. ___. Available, http://www.supremecourt.gov/opinions/14pdf/14a393_08m1.pdf

Vega, Tanzina (2015, October 30). Out of Prison and Out of Work: Jobs Out of Reach for Former Inmates. *CNN Money.* Available, http://money.cnn.com/2015/10/30/news/economy/former-inmates-unemployed/

Veith, Gene (2013, August 27). Making Churches Pay Taxes. *Patheos.* Available, http://www.patheos.com/blogs/geneveith/2013/08/making-churches-pay-taxes/

Velarde, Robert (2008). Prayer Has Its Reasons. *Focus on the Family.* Available, http://www.focusonthefamily.com/faith/faith_in_life/prayer/prayer_has_its_reasons.aspx

Velasquez, Carmen (2014, September 8). Obama Broke His Promise to Latinos. *Politico.* Available, http://www.politico.com/magazine/story/2014/09/after-obamas-punt-maybe-latinos-should-sit-election-out-110728_full.html#.VA_hvvm-2dk

Verdery, C. Stewart (2006, June 19). Prepared Testimony to the U.S. Senate Subcommittee on Immigration, Border Security and Citizenship. *Immigration Enforcement at the Workplace: Learning from the Mistakes of 1996.* U.S. Senate Judiciary website. Available, http://www.judiciary.senate.gov/imo/media/doc/Verdery%20Testimony%20061906.pdf

Veterans Affairs (1997, April 14). *VA Titles and Abbreviations.* Available, http://www.va.gov/vapubs/viewPublication.asp?Pub_ID=39&FType=2

Vitale, Alex S. (2014, August 18). How to End Militarized Policing. *Portside.* Available, http://portside.org/2015-04-28/how-end-militarized-policing

Voice of America (2009, October 27). *Bush: 'You Are Either with Us, or with the Terrorists'—2001-09-21.* Available, http://www.voanews.com/content/a-13-a-2001-09-21-14-bush-66411197/549664.html

Voorhees, Courte C. W., John Vick, John, and Douglas D. Perkins (2007). "Came Hell and High Water": The Intersection of Hurricane Katrina, the News Media, Race and Poverty. *Journal of Community & Applied Social Psychology, 17*(6), 415–429.

Waánatan, Wakínyan (2016, October 25). Muckleshoot Woman Shot and Killed by Police on Muckleshoot Reservation. *The Last Real Indian.* Available, https://www.google.com/webhp?sourceid=chrome-instant&ion=1&espv=2&ie=UTF-8#q=muckleshoot+indian+reservation&*

Walberg, Eric (2017, April 9). Syrian Attack: Trump's Cuban Missile Moment. *American Herald Tribune.* Available, http://ahtribune.com/us/trump-at-war/1602-syria-trump-cuban-missile.html

Wald, Kenneth, Dennis Owen, and Samuel Hill (1988). Churches as Political Communities. *American Political Science Review 82*(2), 531–48.

Wald, Michael S. (2006). Adults' Sexual Orientation and State Determinations Regarding Placement of Children. *Family Law Quarterly 40*(3), 381–434.

Waldman, Michael (2016). *The Fight to Vote.* New York: Simon & Schuster.

Waldman, Paul (2014, April 3). How Barack Obama Trapped the GOP on Health Care. *The American Prospect.* Available, http://prospect.org/article/how-barack-obama-trapped-gop-health-care

Wallace v. Jaffree. 105 S. Ct. 2479 (1985).

Walsh, Joan (2014, April 18). Last Gasps of a Dying Movement: Obamacare Obstructionists' Self-Created Trap. *Salon*. Available, http://www.salon.com/2014/04/18/last_gasps_of_a_dying_movement_obamacare_obstructionists_self_created_trap/

Walz v. Tax Commission of the City of New York. 397 U.S. 664 (1970).

Wang, Marina (2016, July 7). President Obama on Police Shootings: 'Change Has Been Too Slow.' *The Huffington Post*. Available, http://www.huffingtonpost.com/entry/barack-obama-police-brutality_us_577ed1ede4b0c590f7e8af19

War Crimes in Month of Bombing Aleppo (2016, December 1). *Human Rights Watch*. Available, https://www.hrw.org/news/2016/12/01/russia/syria-war-crimes-month-bombing-aleppo

Ward, Clifford (2015, November 12). Failure to be Bonded Out Led Sandra Bland to Suicide, Jail Officials Allege. *Chicago Tribune*. Available, http://www.chicagotribune.com/news/ct-sandra-bland-court-motions-met-20151112-story.html

The Washington Star (1976, February 15). "Welfare Queen" Becomes Issue in Reagan Campaign. *The New York Times*. Available, http://www.nytimes.com/1976/02/15/archives/welfare-queen-becomes-issue-in-reagan-campaign-hitting-a-nerve-now.html?_r=0

Waters, David (2010, April 21). Palin's Christian Nation. *Faith Street*. Available, http://www.faithstreet.com/onfaith/2010/04/21/palins-christian-nation/47

Watkins, Ali (2015, March 26). Chaos in Yemen Gives New Fuel to Critics of Obama's Foreign Policy. *The Huffington Post*. Available, http://www.huffingtonpost.com/2015/03/26/yemen-obama-saudi_n_6950658.html?ncid=fcbklnkushpmg00000013

Watkins, Derek (2015, July 30). What China has been Building in the South China Sea. *The New York Times*. Available, https://www.nytimes.com/interactive/2015/07/30/world/asia/what-china-has-been-building-in-the-south-china-sea.html

Watkins, Eli (2017, April 2). Trump: US will Act Unilaterally on North Korea if Necessary. *CNN Politics*. Available, http://www.cnn.com/2017/04/02/politics/donald-trump-north-korea/

Watts, Eric K. (1997). An Exploration of Spectacular Consumption: Gangsta Rap as Cultural Commodity. *Communication Studies*, *48*(1), 42–58.

Watts, Tim (2011, January 14). I Used to be a Rachel Maddow Fan. *News Focus*. Available, http://www.newsfocus.org/maddow_gaffe.htm

Wax, Amy L. (2005). The Conservative's Dilemma: Traditional Institutions, Social Change, and Same-Sex Marriage. *San Diego Law Review 42*, 1059–1103

WBC [Westboro Baptist Church] (1991). *Compendium of Bible Truth on Fags*. Available, http://www.godhatesfags.com/reports/19910101_fags-compendium.pdf

WBC [Westboro Baptist Church] (2014). Website. Available, www.godhatesfags.com

Weaver, Matthew, Rowena Mason, Martin Chulov, and Emma Graham-Harrison (2017, April 6). Putin Stands by Assad as Firm Evidence of Chemical Attack Mounts. *The Guardian*. Available, https://www.theguardian.com/world/2017/apr/06/postmortems-confirm-syria-chemical-attack-turkey-says

Weber, Paul J. (2016, July 22). Video Shows Officer Slam Woman to Ground, Say Black People Have 'Violent Tendencies.' *Talking Points Memo*. Available, http://talkingpointsmemo.com/news/officer-tells-blacks-have-violent-tendencies

Weber Shandwick (2016). Civility in America 2016: U.S. Facing a Civility Crisis Affecting Public Discourse & Political Action. Available, http://www.webershandwick.com/news/article/civility-in-america-2016-us-facing-a-civility-crisis

Weber Shandwick (2017). *Civility in America VII: The State of Civility*. Available, http://www.webershandwick.com/uploads/news/files/Civility_in_America_the_State_of_Civility.pdf

Webster, Alexander F. C. (1993). Homosexuals in Uniform? *Christianity Today 37*(2), 23.

Weiner, Rachel (2012, September 24). Romney: Uninsured Have Emergency Rooms. *The Washington Post*. Available, http://www.washingtonpost.com/blogs/post-politics/wp/2012/09/24/romney-calls-emergency-room-a-health-care-option-for-uninsured/

Welch, Chris (2014, June 20). Obama Administration Responds to Immigrant Surge by Ramping Up Detention and Deportations. *The Verge*. Available, http://www.theverge.com/2014/6/20/5827594/obama-responds-to-immigrant-crisis-with-detention-deportation.

Welsh, Scott (2013). *The Rhetorical Surface of Democracy: How Deliberative Ideals Undermine Democratic Politics*. Lanham, MD: Lexington Books.

Wesberry v. Sanders (1964). 376 U.S. 1. Available, https://supreme.justia.com/cases/federal/us/376/1/case.html

Wharton, Tony (1998, June 10). Evangelist Robertson Says Gays Bring about Earthquakes, Tornados, Bombs. *Norfolk Virginian-Pilot*. Available, http://www.skeptictank.org/hs/patrob3.htm

Wheeler, Ronald (2016). About Microaggressions. *Law Library Journal, 108*(2), 321–329.

White, Byron (1986). *Bowers v. Hardwick*. 478 U.S. 186 (1986), p. 1–6. Available, http://www.ache.org/pubs/hap_companion/Wing/BowersHardwick.pdf

White, Emily B. (2007). How We Treat Our Guests: Mobilizing Employment Discrimination Protections in a Guest Worker Program. *Berkeley Journal of Employment & Labor Law 28*(1), 269–304.

White House Fact Sheet (2006, October 26). *Fact Sheet: The Secure Fence Act of 2006*. Available, http://georgewbush-whitehouse.archives.gov/news/releases/2006/10/20061026-1.html

Whitley, David (2014, July 12). Liberal Democrats Join Forces with Mexican Invaders. *Eagle Rising*. Available, http://eaglerising.com/7310/liberal-democrats-join-forces-mexican-invaders/

Whitmire, Kyle (2014, May 5). Roy Moore's Twisted History: Islam and Buddhism Don't Have First Amendment Protections. *Alabama.com*. Available, http://www.al.com/opinion/index.ssf/2014/05/roy_moores_twisted_hisotry_isl.html

Wiebe, Carolyn (2010). A General Semantics Approach to Health Care Reform, or, Looking for a Cure for My IFD Disease. *ETC: A Review of General Semantics*, July, 264–279.

Wiebe, Robert H. (2013). Primary Tensions in American Public Life. In Judith Rodin & Stephen P. Steinberg (Eds.), *Public Discourse in America: Conversation and Community in the Twenty-First Century* (pp. 35-39). Philadelphia: University of Pennsylvania Press.

Wiener, Jon (2009, February 2). Rick Warren's court. *The Nation*. Available, http://www.thenation.com/article/rick-warrens-clout#

Wilcox, Clyde, Paul R. Brewer, Shauna Shames, and Celinda Lake (2007). If I Bend this Far I Will Break?: Public Opinion about Same-Sex Marriages. In Craig A. Rimmerman & Clyde Wilcox (Eds.), *The Politics of Same-Sex Marriage* (pp. 215–242). Chicago: University of Chicago Press.

Wilde, Robert (2015, July 25). Huckabee: Obama Marching Israelis to 'Door of Oven.' *Breitbart*. Available, http://www.breitbart.com/big-government/2015/07/25/huckabee-obama-marching-israelis-to-door-of-oven/

Wildman, Sarah (2012, January 5). When 'Anti-Semitism' Is Abused. *Forward*. Available, http://forward.com/opinion/israel/149147/when-anti-semitism-is-abused/

Willer, Robb (2016, September). How to Have Better Political Conversations. *TED Talk*. Available, https://www.ted.com/talks/robb_willer_how_to_have_better_political_conversations

Williams, Kaylene C. (2012). Fear Appeal Theory. *Research in Business and Economics Journal 5*, 1–21.

Williams, Lucinda (2001). Get Right with God. *Essence*. Musical CD produced by Lost Highway.

Williams, Mary Elizabeth (2015, September 4). No, Christians, You're not being "Persecuted"—and Kim Davis Is not a Martyr. *AlterNet*. Available, http://www.alternet.org/no-christians-youre-not-being-persecuted-and-kim-davis-not-martyr?sc=fb

Williams, Timothy (2016, July 7). Study Supports Suspicion that Police Are More Likely to Use Force on Blacks. *The New York Times*. Available, https://www.nytimes.com/2016/07/08/us/study-supports-suspicion-that-police-use-of-force-is-more-likely-for-blacks.html

Williams, Vanessa (2017, May 1). 'Auntie Maxine' and the Quest for Impeachment. *The Washington Post*. Available, https://www.washingtonpost.com/politics/auntie-maxine-and-the-quest-for-impeachment/2017/04/29/38a26816-2476-11e7-a1b3-faff0034e2de_story.html?utm_term=.136ebc0e025b

Williams, Wes (2013, July 20). What the Right Doesn't Want You to Know about Welfare: 9 Myths Exploded. *Addicting Info*. Available, http://www.addictinginfo.org/2013/07/20/what-the-right-doesnt-want-you-to-know-about-welfare-9-myths-exploded/

Willis, Bonnie (2014, April 29). Thoughts on National Day of Prayer. *The Citizen*. Available, http://www.thecitizen.com/blogs/bonnie-willis/04-29-2014/thoughts-national-day-prayer

Wilmouth, Brad (2008, July 31). Olbermann: NRA 'Trying to Increase Deaths,' 2nd Amendment Is for Muskets. *News Busters*. Available, http://newsbusters.org/blogs/brad-wilmouth/2008/07/31/olbermann-nra-trying-increase-deaths-gun-scalia-clown

Wilshire, Peter (2007). Uncovering Michael Moore in Manufacturing Dissent. *Screen Education*, issue 48, 38–45.

Wilson, John K. (2011). *The Most Dangerous Man in America: Rush Limbaugh's Assault on Reason*. New York: St. Martin's Press.

Wilson, John K. (2012, June 21). Rush's 53 Smears against Sandra Fluke. *Daily Kos*. Available, http://www.dailykos.com/story/2012/03/04/1070884/-Rush-s-52-Smears-Against-Sandra-Fluke

Winkler, Adam (2009). Symposium: The Second Amendment and the Right to Bear Arms after *D.C. V. Heller*: Heller's Catch-22. *UCLA Law Review 56*, 1551–1577.

Winkler, Adam (2011). *Gunfight: The Battle over the Right to Bear Arms in America*. New York: W. W. Norton & Co.

Winstanley, Asa (2015, February 13). Israel Is Not a Democracy. *Middle East Monitor*. Available, https://www.middleeastmonitor.com/20150213-israel-is-not-a-democracy/

Wintemute, Garen J. (2013). In Daniel W. Webster & Jon S. Vernick (Eds.), *Reducing Gun Violence in America: Informing Policy with Evidence and Analysis* (pp. 95–107). Baltimore: Johns Hopkins University Press.

Witte, K. (1992). Putting the Fear Back into Fear Appeals: The Extended Parallel Process Model. *Communication Monographs 59*(4), 329–349.

Wolburg, J. M. (2006). College Students' Responses to Antismoking Messages: Denial, Defiance, and Other Boomerang Effects. *Journal of Consumer Affairs 40*(2), 294–323.

Wolf, Sherry (2009). *Sexuality and Socialism: History, Politics, and Theory of GLBT Liberation*. Chicago: Haymarket.

Wolfsfeld, Gadi (2011). *Making Sense of Media & Politics: Five Principles in Political Communication*. New York: Routledge.

Wood, Chip (2014, April 4). Obamacare Is Still a Fraud. *The New American*. Available, http://www.thenewamerican.com/reviews/opinion/item/17985-obamacare-is-still-a-fraud

Wood, Robert W. (2012, September 19). If 47% Don't Pay Taxes, Let's Tax Churches. *Forbes*. Available, http://www.forbes.com/sites/robertwood/2012/09/19/if-47-dont-pay-taxes-lets-tax-churches/

Woodman, Spencer (2016, December 22). A Quarter of Florida's Black Citizens Can't Vote. A New Referendum Could Change That. *The Intercept*. Available, https://theintercept.com/2016/12/22/a-quarter-of-floridas-black-citizens-cant-vote-a-new-referendum-could-change-that/

Woods, Baynard (2016, July 27). Freddie Gray Death: Remaining Charges Dropped against Police Officers. *The Guardian*. Available, https://www.theguardian.com/usnews/2016/jul/27/freddiegraypoliceofficerschargesdropped

Woody, Christopher (2016, October 27). "The Fight Will Be Relentless and It Will Be Sustained": The Body Count in the Philippines' "War on Drugs" Is Mounting. *Business Insider*. Available, http://www.businessinsider.com/philippines-rodrigo-duterte-drug-violence-vigilante-killings-2016-10

Wootson, Cleve R., Jr., Derek Hawkins, and Linsey Bever (2016, September 21). Charlotte Police Shooting Victim Was Armed with a Gun, Chief Says After Night of Violent Protests. *The Washington Post*. Available, https://www.washingtonpost.com/news/morning-mix/wp/2016/09/21/black-man-fatally-shot-by-charlotte-police-was-armed-chief-says-after-night-of-violent-protests/?utm_term=.0e5aaa3e2b0a

Workman, Karen and Jonah Engel Bromwich (2016, October 8). 2 Police Officers Are Shot and Killed in Palm Springs, Calif. *The New York Times*. Available, https://www.nytimes.com/2016/10/09/us/palm-springs-police-officers-shot.html?_r=0

Wu, Frank H. (2002). *Yellow: Race in America beyond Black and White*. New York: Basic Books.

Wucker, Michele (2008, May 29). Security Threats and Immigration Policy. *Atlantic-Community.org*. Available, http://www.atlantic-community.org/index.php/Open_Think_Tank_Article/Security_Threats_and_Immigration_Policy

Yan, Holly, Kristina Sgueglia, and Kylie Walker (2016, December 22). 'Make America White Again': Hate Speech and Crimes Post-Election. *CNN*. Available, http://www.cnn.com/2016/11/10/us/post-election-hate-crimes-and-fears-trnd/

Yang, Alan S. (1997). The Polls—Trends: Attitudes toward Homosexuality. *Public Opinion Quarterly 61*(3), 477–507.

Yerkes, Sarah (2015, October 22). Can We Expect Real Political Reform in the Maghreb Any Time Soon? *The Brookings Institution*. Available, https://www.brookings.edu/blog/markaz/2015/10/22/can-we-expect-real-political-reform-in-the-maghreb-any-time-soon/

Yiannopoulos, Milo (2016, June 12). The Left Chose Islam Over Gays. Now 100 People Are Dead or Maimed in Orlando. *Breitbart*. Available, http://www.breitbart.com/milo/2016/06/12/left-chose-islam-gays-now-100-people-killed-maimed-orlando/

Yoffe, Emily (2012, March 5). How Not to Apologize: Rush Limbaugh's Statement on Sandra Fluke Was a Textbook Example of What Not to Say. *Slate.com*. Available, http://www.slate.com/articles/life/dear_prudence/2012/03/rush_limbaugh_s_apology_to_sandra_fluke_was_awful_here_s_what_he_should_have_said_.html

York, Byron (2014, June 25). Administration: Bush-Era Law Requires US to Slow-Walk Deportations. *Washington Examiner*. Available, http://washingtonexaminer.com/administration-bush-era-law-requires-us-to-slow-walk-deportations/article/2550147

York, Byron (2014, August 25). At Michael Brown Funeral, Al Sharpton's Double-Edged Eulogy Evokes Anger. *Washington Examiner*. Available, http://www.washingtonexaminer.com/at-michael-brown-funeral-al-sharptons-double-edged-eulogy-evokes-anger/article/2552433

Young, Jeffrey (2014, August 5). In States Where It's Wanted, Obamacare Is Working Well. *The Huffington Post*. Available, http://www.huffingtonpost.com/2014/08/05/states-obamacare_n_5650606.html?ncid=fcbklnkushpmg00000013&ir=Politics

Younge, Gary (2015, April 10). White Guilt Won't Fix America's Race Problem. Only Justice and Equality Will. *The Guardian*. Available, https://www.theguardian.com/commentisfree/2015/apr/10/white-guilt-america-walter-scott-us

Yu, Annie Z. (2013, June 9). Boy Scouts' Decision on Gays Tests Loyalty of Members. *The Washington Times*. Available, http://www.washingtontimes.com/news/2013/jun/9/boy-scouts-decision-on-gays-tests-loyalty-of-membe/?page=all

Yusuf, Nadia, Nisreen Al-Banawi, and Hajjah Abdel Rahman Al-Imam (2014). The Social Media as Echo Chamber: The Digital Impact. *Journal of Business & Economics Research*, *12*(1). Available, https://cluteinstitute.com/ojs/index.php/JBER/article/view/8369/8394

Zablocki v. Redhail. 434 U.S. 374 (1978).

Zack, Naomi (2015). *White Privilege and Black Rights*. Lanham, MD. Rowman & Littlefield.

Zadrozny, Brandy (2014, January 20). Study Finds People with Guns More At-Risk for Suicide and Homicide. *The Daily Beast*. Available, http://www.thedailybeast.com/articles/2014/01/20/study-finds-people-with-guns-more-at-risk-for-suicide-and-homicide.html

Zalan, Eszter (2017, February 9). 'Sobering' Poll Finds European Support for Trump's Muslim Ban. *EU Observer*. Available, https://euobserver.com/beyond-brussels/136839

Zallman, Leah, Fernando A. Wilson, James P. Stimpson, Adriana Bearse, Lisa Arsenault, Blessing Dube, David Himmelstein, and Steffie Woolhandler (2015). Unauthorized Immigrants Prolong the Life of Medicare's Trust Fund. *Journal of General Internal Medicine*, *31*(1), 122–127.

Zekman, Pam (2016, October 27). 2 Investigators: Chicago Voters Cast Ballots from Beyond the Grave. *CBS Chicago*. Available, http://chicago.cbslocal.com/2016/10/27/2-investigators-chicago-voters-cast-ballots-from-beyond-the-grave/

Zeleny, Jeff (2013, April 3). $700 Million in Katrina Relief Missing, Report Shows. *ABC News*. Available, http://abcnews.go.com/Politics/700-million-katrina-relief-funds-missing-report-shows/story?id=18870482

Zezima, Katie, and David Nakamura (2014, July 9). Obama Defends Not Visiting Texas Border, Saying He's 'Not Interested in Photo Ops.' *The Washington Post*. Available, http://www.washingtonpost.com/politics/obama-defends-not-visiting-texas-border-saying-hes-not-interested-in-photo-ops/2014/07/09/b7c5d77e-079e-11e4-a0dd-f2b22a257353_story.html

Ziegelmueller, George W. and Jack Kay (1996). *Argumentation: Inquiry and Advocacy*. Boston: Beacon Press.

Zorach v. Clauson. 343 U.S. 306 (1952).

Zorthian, Julia (2015, October 7). Who's Fighting Who in Syria. *Time*. Available, http://time.com/4059856/syria-civil-war-explainer/

Zubiaga, Arkaitz, Damiano Spina, Raquel Martínez, and Victor Fresno (2015). Real-time classification of Twitter trends. *Journal of the Association for Information Science and Technology*, 66(3), 462–73.

Zucca, Lorenzo (2008). Conflicts of Fundamental Rights as Constitutional Dilemmas. Sant'Anna Legal Studies Research Paper, No. 16. In, Eva Brems (Ed.), *Conflicts between Fundamental Rights*. Available, http://papers.ssrn.com/sol3/papers.cfm?abstract_id=1154528

Zurawik, David (2016, July 10). Debating a Reckless Tweet about Black Lives Matter on CNN Today. *The Baltimore Sun*. Available, http://www.baltimoresun.com/entertainment/tv/z-on-tv-blog/bal-reckless-tweet-tomi-lahren-black-lives-matter-cnn-today-20160710-story.html

INDEX

CPSIA information can be obtained
at www.ICGtesting.com
Printed in the USA
LVHW051214131222
735083LV00001B/4